Dr. Ela Sharma's

SAT Math
Manual and Workbook
For the Perfect Score

ISBN: 9798699545391

Published in the United States of America.

Copyright © 2021 Dr. Ela Sharma

All rights reserved.

Version 2.12

Volume discounts are available for schools, teachers, tutors, and learning agencies.

Email: tutorhubllc@gmail.com.

Additional resources and information on this book, including errata, are available at www.tutorhubllc.com.

*SAT is a registered trademark of the College Board, which is not affiliated in the publication of, and does not endorse this book.

To my daughter for her continued support

About the book

To ace the SAT math sections, a student must know how to approach a question and solve it using the least number of steps. This book introduces students to over 1,000 SAT-type questions and covers all the required math areas. It is focused on demonstrating how to quickly solve questions on the SAT math sections using the shortest method (usually one to two steps).

There are 85 categories in this book that are divided into 15 sections. Each category is a question type on the SAT and contains a variety of practice questions on the question type. Key points in each category are the fundamentals required to solve the questions in that category.

The 850 practice questions varying from easy to hard and over 200 examples are based on the prior SAT tests. Answers to the practice questions are written to provide a detailed and a consistent solution that corelates with the steps in the examples.

A student who has diligently completed this book should be able to quickly solve several questions on the SAT math sections without calculation or by using mental math. View at the website which examples from this book can be solved using these techniques (hyperlink available under the Book menu).

How to use the book

Since each category is written to be independent, few key points are repeated across related categories. A student should understand how the key points in a category are used in the examples and apply them in the practice questions.

The mapping of each question on the math sections of the SAT Practice Test 10 released by the College Board to the categories in this book is available on the last page. Students could take this test and focus on the areas of improvement. However, students should keep in mind that the same question type could be presented in several ways on the SAT. Completing all the practice questions in the book is advised for the best score.

Students who are starting SAT math self-study are encouraged to start from the beginning of the book and take time to complete a category. This book will familiarize them with the math topics required for the test and the type of questions that appear on the test.

The "process of elimination" theme is utilized throughout the examples and answers in this book. It is a time saving approach that students are encouraged to utilize on the SAT.

About the author

Teaching, especially in mathematics, has been my passion since my teenage days. Over the course of years, I have helped many students achieve their target scores in SAT and ACT math sections. I have enjoyed every moment of writing this book. I wish good luck to all the students using this book to prepare for the SAT math sections!

Table of Contents

Commonly Used Terminology

xy-plane and ordered pair

xy-plane refers to a coordinate system that has a horizontal x-axis and a vertical y-axis. See figure below. The axes are perpendicular to each other and intersect at a point known as the origin.

Each point in the coordinate system has a coordinate on the x-axis and a coordinate on the y-axis, collectively known as the ordered pair (x, y). For example, in the figure below, the x-coordinate of point A is 3 and the y-coordinate is 1. The ordered pair is $(3, 1)$.

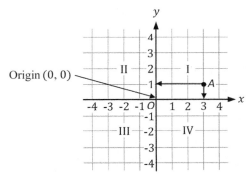

Quadrant

The four sections formed by the intersecting x- and y-axes in the xy-plane are known as quadrants. See figure above. They are numbered 1 to 4 in the counterclockwise direction starting from the upper right quadrant. The quadrant numbers are denoted by Roman numerals.

Line segment

A line segment is a part of a line that has distinct and finite end points. For example, sides of a triangle or a square or any other geometric figure that has distinct end points.

Variable

A variable is a placeholder for a numerical value. It is denoted by an alphabet. For example, in $5x - 7$, x is a variable. The value given to x will determine the value of $5x - 7$.

Constant

A constant is a static number in an equation. For example, in the equation $y = x - 7$, 7 is a constant. Its value will not change in the equation.

A question that denotes an alphabet as a constant will specifically call out the constant. For example, in the equation $y = x - a$, a is a constant.

Coefficient

A coefficient is a constant that is multiplied by a variable. For example, in the equation $2y = 5x - 7$, 2 is the coefficient of the variable y and 5 is the coefficient of the variable x.

Every variable has a coefficient. If a number is not given in front of the variable, then the implicit value of the variable is 1. For example, in the equation $2y = x - 7$, the coefficient of the variable x is 1.

Term

A term refers to a number, a variable, several variables multiplied together, or a number and several variables multiplied together. For example, in the equation $2xy + x + 7 = 3y - 2x$, the terms on the left-side of the equation are $2xy$, x, and 7 and the terms on the right-side of the equation are $3y$ and $2x$.

Expression vs. Equation

The terms on either side of an equation are collectively known as an expression. For example, in the equation $2xy + x + 7 = 3y - 2x$, the two expressions are $2xy + x + 7$ and $3y - 2x$.

Section 1 –
Variables and Expressions in Linear Equations

Category 1 – Solving Variables and Expressions in Linear Equations

Category 1 – Solving Variables and Expressions in Linear Equations

Key Points

- Moving a term from one side of the equation to the other side of the equation reverses the operator. A positive term becomes negative and vice versa. Similarly, multiplication becomes division and vice versa. For example, in the equation $4x - 1 = 2x + 5$, $2x$ moved to the left-side is $-2x$ and -1 moved to the right-side is 1.

$$4x - 1 = 2x + 5 \rightarrow 4x - 2x = 5 + 1 \rightarrow 2x = 6$$

  2 from $2x$ on the left-side of the equation can be removed by dividing the right-side by 2.

$$2x = 6 \rightarrow x = \frac{6}{2}$$

- Fractions can be moved from one side of the equation to the other side of the equation by reversing the addition/subtraction operators. See below.

$$\frac{x}{2} = \frac{1}{2} + \frac{3x}{5} \rightarrow \frac{x}{2} - \frac{3x}{5} = \frac{1}{2}$$

- Fractions can be multiplied by multiplying the numerators and multiplying the denominators. See below.

$$\frac{2x}{3} \times \frac{4}{5} \rightarrow \frac{2x \times 4}{3 \times 5} \rightarrow \frac{8x}{15}$$

- A division operator can be converted to a multiplication operator by flipping the numerator and the denominator of the fraction on the right-side of the division operator. See below.

$$\frac{y}{3} \div \frac{2}{x} \rightarrow \frac{y}{3} \times \frac{x}{2} \rightarrow \frac{y \times x}{3 \times 2} \rightarrow \frac{xy}{6}$$

  A term on the right-side of the division operator can be converted to a fraction by dividing it by 1. See below.

$$\frac{y}{3} \div 5 \rightarrow \frac{y}{3} \div \frac{5}{1} \rightarrow \frac{y}{3} \times \frac{1}{5} \rightarrow \frac{y \times 1}{3 \times 5} \rightarrow \frac{y}{15}$$

- Fractions with the same denominator can be added or subtracted by adding/subtracting the numerators. See below.

$$\frac{5x}{3} - \frac{x}{3} \rightarrow \frac{5x - x}{3} \rightarrow \frac{4x}{3}$$

- Fractions that do not have the same denominator can be added or subtracted by creating the same denominator in the fractions. This can be achieved by determining the lowest common multiple of the denominators. In the example below, the denominators are 2 and 3. The lowest common multiple of 2 and 3 is 6. A common denominator $= 6$ can be obtained by multiplying the fraction $\frac{x}{2}$ by 3 and the fraction $\frac{4x}{3}$ by 2.

$$\frac{x}{2} + \frac{4x}{3} \rightarrow 3\left(\frac{x}{2}\right) + 2\left(\frac{4x}{3}\right) \rightarrow \left(\frac{3 \times x}{3 \times 2}\right) + \left(\frac{2 \times 4x}{2 \times 3}\right) \rightarrow \frac{3x}{6} + \frac{8x}{6} \rightarrow \frac{3x + 8x}{6} \rightarrow \frac{11x}{6}$$

- Cross multiplication refers to multiplying the numerator of the fraction on one side of the equation with the denominator of the fraction on the other side of the equation. Cross multiplication clears the fraction. See below.

$$\frac{x}{3} = \frac{5}{4} \rightarrow \frac{x}{3} \diagdown \diagup \frac{5}{4} \rightarrow x \times 4 = 5 \times 3 \rightarrow 4x = 15$$

- Expressions, such as $a(b + c)$ or $a(b - c)$, that contain added or subtracted terms within parentheses can be simplified by individually multiplying each term within the parentheses with the outside term and then adding or subtracting the multiplied terms. For example, in the expression $3a(x + b)$, x and b can be individually multiplied by $3a$ and then added together. See below.

$$3a(x + b) = (3a \times x) + (3a \times b) = 3ax + 3ab$$

  - Each term within the parentheses must be multiplied with the entire outside term. For example, in the expression $-3a(x - b)$, both x and b must be multiplied with $-3a$ not $3a$.

  - A negative term outside the parentheses multiplied by a negative term inside the parentheses is a positive term. For example, $-3a(-b) = 3ab$.

- Identical expressions in an equation can be added or subtracted as a unit. For example, in the equation $3(4x + 1) + 2(4x + 1) = 9$, $(4x + 1)$ can be considered as a unit. 3 units $+ 2$ units is 5 units. See below.

$$3(4x + 1) + 2(4x + 1) = 9 \rightarrow 5(4x + 1) = 9$$

How to Solve

If an equation has expressions within parentheses, then simplify the parentheses before solving for a variable.

Example 1:

What value of x satisfies the equation $3(x - 2) = x + 2$?

A) 2

B) 4

C) 12

D) 15

Step 1: Simplify the expression within parentheses

$$3(x - 2) = x + 2 \quad \rightarrow \quad (3 \times x) - (3 \times 2) = x + 2 \quad \rightarrow \quad 3x - 6 = x + 2$$

Step 2: Isolate variables on one side of the equation and solve

$$3x - 6 = x + 2 \quad \rightarrow \quad 3x - x = 2 + 6 \quad \rightarrow \quad 2x = 8 \quad \rightarrow \quad x = \frac{8}{2} = 4$$

Correct answer choice is **B**.

Example 2:

$$\frac{\left(\frac{x}{3}\right)}{5} = 8$$

In above the equation what is the value of x?

A) $\frac{5}{3}$

B) $\frac{5}{8}$

C) 40

D) 120

Step 1: Simplify the fraction

In the above fraction, $\frac{x}{3}$ is the numerator (evident by the parentheses) and 5 is the denominator. This is same as $\frac{x}{3} \div 5$.

$$\frac{\left(\frac{x}{3}\right)}{5} = 8 \quad \rightarrow \quad \frac{x}{3} \div 5 = 8 \quad \rightarrow \quad \frac{x}{3} \times \frac{1}{5} = 8 \quad \rightarrow \quad \frac{x}{15} = 8$$

Step 2: Cross multiply and solve

$$\frac{x}{15} = 8 \quad \rightarrow \quad x = 8 \times 15 = 120$$

Correct answer choice is **D**.

Example 3:

If n satisfies the equation $4(n - 3) - 7 = 2(n - 3)$, what is the value of $6(n - 3)$?

Step 1: Isolate all terms of the identical expression on one side of the equation and solve

$$4(n - 3) - 7 = 2(n - 3) \quad \rightarrow \quad 4(n - 3) - 2(n - 3) = 7 \quad \rightarrow \quad 2(n - 3) = 7$$

Since $6(n - 3)$ is triple of $2(n - 3)$, multiplying the equation by 3 will give the value of $6(n - 3)$.

$$(2(n - 3) = 7) \times 3 \quad \rightarrow \quad 6(n - 3) = 21$$

Correct answer is **21**.

Category 1 – Practice Questions (answers on page 330)

No Calculator Questions

1

$$4(x - 3) = 3x - 4$$

What value of x satisfies the equation above?

A) 2

B) 3

C) 8

D) 16

2

If $y + 1 = -3(y - 3)$, what is the value of y?

A) 1

B) 2

C) 4

D) 9

3

$$b - 3b + 2b - b + 3 - 5 = b$$

What value of b satisfies the equation above?

A) 5

B) 3

C) 0

D) −1

4

If $\frac{3a + 2a + a}{5} = 2$, what is the value of a?

A) $\frac{2}{5}$

B) $\frac{6}{5}$

C) $\frac{5}{3}$

D) $\frac{9}{5}$

5

If $\frac{2b}{a} = \frac{5}{11}$, what is the value of $\frac{a}{b}$? ·

A) $\frac{2}{11}$

B) $\frac{5}{22}$

C) $\frac{11}{2}$

D) $\frac{22}{5}$

6

$$\frac{x}{2} - \frac{2}{5} = \frac{3x}{10}$$

What is the value of x in the above equation?

A) $\frac{3}{5}$

B) $\frac{2}{3}$

C) 2

D) 3

7

What is the value of x in the equation $3xy - 10x = 14$, when $y = 4$?

A) 2

B) 4

C) 7

D) 11

8

If $\frac{3x}{y} = \frac{4}{7}$, what is the value of $\frac{4y}{3x}$?

A) $\frac{3}{7}$

B) $\frac{12}{7}$

C) $\frac{21}{4}$

D) 7

9

$$\frac{\left(\frac{x}{7}\right)}{3} = y$$

In the equation above, what is the value of $\frac{y}{x}$?

A) $\frac{1}{21}$

B) $\frac{1}{10}$

C) $\frac{3}{7}$

D) $\frac{7}{3}$

10

If $x + 8 = 11$, which of the following must be true?

A) $x = -3$

B) $3x = 6$

C) $4x = 12$

D) $11x = 8$

11

If $9m + 24 = 15m$, what is the value of $3m$?

A) 4

B) 9

C) 12

D) 24

12

What valve of c satisfies the equation $5c - 8 = 3c$?

A) 2

B) 4

C) 5

D) 10

Calculator Questions

13

If n satisfies the equation
$4(n + 5) - 38 = 3(n + 5)$, what is the value of
$3(n + 5)$?

A) 9

B) 38

C) 114

D) 152

14

$$\frac{2x}{3} = \frac{x}{5} + \frac{7}{5}$$

What value of x satisfies the above equation?

A) 7

B) 3

C) $\frac{3}{5}$

D) $\frac{1}{3}$

15

If $\frac{5}{8}(x - 3) - 42 = \frac{3}{8}(x - 3)$, what is the value of
$x - 3$?

A) 21

B) 42

C) 102

D) 168

16

In the equation $a = \frac{b}{n}$, n is a constant. If $a = 12$
when $b = m$, what is the value of a when $b = 3m$?

Section 2 –
Lines and Linear Functions

Category 2 – Line Equation in Slope-Intercept Form

Key Points

- The equation of a line in the slope-intercept form is written as $y = mx + b$, where m is the slope of the line, b is the y-intercept of the line, and x and y are the coordinates of any point on the line.

- The slope of a line can be negative or positive. On a graph, a line with a positive slope slant upwards from left to right (Fig. 1). A line with a negative slope slant downwards from left to right (Fig. 2).

- The slope of a line can also be written as $\dfrac{\text{rise}}{\text{run}} = \dfrac{\text{change in } y}{\text{change in } x}$ (Fig. 3).

    - For example, in the equation $y = \dfrac{2}{3}x + 5$, slope $= \dfrac{2}{3} = \dfrac{\text{rise}}{\text{run}}$.

    - If the slope is positive, the change in x and y is to the right and upwards, respectively, (Fig. 1 points A and P) or to the left and downwards, respectively, (Fig. 1 points B and P).

    - If the slope is negative, the change in x and y is to the right and downwards, respectively, (Fig. 2 points B and P) or to the left and upwards, respectively, (Fig. 2 points A and P).

- For any two points on a line, the slope can be determined using the slope formula, $m = \dfrac{y_2 - y_1}{x_2 - x_1}$, where m is the slope and (x_1, y_1) and (x_2, y_2) are the two points.

- The slope between any two points on a line is same.

- The slope of a horizontal line is 0.

- The slope of a vertical line is undefined.

- The y-intercept of a line is the point where the line intersects the y-axis (Fig. 1 and 2). At the y-intercept, $x = 0$. The coordinates of the y-intercept are $(0, y)$. Hence, the value of y is referred as the y-coordinate of the y-intercept.

- The x-intercept of a line is the point where the line intersects the x-axis (Fig. 1 and 2). At the x-intercept, $y = 0$. The coordinates of the x-intercept are $(x, 0)$. Hence, the value of x is referred as the x-coordinate of the x-intercept.

- A line passing through origin is a line passing through the point $(0, 0)$ (Fig. 3).

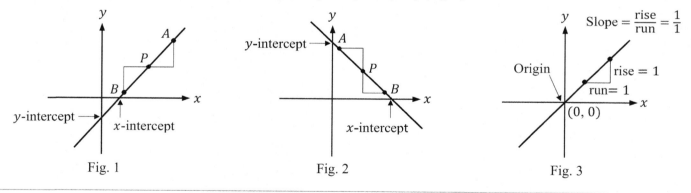

Fig. 1   Fig. 2   Fig. 3

How to Solve

If an equation is given where y is negative or has a constant, then it should be converted to the $y = mx + b$ form before determining the slope. For example, divide equation $-2y = 4x + 10$ by $-2 \rightarrow y = -2x - 5$.

In the slope formula, the results will be same irrespective of whether the two points are entered as $\dfrac{y_2 - y_1}{x_2 - x_1}$ or $\dfrac{y_1 - y_2}{x_1 - x_2}$.

Example 1:

In the xy-plane, a line l passes through the point $(0, 5)$ and has a slope of 2. Which of the following could represent the equation of line l?

A) $y = x + 1$

B) $y = 2x + 5$

C) $y = 2x + 9$

D) $y = 5x + 2$

Step 1: Determine the slope

It is given that the slope of the line is 2. This eliminates answer choices A and D. The slope in answer choice A is 1 and the slope in answer choice D is 5.

Step 2: Determine the y-intercept

The line passes through the point $(0, 5)$. Remember $x = 0$ at the y-intercept. Hence, 5 is the y-intercept of line l. This eliminates answer choice C that has y-intercept $= 9$.

Correct answer choice is **B**.

Example 2:

In the xy-plane, a line n passes through the points $(2, 5)$ and $(4, 7)$. Which of the following could be an equation of line n?

A) $y = x + 1$

B) $y = 2x + 3$

C) $2y = 2x + 6$

D) $2y = 6x + 7$

Step 1: Determine the slope

Set up the slope equation using the points $(2, 5)$ and $(4, 7)$.

$$\frac{y_2 - y_1}{x_2 - x_1} = \frac{7 - 5}{4 - 2} = \frac{2}{2} = 1$$

Note that the answer choices C and D have y with 2 as a constant. Divide the equations by 2. Answer choice C becomes $y = x + 3$ and answer choice D becomes $y = 3x + 3.5$.

This eliminates answer choices B and D. The slope in answer choice B is 2 and the slope in answer choice D is 3.

Step 2: Determine the y-intercept

Plug in the point $(2, 5)$ and slope $= 1$ in the $y = mx + b$ equation. Note that same results will be obtained using the point $(4, 7)$.

$$5 = (1 \times 2) + b$$
$$5 = 2 + b \rightarrow b = 3$$

This eliminates answer choice A that has y-intercept $= 1$.

Correct answer choice is **C**.

Example 3:

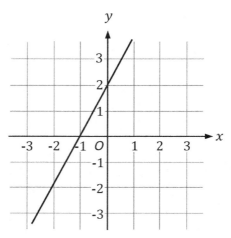

In the xy-plane, the graph of a line is shown above. Which of the following could be an equation of the line?

A) $y = -2x$

B) $y = -x + 2$

C) $y = 2x - 1$

D) $y = 2x + 2$

Step 1: Determine the slope

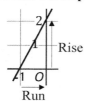

See a portion of the graph in the left figure.

$$\frac{\text{rise}}{\text{run}} = \frac{2}{1} = 2$$

Since the line slants upwards from left to right, the slope of the line is positive. This eliminates answer choices A and B.

Step 2: Determine the y-intercept

The y-intercept can be read from the graph as 2. This eliminates answer choice C.

Correct answer choice is **D**.

Example 4:

In the xy-plane, the slope of line m is $\frac{3}{2}$ and the y-intercept is -6. What is the x-intercept of line m?

A) -3

B) 0

C) 4

D) 6

Step 1: Determine the equation

Plug in slope $= \frac{3}{2}$ and y-intercept $= -6$ in the $y = mx + b$ equation.

$$y = \frac{3}{2}x - 6$$

Step 2: Determine the x-intercept

Since $y = 0$ at the x-intercept, plug in $y = 0$ in the equation and solve for x.

$$0 = \frac{3}{2}x - 6 \;\rightarrow\; \frac{3}{2}x = 6 \;\rightarrow\; 3x = 12 \;\rightarrow\; x = 4$$

Correct answer choice is **C**.

Example 5:

What is the x-coordinate of the x-intercept of a line passing through the points $(4, 4)$ and $(6, 8)$?

Step 1: Determine the x-intercept

When the slope or the y-intercept of a line are not given, the quickest approach is as shown below.

Let the x-intercept of the line $= (x, 0)$. (Remember $y = 0$ at the x-intercept).

Since the slope between any two points on a line is same, set up two slope equations and equate them.

Set up one slope equation using the points $(4, 4)$ and $(6, 8)$. This will give the slope of the line. Set up second slope equation using the points $(x, 0)$ and $(4, 4)$.

$$\frac{8-4}{6-4} = \frac{4-0}{4-x} \rightarrow \frac{4}{2} = \frac{4}{4-x} \rightarrow 2 = \frac{4}{4-x} \rightarrow$$

$$2(4-x) = 4 \rightarrow 8 - 2x = 4 \rightarrow 2x = 4 \rightarrow x = 2$$

Note that same results will be obtained using the points $(x, 0)$ and $(6, 8)$ in the second slope equation.

Correct answer is **2**.

Example 6:

$$y = \frac{1}{2}x + 1$$

The equation of line p in the xy-plane is shown above. If $(2, 2)$ is a point on line p, which of the following could be another point on line p?

A) $(1, 2)$

B) $(2, 4)$

C) $(4, 5)$

D) $(6, 4)$

Step 1: Determine the slope

From the equation, the slope of line p is $\frac{1}{2}$. Slope can also be written as

$$\frac{\text{rise}}{\text{run}} = \frac{1}{2} = \frac{\text{shift in 1 unit of } y}{\text{shift in 2 units of } x}$$

Since the slope is positive, for every 2 units of x from left to right y will move 1 unit upwards or for every 2 units of x from right to left y will move 1 unit downwards.

Step 2: Determine points on the line

Most points in the answer choices are higher than the given point $(2, 2)$. Hence, using $(2, 2)$ as the starting point, determine the next point on the line upwards. See figure on the right.

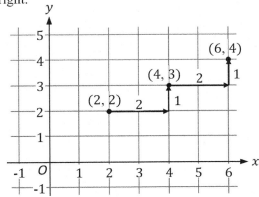

2 units to the right (run) is $2 + 2 = 4$

1 unit upwards (rise) is $2 + 1 = 3$

This gives point $(4, 3)$. This is a not an answer choice.

Using point $(4, 3)$, determine the next point on the line.

2 units to the right (run) is $4 + 2 = 6$

1 unit upwards (rise) is $3 + 1 = 4$

This gives point $(6, 4)$. This is answer choice D.

Correct answer choice is **D**.

(An alternative approach is to plug in the values of x and y from each answer choice in the given equation. Both sides of the equation will be same in the correct answer choice.)

Category 2 – Practice Questions (answers on page 331)

No Calculator Questions

1

A line k, in the xy-plane, passes through the point $(2, 5)$. For every 3 units increase of x from left to right, y increases by 2 units upwards. Which of the following could be an equation of line k?

A) $y = -\frac{2}{3}x + 5$

B) $y = \frac{2}{3}x - \frac{3}{5}$

C) $y = \frac{2}{3}x + \frac{11}{3}$

D) $y = \frac{3}{2}x + 8$

2

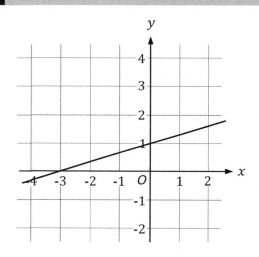

In the xy-plane, the graph of a line is shown above. Which of the following is an equation of the line?

A) $y = \frac{1}{3}x - 1$

B) $y = -x + 1$

C) $3y = -x + 1$

D) $3y = x + 3$

3

In the xy-plane, a line s passes through the points $(-1, 2)$ and $(1, 6)$ and has y-intercept that is twice the slope. Which of the following could be an equation of line s?

A) $y = -2x + 4$

B) $y = 2x + 4$

C) $y = 2x + 6$

D) $y = 3x - 2$

4

$$y = 2x + 4$$

The equation of line l, in the xy-plane, is shown above. If a line p passes through the point $(0, 2)$ and has a slope 3 times that of line l, which of the following could be an equation of line p?

A) $y = 2x + 2$

B) $y = 3x + 4$

C) $y = 6x + 2$

D) $y = 6x + 4$

5

$$y = \frac{2x + 24}{4} - 3$$

What is the x-coordinate of the x-intercept of the line, in the xy-plane, defined by the above equation?

A) -7

B) -6

C) 1

D) 3

If the equation of line q in the xy-plane can be written as $ay = -2ax + ab$, where a and b are constants and $b > 1$, which of the following could be the graph of line q?

A)

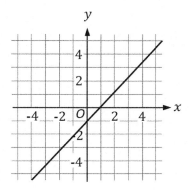

B)

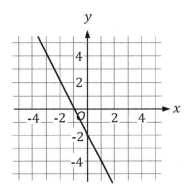

C)

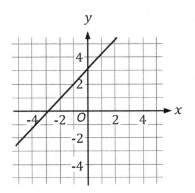

D)

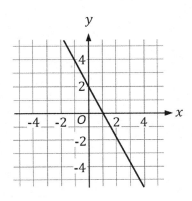

In the xy-plane, a line p passes through the origin and the point $(2, 6)$. Which of the following could represent the equation of line p?

A) $y = 6x$

B) $2y = 6x$

C) $2y = 3x + 1$

D) $2y = 6x + 4$

The y-intercept of line p in the xy-plane is twice the slope. Which of the following could be an equation of line p?

A) $y = 2x + 1$

B) $y = 2x + 2$

C) $2y = 6x + 3$

D) $3y = 3x + 6$

What is the x-coordinate of the x-intercept of a line with the slope of 2 and the y-intercept as -3?

In the xy-plane, a line n has a slope of -3 and passes through the point $(3, -5)$. What is the y-coordinate of the y-intercept of line n?

Category 3 – Line Equation in Standard Form

Key Points

- The equation of a line in the standard form is written as $Ax + By = C$, where A, B, and C are constants and x and y are the coordinates of any point on the line. Constants that appear before x and y are also known as coefficients. A is the coefficient of x and B is the coefficient of y.

    - The slope of a line is $-\dfrac{A}{B}$.

    - The y-coordinate of the y-intercept of a line is $\dfrac{C}{B}$.

- The standard form equation can be converted to the slope-intercept form equation by rearranging the equation. For example, $8x + 2y = 6 \rightarrow 2y = -8x + 6 \rightarrow y = -4x + 3$.

How to Solve

To determine the slope or the y-coordinate of the y-intercept of a line from the standard form equation, remember to include the correct plus/minus operator. For example, in the equation $x - 2y = -5$, $A = 1$, $B = -2$, and $C = -5$. Note that when $B = 1$, the y-coordinate of the y-intercept is the value of C.

The x-coordinate of the x-intercept can be determined by plugging in $y = 0$ in the equation (remember $y = 0$ at the x-intercept).

Example 1:

$$4x - 8y = 6$$

An equation of a line, in the xy-plane, is given above. Which of the following is the y-coordinate of the y-intercept of the line?

A) -6

B) $-\dfrac{3}{4}$

C) $\dfrac{4}{3}$

D) 6

Step 1: Determine the y-intercept

$$\frac{C}{B} = \frac{6}{-8} = -\frac{3}{4}$$

Correct answer choice is **B**.

Example 2:

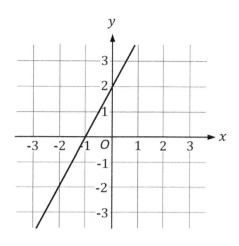

In the xy-plane, which of the following could be an equation of the graph above?

A) $-4x + 2y = 4$

B) $-2x + y = 4$

C) $x + 2y = 4$

D) $4x + 2y = 2$

Step 1: Determine the slope from the graph

Since the line slants upwards from left to right, the slope of the line is positive.

$$\frac{\text{rise}}{\text{run}} = \frac{2}{1} = 2$$

Since the equations in the answer choices are given in the standard form, look for the equation where $-\frac{A}{B} = 2$.

This eliminates answer choices C and D. If unsure, calculate $-\frac{A}{B}$ for each answer choice as shown below.

Answer choice A: $-\frac{A}{B} = -\frac{-4}{2} = 2$.

Answer choice B: $-\frac{A}{B} = -\frac{-2}{1} = 2$.

Answer choice C: $-\frac{A}{B} = -\frac{1}{2}$.

Answer choice D: $-\frac{A}{B} = -\frac{4}{2} = -2$.

(Note that when both A and B are negative or both are positive than the slope will be negative and when one of them is negative than the slope will be positive.)

Step 2: Determine the y-intercept

The y-intercept can be read from the graph as 2. This eliminates answer choice B that has y-intercept $= 4$.

See calculation below.

Answer choice A: $\frac{C}{B} = \frac{4}{2} = 2$.

Answer choice B: $\frac{C}{B} = \frac{4}{1} = 4$.

Correct answer choice is **A**.

Category 3 – Practice Questions (answers on page 332)

No Calculator Questions

1

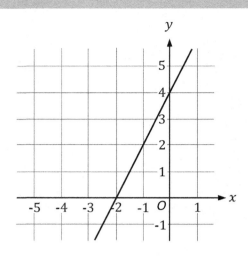

In the xy-plane, which of the following is an equation of the above graph?

A) $6x - 3y = -12$

B) $3x - 6y = -12$

C) $6x + 3y = 12$

D) $2x + 5y = 6$

2

$$6x - 2y = -5$$

What is the y-coordinate of the y-intercept of a line in the xy-plane, defined by the above equation?

A) $\dfrac{1}{2}$

B) $\dfrac{5}{2}$

C) 2

D) 5

3

$$2x + 3y = 4c$$

An equation of a line, in the xy-plane, is shown above, where c is a constant. What are the coordinates at which the line crosses the x-axis?

A) $(-c, 0)$

B) $(c, 0)$

C) $(2c, 0)$

D) $(4c, 0)$

4

A line t, in the xy-plane, has a slope of $-\dfrac{3}{2}$ and intersects the x-axis at 4. Which of the following is an equation of line t?

A) $3x - 2y = 12$

B) $3x + 2y = 8$

C) $2x + 3y = 8$

D) $3x + 2y = 12$

5

$$x - ay = a$$

Equation of a line r, in the xy-plane, is shown above. If line r passes through the point $(4, 1)$, which of the following can be the value of a, where a is a constant in the above equation?

A) 1

B) 2

C) 4

D) 6

Category 4 – Points on a Line with Unknown Coordinates

Key Points

- The slope of any two points on a line is same.

- For any two points on a line, the slope can be determined using the slope formula, $m = \frac{y_2 - y_1}{x_2 - x_1}$, where m is the slope and (x_1, y_1) and (x_2, y_2) are the two points.

- Any three points on a line can be equated in two slope equations. For example, $\frac{y_2 - y_1}{x_2 - x_1} = \frac{y_3 - y_2}{x_3 - x_2}$, where (x_1, y_1), (x_2, y_2), and (x_3, y_3) are the three points.

    - The results will be same irrespective of which two points are used to set up the slope equations. For example, $\frac{y_2 - y_1}{x_2 - x_1} = \frac{y_3 - y_2}{x_3 - x_2}$ is same as $\frac{y_2 - y_1}{x_2 - x_1} = \frac{y_3 - y_1}{x_3 - x_1}$.

- The coordinates of the x-intercept are $(x, 0)$ and the coordinates of the y-intercept are $(0, y)$.

How to Solve

A question may be given where one or more coordinates of one or more points on a line are unknown. The unknown coordinates can be determined by setting up one or two slope equations, depending on the question.

If the slope is given or can be determined, then one slope equation can be set up and equated to the slope.

If the slope is not given, then two slope equations may be required to solve for the missing coordinate(s).

Example 1:

In the xy-plane, a line passes through the points $(0, b)$, $(3, 2b)$, and $(6, 9)$. What is the value of b?

A) 0

B) 3

C) 6

D) 9

Step 1: Set up two slope equations

Since the slope is not given set up two slope equations.

Set up the slope equation using the points $(0, b)$ and $(3, 2b)$.

$$\frac{2b - b}{3 - 0}$$

Set up the slope equation using the points $(3, 2b)$ and $(6, 9)$.

$$\frac{9 - 2b}{6 - 3}$$

Note that same results will be obtained by setting up the slope equation using the points $(0, b)$ and $(6, 9)$.

Step 2: Equate the two equations and solve

$$\frac{2b - b}{3 - 0} = \frac{9 - 2b}{6 - 3} \rightarrow \frac{b}{3} = \frac{9 - 2b}{3} \rightarrow$$
$$b = 9 - 2b \rightarrow 3b = 9 \rightarrow b = 3$$

Correct answer choice is **B**.

Category 4 – Practice Questions (answers on page 332)

No Calculator Questions

1

Line l, in the xy-plane, passes through the points $(2, 2p)$ and $(5, p - 1)$. If the slope of line l is -2, what is the value of $p - 1$?

A) 4

B) 5

C) 7

D) 10

2

In the xy-plane, coordinates $(1, 4)$, $(5, m)$, and $(n, 7)$ lie on a line p. If the slope of line p is 3, what is the value of $m + n$?

A) 12

B) 14

C) 17

D) 18

3

In the xy-plane, a line passes through the points $(1, 3)$, $(4, a)$, and $(7, a + b)$. What is the value of $a - b$?

A) -1

B) 0

C) 3

D) 11

Calculator Questions

4

x	1	s	5
y	2	6	10

A line, in the xy-plane, passes through the (x, y) coordinates shown in the table above. What is the value of s?

A) 2

B) 3

C) 5

D) 8

5

A line l has a slope of 3 and passes through the origin and the point $(3, 3a)$, in the xy-plane. Which of the following is the point $(3, 3a)$?

A) $(1, 3)$

B) $(3, 1)$

C) $(3, 3)$

D) $(3, 9)$

6

In the xy-plane, a line with a slope of $-\frac{1}{2}$ passes through the points $(0, 2)$ and $(x, -2)$. What is the value of x?

Category 5 – Slope of Parallel Lines

Key Points

- Two non-vertical parallel lines have the same slope but different y-intercepts. See figure below of two parallel lines a and b. Vertical parallel lines are excluded since the slope of vertical lines is undefined.

- For any two points on a line, the slope can be determined using the slope formula, $m = \frac{y_2 - y_1}{x_2 - x_1}$, where m is the slope and (x_1, y_1) and (x_2, y_2) are the two points.

- The coordinates of the x-intercept are $(x, 0)$ and the coordinates of the y-intercept are $(0, y)$.

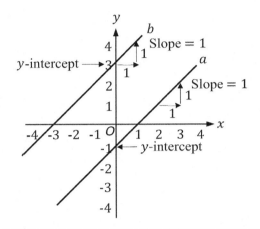

How to Solve

If the slope of one parallel line is given, then the slope of another parallel line will be same.

Example 1:

In the xy-plane, lines r and s are parallel lines. Line r passes through the points $(2, 3)$ and $(3, 5)$. If the point $(1, 9)$ lies on line s, which of the following is an equation of line s?

A) $y = x + 2$

B) $y = 2x + 1$

C) $y = 2x + 7$

D) $y = 4x + 5$

Step 1: Determine the slope

Set up the slope equation for line r using the points $(2, 3)$ and $(3, 5)$.

$$\frac{5 - 3}{3 - 2} = \frac{2}{1} = 2$$

Since line s is parallel to line r, the slope of line $s = 2$. This eliminates answer choices A and D.

Step 2: Determine the y-intercept of line s

Plug in the given point $(1, 9)$ and slope $= 2$ in the $y = mx + b$ equation.

$$9 = (2 \times 1) + b$$
$$9 = 2 + b \ \rightarrow \ b = 7$$

This eliminates answer choice B.

Correct answer choice is **C**.

Category 5 – Practice Questions (answers on page 333)

No Calculator Questions

1

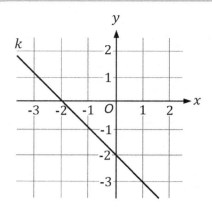

In the xy-plane, lines k and l are parallel lines. The graph of line k is shown above. If line l (not shown) passes through the point $(6, -4)$, which of the following is an equation of line l?

A) $y = -x - 2$

B) $y = -x + 2$

C) $y = x - 2$

D) $y = 3x + 2$

2

$$6x + 3y = 5$$

An equation of line k, in the xy-plane, is shown above. Which of the following could be an equation of a line p parallel to line k?

A) $-3x + 2y = 1$

B) $8x - 4y = 2$

C) $3x + 2y = 1$

D) $8x + 4y = 2$

3

In the xy-plane, line s has a slope of 4. If line t is parallel to line s and passes through the point $(3, 5)$, what are the coordinates of the y-intercept of line t?

A) $(0, -12)$

B) $(0, -7)$

C) $(0, 3)$

D) $(4, 5)$

Calculator Questions

4

Line l, in the xy-plane, passes through the points $(c, 3)$ and $(6, 5)$. Line p is parallel to line l and passes through the points $(c, 1)$ and $(8, 4)$. Which of the following is the value of c?

A) 2

B) 4

C) 5

D) 8

5

In the xy-plane, line p passes through the points $(-2, 3)$ and $(0, 1)$. Line q is parallel to line p and passes through the point $(1, 2)$. Which of the following is the x-coordinate of the x-intercept of line q?

A) -2

B) 0

C) 3

D) 5

Category 6 – Slope of Perpendicular Lines

Key Points

- Two perpendicular lines have negative reciprocal slope. See figure below of two perpendicular lines a and b.
- For any two points on a line, the slope can be determined using the slope formula, $m = \frac{y_2 - y_1}{x_2 - x_1}$, where m is the slope and (x_1, y_1) and (x_2, y_2) are the two points.
- The coordinates of the x-intercept are $(x, 0)$ and the coordinates of the y-intercept are $(0, y)$.

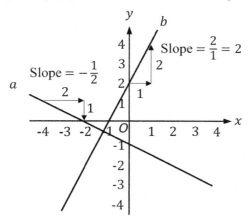

How to Solve

If the slope of a line is given, then the slope of a perpendicular line will be the negative reciprocal.

Example 1:

In the xy-plane, line p passes through the points $(2, 3)$ and $(4, 6)$. Line q is perpendicular to line p and intersects the x-axis at -3. Which of the following could be an equation of line q?

A) $y = -\frac{2}{3}x - 5$

B) $y = -\frac{2}{3}x - 2$

C) $y = \frac{3}{2}x + 1$

D) $y = 3x + 2$

Step 1: Determine the slope

Set up the slope equation for line p using the points $(2, 3)$ and $(4, 6)$.

$$\frac{y_2 - y_1}{x_2 - x_1} = \frac{6 - 3}{4 - 2} = \frac{3}{2}$$

Since line q is perpendicular to line p, the slope of line $q = -\frac{2}{3}$. This eliminates answer choices C and D.

Step 2: Determine the y-intercept of line q

Since line q intersects the x-axis at -3, point $(-3, 0)$ is the x-intercept of the line.

Plug in the point $(-3, 0)$ and slope $= -\frac{2}{3}$ in the $y = mx + b$ equation.

$$0 = \left(-\frac{2}{3} \times -3\right) + b \;\rightarrow\; 0 = 2 + b \;\rightarrow\; b = -2$$

This eliminates answer choice A.

Correct answer choice is **B**.

Category 6 – Practice Questions (answers on pages 333-334)

No Calculator Questions

1

A line p, in the xy-plane, has a slope of 3. If line s is perpendicular to line p and passes through the point $(0, -4)$, which of the following is an equation of line s?

A) $y = -\frac{1}{3}x - 4$

B) $y = -\frac{2}{3}x - 1$

C) $y = -\frac{1}{3}x + 4$

D) $y = \frac{2}{3}x + 1$

2

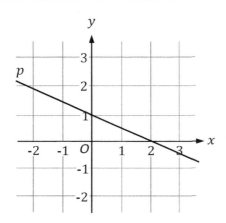

In the xy-plane, the partial graph of line p is shown above. Line t (not shown) is perpendicular to line p and passes through the point $(1, 4)$. Which of the following is the x-coordinate of the x-intercept of line t?

A) -2

B) -1

C) 1

D) 2

3

The points $(-1, 3)$ and $(3, 1)$ are the end points of a line segment l, in the xy-plane. Which of the following could be an equation of a perpendicular line h passing through the line segment l?

A) $y = -\frac{1}{2}x + 2$

B) $y = \frac{1}{2}x + 5$

C) $y = 2x - 2$

D) $y = 2x + 7$

Calculator Questions

4

$$9y + 3x = 3$$

An equation of line s is shown above. If s and t are perpendicular lines, in the xy-plane, and line t passes through the point $(-2, 5)$, which of the following are the coordinates of the y-intercept of line t?

A) $(0, -11)$

B) $(0, -3)$

C) $(0, 9)$

D) $(0, 11)$

5

In the xy-plane, a line m passes through the points $(3, 7)$ and $(4, 9)$. If line n is perpendicular to line m and passes through the origin, which of the following could be an equation of line n?

A) $y = -\frac{1}{2}x - 3$

B) $y = -x + 3$

C) $2y = -x$

D) $4y = x$

Category 7 – Linear Functions

Key Points

- In the xy-plane, each (x, y) pair on a line is a point graphed by a linear function.
- A linear function is written as $f(x) = mx + b$.
  - $f(x)$ is the output value of a function for an input value of x. For example, if $x = 2$, then $f(2) = (m \times 2) + b = $ output value.
  - For any (x, y) point on a line, $f(x) = mx + b$ is same as $y = mx + b$, where $f(x)$ is the value of y.
- A function can be given any name. For example, $g(x)$ or $h(x)$ or $t(x)$.
- For any two points on the graph of a linear function, the slope can be determined using the slope formula,
  $m = \frac{y_2 - y_1}{x_2 - x_1}$, where m is the slope and (x_1, y_1) and (x_2, y_2) are the two points.
- Any three points on a line can be equated in two slope equations. For example, $\frac{y_2 - y_1}{x_2 - x_1} = \frac{y_3 - y_2}{x_3 - x_2}$, where (x_1, y_1), (x_2, y_2), and (x_3, y_3) are the three points.
- The coordinates of the x-intercept are $(x, 0)$ and the coordinates of the y-intercept are $(0, y)$.

How to Solve

Questions on linear functions are solved like the questions on lines.

Remember $y = f(x)$ on the graph of a linear function f. For example, $f(4)$ is the value of y when $x = 4$.

Example 1:

In the xy-plane, the points $(-1, -3)$ and $(2, 6)$ lie on the graph of a linear function f. Which of the following could define the function f?

A) $f(x) = 3x$

B) $f(x) = 2x + 1$

C) $f(x) = 3x + 3$

D) $f(x) = 6x + 4$

Step 1: Determine the slope

Set up the slope equation using the points $(-1, -3)$ and $(2, 6)$.

$$\frac{6 - (-3)}{2 - (-1)} = \frac{9}{3} = 3$$

This eliminates answer choices B and D.

Step 2: Determine the y-intercept

Plug in the point $(2, 6)$ and slope $= 3$ in the $y = mx + b$ equation.

$$6 = (3 \times 2) + b$$
$$6 = 6 + b \rightarrow b = 6 - 6 = 0$$

This eliminates answer choice C.

Note that same results will be obtained by using the point $(-1, -3)$.

Correct answer choice is **A**.

Example 2:

x	$g(x)$
0	-3
2	-7
4	-11
6	-15

Question 1

The above table shows several values of x and the corresponding values of $g(x)$ for the linear function g, where $y = g(x)$. Which of the following is an equation of the function $g(x)$?

A) $g(x) = -2x - 11$

B) $g(x) = -2x - 3$

C) $g(x) = x - 1$

D) $g(x) = 2x + 3$

Step 1: Determine the slope

The points given in the table are some of the points on a line graphed by the linear function g. For any value of x in the table, $g(x)$ is the corresponding y value. Hence, the points from the table are $(0, -3)$, $(2, -7)$, $(4, -11)$, and $(6, -15)$.

Set up the slope equation using any two points. Below slope equation is set up using the points $(2, -7)$ and $(6, -15)$.

$$\frac{-15 - (-7)}{6 - 2} = \frac{-8}{4} = -2$$

This eliminates answer choices C and D.

Step 2: Determine the y-intercept

The table contains a point $(0, -3)$. Remember $x = 0$ at the y-intercept. Hence, -3 is the y-intercept of the function g.

This eliminates answer choice A.

Correct answer choice is **B**.

Question 2

The table above shows several values of x and the corresponding values of $g(x)$ for the linear function g, where $y = g(x)$. What is the value of $g(-9)$?

Step 1: Set up slope equations

The question asks for the value of y when $x = -9$. This point is not given in the table.

Let this point be $(-9, y)$.

Set up two slope equations and equate them. Below equations are set up using the points $(2, -7)$ and $(6, -15)$ and the points $(2, -7)$ and $(-9, y)$.

$$\frac{-15 - (-7)}{6 - 2} = \frac{y - (-7)}{-9 - 2} \rightarrow \frac{-8}{4} = \frac{y + 7}{-11} \rightarrow -2 = \frac{y + 7}{-11} \rightarrow$$

$$-2 \times -11 = y + 7 \rightarrow 22 = y + 7 \rightarrow y = 22 - 7 = 15$$

Hence, $g(-9) = 15$.

Correct answer is **15**.

Category 7 – Practice Questions (answers on page 334)

No Calculator Questions

1

In the xy-plane, the points $(-2, -5)$ and $(2, 3)$ lie on the graph of a linear function f. Which of the following could define the function f?

A) $f(x) = -x - 1$

B) $f(x) = 2x - 1$

C) $f(x) = 2x + 11$

D) $f(x) = 3x + 1$

2

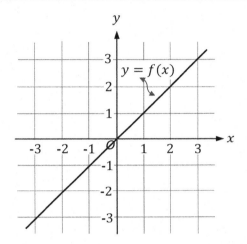

In the xy-plane, the graph of a linear function f, where $y = f(x)$, is shown above. Which of the following defines the graph of the function f?

A) $f(x) = -x + 1$

B) $f(x) = -x$

C) $f(x) = x$

D) $f(x) = 1$

3

The graph of $y = g(x)$, in the xy-plane, passes through the point $(1, 4)$ and has a slope of 3. Which of the following is the value of $g(-2)$?

A) -5

B) -1

C) 2

D) 4

4

In the xy-plane, the points $(-2, 6)$ and $(3, -4)$ lie on the graph of a linear function f, where $y = f(x)$. What is the value of $f(1)$?

A) -1

B) 0

C) 1

D) 4

5

x	$g(x)$
2	6
4	9
6	12

The table above shows several values of x and the corresponding values of $g(x)$ for a linear function g. In the xy-plane, which of the following are the coordinates of the y-intercept of the graph of $y = g(x)$?

A) $(-2, -6)$

B) $(0, -1)$

C) $(0, 0)$

D) $(0, 3)$

Category 8 – Graph Transformations of Linear Functions

Key Points

- Graph transformations could be horizontal (left or right) or vertical (up or down) shifts, or reflection across the x-axis or y-axis. Horizontal and vertical shifts are also known as translations.

- See the horizontal and vertical translation rules below for a line defined by the slope-intercept equation $y = x + 1$, where c is the units by which a horizontal or a vertical translation occurs. Similar rules apply for a line graphed by a linear function $f(x) = x + 1$.

  - Left horizontal shift by c units is $y = (x + c) + 1$.

    - This will shift the x-intercept of the line to the left by c units.

  - Right horizontal shift by c units is $y = (x - c) + 1$.

    - This will shift the x-intercept of the line to the right by c units.

  - Upwards vertical shift by c units is $y = x + 1 + c$.

    - This will shift the y-intercept of the line up by c units.

  - Downwards vertical shift by c units is $y = x + 1 - c$.

    - This will shift the y-intercept of the line down by c units.

- See the reflection rules below for a line defined by the slope-intercept equation $y = x + 1$. Similar transformation rules apply for a line graphed by a linear function $f(x) = x + 1$.

  - Reflection across the x-axis does not change the x values, but the y values change to the opposite sign. $y = x + 1$ will become $-y = x + 1 \rightarrow y = -(x + 1)$.

  - Reflection across the y-axis does not change the y values, but the x values change to the opposite sign. $y = x + 1$ will become $y = -x + 1$.

How to Solve

See example below of line a reflected across the x-axis and the y-axis. Dashed line is the reflected line.

- Reflection across the x-axis is shown in Fig. 1. The x-coordinates of the points on the reflected line remain the same but the y-coordinates have the reverse plus/minus sign. For example, $(2, 2) \rightarrow (2, -2)$ and $(-4, -1) \rightarrow (-4, 1)$.

- Reflection across the y-axis is shown in Fig. 2. The y-coordinates of the points on the reflected line remain the same but the x-coordinates have the reverse plus/minus sign. For example, $(2, 2) \rightarrow (-2, 2)$ and $(-4, -1) \rightarrow (4, -1)$.

Equation of line a:

$$y = \frac{1}{2}x + 1$$

Equation of line a reflected across the x-axis:

$$y = -\left(\frac{1}{2}x + 1\right)$$

Equation of line a reflected across the y-axis:

$$y = -\frac{1}{2}x + 1$$

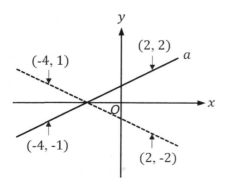

Fig. 1 Reflection of line a across x-axis

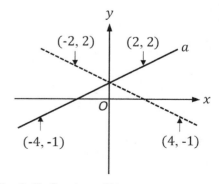

Fig. 2 Reflection of line a across y-axis

Example 1:

$$f(x) = 3x + 5$$

An equation of a linear function f in the xy-plane is given above. Which of the following equations represents the shift of the graph of the function f by 4 units to the left?

A) $f(x) = 3x + 9$

B) $f(x) = 3x + 1$

C) $f(x) = 3(x - 4) + 5$

D) $f(x) = 3(x + 4) + 5$

Step 1: Determine the transformation rule

Since the shift is 4 units to the left, the value of x will become $(x + 4)$.

Note the significance of parentheses. 4 is added within the parentheses such that the equation becomes $f(x) = 3(x + 4) + 5$ not $f(x) = 3x + 4 + 5 = 3x + 9$.

Correct answer choice is **D**.

Example 2:

$$y = 2x - 3$$

In the xy-plane, the graph of the linear equation shown above is reflected across the x-axis. Which of the following could represent the reflected graph?

A)

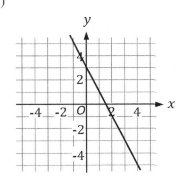

B)

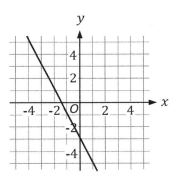

C)

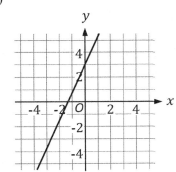

D)

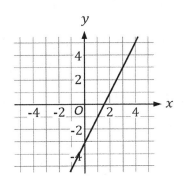

Step 1: Determine the transformation rule

The reflection across the x-axis will result in the following transformation.

$$y = -(2x - 3) \rightarrow y = -2x + 3$$

The transformed equation has negative slope and positive y-intercept. This eliminates answer choices B, C, and D. Answer choices C and D have positive slope. Answer choice B has negative y-intercept.

Correct answer choice is **A**.

Category 8 – Practice Questions (answers on page 334)

No Calculator Questions

Calculator Questions

1

$$f(x) = 2x - 4$$

An equation of a linear function f, in the xy-plane, is given above. Which of the following equations represents the shift of the graph of function f by 3 units to the left and 2 units upwards?

A) $f(x) = 2(x - 1) + 4$

B) $f(x) = 2(x + 1) - 4$

C) $f(x) = 2(x + 3) - 2$

D) $f(x) = 2(x + 3) + 2$

2

$$y = 4x + 1$$

Which of the following equations represents the reflection of the graph of the above equation across the x-axis, in the xy-plane?

A) $y = -4x - 1$

B) $y = -4x + 1$

C) $y = 4x - 1$

D) $y = 4x + 1$

3

In the xy-plane, the function g graphs a line. The y-intercept of the graph of $y = g(x)$ is $(0, -5)$. What is the y-intercept of the graph of $y = g(x) + 3$?

A) $(0, -8)$

B) $(0, -2)$

C) $(0, 2)$

D) $(0, 3)$

4

$$f(x) = x + 2$$

In the xy-plane, which of the following graphs is the reflection of the above function across the y-axis?

A)

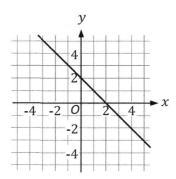

B)

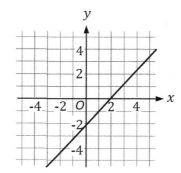

C)

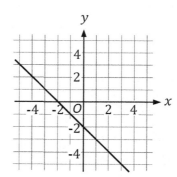

D)

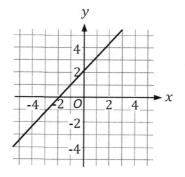

No Calculator Questions

1

In the xy-plane, line k has a slope of 1. If line l is parallel to line k, which of the following could be an equation of line l?

A) $4x - 4y = 12$

B) $8x - 4y = 12$

C) $4x + 4y = 12$

D) $6x + 3y = 12$

2

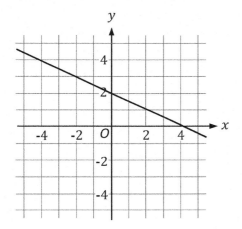

Which of the following could be an equation of the above graph, in the xy-plane?

A) $y = -\frac{1}{2}x - 2$

B) $y = -\frac{1}{2}x + 2$

C) $y = \frac{1}{2}x - 2$

D) $y = \frac{1}{2}x + 2$

3

$$f(x) = 5x - 2$$

If the equation of the above linear function f is transformed to $f(x) = 5(x - 2) + 2$, in the xy-plane, which of the following statements is true?

A) The graph shifts 2 units downwards after the transformation.

B) The graph shifts 2 units to the right and 2 units downwards after the transformation.

C) The graph shifts 2 units to the left and 2 units upwards after the transformation.

D) The graph shifts 2 units to the right and 4 units upwards after the transformation.

4

Which of the following is an equation of a line p, in the xy-plane, passing through the points $(0, -2)$ and $(-2, -5)$?

A) $y = -\frac{3}{2}x - 2$

B) $y = -\frac{3}{2}x + 2$

C) $2y = 3x - 4$

D) $2y = 3x + 4$

5

In the xy-plane, the y-coordinate of the y-intercept of a line s is -6. If $ax - by = 4$ is an equation of line s, where a and b are constants, what is the value of b?

A) $-\frac{1}{2}$

B) $-\frac{2}{3}$

C) $\frac{2}{3}$

D) 4

If the slope of a line p is undefined, which of the following is an equation of line p?

A) $x = 3$

B) $x = -y$

C) $x = y$

D) $y = 2$

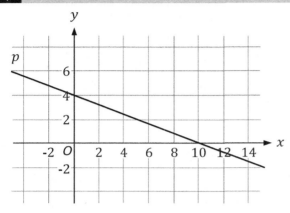

The graph of line p, in the xy-plane, is shown above. Which of the following is an equation of line p?

A) $-x + 5y = 5$

B) $x + 5y = 5$

C) $2x - 5y = 20$

D) $2x + 5y = 20$

x	$f(x)$
-1	-4
-2	-2
-3	0

The table above shows selected values for the linear graph of $y = f(x)$, in the xy-plane. What is the value of $f(-6)$?

A) -8

B) -4

C) 6

D) 10

$$g(x) = 3x + 5$$

The equation for the graph of a linear function $y = g(x)$, in the xy-plane, is given above. If the graph of a linear function $y = f(x)$ is parallel to the graph of function g and passes through the point $(3, 3)$, what is the value of $f(1)$?

A) -6

B) -3

C) 2

D) 8

Two perpendicular lines m and n intersect at the point $(2, 4)$. Line m passes through the origin and line n intersects the x-axis at a point P. Which of the following is the x-coordinate of point P?

A) 2

B) 4

C) 8

D) 10

x	$h(x)$
0	$2k$
3	$3k$
6	$4k$
9	$5k$

For the linear function h, the table above gives several values of x and the corresponding values of $h(x)$, where k is a constant and $y = h(x)$. Which of the following equation could define the function h?

A) $h(x) = \frac{k}{3}x + k$

B) $h(x) = \frac{k}{3}x + 2k$

C) $h(x) = x - k$

D) $h(x) = x + 1$

$$4x + 2y + 5 = 0$$

An equation of line s, in the xy-plane, is given above. If line t is perpendicular to line s and passes through the point $(4, 5)$, what are the x- and y-intercepts of line t?

A) x-intercept is -6 and y-intercept is 3

B) x-intercept is 6 and y-intercept is 3

C) x-intercept is 4 and y-intercept is 2

D) x-intercept is 4 and y-intercept is -4

Number of classes	Monthly cost ($)
4	44.95
8	84.95
12	124.95

A gym charges each member a monthly flat fee, in dollars, for attending yoga classes plus a fixed dollar charge for each yoga class attended. The table above shows the linear relationship between the number of yoga classes attended in a month and the total monthly cost, in dollars. Which of the following function can be used to determine the total monthly cost $f(x)$, in dollars, for attending x yoga classes in a month?

A) $f(x) = 4x$

B) $f(x) = x + 4$

C) $f(x) = 10x + 4.95$

D) $f(x) = 20x + 10.95$

In the xy-plane, the point $(-1, -1)$ lies on the graph of line l defined by $y = 2x + 1$. Which of the following points may also be on the graph of line l?

A) $(-1, 0)$

B) $(0, -1)$

C) $(0, 2)$

D) $(1, 3)$

Calculator Questions

The graph of line l, in the xy-plane, has a slope of $\frac{3}{5}$. If line p is perpendicular to line l and passes through the point $(6, 5)$, which of the following could be an equation of line p?

A) $y = -\frac{3}{5}x - 15$

B) $y = -\frac{5}{3}x + 15$

C) $y = -\frac{5}{3}x + 20$

D) $y = \frac{3}{5}x + 20$

$$2x + 4y = 11$$

The equation of line p, in the xy-plane, is shown above. Line r is perpendicular to line p and is formed by joining two endpoints $M\ (a, b)$ and $N\ (c, d)$. Which of the following could be the coordinates of the points M and N?

A) $(1, -2)$ and $(3, -4)$

B) $(1, 2)$ and $(2, -4)$

C) $(1, 2)$ and $(2, 8)$

D) $(1, 2)$ and $(4, 8)$

$$2y = 5x - 15$$

In the xy-plane, the equation of a line is given above. What is the x-coordinate of the x-intercept of the line?

A) -3

B) 0

C) 3

D) 5

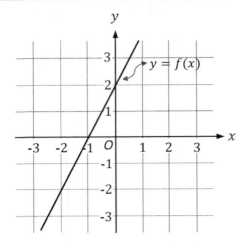

The graph of a linear function $y = f(x)$, in the xy-plane, is shown above. If the graph of $y = g(x)$ (not shown) is perpendicular to the graph of $f(x)$ and passes through the origin, what is the value of $g(4)$?

A) -4

B) -2

C) 1

D) 2

$$f(x) = 3x + 2$$

Equation of a linear function f is given above. Which of the following equations represents the shift of the graph of function f by 3 units to the left and 3 units downwards?

A) $f(x) = 3(x - 3) + 1$

B) $f(x) = 3(x - 3) - 1$

C) $f(x) = 3(x + 3) - 1$

D) $f(x) = 3(x + 3) + 1$

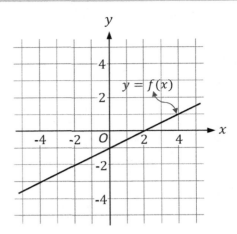

The graph of a linear function $y = f(x)$, in the xy-plane, is shown above. Which of the following equations could be the reflection of the graph of $f(x)$ across the y-axis?

A) $f(x) = -\frac{1}{2}x - 1$

B) $f(x) = -\frac{1}{2}x + 1$

C) $f(x) = \frac{1}{2}x - 1$

D) $f(x) = \frac{1}{2}x + 1$

x	1	4	7	a
$h(x)$	3	b	9	10

The table above shows several values of x and the corresponding values of $h(x)$, for a linear function h. What is the value of $a + b$?

The slope of a line p is $= -\frac{1}{2}$. If a line l is perpendicular to line p and passes through the points $(-2, -2)$ and $(2, k)$, what is the value of k?

Section 3 –
System of Linear Equations and Inequalities

Category 9 – System of Linear Equations and Number of Solutions

Key Points

- Two or more equations of a straight line comprise a system of linear equations.
- A system of equations may have no (zero) solution, exactly one solution, or infinitely many solutions.
  - A system has no solution when the lines of the equations do not intersect (parallel lines that have same slope).
  - A system has exactly one solution when the lines of the equations intersect at exactly one point (x, y).
  - A system has infinitely many solutions when the lines of the equations are the same lines.
- When a system of equations is compared in the standard form $Ax + By = C$, where A, B, and C are constants, the following rules apply for two equations $a_1 x + b_1 y = c_1$ and $a_2 x + b_2 y = c_2$.
  - If $\frac{a_1}{a_2}$, $\frac{b_1}{b_2}$, and $\frac{c_1}{c_2}$ are same, then the system has infinitely many solutions.
  - If $\frac{a_1}{a_2}$ and $\frac{b_1}{b_2}$ are same but $\frac{c_1}{c_2}$ is different, then the system has no solution.
  - If $\frac{a_1}{a_2}$ and $\frac{b_1}{b_2}$ are different, then the system has one solution. The ratio of c does not matter.

How to Solve

Determine the ratios and compare them. Note that the results will be same irrespective of whether the ratios are set up as $\frac{a_1}{a_2}, \frac{b_1}{b_2}, \frac{c_1}{c_2}$ or $\frac{a_2}{a_1}, \frac{b_2}{b_1}, \frac{c_2}{c_1}$. However, $\frac{a_1}{a_2}, \frac{b_2}{b_1}, \frac{c_1}{c_2}$ is incorrect. The numerator and the denominator must belong to the same equation.

If the equations are given in the slope-intercept form, rearrange them in the standard form.

If x or y do not contain a number constant, then the implicit value of the constant is 1. For example, in the equation $3x + y = 9$, $b = 1$.

Example 1:

$$2x + 5y = 3$$
$$4x + 10y = 4$$

For the system of equations given above, how many solutions exist?

A) Zero

B) Exactly one

C) Exactly two

D) Infinitely many

Step 1: Evaluate the ratios

$a_1 = 2.$ $b_1 = 5.$ $c_1 = 3.$

$a_2 = 4.$ $b_2 = 10.$ $c_2 = 4.$

$$\frac{a_1}{a_2} = \frac{2}{4} = \frac{1}{2}$$

$$\frac{b_1}{b_2} = \frac{5}{10} = \frac{1}{2}$$

$$\frac{c_1}{c_2} = \frac{3}{4}$$

Ratios of $\frac{a_1}{a_2}$ and $\frac{b_1}{b_2}$ are same but different than the ratio of $\frac{c_1}{c_2}$. This implies that the system of equations is for parallel lines and has no solution.

Correct answer choice is **A**.

Example 2:

$$3x + 2y = 6$$
$$\frac{1}{2}x + \frac{1}{3}y = 1$$

How many solutions does the above system of equations have?

A)   Zero

B)   Exactly one

C)   Exactly two

D)   Infinitely many

Step 1: Evaluate the ratios

$a_1 = 3$. $b_1 = 2$. $c_1 = 6$.

$a_2 = \frac{1}{2}$. $b_2 = \frac{1}{3}$. $c_2 = 1$.

$$\frac{a_1}{a_2} = \left(3 \div \frac{1}{2}\right) = 3 \times 2 = 6$$
$$\frac{b_1}{b_2} = \left(2 \div \frac{1}{3}\right) = 2 \times 3 = 6$$
$$\frac{c_1}{c_2} = \frac{6}{1} = 6$$

Ratios of $\frac{a_1}{a_2}$, $\frac{b_1}{b_2}$, and $\frac{c_1}{c_2}$ are same. This implies that the system of equations is for the same line and has infinitely many solutions.

Correct answer choice is **D**.

Category 9 – Practice Questions (answers on page 337)

No Calculator Questions

1

$$2x - 3y = -4$$
$$-6x + 9y = 12$$

How many solutions exist for the above system of equations?

A) Zero

B) Exactly one

C) Exactly two

D) Infinitely many

2

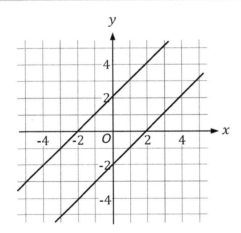

In the xy-plane, the graph of two lines in a system of equations is shown above. How many solutions does the system have?

A) Zero

B) Exactly one

C) Exactly two

D) Infinitely many

3

$$y = 3x - 2$$
$$-y = 3x + 1$$

How many solutions does the above system of equations have?

A) Zero

B) Exactly one

C) Exactly two

D) Infinitely many

Calculator Questions

4

$$4x + 3y = 3$$
$$\frac{1}{3}x + \frac{1}{4}y = \frac{1}{2}$$

For the system of equations above, how many solutions exist?

A) Zero

B) Exactly one

C) Exactly two

D) Infinitely many

5

$$\frac{x}{4} + y = -c$$
$$x + 4y = -4c$$

How many solutions does the above system of equations have, where c is a constant?

A) Zero

B) Exactly one

C) Exactly two

D) Infinitely many

Category 10 – System of Linear Equations with No Solution

Key Points

- A system of linear equations has no solution when the lines described by the equations are parallel lines with the same slope but different y-intercepts.

- When a system of equations is compared in the standard form $Ax + By = C$, where A, B, and C are constants, the following rule applies for two equations $a_1x + b_1y = c_1$ and $a_2x + b_2y = c_2$ to have no solution.

  - If $\dfrac{a_1}{a_2}$ and $\dfrac{b_1}{b_2}$ are same but $\dfrac{c_1}{c_2}$ is different, then the system has no solution.

How to Solve

A question may give equations with one or more unknown constants. To determine the value of a constant, equate the ratios. A constant should be given a value that will make the ratios of a and b same but different than of c.

Example 1:

$$2nx + y = 3$$
$$x + \frac{1}{4}y = 1$$

In the system of equations above n is a constant. For what value of n does the system have no solution?

Step 1: Equate the ratios

$2n$ is the value of a in the top equation. For the system to have no solution, the ratios of a and b must be same. Determine the value of n that will result in the same a and b ratios.

$$\frac{a_1}{a_2} = \frac{b_1}{b_2} \rightarrow \frac{2n}{1} = \left(1 \div \frac{1}{4}\right) \rightarrow 2n = 4 \rightarrow n = 2$$

When $n = 2$, the ratios of a and b are same $= 4$ and the system has no solution.

Correct answer is **2**.

Example 2:

$$3x + 2y = k$$
$$9x + 6y = 3$$

If the above system of equations has no solution, which of the following can NOT be the value of the constant k?

A) -3

B) 0

C) 1

D) 9

Step 1: Equate the ratios

k is the value of c in the top equation. For the system to have no solution, the value of k cannot result in the ratio of c to be same as the ratios of a and b. (Remember that since the system has no solution, ratios of a and b are same.)

Equate the ratio of a or b with c and determine the value of k that makes the ratios same. This cannot be the value of k. Below a is equated with c. (Either a or b could be equated with c, since both ratios are same.)

$$\frac{a_1}{a_2} = \frac{c_1}{c_2} \rightarrow \frac{3}{9} = \frac{k}{3} \rightarrow \frac{1}{3} = \frac{k}{3} \rightarrow k = 1$$

If $k = 1$, then all the ratios will be same. For the system to have no solution $k \neq 1$.

Correct answer choice is **C**.

Category 10 – Practice Questions (answers on pages 337-338)

No Calculator Questions

1

$$2x + 12y = 5$$
$$\frac{1}{6}x + \frac{1}{b}y = 12$$

In the system of equations above, for which of the following value of b the system has no solution, where b is a constant?

A) -6

B) -1

C) 1

D) 8

2

$$y = 4x + 10$$
$$4y = ax + 14$$

In the xy-plane, the graph of the system of equations given above are two parallel lines. Which of the following can be the value of the constant a?

A) 1

B) 4

C) 12

D) 16

3

$$3x + 2y = k$$
$$9x + 6y = 12$$

In the xy-plane, the equations of two parallel lines are given above. Which of the following can NOT be the value of the constant k?

A) 1

B) 3

C) 4

D) 9

4

$$2x - by = 11$$
$$10y + 5x = 16$$

The system of equations above has no solution and b is a constant. What is the value of b?

A) -4

B) -1

C) 1

D) 3

Calculator Questions

5

$$2x + my = n$$
$$5x + 10y = 15$$

If the above system of equations has no solution and m and n are constants, which of the following is true for the values of m and n?

A) $m = 2$ and $n = 1$

B) $m = 2$ and $n = 6$

C) $m = 4$ and $n = 6$

D) $m = 4$ and $n = 8$

6

$$0.2x + 0.3y = 0.1$$
$$ax + 0.6y = 0.3$$

If the above system of equations has no solution, which of the following is the value of a, where a is a constant?

A) 0.2

B) 0.4

C) 2.0

D) 3.1

Category 11 – System of Linear Equations with Infinite Solutions

Key Points

- A system of linear equations has infinitely many solutions when the lines described by the equations are same.
- When a system of equations is compared in the standard form $Ax + By = C$, where A, B, and C are constants, the following rule applies for two equations $a_1 x + b_1 y = c_1$ and $a_2 x + b_2 y = c_2$ to have infinitely many solutions.
  - If $\dfrac{a_1}{a_2}$, $\dfrac{b_1}{b_2}$, and $\dfrac{c_1}{c_2}$ are same, then the system has infinitely many solutions.

How to Solve

A question may give equations with one or more unknown constants. To determine the value of a constant, equate the ratios. A constant should be given a value that will make all the three ratios same. Note that 'infinitely many solutions' may also be worded as 'true for all values of x'.

Example 1:

$$ax + 6y = c$$
$$4x + 2y = 1$$

The system of equations shown above is true for all values of x. What is the value of ac, where a and c are constants?

Step 1: Equate the ratios

For the system to have infinitely many solutions, the ratios of a, b, and c must be same.

$$\frac{a_1}{a_2} = \frac{b_1}{b_2} = \frac{c_1}{c_2} \rightarrow \frac{a}{4} = \frac{6}{2} = \frac{c}{1} \rightarrow \frac{a}{4} = 3 = c$$

Since the ratio of b is 3, it can be equated with a and c to determine their values, respectively.

$$\frac{a}{4} = 3 \rightarrow a = 12$$
$$c = 3$$

Determine ac: $12 \times 3 = 36$.

Correct answer is **36**.

Example 2:

$$ax + by = 2$$
$$\frac{1}{3}x + \frac{1}{4}y = \frac{1}{6}$$

The above system of equations has infinitely many solutions, and a and b are constants. What is the value of $a + b$?

Step 1: Equate the ratios

For the system to have infinitely many solutions, the ratios of a, b, and c must be same.

$$\frac{a_1}{a_2} = \frac{b_1}{b_2} = \frac{c_1}{c_2} \rightarrow \left(a \div \frac{1}{3}\right) = \left(b \div \frac{1}{4}\right) = \left(2 \div \frac{1}{6}\right) \rightarrow 3a = 4b = 12$$

Since the ratio of c is 12, it can be equated with a and b to determine their values, respectively.

$$3a = 12 \rightarrow a = 4$$
$$4b = 12 \rightarrow b = 3$$

Determine $a + b$: $4 + 3 = 7$.

Correct answer is **7**.

Category 11 – Practice Questions (answers on pages 338-339)

No Calculator Questions

1

$$kx - 10y = c$$
$$\frac{1}{2}x - \frac{1}{3}y = 2$$

The system of equations above has infinitely many solutions. What is the value of $c - k$, where c and k are constants?

A) 6

B) 15

C) 30

D) 45

2

$$x + ky = 2$$
$$kx + ty = 2k$$

If the above system of equations has infinitely many solutions, which of the following can NOT be true for the values of k and t, where k and t are constants?

I. $k = 1$ and $t = 1$

II. $k = 2$ and $t = 4$

III. $k = 3$ and $t = 6$

A) I only

B) II only

C) III only

D) I and II only

3

$$mx + 6.25y = 13.75$$
$$nx + 1.25y = 2.75$$

The system of equations above has infinitely many solutions. What is the value of $\frac{m}{n}$, where m and n are constants?

A) 2

B) 5

C) 8

D) 9

4

$$ax + 5y = 5$$
$$x + y = b$$

The above system of equations has infinitely many solutions. What is the value of $a + b$, where a and b are constants?

Calculator Questions

5

$$\sqrt{k}x + y = 2$$
$$2x + cy = \sqrt{k}$$

In the system of equations above, c and k are positive constants. If the system is true for all values of x, what is the value of c?

Category 12 – System of Linear Equations with One Solution

Key Points

- A system of linear equations of two non-parallel and non-identical lines intersects at one point (x, y).
    - The intersection point is the solution to the system and can be solved for the values of x and y.
- When a system of equations is compared in the standard form $Ax + By = C$, where A, B, and C are constants, the following rule applies for two equations $a_1x + b_1y = c_1$ and $a_2x + b_2y = c_2$ to have one solution.
    - If $\frac{a_1}{a_2}$ and $\frac{b_1}{b_2}$ are different, then the system has one solution. The ratio of c does not matter.

How to Solve

A question may give equations with an unknown constant for the value of a or b. A constant should be given a value that will make the ratios of a and b different.

Remember the following for questions that ask to solve for x or y or both:

- A question may ask for combined values of x and y. For example, $x + y$, $x - y$, or $20x + 20y$. In such questions, it is likely that the answer can be obtained without solving for x or y.
- When two equations are given in the slope-intercept form, they can be equated to solve for x. The value of y can be determined by plugging x into either of the equations. The slope-intercept form equations must be in the $y = mx + b$ format. If y is negative or has a constant, it must be removed before equating.
- If the equations are given in a mixed form, such as one equation is in slope-intercept form and the other is in standard form, convert them to one form.

Example 1:

$$2x + 3y = 5$$
$$kx + 15y = 8$$

If the system of equations above intersects at one point, which of the following can NOT be the value of k, where k is a constant?

A)   3

B)   8

C)   10

D)   15

Step 1: Equate the ratios

For the system to have one solution, the ratios of a and b must not be same. Equate the ratios of a and b and determine the value of k that makes the ratios same. This cannot be the value of k.

$$\frac{a_1}{a_2} = \frac{b_1}{b_2} \rightarrow \frac{2}{k} = \frac{3}{15} \rightarrow \frac{2}{k} = \frac{1}{5} \rightarrow k = 2 \times 5 = 10$$

If $k = 10$, then the ratios of a and b will be same. For the system to have one solution $k \neq 10$.

Correct answer choice is **C**.

Example 2:

$$5y = -3x + 6$$
$$2x + 3y = 2$$

Which of the following is the value of (x, y) in the above system of equations?

A) $(-8, 6)$

B) $(-6, 6)$

C) $(3, -5)$

D) $(5, -3)$

Step 1: Determine the approach

Convert $5y = -3x + 6$ to the standard form.

$$5y = -3x + 6 \rightarrow 3x + 5y = 6$$

Make one of the variables same in both the equations.

If the equation $3x + 5y = 6$ is multiplied by 2 and the equation $2x + 3y = 2$ is multiplied by 3, both the equations will have $6x$ that can be cancelled out. It is best to start with the variable that has smaller numbers.

$$\text{Equation 1: } (3x + 5y = 6) \times 2 \rightarrow 6x + 10y = 12$$
$$\text{Equation 2: } (2x + 3y = 2) \times 3 \rightarrow 6x + 9y = 6$$

Step 2: Determine the value of one of the variables

Subtract Equation 2 from Equation 1 to cancel $6x$.

$$\begin{array}{r} 6x + 10y = 12 \\ -(6x + 9y = 6) \end{array} \longrightarrow \begin{array}{r} \cancel{6x} + 10y = 12 \\ -\cancel{6x} - 9y = -6 \\ \hline y = 6 \end{array}$$

Step 3: Determine the value of the second variable

Substitute the value of $y = 6$ in any of the equation. (Best to pick the equation with smaller numbers.)

$$2x + 3y = 2 \rightarrow 2x + (3 \times 6) = 2 \rightarrow$$
$$2x + 18 = 2 \rightarrow 2x = -16 \rightarrow x = -8$$

Correct answer choice is **A**.

Example 3:

$$-3x + 7y = 2$$
$$8x - 6y = 4$$

If (x, y) is the solution to the system of equations shown above, what is the value of $50x + 10y$?

Step 1: Determine the approach

If both the equations are added up, the result is $5x + y = 6$. Multiplying this by 10 will result in $50x + 10y$.

Step 2: Solve

$$\begin{array}{r} -3x + 7y = 2 \\ 8x - 6y = 4 \\ \hline 5x + y = 6 \end{array}$$

Multiply by 10.

$$(5x + y = 6) \times 10$$
$$50x + 10y = 60$$

Correct answer is **60**.

Category 12 – Practice Questions (answers on page 339)

No Calculator Questions

1

$$9x - 6y = 9$$
$$7x - 4y = 3$$

In the above system of equations, what is the value of $x - y$?

A) -6

B) 3

C) 7

D) 9

2

$$4x + y = 7$$
$$4x - 3y = 12$$

The above system of equations has one solution, (x, y). What is the value of $(80x - 20y)$?

A) 19

B) 84

C) 120

D) 190

3

$$4x + by = 7$$
$$8x + 6y = 3$$

In the xy-plane, the lines graphed by the system of equations above intersect at one point. Which of the following could be a value of b, where b is a constant?

I. -3

II. 3

A) I only

B) II only

C) I and II

D) Neither I nor II

4

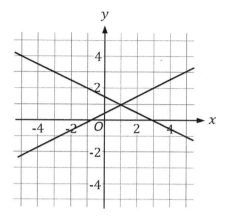

In the xy-plane, the graph of two lines in a system of equations is shown above. Which of the following ordered pairs (x, y) is the solution to the system?

A) $(-1, 1)$

B) $(1, -1)$

C) $(1, 1)$

D) $(2, 2)$

Calculator Questions

5

$$2x - 3y = 4$$
$$3x - 2y = 6$$

Which of the following is the solution to the above system of equations?

A) $(1, 0)$

B) $(1, 1)$

C) $(2, 0)$

D) $(4, 1)$

6

$$2y = -2x + 6$$
$$y = \frac{2}{3}x - 2$$

In the xy-plane, the graph of lines corresponding to the above system of equations intersect at a point (j, k). What is the value of $j + k$?

Category 13 – System of Linear Inequalities

Key Points

- The four inequality symbols are less than ($<$), less than or equal to ($\leq$), greater than ($>$), and greater than or equal to ($\geq$).
- The inequality symbols determine where the solution set to an inequality lies on a graph in the xy-plane (Fig. 1, 2, 3, and 4).
  - The solution set of $y > x$ will be all values above the line of the inequality (Fig. 1).
  - The solution set of $y \geq x$ will be all values on and above the line of the inequality (Fig. 2).
  - The solution set of $y < x$ will be all values below the line of the inequality (Fig. 3).
  - The solution set of $y \leq x$ will be all values on and below the line of the inequality (Fig. 4).
- The inequalities with $\geq$ or $\leq$ symbols have a solid line on the graph and the inequalities with $>$ or $<$ symbols have a dashed line on the graph.
- The solution to a system of two inequalities is the region where the solution set of the two inequalities overlaps.

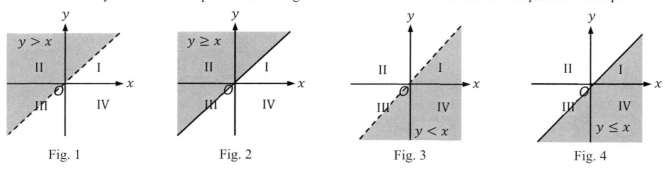

| Fig. 1 | Fig. 2 | Fig. 3 | Fig. 4 |

How to Solve

For questions on the calculator section, use a graphing calculator to graph the inequalities.

Example 1:

$$y \geq -2x + 9$$
$$y > 5x + 2$$

In the xy-plane, which of the following point lies within the solution set of the above system of inequalities?

A) $(0, 6)$

B) $(1, 6)$

C) $(1, 10)$

D) $(3, 8)$

Below solution is based on plugging points from the answer choices in the inequalities. Both inequalities will evaluate true for the correct point. Both inequalities must be checked to be sure. Alternatively, graph the inequalities on paper and evaluate which answer choice is in the overlapping region.

Step 1: Select an answer choice and plug it in the inequalities

Start with answer choice B. Plug in the point $(1, 6)$ in one of the inequalities.
Check $y \geq -2x + 9$:

$$6 \geq -(2 \times 1) + 9 \ \rightarrow \ 6 \geq -2 + 9 \ \rightarrow \ 6 \geq 7$$

Since this evaluation is false, answer choice B can be eliminated.

Step 2: Select another answer choice and plug it in the inequalities

Evaluate answer choice C. Plug in the point $(1, 10)$ in one of the inequalities.

Check $y \geq -2x + 9$:

$$10 \geq -(2 \times 1) + 9 \rightarrow 10 \geq -2 + 9 \rightarrow 10 \geq 7$$

This evaluation is true. Check the second inequality with the point $(1, 10)$.

Check $y > 5x + 2$:

$$10 > (5 \times 1) + 2 \rightarrow 10 > 5 + 2 \rightarrow 10 > 7$$

This evaluation is true.

Correct answer choice is **C**.

Example 2:

$$y > x + 2$$
$$y \leq -2x - 4$$

In the xy-plane, which of the quadrants contain the solution to the above system of inequalities?

A)   I only

B)   II and III only

C)   I, II, and III only

D)   II, III, and IV only

Step 1: Evaluate the slope, the y-intercept, and the inequality symbol

Graphing the inequalities will help.

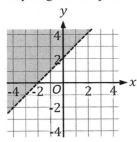

$y > x + 2$:

Since the slope is positive, the line will have an upward slant from left to right. Since the y-intercept is 2, the graph will pass through 2.

Since the inequality symbol is $>$, the solution set will be above the line. See figure on left for the solution to the above equation.

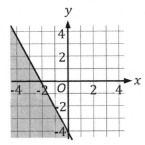

$y \leq -2x - 4$:

Since the slope is negative, the line will have a downward slant from left to right. Since the y-intercept is -4, the graph will pass through -4.

Since the inequality symbol is $\leq$, the solution set will be on or below the line. See figure on left for the solution to the above equation.

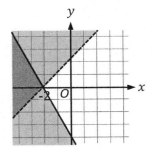

The region on the graph containing the overlapping shaded area is the solution to the system of inequalities. It spans quadrants II and III. See figure on left.

Correct answer choice is **B**.

Example 3:

$$2y \geq 3x + 2$$

$$-y \leq 2x - 1$$

Which of the following graphs, in the xy-plane, could be the solution of the above system of inequalities?

A)

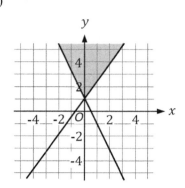

B)

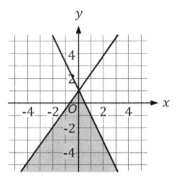

C)

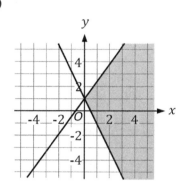

D)

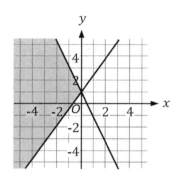

Step 1: Compare the slope, the y-intercept, and the inequality symbol

The value of y cannot be negative or contain a coefficient. Both the equations must be converted to the correct format.

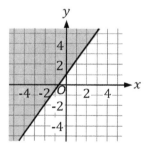

Equation $2y \geq 3x + 2$: Divide both sides by 2.

$$\frac{2}{2}y \geq \frac{3}{2}x + \frac{2}{2} \rightarrow y \geq 1.5x + 1$$

Since the slope is positive, the line will have an upward slant from left to right. Since the inequality symbol is $\geq$, the solution set will be on and above the line. Since the y-intercept is 1, the graph will pass through 1. See figure on left.

This eliminates answer choices B and C that have a line with positive slope but the solution below the line.

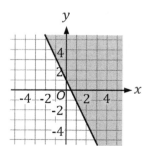

Equation $-y \leq 2x - 1$: Divide both sides by -1 to remove the negative sign from y. When an inequality equation is divided by a negative sign, the inequality symbol gets flipped.

$$-y \leq 2x - 1 \rightarrow y \geq -2x + 1$$

Since the slope is negative, the line will have a downward slant from left to right. Since the inequality symbol is $\geq$, the solution set will be on and above the line. Since the y-intercept is 1, the graph will pass through 1. See figure on left.

This eliminates answer choice D that has a line with negative slope but the solution below the line.

Correct answer choice is **A**.

Category 13 – Practice Questions (answers on page 340)

No Calculator Questions

1

$$y \geq x - 1$$
$$y < -2x + 2$$

Which of the following graphs, in the xy-plane, represents the solution set of the above system of inequalities?

A)

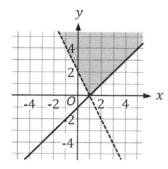

B)

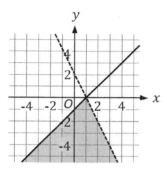

C)

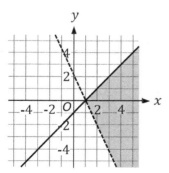

D)

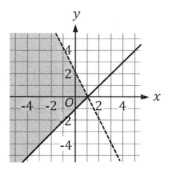

Calculator Questions

2

$$y > x + 2$$
$$y \leq -2x - 3$$

In the xy-plane, which of the following quadrants contain the solution set of the above system of inequalities?

A) I and II only

B) II and III only

C) II, III, and IV only

D) I, II, III, and IV

3

$$y > -2x + 4$$
$$y < 3x + 1$$

Which of the following ordered pair (x, y) satisfies the above system of inequalities?

A) $(-3, 4)$

B) $(1, -2)$

C) $(1, 3)$

D) $(2, 8)$

4

$$y \leq 2x - 4$$
$$y > -x - 1$$

Which of the quadrants do NOT contain the solution set of the system of inequalities shown above?

A) I only

B) II only

C) II and III only

D) I and IV only

Category 14 – Solutions of Linear Expressions

Key Points

- Two linear expressions may or may not be equivalent to each other depending on the values given to the coefficients or constants in the expressions. For example, the equation $3x + k = ax + 2$ has expressions on both sides of the equation, where the values of the coefficient a and the constant k are not known. The values given to a and k will determine if the expressions on both sides of the equation are equal or not.
    - The equation has infinitely many solutions when the expressions on both sides of the equation are equal.
    - The equation has no solution when the expressions on both sides of the equation are unequal.

How to Solve

Unlike the system of equations that have two separate equations with x and y variables, the questions in this category have expressions on both sides of a single equation and have only one variable. They are solved differently than the system of equations.

For an equation to have infinitely many solutions, the coefficients of x and the constants on both sides of the equation must be made equal.

For an equation to have no solution, the coefficients of x and the constants on both sides must not be equal. If the coefficients of x are equal, then the constants must be made unequal. If the constants are equal, then the coefficients of x must be made unequal. This will ensure that the equation will never have a solution.

Example 1:

$$3kx + 6 = 9x + 4 + c$$

In the equation above, c and k are constants and $c \neq k$. If the equation has infinitely many solutions, what is the value of ck?

A) 4

B) 5

C) 6

D) 9

Step 1: Equate the coefficients and the constants of both sides

For the equation to have infinitely many solutions, the expressions on both sides must be equal (see below the corresponding coefficients and constants enclosed in matching shape types on both sides of the equation).

$$\boxed{3k}x + \boxed{6} = \boxed{9}x + \boxed{4 + c}$$

Equate the coefficients of x.

$$3k = 9 \rightarrow k = 3$$

Equate the constants.

$$4 + c = 6 \rightarrow c = 2$$

Determine ck:

$$ck = 2 \times 3 = 6$$

Correct answer choice is **C**.

Example 2:

$$cx + 2(2bx + 3) + 1 = 10x + c + 1$$

If the equation shown above has infinitely many solutions, what is the value of b, where b and c are constants?

Step 1: Equate the coefficients and the constants of both sides

For the equation to have infinitely many solutions, the expressions on both sides must be equal. Before equating, the parentheses must be removed and all x terms and constants must be grouped.

$$cx + 4bx + 6 + 1 = 10x + c + 1$$

$$\boxed{(c + 4b)}x + \textcircled{7} = \boxed{10}x + \overparen{c + 1}$$

First determine the value of c by equating the constants. Then substitute it in the coefficient of the left expression. Equate the constants.

$$7 = c + 1$$
$$c = 6$$

Equate the coefficients of x and substitute $c = 6$.

$$c + 4b = 10$$
$$6 + 4b = 10 \ \rightarrow \ 4b = 4 \ \rightarrow \ b = 1$$

Correct answer is **1**.

Example 3:

$$5bx + 3x + 7 = 18x + 4$$

In the equation above, b is a constant. For what value of b does the equation have no solution?

Step 1: Equate the coefficients and the constants of both sides

Since the constants are not equal in both the expressions, the coefficients must be made equal for the equation to have no solution. Before equating group all terms of x.

$$\boxed{(5b + 3)}x + \textcircled{7} = \boxed{18}x + \textcircled{4}$$

Equate the coefficients to determine the value b that makes both sides of the equation equal.

$$5b + 3 = 18$$
$$5b = 15 \ \rightarrow \ b = 3$$

Correct answer is **3**.

Example 4:

If the equation $0.5ax + 7 = 10x + 7$ has no solution, which of the following can NOT be the value of a?

A)   3

B)   7

C)   10

D)   20

Step 1: Equate the coefficients and the constants of both sides

Since the constants are equal in both the expressions, the coefficients must not be equal. Equate the coefficients to determine the value a that makes both sides of the equation equal. This cannot be the value of a.

$$\boxed{0.5a}x + \textcircled{7} = \boxed{10}x + \textcircled{7}$$

Equate the coefficients.

$$0.5a = 10 \ \rightarrow \ a = 20$$

If $a = 20$, then the expressions on both the sides of the equation will be equal. Hence, $a \neq 20$.

Correct answer choice is **D**.

Category 14 – Practice Questions (answers on pages 340-341)

No Calculator Questions

1

$$5ax - 5 - 2 = 1.25x - 7$$

The equation above is true for all values of x. What is the value of a, where a is a constant?

A) 0.15

B) 0.25

C) 1.25

D) 5.50

2

$$3(bx + 3) + 2 = 8 + c$$

If the above equation has infinitely many solutions, what is the value of b, where b and c are constants?

A) 0

B) 3

C) 5

D) 9

3

$$\frac{6x - a}{3} = 2x - 1$$

If the equation above is true for all values of x and a is a constant, what is the value of a?

A) $-\frac{1}{3}$

B) $\frac{1}{3}$

C) 0

D) 3

4

$$0.2kx = \frac{x + 9}{5}$$

If the above equation has no solution, what is the value of k, where k is a constant?

Calculator Questions

5

$$4ax + x - 20 = 2(x - 2) + 7(x + 2)$$

In the equation above, a is a constant. For what value of a does the equation have no solution?

A) -4

B) 1

C) 2

D) 7

6

$$2(kx + c) + 2 = 10x + 2c + 2$$

In the above equation, c and k are constants and $c \neq k$. If the equation has no solution, which of the following can NOT be the value of k?

A) -5

B) -4

C) 0

D) 5

7

$$5(x + 1) + 3a + 1 = 5x + 18$$

For the above equation to have infinitely many solutions, what is the value of the constant a?

8

If the equation $2(cx + 3) + x = 5x + 7$ has no solution and c is a constant, what is the value of c?

No Calculator Questions

1

$$x - 4y = 4$$
$$4x - 16y = m$$

In the xy-plane, the equations of two parallel lines are shown above. Which of the following can NOT be the value of m, where m is a constant?

A) -4

B) -1

C) 12

D) 16

2

$$2y = 3x + 5$$
$$y = \frac{3}{2}x + 5$$

How many solutions exist for the above system of equations?

A) Zero

B) Exactly one

C) Exactly two

D) Infinitely many

3

$$2(2x + 3kx) + x + 6 = 3(x + cx) + 2c$$

If the above equation has infinitely many solutions, what is the value of k, where c and k are constants and $c \neq k$?

A) -1

B) 0

C) $\frac{1}{2}$

D) $\frac{7}{6}$

4

$$3x = 4x + x(k - 3)$$

In the equation above, k is a constant. If the equation does not have a solution, which of the following can NOT be the value of k?

A) -2

B) 0

C) 1

D) 2

5

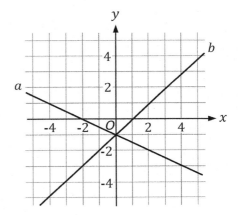

In the xy-plane, the graphs of line a and line b are shown above. Which of the following is the solution (x, y) to the system of equations defined by lines a and b?

A) $(0, -1)$

B) $(0, 0)$

C) $(0, 1)$

D) $(2, 2)$

$$x - y = n$$
$$-mx + 2y = 12$$

In the above system of equations, m and n are constants. For which of the following values of m and n does the above system have no solution?

I. $m = -2$ and $n = 2$

II. $m = 2$ and $n = -6$

III. $m = 2$ and $n = 6$

A)   I only

B)   II only

C)   III only

D)   None of the above

$$4(x + 2ax) + 3(a - x) = 3(x + a) + 2x + 2$$

For what value of a does the above equation has no solution, where a is a constant?

A) -1

B) 0

C) $\dfrac{1}{4}$

D) $\dfrac{1}{2}$

$$2ax + y = b$$
$$4x - 2y = a$$

If the above system of equations is true for all values of x, and a and b are constants, what is the value of b?

A) -2

B) -1

C) $\dfrac{1}{4}$

D) $\dfrac{1}{2}$

$$2x + 3y = a$$
$$\frac{1}{3}x + \frac{1}{2}y = \frac{a}{6}$$

In the xy-plane, which of the following must be true about the lines graphed by the above system of equations?

A)   They are perpendicular lines that intersect at one point.

B)   They are parallel lines with different y-intercepts.

C)   They are the same line.

D)   The information given is inconclusive.

$$2x - 5y = 11$$
$$6x - 3y = 9$$

For the above system of equations, what is the value of $x - y$?

$$(a + 4)x + 4y = 4$$
$$3x + by = 3$$

If the system of equations shown above has infinitely many solutions, where a and b are constants, what is the value of $a + b$?

$$3x + 4y = -5$$
$$x - 10y = 7$$

In the system of equations above, if (x, y) is the solution to the system, what is the value of $40x - 60y$?

13

$$y < -x + 7$$
$$y < 3x + 4$$

In the xy-plane, a point P is contained on the graph of the solution set of the system of inequalities shown above. Which of the following could be point $P\ (x, y)$?

A) $(-3, -2)$

B) $(-2, -1)$

C) $(0, 2)$

D) $(1, 8)$

14

$$y > -2x + 4$$
$$y < 3x + 2$$

In the xy-plane, which of the following quadrants do NOT contain the solution of the above system of inequalities?

A) I only

B) II only

C) I and II only

D) II and III only

15

$$3x - 4y = 5$$
$$3y + 4x = -5$$

What is the value of y in the system of equations given above?

A) -5

B) $-\dfrac{7}{5}$

C) $\dfrac{1}{5}$

D) $\dfrac{1}{2}$

16

$$4(ax + 1) + 3ax + 2 = 6$$

If the above equation has infinitely many solutions, which of the following must be the value of a, where a is a constant?

A) 0

B) 2

C) 3

D) 6

17

$$5y = -x + 3$$
$$2x + 3y = -8$$

What is the solution (x, y) to the above system of equations?

A) $(-8, -2)$

B) $(-7, -2)$

C) $(-7, 2)$

D) $(1, 2)$

18

$$y \geq 2x - 3$$
$$y < x - 1$$

In the xy-plane, which of the following point is within the solution set of the above system of inequalities?

A) $(-1, -6)$

B) $(-1, -3)$

C) $(1, 1)$

D) $(2, 2)$

19

$$\frac{b}{5}x - 2y = 4$$
$$3x - 12y = 7$$

In the above system of equations, b is constant. For what value of b the system has no solution?

Section 4 –
Word Problems on Linear Equations and Inequalities

Category 15 – Word Problems on Linear Equations with One Variable

Key Points

- A word problem may be given that contains a known number and an unknown number.
    - The known number is a constant. For example, a one-time fee or a fixed price service charge of $25. It does not have a variable associated with it.
    - The unknown number is comprised of a fixed number and an associated variable. For example, $4m$, where m is the variable and 4 is the fixed number. The value of the unknown number is determined by the value given to the variable.

How to Solve

Determine the constant and the unknown number in the word problem. Note that not every word problem may have a constant but will have an unknown number.

Example 1:

A yoga club charges an annual membership fee of $25 and $20 for each yoga class attended by members.

Question 1

Which of the following equations represents the total cost C, in dollars, of attending p yoga classes in a year?

A) $C = 25 + p$

B) $C = 20 + 25p$

C) $C = 25 + 20p$

D) $C = 50 + 2p$

Step 1: Determine the constant

It is given that the annual membership fee is $25. This eliminates answer choices B and D.

Step 2: Determine the unknown number/variable

The number of yoga classes in a year $= p$. Cost of each yoga class $= \$20$.

$$\text{cost for } p \text{ classes} = 20p$$

This eliminates answer choice A.

Correct answer choice is **C**.

Question 2

What is the total cost, in dollars, of attending 5 yoga classes in a year?

A) $20

B) $25

C) $100

D) $125

Continue from Step 2 of Question 1.

$p = 5$. Hence,

$$20p = 20 \times 5 = \$100$$

Step 3: Solve:

$$\text{total cost} = \text{constant} + \text{unknown number} = 25 + 100 = \$125$$

Correct answer choice is **D**.

Example 2:

Katie has access to 38 eBooks through an online bookstore. She decides to sign up for a program with the online bookstore that will give her access to a fixed number of new eBooks each week. If the program gives her access to 4 new eBooks each week, which of the following gives the total number of eBooks Katie will have access to at the end of 7 weeks?

A) 28

B) 38

C) 54

D) 66

Step 1: Determine the constant

It is given that Katie has access to 38 eBooks at the beginning of the program.

Step 2: Determine the unknown number/variable

$$4 \text{ eBooks per week for 7 weeks} = 4 \times 7 = 28$$

Step 3: Solve

$$\text{total eBooks} = \text{constant} + \text{unknown number}$$
$$38 + 28 = 66$$

Correct answer choice is **D**.

Example 3:

Tim plans to complete 50 online quizzes within a month. Each quiz takes approximately 45 minutes to complete. If Tim has completed x quizzes within the month, which of the following expressions is the closest representation of the number of hours required to complete the remaining quizzes?

A) $\frac{1}{4}(30x)$

B) $\frac{3}{4}(50 - x)$

C) $50x$

D) $45(50 - x)$

Step 1: Determine the constant

The question does not have a constant.

Step 2: Determine the unknown number/variable

The unknown number = number of quizzes $\times$ 45 minutes.

If Tim completed x quizzes out of 50, then the remaining number of quizzes are $(50 - x)$.

The number of minutes required to complete $(50 - x)$ quizzes are

$$(50 - x) \times 45 \text{ minutes}$$

Since the question asks for the number of hours, divide by 60 to convert minutes to hours.

$$\frac{(50 - x) \times 45}{60} = \frac{(50 - x) \times 3}{4} = \frac{3}{4}(50 - x)$$

Correct answer choice is **B**.

Category 15 – Practice Questions (answers on page 344)

No Calculator Questions

1

For each visit, a roller-skating ring charges an entry fee of $10 and $5 per hour to roller skate. Which of the following equations give the total cost A, in dollars, for each visit to the roller-skating ring for h hours?

A) $A = 10 + 5h$

B) $A = 10 + 10h$

C) $A = 15 + 5h$

D) $A = 5h$

2

Robert rented a power washer from a local hardware store. He was charged a one-time fee of $25 and $20 per hour as the renting fee. If Robert returned the power washer after t hours, which of the following equations can determine the total cost c, in dollars, for renting the power washer for t hours?

A) $c = 20t + 20$

B) $c = 20t + 25$

C) $c = 25t + 20$

D) $c = 45t + 25$

3

Jamie opened a savings account with d dollars. Starting next month, he will make a monthly deposit of $100 in this account for m months. Which of the following equations represents the amount S, in dollars, Jamie will have saved in m months, assuming no withdrawals or interest payments are made during m months?

A) $S = 100m$

B) $S = d + m$

C) $S = m + 100d$

D) $S = d + 100m$

4

For each job, a plumber charges a fixed service fee of s dollars and p dollars for each hour spent on the job. If the plumber charges $360 for a 3 hour job, which of the following equations represents the relationship between p and s?

A) $s = 120 - p$

B) $s = 360 - p$

C) $s = 360 - 3p$

D) $s = 360 + 3p$

5

A car rental company charges a one-time fee of $75 and $55 for each day the car is rented. Which of the following is the total cost of car rental, in dollars, for 4 days?

A) $75

B) $130

C) $220

D) $295

6

A teacher is grading 30 research papers. Each research paper takes 40 minutes to grade. If the teacher has completed grading r research papers, which of the following expressions can determine the number of hours required to grade the remaining research papers?

A) $40(30 - r)$

B) $120 - r$

C) $\frac{2}{3}(r)$

D) $\frac{2}{3}(30 - r)$

Calculator Questions

7

A theater has x tickets to sell in 5 days. On the first day, 400 tickets are sold. If the theater wants to evenly sell the remaining tickets in the next 4 days, which of the following equations represents the number of tickets T that must be sold on each of the 4 days?

A) $T = \frac{x}{5} - 80$

B) $T = \frac{x}{4} - 100$

C) $T = \frac{x+4}{5}$

D) $T = \frac{x}{4}$

8

Samir wants to buy a computer that costs $1,500. He has d dollars saved and plans to save $150 per month. Which of the following equations represents the number of months m Samir will have to save before he can buy the computer?

A) $m = \frac{1,500}{d-150}$

B) $m = 10 - \frac{d}{150}$

C) $m = 1,500 - d$

D) $m = 1,200 + d$

9

The relationship between the height of a plant g, in centimeters, and the number of hours h exposed to sunlight can be modeled by the equation, $g = 0.003h + 0.2$. Which of the following is closest to the height of the plant, in centimeters, after 20 hours of exposure to sunlight?

A) 0.26

B) 0.28

C) 0.50

D) 0.60

10

Raj purchased a monthly data plan from a telephone company. Each month he is charged a flat fee of $25 and $0.20 for each call. If last month Raj made 50 calls, which of the following is the total amount Raj paid to the telephone company last month?

A) $10

B) $25

C) $35

D) $50

11

Tatiana has $35 to spend on the entrance fee and the tickets for rides at a local fair. The entrance fee is $8 and each ride ticket costs $1.50. Which of the following equations can solve for the number of rides r?

A) $35 = 1.50 + r$

B) $35 = 1.50 + 8r$

C) $35 = 8 + r$

D) $35 = 8 + 1.50r$

Category 16 – Word Problems on Linear Equations with Two Variables

Key Points

- A word problem may be given that contains two unknown numbers, each with a separate variable. For example, $4m$ and $10p$. The values of the two unknown numbers are determined by the value given to the variables associated with them.

How to Solve

Determine the two unknown numbers in the word problem.

Example 1:

A bakery owner hires staff on hourly wages. Each staff member is paid $15 per hour and an additional $2.50 for each cake sold. Which of the following equations represents the total earnings E, in dollars, of a staff member working for h hours and selling c cakes?

A) $E = 15 + 2.5c$

B) $E = 15h + 2.5$

C) $E = 15h + 2.5c$

D) $E = 15c + 2.5h$

Step 1: Determine the unknown numbers/variables

Variable 1: The number of hours $= h$. A staff member is paid $15 for each hour of work.

$$\text{earnings for } h \text{ hours} = 15h$$

This eliminates answer choices A and D.

Variable 2: The number of cakes $= c$. A staff member is paid $2.50 for each cake sold.

$$\text{earnings from selling } c \text{ cakes} = 2.5c$$

This eliminates answer choice B.

Correct answer choice is **C**.

Example 2:

Jimena and her friends bought 13 bags of pretzels and 10 bottles of sparkling water for a total of $40.50. If the cost of each bag of pretzels is $1.50, what is the cost of each bottle of sparkling water, in dollars (ignore the dollar sign)?

Step 1: Determine the unknown numbers/variables

In this example, information is given to determine the value of one of the unknown numbers, the cost of pretzels.

Variable 1: Number of bags of pretzels $= 13$. The cost of each bag of pretzel $= \$1.50$.

$$\text{cost of 13 bags of pretzels} = 13 \times 1.50 = \$19.50$$

Variable 2: Number of sparkling water bottles $= 10$. Let the cost of each bottle of sparkling water $= b$.

$$\text{cost of 10 sparkling water bottles} = 10b$$

Step 2: Solve for b

$$\text{total cost} = \text{cost of 13 bags of pretzels} + \text{cost of 10 bottles of sparkling water}$$
$$40.50 = 19.50 + 10b$$
$$10b = 40.50 - 19.50 \rightarrow 10b = 21 \rightarrow b = 2.1 = \$2.10$$

Correct answer choice is $\mathbf{2.1}$ **or** $\mathbf{2.10}$.

Category 16 – Practice Questions (answers on page 345)

No Calculator Question

1

Jessica works two shifts per day at her job. She gets paid $15 per hour for the morning shift and $25 per hour for the night shift. Which of the following expressions represents the amount, in dollars, that Jessica earns per day working m hours in the morning shift and n hours in the night shift?

A) $15m + 25n$

B) $15n + 25m$

C) $15m + 40n$

D) $40m + 40n$

2

Sam works at a restaurant during the day for some hours and is paid $20 per hour. In the night, he works at a hotel for some hours and is paid $35 per hour. If yesterday, Sam worked at the restaurant for x hours and at the hotel for 5 hours, which of the following equations represents his total earnings E, in dollars?

A) $E = 35x + 20$

B) $E = 35x + 175$

C) $E = 20x + 35$

D) $E = 20x + 175$

3

An ice cream truck sells snow cones for c dollars each and frozen yogurt for $c + 1$ dollars each. Casey and her friends spent $40 altogether on snow cones and frozen yogurt. If they bought 4 snow cones and 7 frozen yogurts, which of the following is the value of c?

A) $2

B) $3

C) $10

D) $11

4

A supermarket sells oranges for $1 each and apples for p dollars each. If a school bought 100 oranges and 100 apples from the supermarket and paid a total of $150, which of the following is the cost of one apple, in dollars?

A) $0.50

B) $1.50

C) $1.75

D) $2.50

Calculator Questions

5

Crane A and Crane B are working individually to lift boxes. Crane A can lift 100 boxes per hour and Crane B can lift 75 boxes per hour. If on Friday, Crane A worked for 2 hours and together both the cranes lifted 500 boxes, how many hours did Crane B work?

6

A contractor works as a painter at an hourly rate of $80 and as a landscaper at an hourly rate of $50. If the contractor earned a total of $470 working as a painter for 4 hours and as a landscaper for a hours, what is the value of a?

Category 17 – Word Problems on Interpretation of Linear Equations

Key Points

- A word problem may give a linear equation and ask for the interpretation of any number in the equation. Generally, the components of the linear equation in these word problems are an initial number, an ending number, and an unknown number. The unknown number contains a constant and a variable.

  - The constant in the unknown number determines the average increase or decrease of the initial number. For example, in the equation $P = 2,254 + 45t$, 45 is the average increase each year in the initial population of 2,254 resulting in P population in t years. It is important to note that there is no guarantee that each year the increase will be exactly 45. It could be 42 one year and 47 the following year, and so on. Hence, it is the predicted, estimated, approximate, or plausible average increase modeled by the linear equation.

  - The linear equation will always contain the unknown number. Occasionally, there may be a word problem where instead of a separate initial and an ending number only one number is given. For example, in the linear equation $P = 450w$, 450 is the average increase in the value of P each week for w weeks.

- The above also applies to a linear function. For example, in the linear function $f(t) = 2,254 + 45t$, $f(t)$ is the ending number determined by the value given to the variable t.

How to Solve

Determine the components of the equation and select the correct answer accordingly.

Remember that a positive unknown number represents an average increase, and a negative unknown number represents an average decrease.

Example 1:

$$4,200 = 2,900 + 130t$$

In 1998, the population of crickets in a certain rain forest was 2,900. The above equation models the increase in the population of crickets in t years after 1998, where t satisfies the equation. Which of the following is the best interpretation of the number 130 in the equation?

A) The population of crickets in the rain forest before 1998.

B) The total increase in the population of crickets in the rain forest after 1998 for t years.

C) The difference in the population of crickets in the rain forest from 1998 till present.

D) The average increase in the population of crickets in the rain forest each year after 1998 for t years.

Step 1: Determine the components of the equation

$130 =$ Average increase in the population each year after 1998 for t years.

$2,900 =$ Initial population in 1998.

$4,200 =$ Ending population in t years from 1998.

Correct answer choice is **D**.

(Note that if the equation was $2,900 = 4,200 - 130t$, then 4,200 would be the initial population in 1998, 130 would be the average decrease in the population each year after 1998 for t years, and 2,900 would be the ending population in t years since 1998.)

Example 2:

The equation $s = 6.7 + 0.5583m$ approximates the tusk size s, in inches, of an elephant after one year of birth for m months.

Question 1

Which of the following statements is consistent with the equation?

A) For each year increase in age after one year of birth, the size of an elephant's tusk increases by an average of 0.5583 inches.

B) For each month increase in age after one year of birth, the size of an elephant's tusk increases by an average of 0.5583 inches for m months.

C) For each month increase in age after one year of birth, the size of an elephant's tusk increases by an average of 6.7 inches for m months.

D) For each month increase in age after one year of birth, the size of an elephant's tusk increases by an average of 7.2583 inches for m months.

Step 1: Determine the components of the equation

$0.5583 =$ Average increase in an elephant's tusk size each month after one year of birth for m months.

This can also be phrased as "for each month increase in age after one year of birth, the size of an elephant's tusk increases by an average of 0.5583 inches for m months".

$6.7 =$ Tusk size after one year of birth (initial number).

$s =$ Tusk size in m months after one year of birth (end number).

Correct answer choice is **B**.

Question 2

For what value of m, will the elephant's tusk size increase by 1 inch?

A) 0.083

B) 0.5583

C) $\dfrac{1}{0.67}$

D) $\dfrac{1}{0.5583}$

Step 1: Determine the components of the equation

Continue from Step 1 of Question 1.

For the tusk size to increase by 1 inch, the value of $0.5583m$ must be equal to 1.

$$0.5583m = 1 \;\rightarrow\; m = \frac{1}{0.5583}$$

Note that the value of the variable is the reciprocal of the average increase. Remember this for similar questions that ask for the increase or decrease of the unknown number by 1.

Correct answer choice is **D**.

Category 17 – Practice Questions (answers on page 345)

No Calculator Questions

1

$$R = 58 - 2d$$

Anika is a research assistant at a university. At the beginning of each month, she receives a fixed number of research papers to review during the month. At the end of each day, she can estimate the number of research papers left to review in a month by the above equation, where R is the number of research papers left to review and d is the number of days elapsed in a month. What is the meaning of 2 in this context?

A) Anika receives 2 research papers each day.

B) Anika completes the review of 2 research papers each week.

C) Anika works for 2 weeks as a research assistant.

D) Anika reviews an average of 2 research papers each day.

2

$$g(h) = 15 + 0.0054h$$

A scientist conducted an experiment to study the effect of sunlight on the growth of a certain plant. The growth of the plant, in inches, exposed to h hours of sunlight was modeled by the linear function g, shown above. Which of the following statements best interprets the linear function g in the context?

A) For each 1 hour increase in the exposure to sunlight, the plant grew by an average of 0.0054 inches.

B) For each 1 hour increase in the exposure to sunlight, the plant grew by an average of 1 inch.

C) For each 1 hour increase in the exposure to sunlight, the plant grew by an average of 5.4 inches.

D) For each 1 hour increase in the exposure to sunlight, the plant grew by 15 inches.

Calculator Questions

3

$$R = 1.43w$$

The growth rate R, in pounds, of a baby panda for w weeks after birth can be approximated by the equation above. Which of the following is the best interpretation of the number 1.43 in this context?

A) The weight of a baby panda, in pounds, at birth.

B) The approximate growth rate of a baby panda, in pounds, for w weeks after birth.

C) The average increase in the weight of a baby panda, in pounds, after birth.

D) The average growth rate of a baby panda, in pounds, for w weeks after first year of birth.

4

$$685 = 305 + 7.6t$$

The equation above models the population of certain insects, in thousands, in a rain forest for t years after 1970, where t satisfies the equation. Which of the following is the best interpretation of 7.6 in this context?

A) The number of years for the insect population to increase from 305 to 685, in thousands.

B) The plausible growth rate of the insects each year after 1970 for t years.

C) The plausible average increase in the population of insects, in thousands, each year after 1970 for t years.

D) The population of insects in 7.6 years.

5

$$B = 29.92 - 0.0012a$$

The above equation approximates the barometric pressure B, in inches Hg, exerted by air molecules at an altitude of a feet above the sea surface, where $0 \le a \le 8,000$. At what value of a, in feet, does the barometric pressure decrease by 1 inch Hg?

A) 0.0012

B) 29.92

C) $\dfrac{1}{0.01}$

D) $\dfrac{1}{0.0012}$

Category 18 – Word Problems on Linear System of Equations

Key Points

- A word problem may be given that contains two variables and the values of both the variables are unknown. A single equation cannot solve for the values of both the variables. For example, $x + y = 8$ cannot give the values of the two variables x and y. The word problem will contain information to set up two related equations (system of equations) that can together solve for the variables.

How to Solve

A word problem may either ask to identify the system of equations from the answer choices based on the given information or may require creating two equations to solve for the variables.

(Note that in Category 15 if a question asks to solve for one of the unknown number/associated variable, the question will give information to determine the value of the other unknown number/associated variable. On questions in this category, the values of both the unknown numbers/associated variables are unknown and cannot be determined without setting up a system of equations. This is the main difference between questions in this category and Category 15.)

Example 1:

A gardener ordered a total of 12 butterfly and rose bushes from a garden nursery. The cost of each butterfly bush is $35 and the cost of each rose bush is $55. If the gardener ordered x butterfly bushes and y rose bushes for $520, which of the following systems can determine the number of rose bushes the gardener ordered?

A) $x + y = 12$
    $35x + 55y = 520$

B) $x + y = 12$
    $55x + 35y = 520$

C) $x - y = 12$
    $35x + 55y = 520$

D) $x - y = 12$
    $55x + 35y = 520$

Step 1: Identify the two variables

Variable 1: Butterfly bushes $= x$.

Variable 2: Rose bushes $= y$.

Step 2: Determine the system of equations

Equation 1: It is given that the total number of bushes $= 12$.

$$x + y = 12$$

This eliminates answer choices C and D.

Equation 2: It is given that the total cost of x butterfly bushes and y rose bushes $= \$520$.

$$(\text{cost of each butterfly bush} \times x) + (\text{cost of each rose bush} \times y) = 520$$

$$35x + 55y = 520$$

This eliminates answer choice B.

Correct answer choice is **A.**

Example 2:

An office manager placed an order for 5 boxes of pens and 10 notepads for a total cost of $54.95. The office manager realized that additional pens and notebooks were needed and placed a second order for 15 boxes of pens and 18 notepads for a total cost of $128.85. What is the cost of 1 box of pens and 1 notepad, given that the cost of a box of pens and a notepad was same in both the orders and no sales tax was collected?

A) $3.00

B) $4.25

C) $5.99

D) $7.99

Step 1: Identify the two variables

Variable 1: Let the cost of one box of pens $= x$.

Variable 2: Let the cost of one notebook $= y$.

Step 2: Determine the system of equations

Equation 1: It is given that in the first order the cost of 5 boxes of pens and 10 notepads $= \$54.95$.

$$(\text{cost of each box of pens} \times 5) + (\text{cost of each notepad} \times 10) = 54.95$$

$$5x + 10y = 54.95$$

Equation 2: It is given that in the second order the cost of 15 boxes of pens and 18 notepads $= \$128.85$.

$$(\text{cost of each box of pens} \times 15) + (\text{cost of each notepad} \times 18) = 128.85$$

$$15x + 18y = 128.85$$

Step 3: Solve the system of equations

Multiply equation 1 by 3 and subtract equation 2 from equation 1. This will cancel $15x$ from both the equations.

Equation 1: $3(5x + 10y = 54.95)$ $\cancel{15x} + 30y = 164.85$

Equation 2: $-(15x + 18y = 128.85)$ $-\cancel{15x} - 18y = -128.85$

$$12y = 36 \rightarrow y = 3$$

Determine the value of x by substituting $y = 3$ in any of the equation.

$$5x + (10 \times 3) = 54.95 \rightarrow 5x + 30 = 54.95 \rightarrow 5x = 24.95 \rightarrow x = 4.99$$

One box of pens + one notebook $= x + y = 4.99 + 3 = 7.99$.

Correct answer choice is **D**.

When solving for the two variables it is best to work with small numbers. Note that to eliminate y, equation 1 will have to be multiplied by 9 and equation 2 by 5. This would result in bigger numbers to work with.

Example 3:

A coffee shop cashier is counting the number of pennies and nickels in the cash register. The cashier counts a total of 106 pennies and nickels with a value of $3.14. How many pennies are in the cash register?

Step 1: Identify the two variables

Variable 1: Let the number of pennies $= x$.

Variable 2: Let the number of nickels $= y$.

Step 2: Determine the system of equations

Equation 1: It is given that the total number of pennies and nickels $= 106$.

$$x + y = 106$$

Equation 2: It is given that the total value of the coins $= \$3.14$. Each penny is $0.01 and each nickel is $0.05. Hence,

$$0.01x + 0.05y = 3.14$$

Multiply the equation by 100 to remove the decimals.

$$(0.01x + 0.05y = 3.14) \times 100 \rightarrow x + 5y = 314$$

Step 3: Solve the system of equations

Multiply equation 1 by 5 and subtract equation 2 from equation 1. This will cancel $5y$ from both the equations.

Equation 1: $\qquad 5(x + y = 106) \qquad\qquad 5x + \cancel{5y} = 530$

Equation 2: $\qquad -(x + 5y = 314) \qquad\qquad -x - \cancel{5y} = -314$

$$\rule{4cm}{0.4pt}$$

$$4x \qquad = 216 \rightarrow x = 54$$

Correct answer is **54.**

Example 4:

84 passengers must be seated in an airplane on rows of 2 seats and rows of 3 seats. There is a total of 35 rows. If each seat is occupied by a passenger and all passengers have a seat, how many passengers are seated on rows of 3 seats?

Step 1: Identify the two variables

Variable 1: Let row of 2 seats $= x$.

Variable 2: Let row of 3 seats $= y$.

Step 2: Determine the system of equations

Equation 1: It is given the total number of rows $= 35$.

$$x + y = 35$$

Equation 2: It is given that the total number of passengers seated on x rows and y rows $= 84$.

Each x seats 2 passengers and each y seats 3 passengers. Hence,

$$2x + 3y = 84$$

Step 3: Solve the system of equations

Multiply equation 1 by 2 and subtract it from equation 2. This will cancel $2x$ from both the equations.

Equation 2: $\qquad 2x + 3y = 84 \qquad\longrightarrow\qquad \cancel{2x} + 3y = 84$

Equation 1: $\qquad -2(x + y = 35) \qquad\qquad -\cancel{2x} - 2y = -70$

$$\rule{4cm}{0.4pt}$$

$$y = 14$$

Hence, there are 14 rows of 3 seats. The total passengers on these seats $= 14 \times 3 = 42$.

Correct answer is **42.**

Category 18 – Practice Questions (answers on pages 346-347)

No Calculator Questions

1

At a movie theater, the cost of admission for ages 12 and below is $10 and for ages above 12 is $14. On the opening day of a blockbuster movie, the theater sold 400 tickets and collected a total of $4,600 from ticket sales. If c represents the number of tickets sold to ages 12 and below and a represents the number of tickets sold to ages above 12, which of the following system of equations can be used to determine the values of a and c?

A) $a + c = 400$
    $14a + 10c = 4,600$

B) $a + c = 400$
    $10a + 14c = 4,600$

C) $a + c = 4,600$
    $14a + 10c = 4,600$

D) $a + c = 4,600$
    $10a + 14c = 4,600$

2

A teacher is planning to buy a total of 78 spiral notebooks and pocket folders for her class. Each spiral notebook costs $3 and each pocket folder costs $0.50. If the teacher has $164 to buy n spiral notebooks and p pocket folders, which of the following system of equations the teacher can use to determine the number of spiral notebooks and pocket folders that can be bought, assuming no sales tax was collected?

A) $n + p = 78$
    $0.50n + 3p = 164$

B) $n + p = 78$
    $3n + 0.50p = 164$

C) $n + p = 164$
    $0.50n + 3p = 78$

D) $n + p = 164$
    $3n + 0.50p = 78$

3

Maddie is shopping for a total of 10 shirts and hats for her friends. Each shirt costs $20 and each hat costs half the price of the shirt. If Maddie bought s shirts and h hats for $140, which of the following systems can be used to determine the number of shirts Maddie bought (assuming there is no sales tax)?

A) $8s + 2h = 2(10)$
    $20h + 10s = 140$

B) $s + 8h = 2(10)$
    $20h + 20s = 140$

C) $s + h = 10$
    $20h + 20s = 140$

D) $s + h = 10$
    $20s + 10h = 140$

4

A group of 125 students from a certain high school went on an out-of-town overnight trip. The school reserved a total of 55 rooms in a hotel for the students. The rooms either had 2 beds or 3 beds. If all the beds were occupied, and every student got 1 bed, how many rooms had 3 beds?

A) 10

B) 11

C) 15

D) 25

5

At the present time, the sum of Shannon's age and Tina's age is 42. Three years ago, Tina was twice as old as Shannon. What is Shannon's present age?

6

A furniture company hired a truck driver to deliver furniture from a warehouse to a retail store. The truck driver drove through the back roads for b hours at an average speed of 25 miles per hour and on the highway for h hours at an average speed of 65 miles per hour, The truck driver drove a total distance of 205 miles in 5 hours. Which of the following equations can be used with $b + h = 5$ to determine the distance, in miles, the truck driver drove through the backroads?

A) $b + 5h = 90$

B) $5b + 25h = 90$

C) $65b + 25h = 205$

D) $25b + 65h = 205$

7

A group of friends went to a taco shop and bought 14 fish and chicken tacos for $72. If each fish taco costs $6 and each chicken taco costs $4, how many fish tacos did the group buy?

A)   5

B)   6

C)   8

D)   12

8

A teacher bought 6 boxes of crayons and 4 boxes of pencils for $16. The following week, the teacher bought 3 more boxes of crayons and 7 more boxes of pencils for $13. Which of the following is the price of 1 one box of pencils, assuming the teacher bought the same boxes of crayons and pencils at the same cost and no sales tax was collected?

A) $1.00

B) $1.45

C) $2.00

D) $3.70

9

	20 ounces	50 ounces
Cost	$20	$42

A hair salon sells a certain brand of shampoo in 20 ounces and 50 ounces bottles. The table above shows the cost for each of the 20 ounces and 50 ounces bottle sold by the salon. If a total of 90 shampoo bottles were sold and between $2,900 and $3,120 was collected in sales, which of the following could be the number of 50 ounces bottles sold?

A)   20

B)   42

C)   48

D)   54

10

The sum of two different numbers a and b is 110 and the sum of $3a$ and b is 170. What is number a?

11

Jamal has 40 coins in his piggy bank comprised of quarters and dimes. If the total value of Jamal's coins is $7.60, how many quarters Jamal has in his piggy bank?

12

Rita bought a trays of muffins and b trays of cupcakes for a total of $148. If Rita bought a total of 18 trays of muffins and cupcakes, and each tray of muffin costs $10 and each tray of cupcake costs $6, what is the value of a?

Category 19 – Word Problems on Linear Inequalities

Key Points

- A word problem may be given that evaluates a conditional relationship between two or more numbers, where at least one number is unknown. The unknown number contains a variable that evaluates the condition. For example, $700 \leq 55a$. The value given to the variable a must result in the value of $55a$ equal to or greater than 700.

- When a condition evaluates "greater than", the inequality symbol is $>$. For example, x is greater than y is written as $x > y$.

- When a condition evaluates "less than", the inequality symbol is $<$. For example, x is less than y is written as $x < y$.

- When a condition evaluates "greater than or equal to" (or minimum or at least), the inequality symbol is $\geq$. For example, x is at least y is written as $x \geq y$.

- When a condition evaluates "less than or equal to" (or maximum or at the most), the inequality symbol is $\leq$. For example, x is at the most y is written as $x \leq y$.

How to Solve

Identify the conditional variables and form an equation based on the conditions given in the question.

Example 1:

A lemonade stand owner sells each cup of lemonade for $1.50. The daily cost of the renting the lemonade stand is $83 and the cost of making each lemonade cup is $0.15.

Question 1

Which of the following inequalities can determine the minimum number of lemonade cups c that must be sold each day to cover the daily costs of renting the stand and making lemonade cups?

A) $c \leq \dfrac{83}{1.35}$

B) $c \geq \dfrac{83}{1.35}$

C) $c \leq \dfrac{83}{1.50}$

D) $c \geq \dfrac{83}{1.50}$

Step 1: Determine the variables

Number of lemonade cups $= c$.

Step 2: Determine the conditional relationship

Cost of daily rental $= 83$.

Cost of making c lemonade cups $= 0.15c$.

Earnings from c lemonade cups $= 1.50c$.

Cost of daily rental + cost of making c lemonade cups must be less than or equal to earnings from c lemonade cups.

$$83 + 0.15c \leq 1.50c$$

$$83 \leq 1.50c - 0.15c \;\rightarrow\; 83 \leq 1.35c \;\rightarrow$$

$$\frac{83}{1.35} \leq c \;\rightarrow\; c \geq \frac{83}{1.35}$$

Correct answer choice is **B**.

Question 2

What is the minimum number of lemonade cups that must be sold each day to cover the daily costs, given that each cup is a whole number?

Proceed from Step 2 of Question 1. Solve for c.

$$c \geq \frac{83}{1.35} \rightarrow c \geq 61.48$$

Since a cup is a whole number, the minimum number of lemonade cups = 62.

Correct answer is **62**.

Example 2:

A landscaper has less than \$200 to buy x bags of topsoil and y bags of potting soil. If each bag of topsoil costs \$1.95 and each bag of potting soil costs \$9.99, which of the following inequalities represents the situation in context?

A) $200 > 1.95x + 9.99y$

B) $200 < 1.95x + 9.99y$

C) $200 \geq 9.99x + 1.95y$

D) $200 \leq 9.99x + 1.95y$

Step 1: Determine the variables

Number of topsoil bags $= x$.

Number of potting soil bags $= y$.

Step 2: Determine the conditional relationship

Cost of x bags $= 1.95x$.

Cost of y bags $= 9.99y$.

Total cost $= 1.95x + 9.99y$ should be less than \$200.

$$1.95x + 9.99y < 200 \rightarrow 200 > 1.95x + 9.99y$$

Correct answer choice is **A.**

Example 3:

Betty bought a 16 ounce bottle of sparkling water. She drank x ounces and accidently spilled y ounces. If there is at least 7 ounces of sparkling water left in the bottle, which of the following inequalities represents the plausible amounts of sparkling water left in the bottle, in ounces?

A) $16 + x + y > 7$

B) $16 - x - y > 7$

C) $16 + x + y \geq 7$

D) $16 - x - y \geq 7$

Step 1: Determine the variables

Water drank $= x$.

Water spilled $= y$.

Step 2: Determine the conditional relationship

Total water removed from bottle is drank + spilled $= x + y$.

The ounces of water left after drinking and spilling is $16 - (x + y)$.

The ounces of water left after drinking and spilling is at least 7 ounces (same as greater than or equal to). Hence,

$$16 - (x + y) \geq 7 \rightarrow 16 - x - y \geq 7$$

Correct answer choice is **D.**

Category 19 – Practice Questions (answers on page 348)

No Calculator

1

Niya runs a hot dog stand. Each day, she rents the stand for $68 and sells hot dogs for $4 each. If the cost of making each hot dog is $1.50, which of the following inequalities can determine the least number of hot dogs d Niya must sell each day to cover the costs of renting the stand and making hot dogs?

A) $68 \leq 4d$

B) $68 \leq 2.50d$

C) $68 \geq 4d$

D) $68 \geq 2.50d$

2

Zhang has 15 baseball cards. After he gives a number of cards to his brother and b number of cards to his sister, he has at least 5 baseball cards left. Which of the following inequalities represents the possible number of baseball cards Zhang has after giving to his brother and sister?

A) $15 - a - b \geq 5$

B) $15 + a + b \leq 5$

C) $15 - a - b > 5$

D) $15 + a + b < 5$

3

Joe can spend a maximum of $200 to buy soft pretzels and water bottles for an event. If each soft pretzel costs $3 and each water bottle costs $2, which of the following inequalities correctly determines the total amount Joe can spend on p soft pretzels and b water bottles?

A) $200 \leq 3p + 2b$

B) $200 \leq 3b + 2p$

C) $200 \geq 3p + 2b$

D) $200 \geq 3b + 2p$

4

A farmer sells cherry tomatoes and potatoes every day of the week during the summer. To cover the costs of growing and harvesting, the farmer must sell greater than 12 pounds of cherry tomatoes and potatoes combined each day. If c is the pounds of cherry tomatoes and p is the pounds of potatoes, which of the following inequalities determines the cherry tomatoes and potatoes, in pounds, the farmer must sell per week during the summer?

A) $c + p \geq 12$

B) $c + p \geq 84$

C) $c + p > 12$

D) $c + p > 84$

Calculator Questions

5

Gary's cell phone plan charges a fixed fee of $17.99 per month and $0.16 for each call. If Gary cannot spend more than $25 per month, which of the following is the maximum number of calls Gary can make within a month, where each call is a whole number?

A) 25

B) 42

C) 43

D) 44

6

A party planner can spend a maximum of $24 to buy napkins and candles. Each napkin costs $2 and each candle costs $1.50. If the party planner buys 7 napkins, what is the maximum number of whole candles the party planner can buy, assuming there is no sales tax?

Category 20 – Word Problems on Linear System of Inequalities

Key Points

- A word problem may be given that evaluates a conditional relationship between two sets of unknown variables. A single inequality equation, such as $x + y > 18$, cannot evaluate the conditional relationship between the variables x and y. The word problem will contain information to set up two or more inequality equations (system of inequalities) that together can evaluate the conditional relationship.

How to Solve

Identify the conditional variables and form the system of inequalities based on the conditions given in the question.

Example 1:

A restaurant manager wants to order a combination of at least 96 small and large size plates. The manager does not want to spend more than \$550, but wants to buy at least 50 large plates. The cost of each small size plate is \$4 and the cost of each large size plate is \$6. If the manager decides to order x small size plates and y large size plates, which of the following inequalities represents the situation in context?

A) $x + y \geq 96$

   $4x + 6y \leq 550$

   $x \leq 50$

B) $x + y \geq 96$

   $4x + 6y \leq 550$

   $y \geq 50$

C) $x + y \leq 96$

   $4x + 6y \geq 550$

   $x \leq 50$

D) $6x + 4y \leq 96$

   $x + y \leq 550$

   $y \leq 50$

Step 1: Identify the two variables

Variable 1: Number of small size plates $= x$.

Variable 2: Number of large size plates $= y$.

Step 2: Determine the conditional relationship in the system of inequalities

Equation 1: The total number of small size plates x and large size plates y must be greater than or equal to 96.

$$x + y \geq 96$$

This eliminates answer choices C and D.

Equation 2: The cost of each $x = \$4$ and the cost of each $y = \$6$. The total cost must be less than or equal to \$550.

$$4x + 6y \leq 550$$

Equation 3: It is given that the number of large plates must be at least 50.

$$y \geq 50$$

This eliminates answer choice A.

Correct answer choice is **B.**

Category 20 – Practice Questions (answers on pages 348-349)

No Calculator Questions

1

A truck is loaded with boxes that weigh either 20 pounds or 40 pounds. The truck can carry a maximum of 55 boxes with a total weight of 1,850 pounds or less. Which of the following inequalities represents the allowed capacity of the truck, where m is the number of boxes that weigh 20 pounds and n is the number of boxes that weigh 40 pounds?

A) $m + n \geq 55$
$20m + 40n \geq 1,850$

B) $m + n \leq 55$
$20m + 40n \leq 1,850$

C) $m + n \geq 55$
$40m + 20n \geq 1,850$

D) $m + n \leq 55$
$40m + 20n \leq 1,850$

2

A library has allocated a budget of $680 or less to buy no more than 50 fiction and non-fiction books, combined. The cost of each fiction book c is $12 and the cost of each non-fiction book k is $15. Which of the following systems represents the constraints on c and k?

A) $c + k \geq 50$
$15c + 12k \geq 680$

B) $c + k \geq 50$
$12c + 15k \geq 680$

C) $c + k \leq 50$
$15c + 12k \leq 680$

D) $c + k \leq 50$
$12c + 15k \leq 680$

3

Emma works as a part time tutor. Each week, she provides l hours of on-line tutoring and h hours of in-home tutoring. Emma charges $25 per hour for on-line tutoring and $45 per hour for in-home tutoring. Her schedule does not permit her to provide tutoring for more than 20 hours per week. If Emma must earn at least $600 per week and provide at least 10 hours of in-home tutoring per week, which of the following systems represents the weekly constraints on l and h?

A) $l + h \leq 20$
$45l + 25h \leq 600$
$h \geq 20$

B) $l + h \leq 20$
$25l + 45h \geq 600$
$h \leq 10$

C) $l + h \geq 20$
$45l + 25h \leq 600$
$10 \leq h \leq 20$

D) $l + h \leq 20$
$25l + 45h \geq 600$
$10 \leq h \leq 20$

4

Leena wants to buy at least 12 songs and videos from an online store. Each song costs $0.99 and each video costs $1.99. If Leena must spend less than $21 on x songs and y videos, which of the following system of inequalities accurately represents the situation in context?

A) $x + y > 12$
$0.99x + 1.99y > 21$

B) $x + y > 12$
$0.99x + 1.99y \geq 21$

C) $x + y \geq 12$
$0.99x + 1.99y < 21$

D) $x + y \geq 12$
$0.99x + 1.99y \leq 21$

5

An event planning company is arranging a one-day event with a team of at least 8 staff members present at the event. The staff members will be comprised of c event coordinators and s stewards. The staff must comprise of at least 1 but no more than 3 event coordinators. Each event coordinator will be paid $495 and each steward will be paid $175. If the event planning company has a maximum budget of $2,500 for all the staff members, which of the following systems represents the constraints on the number of event coordinators and the number of stewards that can comprise the team of staff members for the event?

A) $c + s \geq 8$

$495c + 175s \geq 2,500$

$1 \leq c \leq 3$

B) $c + s \geq 8$

$495c + 175s \leq 2,500$

$1 \leq c \leq 3$

C) $c + s \leq 8$

$495c + 175s \geq 2,500$

$1 \leq s \leq 3$

D) $c + s \geq 8$

$495c + 175s \leq 2,500$

$1 \leq s \leq 3$

6

A gym owner has allocated a maximum budget of $28,000 to buy at least 12 new treadmills and exercise bikes. Each treadmill costs $2,600 and each exercise bike costs $1,800. If the gym owner wants to buy t treadmills and b exercise bikes, which of the following systems accurately represents the situation in context?

A) $b + t \geq 12$

$1,800b + 2,600t \leq 28,000$

B) $b + t \leq 12$

$1,800b + 2,600t \geq 28,000$

C) $b + t \geq 12$

$1,800t + 2,600b \leq 28,000$

D) $b + t \leq 12$

$1,800b + 2,600t \geq 28,000$

Category 21 – Word Problems on Equal Variables in Linear Equations

Key Points

- A word problem may be given that contains two linear equations that are equal for some value of a common variable for a certain duration. For example, product price for which cost is equal to profit for d days after New Year's Day, or product quantity for which the supply is equal to the demand for w weeks after product launch, or product price at which the sales of one item equal to the sales of another item for w weeks after a promotion.

How to Solve

Equate the two given equations and solve for the variable that makes them equal.

If the equations are not given, then form the two equations based on the information in the word problem and equate them.

Example 1:

$$S = 122 - \frac{1}{4}P$$

$$D = \frac{1}{2}P + 59$$

In the equations above, S is the number of coffee machines manufactured by a certain manufacturer and D is the number of the coffee machines ordered by customers for m months since the beginning of winter. At what price P, in dollars, the number of coffee machines manufactured were equal to the number of coffee machines ordered by the customers during m months?

A) $21

B) $63

C) $84

D) $101

Step 1: Equate the two equations

$$122 - \frac{1}{4}P = \frac{1}{2}P + 59$$

Step 2: Solve for the variable

$$\frac{1}{2}P + \frac{1}{4}P = 122 - 59$$

$$\frac{3}{4}P = 63$$

$$P = 63 \times \frac{4}{3} = 84$$

Correct answer choice is **C**.

Example 2:

$$a = 5.3 + 0.82d$$

$$p = 8.9 + 0.67d$$

A supermarket recently started selling fresh baked apple pies and pumpkin pies. In the equations above, a and p represent the sales, in dollars, of apple pies and pumpkin pies, respectively, for d days after the supermarket started selling them. Which of the following is closest to the sales of apple pies when they were equal to sales of pumpkin pies?

A) $14

B) $18

C) $23

D) $25

Step 1: Equate the two equations

$$5.3 + 0.82d = 8.9 + 0.67d$$

Step 2: Solve for the variable

$$0.82d - 0.67d = 8.9 - 5.3$$

$$0.15d = 3.6$$

$$d = 24$$

Step 3: Solve the equation

The question asks for the sales of apple pies $= a$. Plug in the value of d in the equation.

$$a = 5.3 + 0.82d \rightarrow a = 5.3 + (0.82 \times 24) = 24.98$$

Correct answer choice is **D**.

Example 3:

A supermarket announced sale on its freshly baked cherry pies. The weekly cost of making cherry pies is $19.20 plus $1.60 per pie. The selling price of each cherry pie is $4.80. How many whole cherry pies must be sold in a week for the cost of making cherry pies to equal the sales from cherry pies, in dollars?

A) 2

B) 6

C) 8

D) 12

Step 1: Determine the two equations

Let the number of cherry pies $= p$.

Let one week cost of making p cherry pies $= c$.

$$c = 19.20 + 1.60p$$

Let one week sales of p cherry pies $= s$.

$$s = 4.80p$$

Step 2: Equate the two equations

$$19.20 + 1.60p = 4.80p$$

Step 3: Solve for the variable

$$19.20 = 4.80p - 1.60p \rightarrow 19.20 = 3.2p \rightarrow p = 6$$

Correct answer choice is **B**.

Category 21 – Practice Questions (answers on page 349)

No Calculator Questions

Calculator Questions

1

$$D = 48 + \frac{1}{4}p$$

$$S = 150 - \frac{1}{2}p$$

In the equations above, S is the quantity of a certain microchip produced by a company and D is the quantity of that microchip in demand by customers for w weeks since the first day of spring. At what price p, in dollars, is the quantity of the microchip produced equal to the quantity of microchip demanded by the customers?

A) $48

B) $95

C) $99

D) $136

2

$$l = 10.50 + 4.50x$$

$$c = 36.50 + 2.50x$$

In the equations above, l and c represent the sales, in dollars, of lemonade and Italian ice, respectively, sold at a certain beach for x weeks last summer. What were the sales for Italian ice when equal to the sales for lemonade, in dollars?

A) $5

B) $13

C) $69

D) $70

3

$$s = 35 + 3p$$

$$d = 75 + p$$

In the equations above, s is the quantity of a certain brand of LED bulbs produced by a manufacturing company and d is the quantity of the LED bulbs ordered by customers. In terms of the product price p, in dollars, at what price is the quantity of the LED bulbs produced same as the quantity of the LED bulbs ordered by the customers?

A) $20

B) $35

C) $55

D) $75

4

$$S = 19,646 + 149W$$

A company that specializes in manufacturing a heart rate monitor watch calculates the quarterly earnings S, in dollars, for W watches sold during a quarter, using the above equation. The company has estimated that in the next quarter the total cost of manufacturing the watches will be $37,750 plus $25 per watch. How many watches W the company must sell next quarter for the total earnings S to equal the total manufacturing costs, in dollars?

A) 98

B) 124

C) 146

D) 158

No Calculator Questions

1

Last week, Samara walked s miles per day for 4 days and Chuck walked p miles per day for 6 days. Which of the following equations represents the total number of miles Samara and Chuck walked last week?

A) $10sp$

B) $4s + p$

C) $4p + 6s$

D) $4s + 6p$

2

An elementary school teacher will be reading a book to the class over the next several days. At the end of each day, the teacher plans to keep a track of the number of pages left to read using the equation $315 = p + 21d$. If p is the number of pages left at the end of each day and d is the number of days the teacher reads the book, which of the following is the best interpretation of the number 315?

A) The total number of pages in the book the teacher will be reading.

B) The number of days it will take the teacher to read the book.

C) The rate at which the teacher will be reading the book each day.

D) The average number of pages the teacher will read each day.

3

Sara burns t calories per minute walking on a treadmill and 6 calories per minute running on it. Which of the following equations represents the total calories C Sara burned after walking on the treadmill for 35 minutes and running on the treadmill for 10 minutes?

A) $C = 45t$

B) $C = 35 + 60t$

C) $C = 35t + 60$

D) $C = 35t + 10t$

4

$$B = 0.2p$$

The equation above can be used to approximate the increase in Body Mass Index B, of a 5 feet tall adult weighing p pounds, where $100 \le p \le 200$. Which of the following statements agrees with the equation?

A) For each increase of 2 pound in weight, B increases by approximately 0.2.

B) For each increase of 0.2 pound in weight, B increases by approximately 1.

C) For each increase of 1 pound in weight, B increases by approximately 0.2.

D) For each increase of 1 pound in weight, B increases by approximately 2.

5

A shipping company charges different rates for shipping packages during peak hours and off-peak hours. The company has several franchises and each franchise is allowed to ship a maximum of 150 packages per day. The number of packages shipped by a franchise during the off-peak hours x cannot be greater than the number of packages shipped during the peak hours y, in a given day. Which of the following inequalities represents the constraints on x and y for each franchise per day?

A) $x + y \le 150$

$x \ge y$

B) $x + y \le 150$

$x \le y$

C) $x + y \ge 150$

$x \ge y$

D) $x + y \ge 150$

$x \le y$

Sita works two shifts as a barista at a 24-hour coffee shop. During the morning shift she earns $18 per hour and during the night shift she earns $34 per hour. Last Friday, Sita worked for a total of 10 hours and earned $276. Which of the following systems can determine the number of hours M Sita worked during the morning shift and the number of hours N Sita worked during the night shift, last Friday?

A) $M + N = 10$

   $18M + 34N = 276$

B) $M + N = 2(10)$

   $34N + 18N = 276$

C) $M + N = 2(10)$

   $18M + 34N = 276$

D) $M + N = 10$

   $18M + 34N = 2(276)$

A high school teacher works in an after school program as an Algebra I tutor and a Spanish tutor for m and n hours per week, respectively. Each week, the teacher is required to teach at least 7 hours of Spanish but no more than 15 hours of Algebra I and Spanish combined. If the teacher charges $50 per hour for teaching Algebra I and $38 per hour for teaching Spanish and must earn a minimum of $500 weekly, which of the following inequalities represents the constraints on m and n?

A) $m + n \leq 7$

   $38m + 50n \geq 500$

   $0 \leq n \leq 7$

B) $m + n \leq 15$

   $38m + 50n \geq 500$

   $7 \leq n \leq 15$

C) $m + n \leq 15$

   $50m + 38n \geq 500$

   $0 \leq n \leq 7$

D) $m + n \leq 15$

   $50m + 38n \geq 500$

   $7 \leq n \leq 15$

The cost of admission to an amusement park for a day is $40 and each ride at the park costs $2. Which of the following expressions can give the total cost, in dollars, of the admission ticket and n rides for a day?

A) $40 + 2n$

B) $40 + 40n$

C) $42 + n$

D) $42n$

$$g(t) = 10 + 0.75t$$

In 2015, Ken planted a 10 feet tall tree in his backyard. The height of the tree, in feet, after t years from 2015 can be modeled by the linear function g shown above. Which of the following is the best interpretation of the equation $g(12) = 19$?

A) The number of years the tree will grow in Ken's backyard after 2015.

B) The height of the tree is predicted to be 19 feet in 12 years from 2015.

C) The average increase in the height of the tree each year is predicted to be 19 feet after 2015.

D) The maximum height of the tree is predicted to be 19 feet.

Teri filled 3.5 gallons of fuel in her car. If her car consumes 1 gallon of fuel for every 19.5 miles, which of the following inequalities represents the maximum number of miles m Teri can drive her car with 3.5 gallons of fuel?

A) $m \geq 3.5$

B) $m \leq 19.5$

C) $m \geq 19.5$

D) $m \leq 68.25$

11

A tutoring center bought c iPads and d desks for a total of \$1,377. The equation $389c + 72d = 1,377$ represents the situation in context. What is the interpretation of $72d$ in this context?

A) The total number of iPads and desks bought by the tutoring center.

B) The total amount, in dollars, the tutoring center spent on buying d desks.

C) The total number of desks bought by the tutoring center.

D) The total amount, in dollars, the tutoring center spent on buying iPads and desks.

12

John has 50 coins in his pocket consisting of nickels and dimes. If the total value of the coins is \$3.50, how many dimes does John have in his pocket?

A) 7

B) 10

C) 20

D) 30

13

A restaurant sells extra-large burgers on the first day of each month. The cost of making the extra-large burgers for the day is \$41.50 plus \$0.45 per extra-large burger. The profit from selling the extra-large burger for the day is \$29.50 plus \$1.95 per extra-large burger. How many extra-large burgers must be sold on the first day of each month for the cost of making the extra-large burgers, in dollars, to equal the profit from the sales, in dollars?

A) 8

B) 11

C) 20

D) 24

14

The advanced tickets for the entrance to a fair were sold at the reduced price of \$9 per ticket. On the day of the fair, the tickets were sold at the regular price of \$29. If a total of 240 tickets were sold and \$4,960 was collected from the ticket sales, which of the following is the number of tickets sold at the regular price?

A) 100

B) 140

C) 200

D) 230

15

This year, a certain school has 52 teachers in total. Over the next 3 years, the school plans to add at least 4, but no more than 9 teachers per year. If g is the number of teachers, which of the following inequalities represents all possible values of the number of teachers at the school by the end of next 3 years?

A) $12 < g < 27$

B) $52 \leq g \leq 64$

C) $64 \leq g \leq 79$

D) $64 \leq g \leq 90$

16

$$g(m) = p + 68m$$

In January 2020, the number of trout fishes in a certain local pond was estimated to be p. The function shown above estimates the number of trout fishes in m months after January 2020. Which of the following is the best interpretation of the number 68 in this context?

A) The total number of trout fishes in m months after January 2020.

B) The average monthly increase in the number of trout fishes before January 2020.

C) The average increase in the number of trout fishes per year after January 2020 for m months.

D) The average increase in the number of trout fishes each month after January 2020 for m months.

In 2015, 176 students were enrolled at a high school. During the next 5 years, the school increased the enrollment by a constant number to a total of 236 in 2020. If, after 2020, the high school continues to enroll the same number of additional students each year for t years, which of the following equations can determine the number of students r enrolled in t years?

A) $r = 176 - 5t$

B) $r = 176 + 12t$

C) $r = 236 + 12t$

D) $r = 412 + 12t$

Sammy opened a bank account with $700. During the next 12 months, Sammy plans to deposit at least $100 but not more than $150 per month in the above bank account for the next two years. Which of the following inequalities represents all possible amounts s, in dollars, in the bank account after 12 months of opening the account, assuming that no withdrawals were made, and no interest was collected?

A) $100 \le s \le 150$

B) $700 \le s \le 1{,}200$

C) $1{,}200 \le s \le 1{,}800$

D) $1{,}900 \le s \le 2{,}500$

A baker has 104 cupcakes to distribute in 6-pack and 14-pack containers. The baker distributes the cupcakes in a total of 12 containers. If each container is full and all the cupcakes have been evenly distributed, how many cupcakes are in the 14-pack containers?

A) 4

B) 8

C) 56

D) 60

$$h = 17 + \frac{t}{2.5}$$

Jasper bought a 17 centimeter tall cactus plant for his garden. In t years, he estimates the height of the cactus h, in centimeters, by the above equation. At what value of t will the height of cactus increase by 1 centimeter?

A) $\frac{1}{17}$

B) $\frac{1}{2.5}$

C) 1

D) 2.5

Casey and her friend Lilian subscribe to separate cell phone data plans. Casey pays a monthly fee of $24.99 and an additional $0.08 per call. Lilian pays a monthly fee of $16.99 and an additional $0.28 per call. For how many calls in a month will the two data plans have the same cost, in dollars?

A trucking company estimates the daily cost C, in dollars, of hiring truck drivers using the equation $C = 500 + 55nh$, where n is the number of truck drivers and h is total number of hours n truck drivers work in a day. If last Monday, the total cost of hiring 3 truck drivers was $3,965, how many total hours did the 3 truck drivers work?

A teacher is packing cookies in paper bags for a school party. If the teacher packs 5 cookies per bag, exactly 4 additional bags will be required to pack the remaining cookies. If the teacher packs 10 cookies per bag, exactly 1 bag will not be used. How many cookies is the teacher packing?

Section 5 –
Polynomial and Undefined Functions

Category 22 – Polynomial Functions as Equations

Key Points

- A polynomial function is an equation containing terms in the form of ax^n, where n is a positive integer. For example, $f(x) = ax^4 + ax^2 + x + 3$.

    - $f(x)$ is the output value of a function for an input value of x. For example, if $x = 2$ in the above equation, then $f(2) = a(2)^4 + a(2)^2 + (2) + 3 =$ output value.

- The input value of x can be referred by any letter. For example, $f(a)$, $f(b)$, or $f(t)$.

- A function can be given any name. For example, $g(x)$, $h(t)$, or $f(a)$, where x, t, and a are the inputs, respectively.

- A function may be evaluated for a single value or multiple values of x. For example, $f(a) + f(b)$ or $\dfrac{f(a)}{f(b)}$, where a and b are two different input values of x for the function f.

How to Solve

In the given equation, plug in the input value of x to determine the corresponding value of y. For example, if the question asks for $f(2)$, then plug in 2 as the value of x in the given equation, and if the questions asks for $f(2x + 3)$, then plug in $2x + 3$ as the value of x in the given equation. Remember that $f(x)$ is the output value of a function. For example, $f(-2) = 8$ means that when $x = -2$, the output value of the function f is 8.

Example 1:

If $f(x) = x^3 - 5x$ for all values of x, what is the valve of $4f(3) - f(4)$?

A)   4

B)   9

C)   12

D)   44

Step 1: Plug in the given value of x in the function

To get the value of $f(3)$, plug in $x = 3$ in the equation.
$$f(3) = 3^3 - (5 \times 3) = 27 - 15 = 12$$
To get the value of $f(4)$, plug in $x = 4$ in the equation.
$$f(4) = 4^3 - (5 \times 4) = 64 - 20 = 44$$

Step 2: Solve for $4f(3) - f(4)$

$$4f(3) - f(4) = (4 \times 12) - 44 = 48 - 44 = 4$$

Correct answer choice is **A**.

Example 2:

For what value of a does $g(a) + h(a) = 1$, where the function g is defined as $g(x) = 7x - 41$ and the function h is defined as $h(x) = 4x + 9$?

Step 1: Solve for a

The input value can be any letter. $g(x) = 7x - 41$ can be written as $g(a) = 7a - 41$ and $h(x) = 4x + 9$ can be written as $h(a) = 4a + 9$. Add the two equations and equate to 1.

$$7a - 41 + 4a + 9 = 1 \quad \rightarrow \quad 11a - 32 = 1 \quad \rightarrow \quad 11a = 33 \quad \rightarrow \quad a = 3$$

Correct answer is **3**.

Category 22 – Practice Questions (answers on page 353)

No Calculator Questions

Calculator Questions

1

For the function f, $f(x) = x^4 - 3x^2 - 4$ for all values of x. What is the value of $f(-2) - f(1)$?

A) -4

B) -2

C) 0

D) 6

2

$$f(x) = \frac{3x - 7}{2}$$

If the function f is defined as shown above, which of the following is the value of $f(2x + 5)$?

A) $x - 6$

B) $3x - 1$

C) $3x + 4$

D) $6x + 8$

3

If $f(x) = 4x + 3$ and $3f(b) = 21$, which of the following is the value of b?

A) 0

B) 1

C) 4

D) 7

4

The function f is defined as $f(x) = 5x + 3$ for all values of x. What is the product of $f(3)$ and $f(9)$?

A) 27

B) 270

C) 864

D) 950

5

$$g(x) = \frac{mx^2 + n}{2}$$

The function g shown above is true for all values of x, and m and n are constants. If $g(10) = 300$ and $g(20) = 1,500$, what is the value of m?

A) 1

B) 8

C) 15

D) 24

6

For what value of t does $g(t) + f(t) = 0$, where the function g is defined as $g(x) = 3x^4 - 2x - 4$ and the function f is defined as $f(x) = -3x^4 + 5x - 5$?

A) -5

B) -3

C) 1

D) 3

Category 23 – Polynomial Functions as Tables and Graphs

Key Points

- A polynomial function may be represented in a table or on a graph.
  - A table contains two columns. For a function f, the x column contains the input values of x and the $f(x)$ column contains the corresponding output values.
  - On the graph of a function f, $f(x)$ is the y-value corresponding to a given value of x on the x-axis.

How to Solve

Remember that $y = f(x)$ on the graph of the function f. For example, $y = f(3) = 8$ means that for $x = 3$ on the graph, the value on the y-axis is 8.

Example 1:

x	$f(x)$
2	3
3	4
4	6
6	12

For the function f, the above table shows selected values of x and the corresponding $f(x)$ values.

Question 1

What is the value of $f(3)$?

A) 2

B) 3

C) 4

D) 12

Step 1: Read the value of $f(x)$ from the table

Since $x = 3$, look for 3 in the x column and read the corresponding value from the $f(x)$ column.

$$f(3) = 4$$

Correct answer choice is **C**.

Remember not to confuse $f(3)$ with $f(x) = 3$.

Question 2

If $f(x) = 3$, what is the value of x?

Step 1: Read the value of x from the table

Since $f(x) = 3$, look for 3 in the $f(x)$ column and read the corresponding value from the x column.

$$x = 2$$

Correct answer is **2**.

Example 2:

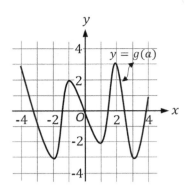

The complete graph of the function g, where $y = g(a)$, is shown above in the xy-plane. How many values of a define $g(-1)$?

A) 1

B) 2

C) 4

D) 5

Step 1: Read the value of y from the graph for the given value of x

The question asks for the number of x values where $y = g(-1)$. The first step is to determine the y value for $x = -1$. Hence, read from the graph the y value where $x = -1$.

$$y = 2$$

Step 2: Count the number of x values from the graph for the y value from Step 1

For ease, draw a line across the graph at $y = 2$ and count the number of points on the line. See figure on the right. There are four values of x that have $y = 2$. In other words, four values of x define $y = 2$.

Correct answer choice is **C**.

Example 3:

x	$f(x)$
2	3
3	4
5	8

For the function f, selected values of x and the corresponding $f(x)$ values are shown in the table above. If $2f(x) = f(x + 2)$ for all values of x, what is the value of $f(4)$?

Step 1: Read the value of $f(x)$ from the table

The table does not contain $x = 4$. Hence, determine a value of x that can give $f(x + 2) = f(4)$ and exists in the table. If $x = 2$, then

$$2f(x) = f(x + 2) \ \rightarrow \ 2f(2) = f(2 + 2) \ \rightarrow \ 2f(2) = f(4)$$

The value of $f(2)$ can be read from the table.

$$f(2) = 3$$

Hence,

$$2f(2) = f(4) \ \rightarrow \ 2 \times 3 = f(4) \ \rightarrow \ 6 = f(4)$$

Correct answer is **6**.

Category 23 – Practice Questions <small>(answers on page 353)</small>

No Calculator Questions

Calculator Questions

(answers on page 353)

1

x	$g(x)$
2	5
4	−2
12	−4

For the function g, selected values of x and the corresponding $g(x)$ values are shown in the table above. If $2g(x) = g(3x)$ for all values of x, which of following is the value of $g(6)$?

A) 3

B) 5

C) 6

D) 10

2

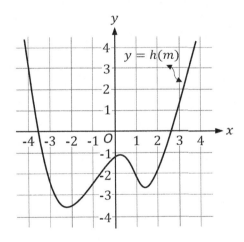

In the xy-plane, the complete graph of the function h is shown above and $y = h(m)$. If c is a constant and $h(m) = c$ has 4 solutions, which of the following can be a value of c?

A) −3

B) −2

C) 0

D) 1

3

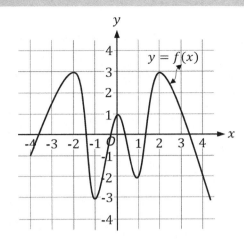

In the xy-plane, the graph of the function f, where $y = f(x)$, is shown above. Which of the following satisfies $f(x) = 3$?

A) $f(-2)$ and $f(2)$

B) $f(-2)$ and $f(3)$

C) $f(-3)$

D) $f(3)$

4

x	3	1	0	−5
$f(x)$	4	2	−1	−4

In the table above, selected values of x and the corresponding $f(x)$ values are given. If $3f(x) = 12$, what is the value of x?

5

x	$f(x)$
1	−3
2	1
3	2
4	4

The table above shows selected values of x and the corresponding $f(x)$ values of the function f. What is the value of $\dfrac{f(2)-f(1)}{f(4)}$?

Category 24 – Polynomial Function within a Function

Key Points

- A polynomial function may be nested in another function.
    - For example, in $g(f(2))$, the function f is nested within the outside function g. The output value of the nested function f becomes the input value of the outside function g. If $f(2) = 5$, then $g(f(2)) = g(5)$.
- A polynomial function may contain another function in its definition.
    - For example, in $g(x) = 5 + 2f(x)$, the function g contains the function f in its definition. The input value of x will be the input value for all the functions in the equation. If $x = 6$, then $g(6) = 5 + 2f(6)$.

How to Solve

Remember that the output value of the nested function must be determined first.

Example 1:

The function f is defined as $f(x) = x^2 + 2x$ and the function g is defined as $g(x) = 5 + 2f(x)$. What is the value of $g(3)$?

Step 1: Plug in the given value of x in all the functions

Plug in $x = 3$ in functions g and f.

$$g(3) = 5 + 2f(3)$$

Plug in the definition of $f(x)$.

$$5 + 2(3^2 + (2 \times 3)) = 5 + 2(15) = 35$$

Correct answer is **35**.

Example 2:

x	-6	-1	3	4
$g(x)$	6	4	0	-6
$f(x)$	12	6	-1	-6

The table above shows some values of x and the corresponding values for functions g and f. What is the value of $f(g(4))$?

A) -6

B) -1

C) 6

D) 12

Step 1: Read the value of $g(x)$ for the nested function

Look for 4 in the x column and read the corresponding value from the $g(x)$ column.

$$g(4) = -6$$

Step 2: Read the value of $f(x)$ for the outside function

Since $g(4) = -6$, the outside function becomes

$$f(g(4)) = f(-6)$$

Look for -6 in the x column and read the corresponding value from the $f(x)$ column.

$$f(-6) = 12$$

Correct answer choice is **D**.

Category 24 – Practice Questions (answers on page 354)

No Calculator Questions

1

x	$f(x)$	$g(x)$
-2	0	-3
-1	-3	7
0	3	5
3	0	4
7	4	2

The above table shows some values of x and the corresponding values of the function f defined as $f(x)$ and the function g defined as $g(x)$. If $g(f(3)) + f(g(-1)) + k = 1$, what is the value of k, where k is a constant?

A) -8

B) -5

C) 1

D) 6

2

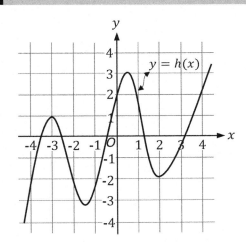

The graph of the function h in the xy-plane is shown above, where $y = h(x)$. If the function g is defined as $g(x) = 2x^4 + 3$, what is the value of $g(h(-3)) - 2$?

A) -2

B) 1

C) 3

D) 5

3

The function g is defined as $g(x) = x^2 + 4$ and the function h is defined as $h(x) = c - g(2)$. For what value of c, $h(x) = -5$?

A) 0

B) 3

C) 8

D) 9

4

The function g is defined as $g(x) = x^3 - 20$ and the function f is defined as $f(x) = x^2 - x$. What is the value of $f(g(3))$?

A) 6

B) 14

C) 27

D) 42

5

If the function f is defined as $f(x) = 4x - 19$ and the function g is defined as $g(x) = 3f(x - 1) - 3$, what is the value of $g(7)$?

A) 2

B) 5

C) 12

D) 15

6

The function g is defined as $g(x) = \frac{2x^3 - 98}{19}$. For the function f, $f(3) = 5$. What is the value of $g(f(3))$?

Category 25 – Polynomial Functions and Zeros

Key Points

- The zeros of a polynomial function are the values of x where the graph of the polynomial function intersects the x-axis. They are also known as the roots, the solutions, or the x-intercepts of the function.

  - If n is the zero of a function, then the factor will be $(x - n)$ when the graph crosses the positive x-axis and $(x + n)$ when the graph crosses the negative x-axis.

  - If the graph touches the x-axis at n and curves back without crossing through the x-axis, then there will be two identical factors for n at that point. On the positive x-axis, the factors will be $(x - n)^2$. On the negative x-axis, the factors will be $(x + n)^2$.

  - For example, the graph below has 3 distinct zeros at $x = -2$, 1 and 3. The corresponding factors are $(x + 2)$, $(x - 1)$ and $(x - 3)^2$. Since the graph curves back at 3, $(x - 3)^2$ are two factors but one distinct x-intercept.

  - The value of y at the x-intercept is 0.

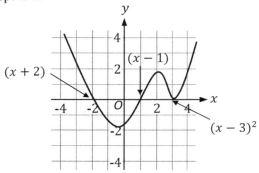

How to Solve

On a graph, read the points where the graph crosses the x-axis or curves back without crossing it.

In a table, look for the values of x that have corresponding output value $= 0$ (the x-intercept).

Example 1:

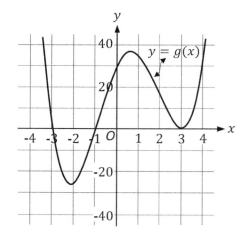

In the xy-plane, the graph of a polynomial function g is shown above. What are the factors of the function g?

A) $g(x) = (x + 3)(x + 1)(x - 3)$

B) $g(x) = (x - 3)(x - 1)(x + 3)$

C) $g(x) = (x + 1)(x + 3)(x - 3)^2$

D) $g(x) = (x - 1)(x - 3)^2$

Step 1: Determine the points on the x-axis where the graph crosses the x-axis

The graph intersects the x-axis at -1 and -3. The corresponding factors are $(x + 1)$ and $(x + 3)$, respectively.

Step 2: Determine the points on the x-axis where the graph touches the x-axis and curves back

The graph touches the x-axis at 3 and curves back. The corresponding factors are $(x - 3)^2$.

Step 3: Select the answer choice with matching factors

The factors are $(x + 1)(x + 3)(x - 3)^2$.

Correct answer choice is **C**.

Example 2:

$$5x(x + 3)(x - 3)^2(x - 1)^2$$

The factors of a polynomial $f(x)$ are shown above. How many distinct zeros does $f(x)$ have?

A) 3

B) 4

C) 5

D) 6

Step 1: Determine the zeros

For $(x + 3)$, the zero is -3.

For $(x - 3)^2$, the distinct zero is 3.

For $(x - 1)^2$, the distinct zero is 1.

For $5x$, the zero is 0. (When a graph passes through the origin, the x-intercept/zero is 0.)

The four distinct zeros are -3, 0, 1, and 3.

Correct answer choice is **B**.

Example 3:

x	$h(x)$
-1	0
0	-3
1	-4
2	2
3	0

In the above table, selected values of a polynomial function h and the corresponding x values are given. What are the x-intercepts of the function h?

A) $\{-3\}$

B) $\{-2, 1\}$

C) $\{-1, 3\}$

D) $\{2, 3\}$

Step 1: Determine the values of x where $y = 0$

At the x-intercept, $y = h(x) = 0$. In the table, look for x values where $h(x) = 0$.

$$x = -1 \text{ and } 3$$

Correct answer choice is **C**.

Category 25 – Practice Questions (answers on page 354)

No Calculator Questions

1

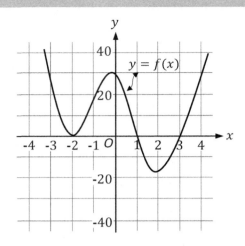

In the xy-plane, the graph of the function f, where $y = f(x)$, is shown above. Which of the following could define the function f?

A) $f(x) = (x + 3)(x + 1)(x - 2)$

B) $f(x) = (x + 2)(x - 3)(x + 1)$

C) $f(x) = (x - 1)(x - 3)(x + 2)^2$

D) $f(x) = (x + 3)(x - 2)^2(x + 1)^2$

2

x	$f(x)$
-2	0
0	-8
4	-2
8	0
0	16

In the above table, selected values of x and the corresponding values of $f(x)$ are given for the function f. What are the zeros of the function f?

A) $\{-8, 16\}$

B) $\{-8, 8\}$

C) $\{-2, 4\}$

D) $\{-2, 8\}$

3

$$x(x - 1)(x - 3)(x + 2)^2$$

The factors of a polynomial $p(x)$ are shown above. Which of the following are the distinct zeros of $p(x)$?

A) $\{-2, 1, 3\}$

B) $\{-2, 0, 1, 3\}$

C) $\{-2, 1, 2, 3\}$

D) $\{0, 1, 2, 3\}$

4

$$p(x) = (x - 4)(x^2 - 4)$$

A polynomial function p is shown above. How many distinct zeros does the function p have?

A) 1

B) 2

C) 3

D) 5

Calculator Questions

5

x	$h(x)$
4	3
2	0
0	-8
5	0
0	-1

In the above table, all the values of a polynomial $h(x)$ are given. What is the product of the zeros of $h(x)$?

Category 26 – Remainder in Polynomial Functions

Key Points

- Remainder Theorem: When a polynomial is divided by a linear expression $x - n$, the remainder can be determined by substituting $x = n$ in the polynomial. For example, for a polynomial function $p(x) = ax^3 + bx + c$, the remainder is $p(n) = an^3 + bn + c$.

- Factor Theorem: When a polynomial is divided by a linear expression $x - n$ and the remainder obtained by substituting $x = n$ in the polynomial is 0, then n is the zero and $x - n$ is a factor of the polynomial. For example, for a polynomial function $p(x) = ax^3 + bx + c$, if $p(n) = an^2 + bn + c = 0$, then $x - n$ is a factor of $p(x)$.

How to Solve

Remember that when a polynomial is divided by $x - n$, then $x = n$ and when a polynomial is divided by $x + n$, then $x = -n$.

Example 1:

$$f(x) = 5x^2 + 15x + 11$$

What is the reminder when the above polynomial $f(x)$ is divided by $x + 2$?

A) -2

B) 1

C) 2

D) 5

Step 1: Plug in the value of x in the equation

Since the equation is divided by $x + 2$, $x = -2$. Plug in $x = -2$ in the equation to determine the remainder.

$$f(-2) = (5 \times (-2)^2) + (15 \times (-2)) + 11 = (5 \times 4) + (-30) + 11 = 20 - 30 + 11 = 1$$

Correct answer choice is **B**.

Example 2:

If $\dfrac{2x^2 - 7x + 8}{x - 3} = 2x - 1 + \dfrac{B}{x - 3}$ where B is a constant, what is the value of B?

Step 1: Plug in the value of x in the equation

The equation can be read as: when $2x^2 - 7x + 8$ is divided by $x - 3$, the quotient is $2x - 1$ and the remainder is B.

Plug in $x = 3$ in the expression $2x^2 - 7x + 8$ to determine the remainder B.

$$B = 2(3)^2 - 7(3) + 8 = 18 - 21 + 8 = 5$$

Correct answer is **5**.

Example 3:

$$p(x) = x^3 + x^2 - ax + 6$$

In the above polynomial $p(x)$, what is the value of a, where a is a constant and $x - 2$ is a factor of $p(x)$?

Step 1: Plug in the value of x in the equation and set the equation to 0

Since $x - 2$ is a factor of the polynomial, for $x = 2$ the reminder is 0.

$$p(2) = 2^3 + 2^2 - 2a + 6 = 0$$

$$8 + 4 - 2a + 6 = 0 \ \rightarrow \ 18 - 2a = 0 \ \rightarrow \ 2a = 18 \ \rightarrow \ a = 9$$

Correct answer is **9**.

Category 26 – Practice Questions (answers on page 355)

Calculator Questions

1

$$p(x) = 3x^3 - 3x^2 - cx + 2$$

If $x - 2$ is a factor of the polynomial $p(x)$ shown above, what is the value of the constant c?

A) 2

B) 7

C) 8

D) 15

2

$$\frac{2x^2 + 9x + 5}{x + 4} = 2x + 1 + \frac{A}{x + 4}$$

In the above equation, what is the value of the constant A?

A) -4

B) -2

C) 1

D) 4

3

When the polynomial $p(x)$ is divided by $(x - 1)$ the remainder is 0. Which of the following could define $p(x)$?

A) $-2x^2 - 3x + 5$

B) $-x^2 - x + 1$

C) $x^2 + x - 1$

D) $2x^2 + x - 1$

4

For a polynomial $p(x)$, if $p\left(-\frac{1}{2}\right) = 0$, which of the following must be true?

A) $x - 1$ is a factor of $p(x)$

B) $x + 2$ is a factor of $p(x)$

C) $2x - 1$ is a factor of $p(x)$

D) $2x + 1$ is a factor of $p(x)$

5

Which of the following is a factor of the polynomial $p(x) = 3x^3 - x^2 - 6x + 2$?

A) $x - 1$

B) $3x - 1$

C) $2x + 1$

D) $2x + 3$

6

For a polynomial $p(x)$, if $p(-5) = 4$, which of the following must be true?

A) $x = -4$ is a zero of $p(x)$

B) $x = 4$ is a zero of $p(x)$

C) $x - 5$ is a factor of $p(x)$

D) $x + 5$ is not a factor of $p(x)$

7

$$f(x) = 3x^3 + 8x^2 + 11$$

What is the reminder when the above polynomial $f(x)$ is divided by $(x + 3)$?

Category 27 – Undefined Functions

Key Points

- A function or a numeric expression is undefined when the denominator is 0.

How to Solve

Set the expression in the denominator to 0 and solve.

Example 1:

$$\frac{5x^2 - x}{2(4x - 8)}$$

For what values of x is the above expression undefined?

A) 1

B) 2

C) 3

D) 8

Step 1: Set the denominator to 0

$$2(4x - 8) = 0$$

Step 2: Solve

$$4x - 8 = 0 \ \rightarrow \ 4x = 8 \ \rightarrow \ x = 2$$

Correct answer choice is **B**.

Example 2:

$$f(x) = \frac{6}{x^2 - 6x + 9}$$

For what values of x is the above function f undefined?

A) -3

B) -2

C) 0

D) 3

Step 1: Set the denominator to 0

$$x^2 - 6x + 9 = 0$$

Step 2: Solve

Factorize.

$$(x - 3)(x - 3) = 0 \ \rightarrow \ x = 3$$

Correct answer choice is **D**.

Category 27 – Practice Questions (answers on page 356)

Calculator Questions

1

$$\frac{5x^3 + 11x}{6x + 2x + 16}$$

For what values of x is the above expression undefined?

A) -2

B) 0

C) 2

D) 5

2

For what values of x is the expression $\frac{2x+4x+9}{3x-12}$ undefined?

A) 1

B) 2

C) 4

D) 6

3

$$f(x) = \frac{8x + 8}{(x^2 - 11x + 27) + (x - 2)}$$

If the function f shown above is undefined, what is value of x?

A) -2

B) 0

C) 3

D) 5

4

$$\frac{(x - 4)^2}{(x + 4)^2 - (16x + 1)}$$

For what values of x is the above expression undefined?

I. -4

II. 3

III. 5

A) I only

B) II only

C) I and II only

D) II and III only

5

$$g(x) = \frac{5x^5 + 2x^3 + 1}{4x - 1}$$

For what values of x is the above function g undefined?

A) $\frac{1}{5}$

B) $\frac{1}{4}$

C) 3

D) 5

No Calculator Questions

1

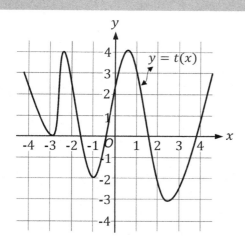

The complete graph of the function t in the xy-plane, where $y = t(x)$, is shown above. If $g(m) = t(-1)$, how many distinct values of m define $g(m)$?

A) 3

B) 4

C) 5

D) 6

2

$$g(x) = (x - 1)(2x - 3)(3x + 2)$$

For the function g defined above, which of the following is NOT an x-intercept of the graph of the function, in the xy-plane?

I.   1

II. $\dfrac{2}{3}$

III. $\dfrac{3}{2}$

A) I only

B) II only

C) III only

D) I and III only

3

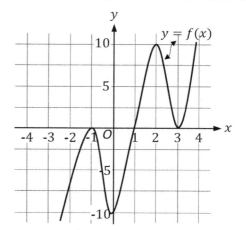

In the xy-plane, which of the following could define the graph of the polynomial $f(x)$ shown above?

A) $f(x) = (x - 1)(x - 3)^2(x + 1)^2$

B) $f(x) = (x - 1)(x + 1)^2(x + 3)^2$

C) $f(x) = (x + 1)(x - 3)^2(x - 1)^2$

D) $f(x) = (x + 1)(x + 3)^2(x - 1)^2$

4

$$y = 2x(x - k)^2(x + k)^2$$

How many distinct zeros does the graph of the above equation in the xy-plane have, where k is a constant?

A) 1

B) 2

C) 3

D) 5

5

$$g(x) = 3x - 6$$

In the xy-plane, the graph of the function g is defined by the equation above. Which of the following is an x-intercept of the graph, where $y = g(x)$?

A) $(-3, g(-3))$

B) $(0, g(0))$

C) $(2, g(0))$

D) $(2, g(2))$

6

If the function f is defined as $f(x) = 3x - 10$ and the function g is defined as $g(x) = 2f(x + 2) - 5$, which of the following is the value of $g(8)$?

A) 15

B) 23

C) 35

D) 40

7

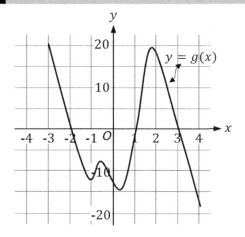

In the xy-plane, the graph of the function g, where $y = g(x)$, is shown above. Which of the following is NOT a factor of $g(x)$?

A) $x - 1$

B) $x - 2$

C) $x - 3$

D) $x + 2$

8

A function f is defined as $f(x) = \dfrac{17.8x^2 + b}{3}$ for all value of x. A function g satisfies $g(b) = 10$. If $f\big(g(b)\big) = 600$ and b is a constant, what is the value of b?

9

For the function f, if $2f(x) = f(x + 2)$ for all values of x and $f(5) = 8$, what is the value of $f(3)$?

Calculator Questions

10

For a polynomial $p(x)$, $p(-\frac{2}{3}) = 0$. Which of the following must be a factor of $p(x)$?

A) $x - 3$

B) $x + 2$

C) $3x - 2$

D) $3x + 2$

11

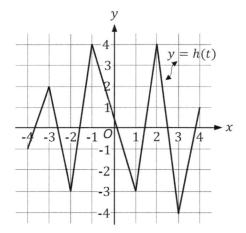

In the xy-plane, the graph of the function h is shown above. If $h(t) = h(2)$, which of the following could be a value of t?

A) -1

B) 0

C) 1

D) 3

12

$$p(x) = 5x^3 + 8x^2 - 3x + 2$$

Which of the following could be a zero of the above polynomial function?

A) -3

B) -2

C) 1

D) 5

13

If the function h is defined as $h(x) = x^3 - a$ for all values of x and a is a constant, what is the value of $h(4) - h(2)$?

A) 8

B) 16

C) 56

D) 64

14

x	-6	-3	2	0	2
$f(x)$	-4	-2	0	1	4

In the table above, values of the function f are given for all values of x. Which of the following is a factor of $f(x)$?

A) $x - 1$

B) $x - 2$

C) $x + 1$

D) $x + 2$

15

x	$f(x)$	$g(x)$
-2	9	-1
0	6	2
1	2	5
4	1	-2
5	-3	4

The table above shows some values of x and the corresponding values of the functions f and g. If k is a constant, and $f\big(g(4)\big) - g\big(f(4)\big) = k$, what is the value of k?

A) 4

B) 5

C) 8

D) 9

16

$$p(x) = x^3 - 7x + 3$$

What is the remainder when the polynomial $p(x)$ shown above is divided by $x - 3$?

A) -2

B) -1

C) 0

D) 9

17

For what values of x is the below expression undefined?

$$\frac{3x^2 + 2x + 5}{(x^2 - x - 9) + 3(x - 2)}$$

A) -3

B) 2

C) -5 and 3

D) -2 and 9

18

$$g(x) = (0.2x + 1)(x - 4)$$

For the function g defined above, what is the value of $g(24)$?

19

For the function h, $h(x) = ax^2 + ax + 4$ and a is a constant. If $h(2) = 10$, what is the value of $h(3)$?

20

The function f is defined by $f(x) = 9x - 1$ and the function h is defined by $h(x) = 5x + 2$. For what value of x does $f(x) - h(x) = 9$?

Section 6 –
Quadratic Equations and Parabola

Category 28 – Quadratic Equations and Factors

Key Points

- A quadratic equation in the standard form is written as $y = ax^2 + bx + c$ where a, b, and c are constants. a and b are also known as coefficients of x^2 and x, respectively. The highest power of x in a quadratic equation is 2.
  - The roots of a quadratic equation in the standard form are the values of x when $y = 0$. A quadratic equation $ax^2 + bx + c = 0$ can be factored to solve for the roots.
  - The roots are also known as the solutions, the zeros, or the x-intercepts of the quadratic equation.
  - The value of c is the product of the two roots of the quadratic equation when $a = 1$.
- A quadratic function is written as $f(x) = ax^2 + bx + c$, where $y = f(x)$ for the input value of x.
- The roots of a quadratic equation can also be determined using the quadratic formula $\frac{-b \pm \sqrt{b^2 - 4ac}}{2a}$.

How to Solve

Use the quadratic formula when factorization is not easily doable or when the answer choices have square root. Factorization is quicker when $a = 1$ and there are multiples of c that add up to the value of b. In the equation below, the two multiples of $c = -10$ that add to $b = -3$ are 2 and -5. Hence the two factors are $(x + 2)$ and $(x - 5)$.

$$x^2 - 3x - 10 = 0 \qquad \text{-----} \ a = 1, b = -3, \text{ and } c = -10$$
$$(x + 2)(x - 5) = 0 \qquad \text{-----} \ c = 2 \times -5 = -10 \text{ and } b = 2 - 5 = -3$$
$$x + 2 = 0 \ \rightarrow \ x = -2$$
$$x - 5 = 0 \ \rightarrow \ x = 5$$

Note that since a factor equates to 0, the value of x will have the opposite plus/minus sign than the factor. Similarly, if the roots of a quadratic equation are -1 and 4, then the corresponding factors are $(x + 1)$ and $(x - 4)$, respectively.

A common multiple in a quadratic equation can be removed to simplify the equation before factoring. For example, $2x^2 + 8x + 4 = 0 \rightarrow 2(x^2 + 4x + 2) = 0 \rightarrow x^2 + 4x + 2 = 0$. If x^2 is negative, then multiply all terms by in the equation by minus. For example, $-x^2 + 4x + 2 = 0 \ \rightarrow \ x^2 - 4x - 2 = 0$.

Example 1:

$$5x^2 - 5x - 1 = 0$$

What are the roots of the above quadratic equation?

A) $\dfrac{5 \pm \sqrt{4}}{5}$

B) $\dfrac{5 \pm 5\sqrt{5}}{10}$

C) $\dfrac{5 \pm 3\sqrt{5}}{10}$

D) $\dfrac{5 \pm \sqrt{5}}{10}$

Step 1: Determine the roots using the quadratic formula

$a = 5$. $b = -5$. $c = -1$.

$$\frac{-(-5) \pm \sqrt{(-5)^2 - (4 \times 5 \times -1)}}{2 \times 5} \rightarrow \frac{5 \pm \sqrt{25 + 20}}{10} \rightarrow \frac{5 \pm \sqrt{45}}{10}$$

Simplify the square root, if possible. Look for multiples of the number within the square root that are perfect square.

$$\frac{5 \pm \sqrt{5 \times 9}}{10} \rightarrow \frac{5 \pm \left(\sqrt{5} \times \sqrt{9}\right)}{10} \rightarrow \frac{5 \pm 3\sqrt{5}}{10}$$

Correct answer choice is **C**.

Category 28 – Practice Questions (answers on page 358)

No Calculator Questions

1

$$2x^2 + 6x - 80 = 0$$

Which of the following is a zero of the above equation?

A) -8

B) -5

C) 2

D) 3

2

$$x^2 - 7x + 12 = 0$$

What are the roots of the above equation?

A) $\{-3, 4\}$

B) $\{3, 4\}$

C) $\{2, 7\}$

D) $\{3, 8\}$

3

$$x^2 + 2x - 5 = 0$$

Which of the following is a solution to the equation above?

A) $-2 - \sqrt{6}$

B) $-2 - \sqrt{24}$

C) $-1 - \sqrt{2}$

D) $-1 - \sqrt{6}$

Calculator Questions

4

The two solutions of an equation in the form $ax^2 + bx + c = 0$ are -8 and 2, where $a = 1$ and b and c are constants. Which of the following is the value of c?

A) -16

B) -8

C) 4

D) 2

5

$$5x^2 - 6x - 3 = 0$$

What are the solutions to the above equation?

A) $\dfrac{\sqrt{2}}{5} \pm \dfrac{\sqrt{3}}{5}$

B) $\dfrac{\sqrt{6}}{5} \pm \dfrac{\sqrt{3}}{5}$

C) $\dfrac{2}{5} \pm \dfrac{\sqrt{3}}{5}$

D) $\dfrac{3}{5} \pm \dfrac{2\sqrt{6}}{5}$

6

$$f(x) = 2x^2 - 5x - 12$$

Which of the following are the factors of the function f shown above?

A) $(x - 2), (x + 2)$

B) $(x - 2), (x + 5)$

C) $(x - 4), (2x + 3)$

D) $(x + 4), (2x - 3)$

Category 29 – Quadratic Equations and Number of Roots

Key Points

- A quadratic equation or a quadratic function may have one, two, or no real solutions.

- In the quadratic formula $\frac{-b\pm\sqrt{b^2-4ac}}{2a}$, the expression $b^2 - 4ac$ is known as the discriminant.

  - $b^2 - 4ac > 0$ indicates two real solutions for the quadratic equation.
  - $b^2 - 4ac = 0$ indicates one real solution for the quadratic equation. This condition happens when both the roots are same.
  - $b^2 - 4ac < 0$ indicates no real solution for the quadratic equation. This condition happens when the values of the roots are negative square root. Negative square roots are not real numbers.

How to Solve

If a question asks for the number of solutions of a quadratic equation or a quadratic function, using the discriminant is the easiest approach. There is no need to solve for the roots by factorization.

Example 1:

$$5x^2 - 12x + 9 = 0$$

How many real solutions does the above equation have?

A) Zero

B) Exactly one

C) Exactly two

D) Infinitely many

Step 1: Determine the number of solutions using the discriminant

$a = 5$. $b = -12$. $c = 9$.

Plug the values in the discriminant.

$$b^2 - 4ac = (-12)^2 - (4 \times 5 \times 9) = 144 - 180 = -36$$

Since discriminant < 0, the equation has no real solution.

Correct answer choice is **A**.

Example 2:

If the quadratic function $f(x) = 4x^2 - 12x + k$ has one solution, what is the value of k, where k is a constant?

A) 0

B) 1

C) 4

D) 9

Step 1: Set the discriminant to 0

$a = 4$. $b = -12$. $c = k$.

Since the quadratic function has one solution the discriminant is 0. Plug in the values in the discriminant and set it to 0.

$$b^2 - 4ac = 0 \rightarrow (-12)^2 - (4 \times 4 \times k) = 0 \rightarrow$$
$$144 - 16k = 0 \rightarrow 16k = 144 \rightarrow k = 9$$

Correct answer choice is **D**.

Category 29 – Practice Questions (answers on pages 358-359)

No Calculator Questions

1

$$3x^2 + 4x + 7 = 0$$

How many real solutions does the above equation have?

A) Zero

B) Exactly one

C) Exactly two

D) Infinitely many

2

$$ax^2 + 6x + c = 0$$

The equation above has one real solution and a and c are constants. Which of the following is the product of a and c?

A) -6

B) 1

C) 6

D) 9

3

$$ax^2 - 8x + 8 = 0$$

The equation above has one real solution. What is the value of a, where a is a constant?

Calculator Questions

4

$$4x^2 - 4x - k = 0$$

In the equation above k is a constant. If the equation has no real solution, which of the following could be a possible value of k?

A) -2

B) -1

C) 0

D) 2

5

$$7x^2 - 10x + 4 = 0$$

Which of the following must be true for the quadratic equation shown above?

A) The equation has exactly two real solutions.

B) The equation has exactly one real solution.

C) The equation has no real solution.

D) The equation has infinitely many solutions.

6

$$9x^2 - 6x + 1 = 0$$

How many real solutions does the above equation have?

A) Zero

B) Exactly one

C) Exactly two

D) Infinitely many

Category 30 – Sum and Product of Quadratic Roots

Key Points

- In a quadratic equation $ax^2 + bx + c = 0$ or a quadratic function $f(x) = ax^2 + bx + c$, the sum and the product of the roots (zeros, solutions, or x-intercepts) can be determined as follows.

  - The sum of the roots $= -\dfrac{b}{a}$.

  - The product of the roots $= \dfrac{c}{a}$.

How to Solve

If a question asks for the sum or the product of the roots of a quadratic equation/function or gives one of the roots and asks for the other, using the above formulas is the easiest approach. There is no need to solve for roots by factorization.

Example 1:

In the quadratic equation $4x^2 + 8x + 3 = 0$, what is the product of the roots?

Step 1: Use the product formula

$a = 4$. $c = 3$.

$$\frac{c}{a} = \frac{3}{4} = 0.75$$

Correct answer is $\dfrac{3}{4}$ or **0.75.**

Example 2:

$$f(x) = 2x^2 + 9x + k$$

If one of the roots of the above quadratic function is -5, which of the following is the other root, where k is a constant?

A) $\dfrac{1}{2}$

B) $\dfrac{3}{2}$

C) 2

D) 5

Step 1: Use the sum formula

Since the value of c is unknown, use the sum formula. (Note that if the value of c is known but the value of b is unknown, then use the product formula.)

$a = 2$. $b = 9$.

$$\text{sum of roots by formula} = -\frac{b}{a} = -\frac{9}{2}$$

Step 2: Determine the second root

It is given that one of the roots $= -5$. Let the second root $= x$. Hence,

$$\text{sum of roots by adding} = -5 + x$$

Equate the two sums of roots.

$$-5 + x = -\frac{9}{2} \rightarrow x = -\frac{9}{2} + 5 = \frac{1}{2}$$

Correct answer choice is **A**.

Category 30 – Practice Questions (answers on page 359)

No Calculator Questions

1

$$2n^2 + 3n - 20 = 0$$

What is the product of all the values of n that satisfy the above equation?

A) -20

B) -10

C) 2

D) 3

2

$$f(x) = 2x^2 - 7x + k$$

If one of the roots of the above quadratic function f is 2, which of the following is the other root, where k is a constant?

A) $\dfrac{3}{2}$

B) $\dfrac{5}{2}$

C) $\dfrac{7}{2}$

D) 3

3

$$2x^2 - bx - 12 = 0$$

If m and n are the two roots of the quadratic equation shown above and b is a constant, which of the following can be the possible values of m and n?

A) $\{-2, -12\}$

B) $\{-2, -6\}$

C) $\{-1, 6\}$

D) $\{1, 6\}$

Calculator Questions

4

$$2x^2 - kx + 9 = 0$$

If one of the roots of the above quadratic equation is 3, which of the following is the other root, where k is a constant?

A) -3

B) -1

C) $\dfrac{3}{2}$

D) $\dfrac{3}{5}$

5

$$3x^2 + 13x + 5 = 0$$

In the above quadratic equation, if n is the sum of the zeros and m is the product of the zeros, what is $m - n$?

A) $\dfrac{3}{5}$

B) $\dfrac{5}{3}$

C) 4

D) 6

Category 31 – Standard Form Equation of a Parabola

Key Points

- A parabola is the graphical representation of a quadratic function (Fig. 1, 2, and 3).
- The standard form equation of a parabola is $f(x) = ax^2 + bx + c$ where a, b, and c are constants.
    - $f(x)$ is the value of y for a particular value of x on the graph of a parabola.
    - The constant c is the y-coordinate of the y-intercept of the parabola.
- A parabola is shaped as an arc. It can open upwards or downwards.
    - If the value of a is positive, the parabola opens upwards (Fig. 1).
    - If the value of a is negative, the parabola opens downwards (Fig. 2).
    - The width of a parabola is determined by the value of a in an inverse relationship. The width increases with the decrease in the value of a and vice versa.
- The tip of a parabola is known as the vertex.
    - In a parabola opening downwards, the y-coordinate of the vertex is the maximum value of the parabola.
    - In a parabola opening upwards, the y-coordinate of the vertex is the minimum value of the parabola.
    - A straight vertical line passing through the vertex is known as the axis of symmetry. The axis of symmetry divides the parabola symmetrically into two equal halves. It is also the x-coordinate of the vertex.
    - In the standard form equation, the x-coordinate of the vertex is $-\frac{b}{2a}$.
- A parabola may intersect the x-axis at one or two points or may not intersect at all. The points where the parabola intersects the x-axis are known as the x-intercepts (same as roots, solutions, or zeros) of a quadratic function.
    - A quadratic function has two x-intercepts when the parabola crosses the x-axis at two points (Fig. 1 and 2). The x-coordinate of the vertex is the midpoint between the two x-intercepts. Midpoint formula is $\frac{x_2+x_1}{2}$, where x_1 and x_2 are the two x-intercepts.
    - A quadratic function has one distinct x-intercept when the parabola touches the x-axis and curves back without crossing through the x-axis (Fig. 3).
    - A quadratic function has no real solution if the parabola does not cross or touch the x-axis (Fig. 3).

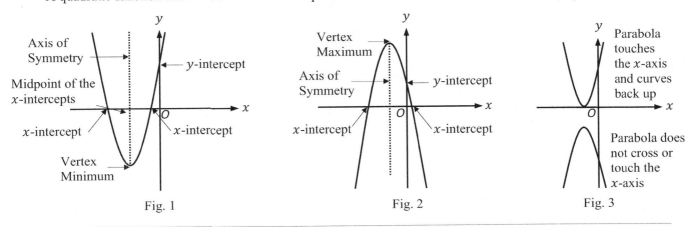

Fig. 1   Fig. 2   Fig. 3

How to Solve

When the equation of a parabola is given in the standard form, it is easiest to determine the x-coordinate of the vertex as $-\frac{b}{2a}$. The y-coordinate of the vertex can be determined by plugging the above value of x in the given equation.

The value of a can be determined by plugging in any point from the graph in the given equation.

When a question refers to the minimum or the maximum values of x and y as constants, it is referring to the vertex.

Remember the following for questions on a ball or a similar object thrown in the air.

- When a ball is thrown up in the air from the ground (Fig. 1) or from a platform (Fig. 2), the movement of the ball in the air and back to the ground is a parabola. The time is along the x-axis and the height is along the y-axis.
  - Note that in Fig. 2 the ball is launched from a 24 feet high platform. This is the y-intercept of the equation. When the ball is launched from the ground, the y-intercept is 0 (Fig. 1).
- The maximum height of the ball in the air is the y-coordinate of the vertex of the parabola.
- The time taken by the ball to reach the maximum height in the air is the x-coordinate of the vertex of the parabola.
- The total time taken by the ball to reach the ground is the positive x-intercept of the parabola.
- The time taken by the ball to reach a specific height can be determined by plugging in the given height as the value of y in the given equation and solving for x.

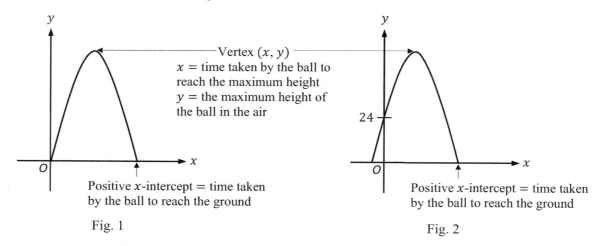

Fig. 1   Fig. 2

Example 1:

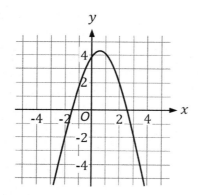

In the xy-plane, which of the following could be an equation of the above graph?

A) $y = -2x^2 + 3x + 2$

B) $y = -x^2 + x + 4$

C) $y = x^2 + 5x - 2$

D) $y = 2x^2 + 3x + 4$

Step 1: Determine if the parabola opens upwards or downwards

Since the parabola opens downwards, a is negative. This eliminates answer choices C and D.

Step 2: Determine the y-intercept

The graph shows that the y-intercept is 4. This eliminates answer choice A.

Correct answer choice is **B**.

Example 2:

$$y = 6x^2 + 12x + 4$$

In the xy-plane, the graph of the above equation is a parabola. Which of the following are the coordinates of the vertex of the parabola?

A) $(-1, -2)$

B) $(-1, 2)$

C) $(2, 2)$

D) $(2, 4)$

Step 1: Determine the x-coordinate of the vertex

$a = 6$. $b = 12$.

$$-\frac{b}{2a} = -\frac{12}{2 \times 6} = -1$$

This eliminates answer choices C and D.

Step 2: Determine the y-coordinate of the vertex

Plug in $x = -1$ in the equation to get the value of y.

$$6(-1 \times -1) + (12 \times -1) + 4 = 6 + (-12) + 4 = -2$$

Correct answer choice is **A**.

Example 3:

$$h(t) = -16t^2 + 32t$$

The equation above models the height of a ball, in feet, t seconds after it is thrown in the air from the ground.

Question 1

If the air resistance is ignored, which of the following gives the maximum height, in feet, of the ball in the air?

A) 1

B) 2

C) 16

D) 32

Step 1: Determine the x-coordinate of the vertex

$a = -16$. $b = 32$.

$$-\frac{b}{2a} = -\frac{32}{2 \times (-16)} = -\frac{32}{-32} = 1$$

Step 2: Determine the y-coordinate of the vertex

Plug in $x = 1$ in the equation to get the value of y.

$$(-16(1 \times 1)) + (32 \times 1) = -16 + 32 = 16$$

Correct answer choice is **C**.

Question 2

How many seconds did it take for the ball to reach the ground?

Step 1: Determine the positive x-intercept of the parabola

Remember at x-intercept, $y = 0$. Plug in $y = 0$ in the equation and solve for x.

$$0 = -16t^2 + 32t \rightarrow 0 = -16t(t - 2) \rightarrow 0 = t - 2 \rightarrow t = 2$$

Correct answer is **2**.

Category 31 – Practice Questions (answers on page 360)

No Calculator Questions

1

In the xy-plane, the parabola defined by a function f, where $y = f(x)$, opens downwards and has a negative y-intercept. Which of the following could define the function f?

A) $f(x) = -3x^2 + 7x - 2$

B) $f(x) = -x^2 + 4x + 3$

C) $f(x) = x^2 + 4x - 3$

D) $f(x) = 2x^2 + 11x + 2$

2

In the xy-plane, the graph of a parabola intersects the x-axis at -5 and 11. Which of the following is the x-coordinate of the vertex?

A)   3

B)   5

C)   6

D)   10

3

$$f(x) = x^2 - 8x + 17$$

The equation shown above graphs a parabola in the xy-plane. Which of the following ordered pair (x, y) is the minimum value of the function f?

A) $(-1, 4)$

B) $(4, 1)$

C) $(4, 4)$

D) $(8, 17)$

4

$$y = -x^2 - 2x + 3$$

Which of the following is the graph of the above equation, in the xy-plane?

A)

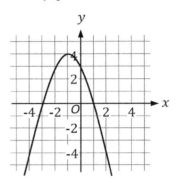

B)

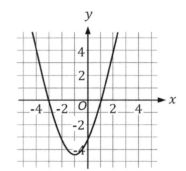

C)

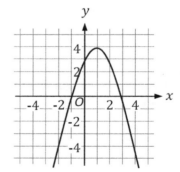

D)

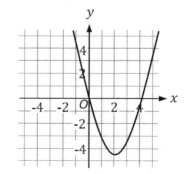

5

$$h(t) = -16t^2 + 48t$$

The height of a ball, in feet, t seconds after it is thrown in the air from the ground is modeled by the above equation. Which of the following is the maximum height of the ball in the air, in feet?

A) 16

B) 26

C) 32

D) 36

6

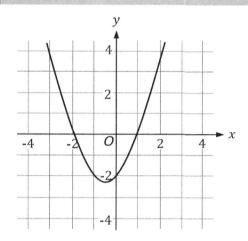

Which of the following could be an equation of the above graph, in the xy-plane?

A) $y = -x^2 + 4x + 2$

B) $y = -x^2 + x - 2$

C) $y = x^2 + x - 2$

D) $y = x^2 + 4x + 2$

7

$$h(t) = -16t^2 + 80t + 96$$

When an object is thrown in the air from a 96 inches high platform, the height of the object in the air after t seconds can be determined by the function h shown above. After how many seconds does the object hit the ground?

8

$$f(x) = -\frac{1}{2}x^2 + 40x - 60$$

A shoe manufacturing company opened a new retail store in a certain shopping mall. The parabola graphed by the above equation models the company's opening day earnings y, in dollars, as a function of the shoe price x, in dollars, where $y = f(x)$. On the opening day, the maximum earnings of the company, in dollars, were for what shoe price, in dollars? (ignore the dollar sign when entering answer)

9

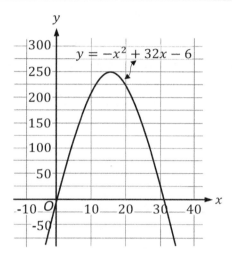

The daily profit y, in dollars, of a bakery selling cakes for the price of x, in dollars, can be modeled by the graph of the above parabola in the xy-plane. If the maximum daily profit of the bakery, in dollars, is p, what is the value of p based on the above graph?

Category 32 – Vertex Form Equation of a Parabola

Key Points

- The highest or the lowest point on the graph of a parabola is known as the vertex.
    - In a parabola opening downwards the vertex is the highest point, also known as the maximum of the parabola.
    - In a parabola opening upwards the vertex is the lowest point, also known as the minimum of the parabola.
- The vertex form equation of a parabola is $f(x) = a(x - h)^2 + k$, where $y = f(x)$ and the constants h and k represent the x- and y-coordinates of the vertex, respectively.
    - Negative a indicates that parabola opens downwards and positive a indicates that parabola opens upwards.
    - Since h is the x-coordinate of the vertex, it is the midpoint of the two x-intercepts of a parabola intersecting the x-axis at two points.

How to Solve

The x- and y-coordinates of the vertex can be directly read from the vertex form equation as the values of (h, k). Remember that the value of h has the opposite sign than in $(x - h)^2$. For example, in the equation $f(x) = a(x - 2)^2 + k, h = 2$ and in the equation $f(x) = a(x + 2)^2 + k, h = -2$.

The y-intercept of the parabola can be determined by plugging in 0 for x in the given equation. (Remember that $x = 0$ at the y-intercept.)

The value of a can be calculated by plugging in any point from the graph in the given equation.

Example 1:

$$f(x) = c(x + 2)^2 + 1$$

The equation above graphs a parabola passing through the point $(-1, 3)$ in the xy-plane, where $y = f(x)$. What is the value of c, where c is a constant?

A) -2

B) -1

C) 2

D) 3

Step 1: Plug in the given point

Plug in the given point $(-1, 3)$ in the equation and solve for c. (Note that a is represented as c in this example.)

$$3 = c(-1 + 2)^2 + 1 \rightarrow 3 = c(1)^2 + 1 \rightarrow 3 = c + 1 \rightarrow c = 2$$

Correct answer choice is **C**.

Example 2:

$$g(x) = -\frac{1}{4}(x - 8)^2 + 20$$

In the xy-plane, the graph of the function g modeled by the above equation is a parabola, where $y = g(x)$. What is the y-coordinate of the y-intercept of the parabola?

Step 1: Determine the y-intercept

Plug in $x = 0$ in the equation and solve for y.

$$y = -\frac{1}{4}(0 - 8)^2 + 20 = \left(-\frac{1}{4} \times 64\right) + 20 = -16 + 20 = 4$$

Correct answer is **4**.

Example 3:

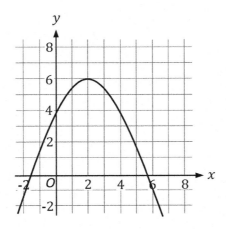

In the xy-plane, the above graph of the quadratic function P models the growth y, in thousands, of a certain species of insects for x days in response to exposure to a certain chemical compound.

Question 1

Which of the following could define P?

A) $P = -\frac{1}{2}(x - 2)^2 + 6$

B) $P = -\frac{1}{2}(x + 2)^2 + 6$

C) $P = \frac{1}{2}(x - 2)^2 + 6$

D) $P = \frac{1}{2}(x + 2)^2 + 4$

Step 1: Determine if the parabola opens upwards or downwards

Since the parabola opens downwards, a is negative. This eliminates answer choices C and D.

Step 2: Determine the vertex from the graph

The vertex is at $(2, 6)$. Hence, $(x - h) = (x - 2)$ and $k = 6$. This eliminates answer choice B.

Correct answer choice is **A**.

Question 2

What is the maximum growth, in thousands, of the insects modeled by the function P?

Step 1: Determine the y-coordinate of the vertex from the graph

The growth is on the y-axis. Hence, the maximum growth is the y-coordinate of the vertex $= 6$.

Correct answer is **6**.

Category 32 – Practice Questions (answers on page 361)

No Calculator Questions

1

$$h(x) = -a(x - s)^2 - t$$

The graph of the above function h is a parabola in the xy-plane, where $y = h(x)$. Which of the following is true about the graph of the function h where the maximum values of s and t appears as constants or coefficients?

A) The vertex is $(-s, -t)$ and the graph opens downwards.

B) The vertex is $(s, -t)$ and the graph opens downwards.

C) The vertex is $(-s, -t)$ and the graph opens upwards.

D) The vertex is $(s, -t)$ and the graph opens upwards.

2

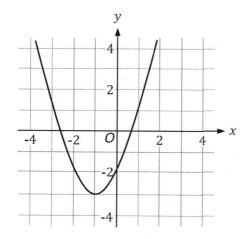

In the xy-plane, the graph of the above parabola is defined by $f(x) = a(x + b)^2 - 3$. What is the value of b in the equation, where a and b are constants?

A) -2

B) -1

C) 1

D) 2

Calculator Questions

3

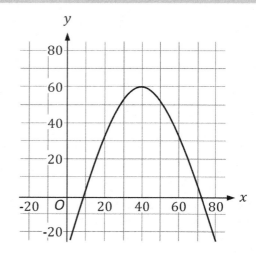

A travel agency in a certain metropolitan city sells city sightseeing tour packages. In the xy-plane, the above graph of the quadratic function T models the number of tour packages y the agency sells daily as a function of tour package price x, in dollars. Which of the following could define function T?

A) $T(x) = -\frac{1}{16}(x - 40)^2 + 60$

B) $T(x) = -\frac{1}{16}(x - 60)^2 + 40$

C) $T(x) = -\frac{1}{16}(x + 40)^2 + 60$

D) $T(x) = -\frac{1}{16}(x + 60)^2 + 40$

4

The graph of the function f, defined as $f(x) = (x - 2)^2 - 4$, intersects the x-axis at points 0 and b, where b is a constant. What is the value of b?

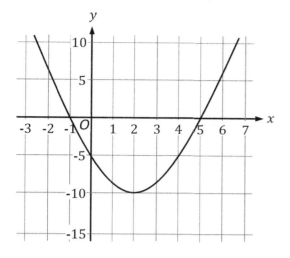

The graph of a parabola, in the xy-plane, is shown above. In which of the following ordered pair (x, y), the minimum values of x and y appears as constants or coefficients?

A) $(-5, -10)$

B) $(-1, -5)$

C) $(2, -5)$

D) $(2, -10)$

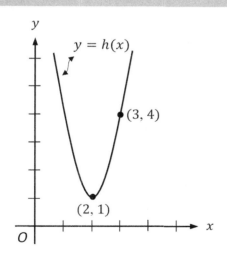

In the xy-plane, the graph of the function h is the parabola shown above. Which of the following could define the function h, where $y = h(x)$?

A) $h(x) = (x - 2)^2 + 1$

B) $h(x) = 2(x - 2)^2 + 1$

C) $h(x) = 3(x - 2)^2 + 1$

D) $h(x) = (x + 2)^2 + 1$

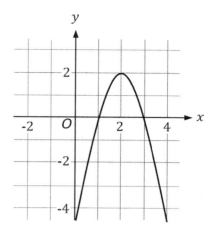

Which of the following could be the equation of the graph of the parabola shown above, in the xy-plane?

A) $y = -(x - 2)^2 + 2$

B) $y = -2(x - 2)^2 + 2$

C) $y = (x + 2)^2 + 2$

D) $y = 2(x + 2)^2 + 2$

$$f(x) = k(x - 3)^2 - 6$$

In the xy-plane, the above function f graphs a parabola passing through the origin, where $y = f(x)$. What is the value of k, where k is a constant?

A) $\dfrac{2}{3}$

B) $\dfrac{5}{6}$

C) 2

D) 6

$$p(x) = -(x - 4)^2 + 22$$

A retail store sells various brands of perfume. In the xy-plane, the parabola graphed by the function p shown above, models the quarterly profit y of the retail store, in thousands of dollars, for the top selling perfume brand as a function of percent discount x offered on that brand. Based on the function p, if q is the quarterly profit, in thousands of dollars, when no discount is offered, what is the value of q, where $y = p(x)$?

Category 33 – Factored Form Equation of a Parabola

Key Points

- The factored form equation of a parabola is $f(x) = a(x - r)(x - s)$, where $y = f(x)$ and the constants r and s are the x-intercepts of the parabola, also known as the factors or the zeros.

  - When the parabola does not intersect the x-axis, the equation cannot be written in the factored form as there are no x-intercepts.

- The x-coordinate of the vertex is the midpoint of the two x-intercepts. It can be determined as $\frac{x_2 + x_1}{2}$, where x_1 and x_2 are the two x-intercepts.

How to Solve

When the equation of a parabola is in the factored form, the x-coordinate of the vertex can be determined by the midpoint formula. The y-coordinate of the vertex can be determined by plugging the value of the x-coordinate of the vertex in the equation.

Remember that if the factor is $(x - n)$, then the x-intercept is n and if the factor is $(x + n)$, then the x-intercept is $-n$.

The value of a can be calculated by plugging in any point from the graph in the given equation.

Example 1:

$$f(x) = (x - 6)(x + 2)$$

In the xy-plane, the equation for the graph of a parabola is given above, where $y = f(x)$. In which of the following ordered pair (x, y), the minimum values of x and y appears as constants?

A) $(2, -2)$

B) $(2, -16)$

C) $(6, -2)$

D) $(16, -2)$

Step 1: Determine the x-coordinate of the vertex

The two x-intercepts from the equation are 6 and -2 . Hence, the x-coordinate of the vertex is

$$\frac{6 + (-2)}{2} = \frac{4}{2} = 2$$

This eliminates answer choices C and D.

Step 2: Determine the y-coordinate of the vertex

Plug in $x = 2$ in the equation to get the value of y.

$$y = (2 - 6)(2 + 2)$$
$$y = -4 \times 4 = -16$$

This eliminates answer choice A.

Correct answer choice is **B**.

Category 33 – Practice Questions (answers on page 362)

No Calculator Questions

1

$$t(x) = -4(x - 1)(x + 1)$$

In the xy-plane, the graph of the function t shown above is a parabola. For which of the following values of (x, y) does the function t reaches its maximum value?

A) $(-4, 0)$

B) $(0, -4)$

C) $(0, 4)$

D) $(4, 4)$

2

$$g(x) = (x + 15)(x - 45)$$

For the function g defined above, which of the following is the distance between the two x-intercepts of the function?

A) 15

B) 20

C) 30

D) 60

3

$$f(x) = -3(x - 5)(x - 7)$$

A manufacturing company specializes in making heavy duty electrical wires. The graph of the above equation in the xy-plane is a parabola and models the company's annual profit y, in millions of dollars, as a function of the product price x, in dollars, where $y = f(x)$. Which of the following is the maximum annual profit of the company, in millions of dollars, based on the above model?

A) 3

B) 5

C) 12

D) 35

Calculator Questions

4

In the xy-plane, the vertex of a parabola is at the point $(-2, -16)$. If the graph of the parabola is defined by $f(x) = (x + n)(x + 6)$, where n is a constant and $y = f(x)$, which of the following is the value of n in the equation?

A) -6

B) -2

C) 2

D) 8

5

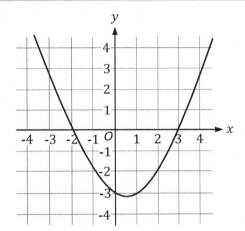

In the xy-plane, the graph of a parabola is shown above. If the equation of the parabola is written as $f(x) = k(x + m)(x + n)$, where $k, m,$ and n are constants, what is the value of k?

A) -2

B) -3

C) $\dfrac{1}{2}$

D) $\dfrac{2}{3}$

Category 34 – Equivalent Standard Form and Vertex Form Equations

Key Points

- The equation of the quadratic function in the standard form is $f(x) = ax^2 + bx + c$, where $y = f(x)$.
  - The x-coordinate of the vertex $= -\dfrac{b}{2a}$.
- The equation of the quadratic function in the vertex form is $f(x) = a(x - h)^2 + k$, where $y = f(x)$.
  - The x- and y-coordinates of the vertex are h and k, respectively (the minimum or the maximum depending on if the parabola opens upwards or downwards, respectively).
- The equivalent standard form and vertex form equations graph the same parabola. For example, equations $f(x) = (x - 3)^2 - 11$ and $f(x) = x^2 - 6x - 2$ are equivalent.
$$f(x) = (x - 3)^2 - 11 = (x - 3)(x - 3) - 11 = x^2 - 6x + 9 - 11 = x^2 - 6x - 2$$
- The value of a is same in equivalent standard form and vertex form equations.

How to Solve

The easiest approach is to determine the x-coordinate of the vertex from the given standard form equation as $-\dfrac{b}{2a}$ and then determine the y-coordinate of the vertex by plugging this value of x in the equation. These vertex coordinates can be matched with (h, k) coordinates in the answer choices.

To match a vertex form equation with an equivalent standard form equation, simply FOIL the vertex form equation.

Example 1:
$$f(x) = 2x^2 + 4x - 1$$

In the xy-plane, the graph of the above function f is a parabola, where $y = f(x)$. Which of the following is an equivalent equation where the minimum values of x and y appears as constants?

A) $f(x) = (x + 1)^2 - 3$

B) $f(x) = 2(x - 2)^2 - 3$

C) $f(x) = 2(x + 1)^2 - 4$

D) $f(x) = 2(x + 1)^2 - 3$

Step 1: Determine the x-coordinate of the vertex

$a = 2$. $b = 4$.

$$-\frac{b}{2a} = -\frac{4}{(2 \times 2)} = -1$$

Since $x = -1$, the factor is $(x + 1)$. This eliminates answer choice B.

Since $a = 2$ in the standard form equation, the equivalent vertex form equation will also have $a = 2$. This eliminates answer choice A.

Step 2: Determine the y-coordinate of the vertex

Plug in $x = -1$ in the equation to get the value of y.

$$y = 2(-1)^2 + (4 \times -1) - 1 = 2 - 4 - 1 = -3$$

This eliminates answer choice C that has the y-coordinate of the vertex $= -4$.

Correct answer choice is **D**.

Category 34 – Practice Questions (answers on pages 362-363)

Calculator Questions

1

$$f(x) = x^2 + 6x + 13$$

In the xy-plane, the parabola of the function f is defined by the above equation, where $y = f(x)$. Which of the following is an equivalent equation of the function f where the minimum values of x and y appears as constants?

A) $f(x) = (x - 3)^2 - 4$

B) $f(x) = (x - 4)^2 + 7$

C) $f(x) = (x + 3)^2 + 4$

D) $f(x) = (x + 3)^2 + 13$

2

$$y = 0.5x^2 + 4x + 1$$

The graph of the above equation is a parabola in the xy-plane. Which of the following equivalent equations include the x- and y-coordinates of the vertex as constants?

A) $y = 0.5(x - 4)^2 + 1$

B) $y = 0.5(x + 4)^2 - 7$

C) $y = (x + 2)^2 + 12$

D) $y = 2(x + 4)^2 + 1$

3

$$y = 1.25x^2 + 7.5x + 1$$

Which of the following is an equivalent form of the above equation, where the minimum values of x and y appears as constants or coefficients?

A) $y = 0.5(x - 3)^2 + 1$

B) $y = 1.25(x - 3)^2 + 8.75$

C) $y = 1.25(x + 3)^2 - 6.5$

D) $y = 1.25(x + 3)^2 - 10.25$

4

$$g(x) = -2(x + 2)^2 + 1$$

In the xy-plane, the graph of the above function g is a parabola. If the equation of the function g is written in the form $g(x) = ax^2 + bx + c$ where a, b, and c are constants and $y = g(x)$, which of the following equations could represent the function g?

A) $g(x) = -ax^2 - bx - 7$

B) $g(x) = -ax^2 + bx + 1$

C) $g(x) = -ax^2 - bx + 1$

D) $g(x) = ax^2 + bx - 7$

5

The graph of $f(x) = -x^2 + 9x - 18$ is a parabola in the xy-plane, where $y = f(x)$. In which of the following equivalent equations the maximum values of x and y appears as constants or coefficients?

A) $f(x) = -(x - 2)^2 + 2.5$

B) $f(x) = -(x - 4.5)^2 + 2.25$

C) $f(x) = (x - 4.5)^2 - 9$

D) $f(x) = (x + 5.5)^2 - 9$

6

In the quadratic equation $y = (x + 2.5)^2 + 2.75$, the minimum values of x and y appears as constants. If the equation is written in the form $y = ax^2 + bx + c$ where a, b, and c are constants, what is the value of c?

Category 35 – Parabola Intersections and System of Equations

Key Points

- The graphs of a vertical parabola and a linear line may intersect at one or two points.

  - A vertical line intersects the parabola at one point (Fig. 1).

  - A horizontal line may intersect the parabola at one or two distinct points (Fig. 2 and 3). A horizontal line that touches the parabola at the vertex without passing through it is a line tangent to the vertex (Fig. 2).

  - A slanting line may intersect the parabola at one or two distinct points (Fig. 4 and 5). A slanting line is tangent to the parabola when it touches the parabola at one point without passing through it (Fig. 4).

- The graphs of two vertical parabolas may intersect at one or two points.

  - When two vertical parabolas intersect at one point, they intersect at the vertex (Fig. 6).

- The equations of an intersecting parabola and a line comprise a system of equations. Similarly, the equations of two intersecting parabolas are a system of equations. The number of solutions or the intersection points (x, y) of the system can be determined by equating the two equations to form one quadratic equation in the form $ax^2 + bx + c = 0$.

  - The number of solutions of the system can be determined by evaluating the discriminant $b^2 - 4ac$.

    - $b^2 - 4ac > 0$ indicates two solutions.

    - $b^2 - 4ac = 0$ indicates one solution.

  - The points of intersection can be determined by solving the quadratic equation for x and y.

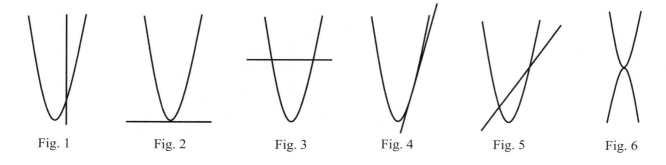

| Fig. 1 | Fig. 2 | Fig. 3 | Fig. 4 | Fig. 5 | Fig. 6 |

How to Solve

The equations in a system must be in the correct form before they can be equated.

- The quadratic equation must be in the $y = ax^2 + bx + c$ form. For example, $y = (x - 2)(x + 5)$ must be converted to $y = x^2 + 3x - 10$ and $y + 2x = 5x^2 - 1$ must be converted to $y = 5x^2 - 2x - 1$.

- The linear equation must be in the $y = mx + b$ form (for more on lines refer to Section 1). For example, $-2y = 4x - 1$ must be converted to $y = -2x + \frac{1}{2}$ and $3x + y = 1$ must be converted to $y = -3x + 1$.

Do not confuse the quadratic system of equations with the linear system of equations in Section 2. They are solved differently. Remember that in a quadratic system of equations at least one of the equations will have x^2 term. Linear system of equations will only have x and y variables.

Example 1:

$$y - 5 = 2x^2 + 7x$$
$$-4x + y = 9$$

How many solutions does the above system of equations have?

A) Zero

B) Exactly one

C) Exactly two

D) Infinitely many

Step 1: Equate the two equations

Convert the equations to the correct form before equating.

$$-4x + y = 9 \rightarrow y = 4x + 9$$
$$y - 5 = 2x^2 + 7x \rightarrow y = 2x^2 + 7x + 5$$

Equate and create one quadratic equation by moving all terms to one side.

$$4x + 9 = 2x^2 + 7x + 5$$
$$2x^2 + 7x + 5 - 4x - 9 = 0 \rightarrow 2x^2 + 3x - 4 = 0$$

Step 2: Set up the discriminant

$a = 2$. $b = 3$. $c = -4$.

$$b^2 - 4ac = 3^2 - (4 \times 2 \times -4) = 9 + 32 = 41$$

Since discriminant > 0, the system has two solutions.

Correct answer choice is **C**.

Example 2:

In the xy-plane, the graph of a parabola defined by the equation $y = x^2 + 7x + 7$ intersects the graph of a straight line defined by the equation $y = 2x + 3$ at two points. Which of the following could be the points of intersection?

A) $\{(-1, -4), (-1, 1)\}$

B) $\{(-1, -4), (-1, -5)\}$

C) $\{(-4, -4), (-1, 1)\}$

D) $\{(-4, -5), (-1, 1)\}$

Step 1: Equate the two equations

$$x^2 + 7x + 7 = 2x + 3$$

Create one quadratic equation by moving all terms to one side.

$$x^2 + 7x + 7 - 2x - 3 = 0 \rightarrow x^2 + 5x + 4 = 0$$

Step 2: Determine the values of x

$$x^2 + 5x + 4 = 0 \rightarrow (x + 4)(x + 1) = 0 \rightarrow x = -4 \text{ and } x = -1$$

The two values of x are -4 and -1. This eliminates answer choices A and B where both values of $x = -1$.

Step 3: Determine the corresponding values of y

Plug in the values of x in either of the equation. Plug it in the linear equation as it is easier to solve.

For $x = -4$:

$$y = (2 \times -4) + 3 = -8 + 3 = -5$$

This eliminates answer choice C since neither of the points in the answer choice have $y = -5$.

Correct answer choice is **D**.

Note that if the above elimination was not possible, then proceed with solving for the second value of x.

Category 35 – Practice Questions (answers on pages 363-364)

No Calculator Questions

1

$$y = x^2 + 2$$
$$8x - y = 9$$

The graphs of the above system of equations in the xy-plane intersect at two points. Which of the following are the x-coordinates of the solutions to the system of equations?

A) $-1 \pm \sqrt{1}$

B) $1 \pm \sqrt{5}$

C) $2 \pm \sqrt{2}$

D) $4 \pm \sqrt{5}$

2

In the xy-plane, the graph of the equation $y + 4x = 2x^2 + 1$ intersects with the graph of the equation $y = (x - 1)(x - 2)$ at how many points?

A) None

B) One

C) Two

D) Infinitely many

3

In the xy-plane, the graph of a line defined by $2y = 4x + 8$ intersects with the graph of a parabola defined by $y = -ax^2 - 4x - 5$ at one point. What is the value of a, where a is a constant?

A) 1

B) 2

C) 4

D) 8

Calculator Questions

4

$$y = x^2 - x - 6$$
$$y = \frac{1}{2}x^2 + 2x + 2$$

If the above system of equations is graphed in the xy-plane, the graphs of the system intersect at which of the following points?

A) $\{(-2, -1), (8, 6)\}$

B) $\{(-2, 0), (8, 50)\}$

C) $\{(2, -4), (10, 20)\}$

D) $\{(3, 4), (10, 20)\}$

5

In the xy-plane, the parabola defined by an equation in the form $y = -(x - m)^2 + n$ includes the maximum values of m and n as constants and intersects the line $y = 9$ at one point. What is the value of n?

6

The graphs of $y = x^2 - 7x + 12$ and $x = y + 4$, in the xy-plane, intersect at a point (s, t). What is the value of s?

7

In the xy-plane, the graph of line l defined by the equation $y - kx = 1$ intersects the graph of the parabola defined by the equation $y = x^2 - kx + 10$ at one point, where k is a constant. If line l has a positive slope, what is the slope of line l?

Category 36 – Graph Transformations of a Parabola

Key Points

- In the vertex form equation $y = a(x - h)^2 + k$, the horizontal shift of the graph of a parabola is the change in the value of h and the vertical shift is the change in the value of k.

- In the standard form equation $y = ax^2 + bx + c$, the horizontal shift of the graph of a parabola is the change in the values of all x terms and the vertical shift is the change in the value of c.

- Reflection of the graph of a parabola across the x-axis does not change the x values, but all the y values change to the opposite sign. For example, the vertex form equation $y = a(x - h)^2 + k$ becomes $-y = a(x - h)^2 + k \rightarrow y = -(a(x - h)^2 + k)$, and the standard form equation $y = ax^2 + bx + c$ becomes $-y = ax^2 + bx + c \rightarrow y = -(ax^2 + bx + c)$.

- Reflection of the graph of a parabola across the y-axis does not change the y values, but all the x values change to the opposite sign. For example, the vertex form equation $y = a(x - h)^2 + k$ becomes $y = a(-x - h)^2 + k$, and the standard form equation $y = ax^2 + bx + c$ becomes $y = a(-x)^2 + b(-x) + c$.

How to Solve

Remember that the right horizontal shift of x by n units is $x - n$ and the left horizontal shift of x by n units is $x + n$. See transformation examples and the figure below for the equivalent vertex form and standard form equations.

Vertex form equation $y = (x - 2)^2 + 2$:

- One unit shift to the right is $y = (x - 2 - 1)^2 + 2 = (x - 3)^2 + 2$.
- One unit shift to the left is $y = (x - 2 + 1)^2 + 2 = (x - 1)^2 + 2$.
- One unit shift upwards is $y = (x - 2)^2 + 2 + 1 = (x - 2)^2 + 3$.
- One unit shift downwards is $y = (x - 2)^2 + 2 - 1 = (x - 2)^2 + 1$.
- Reflection across the x-axis is $y = -((x - 2)^2 + 2) \rightarrow y = -(x - 2)^2 - 2$.
- Reflection across the y-axis is $y = (-x - 2)^2 + 2$.

Standard form equation $y = x^2 - 4x + 6$:

- One unit shift to the right is $y = (x - 1)^2 - 4(x - 1) + 6$.
- One unit shift to the left is $y = (x + 1)^2 - 4(x + 1) + 6$.
- One unit shift upwards is $y = x^2 - 4x + 6 + 1 = x^2 - 4x + 7$.
- One unit shift downwards is $y = x^2 - 4x + 6 - 1 = x^2 - 4x + 5$.
- Reflection across the x-axis is $y = -(x^2 - 4x + 6) \rightarrow y = -x^2 + 4x - 6$.
- Reflection across the y-axis is $y = (-x)^2 - 4(-x) + 6 \rightarrow y = x^2 + 4x + 6$.

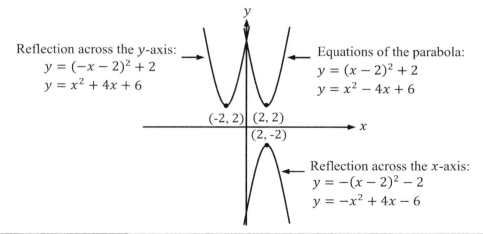

Reflection across the y-axis:
$y = (-x - 2)^2 + 2$
$y = x^2 + 4x + 6$

Equations of the parabola:
$y = (x - 2)^2 + 2$
$y = x^2 - 4x + 6$

(-2, 2) (2, 2)
(2, -2)

Reflection across the x-axis:
$y = -(x - 2)^2 - 2$
$y = -x^2 + 4x - 6$

Example 1:

$$f(x) = x^2 - 4x + 3$$

The function f shown above graphs a parabola in the xy-plane, where $y = f(x)$. Which of the following equations represents the shift in the graph of the parabola by 2 units to the right and 2 units downward?

A) $f(x) = x^2 - 2x + 1$

B) $f(x) = x^2 - 6x + 3$

C) $f(x) = x^2 - 8x + 13$

D) $f(x) = x^2 + 8x + 1$

Step 1: Determine the transformed equation

Since the equation is given in the standard form, 2 units to the right is

$$f(x) = (x - 2)^2 - 4(x - 2) + 3$$

2 units downwards after the above shift is

$$f(x) = (x - 2)^2 - 4(x - 2) + 3 - 2$$

Simplify.

$$f(x) = x^2 - 4x + 4 - 4x + 8 + 1 = x^2 - 8x + 13$$

Correct answer choice is **C**.

Example 2:

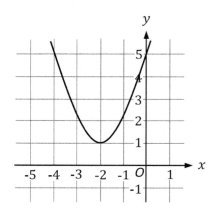

The equation of the graph of the above parabola in the xy-plane can be written as $y = a(x - h)^2 + k$, where the minimum values of h and k appears as constants or coefficients. Which of the following could be the equation of the above parabola shifted 3 units to the left and 4 units upwards?

A) $y = (x - 5)^2 + 1$

B) $y = (x - 1)^2 + 1$

C) $y = (x + 1)^2 + 5$

D) $y = (x + 5)^2 + 5$

Step 1: Determine the transformed vertex from the graph

Since the equation is in the vertex form, the transformed vertex can be directly read from the given graph as shown in the figure on the right.

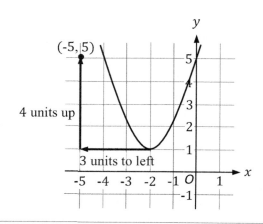

The vertex of the transformed graph is $(-5, 5)$. Hence, the equation of the transformed graph is

$$y = (x + 5)^2 + 5$$

Correct answer choice is **D**.

Category 36 – Practice Questions (answers on page 364)

No Calculator Questions

1

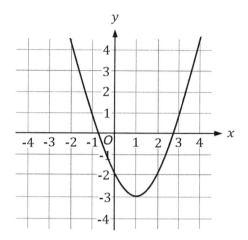

The graph of the parabola shown above in the xy-plane can be written as $y = a(x - h)^2 + k$, where the minimum values of h and k appears as constants. Which of the following could be the equation of the parabola when shifted 4 unit to the left and 5 units upwards?

A) $y = (x - 3)^2 + 4$

B) $y = (x - 3)^2 - 3$

C) $y = (x + 3)^2 + 2$

D) $y = (x + 3)^2 + 5$

2

In the xy-plane, if the graph of the parabola defined by the equation $y = 2(x + 3)^2 - 1$ is reflected across the y-axis, which of the following is the equation of the reflected graph?

A) $y = -2(x + 3)^2 - 1$

B) $y = -2(-x + 3)^2 - 1$

C) $y = 2(x - 3)^2 + 1$

D) $y = 2(-x + 3)^2 - 1$

3

In the xy-plane, the equation $y = x^2 + 4$ graphs a parabola. If the equation is changed to $y = (x - 4)^2$, which of the following statements is true about the graph of the changed equation?

A) The graph will shift 4 units to the left and 4 units upwards.

B) The graph will shift 4 units to the right and 4 units downwards.

C) The graph will shift 4 units to the right.

D) The graph will shift 4 units to the left.

Calculator Questions

4

In the xy-plane, the graph of the parabola defined by the equation $y = (x + 2)^2 - 4$ is reflected across the x-axis and then moved 2 units downwards. Which of the following is the equation of the graph of the transformed parabola?

A) $y = -(x + 2)^2 + 2$

B) $y = (-x + 2)^2 - 6$

C) $y = -(x + 2)^2 - 6$

D) $y = (x - 1)^2 + 2$

5

$$g(x) = x^2 + 5x - 3$$

The function g above graphs a parabola in the xy-plane, where $y = g(x)$. If the parabola is shifted 1 unit to the left and 4 units upwards, which of the following is the equation of the shifted parabola?

A) $g(x) = x^2 + 4x - 7$

B) $g(x) = x^2 + 3x + 1$

C) $g(x) = x^2 + 7x + 3$

D) $g(x) = x^2 + 7x + 7$

Category 37 – Solutions of Quadratic Expressions

Key Points

- Two expressions may or may not be equivalent to each other depending on the values given to one or more coefficients or constants in the expressions. For example, the equation $4x^2 + 8x + k = mx^2 + 8x + 5$ contains expressions on both sides of the equation, where the values of the coefficient m and the constant k are not known. The values given to m and k will determine if the expressions on both sides of the equation are equal or not.

  - The equation has infinitely many solutions when the expressions on both sides are equal.

  - The equation has no solution when the expressions on both sides are unequal.

How to Solve

Note that this category is alike Category 13 on Solutions of Linear Expressions; the difference being the additional x^2 term in the quadratic expressions.

Remember that the two quadratic expressions on either side of an equation are two separate expressions. They cannot be rearranged to form one quadratic equation or considered as system of equations.

For an equation to have infinitely many solutions, the coefficients and the constants on both sides of the equation must be made equal.

For an equation to have no solution, the coefficients and the constants on both sides must be made unequal.

If an equation has the variable x or x^2 on one side only, then the coefficient of that variable on the other side evaluates to 0. For example, in the equation $4ax^2 + 5 = 2x^2 + kx + 5$, the value of $k = 0$ since the left-side expression does not have the variable x. Same is true for constants.

The expressions on both sides must be in the standard form before evaluating for solutions. If either side of the equation is in factored form, then FOIL before evaluating.

Example 1:

$$ax^2 + x(2b + 1) + x + 2 = 5x^2 + 2bx + 2x + 2$$

If the above equation has no solution, and a and b are constants, which of the following can NOT be the value of a?

A) 1

B) 2

C) 5

D) 9

Step 1: Equate the coefficients and constants of both sides

For the equation to have no solution, expressions on both sides must not be equal.

Simplify the left expression.

$$ax^2 + 2bx + x + x + 2 = 5x^2 + 2bx + 2x + 2$$
$$ax^2 + 2bx + 2x + 2 = 5x^2 + 2bx + 2x + 2$$

Group all expressions of x as below. Note that the corresponding coefficients and constants are enclosed in matching shape types on both sides of the equation.

$$\boxed{a}x^2 + \boxed{(2b + 2)}x + ②= \boxed{5}x^2 + \boxed{(2b + 2)}x + ②$$

The coefficients of x and the constants on both sides of the equation are same.

If $a = 5$, then expressions on both sides will be equal and the equation will have infinitely many solutions. Hence, for the equation to have no solution a cannot be 5.

Correct answer choice is **C**.

Example 2:

$$(ax + 2)(bx + 2) = 5x^2 + 4x + 4$$

The equation above is true for all values of x. What is the value of $a + b$, where a and b are constants?

Step 1: Equate the coefficients and constants of both sides

"True for all values of x" implies the equation has infinitely many solutions. Hence, the expressions on both sides of the equation must be equal.

FOIL the left expression.

$$abx^2 + 2ax + 2bx + 4 = 5x^2 + 4x + 4$$

Group all expressions of x.

$$\boxed{ab}\,x^2 + \boxed{(2a + 2b)}\,x + \boxed{4} = \boxed{5}\,x^2 + \boxed{4}\,x + \boxed{4}$$

The question asks for the value of $a + b$. Note that if 2 is factored out from $(2a + 2b)$ it becomes $2(a + b)$.

Hence, equate the coefficients of x.

$$(2a + 2b) = 4$$
$$2(a + b) = 2(2)$$
$$a + b = 2$$

Correct answer is **2**.

Example 3:

If $(mx + 1)(nx + 3) = 3x^2 + kx + 3$ is true for all values of x, which of the following are two possible values of k?

A) $\{1, 3\}$
B) $\{3, 4\}$
C) $\{4, 6\}$
D) $\{6, 10\}$

Step 1: Equate the coefficients and constants of both sides

For the equation to have infinitely many solutions, expressions on both sides of the equation must be equal.

FOIL the left expression.

$$mnx^2 + 3mx + nx + 3 = 3x^2 + kx + 3$$

Group all expressions of x.

$$\boxed{mn}\,x^2 + \boxed{(3m + n)}\,x + \boxed{3} = \boxed{3}\,x^2 + \boxed{k}\,x + \boxed{3}$$

Equate the coefficients of x^2 and x.

$$mn = 3$$
$$3m + n = k$$

Step 2: Determine the value of k

The values of m and n must be determined before the value of k can be solved for.

Get the values of m and n: Since $mn = 3$, m and n are multiples of 3. The only two multiples of 3 are 1 and 3. However, it is not known which multiple is m and which multiple is n. Hence, the possible values of m and n are
$$m = 1 \text{ and } n = 3 \text{ or } m = 3 \text{ and } n = 1$$

Get the values of k: Plug in the above two combinations of m and n values in the equation $3m + n = k$.

For $m = 1$ and $n = 3$: $k = 3m + n = (3 \times 1) + 3 = 6$.

For $m = 3$ and $n = 1$: $k = 3m + n = (3 \times 3) + 1 = 10$.

The two possible values of k are 6 and 10.

Correct answer choice is **D**.

Category 37 – Practice Questions (answers on page 365)

Calculator Questions

1

The expressions $(x + 3)(ax + c)$ and $6x^2 + bx + 9$ are equivalent. What is the value of b, where a, b, and c are constants?

A) 0

B) 3

C) 15

D) 21

2

$$(5x + 2)(bx + 1) = x(5bx + 2b + 5) + k$$

If the equation above has no solution, which of the following can NOT be the value of k, where b and k are constants?

A) 2

B) 5

C) 7

D) 9

3

$$2x^2 + bx^2 + c = (2c + 1)x^2 + 2x^2 + 1$$

If the equation shown above has no solution, which of the following is true about the possible values of b and c, where b and c are constants?

I. $b \neq 3$

II. $b = 3$

III. $c = 1$

A) I only

B) II only

C) I and II only

D) I and III only

4

$$(3ax + 4)(bx + c) = 6x^2 + 4x$$

The equation above has infinitely many solutions, and a, b, and c are constants. Which of the following must be true about the values of a, b, and c?

A) $a = 1, b = 2, c = 0$

B) $a = 2, b = 1, c = 0$

C) $a = 2, b = 2, c = 2$

D) $a = 2, b = 1, c = 4$

5

$$0.6ax^2 + 4cx + 5 = 5.4x^2 + 5$$

If $a = 9$ in the above equation, for what value of c does the equation have infinitely many solutions, where a and c are constants?

A) 0

B) 4

C) 6

D) 9

6

$$0.1ax^2 + k = 1.4x^2 + k$$

For the above equation to have no solution, which of the following can NOT be the value of a, where a and k are constants?

A) 1

B) 4

C) 10

D) 14

7

$$(2x + 3)(2x + 1) = 4x^2 + 8x + c - 2$$

For what value of c, the above equation has infinitely many solutions, where c is a constant?

No Calculator Questions

1

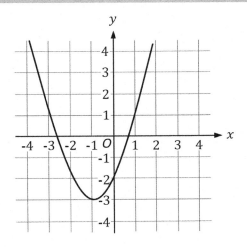

In the xy-plane, if the equation of the above parabola is written in the $y = ax^2 + bx + c$ form, where a, b, and c are constants, which of the following could be the value of c?

A) -1

B) 4

C) 7

D) 8

2

If the graph of the parabola shown above, in the xy-plane, is shifted 2 units to the left and 4 units upwards, which of the following equations represents the shifted graph that includes the minimum values of x and y as constants?

A) $y = 2x^2 + 4$

B) $y = 3(x - 2)^2 + 4$

C) $y = (x + 1)^2 - 3$

D) $y = (x + 3)^2 + 1$

3

In the xy-plane, the graph of the function f is defined by $f(x) = (x - 1)^2 + 2$ and the graph of the function g is defined by $g(x) = (x + 2)^2 - 1$. When $g(x)$ is compared to $f(x)$ which of the following is true about the vertex of the two graphs?

A) The vertex of $g(x)$ is 1 unit to the right and 2 units above the vertex of $f(x)$.

B) The vertex of $g(x)$ is 1 unit to the left and 2 units below the vertex of $f(x)$.

C) The vertex of $g(x)$ is 3 units to the right and 3 units below the vertex of $f(x)$.

D) The vertex of $g(x)$ is 3 units to the left and 3 units below the vertex of $f(x)$.

4

$$y = -5x^2 + 10x - 4$$

In the xy-plane, the above equation graphs a parabola. Which of the following ordered pair (x, y) are the coordinates of the vertex of the parabola?

A) $(1, 0)$

B) $(1, 1)$

C) $(4, 9)$

D) $(5, 4)$

5

The function t is defined as $t(x) = (x + 10.5)(x - 40.5)$. Which of the following is the distance between the two x-intercepts of the function t?

A) 30

B) 40

C) 51

D) 62

6

In the xy-plane, the graph of $x - y = -4$ and the graph of $y = x^2 - 5x + 4$ intersect at two points. Which of the following is a solution to the system for $x > 0$?

A) $(0, -4)$

B) $(6, 4)$

C) $(6, 10)$

D) $(8, 10)$

7

$$x^2 - 5x + 3 = 0$$

Which of the following is a solution to the above quadratic equation?

A) $2.5 - \dfrac{\sqrt{13}}{2}$

B) $2.5 - \dfrac{\sqrt{3}}{2}$

C) $1.5 + \dfrac{\sqrt{5}}{2}$

D) $1 + \dfrac{\sqrt{13}}{2}$

8

$$f(x) = 2x^2 - 7x + 3$$

What is one possible x-intercept of the function f shown above?

9

$$2x^2 + kx + 10 = 0$$

If $(x + 5)$ is a factor of the quadratic equation above, what is the value of the constant k?

10

In the xy-plane, if 2 and k are the x-intercepts of the graph of the equation $y = x^2 - 10x + 16$, what is the value of k, where k is a constant?

Calculator Questions

11

$$y = x^2 - 8x + 13$$

The graph of the equation above is a parabola, in the xy-plane. Which of the following equivalent equations includes the minimum values of x and y as constants or coefficients?

A) $y = (x - 4)^2 - 3$

B) $y = (x - 3)^2 + 2$

C) $y = (x - 4)^2 + 7$

D) $y = (x + 3) + 2$

12

A parabola intersects the x-axis at 2 points and the axis to symmetry is at $x = 2$. Which of the following could be the equation of the parabola?

A) $y = (x - 2)(x - 2)$

B) $y = (x - 1)(x + 5)$

C) $y = (x + 1)(x - 5)$

D) $y = (x + 2)(x + 2)$

13

$$2x(3x + 1) + 2x + c = 6ax^2 + 4x + k$$

If the equation above has no solution, and a, c, and k are constants, which of the following is true about the possible values of a, c, and k given below?

I. $a = 1$

II. $c = k$

III. $c \neq k$

A) I only

B) I and II only

C) I and III only

D) I, II, and III

14

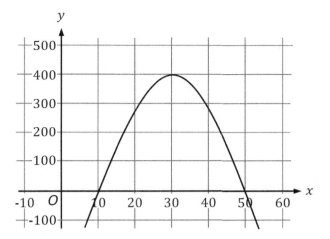

In the xy-plane, the above parabola predicts the weekly profit y, in thousands of dollars, of a furniture store based on the weekly advertising costs x, in hundreds of dollars. Which of the following is the maximum weekly profit, in thousands of dollars, predicted by the parabola?

A) 30

B) 50

C) 200

D) 400

15

$$y = -\frac{1}{12}(x^2 - 36x)$$

An architect designed a 0.3 inches thick arch shaped monument for a park. In the xy-plane, the shape of the arch is a parabola defined by the above equation, where x is the width of the arch, in inches, and y is the height of the arch, in inches. Which of the following is the height of the arch, in inches, excluding the 0.3 inches thickness of the arch?

A) 3

B) 18

C) 27

D) 36

16

In the xy-plane, if the graph of the parabola $y = (x - 3)^2 - 4$ is reflected across the y-axis and then moved 2 units upwards, which of the following is the equation of the transformed graph of the parabola?

A) $y = (-x - 3)^2 - 2$

B) $y = (-x - 3)^2 - 4$

C) $y = -(x - 3)^2 - 2$

D) $y = -(x - 3)^2 - 4$

17

In a controlled laboratory environment, a team of scientists studied the growth rate of a certain species of beetles under varying temperature conditions. In the xy-plane, the graph of the growth rate of beetles y, in response to the temperature x, in °C, is a parabola, where $0°C \leq x \leq 35°C$. If 0 and k are the two x-intercepts of the parabola, where k is a constant, which of the following statements is true about k?

A) It represents the maximum growth rate of beetles.

B) It represents the temperature at which the growth rate of beetles is 0.

C) It represents the temperature at which the growth rate of beetles is maximum.

D) It represents the growth rate of beetles at 0°C.

18

If $(ax + 3)(bx + 4) = 10x^2 + kx + 12$ is true for all values of x and $a + b = 7$, which of the following are the two possible values of k?

A) {2, 26}

B) {12, 26}

C) {23, 23}

D) {23, 26}

19

$$x = y + 2$$
$$x + y = 2x^2 - 2$$

Which of the following is an ordered pair for the above system of equations?

A) $(1, -1)$

B) $(1, -2)$

C) $(1, 1)$

D) $(2, 4)$

20

$$2x^2 - 3x + 6 = 0$$

How many real solutions does the above equation have?

A) Zero

B) Exactly one

C) Exactly two

D) Infinitely many

21

Which of the following functions has a minimum value of n, where $n > 0$?

A) $f(x) = -nx^2$

B) $f(x) = -nx^2 - 5$

C) $f(x) = 2x^2 + n$

D) $f(x) = (x + n)^2$

22

$$f(x) = 2x^2 + 8x + 11$$

The graph of the above function f is a parabola, in the xy-plane. Which of the following equivalent equations includes the x- and y-coordinates of the vertex as constants or coefficients?

A) $f(x) = (x + 2)^2 + 3$

B) $f(x) = (x + 2)^2 + 5$

C) $f(x) = 2(x + 2)^2 + 3$

D) $f(x) = 2(x + 2)^2 + 5$

23

$$ax^2 - 8x + 8 = 0$$

The equation above has one real solution. Which of the following is the value of a, where a is a constant?

24

$$h(t) = -16t^2 + 48t + 64$$

When a ball is launched from a 64 feet projectile, the height of the ball in the air, in feet, after t seconds can be modeled by the above equation. According to the model, how many seconds after launch does the ball reach the ground?

25

$$y = -(x + 2)(x - 12)$$

In the xy-plane, the above equation graphs a parabola. What is the y-coordinate of the vertex of the parabola?

26

$$g(x) = -60x^2 + 4,800x$$

A company sells a specific brand of handbags online. The function g shown above models the company's monthly profit y, in thousands of dollars, as a function of percent discount x offered on the handbags, where $y = g(x)$. If the maximum monthly profit of the company, in thousands of dollars, from selling handbags is at p percent discount, what is p?

Section 7 –
Absolute Value

Category 38 – Absolute Value and Linear Equations

Key Points

- The absolute value of a real number is denoted within two bars and is always a non-negative number. For example, the absolute value of $|x|$ and $|-x|$ is x. Therefore, the absolute value of a number is always non-negative, but the number could be positive or negative.

- The above is also true for absolute value expressions. For example, in the equation $|2x + 5| = 7$ the absolute value of $2x + 5$ is 7, but it is equally possible that the value of $2x + 5$ is -7 or 7. In either situation, the absolute value will always be 7.

- Since the absolute value is always non-negative, an absolute value expression cannot equate to a negative number. For example, the equation $|3x - 8| = -5$ does not have a solution.

How to Solve

An expression within the absolute value sign is solved by removing the absolute value bars and giving the equation two values, one positive and one negative.

If the absolute value expression equates to an expression, for example $|2x + 5| = 7 - x$, then the negative sign must be applied to the entire right expression. To solve for x in the equation $|2x + 5| = 7 - x$, the solutions will be determined as $2x + 5 = (7 - x)$ and $2x + 5 = -(7 - x)$.

The absolute value expression must be on one side of the equation. For example, in the equation $|2x + 5| + 5 = 7$, 5 from the left-side must be moved to the right-side resulting in $|2x + 5| = 7 - 5 \rightarrow |2x + 5| = 2$.

Example 1:

If a and b are the two solutions to the equation $|y + 7| = 3$, which of the following is the value of $|a + b|$?

A) -14

B) -6

C) 6

D) 14

Step 1: Solve for the positive value

$$y + 7 = 3 \rightarrow y = 3 - 7 = -4$$

Step 2: Solve for the negative value

$$y + 7 = -3 \rightarrow y = -3 - 7 = -10$$

Step 3: Solve for $|a + b|$

The two solutions are -4 and -10.

$$|a + b| = |-4 - 10| = |-14| = 14$$

Correct answer choice is **D**.

Example 2:

If $|2x - 3| + 1 = 8$ and $|y + 2| = 5$, what is one possible value of $|x + y|$?

<u>Equation $|2x - 3| + 1 = 8$</u>

Step 1: Solve for the positive value

Before solving move the integer not within absolute value sign to the right-side of the equation.

$$|2x - 3| = 8 - 1 \rightarrow |2x - 3| = 7$$

Solve.

$$2x - 3 = 7 \rightarrow 2x = 10 \rightarrow x = 5$$

If a question asks for one possible solution, then there no need to determine the other value of x. For the purpose of this example, the second value of x is calculated below.

Step 2: Solve for the negative value

$$2x - 3 = -7 \rightarrow 2x = -7 + 3 \rightarrow 2x = -4 \rightarrow x = -2$$

<u>Equation $|y + 2| = 5$</u>

Step 1: Solve for the positive value

$$y + 2 = 5 \rightarrow y = 5 - 2 \rightarrow y = 3$$

There is no need to determine the other value. In this example, the second value of y is shown below.

Step 2: Solve for the negative value

$$y + 2 = -5 \rightarrow y = -5 - 2 = -7$$

Step 3: Solve for $|x + y|$

The possible combinations can be

For $x = 5$ and $y = 3$:

$$|5 + 3| = |8| = 8$$

For $x = 5$ and $y = -7$:

$$|5 - 7| = |-2| = 2$$

For $x = -2$ and $y = 3$:

$$|-2 + 3| = |1| = 1$$

For $x = -2$ and $y = -7$:

$$|-2 - 7| = |-9| = 9$$

The possible values are **1, 2, 8, and 9.** Any of them can be entered for correct answer.

Category 38 – Practice Questions (answers on pages 369-370)

No Calculator Questions

1

$$|x - 4| + 8 = 6$$

How many possible values of x can the above equation have?

A) 0

B) 2

C) 4

D) 6

2

$$|2x - 7| - 2 = 13$$

In the above equation, a and b are the two values of x and $a > b$. What is the absolute value of b?

A) -4

B) 4

C) 11

D) 15

3

$$|2x + 5| - 1 = 6$$

If s and t are the two possible solutions of the above equation and $s = 1$, what is the value of $|t|$?

4

For the equation $|x - 4| + 3 = 6$, what is the sum of the two possible values of x?

Calculator Questions

5

If $|3x - 6| = 2 - x$, which of the following is one possible value of x?

A) 1

B) 2

C) 4

D) 10

6

If m and n are the two solutions of the equation $|2x + 5| = 7$, what is the value of $|m + n|$?

7

For $|x + 3| = 1$ and $|2y - 3| = 5$, what is one possible value of $|xy|$?

8

If $|4x - 3| + 2 = 7$ and $y = -2$, what is one possible value of $|xy|$, where $x > 0$?

9

If $|x + 5| = 3$ and $|y + 2| = 3$, what is one possible value of $|x + y|$, where $y > 0$?

Category 39 – Absolute Value and Linear Inequalities

Key Points

- Absolute value inequalities fall into two types: less than and greater than, for example, $|x| < a$ and $|x| > a$, respectively, where a is a non-negative number.

  - For $|x| < a$, the solution set is any number between $-a$ and a. For example, if $a = 3$, then the solution set of $|x| < 3$ is any number between -3 and 3 and can be written as $-3 < x < 3$.

    If the inequality symbol includes equal to, for example $|x| \leq 3$, then the solution set will include -3 and 3.

  - For $|x| > a$, the solution set is $x > a$ and $x < -a$. For example, if $a = 3$, then the solution set is any number greater than 3 and less than -3 and can be written as $x > 3$ and $x < -3$.

  - The above rules also apply to expressions. For example, $|2x + 1| < 3$ is $-3 < 2x + 1 < 3$, and $|2x + 1| > 3$ is $2x + 1 > 3$ and $2x + 1 < -3$.

- An absolute value inequality can be created for a range of numbers using the following formula, where x is the variable for the range of numbers and a and b are the smallest and the largest values of x, respectively.

  $$|x - \text{midpoint of } a \text{ and } b| < \text{distance of } a \text{ or } b \text{ from the midpoint}$$

  - For example, if the smallest value of x is 10 and the largest value of x is 40, then the midpoint of 10 and 40 is 25 and both 10 and 40 are at distance of 15 from the midpoint. The equation is $|x - 25| < 15$.

How to Solve

See below examples for further explanation on how the solution set of absolute value inequalities is determined.

- $|x| < 3$ represents any number from 0 to less than 3. The three integers that satisfy this condition are 0, 1, and 2. Since the absolute value of -1 is 1 and the absolute value of -2 is 2, these two numbers also satisfy the condition. Hence, the solution set is the distance from 0 in both directions. The solution set to the inequality $|x| < 3$ are five integers, -2, -1, 0, 1, and 2. See darker area on the number line below. For this reason, the solution set is $-3 < x < 3$.

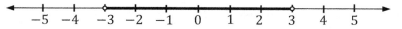

- $|x| > 3$ represents any number greater than 3. However, the absolute values of all the numbers less than -3 is also greater than 3. For example, the absolute value of -4 is 4, the absolute value of -5 is 5, and so on. See the two darker areas on the number line below. For this reason, the solution set is $x > 3$ and $x < -3$.

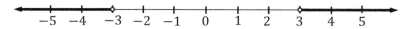

Example 1:

How many integer values of x satisfy the expression $|2x + 3| < 5$?

Step 1: Determine the solution set

Since the absolute value has a less than inequality symbol, the solution set will be

$$-5 < 2x + 3 < 5$$

Isolate x by subtracting 3 from both sides and then dividing both sides by 2.

$$-5 - 3 < 2x + 3 - 3 < 5 - 3 \rightarrow -8 < 2x < 2 \rightarrow$$

$$-\frac{8}{2} < \frac{2x}{2} < \frac{2}{2} \rightarrow -4 < x < 1$$

Since x is greater than -4 and less 1, the integer values of x can be -3, -2, -1, and 0. Hence, there are 4 possible integer values of x.

Correct answer is **4**.

Example 2:

An urgent care clinic determined that between 50 to 80 patients come to the clinic on any given day. Which of the following inequalities give all the possible number of patients p that may come to the clinic on any given day?

A) $|p - 50| < 80$

B) $|p - 80| < 50$

C) $|p - 65| < 15$

D) $|p - 65| = 30$

Step 1: Determine the midpoint of the two numbers

$$\frac{50 + 80}{2} = \frac{130}{2} = 65$$

This eliminates answer choices A and B.

Step 2: Determine the distance of the two numbers from the midpoint

Since 65 is the midpoint of 50 and 80, both the numbers are at a distance of 15 from the midpoint. This eliminates answer choice D.

Correct answer choice is **C**.

Example 3:

$$|2x - 1| > 7$$

Which of the following can NOT be a possible solution of the above inequality?

A) $x = 5$

B) $x = |-4|$

C) $x = |-7|$

D) $x < -4$

Step 1: Determine the solution set

Since the absolute value has a greater than inequality symbol, the solution sets will be

$$2x - 1 > 7 \text{ and } 2x - 1 < -7$$

For $2x - 1 > 7$, isolate x.

$$2x > 7 + 1 \;\rightarrow\; 2x > 8 \;\rightarrow\; \frac{2x}{2} > \frac{8}{2} \;\rightarrow\; x > 4$$

For $2x - 1 < -7$, isolate x.

$$2x < -7 + 1 \;\rightarrow\; 2x < -6 \;\rightarrow\; \frac{2x}{2} < \frac{-6}{2} \;\rightarrow\; x < -3$$

Since x is less than -3 or greater than 4, the integers $-3, -2, -1, 0, 1, 2, 3, 4$ cannot be the values of x.

Evaluate each answer choice. Answer choice B cannot be a value of x since $|-4| = 4$.

Correct answer choice is **B**.

Category 39 – Practice Questions (answers on page 370)

Calculator Questions

1

$$|x + 3| < 2$$

How many integer values of x satisfy the above inequality?

A) 0

B) 2

C) 3

D) 5

2

Giraffes are the tallest land animal in the world. When a baby giraffe is born, it can weigh between 100 and 150 pounds. Which of the following inequalities give all the possible weights w, in pounds, of a newborn baby giraffe?

A) $|w - 125| < 25$

B) $|w - 125| < 50$

C) $|w - 150| < 25$

D) $|w - 150| < 50$

3

If $|a| > 4$, which of the following are true?

I. $a > 4$

II. $a < -4$

III. $-4 < a < 4$

A) I only

B) III only

C) I and II only

D) I and III only

4

$$|r - 79{,}000| \leq 34{,}000$$

Each year, a health care research company mails out surveys to all residents above the age of 50 years in a certain town. The above inequality estimates the number of residents who will complete the survey in any year. Based on the inequality, which of the following could be the maximum number of residents r estimated to complete the survey in a year?

A) 24,000

B) 41,000

C) 45,000

D) 113,000

5

For the inequality $|x - 1| < 4$, which of the following can give all the values of x that satisfy the inequality?

A) $|x| < 3$

B) $-3 < x < 5$

C) $-4 < x < 4$

D) $-1 < x < 4$

6

$$|2x + 3| > 5$$

Which of the following could be the solutions to the above inequality?

I. $|-3|$

II. -2

III. 6

A) II only

B) III only

C) I and II only

D) I and III only

Category 40 – Absolute Value and Functions

Key Points

- The absolute value of a function is always positive. For example, if $f(x) = -2$, then $|f(x)| = |-2| = 2$.

- On the absolute value graph of a function, all the negative y values are converted to positive y values.

- Fig. 1 below shows the graph of a linear function $f(x) = x$. Fig. 2 shows the corresponding absolute value graph where the negative y values (dashed line) are converted to positive values. This gives the absolute value graph a V-shape. The vertex of the graph is at the tip of V.

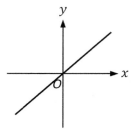

Fig. 1 $f(x) = x$

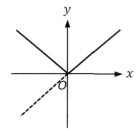

Fig. 2 $f(x) = |x|$

- The linear equation for an absolute value graph is $y = a|x - h| + k$, where h is the x-coordinate of the vertex and k is the y-coordinate of the vertex. In the above example, since the vertex is at origin, both h and k are 0. a determines the width of the V.

- If the above linear graph of $f(x) = x$ is shifted horizontally (right or left) or vertically (up or down), the vertex of the absolute value graph will shift accordingly.

  - In the equation $y = a|x - h| + k$, a negative h indicates a right shift by h units and a positive h indicates a left shift by h units. A negative k indicates downward shift by k units and a positive k indicates an upward shift by k units.

  - For example, if the graph of $f(x) = x$ is moved 2 units to the right and 1 unit downward, the equation of the absolute value graph will be $f(x) = |x - 2| - 1$ and the graph will form a V at the vertex $(2, -1)$.

- The absolute value graph of a non-linear function is not a V-shape. V shape is a characteristic of a linear absolute value graph with the equation in the form $y = a|x - h| + k$.

- Fig. 3 below shows the graph of a non-linear polynomial function. Fig. 4 shows the corresponding absolute value graph. All the negative values of y (dashed lines) are converted to positive values.

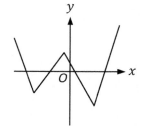

Fig. 3

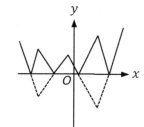

Fig. 4

How to Solve

Remember that for a function f, $f(x)$ is the y value of the function.

Example 1:

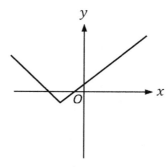

Which of the following could be the equation of the above graph, in the xy-plane?

A) $y = |x| - 1$

B) $y = |x - 2|$

C) $y = |x - 2| + 2$

D) $y = |x + 1| - 1$

Step 1: Determine the shift in the graph

The vertex of the graph is below 0 and to the left. Hence, the y-coordinate of the vertex must be negative and the x-coordinate of the vertex must be positive.

This eliminates answers choices A, B, and C. In correct answer choice D, $x + 1$ is 1 unit shift to the left and the y-coordinate is negative.

Correct answer choice is **D**.

Example 2:

x	-2	0	1	7
$f(x)$	2	1	-5	-2

In the table above, selected values of x and the corresponding $f(x)$ values are given. What is the value of $|f(7) - f(0)|$?

A) -3

B) -1

C) 3

D) 7

Step 1: Read the value of $f(x)$ from the table

To get the value of $f(7)$, look for $x = 7$ in the x column and read the corresponding value from the $f(x)$ column.

$$f(7) = -2$$

To get the value of $f(0)$, look for $x = 0$ in the x column and read the corresponding value from the $f(x)$ column.

$$f(0) = 1$$

Step 2: Solve for $|f(7) - f(0)|$

$$|f(7) - f(0)| = |-2 - 1| = |-3| = 3$$

Correct answer choice is **C**.

Category 40 – Practice Questions (answers on page 371)

No Calculator Questions

1

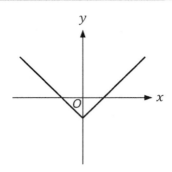

Which of the following could be the equation of the above graph, in the xy-plane?

A) $y = |x| - 2$

B) $y = |x| + 1$

C) $y = |x + 1|$

D) $y = |x + 1| - 1$

2

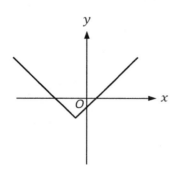

Which of the following could be the equation of the above graph, in the xy-plane, where $y = f(x)$?

A) $f(x) = |x - 1|$

B) $f(x) = |x - 1| - 2$

C) $f(x) = |x + 1| - 2$

D) $f(x) = |x + 1| + 3$

3

In the xy-plane, which of the following could be the graph of $g(x) = |x - 1| + 1$, where $y = g(x)$?

A)

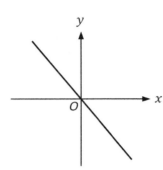

B)

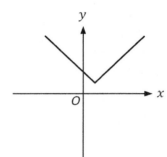

C)

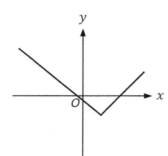

D)

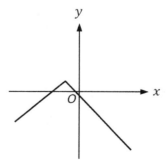

4

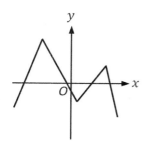

In the xy-plane, the graph of function g is shown above. Which of the following could be the graph of $y = |g(x)|$?

A)

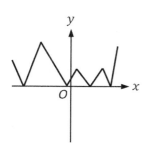

B)

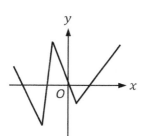

C)

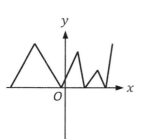

D)

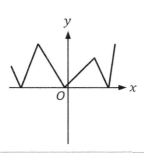

5

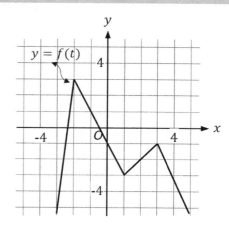

The complete graph of the function f, where $y = f(t)$, is shown above in the xy-plane. For which of the following values of t is $f(t) = |f(t)|$?

A) -4

B) -2

C) 3

D) 4

6

x	4	-2	1	3
$f(x)$	2	0	-2	-1

In the table above, selected values of x and the corresponding values of $f(x)$ are given. What is the absolute value of $2f(1) - f(3)$?

A) -3

B) -2

C) 3

D) 6

7

The function f can be defined by $f(-2) = -10$ and the function g can be defined as $g(x) = 3x - 10$. Which of the following is the value of $|f(-2) + g(5)|$?

A) -5

B) -2

C) 2

D) 5

No Calculator Questions

1

$$|x - 3| > 5$$

Which of the following could be the solution of the above inequality?

A) $x = |-1|$

B) $x = |-3|$

C) $x = -5$

D) $x = 6$

2

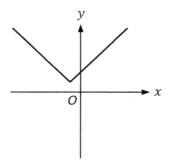

Which of the following could be the equation of the above graph, in the xy-plane?

A) $y = |x - 1| + 1$

B) $y = |x - 2| - 2$

C) $y = |x + 2| - 1$

D) $y = |x + 1| + 1$

3

$$|6 - x| = 4$$

The above equation has two solutions, s and t. If $s = 10$, what is the value of t?

Calculator Questions

4

The height of trees in a certain wildlife conservation is between 40 and 70 feet. Which of the following inequalities give all the possible heights h, in feet, of a tree in the wildlife conservation?

A) $|h - 55| < 15$

B) $|h - 70| < 30$

C) $|h - 55| < 30$

D) $|h - 40| < 70$

5

A spotted female deer can weigh between 25 to 45 kilograms. Which of the following inequalities give all the possible weights w, in kilograms, of a spotted female deer?

A) $|w - 25| < 45$

B) $|w - 35| < 10$

C) $|w - 45| < 25$

D) $|w + 35| < 65$

6

For the inequality $|2x - 1| < 3$, which of the following can give all the values of x that satisfy the inequality?

A) $|x| < 2$

B) $-3 < x < 3$

C) $-2 < x < 4$

D) $-1 < x < 2$

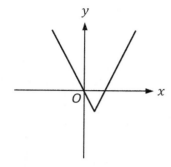

In the xy-plane, which of the following could be the equation of the above graph?

A) $y = |x - 1|$

B) $y = |x + 1| - 1$

C) $y = 2|x - 1| - 2$

D) $y = 2|x + 1| + 1$

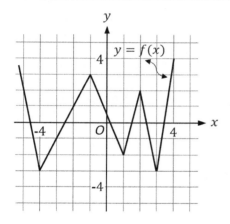

The complete graph of the function f is shown above, in the xy-plane, and $y = f(x)$. Which of the following is the sum of the absolute values of x that define the function $f(3)$?

A) -3

B) 1

C) 4

D) 7

$$|l - 38| \le 16$$

The above inequality estimates the length, in inches, of garden snakes in a wooded area of a certain state park. Based on the inequality, which of the following could be the length l, in inches, of the smallest garden snake in the wooded area of the state park?

A) 16

B) 22

C) 38

D) 54

If the function g defined as $g(x) = x^2 - 2x - 11$ is true for all values of x, which of the following is the absolute value of $g(3) - g(5)$?

A) 2

B) 4

C) 12

D) 16

$$|2x + 7| + 1 = 4$$

If a and b are the two solutions to the equation above, what is the value of $|a + b|$?

For $|2x + 1| = 3$ and $|2y + 3| = 7$, what is one possible value of $x + y$, where $y > x > 0$?

Section 8 –
Ratio, Proportion, and Rate

Category 41 – Ratio and Proportion

Key Points

- A ratio is a comparison of two numbers.
    - A ratio may compare the parts of two or more numbers within the total. For example, if there are a total of 5 oatmeal and sugar cookies, of which 2 are oatmeal and 3 are sugar, then the ratio of the number of oatmeal cookies to the number of sugar cookies is $2:3$.
    - A ratio may compare a part within the total. From the above example, the ratio of the number of oatmeal cookies to the total number of cookies is $2:5$ and the ratio of the number of sugar cookies to the total number of cookies is $3:5$.
    - A ratio can also be written as a fraction. The fraction of oatmeal cookies is $\frac{2}{5}$ and the fraction of sugar cookies is $\frac{3}{5}$.
- A proportion equates equal ratios. If one number of the ratio increases, then the other numbers increase proportionally. For example, if the number of oatmeal and sugar cookies (from the above example) were proportionally increased three times, then the ratio would be $(2:3) \times 3 = 6:9$.

    As a fraction, the proportion can be written as $\frac{2}{3} = \frac{6}{9}$.

How to Solve

The numerator and the denominator of a proportion must represent the same thing. For example, in the below proportions all the numerators represent the oatmeal cookies, and all the denominators represent the total cookies.

$$\frac{\text{oatmeal cookies}}{\text{total cookies}} = \frac{2}{5} = \frac{4}{10} = \frac{6}{15} = \frac{8}{20}$$

In the above example, the ratios are $2:5 = 4:10 = 6:15 = 8:20$. The lowest ratio is $2:5$. Any ratio in a proportion can be simplified to the lowest ratio. Look for common multiples. For example, both the numbers in the ratio $6:15$ can be divided by 3, resulting in

$$\frac{6}{3} : \frac{15}{3} = 2:5$$

Example 1:

In a certain school, the total number of students on the wrestling and karate teams is 60. If there are 24 students in the wrestling team, what is the ratio of the number of students in the wresting team to the number of students in the karate team?

A) $2:3$

B) $2:5$

C) $3:2$

D) $8:15$

Step 1: Determine the ratio

Number of students in wrestling team $= 24$.

Number of students in karate team $=$ total students in both teams − number of students in wrestling team.

$$60 - 24 = 36$$

$$\text{students in wrestling team} : \text{students in karate team} = 24:36 = 2:3$$

Note that the ratios in the answer choices are usually given as the lowest ratio.

Correct answer choice is **A.**

Example 2:

Hyperion dwarf is a 379.7 feet tall redwood tree discovered in 2006. What is the equivalent height of Hyperion dwarf tree in meters, rounded to the nearest tenth? (1 meter = 3.28084 feet)

A) 88

B) 92.4

C) 115.7

D) 155.8

Step 1: Set up a proportion

Let the height of tree in meters $= x$.

It is given that 1 meter = 3.28084 feet. Set up a proportion for feet and meters as follows.

$$\frac{\text{feet}}{\text{meters}} = \frac{3.28084}{1} = \frac{379.7}{x}$$

Step 2: Solve

Cross multiply.

$$3.28084x = 379.7 \rightarrow x = 115.73 = 115.7$$

Correct answer choice is **C**.

Example 3:

A farmer sells apples and oranges at a local market during the summer. Last week, the ratio of oranges sold to apples sold, in pounds, was $4:7$. If 112 pounds of apples were sold last week, how many pounds of oranges were sold last week?

Step 1: Set up a proportion

Let the pounds of oranges sold $= x$.

Set up a proportion for pounds of oranges sold and pounds of apples sold as follows.

$$\frac{\text{pounds of oranges sold}}{\text{pounds of apples sold}} = \frac{4}{7} = \frac{x}{112}$$

Step 2: Solve

Cross multiply.

$$7 \times x = 4 \times 112 \rightarrow 7x = 448 \rightarrow x = 64$$

Correct answer is **64**.

Example 4:

An architect created a scaling system for a building. Every 10 feet represent 0.2 centimeters on the scale. If the architect draws the height of a building as 9 centimeters on the scaling system, what is the height of the building in feet?

Step 1: Set up a proportion

Let the height in feet $= x$.

Set up a proportion for feet and centimeters as follows.

$$\frac{\text{feet}}{\text{centimeters}} = \frac{10}{0.2} = \frac{x}{9}$$

Step 2: Solve

Cross multiply.

$$0.2 \times x = 9 \times 10 \rightarrow 0.2x = 90 \rightarrow x = 450$$

Correct answer is **450**.

Category 41 – Practice Questions (answers on pages 373-374)

Calculator Questions

1

An elementary school offers music and drama classes to all students enrolled in the school. A student must select either a music or a drama class in a given school year. In the current school year, the ratio of the number of students in the music class to the number of students in the drama class is $2:5$. If 120 students selected drama, how many students are enrolled in the school in the current school year?

A) 48

B) 120

C) 142

D) 168

2

Kara is mixing ingredients to bake 4 trays of muffins and 7 trays of cookies. She requires $5\frac{1}{2}$ cups of butter in total. If the same amount of butter is required for each tray of muffin and cookie, how many cups of butter is required for 4 trays of muffins?

A) $\frac{4}{7}$

B) $\frac{11}{8}$

C) 2

D) 11

3

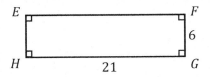

What is the ratio of GH to FG?

A) 21 to 6

B) 15 to 4

C) 6 to 21

D) 3 to 1

Questions 4 and 5 refer to the following information.

Company X and Company Y both sell Product A and Product B. The table below shows the number Product A and Product B sold at each company last month.

	Company X	Company Y	Total
Product A	502	1,004	1,506
Product B	710	800	1,510
Total	1,212	1,804	3,016

4

Which of the following is closest to the ratio of the total number of the two products sold at Company X to the total number of the two products sold at Company X and Company Y last month?

A) $1:3.1$

B) $1:2.5$

C) $2.1:3.5$

D) $3.1:5.3$

5

Of the total number of Product A sold at Company X and Company Y last month, which of the following is closest to the fraction of Product A sold at Company X last month?

A) $\frac{1}{3}$

B) $\frac{1}{2}$

C) $\frac{2}{3}$

D) $\frac{3}{5}$

6

A city council created a new scaling system for the city map. Every 2 meters are scaled to 0.04 inches. How many inches do 2,500 meters represent on the scale?

A) 20

B) 40

C) 50

D) 100

7

If the ratio $a:5:12$ is equivalent to $3:b:24$, what is the value of $2(a + b)$?

A) 3

B) 10

C) 11

D) 23

8

One box of 50 mini muffins contain bran and corn muffins in the ratio of $2:3$, respectively. How many more corn muffins are in the box than bran muffins?

A) 10

B) 12

C) 20

D) 30

9

Aiko bought 48 ounces of regular sugar cookies and 48 ounces of low sugar cookies. The regular sugar cookies come in packets of 12 ounces and each packet contain 8 cookies. The low sugar cookies come in packets of 8 ounces and each packet contain 12 cookies. If L is the number of low sugar cookies in 48 ounces and R is the number of regular sugar cookies in 48 ounces, what is $L - R$?

A) 4

B) 40

C) 48

D) 64

10

A baker uses the same proportion of ingredients to bake cakes of assorted sizes. For the first cake, the baker added 10 grams of butter and 2 grams of sugar. For the second cake, if the baker plans to add 25 grams of butter, which of the following is true about the grams of sugar that must be added?

A) Twice the amount as in the first cake.

B) Same amount as the first cake.

C) Half the amount of butter added to the first cake.

D) 10 grams.

11

Anula mixes $\frac{1}{4}$ cup of melted butter with $2\frac{3}{4}$ cup of flour batter in a large container. What is the fraction of butter in each cup of the mixture?

A) $\frac{1}{12}$

B) $\frac{1}{8}$

C) $\frac{1}{4}$

D) 1

12

There are 600 students in a high school. At the end of the school day, 80 students walk home, 160 students go home with a parent, and the remaining students take the school bus. What is the ratio of the number of students who go home with a parent to the number of students who take the school bus?

A) $1:5$

B) $2:5$

C) $2:7$

D) $4:9$

Questions 13 and 14 refer to the following information.

The number of trees planted in a certain community over the last 8 years is shown in the table below.

Years since trees planted	Number of trees planted
1	5
2	3
3	12
4	8
5	11
6	2
7	6
8	3

13

Out of the trees that were planted 4 or more years ago, what fraction were planted more than 6 years ago?

A) $\dfrac{3}{10}$

B) $\dfrac{11}{30}$

C) $\dfrac{5}{8}$

D) $\dfrac{3}{4}$

14

What is the ratio of the number of trees planted within the last 3 years to the number of trees planted over the last 8 years?

A) $1:8$

B) $2:5$

C) $3:8$

D) $3:5$

15

Laura mixes $\dfrac{1}{4}$ cup of protein mix A with $\dfrac{3}{4}$ cup of protein mix B. If protein mix A contains 28 grams of protein per cup and protein mix B contains 20 grams of protein per cup, how many grams of protein is in one cup of the protein mix Laura created?

A) 7

B) 12

C) 22

D) 48

16

On a map the distance between two airports in a certain city is 7.5 inches. If 0.5 inches on the map corresponds to an actual distance of 14 miles, how many miles far apart are the two airports?

17

A healthy baby elephant can weigh approximately 200 pounds at birth. If the weight is measured in kilograms, what would be the approximate weight of a healthy baby elephant at birth, rounded to the nearest tenth? (1 kilogram = 2.20462 pounds)

18

An 8 feet long pole casts a 20 feet long shadow on the ground. What is the difference, in feet, between the length of the shadow casted on the ground by a 20 feet long pole and the length of the shadow casted on the ground by an 8 feet long pole, assuming that the shadows are proportional?

Category 42 – Rate

Key Points

- A rate is a ratio of two units of measurement. For example, 35 miles per hour. The two units of measurement are miles and hour. The ratio can be written as 35 miles:1 hour or $\frac{35 \text{ miles}}{1 \text{ hour}}$. Similarly, 35 miles per gallon is 35 miles:1 gallon or $\frac{35 \text{ miles}}{1 \text{ gallon}}$.

- When two rates are compared, both the units in the two rates must be compared, respectively. For example, when comparing the speed of a car in miles per hour to the speed in kilometers per second, miles must be compared to kilometers and per hour to per second. Comparing miles per hour to kilometers per hour is incorrect.

How to Solve

Question on rates can be solved using conversion factors or by setting up a proportion.

Conversion factors are a quicker method when working with several units of measurements.

- It is important to determine what the starting and the ending units should be in the conversion process.
- When working with time units, a shortcut approach is to convert all time units to the smallest time unit before solving (see Alternative 1 in Example 1 below).

In this book, most questions on rates are solved using conversion factors. However, some questions may be quickly solved with simpler calculations. For example, if a car is traveling at a speed of 40 miles per hour, then in 15 minutes (one-fourth of an hour) the car will travel one-fourth the distance = 10 miles.

Example 1:

If a bus is driving at an average speed of 36 kilometers per hour, what is the equivalent speed in feet per second, rounded to the nearest tenth? (1 kilometer = 3,280 feet)

A) 10.5 feet per second

B) 32.8 feet per second

C) 36.0 feet per second

D) 60.0 feet per second

Step 1: Use the conversion factors

Conversion factors should be set up such that the units cancel from left to right. The question is asking to convert kilometers per hour to feet per second. Hence, the starting units should be kilometers per hour and the ending units should be feet per second.

Converting hour to seconds requires two conversion factors, minutes per hour and seconds per minute.

$$\frac{36 \text{ kilometers}}{1 \text{ hour}} \times \frac{1 \text{ hour}}{60 \text{ minutes}} \times \frac{1 \text{ minute}}{60 \text{ seconds}} \times \frac{3,280 \text{ feet}}{1 \text{ kilometer}}$$

Cancel units from left to right.

$$\frac{36 \ \cancel{\text{kilometers}}}{1 \ \cancel{\text{hour}}} \times \frac{1 \ \cancel{\text{hour}}}{60 \ \cancel{\text{minutes}}} \times \frac{1 \ \cancel{\text{minute}}}{60 \text{ seconds}} \times \frac{3,280 \text{ feet}}{1 \ \cancel{\text{kilometer}}} = \frac{36 \times 3,280 \text{ feet}}{60 \times 60 \text{ seconds}} = \frac{32.8 \text{ feet}}{\text{seconds}} = 32.8 \text{ feet per second}$$

In the first conversion factor, the ratio is written as 36 kilometers:1 hour. Hence, hour is in the denominator.

The second conversion factor converts an hour to minutes. Since the hour in the first and the second conversion factors must cancel out, hour must be in the numerator of the second conversion factor. Hence, the ratio can be written as 1 hour:60 minutes (hour in the numerator). Writing it as 60 minutes:1 hour is incorrect as the hours will not cancel.

Similarly, in the third conversion factor the ratio must be written as 1 minute:60 seconds (minute in the numerator) so the minutes of the second and the third conversion factor can cancel.

Correct answer choice is **B**.

Alternative 1: Having one time unit during the conversion process can save time and avoid confusion with conversion factors. Since 1 hour = 3,600 seconds, replace 1 hour with 3,600 seconds.

$$\frac{36 \; \cancel{\text{kilometers}}}{3,600 \text{ seconds}} \times \frac{3,280 \text{ feet}}{1 \; \cancel{\text{kilometer}}} = \frac{36 \times 3,280 \text{ feet}}{3,600 \text{ seconds}} = 32.8 \text{ feet per second}$$

Alternative 2: See the solution below using proportion.

Start with converting kilometers per hour to feet per hour. Set up a proportion for kilometers and feet.

Let the unknown feet = x.

$$\frac{\text{kilometers}}{\text{feet}} \; \rightarrow \; \frac{36}{x} = \frac{1}{3,280}$$

$$x = 36 \times 3,280 \text{ feet per hour}$$

To convert feet per hour to feet per second divide by 3,600.

$$\frac{36 \times 3,280}{3,600} = 32.8 \text{ feet per second}$$

Example 2:

Taxi A and Taxi B pick up passengers from the same taxi stand and leave at the same time in opposite directions on a straight path. Taxi A is going at the average speed of 40 miles per hour. Taxi B is going at the average speed of 30 miles per hour. How many miles apart the taxis will be in 15 minutes?

Step 1: Use the conversion factors

Since the taxis are traveling in opposite directions, the distance between them is the sum of the distance traveled by each taxi in 15 minutes. Since miles traveled in 15 minutes must be determined, the starting unit should be 15 minutes and the ending unit should be miles.

Taxi A: 40 miles per hour = 40 miles in 60 minutes.

$$15 \; \cancel{\text{minutes}} \times \frac{40 \text{ miles}}{60 \; \cancel{\text{minutes}}} = \frac{15 \times 40 \text{ miles}}{60} = 10 \text{ miles}$$

Taxi B: 30 miles per hour = 30 miles in 60 minutes.

$$15 \; \cancel{\text{minutes}} \times \frac{30 \text{ miles}}{60 \; \cancel{\text{minutes}}} = \frac{15 \times 30 \text{ miles}}{60} = 7.5 \text{ miles}$$

The distance between taxi A and taxi B = $10 + 7.5 = 17.5$ miles.

Correct answer is **17.5.**

Example 3:

Preena drove 44 miles from her home to a shopping mall. The fuel consumption of Preena's car is 28 miles per gallon and the cost of fuel is $2.89 per gallon. What is the cost, in dollars, of the fuel consumed during Preena's drive from her home to the shopping mall, rounded to the nearest hundred?

A) $0.50

B) $2.01

C) $3.52

D) $4.54

Step 1: Use the conversion factors

Since the dollar cost of 44 miles must be determined, the starting unit should be 44 miles and the ending unit should be dollars. (This is an example when using conversion factors is the quickest approach to solve a question.)

$$44 \; \cancel{\text{miles}} \times \frac{1 \; \cancel{\text{gallon}}}{28 \; \cancel{\text{miles}}} \times \frac{2.89 \text{ dollars}}{1 \; \cancel{\text{gallon}}} = \frac{44 \times 2.89 \text{ dollars}}{28} = 4.54 \text{ dollars}$$

Correct answer is **4.54.**

Category 42 – Practice Questions (answers on pages 375-376)

No Calculator Questions

Calculator Questions

1

A car driving at an average speed of 30 miles per hour will travel how many miles in 10 minutes?

A) 3

B) 5

C) 10

D) 30

2

A wheel is rolling at an average speed of x inches per minute. Which of the following equations represents the time, in seconds, it will take for the wheel to roll y inches, where x and y are constants?

A) xy

B) $60xy$

C) $\dfrac{12x}{y}$

D) $\dfrac{60y}{x}$

3

Sam drove at an average speed of 45 miles per hour for a total of 140 minutes. How many miles did Sam drive?

4

Casper drove his truck on a certain highway for 2 hours at the average speed of 50 miles per hour. If the fuel consumption of Casper's truck on the highway is 20 miles per gallon and the cost of fuel is $3 per gallon, which of the following is the cost, in dollars, of the fuel consumed during the 2 hour drive on the highway, if Casper did not stop during the 2 hours?

A) $3

B) $12

C) $15

D) $20

5

Water flows from a tank at the rate of 768 ounces per minute. Which of the following is equivalent to the rate of water flow in gallons per second? (1 gallon = 128 ounces)

A) 0.1 gallon per second

B) 0.5 gallon per second

C) 1 gallons per second

D) 6 gallons per second

6

Jolie and Charlie started bicycling from the same point in a straight line in opposite directions. Jodie rides the bicycle at an average speed of 10 miles per hour. Charlie rides the bicycle at an average speed of 18 miles per hour. In 15 minutes from start, Jolie and Charlie are how many miles apart?

A) 2

B) 3

C) 5

D) 7

Jerry took a non-stop flight from New York to London. The total flight distance was 3,459 miles. The plane flew for 4 hours at an average speed of 526 miles per hour and for the remaining x minutes at an average speed of 420 miles per hour. Ignoring the air resistance, which of the following is closest to the value of x?

A) 3

B) 27

C) 102

D) 194

Two birds take off from a tree at the same time in a straight line and the same direction. If bird A is flying at an average speed of 18 miles per hour and bird B is flying at an average speed of 24 miles per hour, how far behind, in miles, is bird A from bird B in 10 minutes?

A) 1.0

B) 1.5

C) 3.1

D) 4.5

A farmer has set up a watering system to irrigate the farmland. A water tank pumps out water at the rate of 36 gallons per hour and sprays around the farmland. How many ounces of water is pumped out per second? (1 gallon = 128 ounces)

A) 0.01

B) 0.92

C) 1.28

D) 3.60

Rosario drove from her home to a shopping mall for 45 minutes. For the first 15 minutes, she drove at an average speed of 60 miles per hour. For the remaining 30 minutes, she drove at an average speed of 40 miles per hour. How many miles did Rosario drive from her home to the shopping mall?

A) 30

B) 35

C) 55

D) 90

A train traveling at the average speed of 180 kilometers per hour, travels how many meters in 1 second? (1 kilometer = 1,000 meters)

If Maria rides her bicycle at an average speed of 20 miles per hour, how many minutes will it take her to ride 4 miles?

John drives 100 miles on each working day. The fuel consumption of his car is 30 miles per gallon. In 4 working days, how many liters of fuel is consumed by John's car, rounded to the nearest tenth? (1 gallon = 3.8 liters)

No Calculator Questions

1

If Samantha rides her bike at the average speed of 30 kilometers per hour, how many minutes will it take her to ride 10 kilometers?

A) 10

B) 20

C) 55

D) 60

2

Sara reads p pages in m minutes. Which of the following expressions could represent the number of pages Sara reads in 3 hours in terms of p and m?

A) $3pm$

B) $180pm$

C) $\dfrac{3p}{m}$

D) $\dfrac{180p}{m}$

Calculator Questions

3

A bald eagle can achieve a flying speed of 30 miles per hour using powerful wingbeats and up to 100 miles per hour when diving straight down to catch a prey. If a bald eagle dives down straight at the speed of 60 miles per hour to catch a prey 0.2 miles away, how many seconds will it take the eagle to catch the prey?

A) 4

B) 5

C) 12

D) 30

4

A mixture contains 20 grams of salt in 500 milliliters of water. If a second mixture is created in the same proportion, which of the following could be the ratios of salt to water in the second mixture?

I. $1:25$

II. $3:50$

III. $5:125$

A) II only

B) III only

C) I and III only

D) II and III only

5

A meteorologist report showed that in a certain city in 2019, the ratio of the total annual rainfall, in inches, to the ratio of the rainfall, in inches, in the month of March was 12.4 to 3.1. If r is the total inches of annual rainfall in 2019, which of the following expressions represent the rainfall, in inches, in March in terms of r?

A) $\dfrac{r}{4}$

B) $\dfrac{12}{r}$

C) $3.1r$

D) 12.4

6

If a train is travelling at an average speed of 120 miles per hour, what is the equivalent average speed of the train in feet per second? (1 mile is 5,280 feet)

A) 44 feet per second

B) 52 feet per second

C) 120 feet per second

D) 176 feet per second

7

A painter takes 8 hours to paint 140 square feet area. For every 100 square feet of area, the painter earns $250. How many hours will it take the painter to earn $1,400?

A) 20

B) 32

C) 44

D) 100

8

A study revealed that in 15 minutes a pilot whale can dive up to a depth of 3,280 feet to catch squids. What is the approximate equivalent depth, in miles? (1 mile = 5,280 feet)

A) 0.6

B) 1.1

C) 1.6

D) 16.2

9

Plane A and Plane B are flying from California to Sydney. Plane A is flying at an average speed of 600 miles per hour and Plane B is flying at an average speed of 500 miles per hour. If the two planes continue to fly at the above speed for the next hour, how many more miles would Plane A travel than Plane B in 30 minutes, ignoring the wind speed?

10

A hiker is following a map of a hiking trail. Each mile on the map is scaled to 0.2 centimeters. If the hiking trail is 30 miles, how many centimeters does it represent on the map?

Questions 11, 12, and 13 refer to the following information.

Bentley is planning to visit his grandparents. On a map, Bentley measures the distance he will be driving on various roads and highways. The map represents 24 miles as $\frac{1}{2}$ centimeter. The table below shows the names of the roads and the highways, and the distance on the map, in centimeters, Bentley will be traveling on each of them.

Names of roads and highways	Distance in centimeter
State Road 27	$\frac{1}{8}$
Highway 2	$1\frac{1}{4}$
Highway 17	$\frac{1}{4}$
State Road 4	$\frac{3}{4}$

11

What is the total distance, in miles, Bentley will be driving on all the roads and highways?

12

If Bentley plans to drive on Highway 2 at an average speed of 40 miles per hour, for how many minutes will Bentley drive on Highway 2?

13

If Bentley estimates that the fuel consumption of his car on State Road 27 and State Road 4 will be 28 miles per gallon, how many gallons of fuel will be consumed driving on both these roads?

Section 9 – Percent

Category 43 – Percent of a Number and Percent Increase/Decrease

Key Points

- Percent (%) refers to parts of a number per 100. For example, 32 parts per 100 is 32%. It can also be written as $\frac{32}{100}$ or 0.32. Similarly, 260 parts per 100 is 260% or $\frac{260}{100}$ or 2.6.

- A percent decrease refers to a decrease in parts of a number per 100. For example, 20% decrease of number n is $100 - 20 = 80\%n$ or $\frac{80}{100}n$ or $0.8n$.

- A percent increase refers to an increase in parts of a number per 100. For example, 20% increase of number n is $100 + 20 = 120\%n$ or $\frac{120}{100}n$ or $1.2n$. Similarly, 250% increase of number n is $100 + 250 = 350\%n$ or $3.5n$.

- Multiple increases and decreases can be multiplied together. For example, a 20% increase (1.2) of a number n, followed by a 10% increase (1.1) and then followed by a 25% decrease (0.75) is $(1.2 \times 1.1 \times 0.75)n = 0.99n$.

  - The order of multiplication does not matter. $(0.75 \times 1.2 \times 1.1 \times n)$, or $(1.1 \times 0.75 \times 1.2 \times n)$, or $(n \times 1.2 \times 0.75 \times 1.1)$ will give the same answer.

How to Solve

The quickest approach to determining the percent of a number or percent increase/decrease of a number is to convert the percent to a decimal and multiply it with the given number. For example,

- 10% of $50 = 0.1 \times 50 = 5$.

- 10% increase of $50 = 1.1 \times 50 = 55$.

- 10% decrease of $50 = 0.9 \times 50 = 45$.

Note that when a percent is converted to a decimal, it is divided by 100. For example, 10% increase is $100 + 10 = 110\% = 1.1$. This is same as $1 + 0.1 = 1.1$. Similarly, 10% decrease is $100 - 10 = 90\% = 0.9$. This is same as $1 - 0.1 = 0.9$. Hence, when converting percent increase/decrease to a decimal it is more efficient to start with 1 instead of 100.

Remember that incremental percent increases and decreases are multiplied not added. For example, a 10% increase followed by a 20% increase is (1.1×1.2) not $(1.1 + 1.2)$.

The distinction between percent of a number and percent increase of a number is important to remember, especially when the percent increase is greater than 100. For example, 300% of 50 is $3 \times 50 = 150$, whereas 300% increase of 50 is $(1 + 3) \times 50 = 4 \times 50 = 200$.

Example 1:

What is 6% of 150% of 80% of 50?

Step 1: Convert percent to decimal

$$80\% = 0.8$$

$$150\% = 1.5$$

$$6\% = 0.06$$

Step 2: Determine the final value

Multiply all decimals and the given number.

$$0.8 \times 1.5 \times 0.06 \times 50 = 3.6$$

Correct answer is **3.6**.

Example 2:

In 2015, 80 students were enrolled in a music club at a certain high school. In 2016, the number of students enrolled in the music class increased by 10%. In 2017, 25% less students enrolled in the music club than in 2016. How many students were enrolled in the music class in 2017?

A) 52

B) 66

C) 88

D) 108

Step 1: Convert percent to decimal

$$10 \text{ percent increase in } 2016 = 1 + 0.1 = 1.1$$
$$25 \text{ percent less in } 2107 = 25 \text{ percent decrease in } 2107 = 1 - 0.25 = 0.75$$

Step 2: Determine the final value

$$1.1 \times 0.75 \times 80 = 66$$

Correct answer choice is **B**.

Example 3:

A garden center has discounted the price of each rose bush by 14% for the entire month of June. Each Sunday during June, an additional 23% discount is offered on the already discounted price. If the original price of a rose bush is $39.99 and no sales tax is collected, which of the following expressions represents the discounted price of a rose bush, in dollars, on a Sunday in June?

A) $(39.99)(0.14)(0.23)$

B) $(39.99)(0.86)(0.23)$

C) $(39.99)(0.86)(0.77)$

D) $(39.99)(1.14)(1.23)$

Step 1: Convert percent to decimal

$$14 \text{ percent discount } = 14 \text{ percent decrease in price} = 1 - 0.14 = 0.86$$
$$23 \text{ percent discount } = 23 \text{ percent decrease in price} = 1 - 0.23 = 0.77$$

Step 2: Determine the final value

Original price $= \$39.99$.

Total percent discount $= (0.86)(0.77)$.

$$\text{final price} = (39.99)(0.86)(0.77)$$

Correct answer choice is **C.**

Category 43 – Practice Questions (answers on page 378)

Calculator Questions

1

The value of a number k is decreased by 25% and then increased by 6%. Which of the following expressions represents the final value of k?

A) $(0.75)(1.06)(k)$

B) $(0.75)(1.6)(k)$

C) $(1.25)(0.4)(k)$

D) $(1.25)(1.6)(k)$

2

If the value of number 72 is decreased by 25% and then increased by 150%, which of the following is closest to the final value of 72?

A) 54

B) 81

C) 90

D) 135

3

John analyzes his stock portfolio each week on Friday night. Last week, the starting balance of the portfolio on Monday was s dollars. If the portfolio increased by 55% on Tuesday, decreased by 13% on Wednesday, increased by 117% on Thursday, and remained unchanged on Monday and Friday, which of the following expressions represents the ending balance of John's stock portfolio last week on Friday night?

A) $(1.55)(0.87)(1.17)(s)$

B) $(1.55)(0.87)(2.17)(s)$

C) $(1.55)(1.13)(0.83)(s)$

D) $(4.59)(s)$

4

A library uses a computer system to check-in and check-out books. The librarian monitors the inventory of books each morning before opening the library and each evening after closing the library. Last Monday, the library had a total of 1,040 books before opening. After closing, 20% of books were checked out and 125 books were returned. Which of the following was the number of books in the library last Monday after closing?

A) 333

B) 832

C) 957

D) 1,248

5

An electronic store is offering 35% discount on the television that Jenny wants to buy. She has a coupon for an additional 12% discount to be applied on the already discounted price of the television. If p dollars is the price of the television without any discount, which of the following expressions represents the total amount, in dollars, Jenny will pay after both the discounts are applied and 8% sales tax is added to the final price?

A) $(0.65)(0.88)(1.08)(p)$

B) $(0.65)(1.12)(1.8)(p)$

C) $(1.35)(0.88)(0.92)(p)$

D) $(1.35)(1.12)(1.08)(p)$

6

Jane has a collection of 125 music CDs. She is planning on giving 20% of the collection to her brother and 35% to her cousin. How many CDs will be left with Jane after she gives to her brother and cousin?

A) 56

B) 65

C) 70

D) 110

7

What is 200% of 30% of 25% of 60?

A) 9

B) 54

C) 68

D) 150

8

In the current school year, 200 students are enrolled in chemistry honors course at a certain high school. The school administration has projected an increase of 10% enrollment in chemistry honors course each year for the next 2 academic years. Which of the following is closest to the total number of students projected to be enrolled in the chemistry honors course by the end of next 2 academic years?

A) 210

B) 220

C) 240

D) 242

9

An independent research company projected that by 2025 the number of residents in a remote island will increase by 160%. If currently there are 3,680 residents on the remote island, how many additional residents are projected by 2025?

A) 1,000

B) 2,208

C) 5,888

D) 9,568

10

In 2019, Rita received 6% more bonus than the estimated bonus of d dollars. How much bonus did Rita receive in 2019 in terms of d?

A) $1.06d$

B) $1.6d$

C) $d + 1.06$

D) $d + 6$

11

Tom took three history tests during the first semester of school. In the first test he scored an 80. In the second test, he scored 20% less than the first test and in the third test he scored 25% more than the second test. What was the score of the third history test?

12

A bus left the bus terminal with a total of 48 passengers. At the first stop, 25% of the passengers got off the bus and no one boarded. At the second stop, 50% of the remaining passengers got off the bus and 2 passengers boarded the bus. How many passengers are on the bus after the second stop?

Category 44 – The Original Number before a Percent Increase/Decrease

Key Points

- When a number is modified by percent increase or decrease, the original number (before the increase or decrease) can be determined as follows, where end number is the number after percent increase/decrease.

$$\text{original number} = \frac{\text{end number}}{1 \pm \text{percent increase or decrease as decimal}}$$

- If the original number was decreased by a certain percent, then the denominator will be $1 -$ percent decrease. For example, the denominator for 30% decrease will be $1 - 0.3 = 0.7$.

- If the original number was increased by a certain percent, then the denominator will be $1 +$ percent increase. For example, the denominator for 30% increase will be $1 + 0.3 = 1.3$.

- Multiple increases and decreases can be multiplied. For example, if the original number was decreased by 30% and then increased by 20%, the denominator will be (0.7×1.2).

How to Solve

If a question gives a dollar cost with sales tax, remember to include it in the denominator as percent increase.

Example 1:

Tina bought a shirt at 15% discount. The price of the shirt after the discount and addition of 6% sales tax was $18.02.

Question 1

If the original price of the shirt before the sales tax and the discount was a dollars, which of the following expressions represents the value of a?

A) $\dfrac{18.02}{(0.85)(0.6)}$

B) $\dfrac{18.02}{(0.85)(1.06)}$

C) $(0.85)(0.94)18.02$

D) $(0.85)(1.6)18.02$

Step 1: Convert percent to decimal

$$\text{discount} = 15\% \text{ decrease} = 1 - 0.15 = 0.85$$
$$\text{sales tax} = 6\% \text{ increase} = 1 + 0.06 = 1.06$$

Step 2: Determine the original value

End price = $18.02. Total increase/decrease = $(0.85)(1.06)$.

$$\text{original price} = \frac{18.02}{(0.85)(1.06)}$$

Correct answer choice is **B.**

Question 2

What was the original price of the shirt, in dollars, excluding the sales tax?

Proceed from Step 2 of Question 1 and solve the equation for the original price.

$$\frac{18.02}{0.85 \times 1.06} = 20$$

Correct answer is **20**.

Category 44 – Practice Questions (answers on page 379)

Calculator Questions

1

The number n when decreased by 20% and then increased by 5% is 42. Which of the following expressions represents the number n?

A) $\dfrac{42}{(0.8)(1.05)}$

B) $\dfrac{42}{(1.2)(1.05)}$

C) $(0.8)(1.05)42$

D) $(0.8)(0.95)42$

2

A retail company plans to close 27% of its worldwide stores between January 2022 and December 2025. At the end of December 2025, the company will have 584 remaining stores open. How many stores does the retail company have worldwide before the closing begins in January 2022?

A) 426

B) 700

C) 742

D) 800

3

Yulana bought a shirt at 40% discount. If Yulana paid $15.90 inclusive of 6% sales tax for the shirt, what was the original price of the shirt before the sales tax was collected and the discount was applied?

A) $6

B) $10

C) $25

D) $28

4

When the number p is increased by 20% and then decreased by 10%, the value of p is 378. What is number p?

A) 302

B) 350

C) 378

D) 416

5

A bookstore has discounted all the books by 30% of the original price. Sam's library membership card allows 5% discount over the discounted price. If Sam paid $5.32 for a book and no sales tax was collected, what was the original price of the book?

A) $3

B) $5

C) $8

D) $10

6

A manufacturing company's profit for the year 2018 was 10.5 million dollars. This was 25% higher than the profit of 2017. The profit of 2017 was 20% higher than the profit of 2016. Which of the following is closest to company's profit in 2016, in millions of dollars?

A) 7

B) 8

C) 10

D) 19

Category 45 – A Number Percent of Another Number

Key Points

- If x and y are two numbers, then x is what percent of y (also worded as what percent of y is x) can be determined as follows.

$$\frac{x}{y} \times 100$$

How to Solve

Translate the question as 'x is what percent of y' and solve. It is important to identify the numerator and the denominator correctly.

Example 1:

In 1980, about 3 million geese migrated to the central part of United States during winter.

Question 1

In 2015, the number of geese that migrated increased to about 15 million. In 1980, the geese migration was what percent of geese migration in 2015?

A) 12%

B) 20%

C) 33%

D) 50%

Step 1: Translate question into 'x is what percent of y'

Geese migration in 1980 = 3. Geese migration in 2015 = 15.

The question is asking 'geese migration in 1980 was what percent of geese migration in 2015'. This is same as '3 is what percent of 15'. Hence, numerator = 3 and denominator = 15.

$$\frac{3}{15} \times 100 = 20\%$$

Correct answer choice is **B.**

Question 2

In 2015, this number increased by 400%. In 1980, the geese migration was what percent of geese migration in 2015?

A) 12%

B) 20%

C) 33%

D) 50%

Step 1: Determine the number of geese in 2015

The number of geese in 2015 must be determined before solving.

$$400\% \text{ percent increase} = 1 + 4 = 5$$
$$\text{number of geese } 3 \times 5 = 15$$

Step 2: Translate question into 'x is what percent of y'

This is Step 1 of Question 1.

Correct answer choice is **B.**

Category 45 – Practice Questions (answers on pages 379-380)

Calculator Questions

1

What percent of 30 is 12?

A) 35%

B) 40%

C) 60%

D) 75%

2

An office manager is shopping for a new table for the office lobby. The original price of the table the office manager wants to buy is $250. Store A is selling the table for the discounted price of $215. Another store, Store B, is selling the same table for the discounted price of $200. What is the difference in the percent discount of the table at Store A and Store B?

A) 6%

B) 9%

C) 15%

D) 35%

3

If a number p is increased by 25%, what percent is p of the increased number, where $p = 72$?

A) 25%

B) 75%

C) 77%

D) 80%

4

Jeremy bought a computer for $1,200 from Store A. No sales tax was collected. At Store B, the same computer was advertised for $1,180 and an additional 10% in-store discount. If a is the price of the computer, in dollars, at store B after the 10% in-store discount on the advertised price, what percent of $1,200 is a?

A) 85.5%

B) 88.5%

C) 90.0%

D) 98.5%

5

Chris went to a local fair with his friends and bought a ride pass for $40. For each ride, $3.20 is deducted from the value of the ride pass. What percent of the initial value of the ride pass is the cost of one ride?

A) 3.2%

B) 4.5%

C) 7%

D) 8%

6

Neena bought a pair of shoes for $43.20 inclusive of 8% sales tax. When she returned the shoes after 3 months, she was refunded $36, which included the full refund of 8% sales tax. The return price is what percent of the original price, excluding the sales tax?

A) 21%

B) 80%

C) 82%

D) 84%

Category 46 – Percent Change

Key Points

- Percent change is the percent by which a number is changed (increased or decreased).
  - The number before the change is referred to as the "old value" and the number after the change is referred to as the "new value".
  - When the new value is higher than the old value, the percent change is an increase and is positive. When the new value is lower than the old value, the percent change is a decrease and is negative.
  - The formula for percent change is

$$\% \text{ change} = \frac{\text{new value} - \text{old value}}{\text{old value}} \times 100$$

How to Solve

When the percent change is negative ignore the negative sign. It simply means that the percent change is a decrease.

Example 1:

Last year, Natalie saved $6,340. This year she plans to save $5,200. Which of the following is closest to the percent change in Natalie's savings from last year to this year?

A) 18%

B) 25%

C) 76%

D) 81%

Step 1: Determine old value and new value

Old value is the amount Natalie saved last year = $6,340.

New value is the amount Natalie plans to save this year = $5,200.

Step 2: Determine percent change

$$\frac{5,200 - 6,340}{6,340} \times 100 = \frac{-1,140}{6,340} \times 100 = -17.98\%$$

The percent change is negative, indicating a decrease of 17.98%. Answer choice A is closest.

Correct answer choice is **A**.

Category 46 – Practice Questions (answers on page 380)

Calculator Questions

1

In 2015, a car dealership reported a profit of 1.2 million dollars. In 2017, the profit increased to 1.6 million dollars. Which of the following is the percent change in the profit, rounded to the nearest tenth?

A) 25.0%

B) 33.3%

C) 65.5%

D) 80.5%

2

The original price of a scarf is $20. The final price after the discount is $8, excluding sales tax. What is the percent change in the price of the scarf after the discount?

A) 35%

B) 40%

C) 60%

D) 80%

3

An online retailer has reduced the sale price of a certain computer from $3,200 to $2,300. The original and reduced prices are inclusive of $200 warranty that is not affected by the price reduction. What is the percent change in the price of the computer, rounded to the nearest whole number?

A) 28%

B) 30%

C) 41%

D) 60%

Questions 4 and 5 refer to the following information.

A certain school offers monthly meal plan to all the students at the school. The table below shows the total number of students enrolled in the monthly meal plan over a five-month period in 2020.

Month	Number of students
January	80
February	88
March	110
April	120
May	132

4

Based on the table, during which two months was the percent change in the number of students the greatest?

A) From January to February

B) From February to March

C) From March to April

D) From April to May

5

Based on the table, the number of students enrolled in March was p% greater than the number of students enrolled in February. What is the value of p? (Ignore the % sign when entering your answer.)

Calculator Questions

1

Makenna got a $75 clothing store gift card on her birthday. If Makenna bought a shirt for $9 and a jacket for $17.25 using the gift card, the remaining balance on the gift card is what percent of the starting value of the gift card?

A) 35%

B) 55%

C) 65%

D) 80%

2

Last year, a company gave its employees 12 paid vacation days in a year. This year, the company announced that the employees will get 14 paid vacation days in a year. By what percent did the number of vacation days change from last year to this year?

A) Decreased by 11.66%

B) Decreased by 20%

C) Increased by 11.66%

D) Increased by 16.66%

3

Juana paid d dollars for a hat after 15% discount and addition of 8% sales tax. Which of the following expressions represents the price of the hat before the 15% discount and excluding the 8% sales tax?

A) $\dfrac{d}{(0.85)(1.08)}$

B) $\dfrac{d}{(1.15)(1.08)}$

C) $(0.85)(0.92)d$

D) $(1.15)(0.92)d$

4

An environmental research company is studying the population of two species of birds, Bird A and Bird B, in a certain forest. In 2019, the populations of Bird A and Bird B were same. From 2016 to 2019, the population of Bird A increased by 5% and the population of Bird B increased by 20%. If the population of Bird A in 2016 was 6,000, what was the population of Bird B in 2016?

A) 4,800

B) 5,250

C) 6,300

D) 7,200

5

If the beginning value of a number is $2k$ and the ending value is $0.6k$, what is the percent change in the value of k, where k is a constant?

A) 30%

B) 60%

C) 70%

D) 140%

6

The population of a certain species of fish decreased by 6% from 1999 to 2004. From 2005 to 2009 the population of fish increased by 19%, and from 2010 to 2015 the population of fish increased by 22%. If s was the population of fish in 1999, which of the following expressions represents the change in the population of fish from 1999 to 2015?

A) $(0.94)(0.81)(0.78)(s)$

B) $(0.94)(1.19)(1.22)(s)$

C) $(0.94)(1.41)(s)$

D) $(1.35)(s)$

Questions 7 and 8 refer to the following information.

Of all the members enrolled in a certain fitness club, 140 members participate in the yoga or the karate class. The table below shows the number of members participating in the yoga class or the karate class, categorized in 4 age groups. Each member can participate either in the yoga class or the karate class.

Age group	Yoga	Karate	Total
21 - 30	6	14	20
31 - 40	14	16	30
41 - 50	28	15	43
51 and up	35	12	47
Total	83	57	140

7

Based on the above table, of all the members of ages 41 and up, what is the difference between the percentage of members who participate in the yoga class and the members who participate in the karate class?

A)   20%

B)   40%

C)   60%

D)   75%

8

If the members of all ages participating in the karate class and the yoga class are 40% of all the members enrolled in the fitness club, how many total members are enrolled in the fitness club?

A)   52

B)   140

C)   210

D)   350

9

Jim went to an amusement arcade with his friends. At the arcade, he bought a cashless card worth $20 to play his favorite game. If Jim played 36 rounds of his favorite game and for every 3 rounds of games played $0.50 was deduced from the cashless card, the dollar amount remaining on the cashless card is what percent of the starting amount of $20?

A)   30%

B)   40%

C)   60%

D)   70%

10

A supermarket chain closed 20% of its stores between 2015 and 2018. In 2018, 112 stores were open. How many stores were open in 2015?

11

A number n when decreased by 10% is equal to x. A number p when increased by 20% is equal to x. If number n is 40, what is number p?

12

Last Friday, Kamla rented a concert hall for a dance performance. Her total earnings from the performance were x dollars. If she had $784 left after paying 20% in miscellaneous costs, what is x?

13

The students at a certain high school are given the option to join an annual cooking club. In the current academic year, 40% of the students joined the cooking club. If the number of students who joined the club is 96 less than the number of students who did not join the club, how many students attend the high school in the current academic year?

Section 10 –
Exponents and Exponential Functions

Category 47 – Exponents

Key Points

- When a number is multiplied by itself several times, such as $3 \times 3 \times 3 \times 3$, the number is called the base and the number of times it is multiplied by itself is called the exponent. Since 3 is multiplied by itself 4 times, 3 is the base and 4 is the exponent. It can be written as 3^4. The same applies for an expression. For example, $3abk \times 3abk \times 3abk \times 3abk \times 3abk$ can be written as $(3abk)^5$, where $3abk$ is the base and 5 is the exponent. All numbers and expressions within parentheses are the base of the exponent.

- When a number or an expression has a negative sign that is not within the parentheses, then the negative sign is not part of the base. When the negative sign is within the parentheses, then it is part of the base. For example, $-a^3$ is $-(a \times a \times a)$ and $(-a)^3$ is $(-a \times -a \times -a)$.

- Following are the exponent rules (also known as the laws of exponents).

  - $x^0 = 1$

  - $x^a \times x^b = x^{a+b}$

  - $\dfrac{x^a}{x^b} = x^{a-b}$

  - $x^{a^b} = x^{ab}$

  - $(xy)^a = x^a y^a$

  - $\left(\dfrac{x}{y}\right)^a = \dfrac{x^a}{y^b}$

  - $x^{-a} = \dfrac{1}{x^a}$

- When a number or an expression is within a root (square root, cube root, and so on), the root can be removed and replaced with a fractional exponent. The value of the root is the denominator of the fraction. The entire expression within the root must be to the power of the fractional exponent. For example,

  - $\sqrt{x} = x^{\frac{1}{2}}$

  - $\sqrt[3]{x^3} = x^{\frac{3}{3}} = x$

  - $\sqrt[4]{x^5} = x^{\frac{5}{4}}$

  - $\sqrt[6]{xy} = (xy)^{\frac{1}{6}}$

  - $\sqrt[4]{x^3 y^3} = \sqrt[4]{(xy)^3} = (xy)^{\frac{3}{4}}$

  - $\sqrt[3]{3y^3} = (3y^3)^{\frac{1}{3}} = 3^{\frac{1}{3}} \times y^{\frac{3}{3}} = 3^{\frac{1}{3}}y$

- When the bases of two numbers or expressions are same, the exponents can be equated. For example, if $xy^a = xy^b$, then $a = b$.

How to Solve

A question may require equating two exponents that do not have the same base, but the bases are multiples of the same number. For example, $4^2 = 2^x$ cannot give the value of x. When 4^2 is rewritten as $(2^2)^2$, the equation becomes $2^4 = 2^x$. Since the bases are now same, the exponents can be equated. Hence, $x = 4$. In such questions, being able to recognize multiples can be helpful. See few examples of multiples below.

- $4 = 2^2, 8 = 2^3, 16 = 4^2 = 2^4, 32 = 2^5, 64 = 4^3 = 2^6$.

- $9 = 3^2, 27 = 3^3, 81 = 9^2 = 3^4$.

- $25 = 5^2, 125 = 5^3$.

Example 1:

Which of the following expression is equivalent to $\frac{m^4 n^5}{m^2 n^2} \times n^{-2}$, where m and n are positive?

A) $m^6 n^5$

B) $m^2 n$

C) $\frac{m^4 n^3}{m^{-2} n^{-2}}$

D) $\frac{m^{-2} n^{-1}}{m^2 n^2}$

Step 1: Simplify by applying rules

Apply $\frac{x^a}{x^b} = x^{a-b}$ rule to m and n and simplify.

$$(m^{4-2} n^{5-2}) \times n^{-2} \rightarrow m^2 n^3 \times n^{-2}$$

Apply $x^a \times x^b = x^{a+b}$ rule to n.

$$m^2 n^{3-2} \rightarrow m^2 n$$

Correct answer choice is **B**.

Example 2:

Which of the following expression is equivalent to $\frac{\sqrt[3]{x^4}}{\sqrt[4]{x^5}}$, where $x > 0$?

A) $x^{\frac{3}{4}}$

B) $x^{\frac{4}{5}}$

C) $x^{\frac{3}{5}}$

D) $x^{\frac{1}{12}}$

Step 1: Simplify by applying rules

Replace roots with fractional exponents.

$$\frac{x^{\frac{4}{3}}}{x^{\frac{5}{4}}}$$

Apply $\frac{x^a}{x^b} = x^{a-b}$ rule and simplify the fractional exponent.

$$x^{\frac{4}{3} - \frac{5}{4}} \rightarrow x^{\frac{16-15}{12}} \rightarrow x^{\frac{1}{12}}$$

Correct answer choice is **D**.

Example 3:

What is the value of m in the equation $\sqrt{16t^4} = (2t)^{m-1}$, where m is positive?

Step 1: Simplify by applying rules

In the left expression, replace root with fractional exponent and write 16 as 2^4. This will result in same bases on both sides of the equation.

$$(16t^4)^{\frac{1}{2}} = (2t)^{m-1} \rightarrow (2^4 t^4)^{\frac{1}{2}} = (2t)^{m-1} \rightarrow (2t)^{4 \times \frac{1}{2}} = (2t)^{m-1} \rightarrow (2t)^2 = (2t)^{m-1}$$

Since the base $(2t)$ is same on both sides, the exponents can be equated.

$$m - 1 = 2 \rightarrow m = 3$$

Correct answer is **3**.

Category 47 – Practice Questions (answers on page 382)

No Calculator Questions

1

Which of the following is equivalent to $3^2 \times 27^4$?

A) 3

B) 51

C) 3^{14}

D) 27^6

2

Which of the following expression is equivalent to $\sqrt{16x^4}$?

A) $4x$

B) $4\sqrt{4x^4}$

C) $4x^2\sqrt{4x^2}$

D) $4x^2$

3

If $(9^3)^{n+1} = (81)^3 \times 3^{3n}$, what is the value of n?

A) 2

B) 3

C) 6

D) 8

4

If $4^{3a-1} = 2^{3+a} \times 32^b$, which of the following could represent the value of b in terms of a?

A) a

B) $a - 1$

C) $a - b$

D) $ab + 1$

5

Which of the following expression is equivalent to $(16x^5y^3)^{\frac{1}{2}}$, where x and y are positive?

A) $4\sqrt{x^4y^2}$

B) $4x^5y^3\sqrt{x^5y^3}$

C) $4\sqrt{x^5y}$

D) $4x^2y\sqrt{xy}$

6

Which of the following expression is equivalent to $(3y)^{\frac{3}{a}}$, where $y > 0$?

A) $\sqrt[a]{3y^3}$

B) $\sqrt[3]{27y^a}$

C) $\sqrt[a]{27y^3}$

D) $ay^{\frac{3}{2}}$

7

$$\frac{\sqrt{5a^4}}{\sqrt[4]{5a^3}}$$

If the above expression is equivalent to k, which of the following expressions can represent k?

A) $a^{\frac{4}{3}}$

B) $5a^7$

C) $\sqrt[4]{5a^5}$

D) $\sqrt[5]{5a^3}$

8

Which of the following expression is equivalent to $(27a^9)^{\frac{1}{3}}$?

A) $a^{\frac{5}{2}}$

B) $3a^3$

C) $\sqrt[3]{3a^6}$

D) $\sqrt[2]{27a^9}$

9

Which of the following is equivalent to $\sqrt{r}\ \sqrt[3]{r}$, where $r > 0$?

A) $r^{\frac{5}{6}}$

B) r^4

C) $2r^{\frac{1}{3}}$

D) r

10

If $2^a y^4 = 80$ and $2^b y^4 = 5$, which of the following can be the value of $a - b$?

A) -2

B) 0

C) 2

D) 4

Calculator Questions

11

$$\frac{x^5 y^{-2}}{x^{-2} y^3} \times x^{-6} y^6$$

Which of the following expressions is equivalent to the above expression, where x and y are positive real numbers?

A) xy

B) $x^{-5}y$

C) $\dfrac{x^3 y}{x^{-2}}$

D) $\dfrac{x^3 y^4}{x^2 y^2}$

12

If $\sqrt[3]{64m^3} = 20$, what is the value of m, where $m > 0$?

13

$$\frac{\sqrt{s^3 s^5}}{\sqrt[5]{s^2}} = s^{\frac{x}{y}}$$

What is the value of $\dfrac{x}{y}$ in the above expression for all positive values of s?

14

If $a^2 = 10$ and $b^5 = 50$, what is the value of $a^6 \times b^{-5}$?

Category 48 – Linear Versus Exponential Growth and Decay

Key Points

- A linear increase or decrease occurs at a constant rate. An exponential growth starts slow followed by a rapid increase. An exponential decay starts with a rapid decrease followed by a slower decrease. See examples below.

  - If the number 400 is increased by 2 each day, then the increase each day is same. For example, on the first day of increase the number will be 402 and then 404 the day after, 406 the day after, 408 the day after, and so on. This is linear increase (or increasing linear). If the number 400 is doubled each day, then the increase each day is significantly greater. For example, on the first day of increase the number will be 800 and then 1,600 the day after, 3,200 the day after, 6,400 the day after, and so on. This is exponential growth (increase).

  - If the number 400 is decreased by 2 each day, then the decrease each day is same. For example, on the first day of decrease the number will be 398 and then 396 the day after, 394 the day after, 392 the day after, and so on. This is linear decrease (or decreasing linear). If the number 400 is decreased by half each day, then the decrease each day is significantly greater. For example, on the first day of decrease the number will be 200 and then 100 the day after, 50 the day after, 25 the day after, and so on. This is exponential decay (decrease).

- The graph of linear increase and linear decrease is a straight line (Fig. 1 and 2, respectively). The graph of exponential growth rises slowly from left to right followed by a sharp curve upwards (Fig. 3). The graph of exponential decay drops sharply from left to right as a curve followed by a slower decrease (Fig. 4).

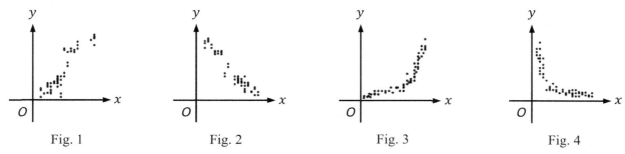

| Fig. 1 | Fig. 2 | Fig. 3 | Fig. 4 |

How to Solve

Words/phrases like "double", "half", "x percent more than the preceding year" refer to an exponential growth/decay.

Example 1:

In which of the following tables is the relation between the values of m and their corresponding n values non-linear?

A)

m	3	5	7	9
n	4.5	5.9	7.3	8.7

B)

m	0.5	1	1.5	2
n	3	9	27	81

C)

m	6	4.5	3	1.5
n	21	15	9	3

D)

m	1	2	3	4
n	0	2	4	6

Step 1: Determine the relationship between the two variables

In tables A, C, and D, the change in the value of n in response to the change in the value of m is by a constant number. This corresponds to a linear relationship. In table B, the value of n increases 3 times for every 0.5 increase in the value of m. This is exponential increase/growth.

Alternatively, determine the slope between 2 sets of points in each table. If the slope is same, then the relationship is linear (see Section 1 for further details on lines and slope).

Correct answer choice is **B**.

Category 48 – Practice Questions (answers on page 383)

Calculator Questions

1

In which of the following tables is the relation between the values of x and their corresponding y values non-linear?

A)

x	0.3	0.6	0.9	1.2
y	2	4	6	8

B)

x	1	3	5	7
y	2	8	32	128

C)

x	20	40	60	80
y	13	9	5	1

D)

x	3	6	9	12
y	4.5	6	7.5	9

2

A colony of bacteria doubles every 30 minutes. Which of the following most accurately describes the relationship between time and bacterial growth?

A) Every 30 minutes there are 2 more colonies of bacteria.

B) Every 30 minutes there are 2 less colonies of bacteria.

C) Every 30 minutes there are twice fewer colonies of bacteria.

D) Every 30 minutes there are twice more colonies of bacteria.

3

The results of a survey conducted in 2002 in a city in the United States showed that the population of the city is expected to decrease by 1, 600 each year. Which of the following describes the relationship between time in years and the population of the city?

A) Decreasing linear

B) Increasing linear

C) Exponential decay

D) Exponential growth

4

The population of a certain city is projected to grow exponentially each year for 10 years starting from 2019. Which of the following could describe how the population of the city changes each year?

A) Each year, the population of the city is 5,000 more than the previous year.

B) Each year, the population of the city is 2.5% more than the previous year.

C) Each year, the population of the city is 2,000 less than the previous year.

D) Each year, the population of the city is 4% less than the previous year.

5

Team A and Team B are competing in a 2 hour boat race. Team A is ahead of Team B by one-fourth the amount every 20 minutes than the preceding 20 minutes. Which of the following best describes the relationship between time in minutes and distance of Team A in relation to Team B?

A) Decreasing linear

B) Increasing linear

C) Exponential decay

D) Exponential growth

Category 49 – Exponential Growth and Decay

Key Points

- The formula for exponential growth or decay is $y = a(b)^x$. The components of the equation are:
    - a is the initial number and is greater than 0.
    - b is the rate of change in the value of a.
    - x is the number of time intervals when the change occurs.
    - y is the accumulated number after x time intervals.
- The rate of change in exponential growth and decay can be calculated as follows:
    - In exponential growth, $b = 1 + r$, where r is the percent growth rate as decimal. For example, if the growth rate is 20%, then $b = 1 + 0.2 = 1.2$. The value of b will always be greater than 1.
    - In exponential decay, $b = 1 - r$, where r is the percent decay rate as decimal. For example, if the decay rate is 20%, then $b = 1 - 0.2 = 0.8$. The value of b will always be less than 1 but greater than 0.
- The exponential growth or decay function is $f(x) = a(b)^x$, where $f(x)$ is the y value for an input value of x.
- When an interest rate is compounded on a monetary amount (for example, 6% interest compounded every 3 months on the dollar amount in a savings account), the growth of the monetary amount over time is exponential.
    - The formula for compound interest is $A = P\left(1 + \frac{r}{n}\right)^{nt}$. The components of the equation are:
        - P is the principal amount (the initial amount).
        - r is the compounded percent interest rate as decimal.
        - t is the number of years.
        - n is the number of times the interest is compounded per year.
        - A is the amount accumulated after t years.
    - When the interest rate is compounded annually, then $n = 1$ and the formula is simplified to $A = P(1 + r)^t$.

How to Solve

It is important to interpret the time interval correctly. For example, if an increase occurs twice per year, then the time interval is $2t$ in t years. If an increase occurs once in every 2 years, then the time interval is $\frac{t}{2}$ in t years.
Time interval could be t years, m months, w weeks, s seconds, and so on.

Example 1:

From 1960 to 1990, the population of an endangered species of insect decreased exponentially every 3 years by 7%. If the population of the endangered species of insect was 1,980 in 1960, which of the following models the decrease D in the population of the endangered species of insect 15 years after 1960?

A) $D = 1,980\,(0.7)^3$

B) $D = 1,980\,(0.93)^{3t}$

C) $D = 1,980\,(0.93)^5$

D) $D = 1,980\,(1.07)^t$

Step 1: Determine the components of the exponential equation

Since the question states 'species decreased exponentially every 3 years by 7%', the question is on exponential decay.
$a = 1,980$. $r = 7\% = 0.07$. $b = 1 - r = 1 - 0.07 = 0.93$. $y = D$.

Time interval = every 3 years. In 15 years, the decrease will occur $\frac{15}{3} = 5$ times. Hence, $x = 5$.

$$y = a(b)^x \;\rightarrow\; D = 1,980\,(0.93)^5$$

Correct answer choice is **C**.

Example 2:

Kara started a new job in 2010 at an annual salary of $90,000. Each year, her salary increased by 2% than the preceding year.

Question 1 (mental math)

Which of the following equations models Kara's salary S, in dollars, t years after 2010?

A) $S = 90,000(0.92)^t$

B) $S = 90,000(1.2)^t$

C) $S = 90,000(1 + 8)^t$

D) $S = 90,000(1.02)^t$

Step 1: Determine the components of the exponential equation

Since each year, the salary increased by 2% of the preceding year, the question is on exponential growth.

$a = 90,000$. $r = 2\% = 0.02$. $b = 1 + r = 1.02$. $y = S$. Since time interval = once per year, in one year the increase will occur one time. Hence, in t years the increase will occur t times.

$$y = a(b)^x \rightarrow S = 90,000(1.02)^t$$

Correct answer choice is **D**.

Question 2

Which of the following is closest to the increase in Kara's salary in 3 years after 2010, in dollars?

A) $5,400

B) $5,508

C) $8,000

D) $9,600

Continue from Step 1 of Question 1. Solve the equation for $t = 3$.

$$90,000(1.02)^3 = 90,000(1.02)(1.02)(1.02) = 95,508.72 = \$95,508$$

Salary increase in 3 years = $95,508 - 90,000 = \$5,508$.

Correct answer choice is **B**.

Example 3:

Janice deposited $2,000 dollars in a savings account at an annual interest rate of 6% compounded monthly. Which of the following equations models the accumulated amount A, in dollars, after 4 years, assuming no deposits or withdrawals were made after the initial deposit?

A) $A = 2,000(1.6)^t$

B) $A = 2,000(1.06)^4$

C) $A = 2,000(1.06)^{4t}$

D) $A = 2,000(1.005)^{48}$

Step 1: Determine the components of the compound interest rate equation

Since the interest is compounded monthly, use the complete compound interest rate formula.

$P = 2,000$. $r = 6\% = 0.06$. $t = 4$ years. $n = 12$ (since the interest is compounded each month and there are 12 months in a year, $n = 12$).

Plug in the values in the formula.

$$A = P\left(1 + \frac{r}{n}\right)^{nt} \rightarrow A = 2,000\left(1 + \frac{0.06}{12}\right)^{12\times4} \rightarrow A = 2,000(1 + 0.005)^{48} \rightarrow A = 2,000(1.005)^{48}$$

Correct answer choice is **D**.

Note that if the savings account was compounded annually, then $n = 1$ and $A = P(1 + r)^t \rightarrow A = 2,000(1.06)^4$.

Category 49 – Practice Questions (answers on pages 383-384)

No Calculator Questions

1

$$P(t) = 3.2(1.06)^t$$

The function P above estimates the population, in millions, of a certain city t years after 1990. Which of the following is the best interpretation of the number 3.2 in this context?

A) The estimated population of the city after 1990.

B) The estimated population of the city t years after 1990.

C) The estimated population of the city in 1990.

D) The estimated population of the city in 3.2 years.

2

The function $G(n) = 23,000(k)^n$ models the growth of Roma's savings account, in dollars, in n years. If the interest rate is compounded each year by 12%, what is the value of k?

A) 0.12

B) 0.88

C) 1.01

D) 1.12

3

$$P = 550(1.16)^{\frac{t}{2}}$$

The equation above models the number of products P sold by an online retail company t years after 2015. Which of the following is most appropriate interpretation about the value of P after 2015?

A) Each year after 2015, the value of P increases by 1.16%.

B) Each year after 2015, the value of P increases by 6%.

C) Every 2 years after 2015, the value of P increases by 1.16%.

D) Every 2 years after 2015, the value of P increases by 16%.

4

A scientist is testing the effect of a chemical on the growth of 200,000 bacterial colonies. If the treatment with the chemical compound results in 50% reduction of bacterial colonies every 10 minutes, how many bacterial colonies remain after 30 minutes of treatment?

A) 25,000

B) 50,000

C) 70,000

D) 75,000

5

A radioactive material of mass 150 grams decays exponentially at the rate of 1% every 4 months. Which of the following equations represents the decay D, in grams, in m months?

A) $D = 150(0.1)^m$

B) $D = 150(0.9)^{4m}$

C) $D = 150(0.99)^m$

D) $D = 150(0.99)^{\frac{m}{4}}$

6

$$R = 1080(k)^t$$

The equation above models the revenue of a manufacturing company t years after 2015. The model forecasts the revenue to increase 9% each year than the preceding year. Which of the following is the value of k?

A) 0.94

B) 1.00

C) 1.09

D) 1.94

7

Sam deposited $2,000 in a bank account earning 8% interest rate compounded quarterly. Which of the following equations represents the accumulated amount A, in dollars, at the end of 3 years, assuming no deposits or withdrawals were made after the initial deposit of $2,000? (3 months = 1 quarter).

A) $A = 2,000(0.97)^3$

B) $A = 2,000(1.02)^{12}$

C) $A = 2,000(1.03)^{12}$

D) $A = 2,300(1.3)$

8

$$M = 400(2)^m$$

$$Q = 2,100(3)^q$$

A manufacturing company has created two models to predict the sales, in thousands of dollars, of a new product to be launched soon. The two models are shown above. M is sales per month for m months after the product launch. Q is sales per quarter for q quarters after the product launch. How many more sales, in thousands of dollars, are predicted by model M than by model Q, in 6 months after the product launch? (3 months = 1 quarter)

A) 6,700

B) 9,050

C) 18,900

D) 25,600

9

A team of scientists concluded that since 1900 the number of trees in a certain forest doubled every 29 years. If a is the approximate number of trees in 1900, which of the following equations most appropriately models the number of trees n in t years since 1900?

A) $n = a(1.2)^{29t}$

B) $n = a(2)^{\frac{t}{a}}$

C) $n = a(2)^{\frac{t}{29}}$

D) $n = 29(2)^t$

10

The per pound price of a certain brand of coffee beans increased exponetially by 8% for 4 consecutive months. If the price of the coffee beans before the increase was $12 per pound, what is the approximate per pound price of the coffee beans, in dollars, after 4 months?

A) $12

B) $16

C) $31

D) $40

11

Sara and Jenny invested d dollars at the same time for a period of 4 years. Sara's investment earned 5% interest rate compounded annually. Jenny's investment earned 6% interest rate compounded semi-annually. If X is Jenny's accumulated investment earnings, in dollars, in 4 years and Y is Sara's accumulated investment earnings, in dollars, in 4 years, which of the following expressions represents $X - Y$, assuming no deposits or withdrawals were made during 4 years?

A) $d(1.01)^4$

B) $d(1.11)^{4t}$

C) $d(1.06)^4 - d(1.05)^4$

D) $d(1.03)^8 - d(1.05)^4$

12

In 2015, Kavita opened a new bank account and deposited d dollars at the interest rate of 10% compounded annually. At the end of 3 years, in 2018, Kavita had $1,331 in her bank account. Which of the following is the value of d, in dollars, assuming no deposits or withdrawals were made from 2015 to 2018?

A) $931

B) $988

C) $1,000

D) $1,210

Category 50 – Graphs of Exponential Growth and Decay Functions

Key Points

- In the xy-plane, the graph of an exponential growth or decay function is defined by $f(x) = a(b)^x$. When $a = 1$, the function simplifies to $f(x) = (b)^x$. For example, in $f(x) = 4(3)^x$, $a = 4$ and in $f(x) = (3)^x$, $a = 1$.
  - The coordinates of the y-intercept are $(0, a)$, where a is the y-coordinate of the y-intercept.
  - The graph always passes through the points $(0, a)$ and $(1, ab)$. For $a = 1$, these points are $(0, 1)$ and $(1, b)$.
  - The graph is increasing (growth) when $b > 1$ and decreasing (decay) when $0 < b < 1$.
- The graph of $f(x) = a(b)^x$ can be shifted vertically upwards or downwards. For example, $f(x) = a(b)^x + c$ will shift the graph upwards by c units and $f(x) = a(b)^x - c$ will shift the graph downwards by c units. The y-coordinate of the y-intercept of the graph will shift proportionally.
- The graph of $f(x) = a(b)^x$ reflected across the y-axis is $f(x) = a(b)^{-x}$. The reflected graph will pass through the points $(0, a)$ and $(-1, ab)$ instead of $(0, a)$ and $(1, ab)$. This is important to remember.

How to Solve

To match the equation of a given exponential function with the graphs in the answer choices, substitute the values of a and b in the points $(0, a)$ and $(1, ab)$ and look for the graph with these points.

The presence of a constant in an exponential function indicates that the graph has been shifted vertically. The value of the constant is the change in the y-coordinate of the y-intercept of the shifted graph when compared with the value of a. For example, if the equation is $f(x) = 3(4)^x - c$ and the y-coordinate of the y-intercept of the shifted graph is 1, then the graph is shifted downwards from $(0, 3)$ to $(0, 1)$. Hence, $c = 2$.

Example 1:

Which of the following is the graph of the equation $y = 2(2)^x$?

A) 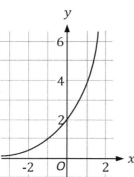 B) 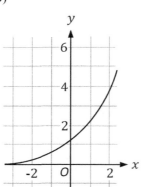 C) 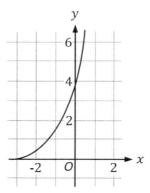 D)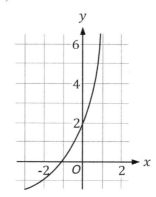

Step 1: Determine values of a and b from the equation

$a = 2$. $b = 2$.

Step 2: Determine the graph that passes through the points $(0, a)$ and $(1, ab)$

$(0, a) = (0, 2)$.

$(1, ab) = (1, 2 \times 2) = (1, 4)$.

Only the graph in answer choice A passes through the above points.

Correct answer choice is **A.**

Note that if the graph in answer choice A is shifted downwards by 3 units, then the equation would be $y = 2(2)^x - 3$ and the y-intercept of the shifted graph would be $(0, a - 3) = (0, 2 - 3) = (0, -1)$.

Category 50 – Practice Questions (answers on page 384)

No Calculator Questions

1

Which of the following is the graph of the equation $y = (3)^x$?

A)

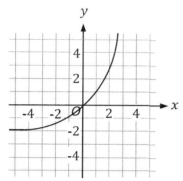

B)

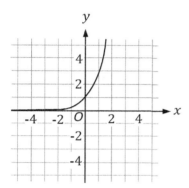

C)

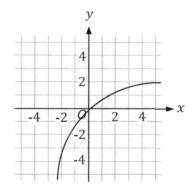

D)

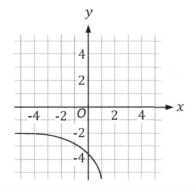

2

In the xy-plane, the graph of the exponential decay function g has a y-intercept of 575, where $y = g(m)$. Which of the following equations could define the function g?

A) $g(m) = -250(5)^m$

B) $g(m) = 250(0.87)^m$

C) $g(m) = 575(0.95)^m$

D) $g(m) = 575(1.05)^m$

Calculator Questions

3

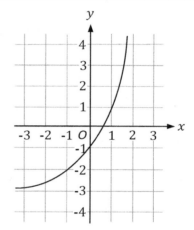

The graph of $y = 2(2)^x - n$ is shown above, where n is a constant. What is the value of n?

A) -1

B) 0

C) 1

D) 3

4

The graph of the equation $y = f(x)$ in the xy-plane, passes through the points (m, n) and $(m + 1, 4n)$. Which of the following equations could define f?

A) $f(x) = 2(4)^x$

B) $f(x) = 4(2)^x$

C) $f(x) = \frac{1}{4}(1.4)^x$

D) $f(x) = \frac{1}{4}(1)^x$

No Calculator Questions

1

$$P = 12(1.03)^t$$

The equation above models the exponential increase in price P, in dollars, of one pound of wheat by k percent for t years. Which of the following is value of k as percent?

A) 3%

B) 5%

C) 6%

D) 12%

2

An environmental scientist studied the population of flies in a certain forest for d days. The scientist found that the population, in hundreds, decreased by 3% every 8 days. If the population of flies at the start of the scientist's study is n, which of the following represents the population P of flies, in hundreds, in the forest in d days?

A) $P = n(0.97)^{8t}$

B) $P = n(0.97)^{\frac{d}{8}}$

C) $P = n(0.03)^d$

D) $P = n - (0.03)^d$

3

$$f(t) = a(b)^t$$

Which of the following appropriately describes the relationship between a and t modeled by the exponential function f shown above, where t is a positive integer, b is a constant, and $0 < b < 1$?

A) Increase in the value of a causes increase in the value of t.

B) Increase in the value of t does not change the the value of a.

C) Increase in the value of t causes increase in the value of a.

D) Increase in the value of t causes decrease in the value of a.

4

$$(x^3 y^5)^{\frac{2}{5}}$$

Which of the following is equivalent to the above expression?

A) $-x \times \sqrt[5]{xy}$

B) $x \times \sqrt[5]{xy^2}$

C) $xy^2 \times \sqrt[5]{x}$

D) $y^2 \times \sqrt[5]{xy}$

5

$$\sqrt[4]{x^2 - 1}$$

If $x - 1 = 16$, which of the following is equivalent to the above expression, where $x > 0$?

A) 2

B) 4

C) $2(x + 1)^{\frac{1}{4}}$

D) $4(x + 1)^4$

6

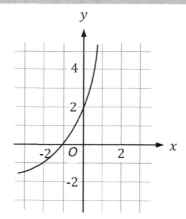

The graph of $y = 4(2)^x - c$ is shown above, where c is a constant. What is the value of c?

A) -1

B) 0

C) 2

D) 4

7

$$(x^2)^3\left(\sqrt[4]{x^3}\right) = x^a$$

What is the value of a in the above equation, where $x > 0$?

8

$$\frac{\sqrt[3]{x^7}}{\sqrt[3]{x^4}}$$

If the above expression is equivalent to x^{mn} for all positive values of x, what is the value of mn?

Calculator Questions

9

Tim opened a savings account and deposited d dollars at an interest rate of 10% compounded annually. After 3 years, he had $1,655 more than the original deposit of d dollars in his savings account. Assuming no withdrawals or deposits were made in 3 years, which of the following is the value of d?

A) $1,695

B) $2,164

C) $4,995

D) $5,000

10

Ramona deposited $2,000 dollars in a savings account at an annual rate of 8% compounded quarterly. Which of the following equations models the amount A, in dollars, in Ramona's savings account after t years? (1 quarter = 3 months)

A) $A = 2,000(1.0075)^{2t}$

B) $A = 2,000(1.08)^3$

C) $A = 2,000(1.08)^{2t}$

D) $A = 2,000(1.02)^{4t}$

11

The function $A(m) = a(0.5)^{\frac{m}{20}}$ models the number of bacterial colonies over time since the start of a laboratory experiment. a is the number of bacterial colonies at the start of the experiment, m is the time in minutes, and $A(m)$ is the number of bacterial colonies in m minutes. What is the best interpretation of $(0.5)^{\frac{m}{20}}$?

A)   The number of bacterial colonies reduced by 5% every minute.

B)   The number of bacterial colonies reduced by half every 20 minutes.

C)   The number of bacterial colonies increased by 5% every minute.

D)   The number of bacterial colonies increased by 20 every minute.

12

The population of beetles y in a certain city decreases exponentially each year x, for t years. In the xy-plane, which of the following graphs could represent this relationship between x and y?

A)

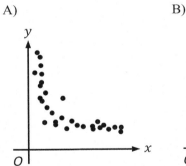

B)

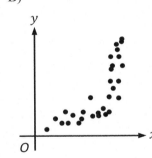

C)

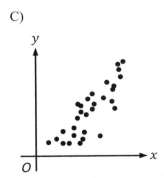

D)

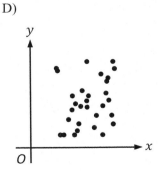

Section 11 – Manipulating Expressions and Equations

Category 51 – Fractions with Expressions in the Denominator

Key Points

- An equation may contain fractions that have expressions in the denominator. The key to solving these equations is to determine the strategy that will simplify or remove the expressions from the denominator.
- The following factors are helpful to remember.
  - $(x + y)(x + y) = x^2 + 2xy + y^2$
  - $(x - y)(x - y) = x^2 - 2xy + y^2$
  - $(x - y)(x + y) = x^2 - y^2$
    - $(x - 1)(x + 1) = x^2 - 1$
    - $(x - 2)(x + 2) = x^2 - 4$
    - $(x - 3)(x + 3) = x^2 - 9$

How to Solve

If the expressions in the denominators of two or more fractions are same, then the numerators can be added/subtracted to create one fraction.

If an equation is a mix of fractions and numbers, then collect the numbers on one side and the fractions on the other side of the equation.

Remember that multiplying and dividing a fraction by the same number or expression does not alter the value of the fraction. For example, $\frac{x}{x+2}$ is same as $\frac{8(x)}{8(x+2)}$ or $\frac{(x+5)(x)}{(x+5)(x+2)}$, and so on.

Example 1:

$$\frac{2(x + 2)}{x + 3} = 3 - \frac{6}{x + 3}$$

In the above equation, what is the value of x?

A) -3

B) -1

C) 1

D) 3

Step 1: Determine the strategy

Since the denominators of the fractions have the same expression, the numerators can be added to create one fraction that equates to 3.

Step 2: Solve

Collect fractions on one side of the equation.

$$\frac{2(x + 2)}{x + 3} + \frac{6}{x + 3} = 3$$

Create one fraction.

$$\frac{2(x + 2) + 6}{x + 3} = 3 \;\rightarrow\; \frac{2x + 4 + 6}{x + 3} = 3 \;\rightarrow\; \frac{2x + 10}{x + 3} = 3$$

Cross multiply and solve.

$$2x + 10 = 3(x + 3) \;\rightarrow\; 2x + 10 = 3x + 9 \;\rightarrow\; 3x - 2x = 10 - 9 \;\rightarrow\; x = 1$$

Correct answer choice is **C**.

Example 2:

$$\frac{x}{x-3} - \frac{2x+13}{x^2-9}$$

If the above expression is equivalent to 1, which of the following value of x satisfies the above expression?

A) 3

B) 4

C) 5

D) 9

Step 1: Determine the strategy

The two factors of $x^2 - 9$ are $(x+3)$ and $(x-3)$. Multiplying and dividing the left fraction by $(x+3)$ will result in the same denominator for the two fractions. The numerators can then be added to create one fraction.

Step 2: Solve

Multiply the numerator and denominator of the left fraction by $(x+3)$ and equate the expression to 1.

$$\frac{(x+3)x}{(x+3)(x-3)} - \frac{2x+13}{x^2-9} = 1 \;\rightarrow\; \frac{x(x+3)}{x^2-9} - \frac{2x+13}{x^2-9} = 1$$

Create one fraction.

$$\frac{x(x+3)-(2x+13)}{x^2-9} = 1 \;\rightarrow\; \frac{x^2+3x-2x-13}{x^2-9} = 1 \;\rightarrow\; \frac{x^2+x-13}{x^2-9} = 1$$

Cross multiply and solve.

$$x^2+x-13 = x^2-9 \;\rightarrow\; x = -9+13 \;\rightarrow\; x = 4$$

Correct answer choice is **B**.

Example 3:

$$\frac{12}{x-y} + \frac{10}{x^2-y^2}$$

What is the value of the above expression if $x - y = 2$ and $x + y = 5$?

Step 1: Determine the approach

The two factors of $x^2 - y^2$ are $(x-y)$ and $(x+y)$. The values of both the factors are given to solve the equation.

Step 2: Solve

$$\frac{12}{x-y} + \frac{10}{(x-y)(x+y)}$$

Plug in the given values of $(x-y)$ and $(x+y)$ and solve.

$$\frac{12}{2} + \frac{10}{(2)(5)} = 6 + \frac{10}{10} = 6 + 1 = 7$$

Correct answer is **7**.

Category 51 – Practice Questions (answers on page 386)

No Calculator Questions

1

$$\frac{3(x+1)}{x-2} - \frac{3x+4}{x-2}$$

The expression above is equivalent to 1. What is the value of x?

A) -1

B) -2

C) 1

D) 2

2

$$\frac{6m-10}{m^2-n^2} - \frac{3}{m-n} = \frac{m}{m-n}$$

If $m + n = 2$, which of the following is the value of mn in the above equation?

A) -10

B) -8

C) 6

D) 12

3

$$\frac{6}{x+5} + \frac{3}{x-2} = \frac{7x+9}{(x+5)(x-2)}$$

In the above equation, what is the value of x?

A) 3

B) 6

C) 9

D) 15

4

$$\frac{3}{x-1} + \frac{k}{x^2-1} = \frac{3x+8}{x^2-1}$$

In the above equation, what is the value of k, where k is a constant?

A) -2

B) -1

C) 2

D) 5

5

$$\frac{3a^2+7ab}{(a+b)} = 9 + \frac{ab-3b^2}{(a+b)}$$

In the above equation, what is the value of $a + b$?

6

$$\frac{2}{x-y} + \frac{5}{x^2-y^2}$$

If $x^2 - y^2 = 3$ and $x + y = 11$, what is the value of the above expression?

7

$$\frac{y^2-9}{y+3} = 5$$

What is the value of y in the above equation?

Category 52 – Rearranging Variables in an Equation

Key Points

- The variables in an equation can be rearranged to isolate one variable from the others. For example, in the equation $a + h = yc - t(b + s)$, the variable h can be isolated by removing a from the left-side. This will express the variables $a, b, c, s, t,$ and y in terms of the variable h. Any variable in the equation can be isolated by rearranging the variables.

How to Solve

Determine which variable must be isolated. Most likely, this will be mentioned in the last sentence of the question.

Note that a question may be based on a formula and the question may give the explanation of the formula that is irrelevant to solving the question.

If a question contains a fraction the numerator of a fraction also a fraction, then simplify the fraction as shown below. In the example below, the numerator is $\frac{x}{5}$ and the denominator is 8, which is same as $\frac{x}{5}$ divided by 8.

$$\frac{\left(\frac{x}{5}\right)}{8} \rightarrow \frac{x}{5} \div 8 \rightarrow \frac{x}{5} \times \frac{1}{8} \rightarrow \frac{x}{40}$$

Example 1:

Kinetic energy of an object can be calculated using the equation $E_K = \frac{1}{2}mv^2$, where E_K is the kinetic energy, m is the mass of the object, and v^2 is the square of its velocity. Which of the following expresses the mass of the object m, in terms of the kinetic energy and the squared velocity?

A) $m = \dfrac{2E_K}{v^2}$

B) $m = \dfrac{E_K}{2v^2}$

C) $m = E_K - 2v^2$

D) $m = 2E_K v^2$

Step 1: Rearrange

This is an example of a simple rearrange. Multiplying both sides by 2 and dividing both sides by v^2 will remove $\frac{1}{2}v^2$ from the right expression and isolate m.

$$\frac{2}{v^2} \times E_K = \frac{1}{2}mv^2 \times \frac{2}{v^2} \rightarrow$$

$$\frac{2}{v^2} \times E_K = \frac{1}{\cancel{2}}m\cancel{v^2} \times \frac{\cancel{2}}{\cancel{v^2}} \rightarrow$$

$$\frac{2}{v^2} \times E_K = m \rightarrow$$

$$m = \frac{2E_K}{v^2}$$

Correct answer choice is **A**.

Example 2:

$$S = 5 + \left(\frac{2Mt + Et}{t^2}\right)$$

Raj has created the above equation to determine his running speed, where S is the speed in kilometers per hour, M and E are variables, and t is the time in hours. Which of the following expresses the time t, in terms of the speed, M, and E?

A) $t = \sqrt{\frac{2M+E}{S-5}}$

B) $t = \frac{2M+E}{S-5}$

C) $t = \frac{S-5}{2MT+Et}$

D) $t = \frac{2Mt+Et}{S-5}$

Step 1: Rearrange

t must be removed from the denominator and isolated on one side of the equation.

The process of rearranging the equation to isolate t consists of 4 steps shown below.

$$S - 5 = \frac{2Mt + Et}{t^2}$$

$$S - 5 = \frac{(2M + E)}{t}$$

$$t(S - 5) = (2M + E)$$

$$t = \frac{2M + E}{S - 5}$$

See below for the details of each step.

Step 1: Subtract 5 from both sides of the equation to remove it from the right expression.

$$S - 5 = \cancel{5} + \left(\frac{2Mt + Et}{t^2}\right) - \cancel{5} \;\rightarrow\; S - 5 = \frac{2Mt + Et}{t^2}$$

Step 2: Factor t in the right expression and cancel it from the numerator and the denominator.

$$S - 5 = \frac{t(2M + E)}{t \times t} \;\rightarrow\; S - 5 = \frac{\cancel{t}(2M + E)}{\cancel{t} \times t} \;\rightarrow\; S - 5 = \frac{(2M + E)}{t}$$

Step 3: Multiply both sides by t to move it to the numerator.

$$t(S - 5) = \frac{(2M + E) \times \cancel{t}}{\cancel{t}} \;\rightarrow\; t(S - 5) = (2M + E)$$

Step 4: Divide both sides by $(S - 5)$ to isolate t.

$$\frac{t\cancel{(S-5)}}{\cancel{(S-5)}} = \frac{(2M + E)}{(S - 5)} \;\rightarrow\; t = \frac{2M + E}{S - 5}$$

Correct answer choice is **B**.

Category 52 – Practice Questions (answers on page 387)

No Calculator Questions

1

The law of universal gravitation states that every point mass attracts every other point mass in the universe with a force that is directly proportional to the product of their masses and inversely proportional to the square of the distance between their centers. The formula is written as $F = G\frac{m_1 m_2}{r^2}$, where F is the gravitational force, m_1 and m_2 are the two masses, r is the distance between the center of the two masses, and G is the gravitational constant. Which of the following expresses the distance between the center of the two masses r in terms of the masses of the two objects, the gravitational force, and the gravitational constant?

A) $r = F\frac{m_1 m_2}{G}$

B) $r = \sqrt{G\frac{m_1 m_2}{F}}$

C) $r = G\sqrt{\frac{m_1 m_2}{F}}$

D) $r = F\sqrt{\frac{m_1 m_2}{G}}$

2

$$R = \frac{(8 \times \mu)l}{\pi \times r^4}$$

Pressure of a fluid as it travels through a cylindrical pipe can be calculated by the above formula. R is the airway resistance, μ is the dynamic viscosity, l is the length of the pipe, r is the radius of the pipe, and π is pi. Which of the following gives the dynamic viscosity μ in terms of the length of the pipe, the radius of the pipe, the airway resistance, and pi?

A) $\mu = \frac{R\pi r^4}{8l}$

B) $\mu = \frac{R\pi r^4}{8l^2}$

C) $\mu = R\pi r^4 - 8l$

D) $\mu = R\pi r^4 8l^2$

3

$$A = \frac{a+b}{2}h$$

The above formula is for the area A of a trapezoid in terms of its height h and the two parallel bases a and b. Which of the following expresses the height h of the trapezoid in terms of the area and the two parallel bases?

A) $h = 2A(a + b)$

B) $h = 2Aab$

C) $h = \frac{A}{2a+2b}$

D) $h = \frac{2A}{a+b}$

4

$$\frac{ut + 2u + 1}{u + 1} = 1 + \frac{us - ut^2}{u + 1}$$

Which of the following is equivalent to the expression above?

A) $s = \frac{u+t-1}{u}$

B) $s = \frac{t^2+t+1}{u}$

C) $s = t^2 + t + 1$

D) $s = u^2 + t^2 + 1$

5

$$(1 + i) = (1 + r)(1 + \pi)$$

The above formula determines the relationship between real and nominal interest rates during inflation, where i is the nominal interest rate, r is the real interest rate, and π is the inflation rate. Which of the following expresses the nominal and the real interest rates in terms of the inflation rate π?

A) $\pi = \frac{1+i}{1+r} - 1$

B) $\pi = \frac{1+i}{1+r} + 1$

C) $\pi = (1 + i) - (1 + r)$

D) $\pi = (1 + i) + (1 + r)$

Category 53 – Combining Like Terms

Key Points

- Like terms have the same variable(s) with the same exponent. For example, $3x^2$ and x^2 are like terms. They have the same variable x and the exponent 2. Similarly, x^3y^2 and $4x^3y^2$ are like terms since the variables are same and have the same exponent. x^3y^2 and $4x^2y^2$ are not like terms since the exponents of the variable x are different.

- Like terms can be added or subtracted. For example, in the expression $2x^2 + xy + x^2 + 5xy$, the like terms $2x^2$ and x^2 can be added to give $3x^2$, and the like terms xy and $5xy$ can be added to give $6xy$.

How to Solve

If the expression has parentheses, then simplify before solving. Use the laws of exponents to multiply the variables. If the answer choices are given in the factored form, then factor out the common terms.

Example 1:

Which of the following is equivalent to $3x(x^2 - x) + 7x^2 - 2x^3$?

A) $-4x^2 - x^3$

B) $4x^2 - x^3$

C) $x + 3x^2 - x^3$

D) $x + x^2 - 2x^3$

Step 1: Simplify the expression within the parentheses and add/subtract like terms

$$3x(x^2 - x) + 7x^2 - 2x^3 \rightarrow (3x \times x^2) - (3x \times x) + 7x^2 - 2x^3 \rightarrow$$
$$3x^3 - 3x^2 + 7x^2 - 2x^3 \rightarrow 4x^2 - x^3$$

Correct answer choice is **B**.

Category 53 – Practice Questions (answers on page 387)

No Calculator Questions

1

Which of the following is equivalent to $2(x^2 - 1) + 10x^3 - 2x^2$?

A) $10x^3$

B) $10x^3 - 2$

C) $2x^2 - 10x^3 - 2$

D) $2x^2 + 6x^3 - 1$

2

Which of the following is equivalent to $4x(x^3 + 3x^2) - 3(x^4 - 2x^3) + x^4$?

A) $2x^3(x + 9)$

B) $2(x^4 + 3x^3)$

C) $2x(x + 9x^3)$

D) $2x^3(x^3 - x^2) - 12x^3$

3

Which of the following is equivalent to $m^2 + 3n^3 - 2mn - m(m - 2)$?

A) $3n^3$

B) $3n^3 + m^2 - 2mn$

C) $3n^3 - m^2 + 2m$

D) $3m^3 - 2mn + 2m$

4

Which of the following is equivalent to the sum of $s^2 - 3t^3$ and $3s^2 + 5t^3 + t$?

A) $-s^2 + t^2$

B) $4s^3 + 2t^3$

C) $4s^2 + 2t^3 + t$

D) $4s^2 + t^2 + 2t$

Category 54 – Expressions with Square Root

Key Points

- When an equation contains a square root expression, the square root can be removed by squaring both sides of the equation. For example, squaring both sides of $\sqrt{2x+1} = 2$ will result in $2x+1 = 2^2$ and squaring both sides of $\sqrt{2x+1} = \sqrt{x+3}$ will result in $2x+1 = x+3$.

- Working with square root expressions may result in a solution that does not solve the equation, also known as an extraneous solution. Equations that have 2 solutions are more likely to have extraneous solution.

How to Solve

Collect all the integers and variables that are not under the square root on one side. For example,
$\sqrt{2x+1} - 3 = 2 + x \rightarrow \sqrt{2x+1} = 2 + 3 + x \rightarrow \sqrt{2x+1} = 5 + x$.

The entire expression on each side must be squared. For example, $\sqrt{2x+1} = 5 + x \rightarrow \left(\sqrt{2x+1}\right)^2 = (5+x)^2$ and $\sqrt{2x+1} = 5\sqrt{x-1} \rightarrow \left(\sqrt{2x+1}\right)^2 = \left(5\sqrt{x-1}\right)^2$.

If the solution is a perfect square, for example $x^2 = 9$, then the variable will have two values: a negative value and a positive value. For $x^2 = 9$, the value of x can be -3 or 3, since both will give 9 when squared.

When there are two values of x, plug them in the given equation to check for an extraneous solution. The values must be plugged in the given equation, not in any equation formed during the calculation process.

Example 1:

$$\sqrt{7x+3} = 2\sqrt{x+6}$$

What value of x satisfies the equation above?

A) 2

B) 3

C) 7

D) 9

Step 1: Square both sides

$$\left(\sqrt{7x+3}\right)^2 = \left(2\sqrt{x+6}\right)^2 \rightarrow 7x+3 = 4(x+6)$$

Step 2: Solve

$$7x + 3 = 4x + 24 \rightarrow 3x = 21 \rightarrow x = 7$$

Correct answer choice is **C**.

Example 2:

$$\sqrt{12 - 2x} + 2 = x$$

Which of the following are the solutions of x, in the above equation?

A) $\{-4, 2\}$

B) $\{-2, 4\}$

C) -2

D) 4

Step 1: Square both sides

Move 2 to the right-side and square both sides.

$$\sqrt{12 - 2x} = x - 2 \rightarrow \left(\sqrt{12 - 2x}\right)^2 = (x - 2)^2 \rightarrow 12 - 2x = (x - 2)^2$$

Step 2: Solve

FOIL the right expression and create a quadratic equation.

$$12 - 2x = x^2 - 4x + 4$$

$$x^2 - 4x + 4 + 2x - 12 = 0$$

$$x^2 - 2x - 8 = 0$$

Factorize the above equation.

$$(x - 4)(x + 2) = 0$$

The two solutions of x are -2 and 4.

Step 3: Check for extraneous solution

Plug in $x = -2$ into the given equation.

$$\sqrt{12 - 2x} + 2 = x \rightarrow \sqrt{12 - 2(-2)} + 2 = -2 \rightarrow \sqrt{12 + 4} + 2 = -2 \rightarrow$$

$$\sqrt{16} + 2 = -2 \rightarrow 4 + 2 = -2 \rightarrow 6 = -2$$

When $x = -2$, the two sides of the equation do not have the same value. Hence, -2 is an extraneous solution.

Plug in $x = 4$ into the given equation.

$$\sqrt{12 - 2x} + 2 = x \rightarrow \sqrt{12 - 2(4)} + 2 = 4 \rightarrow \sqrt{12 - 8} + 2 = 4 \rightarrow$$

$$\sqrt{4} + 2 = 4 \rightarrow 2 + 2 = 4 \rightarrow 4 = 4$$

When $x = 4$, the two sides of the equation have the same value. Hence, 4 is the real solution.

Correct answer choice is **D**.

Note that if one of the solutions is negative, then it is likely that the negative solution is the extraneous solution.

Category 54 – Practice Questions (answers on page 388)

No Calculator Questions

1

$$\sqrt{x + 5} - 2 = 3$$

What value of x satisfies the above equation?

A) 0

B) 7

C) 9

D) 20

2

$$\sqrt{\frac{27}{x}} + 1 = 4$$

Which of the following can be the value of x in the above equation?

A) 2

B) 3

C) 5

D) 9

3

$$\sqrt{x^2 + 5} = 3$$

What value of x satisfies the above equation, where $x > 0$?

A) -1

B) 1

C) 2

D) 4

4

If $\sqrt{5x - 1} = 3\sqrt{x - 1}$, what is the value of x?

A) -5

B) -2

C) 2

D) 5

5

$$3\sqrt{x + 2} - \sqrt{x + 26} = 0$$

What value of x can satisfy the equation above?

6

$$\frac{1}{2}\sqrt{x + 5} + 1 = 3$$

In the above equation, what is a value of x?

Calculator Questions

7

$$\sqrt{7 - 2x} + 2 = x$$

Which of the following are the solutions of the above equation?

I. -1

II. 1

III. 3

A) I only

B) III only

C) I and III only

D) II and III only

No Calculator Questions

1

$$\frac{1}{(a - b)(a^2 - b^2)}$$

If $a - b = 2$ and $a + b = 3$, what is the solution to the above expression?

A) $\frac{1}{12}$

B) $\frac{1}{6}$

C) 6

D) 7

2

$$m = \frac{1}{2}am + 4$$

The ideal body weight for a child less than one year old can be calculated by the above formula, where m is the child's weight in kilograms and a is the child's age in months. Which of the following represents child's age a in terms of m?

A) $a = 8m$

B) $a = 2 - \frac{8}{m}$

C) $a = m - \frac{4}{m}$

D) $a = 2 + \frac{8}{m}$

3

$$K = \frac{1}{2}(D^2 + H) + D^2$$

In terms of H, which of the following is equivalent to the equation above, where D, H, and K are variables?

A) $2K + D$

B) $K + 2D^2$

C) $K - 3D^2$

D) $2K - 3D^2$

4

$$\frac{2y^2 + y}{y - 2} - \frac{y^2 + 5y - 4}{y - 2}$$

If the above expression is equal to 3, which of the following can be the value of y?

A) 2

B) 4

C) 5

D) 12

5

$$s = \frac{at^2}{2} + v_o t + s_o$$

The equation above is the second equation of motion for position-time relationship. It applies to a particle moving linearly in a straight line with constant acceleration, where s is the final position, a is the acceleration, t is the time, v_o is the initial linear velocity, and s is the initial position. Which of the following gives the initial linear velocity v_o in terms of the acceleration, the time, the initial position, and the final position?

A) $v_o = \frac{s - s_o}{t} - \frac{at}{2}$

B) $v_o = \frac{s - s_o - at}{2t}$

C) $v_o = s - \frac{at^2 - s_o}{2}$

D) $v_o = s - \frac{at^2}{2} - t + s_o$

6

$$\sqrt{2k + 17} = 7$$

What value of k satisfies the above equation?

A) -5

B) -1

C) 11

D) 16

$$\sqrt{5c^2 - 4} = 2c$$

What values of c satisfy the above equation?

I. -2

II. -1

III. 2

A)   II only

B)   III only

C)   I and II only

D)   I and III only

$$\frac{2}{\dfrac{1}{x+2} + \dfrac{1}{x-2}} = x - 1$$

Which of the following is the value of x in the above equation?

A)   0

B)   1

C)   4

D)   12

$$\sqrt{\frac{36}{4x^2} - 1} = 0$$

Which of the following is one possible value of x in the above equation?

A)   0

B)   3

C)   4

D)   6

$$a^2 - b^2 = \frac{2a^2 + 4ab + 2b^2}{a + b}$$

What is the value of $a - b$ in the above equation?

Which of the following is equivalent to $4a(a^2 + b) - 2a^2 - ab$?

A) $2a^2 - ab$

B) $2a^2 - 2ab$

C) $2a^3 - 2a^2 + 3ab$

D) $4a^3 - 2a^2 + 3ab$

Which of the following is equivalent to $x(2x^2 + y) - 2x(x^2 - y^2)$?

A) $2(x - 2y^2)$

B) $xy(1 + 2y)$

C) $xy^2(2 + x)$

D) x^2y^2

Calculator Questions

$$\frac{x^2 - 9}{2(x - 3)} = 4$$

In the above equation, what is the value of x?

$$\frac{1}{3}\sqrt{5x + 6}$$

If the above expression is equal to 2, what is the value of x?

Section 12 –
Data Analysis and Interpretation

Category 55 – Probability

Category 56 – Graphs with Line Segments and Curves

Category 57 – Scatter Plots and Line of Best Fit

Category 58 – Bar Graphs

Category 59 – Histograms and Dot Plots

Category 60 – Mean

Category 61 – Histograms, Dot Plots, and Mean

Category 62 – Median

Category 63 – Histograms, Dot Plots, Bar Graphs, and Median

Category 64 – Box Plots and Median

Category 65 – Mode

Category 66 – Standard Deviation and Range

Category 67 – Comparing Mean, Median, Mode, SD, and Range

Category 68 – Interpretation of Sample Data in Studies and Surveys

Section 12 – Review Questions

Category 55 – Probability

Key Points

- Probability is the likelihood of achieving certain or desired outcomes from the total possible outcomes, at random.

$$\text{probability} = \frac{\text{number of certain/desired outcomes}}{\text{number of total possible outcomes}}$$

How to Solve

It is important to identify the numerator and the denominator correctly. For example, if a red or a blue color marble is desired from a bag containing marbles of various colors, then the desired outcomes must consider all the red marbles and all the blue marbles that are in the bag and the total possible outcomes must consider all the marbles in the bag.

$$\text{probability} = \frac{\text{all red marbles} + \text{all blue marbles}}{\text{all marbles}}$$

Similarly, if a red marble is desired out of red, blue, green, and white marbles, then desired outcomes = all red marbles and total outcomes = all red marbles + all blue marbles + all green marbles + all white marbles.

Example 1:

The table below shows the number of freshman, sophomore, junior, and senior class students enrolled in various sports teams at a certain high school. Each student is enrolled in one team.

Team	Freshman	Sophomore	Junior	Senior	Total
Baseball	21	25	12	29	87
Football	15	22	15	30	82
Wrestling	7	28	30	2	67
Boxing	5	11	9	7	32
Total	48	86	66	68	268

Question 1

If one of the students is selected at random, what is the probability that the student is on the boxing team?

A) $\dfrac{7}{52}$

B) $\dfrac{8}{67}$

C) $\dfrac{12}{67}$

D) $\dfrac{11}{268}$

Step 1: Determine the probability

desired outcomes = all students on boxing team.

total possible outcomes = all students.

$$\text{probability} = \frac{\text{all students on boxing team}}{\text{all students}} = \frac{32}{268} = \frac{8}{67}$$

Note that the phrase "one of the students is selected" implies that the selection of a student on the boxing team is out of all the students. Hence, all freshman, sophomore, junior, and senior students are considered in total possible outcomes.

Correct answer choice is **B**.

Question 2

Which of the following is closest to the probability that a randomly selected junior or senior student is on the football or wrestling team?

A)   0.28

B)   0.36

C)   0.39

D)   0.57

Step 1: Determine the probability

Note that the phrase "randomly selected junior or senior student" implies that the selection of a student on football or wrestling team is from junior or senior students. Hence, including freshmen or sophomores in the total possible outcomes will be incorrect. This is important to look out for in Probability questions.

desired outcomes = all juniors on football team, all juniors on wrestling team, all seniors on football team, and seniors on wrestling team.

total possible outcomes = all junior students and all senior students.

$$\text{probability} = \frac{\text{all juniors on football} + \text{all juniors on wrestling} + \text{all seniors on football} + \text{all seniors on wrestling}}{\text{all juniors} + \text{all seniors}}$$

$$\frac{15 + 30 + 30 + 2}{66 + 68} = \frac{77}{134} = 0.57$$

Correct answer choice is **D**.

Example 2:

The table below shows the number of medium and large sized jackets in two colors at a department store. If one jacket is selected at random, the probability of selecting a large red color jacket is $\frac{1}{6}$. What is the value of x?

Color	Jacket size	
	Medium	Large
Black	4	5
Red	11	x

Step 1: Determine the probability

It is given that the probability of selecting a large red jacket from all the jackets is $\frac{1}{6}$. Hence,

desired outcomes = all large red jackets.

total possible outcomes = all jackets.

$$\text{probabiliy} = \frac{\text{all large red jackets}}{\text{all jackets}} = \frac{1}{6}$$

$$\frac{x}{4 + 5 + 11 + x} = \frac{1}{6} \;\rightarrow\; \frac{x}{20 + x} = \frac{1}{6}$$

Cross multiply.

$$6x = 20 + x \;\rightarrow\; 5x + 20 \;\rightarrow\; x = 4$$

Correct answer is **4**.

Category 55 – Practice Questions (answers on page 391)

Calculator Questions

1

Color	Electric cars	Gas cars	Total
White	25	151	176
Red	136	152	288
Blue	311	205	516
Total	472	508	980

The above table summarizes the number of electric and gas cars available in three different colors at a car dealership. If a blue car is selected at random, what is the probability that the blue car will be electric?

A) $\dfrac{205}{516}$

B) $\dfrac{311}{472}$

C) $\dfrac{311}{516}$

D) $\dfrac{311}{980}$

2

| School district | Response | | | Total |
	Yes	No	Not Sure	
District A	11	4	5	20
District B	15	4	1	20
District C	11	4	5	20
Total	37	12	11	60

Three school districts conducted a survey to determine if the teachers were in favor of changes in the school curriculum. 20 teachers were selected at random from each school district for the survey. The above table categorizes the results of the survey by the school district and the response of the teachers as "Yes", "No", or "Not Sure". Which of the following is closed to the probability that a randomly selected response from District A or District C is "Yes" or "Not Sure"?

A) 0.37

B) 0.46

C) 0.55

D) 0.80

Questions 3 and 4 refer to the following information.

Answer choice	Number of responses
Yes	72
Maybe	84
No	32
Do not wish to answer	21
Total	209

A perfume company sent out a small perfume sample to all the residents in a certain small town. The company included a questionnaire with the sample and requested the residents to mail the completed questionnaire to the company. One of the questions asked the residents whether they would buy the perfume. Four answer choices were given for the question. The number of responses to each answer choice for the question are shown in the above table for 209 residents.

3

Based on the information in the table, which of the following is closest to the probability that if an answer choice is selected at random, the answer choice is "No", given that the answer choice "Do not wish to answer" was not considered?

A) 0.15

B) 0.17

C) 0.22

D) 0.83

4

If a "Yes" or "Maybe" answer choice is selected at random, which of the following is closest to the probability that the answer choice is "Yes"?

A) 0.18

B) 0.34

C) 0.46

D) 0.54

Takiyah bought a bag of 100 marbles of assorted colors and sizes. The table below shows the distribution of the marbles by color and size.

Size	Color			
	Red	Green	Blue	Total
Small	18	6	9	33
Medium	8	30	11	49
Large	6	10	2	18
Total	32	46	22	100

If all large size marbles are removed from the bag, which of the following is closest to the probability that a marble selected at random will be a small size green marble or a small size blue marble?

A) $\dfrac{15}{82}$

B) $\dfrac{15}{68}$

C) $\dfrac{68}{100}$

D) $\dfrac{82}{100}$

A library bought a total of 140 novels. $\dfrac{4}{7}$ were mystery novels and the remaining were either adventure novels or science fiction novels. If one of the 140 novels is selected at random, the probability of selecting an adventure novel is $\dfrac{1}{10}$. How many science fiction novels did the library buy?

A) 10

B) 14

C) 46

D) 80

	No flexible hours	Flexible hours	Total
Did not work from home	200	140	340
Worked from home once a week	60	50	110
Total	260	190	450

A small company of 450 employees offer two types of flexible working options to all the employees from June to August each year. One option allows an employee to work flexible hours and the other option allows an employee to work from home once a week. An employee may choose one option, both options, or neither option. For 2018, the distribution of the employees based on the flexible working options is shown in the above table. If x is the probability that a randomly selected employee worked flexible hours and worked from home once a week and y is the probability that a randomly selected employee did not work flexible hours and did not work from home once a week, what percent is x of y?

A) 12%

B) 25%

C) 42%

D) 75%

	Team A	Team B	Team C
Coffee Brand A	6	2	5
Coffee Brand B	a	5	6

The above table shows the number of participants in three teams assigned to test two different brands of coffee. If one of the participants is selected at random, the probability that the participant belongs to Team A and assigned to test Coffee Brand B is $\dfrac{1}{9}$. What is the value of a?

Category 56 – Graphs with Line Segments and Curves

Key Points

- A graph illustrates the relationship between two variables plotted as data points. One variable is represented on the horizontal axis and the other variable is represented on the vertical axis. Each data point is represented as a dot and corresponds to a value on the horizontal axis and a value on the vertical axis.

- The data points may be connected by straight line segments or by curves.

How to Solve

The value of a data point can be determined by reading the value of that dot on the horizontal and the vertical axes. Use best approximation when reading data points not on the graph grid lines.

Example 1:

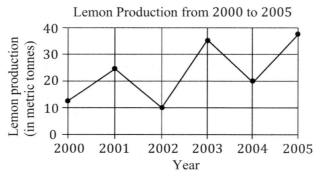

The above graph shows the lemon production, in metric tonnes, at an orchard in the United States from 2000 to 2005. During which of the following one-year period was the greatest increase in lemon production, in metric tonnes?

A)   2000 to 2001

B)   2002 to 2003

C)   2003 to 2004

D)   2004 to 2005

Step 1: Read the data points from the graph

Each data point represents the lemon production in a year. It can be seen from the graph that the greatest difference in the increase of lemon production is from 2002 to 2003. If unsure, evaluate each answer choice as shown below.

Answer choice A: In 2000, lemon production = 12. In 2001, lemon production = 24. Difference = $24 - 12 = 12$.

Answer choice B: In 2002, lemon production = 10. In 2003, lemon production = 35. Difference = $35 - 10 = 25$.

Answer choice C: In 2003, lemon production = 35. In 2004, lemon production = 20. Difference = $20 - 35 = -15$.

Answer choice D: In 2004, lemon production = 20. In 2005, lemon production = 38. Difference = $38 - 20 = 18$.

Correct answer choice is **B**.

See below for the corresponding curve graph.

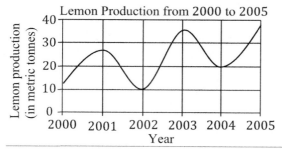

Example 2:

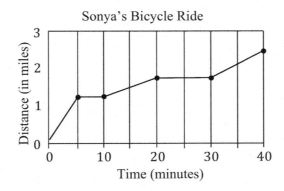

Sonya's Bicycle Ride

Sonya rode on a bicycle from her home to a park. On the way, she stopped at the library to get a book and then rode to a bakery. After stopping at the bakery for few minutes, she continued to ride to the park. The graph above shows the total time it took Sonya to reach the park after leaving her home. Based on the graph, how many minutes did Sonya ride on the bicycle?

A) 25

B) 28

C) 30

D) 40

Step 1: Read the data points from the graph

The change in distance with time indicates movement. This will be an upward slanting line on the graph. A horizontal line indicates that the distance did not change with time, hence, no movement. The graph shows that the distance changed with time between 0 to 5 minutes (5 minutes of movement), 10 to 20 minutes (10 minutes of movement), and 30 to 40 minutes (10 minutes of movement). This represents the duration when Sonya rode her bicycle. Hence, the total minutes Sonya rode her bicycle are

$$5 + 10 + 10 = 25$$

Correct answer choice is **A**.

Example 3:

Sonya rode on a bicycle from her home to a park. On the way, she stopped at the library to get a book and then rode to a bakery. After stopping at the bakery for few minutes, she continued to ride to the park. Which of the following graphs represents the situation in context?

A)

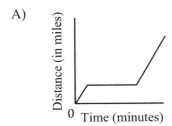

B)

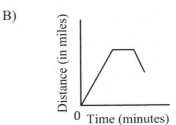

C)

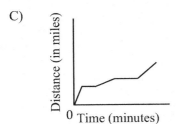

D)

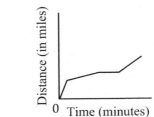

Match the sequence of events in the question to the flow of events on the graphs. Since Sonya made two stops, the graph should have two horizontal lines corresponding to no movement. This eliminates answer choices A, B, and D.

Correct answer choice is **C**.

Category 56 – Practice Questions (answers on page 392)

Calculator Questions

1

Every Monday, Quinn buys a 50 ml bottle of protein shake and drinks it over a period of 90 minutes. Last Monday, Quinn finished half the protein shake within 30 minutes of opening the bottle and the remaining half 30 minutes later over a period of 30 minutes. Which of the following graphs show the situation in context?

A)

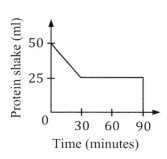

B)

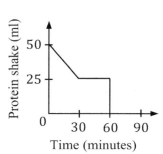

C)

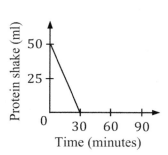

D)

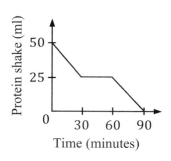

2

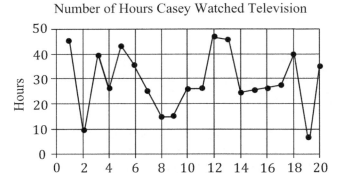

The graph above shows the number of hours Casey watched television each week over a period of 20 weeks. During which two consecutive weeks did Casey watch the least hours of television?

A)   Week 1 and week 2

B)   Week 7 and week 8

C)   Week 8 and week 9

D)   Week 18 and week 19

3

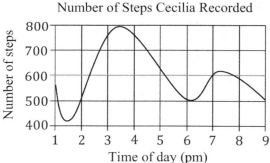

The graph above shows the number of steps Cecilia recorded using a step tracker watch between 1 pm and 8 pm last Sunday. For which of the following one-hour period is the difference between the number of steps the greatest?

A)   From 2 pm to 3 pm

B)   From 3 pm to 4 pm

C)   From 4 pm to 5 pm

D)   From 6 pm to 7 pm

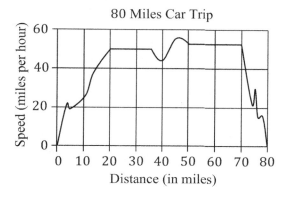

80 Miles Car Trip

During an 80 miles car trip, Geeta drove at varying speeds, in miles per hour, as shown in the above graph. According to the graph, for approximately how many miles Geeta maintained a constant speed?

A) 15

B) 20

C) 35

D) 50

5

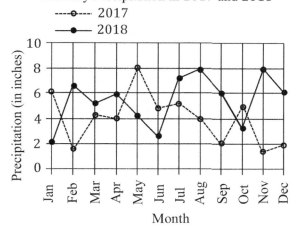

Monthly Precipitation in 2017 and 2018

The above line graph shows the monthly precipitation in a city in 2017 and 2018. According to the graph, in which month was the precipitation in 2018 twice that of 2017?

A) May

B) August

C) September

D) December

Questions 6 and 7 refer to the following information.

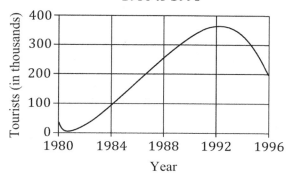

Number of Tourists in an Island from 1980 to 1996

The above graph shows the number of tourists, in thousands, visiting a certain island from 1980 to 1996.

6

During which four-year period, the increase in the number of tourists was greatest?

A) 1980 to 1984

B) 1984 to 1988

C) 1988 to 1992

D) 1992 to 1996

7

The tourists who visited the island in 1984 were approximately what percent of the tourists who visited the island in 1996?

A) 22%

B) 42%

C) 50%

D) 200%

Questions 8 and 9 refer to the following information.

Online Sales of Action Figures

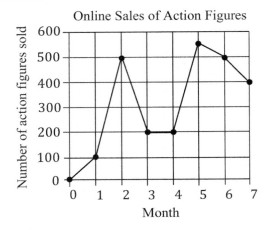

An action figure manufacturing company launched a website to sell action figures online. The above graph shows the number of action figures sold online during the first 7 months of launching the website.

8

Based on the graph above, how many action figures were sold within the first 4 months of launching the website?

A)   600

B)   750

C)   800

D)   1,000

9

What was the percent change in the number of action figures sold from month 6 to month 7?

A)   20%

B)   25%

C)   50%

D)   400%

10

Number of Customers at a Coffee Shop

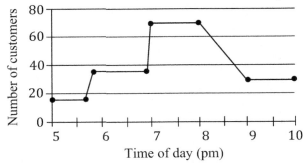

The graph above shows the number of customers at a coffee shop between 5 pm and 10 pm last Friday. Which segment of the graph shows the greatest number of customers?

A)   The segment from (7, 70) to (7, 80)

B)   The segment from (7, 70) to (8, 70)

C)   The segment from (8, 70) to (9, 30)

D)   The segment from (9, 30) to (10, 30)

11

12 Month Weight Loss Program

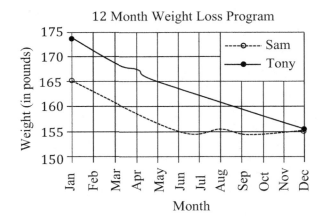

Last year, Tony and Sam enrolled in a 12 month weight loss program from January through December. Their monthly weight, in pounds, from the start to the end of the program is represented by the above line graph. Based on the graph, which of the following statements must be true?

A)   At the end of the program, Tony and Sam lost the same amount of weight, in pounds.

B)   At the end of the program, Sam lost greater weight than Tony, in pounds.

C)   At the end of the program, Tony lost greater weight than Sam, in pounds.

D)   At the end of the program, neither Tony nor Sam lost any weight, in pounds.

Category 57 – Scatter Plots and Line of Best Fit

Key Points

- A scatter plot shows the correlation between two variables plotted as data points. One variable is represented on the horizontal axis and the other variable is represented on the vertical axis. Each data point is represented as a dot and corresponds to a value on the horizontal axis and a value on the vertical axis. See Fig. 1, 2, and 3 below.

    - In a positive correlation, the increase in the value of one variable increases the value of the other variable.

    - In a negative correlation, the increase in the value of one variable decreases the value of the other variable.

    - When the data points are scattered all over the graph, there is no correlation between the two variables.

- A line of best fit on a scatter plot expresses the linear relationship between the data points and can be used to make predictions. It is a straight line drawn through the maximum number of data points on a scatter plot.

    - When the data points are concentrated around the line of best fit, the correlation is high (strong) (Fig. 1).

    - When the data points are spread out around the line of best fit, the correlation is low (weak) (Fig. 2).

    - The actual value of a data point is the value of the dot on the scatter plot. The predicted value of the same data point is the value on the line of best fit. The points that lie on the line of best fit are the points for which the predictions are most accurate. In Fig. 4 below, the prediction is accurate for point B. The predicted value of point A is higher (overestimated) and the predicted value of point C is lower (underestimated).

    - The equation of the line of best fit is the slope-intercept equation, $y = mx + b$. The point where the line of best fit intersects the y-axis (vertical axis) is the y-intercept of the line. At y-intercept, x (horizontal axis) $= 0$.

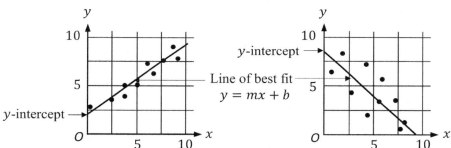

Fig. 1 Positive Correlation   Fig. 2 Negative Correlation   Fig. 3 No Correlation

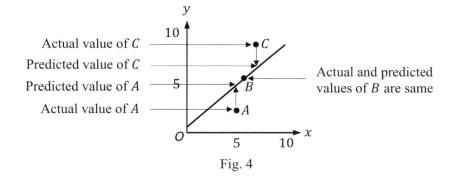

Fig. 4

How to Solve

The slope of the line of best fit can be determined by selecting any two points on the line and using the slope formula shown below, where m is the slope and (x_1, y_1) and (x_2, y_2) are the two points on the line of best fit. It is easiest to select points that are on the grid lines of the graph. (For further information on slope, refer to Section 1 on Lines.)

$$m = \frac{y_2 - y_1}{x_2 - x_1}$$

Remember that the data points below the line are overestimated and the data points above the line are underestimated.

Example 1:

Carbohydrate and Sugar in 10 Milk Shakes

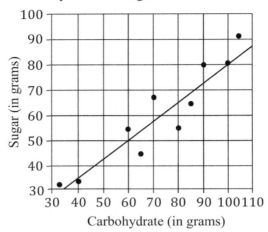

The graph above shows the grams of carbohydrate and sugar in 10 milkshakes. A line of best fit for the data is also shown.

Question 1

Which of the following is the sugar, in grams, predicted by the line of best fit in a milk shake containing 60 grams of carbohydrate?

A)   50

B)   70

C)   81

D)   100

Step 1: Read the data point on the line of best fit

60 grams of carbohydrate (horizontal axis) correspond to 50 grams of sugar (vertical axis).

Correct answer choice is **A**.

Question 2

Which of the following is the approximate difference between the sugar, in grams, predicted by the line of best fit and the actual sugar, in grams, in a milk shake containing 70 grams of carbohydrate?

A)   0

B)   4

C)   5

D)   10

Step 1: Read the data point on the line of best fit

70 grams of carbohydrate (horizontal axis) correspond to approximately 58 grams of sugar (vertical axis).

Step 2: Read the data point on the scatter plot

Look for the dot on the scatter plot that corresponds to 70 grams of carbohydrate (horizontal axis). Read the corresponding grams of sugar (vertical axis). The corresponding amount of sugar is approximately 68 grams.

Step 3: Calculate the difference

$$68 - 58 = 10$$

Correct answer choice is **D**.

The graph is repeated for Questions 3 and 4.

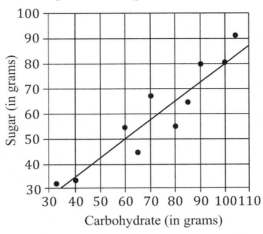

Carbohydrate and Sugar in 10 Milk Shakes

Question 3

Which of the following could be an equation of a line of best fit?

A) $y = \frac{1}{2}x + 10$

B) $y = \frac{1}{2}x - 2$

C) $y = \frac{3}{4}x + 1$

D) $y = \frac{3}{4}x + 50$

Step 1: Determine the slope of the line of best fit

The slope is determined below using the points (60, 50) and (100, 80) on the line of best fit.

$$m = \frac{y_2 - y_1}{x_2 - x_1} = \frac{80 - 50}{100 - 60} = \frac{30}{40} = \frac{3}{4}$$

This eliminates answer choices A and B. From the graph, it is seen that the y-intercept is less than 30. This eliminates answer choice D.

Correct answer choice is **C**.

Question 4

Based on the line of best fit, which of the following best interprets the relationship between the amount of sugar and the carbohydrate, in grams, in the 10 milk shakes?

A) For every 1 gram of sugar, the predicted increase in carbohydrate is approximately 1.3 grams.

B) For every 1 gram of carbohydrate, the predicted increase in sugar is approximately 1.4 grams.

C) For every 1 gram of carbohydrate, the predicted increase in sugar is 5 grams.

D) For every 1 gram of sugar, there is no change in carbohydrate.

Step 1: Determine the slope of the line of best fit

The relationship between sugar and carbohydrate is defined by the slope of the line of best fit. See question 3 above for calculation of the slope.

$$\text{slope} = \frac{\text{rise (change in } y)}{\text{run (change in } x)} = \frac{3}{4} = \frac{3 \text{ grams of sugar}}{4 \text{ grams of carbohydrate}} = \frac{1 \text{ gram of sugar}}{1.33 \text{ grams of carbohydrate}}$$

Since the slope is positive, for every 1 gram of sugar, carbohydrate increases approximately by 1.3 grams.

Correct answer choice is **A**.

Category 57 – Practice Questions (answers on page 393)

Calculator Questions

1

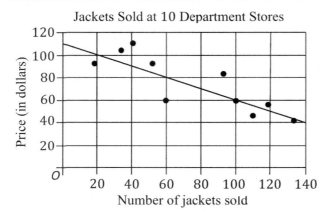

Jackets Sold at 10 Department Stores

The scatter plot above shows the price of jackets, in dollars, and the number of jackets sold per month at 10 department stores. A line of best fit is also shown. Which of the following could be an equation of the line of best fit?

A) $y = -0.5x + 112$

B) $y = -2x + 20$

C) $y = 0.5x + 110$

D) $y = 2x + 115$

2

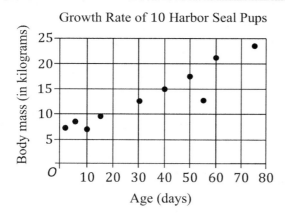

Growth Rate of 10 Harbor Seal Pups

The above scatter plot shows the body mass, in kilograms, of 10 harbor seal pups from ages 1 to 80 days. Based on the graph, which of the following best estimates the increase in body mass, in kilograms, for every 20 days increase in age?

A) 2

B) 5

C) 8

D) 10

Questions 3 and 4 refer to the following information.

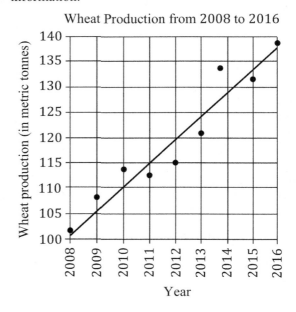

Wheat Production from 2008 to 2016

The scatter plot above shows the amount of wheat production, in millions of metric tonnes, in a certain country from 2008 to 2016. A line of best fit for the data is also shown.

3

Based on the above graph, which of the following is the approximate amount of wheat production, in millions of metric tons, predicted by the line of best fit in 2014?

A) 110

B) 118

C) 125

D) 128

4

Which of the following best estimates the amount, in millions of metric tons, by which the line of best fit underestimates the wheat production in 2010?

A) 4

B) 9

C) 14

D) 20

Questions 5 and 6 refer to the following information.

Time Spent on Advertising at 10 Companies

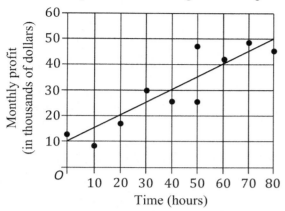

The above scatter plot shows the monthly profit, in thousands of dollars, of 10 companies and the number of hours the companies spend on advertising each month. A line of best fit for the data is also shown.

5

Which of the following is the best interpretation of the *y*-intercept of the line of best fit?

A) The predicted monthly profit of a company, in thousands of dollars, when unlimited time is spent on advertising each month.

B) The predicted monthly profit of a company, in thousands of dollars, when 10 hours are spent on advertising each month.

C) The predicted monthly profit of a company, in thousands of dollars, when 80 hours are spent on advertising each month.

D) The predicted monthly profit of a company, in thousands of dollars, when no time is spent on advertising each month.

6

If *k* is the monthly profit, in thousands of dollars, when 40 hours are spent on advertising each month by a company, which of the following could be the value of *k* predicted by the line of best fit?

A) 10

B) 24

C) 30

D) 60

Questions 7 and 8 refer to the following information.

Weight Loss of 10 Participants

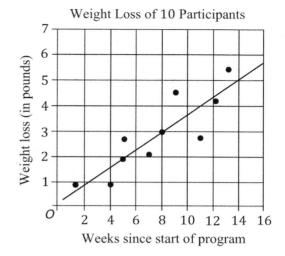

10 participants joined a weight loss program at a health club. The above scatter plot shows the weight loss, in pounds, of the 10 participants and the number of weeks since start of the program. A line of best fit is also shown.

7

Based on the line of best fit shown in the above graph, which of the following best interprets the relationship between the weeks in the program and the weight loss in pounds?

A) For every 1 week in the program, the predicted weight loss is 0.33 pounds.

B) For every 1 week in the program, the predicted weight loss is 2 pounds.

C) For every 1 week in the program, the predicted weight loss is 3.33 pounds.

D) For every 1 week in the program, there is no predicted weight loss.

8

Based on the line of best fit, which of the following is the predicted weight loss, in pounds, for participants who continue the program till week 30?

A) 7.5

B) 10.3

C) 18.2

D) 40.0

Category 58 – Bar Graphs

Key Points

- A bar graph shows data grouped into categories. For example, book genre, year, color, height, and so on. The data is represented as rectangular bars that can be horizontal or vertical. The height or the length of a bar determines the number of data points in a category.

- A bar graph may contain sub-groups within each category. For example, if the category is department, then each department may have sub-groups for expense type. Sub-groups may be displayed side by side as bars within each category or may be stacked on each other as a column.

How to Solve

Determine the number of data points in each category or sub-group by reading the height of a vertical bar or the length of a horizontal bar. The correct answer may sometimes be apparent by looking at the graph.

Example 1:

New Employees at a Company

The above graph shows the number of new employees hired at Branch 1 and Branch 2 of a company from January to May. During which of the following months, the greatest number of new employees were hired at Branch 1 and Branch 2 combined?

A) January

B) February

C) April

D) May

Step 1: Read the height of each bar

This is an example of sub-groups displayed side by side. The category is month, and the sub-group is branch.

The graph shows that January and May have relatively shorter bars indicating fewer new employees. Hence, answer choices A and D can be eliminated. Determine the total number of new employees for the remaining answer choices.

February: In Branch 1, the number of new employees = 6. In Branch 2, the number of new employees = 15.

$$6 + 15 = 21$$

April: In Branch 1, the number of new employees = 10. In Branch 2, the number of new employees = 13.

$$10 + 13 = 23$$

Correct answer choice is **C**.

Example 2:

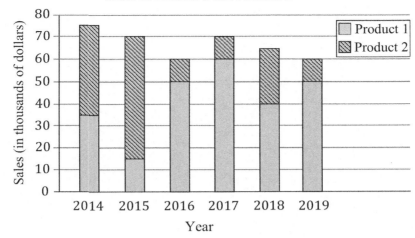

Sales of Product 1 and Product 2

The above bar graph shows the sales, in thousands of dollars, of Product 1 and Product 2 at a certain company from 2014 to 2019. Based on the graph, Product 1 sales, in thousands of dollars, are what fraction of the total sales of Product 1 and Product 2 combined, in thousands of dollars, from 2014 to 2019?

A) $\frac{3}{8}$

B) $\frac{5}{8}$

C) $\frac{3}{5}$

D) $\frac{2}{3}$

Step 1: Read the height of each bar

This is an example of a stacked bar graph. The category is year. The two sub-groups are Product 1 and Product 2. The Product 2 bar is stacked on the Product 1 bar. The height of each sub-group bar must be read from the bottom of each bar.

Product 1: Read the vertical axis from the bottom of the bar to the top of the bar. Since Product 1 is the lower bar, it starts from 0.

$2014 = 35$. $2015 = 15$. $2016 = 50$. $2017 = 60$. $2018 = 40$. $2019 = 50$.

$$35 + 15 + 50 + 60 + 40 + 50 = 250$$

Product 2: Read the vertical axis from the bottom of the Product 2 bar to the top of the Product 2 bar. The height of this bar is the difference between the two numbers. (Remember that the top bar does not start from 0.)

2014 bar is from 35 to 75. The difference is $75 - 35 = 40$.

2015 bar is from 15 to 70. The difference is $70 - 15 = 55$.

2016 bar is from 50 to 60. The difference is $60 - 50 = 10$.

2017 bar is from 60 to 70. The difference is $70 - 60 = 10$.

2018 bar is from 40 to 65. The difference is $65 - 40 = 25$.

2019 bar is from 50 to 60. The difference is $60 - 50 = 10$.

$$40 + 55 + 10 + 10 + 25 + 10 = 150$$

Step 2: Determine the fraction

$$\frac{\text{Product 1 sales}}{\text{Product 1 sales} + \text{Product 2 sales}} = \frac{250}{250 + 150} = \frac{250}{400} = \frac{5}{8}$$

Correct answer choice is **B**.

Category 58 – Practice Questions (answers on page 394)

Calculator Questions

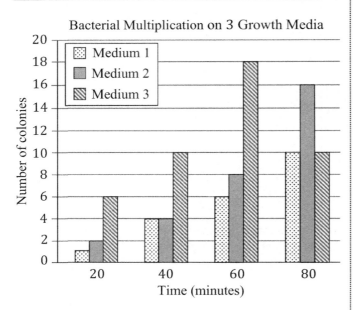

The graph above shows the bacterial multiplication on 3 different types of growth media: Medium 1, Medium 2, and Medium 3. The growth of a single colony of bacteria on each growth medium was observed every 20 minutes for 80 minutes. Based on the data represented in the graph, on which of the following media the bacterial colonies doubled every 20 minutes?

I.   Medium 1

II. Medium 2

III. Medium 3

A)   I only

B)   II only

C)   I and II only

D)   II and III only

Questions 2 and 3 refer to the following information.

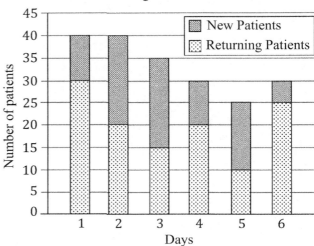

The above graph shows the daily number of returning and new patients at a certain medical center for 6 consecutive days.

2

Based on the data in the graph, how many new patients came to the medical center in 6 consecutive days?

A)   40

B)   65

C)   70

D)   80

3

On day 5, what percent of all patients were returning patients?

A)   24%

B)   35%

C)   40%

D)   60%

4

Study Hours

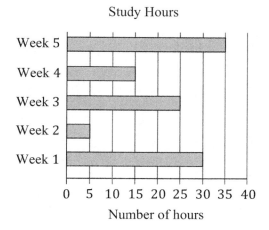

The above graph shows the number of hours Payton studied each week for 5 consecutive weeks. Based on the data in the graph, during which of the following period the number of hours changed the greatest?

A) From week 1 to week 2

B) From week 2 to week 3

C) From week 3 to week 4

D) From week 4 to week 5

5

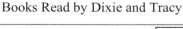

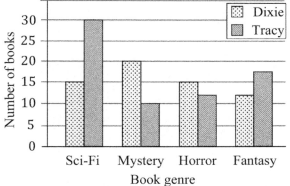

The above bar graph shows the number of books Dixie and Tracy read by genre during the last 6 months. For which book genre, Dixie read double the number of books than Tracy?

A) Sci-Fi

B) Mystery

C) Horror

D) Fantasy

Questions 6 and 7 refer to the following information.

Cafeteria Lunch Satisfaction

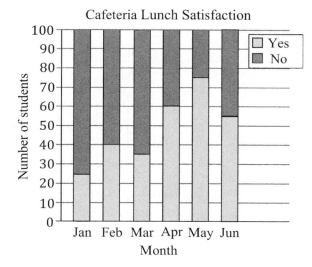

A high school surveyed 100 students each month, from January to June, to determine if the students were satisfied with the lunch offered at the school cafeteria. The above graph summarizes the responses of the 100 students for each month as "Yes" or "No".

6

Based on the above graph, during which of the following months was the difference between "Yes" and "No" the least?

A) February

B) March

C) April

D) June

7

Based on the graph, what percent of students responded "No" in May?

A) 25%

B) 45%

C) 50%

D) 75%

Category 59 – Histograms and Dot Plots

Key Points

- A histogram shows the distribution of data points in defined groups. Groups are generally represented on the horizontal axis and the number of data points (also known as frequency) on the vertical axis. The number of data points (or frequency) in each group is represented by a rectangular bar. The data distribution is continuous without any gaps between the bars (difference from bar graphs where data is grouped in categories and is not continuous).

  - A histogram bar may represent a single group. For example, if the horizontal axis is number of servings then the first bar is 1, the second bar is 2, the third bar is 3, and so on.

  - A histogram bar may represent a group in increments. For example, the first bar is 0-5, the second bar is 5-10, the third bar is 10-15, and so on. The lower number is on the left corner of the bar and the higher number is on the right corner of the bar.

- A dot plot is used to show the distribution of relatively small data sets. Data points are represented using dots. The horizontal axis represents the group and the number of dots on each group represent the number of data points in that group.

How to Solve

In a histogram, determine the frequency in each group by reading the height of a vertical bar or the length of a horizontal bar.

In a dot plot, count the number of dots in each group.

Example 1:

Daily Homework Time of 24 Students

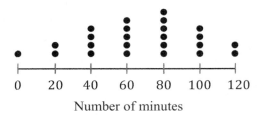

Number of minutes

The above dot plot shows the distribution of the number of minutes 24 students spend on daily homework. Based on the data in the dot plot, how many students spend 80 or more minutes on daily homework?

A) 7

B) 8

C) 12

D) 24

Step 1: Count the number of dots in each group

Each student is represented by a dot. The question asks for number of students who spend 80 or more minutes. Count the number of dots for 80, 100, and 120 minutes.

For 80 minutes, there are 6 dots = 6 students.

For 100 minutes, there are 4 dots = 4 students.

For 120 minutes, there are 2 dots = 2 students.

Step 2: Determine the total

$$6 + 4 + 2 = 12$$

Correct answer choice is **C**.

Example 2:

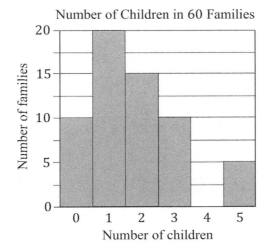

Number of Children in 60 Families

The above histogram shows the distribution of the number of children in 60 families.

<u>Question 1</u>

If a is the number of families with 3 or more children and b is the total number of families, what is $a:b$?

A) $1:4$

B) $1:3$

C) $2:3$

D) $3:4$

Step 1: Read the height of each bar

Determine the number of families with 3, 4, and 5 children and add them. The number of families is the height of the vertical bar and can be read from the vertical axis.

For the bar corresponding to 3 children, there are 10 families.

For the bar corresponding to 4 children, there are 0 families.

For the bar corresponding to 5 children, there are 5 families.

$$10 + 0 + 5 = 15$$

Step 2: Determine $a:b$:

$$a:b = \text{families with 3 or more children}:\text{total number of families} = 15:60 = 1:4$$

Correct answer choice is **A**.

<u>Question 2</u>

Based on the data in the histogram above, what is the total number of children in 60 families?

A)   80

B)   105

C)   115

D)   120

Step 1: Determine the total

The total number of children is the sum of children in all the 60 families. Multiply the number of children in each bar with the corresponding number of families (height of the vertical bar) and add the numbers.

$$(0 \times 10) + (1 \times 20) + (2 \times 15) + (3 \times 10) + (4 \times 0) + (5 \times 5) = 0 + 20 + 30 + 30 + 0 + 25 = 105$$

Correct answer choice is **B**.

Category 59 – Practice Questions (answers on page 394)

Calculator Questions

1

Dinner Per Week of 22 Families

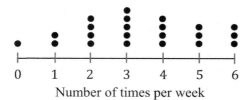

Number of times per week

The above dot plot shows the distribution of the number of times 22 families go out for dinner during a week. Based on the data in the data plot, how many families go out for dinner 3 to 4 times per week?

A) 9

B) 10

C) 15

D) 22

2

Calls Made by 20 Customers

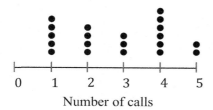

Number of calls

The above dot plot shows the distribution of the number of service calls made by 20 customers to a cable subscription company during a certain month. Based on the dot plot, which of the following is the total number of calls made by the 20 customers during that month?

A) 6

B) 20

C) 56

D) 90

Questions 3 and 4 refer to the following information.

Daily Servings of Vegetables for 70 People

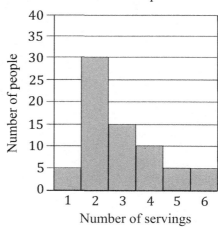

Number of servings

70 people at a nutrition center were asked how many servings of vegetables they eat per day. The histogram above summarizes the distribution of the number of servings for the 70 people.

3

According to the data in the histogram, what is the total number of daily vegetable servings 70 people ate?

A) 21

B) 70

C) 120

D) 205

4

Based on the distribution of the data in the histogram, what percent of people ate at least 3 daily servings of vegetables?

A) 30%

B) 50%

C) 75%

D) 90%

Questions 5 and 6 refer to the following information.

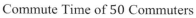

Commute Time of 50 Commuters

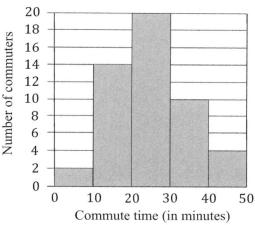

The histogram above summarizes the distribution of the commute time, in minutes, of 50 commuters from home to work. The first bar represents the commute time of less than 10 minutes, the second bar represents the commute time of at least 10 minutes but less than 20 minutes, and so on.

5

Which of the following is the number of commuters with a commute time of 20 minutes or greater but less than 40 minutes?

A)   10

B)   14

C)   30

D)   34

6

Based on the data in the histogram, what percent of total commuters had a commute time of 30 minutes or greater?

A)   20%

B)   28%

C)   50%

D)   68%

7

Height of 30 Adults

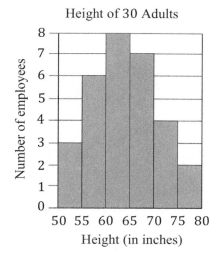

The histogram above shows the distribution of the height of 30 adults in increments of 5 inches. The first bar represents at least 50 inches but less than 55 inches, the second bar represents at least 55 inches but less than 60 inches, and so on. Based on the data in the histogram, which of the following is the number of adults who are 70 inches or greater, in height?

A)   6

B)   11

C)   17

D)   21

8

20 Students Enrolled in Clubs at School

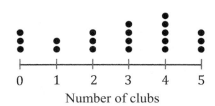

The above dot plot shows the distribution of the number of clubs 20 students are enrolled in at a certain middle school. Based on the data in the dot plot, the maximum number of students are enrolled in how many clubs?

A)   0

B)   3

C)   4

D)   5

Category 60 – Mean

Key Points

- The average is the sum of numbers in a data set divided by the total count of numbers in the data set. Mean is a method of describing the average. The terms are used interchangeably.

$$\text{mean} = \frac{\text{sum of numbers}}{\text{total count of numbers}}$$

How to Solve

When the mean of a set of numbers is given, the sum of the numbers can be determined as (mean × count of numbers). For example, if 7.5 is the mean of a set of 4 numbers, then the sum of the numbers is $4 \times 7.5 = 30$.

When grouped numbers are given, the sum of numbers in each group must be determined before calculating the mean. For example, if 7 students are 150 inches tall and 3 students are 165 inches tall, then the total height of $7 + 3 = 10$ students is $(7 \times 150) + (3 \times 165)$. Dividing this total by 10 will give the mean height of the 10 students.

Example 1:

A team scored 12, 10, 8, 6, and 9 points in 5 games.

Question 1

What is the mean score of the team in 5 games?

Step 1: Determine the mean

Total count of numbers = 5.

5 numbers are 12, 10, 8, 6, 9.

$$\frac{12 + 10 + 8 + 6 + 9}{5} = \frac{45}{5} = 9$$

Correct answer is **9**.

Question 2

If the team wants a mean score of 10 by the end of the 6th game, what should be the score of the 6th game?

Step 1: Set up the mean

Total count of numbers after 6th game = 6.

Let the score of 6th game = x.

The 6 numbers are 12, 10, 8, 6, 9, x.

Since the mean of the 6 numbers should be 10, set up the mean and equate it to 10.

$$\frac{12 + 10 + 8 + 6 + 9 + x}{6} = 10 \rightarrow \frac{45 + x}{6} = 10$$

Cross multiply.

$$45 + x = 10 \times 6 \rightarrow x = 60 - 45 = 15$$

Correct answer is **15**.

Example 2:

Weight (pounds)	Number of packets
1	10
2	4
3	4
5	2

The table above shows the number of almond packets Karina bought and their weight in pounds. What is the mean weight, in pounds, of all the almond packets Karina bought?

Step 1: Determine the sum of numbers

Total number of packets are $10 + 4 + 4 + 2 = 20$. Hence, the total count of numbers is 20.

The total weight of the 20 packages must be added up and then divided by 20.

The total weight of 10 packets that weigh 1 pound each is $10 \times 1 = 10$.

The total weight of 4 packets that weigh 2 pounds each is $4 \times 2 = 8$.

The total weight of 4 packets that weigh 3 pounds each is $4 \times 3 = 12$.

The total weight of 2 packets that weigh 5 pounds each is $2 \times 5 = 10$.

$$\text{total weight of 20 packets} = 10 + 8 + 12 + 10 = 40$$

Step 2: Determine the mean

$$\frac{40}{20} = 2$$

Correct answer is **2**.

Example 3:

The average weight, in pounds, of 12 students in class A is 115 pounds. The average weight, in pounds, of 18 students in class B is 110 pounds. What is the average weight of all the students in class A and class B?

Step 1: Determine the sum of numbers

Total number of students in both the classes are $12 + 18 = 30$. Hence, the total count of numbers is 30.

The total weight of the 30 students must be added up and then divided by 30.

The total weight of 12 students in class A is $12 \times 115 = 1,380$.

The total weight of 18 students in class B is $18 \times 110 = 1,980$.

$$\text{total weight of 30 students} = 1,380 + 1,980 = 3,360$$

Step 2: Determine the mean

$$\frac{3,360}{30} = 112$$

Correct answer is **112**.

Category 60 – Practice Questions (answers on page 395)

Calculator Questions

1

The average (arithmetic mean) score of Mr. Daniel's class of 40 students is a and the average score of Mr. Power's class of 20 students is b. In terms of a and b, which of the following represents the average score of all the students in both the classes?

A) $\frac{1}{6}(a+b)$

B) $\frac{1}{3}(2a+b)$

C) $40a + 20b$

D) $30ab$

2

$$50, 120, 230, 80, 220$$

If a number y is added to the above set of 5 numbers, the mean of the set becomes 134. What is number y?

3

Gianna took 4 biology tests and scored 85, 88, 87, and 92. Given that all the scores are integers out of 100 and all the tests are equally weighed, what is the minimum score Gianna will need on the fifth biology test for a mean score of at least 90 for the 5 biology tests?

4

The mean of two numbers is 32. If one of the numbers is three times the other number, what is the value of the lesser number?

5

In a set of 12 integers, two of the integers are 11 and 15. The mean of the 12 integers is 38. If 11 and 15 are removed from the set, what is the mean of the remaining 10 integers in the set?

6

Daisy took 7 tests in the first semester of school. The mean score of the 7 tests is 92. If the mean score of the first 5 tests is 96, what is the mean score of the last 2 tests?

7

Weight (pounds)	Number of dumbbells
5	6
10	10
20	4

Rita bought dumbbells of three different weights, in pounds. The table above shows the weight of the dumbbells, in pounds, and the number of dumbbells for each weight Rita bought. What is the mean weight of the dumbbells, in pounds?

8

In a data set of 11 integers, the mean of 3 integers is 210, the mean of 4 integers is 148, and the mean of the 4 remaining integers is 74. What is the mean of all the 11 integers in the data set?

Category 61 – Histograms, Dot Plots, and Mean

Key Points

- The mean of the data in a histogram or a dot plot is the sum of values in all the groups divided by the number of the data points.

How to Solve

For each bar in a histogram, multiply the height of the bar with the value of the group. Sum the numbers for all the bars and divide by the number of data points.

In a dot plot, count the number of dots in each group and multiply the count by the value of the group. Sum the numbers and divide by the number of data points.

Example 1:

The histogram above shows the distribution of the number of fruit servings 44 people ate in a week. What is the mean number of fruit servings per person?

Step 1: Determine the total

Multiply the height of each bar with the number of fruit servings for that bar. Add all the numbers.

The bar for 1 serving has 6 people. The total servings are $(1 \times 6) = 6$.

The bar for 2 servings has 10 people. The total servings are $(2 \times 10) = 20$.

The bar for 4 servings has 14 people. The total servings are $(4 \times 14) = 56$.

The bar for 5 servings has 12 people. The total servings are $(5 \times 12) = 60$.

The bar for 6 servings has 2 people. The total servings are $(6 \times 2) = 12$.

$$\text{total servings of all 50 people} = 6 + 20 + 56 + 60 + 12 = 154$$

Step 2: Determine the mean

Total servings = 154. Total people = 44.

$$\frac{154}{44} = 3.5$$

Correct answer is **3.5**.

Example 2:

Number of Rides for 14 Kids

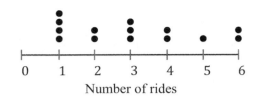

Number of rides

The dot plot above shows the number of rides 14 kids rode at a fair. What is the mean number of rides per kid?

A) 1

B) 3

C) 4

D) 7

Step 1: Determine the total

To determine the total number of rides for all the 14 kids, multiply the number of rides with the number of dots on it. Add all the numbers.

$$(1 \times 4) + (2 \times 2) + (3 \times 3) + (4 \times 2) + (5 \times 1) + (6 \times 2) =$$
$$4 + 4 + 9 + 8 + 5 + 12 = 42$$

Step 2: Determine the mean

Total rides = 42. Total kids = 14.

$$\frac{42}{14} = 3$$

Correct answer choice is **B**.

Category 61 – Practice Questions (answers on page 396)

Calculator Questions

1

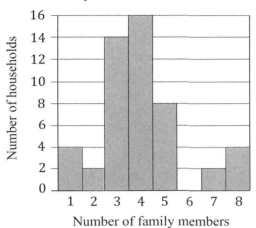

Family Members in 50 Households

The histogram above shows the distribution of the number of family members in a household for 50 households. Based on the data in the histogram, which of the following is the mean number of family members per household?

A) 1

B) 3

C) 4

D) 5

2

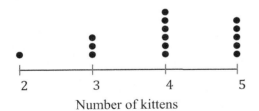

Kittens of 15 Cats

The dot plot above shows the distribution of the number of kittens born to 15 cats. Based on the data in the dot plot, which of the following is the mean number of kittens per cat?

A) 3

B) 4

C) 12

D) 30

3

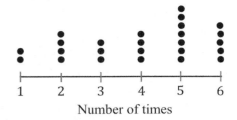

25 School Buses Late to School

The dot plot above shows the number of times 25 school buses were late to school last week. Based on the above dot plot, what is the average number of times a school bus was late to school last week?

4

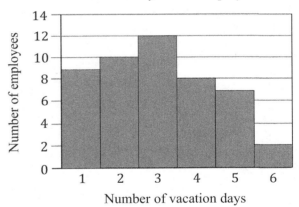

Vacation Days of 48 Employees

The histogram above shows the distribution of the number of vacation days taken by 48 employees at a certain company in January 2015. Based on the histogram, what is the mean number of vacation days per employee?

Category 62 – Median

Key Points

- In a data set of sorted numbers, the median is determined based on the count of numbers in the set.
  - If the data set contains an odd count of numbers, then the median is the middle number. For example, in a set of 5 numbers, the 3rd number is the middle number and the median.
  - If the data set contains an even count of numbers, then the median is the average of the two middle numbers. For example, in a set of 6 numbers, the 3rd and the 4th numbers are the middle numbers. The median is the average of the 3rd and the 4th numbers.
- In a grouped set of data, the group that includes the median number of the data set is the median group. For example, if there are 27 students in a data set, then the medium is in the group that includes the 14th student. The median can be any number in the median group.

How to Solve

Remember to sort the numbers in a data set, if not already sorted.

Example 1:

$$1, 12, 4, 18, 16, 14, 10, 25, 6, 20$$

What is the median of the above set of numbers?

Step 1: Sort the numbers from least to greatest

1, 4, 6, 10, 12, 14, 16, 18, 20, 25

Step 2: Determine the middle number

Since there are 10 numbers in the set, the median is the average of the two middle numbers (5th and 6th numbers).

$$\frac{12 + 14}{2} = \frac{26}{2} = 13$$

Correct answer is **13**.

Example 2:

Year	2012	2013	2014	2015	2016
Number of students	163	171	154	165	150

The table above shows the number of students enrolled in an elementary school from 2012 to 2016. Which of the following year contains the median number of students enrolled from 2012 to 2016?

A) 2012

B) 2014

C) 2015

D) 2016

Step 1: Sort the number of students from least to greatest

150, 154, 163, 165, 171

Step 2: Determine the middle number

Since there are 5 numbers in the data set, the median is the 3rd number = 163. The corresponding year is 2012. Correct answer choice is **A**.

Example 3:

The table below shows the score range of 21 students in a class, where each score is an integer.

Score range	Number of students
51 - 60	1
61 - 70	4
71 - 80	3
81 - 90	8
91 - 100	5

Question 1

The median score of the students in the class falls into which of the following score range?

A) 51 - 60

B) 61 - 70

C) 81 - 90

D) 91 - 100

Step 1: Determine the median

The questions on grouped data are generally sorted by the group from least to greatest.

The scores in the above table are grouped in increments of 10.

There are 21 students in the class. The median of 21 students from 1 to 21 is 11. Hence, the score range that contains the 11th student is the medium score range.

Starting from the top of the table, continue a cumulative count of the number of students till the 11th student is reached. See table below. 11th student is in the 81 - 90 score range.

Score range	Number of students	Cumulative count of students
51 - 60	1	1st student.
61 - 70	4	2nd, 3rd, 4th, and 5th student.
71 - 80	3	6th, 7th, and 8th student.
81 - 90	8	9th, 10th, **11th**, 12th, 13th, 14th, 15th, and 16th student.
91 - 100	5	17th, 18th, 19th, 20th, and 21st student.

Correct answer choice is **C**.

Question 2

Which of the following could be a median score of the class?

A) 69

B) 72

C) 80

D) 90

Continue from Step 1 of Question 1. Any score in the median score range can be the median. Hence, any score between 81 and 90 could be a median score.

This eliminates answer choices A, B, and C.

Correct answer choice is **D**.

Category 62 – Practice Questions (answers on page 396)

Calculator Questions

1

The table below shows the annual rainfall, in inches, in New York City from 2010 to 2014.

Year	2010	2011	2012	2013	2014
Rainfall (in inches)	49.37	72.81	38.51	46.32	53.79

The median annual rainfall, in inches, in New York City from 2010 to 2014 was in which of the following years?

A) 2010

B) 2011

C) 2012

D) 2014

2

In a small company of 27 total employees, 15 employees receive an annual salary between $40,000 - $60,000, 9 employees receive an annual salary between $61,000 - $75,000, and 3 employees receive an annual salary between $76,000 - $90,000. Which of the following could be a median salary of the 27 employees?

A) $30,000

B) $54,000

C) $68,000

D) $78,000

3

Set 1	12.5	10.1	5.2	17.5	15.3	14.5	13.5
Set 2	49.5	72.8	38.5	47.5	12.5	50.1	48.5

The table above shows two sets of numbers. If the median of Set 1 is A and the median of Set 2 is B, by how much does B exceed A?

A) 17

B) 20

C) 34

D) 35

4

$$y, 8, 15, 5, 11$$

In the above set of 5 integers, y is the median. Which of the following could be the values of y?

I.   8

II. 10

III. 12

A) I only

B) III only

C) I and II only

D) II and III only

5

Number of books	Number of students
1 - 3	11
4 - 6	16
7 - 9	3
10 - 12	18
13 - 15	1

The bookstore at a certain elementary school sells children books throughout the year. Last year, 49 students bought one or more books from the school bookstore. The above table shows the number of books, grouped in increments of 3, and the corresponding number of students. Which of the following could be a median number of books bought by the 49 students from the school bookstore, last year?

A) 4

B) 8

C) 11

D) 16

6

$$8.2, 29.0, 5.1, 24.3, 42.7, 25.7$$

What is the median of the above set of numbers?

Category 63 – Histograms, Dot Plots, Bar Graphs, and Median

Key Points

- In a histogram, the bar that includes the median data point of the data set is the median group. For example, if there are 51 data points, then the medium is in the bar that includes the 26th data point. The median can be any number in the median bar.

- In a dot plot, the median is in the group that includes the dot corresponding to the median data point.

- In a bar graph, the median is the middle number of the height of the bars, ordered least to greatest. For example, in a bar graph of 5 bars if the heights of the bars starting from left to right are 2, 8, 19, 5, 11, then the median is 8.

How to Solve

In a histogram, continue a cumulative count of data points from left to right (or right to left) till the bar that contains the median data point is reached.

In a dot plot, count the dots from left to right till the dot corresponding to the median data point is reached.

In a bar graph, determining the median is simpler since the data is not continuous. Read the height of each vertical bar or the width of each horizontal bar and order the numbers least to greatest. The middle number is the median.

Example 1:

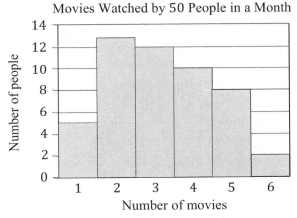

The histogram above shows the distribution of the number of movies 50 people watched in a certain month. Based on the histogram, what is the median number of movies watched by the 50 people in the month?

A) 1

B) 3

C) 6

D) 25

Step 1: Determine the median

Since there are 50 people, the bar that includes the 25th and 26th person contains the median number of movies. Starting from the left bar, continue a cumulative count of the number of people for each bar till the bar containing the 25th to 26th person is reached.

The bar for 1 movie has 5 people. This bar includes 1st to 5th person.

The bar for 2 movies has 13 people. This bar includes 6th to 18th person.

The bar for 3 movies has 12 people. This bar includes 19th to 30th person and, hence, the median data point.

The median number of movies is **3**.

Correct answer choice is **B**.

Note that if the question asked, "how many people watched the median number of movies in a month", then the answer would be 12 since the median bar has 12 people.

Example 2:

Number of Times 40 Adults Went to
Movie Theater in a Year

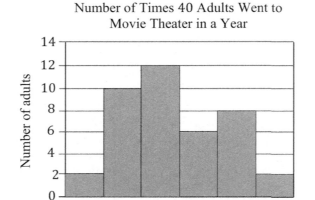

The above histogram shows the distribution of the number of times 40 adults went to a movie theater in a year. The first bar represents less than 5 times in a year, the second bar represents at least 5 times but less than 10 times in a year, and so on. What is one possible integer value of the median number of times 40 adults went to a movie theater in a year?

Step 1: Determine the median

Since there are 40 adults, the bar that includes the 20th and 21st adult contains the median number of times.

Each bar represents a group of numbers in increments of 5. The question mentions that the value of each bar is from the number at the left corner to any number till the right corner but excluding the number at the right corner. For example, the bar between 10 and 15 can be any number from 10 to less than 15.

Starting from the left bar, continue a cumulative count of the number of adults for each bar till the bar containing the 20th to 21st adult is reached.

The bar between 0 and 5 has 2 adults. This bar includes 1st to 2nd adult.

The bar between 5 and 10 has 10 adults. This bar includes 3rd to 12th adult.

The bar between 10 and 15 has 12 adults. This bar includes 13th to 24th adult and, hence, the median data point. The median can be any integer between 10 and 14.

Correct answer is **10, 11, 12, 13,** or **14**.

Example 3:

Number of Rides by 21 Kids

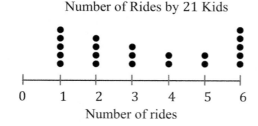

The dot plot above shows the number of rides 21 kids rode at a fair. What is the median number of rides?

Step 1: Determine the median

Since there are 21 kids, the group that includes the 11th dot (kid) is the median number of rides.

Count dots from left to right until the 11th dot is reached. 11th dot is on number of rides $= 3$.

Correct answer is **3**.

Category 63 – Practice Questions (answers on page 397)

Calculator Questions

1

Monthly Car Expense of 100 Households

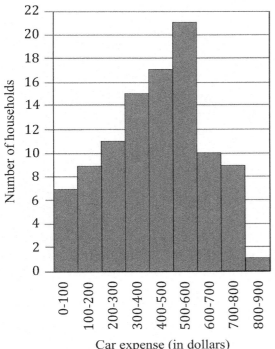

Car expense (in dollars)

The histogram above shows the distribution of the monthly car expense, in dollars, of 100 households. Based on the data in the histogram, which of the following statements are true about a median car expense, in dollars, of the 100 households?

I.   The median car expense of the 100 households is between 500 - 600 dollars per month.

II. One possible value of a median car expense of the 100 households is $445.

A)   I only

B)   II only

C)   I and II only

D)   Neither

2

Highway Speed Limit Preference of 85 Adults

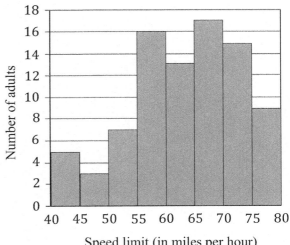

Speed limit (in miles per hour)

85 adults in a certain neighborhood were asked on their preference on the speed limit, in miles per hour, on a highway close to their home. The above graph shows the distribution of the response of the 85 adults. Speed limit was categorized in groups of 5 miles, from 40 miles per hour to 80 miles per hour. The first bar represents at least 40 miles per hour but less than 45 miles per hour, the second bar represents at least 45 miles per hour but less than 50 miles per hour, and so on. Based on the data in the graph, which of the following could be a median speed limit, in miles per hour, preferred by the 85 adults?

A)   50

B)   58

C)   62

D)   65

Weight of 15 Baby Dolphins

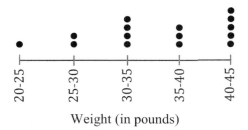

Weight (in pounds)

The above dot pot shows the weight, in pounds, of 15 baby dolphins. Which of the following could be a median weight, in pounds, of the 15 baby dolphins?

A) 30

B) 36

C) 41

D) 42

Number of College Degrees for 60 Employees

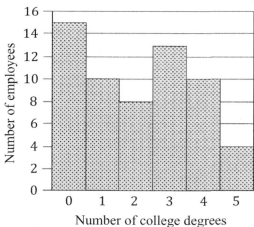

Number of college degrees

The above histogram shows the distribution of the number of college degrees held by 60 employees at a certain company. What is the median number of degrees held by the 60 employees at the company?

Student Scores on 21 Quizzes

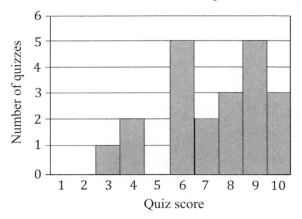

Quiz score

The histogram above shows the scores of 21 quizzes taken by students in Ms. Debbie's class. Based on the distribution of the data in the histogram, in how many quizzes taken by the students was the quiz score equal to the median quiz score?

Length of 49 Newborn Babies

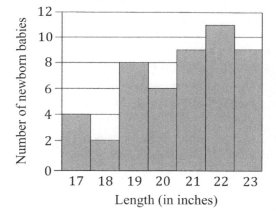

Length (in inches)

The graph above shows the distribution of the length, in inches, of 49 newborn babies. In what number of newborn babies was the length, in inches, equal to the median length, in inches, of the 49 newborn babies?

Category 64 – Box Plots and Median

Key Points

- A box plot (also known as box and whisker plot) distributes the numbers in a data set from least to greatest into 4 sections. Each section contains approximately 25% of the numbers. See figure below.

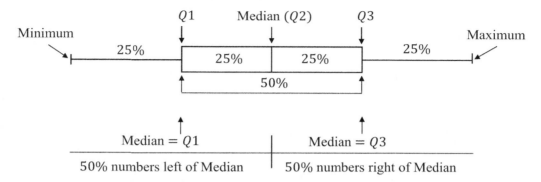

- The middle 50% of the numbers are represented in a box. The median is the middle number of the data set in the box and shown by a vertical line.

- The number at the left end of the box is known as the First Quartile ($Q1$). It is the median of the 50% of the numbers to the left of the median.

- The number at the right end of the box is known as the Third Quartile ($Q3$). It is the median of the 50% numbers to the right of the median.

- The minimum is the lowest number in a data set and the maximum is the highest number in a data set.

- The line between the minimum and $Q1$ and the line between the maximum and $Q3$ is known as the whiskers.

- The distance between the minimum and the maximum is the range of numbers in a data set.

- The box is larger when the middle 50% numbers are spread out farther from each other (see Fig. 1 below). The box is smaller when the middle 50% numbers are closer to each other (see Fig. 2 below).

| Fig. 1 | Fig. 2 |

How to Solve

Note that the actual data or the frequency of the data in a data set is not known from a box plot. The numbers that can be read from a boxplot are minimum, $Q1$, median, $Q2$, and maximum.

Since the actual numbers are not known, the mean of the data in a data set cannot be determined from a box plot.

Example 1:

Monthly Rainfall in New York City from 2018 to 2019

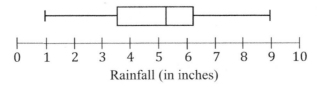

Rainfall (in inches)

The above box plot shows the monthly distribution of rainfall, in inches, in New York City from January 2018 to December 2019. Which of the following statements about the data shown in the box plot must be true?

A) The median of the data is 6.2.

B) There is more data between 1 and 4.

C) Approximately 50% of the data is between 3.5 and 6.2.

D) Approximately 50% of the data is between 1 and 9.

Step 1: Compare the answer choices with the data in the box plot

The box plot shows that the median is around 5.2. This eliminates answer choice A.

It is apparent that data is not more between 1 and 4. This eliminates answer choice B.

The box plot shows that the data in the box (about 50% data) is approximately between 3.5 and 6.2. This eliminates answer choice D.

Correct answer choice is **C.**

Example 2:

Rides	1	2	3	4	5	6	7	8	9	10
Number of adults	5	22	11	11	8	5	0	14	2	1

The table above shows the distribution of the number of rides 79 adults rode at an amusement park? Which of the following box plots is the closest representation of the data in the table?

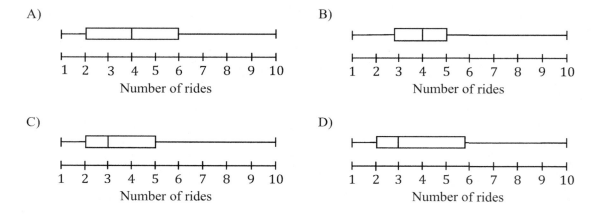

Step 1: Determine the median

Since there are 79 adults, the median is in the number of rides for the 40th adult. Staring from the left of the table continue a cumulative count of the number of adults till the 40th adult is reached. The 40th adult is in the number of rides = 4. Hence, median = 4. This eliminates answer choices C and D that have median = 3.

Step 2: Determine $Q1$

Since the answer choices with the correct median have different $Q1$ and $Q3$, one of these numbers must be determined for further elimination. Start with $Q1$.

Since there are 79 adults, each side of the median has half the data = 39. Hence, the 50% left-side of the median has 39 adults. The median = $Q1$ is in the number of rides for the 20th adult.

Starting from the left of the table continue a cumulative count of the number of adults till the 20th adult is reached. The 20th adult is in the number of rides = 2. Hence, median = $Q1 = 2$. This eliminates answer choice B that has $Q1 = 3$.

Correct answer choice is **A.**

Note that to determine $Q3$, the easiest approach is to continue a cumulative count of numbers from Right to Left till the median number is reached. In the above example, from right to left continue a cumulative count of the number of adults till the 20th adult is reached. This is in number of rides = 6.

Category 64 – Practice Questions (answers on page 397)

Calculator Questions

1

Head Mass of 32 Adult Giraffes

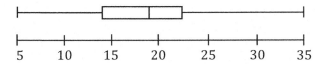

The above box plot summarizes the distribution of the head mass, in kg, of 32 adult giraffes. Based on the box plot, which of the following is the best estimate of the median head mass, in kg, of the 32 adult giraffes?

A) 8

B) 15

C) 19

D) 21

2

20 Survey Questions

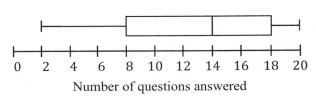

Number of questions answered

An independent research company sent out a survey containing 20 questions to 1,220 residents in a certain city. The above box plot shows the distribution of the number of questions answered by 582 residents who responded to the survey. Which of the following statements about the data shown in the above box plot must be true?

A) The median number of questions answered by the 582 residents are 8.

B) Approximately 50% of the 582 residents who responded to the survey answered between 8 and 18 questions.

C) Approximately 50% of the 582 residents who responded to the survey answered more than 8 questions.

D) The 582 residents who responded to the survey answered 18 questions.

3

Distribution of 300 Integers

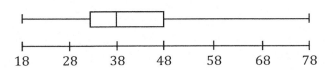

The above box plot shows the distribution of 300 integers between 18 and 78. Which of the following statements about the data shown in the box plot must be true?

A) The greatest number in the data is 48.

B) There is more data between 48 and 78.

C) 50% of the data is greater than 48.

D) The median is 38.

4

Number of Customers Per Day at 2 Bakeries

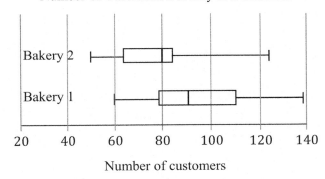

Number of customers

The above box plot summarizes the distribution of the number of customers at two separate bakeries, each day for a certain month. How does the median number of customers at Bakery 1, a, compare to the median number of the customers at Bakery 2, b?

A) $a = b$

B) $a > b$

C) $a < b$

D) There is not enough information to compare the medians.

Rating	1	2	3	4	5	6	7	8	9	10
Number of responses	9	50	27	41	23	10	9	9	11	3

A random survey of 192 commuters was conducted at a certain train station. The commuters were asked to rate the satisfaction of the train service at that station on a scale of 1 to 10. The above table shows the number of responses for each rating. Based on the data in the table, which of the following box plots could represent the distribution of the ratings of the 192 commuters?

A)

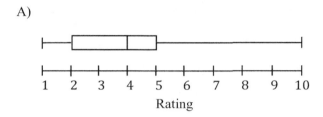

B)

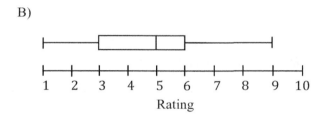

C)

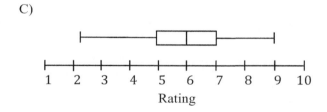

D)

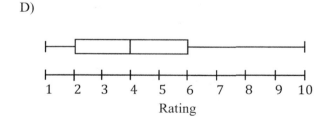

Monthly Salary of 950 Employees at a Company

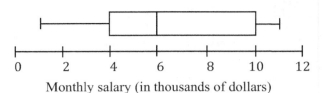

Monthly salary (in thousands of dollars)

The box plot above shows the spread of the monthly salary, in thousands of dollars, of 950 employees at a certain company. Which of the following statements about the distribution of the monthly salary of the 950 employees shown in the box plot is not true?

I.   The median monthly salary is approximately $6,000.

II. Approximately 50% of the monthly salaries are between $4,000 and $10,000.

III. The monthly salaries are greater than $4,000.

A) I only

B) II only

C) III only

D) I and II only

Grade Point Average of Senior Year Students

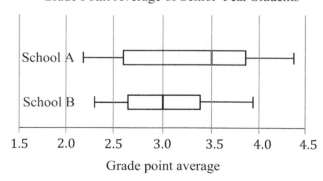

Grade point average

The above box plot summarizes the distribution of the grade point average of 184 senior year students at School A and of 168 senior year students at School B. By how much, does the median grade point average of senior year students at School A exceeds the median grade point average of senior year students at School B?

Category 65 – Mode

Key Points

- The mode is the number that occurs most often in a data set. If a data set does not contain repeated numbers, then there is no mode in the data set.

How to Solve

Remember to sort the numbers in a data set, if not already sorted.

Example 1:

$$1, 6, 4, 10, 16, 4, 10, 25, 4, 20$$

What is the mode in the above set of numbers?

Step 1: Sort the numbers least to greatest

1, 4, 4, 4, 6, 10, 10, 16, 20, 25

Step 2: Determine the most often occurring number

1, 16, 20, and 25 occur once.

10 occurs 2 times.

4 occurs 3 times.

Correct answer is **4**.

Category 65 – Practice Questions (answers on page 398)

Calculator Questions

1

Set 1	15.1	20.5	17.2	20.5	35.3	50.1
Set 2	35.3	72.8	15.1	47.5	20.5	50.1

The table above shows two sets of numbers. Which of the following is the mode of all the numbers in Set 1 and Set 2?

A) 15.1

B) 20.5

C) 35.3

D) 50.1

2

Year	Snowfall (feet)
2010	8.1
2011	21.2
2012	15.2
2013	9.5
2014	10.7
2015	9.4
2016	21.2
2017	9.3
2018	15.1
2019	21.1

The above table shows the average annual snowfall, in feet, for a certain city from 2010 to 2019. Based on the table, what is the mode of the data?

A) 9.3

B) 15.1

C) 21.1

D) 21.2

3

2, 4, 9, 7, 1, 9, 2, 7, 4, 5, 1, 2, 3, 7

Which of the following is the mode of the above data set?

I.   2

II. 7

III. 9

A) I only

B) III only

C) I and II only

D) None of the above

4

10.1, 10.2, 15.1, 15.3, 10.2, 10.6, 15.4, 15.3, 10.2

What is the mode in the above set of numbers?

Category 66 – Standard Deviation and Range

Key Points

- The standard deviation is the spread of numbers in a data set from the mean.
  - When the numbers in a set are closer to the mean, the standard deviation is low.
  - When the numbers in a set are farther from the mean, the standard deviation is high.
- The range is the difference between the lowest number and the highest number in a data set.

How to Solve

When comparing the standard deviation between two sets of data, the comparative spread of the numbers is usually evident by looking at the numbers in the data sets. Calculating the mean is not required.

Example 1:

Set A	40.1	60.8	52.5	82.5	11.2	90.8
Set B	52.3	55.8	32.7	65.9	62.4	45.6

Question 1

The table above shows two sets of data. Which of the following statements is true about the range of the two sets?

A)   The range of Set A is equal to the range of Set B.

B)   The range of Set A is greater than the range of Set B.

C)   The range of Set B is greater than the range of Set A.

D)   The range of Set A and Set B cannot be compared.

Step 1: Compare the range

Set A: The lowest number is 11.2 and the highest number is 90.8. The range is $90.8 - 11.2 = 79.6$.

Set B: The lowest number is 32.7 and the highest number is 65.9. The range is $65.9 - 32.7 = 33.2$.

The range of Set A is greater than the range of Set B.

Correct answer choice is **B.**

Question 2

The table above shows two sets of data. Which of the following statements is true about the standard deviation of the two sets?

A)   The standard deviation of Set A is equal to the standard deviation of Set B.

B)   The standard deviation of Set A is lower than the standard deviation of Set B.

C)   The standard deviation of Set A is greater than the standard deviation of Set B.

D)   The standard deviation of Set A and Set B cannot be compared.

Step 1: Compare the standard deviation

It can be seen from the data that the numbers in Set A are spread out farther than the numbers in Set B.

In Set A, the numbers are spread between 11.2 and 90.8.

In Set B, the numbers are spread between 32.7 and 65.9. This spread is lower than the spread in Set A.

Hence, Set A has a greater standard deviation than Set B.

Correct answer choice is **C.**

Category 66 – Practice Questions (answers on page 398)

Calculator Questions

1

Group A	915	810	816	825	790	744
Group B	495	546	490	369	100	101

The table above shows two groups of data. Which of the following statements is true about the range of the two groups?

A)   The range of Group A is equal to the range of Group B.

B)   The range of Group A is less than the range of Group B.

C)   The range of Group A is greater than the range of Group B.

D)   The range of Group A and Group B cannot be determined.

2

12, 18, 31, 20, 6, 10, 23, 16

If a number x is added to the above set of numbers and is given the value of 52, how will the standard deviation of the set change?

A)   The standard deviation of the set will be unchanged.

B)   The standard deviation of the set will be lower.

C)   The standard deviation of the set will be higher.

D)   The standard deviation of the set cannot be compared.

Questions 3 and 4 refer to the following information.

The table below shows the number of students enrolled in Lacrosse and Soccer teams at a certain high school, from 2010 to 2018.

	Number of students	
Year	Lacrosse	Soccer
2010	12	47
2011	55	52
2012	43	41
2013	4	55
2014	0	46
2015	4	58
2016	18	51
2017	9	48
2018	4	50

3

Based on the information given in the table above, which of the following statements is true about the standard deviation of the number of students enrolled in the two teams from 2010 to 2018?

A)   The standard deviation of the number of students enrolled in the Soccer team is less than the standard deviation of the number of students enrolled in the Lacrosse team.

B)   The standard deviation of the number of students enrolled in the Soccer team is higher than the standard deviation of the number of students enrolled in the Lacrosse team.

C)   The standard deviation of the number of students enrolled in the Soccer team is same as the standard deviation of the number of students enrolled in the Lacrosse team.

D)   The standard deviation shows that too many students were enrolled in the Soccer team.

4

If a is the range of the number of students enrolled in the Lacrosse team from 2010 to 2018 and b is the range of the number of students enrolled in the Soccer team from 2010 to 2018, what is $a - b$?

Category 67 – Comparing Mean, Median, Mode, SD, and Range

Key Points

- Adding a constant number to or subtracting a constant number from each number in a data set will change the mean, the median, and the mode. The range and the standard deviation will not change.

- Adding a number to or removing a number from a data set will change the mean. The other measures may or may not change depending on which number is removed.

- Multiplying or dividing each number in a data set by a constant number will change the mean, the median, the mode, the range, and the standard deviation by the same scale. For example, if each number in a data set is multiplied by 3, then each measure will triple.

How to Solve

Note: SD in the category heading is referring to standard deviation.

Evaluate each measure given in the answer choices.

Example 1:

Set A	5	18	24	26	35	40
Set B	23	23	24	25	26	27

The above table shows two groups of numbers. Which of the following is a true statement when comparing Set A and Set B?

A)   The means are same, and the medians are same.

B)   The means are same, and the standard deviations are same.

C)   The means are same, and the standard deviations are different.

D)   The medians are same, and the standard deviations are different.

Step 1: Evaluate each measure

Mean:

Mean of Set A is

$$\frac{5 + 18 + 24 + 26 + 35 + 40}{6} = \frac{148}{6} = 24.66$$

Mean of Set B is

$$\frac{23 + 23 + 24 + 25 + 26 + 27}{6} = \frac{148}{6} = 24.66$$

The means of the two data sets are same.

Median:

The median of Set A is the average of 24 and 26 = 25.

The median of Set B is the average of 24 and 25 = 24.5.

The medians are different. This eliminates answer choices A and D.

Standard deviation: In Set A, the numbers are spread from 5 to 40. In Set B, the numbers are spread from 23 to 27. Hence, the numbers in Set A have a greater standard deviation. This eliminates answer choice B.

Correct answer choice is **C**.

Example 2:

$$38, 51, 12, 9, 38, 56, 78$$

Question 1

If 3 is subtracted from each number of the above data set, which of the following statements is true about the mean, the median, and the range of the modified set?

A)   The mean will increase by 3.

B)   The median will decrease by 3.

C)   The range will decrease by 3.

D)   All of them will remain unchanged.

Step 1: Evaluate each measure

The original data set ordered from least to greatest is 9, 12, 38, 38, 51, 56, 78.

After subtracting 3 from each number, the modified data set will be 6, 9, 35, 35, 48, 53, 75.

Mean: Subtracting each number by 3, will reduce the mean. This eliminates answer choices A and D.

Median: The middle number 38 will decrease by 3. Answer choice B is correct.

Note that the range will be unaffected since the least number and the greatest number will be reduced by 3, resulting in the same difference.

Correct answer choice is **B**.

Question 2

If 56 is removed from the above data set, which of the following measures will NOT change?

A)   The mean and the median.

B)   The mean and the range.

C)   The median and the range.

D)   All of them will change.

Step 1: Evaluate each measure

The original data set ordered from least to greatest is 9, 12, 38, 38, 51, 56, 78.

After removing 56, the modified data set will be 9, 12, 38, 38, 51, 78.

Mean: Removing 56 from the data set will change the mean. This eliminates answer choices A and B.

Median: In the original data set, the median = 38. After removing 56, the median remains the same.

Range: The range will be unaffected since the least number, or the greatest number is not being removed.

Hence, the median and the range will not change. This eliminates answer choice D.

Correct answer choice is **C**.

Category 67 – Practice Questions (answers on pages 398-399)

Calculator Questions

1

3, 95, 52, 204, 16, 152, 101

If 5 is added to each number of the above data set, which of the following measures will remain unchanged?

A) Mean

B) Median

C) Range

D) All of them will remain unchanged.

2

Day of week	Rainfall (inches)
Sunday	0.2
Monday	1.1
Tuesday	0
Wednesday	2.5
Thursday	0.2
Friday	4.8
Saturday	0

The table above shows a report produced by a meteorologist for the rainfall, in inches, in a certain city last week. The meteorologist realized that incorrect rainfall was reported for Friday. The correct rainfall was 0.8 inches. The mean, the median, the standard deviation, and the range were recalculated with the corrected rainfall measurements. Which of the following were unaffected after the correction?

A) Mean

B) Median

C) Range

D) Standard deviation

3

A biologist bought 21 plants of varying heights to study the effect of sunlight on the growth of plants. The shortest plant in the study is 14 inches tall. The biologist decides to buy another plant of height 4 inches to include in the study. If the mean, the median, the mode, and the range of the height of the plants are compared before and after including the 4 inch plant in the study, which of the following values must increase by 10?

A) Mean

B) Median

C) Mode

D) Range

4

Distribution of 200 Numbers

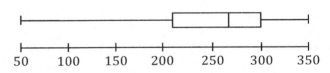

The above box plot shows the distribution of a set of 200 numbers between 50 and 350. If a new set of numbers is created by removing the numbers between 50 and 125, which of the following measurements must change when comparing the original set of numbers with the new set of numbers?

I. Median

II. Range

III. Standard deviation

A) I only

B) III only

C) II and III only

D) I, II, and III

Questions 5 and 6 refer to the following information.

The table below shows 2018 and 2019 bonus, in dollars, of 5 employees at a small company.

Employee name	2018 bonus (dollars)	2019 bonus (dollars)
Josie	7,500	8,500
Tammy	7,800	8,800
Kamal	6,500	9,100
Joe	8,100	12,500
Aniyah	18,000	9,000

5

If the 2020 bonus (not shown) of each employee in the above table is 10% greater than the 2019 bonus, which of the following is a true statement when comparing the 2019 bonus and the 2020 bonus, in dollars, of the 5 employees?

A) The means are same, and the medians are same.

B) The means are same, and the medians are different.

C) The means are different, and the medians are different.

D) The means and the medians cannot be compared.

6

If Aniyah's bonus is removed from the 2018 bonuses, and the mean and the median are recalculated, which of the following correctly represents the change in the mean and the median of the 2018 bonuses?

A) The mean and the median will change, and the mean will decrease less than the median.

B) The mean and the median will change, and the mean will decrease greater than the median.

C) The mean and the median will change equally.

D) The mean and the median will not change.

7

Group A	15	24	26	18	35	32
Group B	27	26	25	23	26	23

The above table shows two groups of numbers. Which of the following is true when comparing the mean, the median, and the range of Group A and Group B?

A) The means are same, the medians are same, and the ranges same.

B) The means are same, the medians are same, and the ranges are different.

C) The means are same, the medians are different, and the ranges are different.

D) The means are different, the medians are different, and the ranges are different.

8

Scores in 20 Games

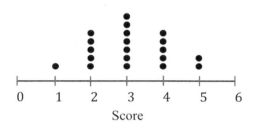

The above dot plots show the distribution of scores for 20 games played by a team. If in the next 5 games the score of the team is consistently 6, which of the following measures will change when the mean, the median, and the range of the scores is recalculated after these 5 games?

I.   Mean

II. Median

III. Range

A) I only

B) III only

C) I and II only

D) I and III only

Category 68 – Interpretation of Sample Data in Studies and Surveys

Key Points

- Studies and surveys are conducted using a random sample from the sample population.

  - For example, if a survey is to be conducted on the satisfaction of train service at a certain train station, then it is not practical to survey every single person coming in and out of that train station. A random sample of appropriate size will be surveyed such that the results reflect the true average of the sample population. This process is known as random sampling. In this example, the sample population is all the people coming in and out of that train station.

- If the sample is not random, or is small, or deviates from the sample population, then the study or the survey is flawed.

  - In the above example, if a survey is conducted on the first 50 people at the train station from 9 am to 11 am on Monday and Friday each week, then the sample is not random and is small. It will not represent the true average of the sample population. Similarly, if random people at a coffee shop outside the train station are also included in the survey, then the sample no longer represents the correct sample population.

- A margin of error is the variability by which the results obtained from a random sample are expected to differ from that of the sample population. It is the positive and the negative deviation from the results.

  - In the above example, if 62% of the people surveyed in a random sample were satisfied with a margin of error of 4%, then it is plausible that between $62\% - 4\% = 58\%$ and $62\% + 4\% = 66\%$ of the people at that train station will respond similarly.

  - Increasing the random sample size can reduce the margin of error.

- A confidence level is how often the results obtained from a random sample will deviate from another random sample from the same population for the same study or survey.

  - For example, 95% confidence level of a team conducting a survey indicates that the team is 95% confident that if the survey is repeated as many times, the same results will be obtained 95% of the time and will reflect the true average of the sample population.

- Generalization is applying the results obtained from a random sample to the sample population.

  - The largest population the results can be generalized to is the sample population. In the above example of the train station, the largest population the survey can be generalized to is all the people at that train station. It will be incorrect to generalize the results to people at any other train station.

- An association (or correlation) is the relationship between variables in a study. Note that association is different from cause-and-effect relationship where change in one variable directly causes the change in the other variable.

  - For example, a random sample of people with chronic headache is randomly divided into two groups. One group is asked to spend at least 4 hours in a park each week reading a book. The other group is asked not to make any change in the regular activities. After six months, both the groups are surveyed. The results show that the group who spend at least 4 hour in a park each week reading a book reported improvement in headache. This shows an association between improvement in headache and reading a book in the park but not necessarily a cause-and-effect relationship. (If the people with headache took pain medication specifically to reduce headache, then it is a cause-and-effect-relationship.)

  - To generalize the results of an association, the samples must be randomly divided into groups.

How to Solve

Note that the questions test the knowledge on the above concepts not the statistical calculations on margin of error, or confidence level, or sampling, or designing studies, or analyzing cause-and-effect relationships.

Use the process of elimination based on the above key points.

Example 1:

A hospital wants to conduct a survey to determine if the admitted patients are satisfied by the meal choices offered to them. Which of the following sampling method is most appropriate to estimate the satisfaction of the admitted patients on the meal choices offered at the hospital?

A) Selecting 300 random family members of the patients admitted at the hospital and surveying them.

B) Selecting 800 random patients from 10 hospitals in the city and surveying them.

C) Selecting 250 random patients admitted at the hospital and surveying them.

D) Selecting 350 patients admitted at the hospital every Monday and Tuesday mornings and surveying them.

Step 1: Process of elimination

The correct sample should be a random sample of patients admitted at the hospital. This is answer choice C.

Answer choices A and B are incorrect since the samples do not represent the correct sample population. Answer choice D is incorrect since the sample is not random.

Correct answer choice is **C**.

Example 2:

The board of education in a certain city interviewed a random sample of 800 residents from the most populated area of the city. Each randomly selected resident was asked whether they are in support of two new elementary schools in the city. Based on the results of these interviews, the board of education concluded that 70% residents of the city are in support of two new elementary schools in the city. Which of the following most accurately describes why the board of education's conclusion is flawed?

A) The survey should have been conducted on random residents with small children.

B) The residents surveyed did not represent a random sample of the residents in the city.

C) The residents surveyed did not include families that are planning on relocating to the city.

D) Letters should have been sent out to all the residents of the city before reaching a conclusion.

Step 1: Process of elimination

Limiting the sample to one area of the city does not represent a random sample of the residents in the city. The correct sample should be a random sample from all the residents in the city. Answer choice B correctly states that the sample did not represent a random sample of the residents in the city.

Answer choice A is incorrect since the sample is being restricted to residents with small children. Answer choice C does not represent the correct sample population. Answer D is not relevant to the question.

Correct answer choice is **B**.

Example 3:

250 employees at a company were selected at random and asked if they were in support of redesigning the office space. The results of the survey showed that 73% employees were in support of the redesign, with a margin of error of 4.5%. Which of the following is most appropriate interpretation of the survey results?

A) At least 73% of the employees were in support of the redesign of the office space.

B) At the most 73% of the employees were in support of the redesign of the office space.

C) It is plausible that between 73% and 77.5% employees were in support of the redesign of the office space.

D) It is plausible that between 68.5% and 77.5% employees were in support of the redesign of the office space.

Step 1: Process of elimination

The 4.5% margin of error indicates that likely between $73\% - 4.5\% = 68.5\%$ and $73\% + 4.5\% = 77.5\%$ employees at the company were in support of the redesign of the office space. This matches answer choice D.

Answer choices A and B are incorrect since they are limiting the results to at least or at the most 73% employees, respectively. Answer choice C is incorrect since it does not have the correct margin of error.

Correct answer choice is **D**.

Category 68 – Practice Questions (answers on page 399)

Calculator Questions

1

A school district wants to access if the teachers within all the district schools are satisfied with their salary. The school district has put together a scoring system that allows the teachers to score their salary satisfaction. The scoring system has a scale of 1 to 10, where 1 is the lowest satisfaction and 10 is the highest satisfaction. Which of the following sampling method is most appropriate to estimate the salary satisfaction of the teachers in all the district schools?

A)   Selecting one of the schools in the district at random and asking all the teachers in that school to score salary satisfaction.

B)   Selecting 25 teachers at random from each school in the district and asking them to score salary satisfaction.

C)   Selecting 50 teachers at random from the school that has the highest number of teachers and asking them to score salary satisfaction.

D)   Selecting 100 teachers who are available and asking them to score salary satisfaction.

2

The owners of a shopping mall surveyed a random sample of mall visitors on how many items they purchase during a single visit to the mall. Using the sample data, the owners estimated that 52% of the mall visitors purchased at least one item during a visit. The margin of error was 4.5%. Which of the following is most appropriate conclusion based on the survey and the margin of error?

A)   More than 52% of the mall visitors purchase at least one item on their visit to the mall.

B)   It is probable that at least 47.5%, but no more than 52% of the mall visitors purchase at least one item on their visit to the mall.

C)   It is probable that between 47.5% and 56.5% of the mall visitors purchase at least one item on their visit to the mall.

D)   Less than 52% of the mall visitors do not purchase anything on their visit to the mall.

3

A large auto dealership wanted to determine if the visitors to the dealership were satisfied with the number of cars on display in the showroom. The dealership conducted a survey on the first 50 visitors on four consecutive Saturdays. 74% of all the visitors who were surveyed responded that were satisfied with the number of cars on display in the showroom. The dealership concluded that the visitors to their dealership were satisfied with the number of cars on display in the showroom. Which of the following best describes why the auto dealership's conclusion is flawed?

A)   The visitors surveyed did not represent a random sample of the visitors coming to the auto dealership.

B)   Saturday is not a good day to conduct a survey.

C)   The auto dealership did not consult other auto dealerships in the area.

D)   At least 200 visitors to the auto dealership should have been surveyed each Saturday.

4

A wild life reasearch company conducted a study on a random sample of 85 male African elephants to determine the average size of their tusk. The company concluded that the average length of their tusk has 95% confidence level of 5.8 to 6.3 feet. Based on the confidence level, which of the following is the most appropriate conclusion?

A)   95% of all the elephants have tusk length between 5.8 to 6.3 feet.

B)   95% of all male African elephants have tusk length between 5.8 to 6.3 feet.

C)   It is probable that the true average length of the tusk of a male African elephant is between 5.8 to 6.3 feet.

D)   It is probable that the true average length of the tusk of an African elephant is between 5.8 to 6.3 feet.

A random sample of 140 students at a certain high school were asked how much time they spend on homework each day. Based on the responses, the estimated time was 80 minutes, with an associated margin of 15 minutes. Which of the following best summarizes the conclusions from the data?

A)   The students like to complete homework.

B)   The students who spend at least 95 minutes per day on homework do well at school.

C)   It is plausible that the students spend less than 95 minutes each day on homework.

D)   It is plausible that the students spend between 65 and 95 minutes each day on homework.

A scientist studied the effect of an organic fertilizer on 44 randomly selected miniature hybrid tea roses from a certain geographic region. The scientist concluded that the fertilizer promoted growth in 40 of the 44 miniature hybrid tea roses. What is the largest group the results of the scientist's experiment can be applied to?

A)   44 miniature hybrid tea roses the scientist studied.

B)   All roses in the geographic region.

C)   All miniature hybrid tea roses in the geographic region.

D)   All hybrid tea roses.

The home association in a certain community is planning on reducing the size of the recreation area to extend the playground. The association hires two independent teams, Team A and Team B, to conduct a survey and access the support of the residents on the plan. Both teams selected random samples from the same sample population of the residents and calculated the margin of error using the same method. Team A concluded that 55% residents are in support with a margin of error of 5.5%. Team B concluded that 49.5% residents are in support with a margin of error of 2.1%. Which of the following is the most appropriate reason for the smaller margin of error in the survey conducted by Team B when compared to the survey conducted by Team A?

A)   Team B selected a larger sample size.

B)   Team B selected a smaller sample size.

C)   Team B worked longer hours.

D)   Team B selected residents with small children.

A senior rehabilitation center offers daily yoga classes to all the seniors at the rehabilitation center. The seniors who took daily yoga classes were able to walk on a treadmill for 15 minutes without fatigue when compared with the seniors who did not take any yoga class. Based on the results which of the following is the most appropriate conclusion?

A)   Taking yoga classes does not help all the seniors.

B)   Taking yoga classes will help every senior at the rehabilitation center to walk longer on a treadmill without fatigue.

C)   The relationship between taking yoga classes and walking on treadmill for 15 minutes without fatigue is likely a cause-and-effect relationship.

D)   There is likely an association between taking yoga classes and walking on treadmill for 15 minutes without fatigue, but is not necessarily a cause-and-effect relationship.

A nutrition company conducted a study to test the effect of their new herbal pill on improving sleep in adults 50 years and older. 600 adults of ages 50 years and older with sleep problems were randomly selected and divided into two groups. One group consisted of adults from ages of 50 to 65 years. This group was asked to take the herbal pill with a full glass of warm water daily after dinner. The second group consisted of adults 65 years and older. This group was asked to drink a full glass of warm water daily after dinner. After 6 months, the adults in both the groups were asked about the improvement in sleep. Based on the responses, the company concluded that in adults 50 years and older there is likely an association between taking the herbal pill daily after dinner and improvement in sleep. Which of the following most appropriately describes why the nutrition company's conclusion is flawed?

A)   The two groups were not randomly selected.

B)   The sample size was small.

C)   Separate studies should have been conducted on men and women.

D)   Younger adults were not included in the study.

Calculator Questions

1

The mean of x and 11 is a and the mean of $3x$ and 5 is b. Which of the following is the mean of a and b in terms of x?

A) $x + 4$

B) $2x + 1$

C) $2x + 8$

D) $4x + 16$

2

The apple production at a certain orchard has decreased at a constant rate each year over an 8-year period. In the xy-plane, if the x-axis represents year and the y-axis represents apple production, which of the following scatter plots could represent the apple production over the 8 year period?

A)

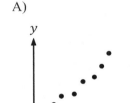

B)

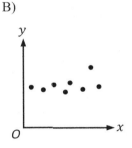

C)

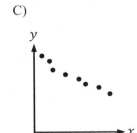

D)

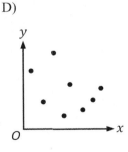

Questions 3 and 4 refer to the following information.

	Transportation mode			Total
Age group	Bus	Car	Train	
18 - 28 years old	124	28	48	200
29 - 40 years old	55	103	42	200
41 - 55 years old	20	89	91	200
56 - 70 years old	121	65	14	200
71 years and older	140	45	15	200
Total	460	330	210	1,000

An independent research company conducted a survey to determine the main transportation mode of residents in a metropolitan city. 1,000 residents from ages 18 years and up were randomly selected. The table above summarizes the results categorized by resident's age group and the main transportation mode.

3

Based on the information in the above table, which of the following is closest to the probability that if a resident from ages 18 to 40 years is selected at random the main transportation mode of the resident is "Bus"?

A)   0.12

B)   0.25

C)   0.39

D)   0.45

4

Based on the information in the above table, which of the following is closest to the probability that if a resident is selected at random who's main transportation mode is "Car" or "Train", the resident is 71 years and older?

A) $\dfrac{1}{9}$

B) $\dfrac{3}{10}$

C) $\dfrac{5}{39}$

D) $\dfrac{7}{50}$

Questions 5 and 6 refer to the following information.

In 2017, an advertising company sent out two different surveys, Survey 1 and Survey 2, to residents in a small town. Each survey was sent out to 500 residents and each resident received only one survey. 78 residents responded to Survey 1 and 104 residents responded to Survey 2. The table below summarizes the number of responses to each survey, categorized in 5 age groups of the residents. The age is a whole number determined by resident's age in 2017.

Age group	Number of responses	
	Survey 1	Survey 2
18 - 25 years old	8	16
26 - 40 years old	32	34
41 - 55 years old	18	24
56 - 64 years old	9	20
65 and older	11	10

5

If Survey 1 is x and Survey 2 is y, which of the following statements is true?

A) The median age group of the residents who responded to x and y is between age 26 - 40.

B) The median age group of the residents who responded to x is between age 18 - 25 and the median age group of the residents who responded to y is between age 26 - 40.

C) The median age group of the residents who responded to x is between age 26 - 40 and the median age group of the residents who responded to y is between age 41 - 55.

D) The median age group of the residents who responded to x is between age 41 - 55 and the median age group of the residents who responded to y is between age 26 - 40.

6

The ratio of the number of responses that correspond to the median age group in Survey 1 to the number of responses that correspond to median age group in Survey 2 is 4: a. What is the value of a?

7

A skating ring charges a flat fee of $25 per month inclusive of 20 free visits and $2 for each additional visit during a month. Which of the following graphs could represent the number of visits in terms of the monthly cost?

A)

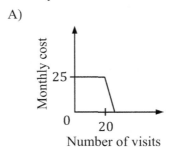

B)

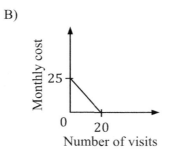

C)

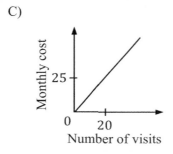

D)

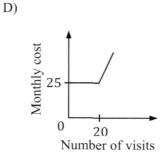

Questions 8 and 9 refer to the following information.

Commercial Time of 12 Companies

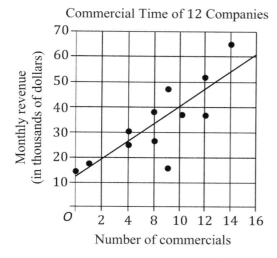

The above scatter plot shows the monthly revenue, in thousands of dollars, of 12 companies, based on the number of commercials each company plays per day on television. A line of best fit for the data is also shown.

Which of the following is the best interpretation of the y-intercept of the line of best fit?

A) The predicted monthly revenue, in thousands of dollars, when a company has unlimited number of commercials playing on television in a day.

B) The predicted monthly revenue, in thousands of dollars, when a company does not have commercials playing on television in a day.

C) The predicted monthly revenue, in thousands of dollars, when a company has 12 commercials playing on television in a day.

D) The predicted monthly revenue, in thousands of dollars, of 12 companies.

9

Which of the following could be an equation of the line of best fit?

A) $y = \frac{5}{2}x + 12$

B) $y = \frac{5}{2}x + 45$

C) $y = \frac{7}{2} + 8$

D) $y = 1.6x$

10

Chess Matches at a Middle School

		5th grade shirt color		
		Blue	Green	Total
6th grade shirt color	Blue	3	11	14
	Green	13	5	18
	Total	16	16	32

Chess matches were held between 5th grade students and 6th grade students at a middle school. The students participating in the competition were asked to wear either a blue or a green color shirt. Each match was played by one student from 5th grade and one student from 6th grade. A total of 32 matches were played. The table above shows the distribution of the 32 matches by the shirt color of the two students in a match. If a match is selected at random, which of the following is the probability that the two students in a match wore different color shirts?

A) 0.25

B) 0.40

C) 0.66

D) 0.75

11

If one number between 1 and 100 is selected at random, what is the probability that the number is a multiple of 11?

A) $\frac{9}{100}$

B) $\frac{11}{100}$

C) $\frac{11}{50}$

D) $\frac{9}{11}$

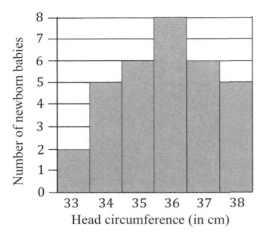

Head Circumference of 32 Newborn Babies

The histogram above summarizes the distribution of the head circumference, in cm, of 32 newborn babies. Which of the following could be the mean of the data shown in the histogram?

A) 34.7

B) 35.8

C) 36.5

D) 37.0

An environmental company wants to conduct a survey to determine the chemicals in the water of 6 lakes in the 200 mile vicinity of a manufacturing plant. Which of the following sampling method is most appropriate to provide most accurate results?

A) Selecting 210 random water samples from 1 of the lakes within the 200 mile vicinity of the manufacturing plant.

B) Selecting 100 random water samples from 2 of the lakes within the 200 mile vicinity of the manufacturing plant.

C) Selecting 50 random water samples from each of the 6 lakes within the 200 mile vicinity of the manufacturing plant.

D) Selecting 200 random water samples from 10 lakes around the country.

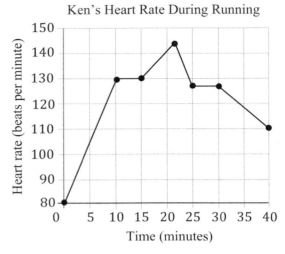

Ken's Heart Rate During Running

The above graph shows Ken's heart rate during a 40 minute run. Based on the graph, which of the following statements can NOT be true?

A) Ken's heart rate increased rapidly during the first 10 minutes of running.

B) Ken's heart rate was constant for 15 minutes during the 40 minute run.

C) Ken's heart rate stayed over 130 for approximately 9 minutes.

D) Ken's heart rate decreased constantly during the last 10 minutes of running.

Height of 20 Elephants

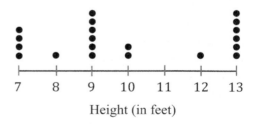

Height (in feet)

The dot plot above shows the height, in feet, of 20 elephants. Which of the following is true about the mean and the median of the data?

A) Mean = 9 and Median = 9

B) Mean = 9 and Median = 10

C) Mean = 10 and Median = 9

D) Mean = 10 and Median = 13

Number of New Employees Hired at 2 Companies
from January to June

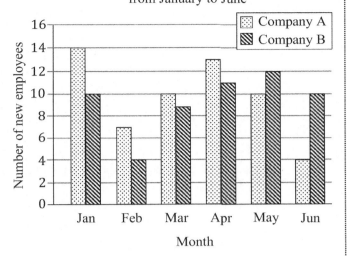

The above bar graph shows the number of new employees hired at two companies, Company A and Company B, from January to June last year. Based on the graph, which of the following statements is true about the median number of new employees hired at Company A and the median number of new employees hired at Company B from January to June last year?

A) The median number of new employees at Company A is same as the median number of new employees at Company B.

B) The median number of new employees at Company A is less than the median number of new employees at Company B.

C) The median number of new employees at Company A is greater than the median number of new employees at Company B.

D) The median number of new employees cannot be determined.

5, 10, 5, 3, 8, 11, 3, 121, 5, 23, 7, 10

What is the mode of the above set of numbers?

A) 3

B) 5

C) 10

D) 11

Number of Times 30 Adults
Exercise Per Month

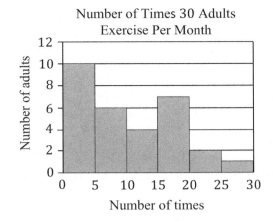

The histogram above summarizes the distribution of the number of times 30 adults exercise per month. The first bar represents less than 5 times per month, the second bar represents at least 5 times but less than 10 times per month, and so on. Which of the following could be the mean and the median of the above graph?

A) Mean = 7 and Median = 8

B) Mean = 9 and Median = 10

C) Mean = 9 and Median = 8

D) Mean = 12 and Median = 12

Distribution of 100 Numbers

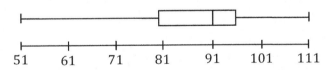

The above box plot shows the distribution of a set of 100 numbers from 51 to 111. If a new box plot is created by adding 127 numbers between 51 and 70 to the data set of the above box plot and the mean, the median, and the range are recalculated, which of the following will change?

A) The mean and the median.

B) The mean and the range.

C) The median and the range.

D) None of them will change.

Questions 20 and 21 refer to the following information.

Average Weekly Cost of Air Conditioning for 14 Households

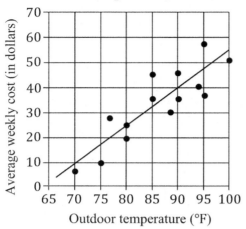

The above scatter plot shows the average weekly air conditioning cost, in dollars, for 14 households at varying outdoor temperatures, in °F. A line of best fit for the data is also shown.

20

For how many households the line of best fit predicts a value greater than the actual value?

A)   1

B)   5

C)   8

D)   9

21

According to the line of best fit, which of the following is closest to the predicted increase in the average weekly air conditioning cost, in dollars, for every 1°F increase in temperature?

A) $1.50

B) $4.10

C) $8.51

D) $10.24

22

A company of 1,550 employees offers complimentary coffee at the company cafeteria. The head of the sales department was interested in determining if the employees in her department liked the complimentary coffee. She selected 175 random employees from her department and asked them about their liking. Based on the responses she concluded that 44% of the 175 employees liked the coffee. What is the largest group to which the above conclusion can be generalized?

A)   175 employees at the company who were asked about their liking of the complimentary brand of coffee.

B)   44% of the employees at the company.

C)   All the employees at the company.

D)   All employees in the sales department at the company.

23

A restaurant manager wanted to determine if the customers have a happy customer service experience at the restaurant. On a Friday night, 80 customers were asked if they were happy with the customer service offered to them. 80% of the customers responded that they were happy. The restaurant manager concluded that the customers have a happy customer service experience at the restaurant. Which of the following best describes why the restaurant manager's conclusion is flawed?

A)   Only 80 customers were asked if they were happy with the customer service experience.

B)   Friday night is terribly busy and not a good time to ask customers on their experience.

C)   The customers surveyed did not represent a random sample of the customers coming to the restaurant.

D)   The happy customers did not get a free meal.

24

3, 121, x, y, z

In the above set of numbers, 3 is the minimum number and 121 is the maximum number. If the mean, the median, the mode, and the range were calculated for any integer values of x, y, and z, which of the following will NOT change?

A) Mean

B) Median

C) Mode

D) Range

25

The table below shows the distribution of junior and senior year students enrolled in physics and chemistry classes at a certain high school.

	Physics	Chemistry	Total
Junior	11	17	28
Senior	x	y	12

If one of the students is selected at random, the probability that the student is a senior enrolled in physics is $\frac{1}{5}$. What is the value of y?

26

The mean of 7 numbers in a data set is 92. If the lowest number is removed, the mean of the remaining 6 numbers is 94. What is the lowest number in the data set?

27

126, 90, 41, 135, 44, 87, 127, 139

What is the median of the above set of numbers?

Questions 28 and 29 refer to the following information.

A smart phone distributor makes weekly deliveries of smart phones to retail stores. The delivery of smart phones to two retail stores, Retail Store A and Retail Store B, during the first 10 weeks of 2017 is shown in the figures below. The distribution of the number of smart phones delivered weekly to Retail Store A is shown in the box plot below. The number of smart phones delivered weekly to Retail Store B is shown in the bar graph below, where each bar represents a week.

Delivery of Smart Phones to Retail Store A

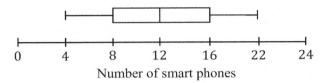

Number of smart phones

Delivery of Smart Phones to Retail Store B

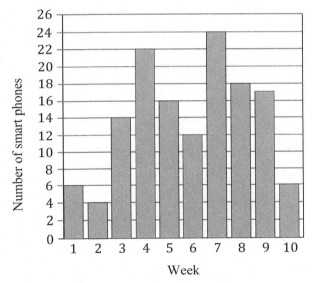

28

During the first 10 weeks of 2017, what is the maximum number of smart phones delivered to Retail Store A in a week?

29

If a is the median number of smart phones delivered to Retail Store A weekly, and b is the median number of smart phones delivered to Retail Store B weekly, by how much does b exceed a?

Section 13 – Geometry

Category 69 – Area and Angles of a Circle

Key Points

- A radius of a circle is a straight-line segment from the center of the circle to a point on the circle. In the figure below, AO and CO are two radii of a circle.

- A diameter of a circle is a straight-line segment from one point on the circle to another point on the circle and passes through the center of the circle.

- The length of the diameter is twice the length of the radius of a circle.

- A chord in a circle is a straight-line segment from one point on the circle to another point on the circle and does not pass through the center of the circle. See figure below for chords AB and BC. A perpendicular line from the center of the circle to a chord, divides the chord into two equal halves.

- An angle formed between two radii of a circle is known as a central angle. See angle AOC in figure below.

- An angle formed between two chords originating from the same point on a circle is known as an inscribed angle. See angle ABC in figure below. An inscribed angle is half the measure of its corresponding central angle.

- The measure of an angle may be given in π radians or degrees. One π radian is equal to $180°$.

  - An angle in π radians can be converted to degrees by multiplying with $\frac{180}{\pi}$.

  - An angle in degrees can be converted to π radians by multiplying with $\frac{\pi}{180}$.

- The area of a circle is πr^2, where r is the radius of the circle and π is approximately 3.14.

- The area enclosed between two radii is known as a sector. See figure below for a sector enclosed by AO and CO.

  - When the central angle is given in radians, the area of the sector can be determined as $\frac{1}{2}r^2\theta$, where r is the radius of the circle and θ is the central angle in π radians.

  - When the central angle is given in degrees, the area of the sector can be determined as $\frac{\theta}{360} \times \pi r^2$, where r is the radius of the circle and θ is the central angle in degrees.

  - The proportion relationship between the area of a sector and the area of the circle is

  $$\frac{\text{area of a sector}}{\text{area of the circle}} = \frac{\text{degree measure of central angle}}{360°}$$

- When a circle is divided into two equal halves, each half is known as a semicircle and the area of each semicircle is half the area of the circle.

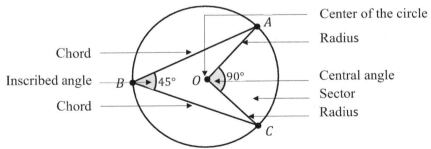

How to Solve

If the area of a circle is given, then the radius can be determined by equating it to πr^2. Note that the square root of r^2 will have two values: a positive value and a negative value. Since the radius is always positive, the negative value can be ignored. For example, if the area of a circle is 9π, then the radius can be determined as follows.

$$\pi r^2 = 9\pi \;\rightarrow\; r^2 = 9 \;\rightarrow\; r = \pm 3 \;\rightarrow\; r = 3$$

Note that a line segment name may be designated with an accent on the top of the name. For example, line segment AB can be written as $\overline{AB}$.

Example 1:

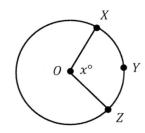

Note: Figure not drawn to scale.

Point O is the center of the circle shown above and the central angle x is $108°$.

Question 1

The area of the sector formed by angle x is what fraction of the area of the circle?

A) $\dfrac{1}{3}$

B) $\dfrac{2}{5}$

C) $\dfrac{3}{10}$

D) $\dfrac{5}{12}$

Step 1: Set up a proportion

Central angle $x = 108°$.

$$\frac{\text{area of a sector}}{\text{area of the circle}} = \frac{\text{degree measure of central angle}}{360°} = \frac{108°}{360°} = \frac{3}{10}$$

Correct answer choice is **C.**

Question 2

If the area of the circle is 25π, what is the area of the sector formed by the central angle x?

A) 5π

B) 7.5π

C) $\dfrac{\pi}{2.5}$

D) $\dfrac{2\pi}{3}$

Step 1: Set up a proportion

Central angle $x = 108°$.

Area of the circle $= 25\pi$.

$$\frac{\text{area of a sector}}{\text{area of the circle}} = \frac{\text{degree measure of central angle}}{360°} \rightarrow \frac{\text{area of a sector}}{25\pi} = \frac{108°}{360°}$$

$$\text{area of a sector} = \frac{108° \times 25\pi}{360°} = 7.5\pi$$

Correct answer choice is **B.**

Example 2:

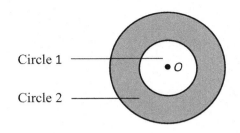

Note: Figure not drawn to scale.

The figure above shows 2 circles with center O. The radius of circle 1 is 1 inch. Circle 2 is outside of Circle 1 and has a radius of 2 inches. What is the area of the shaded region, in square inches?

A) π

B) 3π

C) $\dfrac{2\pi}{3}$

D) $\dfrac{3\pi}{2}$

Step 1: Determine the area of the circles

Circle 1 is smaller and covers a portion of the larger Circle 2. Both the circles have the same center O. The shaded area is the area of Circle 2 minus the area of Circle 1.

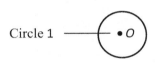 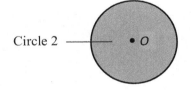 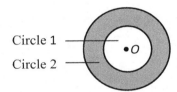

Area of Circle 1: $r = 1$.

$$\pi \times 1 \times 1 = \pi$$

Area of Circle 2: $r = 2$.

$$\pi \times 2 \times 2 = 4\pi$$

Step 2: Determine the area of the shaded region

$$4\pi - \pi = 3\pi$$

Correct answer choice is **B.**

Category 69 – Practice Questions (answers on page 403)

No Calculator Questions

1

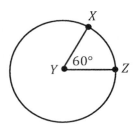

Note: Figure not drawn to scale.

Point Y is the center of the circle shown above. What is the measure of the angle XYZ, in radians?

A) $\dfrac{\pi}{3}$

B) $\dfrac{\pi}{2}$

C) π

D) 2π

2

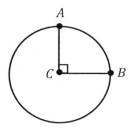

Note: Figure not drawn to scale.

The area of the above circle with center C is 12π. Which of the following is the area enclosed by the right angle ACB?

A) π

B) 3π

C) $\dfrac{\pi}{12}$

D) $\dfrac{\pi}{3}$

3

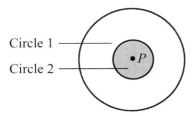

The above figure shows two circles, each drawn from the center P. Circle 2 is drawn within circle 1. Circle 1 has a radius of 5 centimeters and Circle 2 has a radius of 2 centimeters. Which of the following is the closest ratio of the area, in square centimeters, of Circle 1 to the area, in square centimeters, of Circle 2?

A) $2:3$

B) $2:5$

C) $2.5:5$

D) $6.3:1$

4

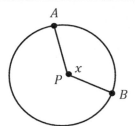

Note: Figure not drawn to scale.

Point P is the center of the circle shown above and the central angle x is $\dfrac{2\pi}{3}$ radians. The area of the sector formed by angle x is what fraction of the area of the circle?

A) $\dfrac{1}{2}$

B) $\dfrac{1}{3}$

C) $\dfrac{2}{5}$

D) $\dfrac{3}{8}$

Calculator Questions

5

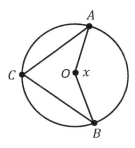

Note: Figure not drawn to scale.

As shown in the figure above, the chords AC and BC intersect the circle with center O at point C. If $x = 150°$, what is the measure of the inscribed angle ACB, in radians?

A) π

B) 5π

C) $\dfrac{\pi}{12}$

D) $\dfrac{5\pi}{12}$

6

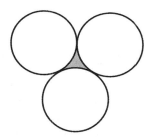

Note: Figure not drawn to scale.

The above figure shows 3 identical circles that are tangent to each other. The radius of each circle is 3 inches. The total area of the 3 circles and the shaded region is 88 square inches. Which of the following is closest to the area of the shaded region, in square inches, rounded to the nearest hundredth?

A) 0.64

B) 2.09

C) 3.22

D) 12.50

7

Which of the following is closest to the area of a circle with a diameter of 5, rounded to the nearest tenth?

A) 19.6

B) 22.5

C) 35.4

D) 78.5

8

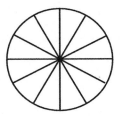

Note: Figure not drawn to scale.

The above figure shows a circle divided into 12 equal sectors. If the diameter of the circle is 12, what is the area of each sector?

A) π

B) 3π

C) 5π

D) 12π

9

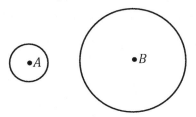

Note: Figure not drawn to scale.

The area of circle B is four times the area of circle A. If the area of circle A is 4π, what is the radius of circle B?

Category 70 – Circumference and Arc of a Circle

Key Points

- The circumference of a circle is $2\pi r$, where r is the radius of the circle and π is approximately 3.14.

- In degrees, the circumference of a full circle is $360°$.

- An arc is the portion of the circumference enclosed between the endpoints of two chords or radii on the circumference. In the figure below, arc ABC is enclosed between the endpoints of radii AO and CO and between the endpoints of chords AP and CP.

  - An arc less than a semicircle is known as a minor arc. An arc greater than a semicircle is known as a major arc.

  - The degree measure of an arc is equal to the degree measure of its central angle and twice the degree measure of its inscribed angle. See figure below.

  - When the central angle is given in radians, the length of the arc can be determined as $s = r\theta$, where s is the length of the arc, r is the radius of the circle, and θ is the central angle in π radians.

  - When the central angle is given in degrees, the length of the arc can be determined as $s = 2\pi r \times \dfrac{\theta}{360}$, where s is the length of the arc, r is the radius of the circle, and θ is the central angle in degrees.

- The proportion relationship between an arc length and the circumference is

$$\frac{\text{arc length}}{\text{circumference}} = \frac{\text{degree measure of central angle}}{360°}$$

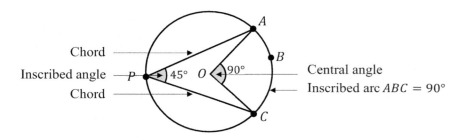

How to Solve

When the circumference of the circle is given and the central angle is in degrees, using the proportion relationship is the easiest method to determine the length of an arc.

Note that an arc name may be designated with an accent on the top of the name. For example, arc ABC can be written as $\overset{\frown}{ABC}$.

Example 1:

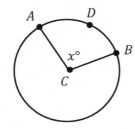

Segments AC and BC are the radii of the circle shown above. Arc ADB has a length of 3π and $\overline{AC} = 5$. What is the degree measure of x?

Step 1: Determine the central angle in degrees

$s = 3\pi$. $r = 5$.

$$s = \frac{\theta}{360} \times 2\pi r \rightarrow 3\pi = \frac{\theta}{360} \times 2\pi \times 5 \rightarrow 3 = \frac{10\theta}{360} \rightarrow 3 = \frac{\theta}{36} \rightarrow \theta = 108°$$

Correct answer is **108**.

Example 2:

The inscribed angle ACB in the figure above is $\frac{\pi}{6}$ radians. The circumference of the circle is 24 centimeters. What is the length of $\widehat{ADB}$, in centimeters?

A) 3

B) 4

C) 6

D) 10

Step 1: Determine the central angle in degrees

See figure on the right. The inscribed angle in degrees is

$$\frac{\pi}{6} \times \frac{180}{\pi} = 30°$$

The central angle in degrees is

$$30° \times 2 = 60°$$

Step 2: Determine the length of arc $\widehat{ADB}$

Circumference $= 24$.

Central angle $= 60°$.

$$\frac{\text{arc length}}{\text{circumference}} = \frac{\text{degree measure of central angle}}{360°} \rightarrow \frac{\text{Arc Length}}{24} = \frac{60°}{360°} \rightarrow$$

$$\text{Arc Length} = \frac{60° \times 24}{360°} = 4$$

Correct answer choice is **B**.

Category 70 – Practice Questions (answers on pages 403-404)

No Calculator Questions

1

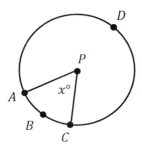

Note: Figure not drawn to scale.

In the circle shown above, P is the center, $x = 60$, and the arc $ABC = 3\pi$. What is the length of arc ADC?

A) 6π

B) 15π

C) $\dfrac{12\pi}{5}$

D) $\dfrac{15\pi}{6}$

2

A circle with radius 2 has a minor arc equal to $\dfrac{2\pi}{5}$ radians. The minor arc is what fraction of the circumference of the circle?

A) $\dfrac{1}{10}$

B) $\dfrac{2}{5}$

C) $\dfrac{1}{2}$

D) $\dfrac{3}{8}$

3

Sheela is learning to ride a bicycle. The radius of the circular wheels of the bicycle is 0.5 feet. She starts riding in a straight line and the wheels make 7 complete revolutions before she comes to a complete stop. What is the total distance Sheela traveled, in feet, rounded to the nearest whole number?

4

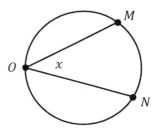

Note: Figure not drawn to scale.

In the figure above, the inscribed angle x is $\dfrac{\pi}{4}$ radians and the circumference of the circle is 32 inches. What is the length of the minor arc MN, in inches?

5

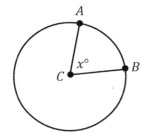

Note: Figure not drawn to scale.

The center of the above circle is C, the radius is 12, and $\widehat{AB}$ is 5π. What is the value of x?

6

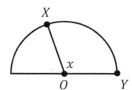

Note: Figure not drawn to scale.

In the above figure, segments OX and OY are the radii of the semicircle, angle x is $\dfrac{2\pi}{3}$ radians, and $\widehat{XY}$ is 2π. What is the length of $\overline{OX}$?

Category 71 – Equation of a Circle

Key Points

- The equation of a circle in the standard form is written as $(x - h)^2 + (y - k)^2 = r^2$.
  - r is the radius of the circle.
  - (h, k) are the coordinates of the center of the circle.
  - (x, y) are the coordinates of any point on the circumference of the circle.
- The equation of a circle in the general form is written as $x^2 + y^2 + Ax + By + C = 0$, where A, B, and C are constants. A and B are also known as coefficients of x and y, respectively.
  - The general form of the equation can be converted to the standard form by "completing the square" method.
- The center of the circle is the midpoint of the diameter. When two ends of a diameter are given, the center of the circle can be determined by the midpoint formula.
  - If (x_1, y_1) and (x_2, y_2) are the two end points of the diameter, then the x-coordinate of the center is $\frac{x_1 + x_2}{2}$ and the y-coordinate of the center is $\frac{y_1 + y_2}{2}$.
- If the distance of a point from the center of a circle is less than the radius, then the point is inside the circle. If the distance of a point from the center of a circle is greater than the radius, then the point is outside to the circle.

How to Solve

The center and the radius of a circle can be directly read from the standard form equation. For example, in the equation $(x + 1)^2 + (y - 3)^2 = 36$, the center is $(-1, 3)$ and the radius is $\sqrt{36} = 6$. Note that if the equation of the circle is $(x)^2 + (y - k)^2 = r^2$, then the x-coordinate of the center of the circle is 0. Similarly, in $(x - h)^2 + (y)^2 = r^2$, the y-coordinate of the center of the circle is 0.

The radius or the center of a circle cannot be determined from the general form equation. It must be converted to the standard form.

In the general form equation, if the coefficients of x^2 and y^2 are greater than 1, then divide the entire equation with the value of the coefficients before proceeding with "completing the square". Keep the value of C to the right-side of the equation. For example, in the equation $3x^2 - 12x + 3y^2 + 42y - 33 = 0$ move 33 to the right-side and divide the equation by 3. (Note that in a general form equation of a circle, the coefficients of x^2 and y^2 will always be same.)

Example 1:

The center of a circle in the xy-plane is $(0, 7.5)$ and the radius is 4. Which of the following is an equation of the circle?

A) $(x)^2 + (y - 7.5)^2 = 4$

B) $(x)^2 + (y - 7.5)^2 = 16$

C) $(x - 7.5)^2 + (y + 7.5)^2 = 4$

D) $(x - 7.5)^2 + (y + 7.5)^2 = 16$

Step 1: Determine the equation

Since the center is $(0, 7.5)$, the corresponding factors are $(x)^2$ and $(y - 7.5)^2$. This eliminates answer choices C and D.

Since $r = 4$, $r^2 = 16$. This eliminates answer choice A.

It is important not to confuse r and r^2. The right-side of the equation should always be considered as r^2.

Correct answer choice is **B**.

Example 2:

The points $(3, -2)$ and $(-5, 4)$ are the endpoints of a diameter of a circle in the xy-plane. Which of the following is an equation of the circle?

A) $(x - 1)^2 + (y + 1)^2 = 5$

B) $(x + 1)^2 + (y - 1)^2 = 5$

C) $(x + 1)^2 + (y - 1)^2 = 25$

D) $(x + 1)^2 + (y + 1)^2 = 25$

Step 1: Determine the coordinates of the center

Plug in the diameter endpoints in the midpoint formula.

$$x = \frac{-5 + 3}{2} = \frac{-2}{2} = -1$$

$$y = \frac{4 - 2}{2} = \frac{2}{2} = 1$$

Hence, the coordinates of the center are $(-1, 1)$. The corresponding the factors are $(x + 1)^2$ and $(y - 1)^2$. The equation can be written as $(x + 1)^2 + (y - 1)^2 = r^2$. This eliminates answer choices A and D.

Step 2: Determine the radius

Plug in any of the two given points in the above equation. Point $(3, -2)$ is plugged in below.

$$(3 + 1)^2 + (-2 - 1)^2 = r^2$$

$$r^2 = 4^2 + (-3)^2 = 16 + 9 = 25$$

Correct answer choice is **C.**

Example 3:

In the xy-plane, the graph of $3x^2 - 12x + 3y^2 + 42y - 33 = 0$ is a circle. What is the radius of the circle?

Step 1: Determine the factors for the complete squares of x and y

The quickest approach to determine the factors is to divide the coefficients of x and y by 2. It is important to remember that whatever number is obtained after diving by 2 becomes the factor (the signs do not get reversed).

Before proceeding, move 33 to the right-side and divide the entire equation by 3.

$$\frac{3x^2 - 12x + 3y^2 + 42y = 33}{3} \rightarrow x^2 - 4x + y^2 + 14y = 11$$

Factor for x: Coefficient of $x = -4$.

$$\frac{-4}{2} = -2$$

Hence, the complete square for x is $(x - 2)^2$.

Factor for y: Coefficient of $y = 14$.

$$\frac{14}{2} = 7$$

Hence, the complete square for y is $(y + 7)^2$.

Step 2: Complete the equation

Left side: Replace $x^2 - 4x + y^2 + 14y$ with $(x - 2)^2 + (y + 7)^2$.

Right side: Square both the factors obtained from Step 1 and add them to the right-side of the equation.

$$(x - 2)^2 + (y + 7)^2 = 11 + (-2)^2 + 7^2$$

$$(x - 2)^2 + (y + 7)^2 = 11 + 4 + 49$$

$$(x - 2)^2 + (y + 7)^2 = 64$$

Since $r^2 = 64$, $r = 8$.

Correct answer is **8.**

Category 71 – Practice Questions (answers on page 404)

No Calculator Questions

1

The center of a circle in the xy-plane is $(-7, 0)$ and the radius is 6. Which of the following is the equation of the circle?

A) $(x - 7)^2 + y^2 = 6$

B) $(x + 7)^2 + y^2 = 6$

C) $(x - 7)^2 + y^2 = 36$

D) $(x + 7)^2 + y^2 = 36$

2

In the xy-plane, points $(-1, -6)$ and $(1, -2)$ are the endpoints of a diameter of a circle. Which of the following represents the equation of the above circle?

A) $x^2 + (y + 4)^2 = 5$

B) $x^2 + (y + 4)^2 = 25$

C) $(x + 1)^2 + (y - 2)^2 = 5$

D) $(x + 4)^2 + (y + 2)^2 = 25$

3

In the xy-plane, point $(-2, -4)$ is the center of a circle. If the endpoint of a radius on the circle is $(0.5, -2)$, which of the following is the equation of the circle?

A) $(x - 2)^2 + (y - 4)^2 = 5.5$

B) $(x + 2)^2 + (y + 4)^2 = 5.5$

C) $(x - 2)^2 + (y - 4)^2 = 10.25$

D) $(x + 2)^2 + (y + 4)^2 = 10.25$

Calculator Questions

4

If the equation of a circle in the xy-plane is $(x - 2)^2 + (y + 3)^2 = 36$, which of the following points lie in the interior of the circle?

I. $(-2, 0)$

II. $(-5, 1)$

III. $(3, 3)$

A) I only

B) I and III only

C) II and III only

D) I, II, and III

5

$$2x^2 - 32x + 2y^2 + 12y - 16 = 0$$

The equation of the circle in the xy-plane is given above. What is the radius of the circle?

6

The graph of $x^2 - x + y^2 + 13y = -34$ in the xy-plane is a circle. What is the x-coordinate of the center of the circle?

Category 72 – Parallel and Intersecting Lines

Key Points

- At any point on a line, the sum of angles is 180°. For example, in Fig. 1 below, $\angle 1 + \angle 2 + \angle 3 = 180°$.

- Two angles that add up to 180° are known as supplementary angles.

- Two angles that add up to 90° are known as complimentary angles.

- Two intersecting lines form four angles. Each opposite pair are called vertical angles and are congruent. For example, in Fig. 2 below, lines c and p are intersecting lines. $\angle 1 = \angle 4$ and $\angle 2 = \angle 3$.

- When a straight line cuts across two parallel lines, several types of angles are formed. In Fig. 2, parallel lines c and d are intersected by line p. The types of angles and their position identified by numbers is shown in the figure.

  - Corresponding angles are congruent. $\angle 1 = \angle 5$, $\angle 2 = \angle 6$, $\angle 3 = \angle 7$, and $\angle 4 = \angle 8$.

  - Alternate interior angles are congruent. $\angle 4 = \angle 5$ and $\angle 3 = \angle 6$.

  - Alternate exterior angles are congruent. $\angle 1 = \angle 8$ and $\angle 2 = \angle 7$.

  - Same side interior angles are supplementary angles. $\angle 3 + \angle 5 = 180°$ and $\angle 4 + \angle 6 = 180°$.

  - Same side exterior angles are supplementary angles. $\angle 1 + \angle 7 = 180°$ and $\angle 2 + \angle 8 = 180°$.

- When two or more parallel lines are intersected by two or more non-parallel lines, the ratio of any two segments on one non-parallel line are equal to the ratio of the corresponding segments on the other non-parallel line. In Fig. 3 below, lines l, m, and n are parallel lines and lines p and q are non-parallel lines. $\frac{AC}{AE} = \frac{BD}{BF}$ and $\frac{CE}{AE} = \frac{DF}{BF}$.

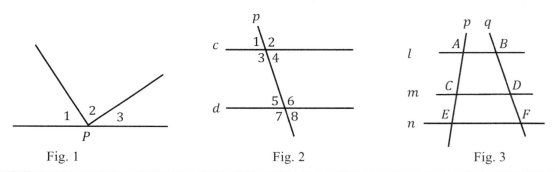

| Fig. 1 | Fig. 2 | Fig. 3 |

How to Solve

Remember the different types of angles and identify them appropriately in a question.

Example 1:

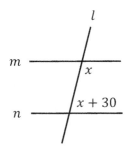

In the figure above, lines m and n are parallel lines. What is the value of x in degree measure?

Step 1: Identify the types of angles

Since lines m and n are parallel lines, angles x and $x + 30$ are the same side interior supplementary angles.

$$x + x + 30 = 180 \rightarrow 2x = 150 \rightarrow x = 75$$

Correct answer is **75**.

Example 2:

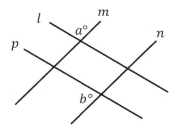

In the above figure, line l is parallel to line p and line m is parallel to line n. If a measures $80°$, what is the degree measure of b?

Step 1: Identify the types of angles

See figure below for explanation.

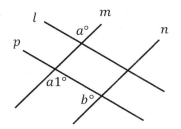

Since lines l and p are parallel lines, a and $a1$ are alternate exterior angles.

$$a = a1 = 80$$

Since lines m and n are parallel lines, $a1$ and b are same side interior supplementary angles.

$$a1 + b = 180 \rightarrow 80 + b = 180 \rightarrow b = 100$$

Correct answer is **100**.

Example 3:

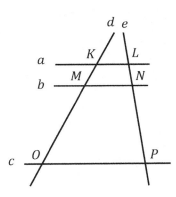

In the figure above, lines d and e intersect parallel lines a, b, and c. Points K and L are on line a, points M and N are on line b, and points O and P are on line c. If $KM = 3$, $KO = 16$, and $LN = 2.2$, what is the length of $\overline{LP}$, rounded to the nearest tenth?

Step 1: Set up segment proportion and solve

$KM = 3$. $KO = 16$. $LN = 2.2$.

The length of LP can be calculated by setting up the following proportion.

$$\frac{KO}{KM} = \frac{LP}{LN} \rightarrow \frac{16}{3} = \frac{LP}{2.2} \rightarrow$$

$$3 \times LP = 16 \times 2.2$$

$$LP = 11.73$$

Correct answer is **11.7**.

Category 72 – Practice Questions (answers on page 405)

No Calculator Questions

1

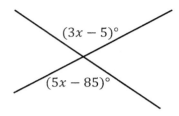

Note: Figure not drawn to scale.

The figure above shows two intersecting lines. What is the value of x?

A) 10

B) 30

C) 40

D) 75

2

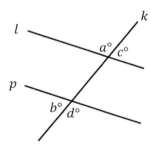

In the figure above, line k intersects parallel lines l and p. For angles a, b, c, and d, which of the following must be true?

I. $a + b = 180$

II. $a + c = 180$

III. $b + c = 180$

A) I only

B) I and II only

C) I and III only

D) I, II, and III

3

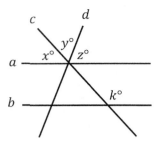

Note: Figure not drawn to scale.

In the figure above, lines c and d intersect parallel lines a and b. Lines c and d intersect line a at the same point. Which of the following must be true about angles k, x, y, and z?

A) $k = y + z$

B) $k = x + y$

C) $k = y - z$

D) $k = x - z$

4

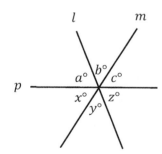

Note: Figure not drawn to scale.

Lines l, m, and p intersect at one point. If $a + b = 120°$, which of the following must be true?

I. $a + y = 120$

II. $b + z = 120$

III. $c + x = 120$

A) I and II only

B) I and III only

C) II and III only

D) I, II, and III

5

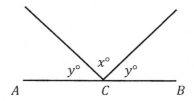

In the figure above, point C lies on $\overline{AB}$. If $38 < y < 42$, what is one possible integer value of x?

6

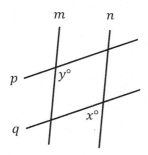

Note: Figure not drawn to scale.

In the figure above, lines m and n and lines p and q are parallel lines. If $y° = x° + 50°$, what is the degree measure of x?

7

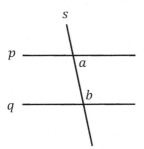

Note: Figure not drawn to scale.

Line s intersects two parallel lines p and q, as shown in the above figure. If $a° = 3x + 6$ and $b° = 4x - 1$, what is the value of x?

Calculator Questions

8

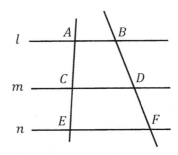

Note: Figure not drawn to scale.

In the above figure, l, m, and n are parallel lines. Points A and B are on line l, points C and D are on line m, and points E and F are on line n. If $AE = 8.1$, $BD = 4$, and $DF = 5$, which of the following ranges contain the length of $\overline{CE}$?

A) 4.2 to 4.4

B) 4.4 to 4.6

C) 4.6 to 4.8

D) 4.8 to 5.1

9

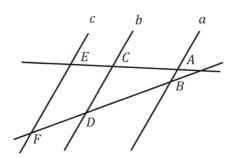

Note: Figure not drawn to scale.

In the above figure, a, b, and c are parallel lines. Points A and B are on line a, points C and D are on line b, and points E and F are on line c. If $AC = 10$, $CE = 6$, and $BD = 15$, what is length of $\overline{DF}$?

Category 73 – Polygons

Key Points

- A polygon is a geometric shape enclosed by straight line segments. In the Fig. 1 below, $ABCDEF$ is a 6 sided polygon.
- Each corner of a polygon is known as a vertex. Number of vertices is equal to the number of sides in a polygon.
- A polygon that has all the sides of equal length and all the angles of same measure is known as a regular polygon. For example, an equilateral triangle or a square.
- A polygon that does not have all the side lengths and the angles same is known as an irregular polygon.
- The perimeter of a polygon is the sum of the length of all sides.
  - For a regular polygon, the sum is the length of a side × the number of sides (since all the sides are of equal length).
- The sum of the degree measure of the interior angles of any polygon is $180(n - 2)$, where n is the number of sides. For example, in Fig. 2 below m, n, o, p, q, and r are the interior angles of a 6 sided polygon. The total degree measure of these angles is $180(6 - 2) = 720°$.
- The average degree measure of an interior angle of a polygon with n sides is $\frac{180(n-2)}{n}$. For example, in the figure below, the average degree measure of an interior angle is $\frac{720°}{6} = 120°$.
- The sum of the degree measure of the exterior angles of any polygon is always $360°$. In Fig. 2 below, a, b, c, d, e, and f are exterior angles (shown by extended lines) of a 6 sided polygon and their sum is $360°$.
  - The average degree measure of any exterior angle of a polygon with n sides is $\frac{360}{n}$.

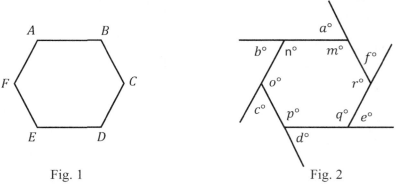

Fig. 1   Fig. 2

How to Solve

Remember that in a regular polygon, the average degree measure of the interior or the exterior angles is same as each individual angle. This is not true for an irregular polygon since each angle is not same.

Note that quadrilateral is a term used for polygons with 4 sides. For example, a rectangle, a trapezoid, a parallelogram. The sum of the interior angles of a quadrilateral is $360°$.

Example 1:

If the sum of the degree measure of interior angles of a regular polygon with n sides is $540°$, what is the value of n?

Step 1: Determine the number of sides

Sum of the degree measure of interior angles $= 540$. Hence,

$$180(n - 2) = 540 \rightarrow 180n - 360 = 540 \rightarrow 180n = 900 \rightarrow n = 5$$

Correct answer is **5**.

Example 2:

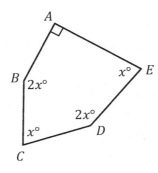

In the figure above, $ABCDE$ is a polygon with 5 sides. What is the value of $2x$?

A) 75

B) 90

C) 125

D) 150

Step 1: Determine the sum of interior angles

This is an example of an irregular polygon.

$n = 5$. Hence, the sum of the degree measure of all interior angles is

$$180(5-2) = 180 \times 3 = 540$$

Step 2: Determine the interior angles

Sum of angles $= 540°$.

$$\angle A + \angle B + \angle C + \angle D + \angle E = 90 + 2x + x + 2x + x = 540 \rightarrow$$
$$90 + 6x = 540 \rightarrow 6x = 450 \rightarrow 2x = 150$$

Correct answer choice is **D**.

Category 73 – Practice Questions (answers on page 406)

Calculator Questions

1

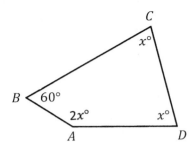

Note: Figure not drawn to scale.

In the figure above, ABCD is a quadrilateral. What is the value of x?

A)   60

B)   75

C)   120

D)   150

2

The average measure of each exterior angle of a regular polygon is 30°. What is the average degree measure of an interior angle of the polygon?

A)   30

B)   100

C)   150

D)   180

3

If a is the average degree measure of an exterior angle of a regular polygon with 10 sides, what is a?

4

The sum of the degree measure of the interior angles of a regular polygon with n sides is 900°. What is the value of n?

5

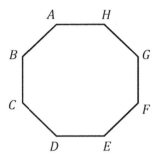

The regular polygon shown above has 8 sides. If the length of line segment $\overline{AB}$ is 5 inches, what is the perimeter of the polygon, in inches?

6

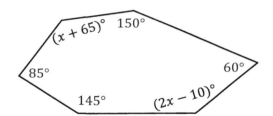

Note: Figure not drawn to scale.

In the polygon above, what is the value of x?

Category 74 – Angles, Sides, and Area of a Triangle

Key Points

- A triangle has three sides, three angles, and three vertices (corners).
    - The sum of the degree measure of the three angles is 180°.
    - The sum of the lengths of any two sides of a triangle is greater than the length of the third side. For example, if x, y, and z are the three sides of a triangle, then $x + y > z$, $x + z > y$, and $y + z > x$.
- An exterior angle is formed when any side of a triangle is extended. It is equal to the sum of the two non-adjacent angles. In Fig. 1 below, c is the exterior angle, and a and b are the two non-adjacent angles. $c° = a° + b°$.
- An equilateral triangle has all the three sides and all the three angles equal. Since the total of the three angles of a triangle is 180°, each angle of an equilateral triangle is 60°. A perpendicular line segment from any corner to the opposite side (also known as the perpendicular bisector) divides the equilateral triangle into two equal 30°-60°-90° triangles (Fig. 2 below).
- An isosceles triangle has two sides of equal length. The angles opposite to these sides are equal (Fig. 3 below).
- A right triangle has one of the angles as 90°, also known as the right angle. The other two angles are known as acute angles and their sum is 90° (Fig. 4, 5, and 6 below).
    - The side opposite to the right angle is known as the hypotenuse and is the longest side. The other two sides are known as the legs and meet at the 90° angle (Fig. 4 below).
    - In an isosceles right triangle, the measure of each acute angle is 45° (Fig. 5 below). It is also known as a 45°-45°-90° triangle.
    - The right triangles with degree measure of 45°-45°-90° and 30°-60°-90° have known side length relationship.
        - In Fig. 5 below, a are the sides opposite to 45° angles and $a\sqrt{2}$ is the side opposite to 90° angle. The ratio of the side lengths in relation to the opposite angles is $45°:45°:90° \rightarrow a:a:a\sqrt{2}$.
        - In Fig. 6 below, a is the side opposite to 30° angle, $a\sqrt{3}$ is the side opposite to 60°, and $2a$ is the side opposite to 90° angle. The ratio of the side lengths in relation to the opposite angles is $30°:60°:90° \rightarrow a:a\sqrt{3}:2a$.
    - If the lengths of any two sides of a right triangle are known, the length of the third side can be calculated using the Pythagorean Theorem. Pythagorean Theorem is written as $a^2 + b^2 = c^2$, where c is the hypotenuse and a and b are the two legs of the right triangle.
    - When the lengths of all three sides of a right triangle are integers, their lengths are collectively known as Pythagorean triples. Common Pythagorean triples are $3:4:5$, $5:12:13$, and $8:15:17$ or any of their multiples. The largest ratio corresponds to the hypotenuse and the smallest ratio corresponds to the smallest side.
- The area of any triangle can be determined as $\frac{1}{2}bh$, where b is the length of the base and h is the height.
- The area of an equilateral triangle can also be determined as $\frac{\sqrt{3}}{4}a^2$, where a is the length of each side.

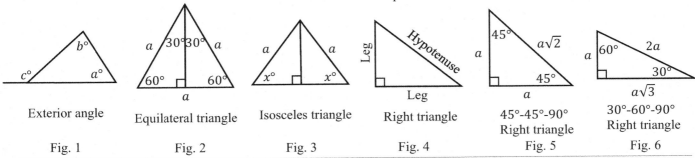

Exterior angle	Equilateral triangle	Isosceles triangle	Right triangle	45°-45°-90° Right triangle	30°-60°-90° Right triangle
Fig. 1	Fig. 2	Fig. 3	Fig. 4	Fig. 5	Fig. 6

How to Solve

In a right triangle, if a question gives the lengths of two sides as integers, check for Pythagorean triples before using the Pythagorean Theorem to determine the length of the third side.

Example 1:

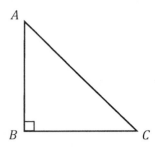

In the right triangle ABC shown above, $AB = BC$ and $AC = 6\sqrt{2}$. What is the area of the triangle ABC?

A) 12

B) 18

C) 25

D) 26

Step 1: Determine the base and the height

The base BC and the height AB are not given. Determine them as shown below.

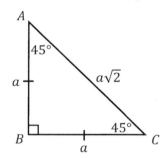

Since $AB = BC$ and angle $ABC = 90°$, triangle ABC is a right isosceles 45°-45°-90° triangle with side relationship seen in the left figure.

$$AB:BC:AC = a:a:a\sqrt{2}$$

It is given that $AC = 6\sqrt{2}$. Hence,

$$AC = 6\sqrt{2} = a\sqrt{2} \rightarrow a = 6$$
$$AB = BC = a = 6$$

Step 2: Determine the area

Base $= BC = 6$. Height $= AB = 6$.

$$\frac{1}{2}bh = \frac{1}{2} \times 6 \times 6 = 18$$

Correct answer choice is **B**.

Example 2:

The perimeter of an equilateral triangle XYZ is 24 inches. What is the area of the triangle XYZ, in square inches?

A) 8

B) 12

C) $8\sqrt{3}$

D) $16\sqrt{3}$

Step 1: Determine the length of the sides

Since the three sides of an equilateral triangle are same, divide the perimeter by 3 to get the length of each side.

$$\frac{24}{3} = 8$$

Step 2: Determine the area

$$\frac{\sqrt{3}}{4}a^2 = \frac{\sqrt{3}}{4} \times 8 \times 8 = 16\sqrt{3}$$

Correct answer choice is **D**.

Example 3:

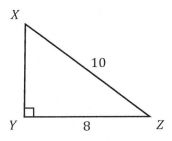

In the right triangle XYZ shown above, $YZ = 8$ and $XZ = 10$. What is the area of triangle XYZ?

Step 1: Determine the length of XY

The base of the triangle $YZ = 8$. The height XY is not given.

The ratio of the sides $YZ : XZ$ is $8 : 10 = 2(4 : 5)$. This is the ratio of the Pythagorean triple $2(3 : 4 : 5) = 6 : 8 : 10$ in a right triangle.

Since YZ and XZ correspond to the ratio components 8 and 10, respectively, the third side XY must correspond to the ratio component 6. Hence,

$$XY : YZ : XZ = XY : 8 : 10 = 6 : 8 : 10$$
$$XY = 6$$

Step 2: Determine the area

Base $= YZ = 8$. Height $= XY = 6$.

$$\frac{1}{2}bh = \frac{1}{2} \times 8 \times 6 = 24$$

Correct answer is **24**.

Example 4:

In a triangle DEF, if the lengths of $\overline{DE}$ and $\overline{EF}$ are 2 and 7, respectively, which of the following could be a possible length of the third side $\overline{DF}$?

A) 3

B) 4

C) 6

D) 9

Step 1: Compare the lengths of the sides

The sum of the lengths of two sides is greater than the third side. Drawing a figure may help visualize. See figure below.

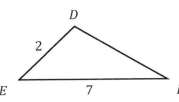

The three combinations for lengths are
$$2 + 7 > DF \;\rightarrow\; 9 > DF$$
$$2 + DF > 7 \;\rightarrow\; DF > 5$$
$$DF + 7 > 2 \;\rightarrow\; DF > -5$$

Since a line cannot have a negative length, $DF > -5$ can be ignored. The remaining two combinations are $9 > DF$ and $DF > 5$. This can be written as $9 > DF > 5$. Hence, DF can have three values: 6, 7, or 8.

Correct answer choice is **C**.

Category 74 – Practice Questions (answers on pages 406-407)

No Calculator Questions

1

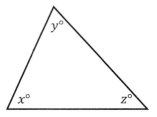

In the triangle above, which of the following expresses x in terms of y and z?

A) $x = \dfrac{y+z}{180}$

B) $x = \dfrac{y-z}{180}$

C) $x = 180 - y - z$

D) $x = 180 - y + z$

2

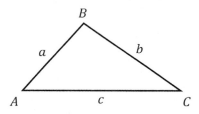

Note: Figure not drawn to scale.

In the triangle ABC above, if side $a = 2$ and side $b = 5$, which of the following are NOT true about all the possible lengths of side c?

I. $5 > c > 1$

II. $7 > c > 3$

III. $c = 8$

A) I and II only

B) I and III only

C) II and III only

D) I, II, and III

3

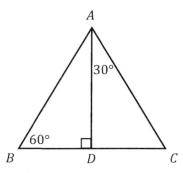

Note: Figure not drawn to scale.

In the figure above, $AD = 2\sqrt{3}$ bisects $\overline{BC}$ at point D. What is the length of $\overline{AC}$?

4

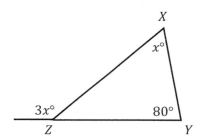

Note: Figure not drawn to scale.

In the figure above, what is the value of $3x$?

5

In a triangle with sides a, b, and c, $a = 3$ and $b = 7$. If $c > 7$, what can be one possible integer value of c?

6

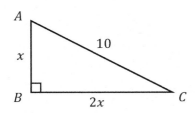

Note: Figure not drawn to scale.

Which of the following is the perimeter of the right triangle ABC shown above?

A) $2\sqrt{2} + 10$

B) $4\sqrt{5} + 4$

C) $6\sqrt{5} + 10$

D) 21

7

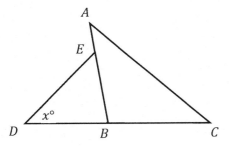

In the figure above, $AB = BC$, $BD = BE$, and angle $BAC = 40°$. Which of the following is the value of x?

A) 30

B) 40

C) 48

D) 50

8

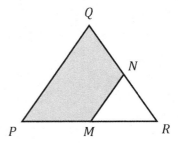

In the figure above, triangle PQR is an equilateral triangle with each side measuring 4 centimeters. If M is the midpoint of $\overline{PR}$ and N is the midpoint of $\overline{QR}$, and $MN = 2$ centimeters, what is the area of the shaded region in the figure, in square centimeters?

A) $2\sqrt{5}$

B) $3\sqrt{3}$

C) $4\sqrt{2}$

D) 4

9

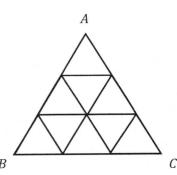

Keisha is creating designs for her art project. She puts together 9 small congruent equilateral triangles adjacent to each other to form one large equilateral triangle ABC shown in the above figure. If the area of each small congruent equilateral triangle is $\sqrt{3}$ square inches, which of the following is the perimeter, in inches, of the equilateral triangle ABC?

A) 6

B) 18

C) $18\sqrt{3}$

D) $27\sqrt{3}$

Triangle ABC is an isosceles triangle with $AB = AC$ and angle $B = 50°$. What is the value of angle A in radians?

A) $\dfrac{4\pi}{9}$

B) $\dfrac{\pi}{3}$

C) $\dfrac{3\pi}{2}$

D) 2π

The area of an equilateral triangle is $\sqrt{3}$ square inches. What is the perimeter of the triangle, in inches?

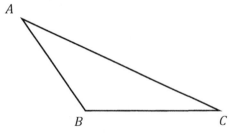

Note: Figure not drawn to scale.

An artist plans to present artwork on a wooden sculpture in the shape shown above. The base of the sculpture BC is 5 feet and sits on a flat surface. If the height of the sculpture is 4 feet from point A to the flat surface, how much area, in square feet, is available to the artist on the wooden sculpture?

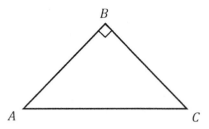

In the triangle ABC, $AB = BC$ and $AC = 4\sqrt{2}$. What is the length of $\overline{AB}$?

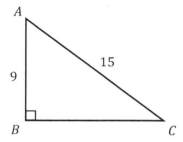

What is the area of the triangle ABC shown in the figure above?

Category 75 – Similar Triangles

Key Points

- In two similar triangles, the corresponding angles are congruent, and the corresponding sides are in proportion.

  - For example, if in two similar triangles ABC and DEF, the corresponding sides are AB and DE, BC and EF, and AC and DF, then $AB:DE = BC:EF = AC:DF$, $\angle A = \angle D$, $\angle B = \angle E$, and $\angle C = \angle F$.

- When a triangle is modified by proportionally shrinking or enlarging each side, the original and the modified triangles are similar triangles. The perimeter and the area of the modified triangle will change and all the three sides will proportionally decrease or increase in length. However, the corresponding angles and the side proportions of the corresponding sides in the original and the modified triangles will not change.

How to Solve

See below for similar triangle figures and how to identify them. It is important to identify the correct corresponding sides in similar triangles.

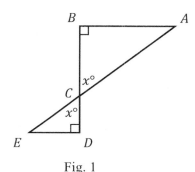

Fig. 1

Three angles are congruent

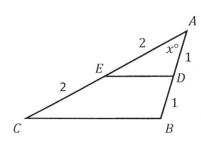

Fig. 2

Two sides are in proportion and share the same angle

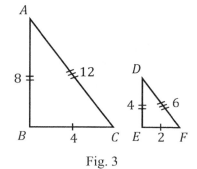

Fig. 3

Three sides are in proportion

- When all the three angles of two given triangles are congruent, then the two triangles are similar.

  In Fig. 1, ABC and EDC are right angle triangles. Angles x are congruent vertical angles and the right angles B and D are congruent. Since the sum of three angles of any triangle is 180°, the third angle (angle A in a triangle ABC and angle E in triangle EDC) must also be congruent. Hence, the two triangles are similar.

  The corresponding sides are between the corresponding angles. BC and CD are between angles $x°$ and 90°. Hence, they are corresponding sides. Similarly, AB and DE, and AC and CE are corresponding sides.

- When two given triangles have two sides in proportion and share an angle between these sides, then the two triangles are similar.

  In Fig. 2, ABC and ADE are two triangles. The ratios $AB:AD$ (2: 1) and $AC:AE$ (4: 2 = 2: 1) are same and the sides share the same angle x. Hence, the two triangles are similar.

  Since triangle ADE is within triangle ABC, the shared sides are the corresponding sides. Hence, AB and AD are corresponding sides and AC and AE are corresponding sides. The remaining sides BC and DE must be the third set of corresponding sides.

- When two given triangles have all three sides in proportion, then the two triangles are similar.

  In Fig. 3, the three sides of triangles ABC and DEF are in proportion. The ratios $AB:DE$ (8: 4 = 2: 1), $BC:EF$ (4: 2 = 2: 1), and $AC:DF$ (12: 6 = 2: 1) are same. Hence, the two triangles are similar.

  Note that in these types of similar triangles the question will give the corresponding vertices of the two triangles so the corresponding sides can be matched. For example, the question will mention that in triangles ABC and DEF, vertices A, B, and C correspond to vertices D, E, and F, respectively.

  The corresponding sides are between the corresponding vertices. Hence, the corresponding sides are AB and DE, BC and EF, and AC and DF.

Example 1:

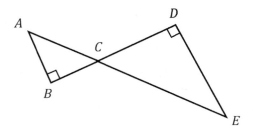

Note: Figure not drawn to scale.

In the figure above, ABC and EDC are right triangles. If $AB = 6$, $DE = 21$, and $CE = 35$, what is the length of segment AE?

Step 1: Identify similar triangles

It is given that both triangles have a right angle. Angles ACB and DCE are congruent vertical angles. Hence, triangles ABC and EDC are similar triangles with corresponding sides in proportion, $AB:DE = BC:CD = AC:CE$.

Step 2: Set up proportion for corresponding sides

$$AE = AC + CE = AC + 35$$

The length of AC can be determined by setting up the following proportion.

$$\frac{AB}{DE} = \frac{AC}{CE} \rightarrow \frac{6}{21} = \frac{AC}{35} \rightarrow$$

$$21 \times AC = 6 \times 35 \rightarrow 21 \times AC = 210 \rightarrow AC = 10$$

Determine AE:

$$AE = 10 + 35 = 45$$

Correct answer is **45**.

Example 2:

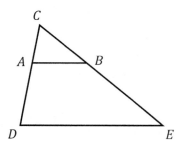

Note: Figure not drawn to scale.

In the figure above, $\overline{AB}$ is parallel to $\overline{DE}$. If $AB = 5$, $DE = 20$, and $CE = 32$, what is the length of segment BC?

Step 1: Identify similar triangles

Since AB is parallel to DE, angles CAB and CDE and angles CBA and CED are corresponding angles. Hence, triangles ABC and DEC are similar triangles with corresponding sides in proportion, $AB:DE = BC:CE = AC:CD$.

Step 2: Set up proportion for corresponding sides

Note that the ratio of the corresponding sides $AB:DE = 5:20 = 1:4$. Hence, the ratio of the corresponding sides $BC:CE$ will also be $1:4$. Since $CE = 32$, BC must be 8 for the ratio to be $1:4$. See below calculation using proportion.

$$\frac{AB}{DE} = \frac{BC}{CE} \rightarrow \frac{5}{20} = \frac{BC}{32} \rightarrow \frac{1}{4} = \frac{BC}{32} \rightarrow$$

$$4 \times BC = 32 \rightarrow BC = 8$$

Correct answer is **8**.

Category 75 – Practice Questions (answers on pages 407-408)

No Calculator Questions

1

A

B   C

E   F

D

$x°$

$x°$

Note: Figure not drawn to scale.

The figure above shows two similar right triangles. Which of the following is equal to the ratio of $\dfrac{BC}{DE}$?

A) $\dfrac{AC}{EF}$

B) $\dfrac{AC}{DF}$

C) $\dfrac{DE}{EF}$

D) $\dfrac{EF}{DE}$

2

Triangles ABC and DEF are congruent triangles where vertices A, B, and C correspond to vertices D, E, and F, respectively. If each side of the triangle ABC is four times the length of the corresponding side of the triangle DEF, which of the following statements is NOT true?

A) Angle C is congruent to angle F.

B) The sum of measure of all the angles of triangle ABC and the sum of measure of all the angles of triangle DEF is same.

C) The measure of angle B is four times the measure of angle E.

D) The length of $\overline{AB}$ is four times the length of $\overline{DE}$.

Calculator Questions

3

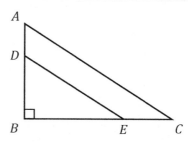

Note: Figure not drawn to scale.

In the figure above, $\overline{DE}\|\overline{AC}$, $AC = 9$, and the length of $\overline{BE}$ is double the length of $\overline{CE}$. What is the length of $\overline{DE}$?

4

A triangle XYZ is proportionally shrunk to form the triangle ABC. Each side of triangle ABC is half the length of the corresponding side of the triangle XYZ and vertices A, B, and C correspond to vertices X, Y, and Z, respectively. In triangle ABC, angle B measures $70°$ and angle C measures $32°$. If the difference in the degree measure of angle X and angle Z is a, what is the value of a?

5

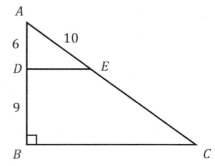

Note: Figure not drawn to scale.

In the figure above, $\overline{BC}$ and $\overline{DE}$ are parallel to each other. If $AD = 6$, $BD = 9$, and $AE = 10$, what is the length of line segment BC?

Category 76 – Squares and Cubes

Key Points

- A square has four equal edges and four 90° angles (Fig. 1). For a square of edge s, see the following formulas.
  - Perimeter $= 4s$.
  - Area $= s^2$.
  - Diagonal $= s\sqrt{2}$.

- A cube is a three-dimensional figure bounded by 6 square faces and 12 edges (Fig. 2). Each angle is 90°. For a cube of edge s, see the following formulas.
  - Surface area $= 6s^2$.
  - Surface area of each square face $= s^2$.
  - Volume $= s^3$.
  - Diagonal $= s\sqrt{3}$.

Fig. 1   Fig. 2

How to Solve

Apply the appropriate formula, depending on the question. Note that an edge is referred to a side.

Example 1:

The length of the diagonal of a square is $6\sqrt{2}$ centimeters. What is the area of the square, in square centimeters?

Step 1: Determine the length of edge

$$s\sqrt{2} = 6\sqrt{2} \ \rightarrow \ s = 6$$

Step 2: Determine the area

$$s^2 = 6 \times 6 = 36$$

Correct answer is **36.**

Example 2:

If the surface area of a cube is 54 square feet, which of the following is the volume of the cube, in cubic feet?

A) 6

B) 9

C) 27

D) 36

Step 1: Determine the length of edge

$$6s^2 = 54 \ \rightarrow \ s^2 = 9 \ \rightarrow \ s = 3$$

Step 2: Determine the volume

$$s^3 = 3^3 = 27$$

Correct answer choice is **C.**

Category 76 – Practice Questions (answers on page 408)

Calculator Questions

1

The surface area of a cube is 96 square feet. Which of the following is the volume of the cube, in cubic feet?

A) 12

B) 16

C) 32

D) 64

2

The volume of a cube, in cubic centimeters, of edge length 5 centimeters is how much greater than the volume of a cube, in cubic centimeters, of edge length 2 centimeters?

A) 27

B) 81

C) 117

D) 120

3

If the area of a square is $\dfrac{b^2}{4}$, where b is a positive constant, which of the following is the perimeter of the square in terms of b?

A) $2b$

B) b

C) $\dfrac{b}{2}$

D) $\dfrac{b}{4}$

4

The volume of a cube is 27 cubic millimeters. Which of the following is the surface area of the cube, in square millimeters?

A) 3

B) 12

C) 54

D) 60

5

The surface area of a cube is $6\left(\dfrac{1}{2}\right)^2$ square inches. What is the surface area of one face of the cube, in square inches?

6

If the diagonal of a cube is $5\sqrt{3}$ inches, what is the surface area of the cube, in square inches?

7

The volume of a cube is 64 cubic feet. The area of one face of the cube is how many square feet less than the surface area of the cube?

8

If the surface area of a cube is 150 square centimeters, what is the volume of the cube, in cubic centimeters?

Category 77 – Rectangles and Right Rectangular Prisms

Key Points

- A rectangle has four edges and four 90° angles (Fig. 1). The opposite facing edges of a rectangle are equal. For a rectangle with length l and width w, see the following formulas.
    - Perimeter $= 2(l + w)$.
    - Area $= lw$.
- In two similar two-dimensional figures, such as a rectangle, the ratio of their area is the square ratio of their corresponding linear sides.
- A right rectangular prism is a three-dimensional rectangle, such as a box (Fig. 2). Each angle is 90°. It has 6 rectangular faces and 12 edges. The opposite faces are equal. For a right rectangular prism with length l, width w, and height h, see the following formulas.
    - Surface area $= 2(lw + lh + wh)$.
    - Volume $= lwh$.
- In two similar three-dimensional figures, such as a right rectangular prism, the ratio of their volumes is the cube ratio of their corresponding linear sides.

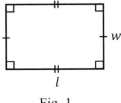

Fig. 1

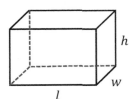

Fig. 2

How to Solve

Example 1:

Jasper dug a 7 feet by 5 feet by 1 foot rectangular flower bed in his garden. What is the surface area of the rectangular flower bed, in square feet?

Step 1: Determine the surface area

$l = 7$. $w = 5$. $h = 1$.

$$2(lw + lh + wh) = 2\big((7 \times 5) + (7 \times 1) + (5 \times 1)\big) = 2(35 + 7 + 5) = 2 \times 47 = 94$$

Correct answer is **94**.

Example 2:

The area of rectangle $ABCD$ is 16 square inches. The area of a similar rectangle $MNOP$ is 144 square inches. $\overline{MN}$ is 6 inches and corresponds to $\overline{AB}$. What is the length of $\overline{AB}$, in inches?

Step 1: Determine the square ratio of the areas

$$\text{area of } ABCD : \text{area of } MNOP = 16 : 144 = 1 : 9 = 1^2 : 3^2$$

Hence, the ratio of the corresponding sides (linear length) $= AB : MN = 1 : 3$ (Remember that the square of 1 is also 1).

Step 2: Set up a proportion

$$AB : MN = 1 : 3 = AB : 6 \quad \rightarrow \quad AB = 2$$

Correct answer is **2**.

(If a question gives the volume of two similar three-dimensional figures, then determine the cube ratio of the volumes.)

Category 77 – Practice Questions (answers on page 409)

No Calculator Questions

Calculator Questions

1

The dimensions of a right rectangular prism are 8 inches by 5 inches by 3 inches. Which of the following is the surface area of the prism, in square inches?

A) 63

B) 120

C) 158

D) 179

2

The area of a rectangular courtyard is 147 square meters. If the length of the courtyard is 3 times the width, how much shorter is the width of the courtyard than the length of the courtyard, in meters?

A) 14

B) 21

C) 37

D) 49

3

The length of a right rectangular prism is two times the height and the height is three times the width. Which of the following expresses the volume V in terms of the width w?

A) $V = 5w^2$

B) $V = 18w^3$

C) $V = 5w$

D) $V = 12w$

4

Naniya must paint the entire surface area of a right rectangular box for her art project. The length of the box is 7 inches, the width is 5 inches, and the height is 2 inches. What is the surface area Naniya must paint, in square inches?

A) 59

B) 118

C) 140

D) 145

5

Sam and Molly must summarize the findings of their school science project on a rectangular size charting paper. Molly selects a 12 inches by 16 inches sized paper. Sam selects a paper that is double in dimensions than the paper Molly selected. The area, in square inches, of the paper Molly selected is what percent of the area, in square inches, of the paper Sam selected?

A) 25%

B) 50%

C) 200%

D) 400%

6

The volume of a right rectangular prism is 1,000 cubic feet and the height is 4 feet. The volume of a similar right rectangular prism is 64 cubic feet and the height is h feet. What is the value of h?

Category 78 – Trapezoids and Parallelograms

Key Points

- A trapezoid is a quadrilateral with one pair of opposite sides parallel (Fig. 1).

  - The area of a trapezoid is $\frac{1}{2}(a+b)h$, where a and b are the two parallel bases and h is the height (the perpendicular distance between the two parallel sides) of the trapezoid.

- A parallelogram is a quadrilateral with opposite sides parallel and equal in length (Fig. 2).

  - The area of a parallelogram is bh, where b is the base and h is the height (the perpendicular distance between two parallel sides where one of the sides is the base) of the parallelogram.

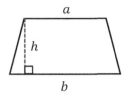

Fig. 1

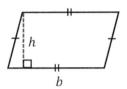

Fig. 2

How to Solve

When the height of a trapezoid or a parallelogram is not given, it can most likely be determined using the ratio of Pythagorean triples, or the side ratio of 30°-60°-90° triangle or 45°-45°-90° triangle.

Example 1:

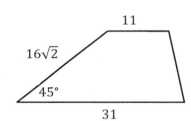

Note: Figure not drawn to scale.

What is the area of the trapezoid shown in the figure above?

Step 1: Determine the height of the trapezoid

The two bases are given but the height is unknown. See figure below to determine the height AC.

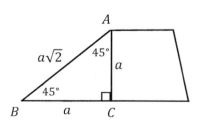

A perpendicular line from point A forms a right angle at point C. Since angle $ACB = 90°$ and angle $ABC = 45°$, angle BAC must be 45°. Hence, triangle ABC is a 45°-45°-90° triangle with side ratio as follows.

$$BC:AC:AB = a:a:a\sqrt{2}$$

It is given that $AB = 16\sqrt{2}$, Hence,

$$a\sqrt{2} = 16\sqrt{2} \quad \rightarrow \quad a = 16$$

$$\text{Height} = AC = a = 16$$

Step 2: Determine the area of the trapezoid

$$\frac{1}{2}(11+31)16 = 42 \times 8 = 336$$

Correct answer is **336**.

Category 78 – Practice Questions (answers on page 409)

Calculator Questions

1

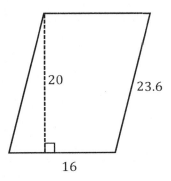

Note: Figure not drawn to scale.

The above figure shows the length of the sides and the height of a parallelogram, in inches. What is the area of the parallelogram, in square inches?

2

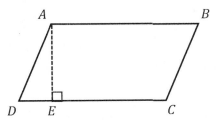

Note: Figure not drawn to scale.

In the above parallelogram, $AE = 24$ centimeters and $DE = 10$ centimeters. If the perimeter of the parallelogram is 162 centimeters, what is the length of $\overline{AB}$, in centimeters?

3

The area of a trapezoid is 110 square feet and the lengths of the two bases are 6.5 feet and 15.5 feet. What is the height, in feet, of the trapezoid?

4

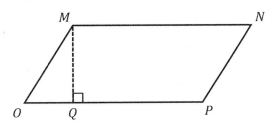

Note: Figure not drawn to scale.

In the above parallelogram, angle MOQ is 60°, the length of $\overline{MQ}$ is $3\sqrt{3}$ feet, and the length of $\overline{QP}$ is 9 feet. What is the length of $\overline{MN}$, in feet?

5

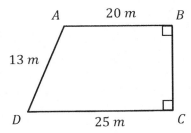

Note: Figure not drawn to scale.

A playground is designed in the form of a trapezoid, as shown in the figure above. What is the area of the playground, in square meters? (m = meters).

Category 79 – Volume of Cylinders, Spheres, Cones, Pyramids, Prisms

Key Points

- The volume of a right cylinder is $\pi r^2 h$, where r is the radius and h is the height of the cylinder (Fig. 1).
  - The volume can also be written as area of the circular base $(\pi r^2) \times h$.
- The volume of a sphere is $\frac{4}{3}\pi r^3$, where r is the radius of the sphere (Fig. 2).
- The volume of a right circular cone is $\frac{1}{3}\pi r^2 h$, where r is the radius and h is the height of the cone (Fig. 3).
  - The volume can also be written as $\frac{1}{3} \times$ area of the circular base $(\pi r^2) \times h$.
- The volume of a right pyramid with a rectangular base is $\frac{1}{3}lwh$, where l is the base length, w is the base width, and h is the height of the pyramid (Fig. 4).
  - The volume can also be written as $\frac{1}{3} \times$ area of the rectangular base $(lw) \times h$. If the base is a square, then l and w will be same.
- The volume of a right triangular prism is the area of the triangular base $\times\ l$, where l is the base length of the prism (Fig. 5).

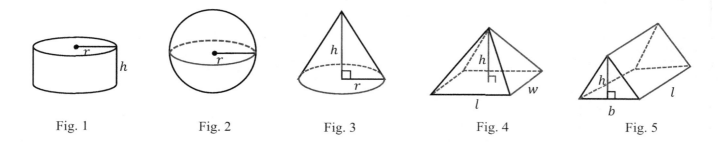

Fig. 1	Fig. 2	Fig. 3	Fig. 4	Fig. 5

How to Solve

Apply the appropriate formula, depending on the question.

In a right triangular prism, if the triangle is an isosceles right triangle, then use the 45°-45°-90° triangle side relationship to determine the base and height of the triangle. If the triangle is an equilateral triangle, then the area of the triangle can be directly determined using the area formula of an equilateral triangle.

Example 1:

The area of the base of a right circular cone is 9π square centimeters and the volume is 60π cubic centimeters. What is the height of the cone, in centimeters?

Step 1: Determine the height of the cone

Volume $= 60\pi$. Area of circular base $= \pi r^2 = 9\pi$.

$$\text{volume} = \frac{1}{3}\pi r^2 h \ \rightarrow\ 60\pi = \frac{1}{3} \times 9\pi \times h \ \rightarrow\ 60 = 3h \ \rightarrow\ h = 20$$

Correct answer is **20**.

Example 2:

The area of the base of a right cylindrical container is 14 square inches. If the height of the cylindrical container is 7 inches, what is the volume of the cylindrical container, in cubic inches?

A)   14

B)   21

C)   52

D)   98

Step 1: Determine the volume of the cylinder

$h = 7$.   Area of circular base $= \pi r^2 = 14$.

$$\pi r^2 h = 14 \times 7 = 98$$

Correct answer choice is **D**.

Example 3:

An art teacher is creating a pyramid with a rectangular base. If the teacher wants the volume of the pyramid to be 72 cubic inches and the dimensions of the base to be 3 inches in length and 6 inches in width, what should be the height of the pyramid?

Step 1: Determine the height of the rectangular pyramid

Volume $= 72$. $l = 3$. $w = 6$.

$$\text{volume} = \frac{1}{3}lwh \;\rightarrow\; 72 = \frac{1}{3} \times 3 \times 6 \times h \;\rightarrow\; 72 = 6h \;\rightarrow\; h = 12$$

Correct answer is **12**.

Example 4:

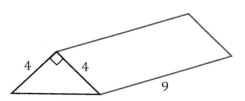

Note: Figure not drawn to scale.

What is the volume, in cubic units, of the right triangular prism shown above?

Step 1: Determine the area of the triangular base

See figure below for calculation of the base AC and height BD of the triangular base of the prism.

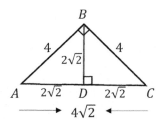

Determine AC: Since $AB = BC$ and angle $ABC = 90°$, triangle ABC is a right isosceles 45°-45°-90° triangle with side relationship seen in the left figure.

$$AB: BC: AC = a: a: a\sqrt{2} = 4: 4: 4\sqrt{2} \;\rightarrow\; AC = 4\sqrt{2}$$

Determine BD: The perpendicular bisector BD divides the triangle ABC into two equal 45°-45°-90° triangles. Hence, $AD = CD = \frac{1}{2} \times 4\sqrt{2} = 2\sqrt{2}$ and $BD = 2\sqrt{2}$.

Determine the area of triangle ABC:

$$\frac{1}{2} \times AC \times BD = \frac{1}{2} \times 4\sqrt{2} \times 2\sqrt{2} = 8$$

Step 2: Determine the volume of the prism

$$\text{area of triangular base} \times 9 = 8 \times 9 = 72$$

Correct answer is **72**.

Category 79 – Practice Questions (answers on page 410)

No Calculator Questions

Calculator Questions

1

A manufacturing company produces right cylindrical cones in several sizes. The company conducted research to determine the size of the cone in highest demand. The results showed that the cone with the height three times the size of the radius is in highest demand. Which of the following expresses the volume V in terms of the radius r of the cone that is highest in demand?

A) $V = \frac{1}{3}\pi r^3$

B) $V = \pi r^3$

C) $V = \pi r^2$

D) $V = 3\pi r^2$

2

A right circular cone has a volume of $\frac{1}{6}\pi$. If the radius of the cone is twice the height, which of the following is the height of the cone?

A) $\frac{1}{2}$

B) $\frac{2}{3}$

C) $\sqrt{4}$

D) $3\sqrt{4}$

3

An ice ball of radius 3 centimeters is dropped in a tank containing 108π cubic centimeters of water. Which of the following is the ratio of the volume of the water in the tank before the ice ball was dropped and after the ice ball was dropped and melted?

A) $1:3$

B) $2:3$

C) $3:4$

D) $3:5$

4

Isa is finalizing the dimensions of a cone for her school project. She wants the height of the cone to be 12 inches, the diameter to be between 7 to 10 inches, and the volume to be less than or equal to 64π cubic inches. Based on the above dimensions, which of the following can NOT be the radius of the cone, in inches?

A) 3.5

B) 3.7

C) 3.9

D) 4.1

5

Cory has two right cylindrical containers of different sizes. The volume of the smaller container is x cubic inches and the volume of the larger container is y cubic inches. If the radius and the height of the larger container, in inches, is twice that of the smaller container, what is $\frac{x}{y}$?

A) $\frac{1}{4}$

B) $\frac{1}{8}$

C) 2

D) 4

6

A circular cone of volume 6π cubic inches has a height of 2 inches. If the radius and the height of the circular cone are doubled to create a new circular cone, which of the following statements is true when the volume of the new cone is compared with the volume of the original cone?

A) The volume of the new cone increases 2 times.

B) The volume of the new cone increases 4 times.

C) The volume of the new cone increases 8 times.

D) The volume of the new cone decreases 4 times.

7

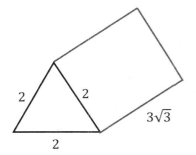

Note: Figure not drawn to scale.

The triangular base of the right triangular prism shown in above figure is an equilateral triangle. What is the volume, in cubic units, of the right triangular prism?

A) 9

B) 12

C) $8\sqrt{3}$

D) $24\sqrt{3}$

8

Suman bought an inflatable ball that has a diameter of 6 inches when fully inflated. How many cubic inches of air must be filled in the ball for it to fully inflate, rounded to the nearest whole number?

9

A right cylindrical bottle occupies 7 square centimeters of area when kept on a flat surface. If the height of the bottle is 6 centimeters, what is the volume of the bottle, in cubic centimeters?

10

Fred built a wooden sculpture in the shape of a right pyramid with a square base. The perimeter of the base is 12 inches and the volume of the pyramid is 42 cubic inches. What is the height, in centimeters, of the pyramid Fred built?

11

Jasmine has several right cylindrical containers with the height twice the length of the radius, in inches. If one such container has a volume of 54π cubic inches, what is the height of the container, in inches?

12

The volume of a right cylindrical cone is $27\pi h$ cubic inches, where h is the height of the cone in inches. What is the radius, in inches, of the cone?

13

If the volume of a sphere is $\frac{32}{3}\pi$ cubic feet, what is the diameter of the sphere, in feet?

14

The volume of a pyramid with a rectangular base is 32 cubic feet. If the height of the pyramid is 6 feet, what is the area of the rectangular base, in square feet?

Category 80 – Combined Geometric Figures

Key Points

- A geometric figure may be comprised of one or more geometric shapes. The geometric shapes may be adjacent to each other sharing a common side (for example, a semicircle and a rectangle with a common side, a triangle and a square with a common side, tangent circles, and so on) or may be contained within another (for example, triangle in a circle, square in a circle, rectangle in a square, rectangle in a semicircle, and so on).

- See few examples below that are good to remember.
    - A regular hexagon is comprised of six congruent equilateral triangles. Total area of a hexagon is the sum of the area of the six equilateral triangles (Fig. 1).
    - A rectangle is made up of two equal right triangles with a common diagonal (Fig. 2).
    - A triangle formed within a circle with two sides as radii is an isosceles triangle (Fig. 3).
    - A triangle formed within a circle with one side as the diameter of the circle and the other two sides as chords, has a right angle where the two chords meet (Fig. 4).
    - An angle formed by the radius of a circle and a line segment tangent to the circle is a right angle (Fig. 5).
    - Two line segments tangent to a circle form a quadrilateral as shown in Fig. 5.

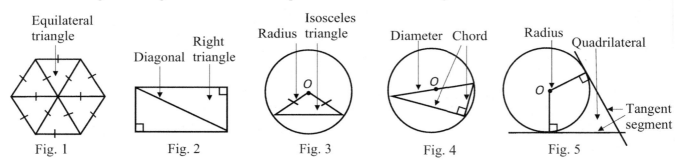

| Fig. 1 | Fig. 2 | Fig. 3 | Fig. 4 | Fig. 5 |

How to Solve

It is important to determine an approach before solving the questions on combined geometric shapes.

Example 1:

What is the perimeter of a regular hexagon with an area of $24\sqrt{3}$?

Step 1: Determine the approach

The area of each equilateral triangle of the hexagon is the total area of the hexagon divided by 6. Using the equilateral triangle area formula, the length of a side can be determined. The perimeter will be 6 × length of a side.

Step 2: Determine the length of each side of the equilateral triangle

$$\text{area of each equilateral triangle} = \frac{24\sqrt{3}}{6} = 4\sqrt{3}$$

Hence,

$$\frac{\sqrt{3}}{4}a^2 = 4\sqrt{3} \rightarrow a^2 = 4 \times 4 = 4^2 \rightarrow a = 4$$

Step 3: Determine the perimeter

$$6 \times 4 = 24$$

Correct answer is **24**.

Example 2:

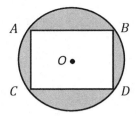

Note: Figure not drawn to scale.

In the figure above, point O is the center of the circle shown. Points A, B, C, and D lie on the circle and form the inscribed rectangle $ABCD$. The diagonals AD and BC (not shown) of the rectangle $ABCD$ pass through the point O and each measure 10 inches. If the width of the rectangle BD is 6 inches, what is the area of the shaded region, in square inches, rounded to the nearest tenth?

A)   12.2

B)   30.5

C)   48.0

D)   78.5

Step 1: Determine the approach

$$\text{area of the shaded region } = \text{area of the circle } - \text{area of the rectangle}$$

See figure below for the approach to determine the length of the rectangle and the radius of the circle.

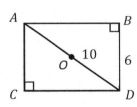

Rectangle: The diagonal AD divides the rectangle $ABCD$ into two equal right triangles. Either of these triangles can be used to determine the width and the length of the rectangle.

In the triangle ABD, AB is the length of the rectangle and BD is the width of the rectangle. The length of BD is given but AB is unknown. Since the lengths of BD and AD are the ratio of the Pythagorean triple $6{:}8{:}10$, the length of AB can be determined.

Circle: The diagonal of the rectangle AD passes through the center of the circle. Hence, AD is the diameter of the circle $= 10$. Radius will be half of the diameter.

Step 2: Determine the area of the rectangle

$$BD{:}AB{:}AD = 6{:}AB{:}10 = 6{:}8{:}10 \rightarrow AB = 8$$
$$\text{area} = lw = AB \times BD = 8 \times 6 = 48$$

Step 3: Determine the area of the circle

Since diameter $= 10$, radius $= 5$.

$$\pi r^2 = \pi \times 5 \times 5 = 25\pi = 25 \times 3.14 = 78.5$$

Step 4: Determine the area of the shaded region

$$\text{area of the circle} - \text{the area of the rectangle } = 78.5 - 48 = 30.5$$

Correct answer choice is **B**.

Category 80 – Practice Questions <small>(answers on pages 411-412)</small>

No Calculator Questions

1

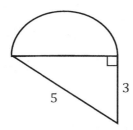

Note: Figure not drawn to scale.

An ice cream company is redesigning the company logo as shown in the figure above. The design consists of a semicircle on top of a right triangle. The lengths of two sides of the triangle are given in the above figure. Which of the following is the area of the semicircle?

A) 2π

B) 3π

C) 4π

D) 8π

2

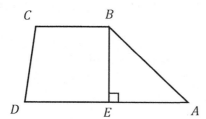

Note: Figure not drawn to scale.

A building architect is designing a roof in the form of the trapezoid $ABDC$ shown above. If $AE = BE$, and the degree measure of angle B is $y°$, what is the value of y?

A) 100

B) 110

C) 125

D) 135

3

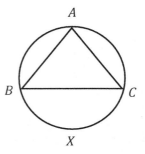

Note: Figure not drawn to scale.

In the figure above, triangle ABC is inscribed in a circle. If arcs AB and AC are congruent and the degree measure of arc BXC is 160°, what is the degree measure of angle B?

A) 20

B) 50

C) 80

D) 120

4

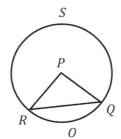

Note: Figure not drawn to scale.

Point P is the center of the circle shown above. If angle PQR is 40°, what fraction is arc QOR of arc QSR?

A) $\dfrac{1}{4}$

B) $\dfrac{2}{5}$

C) $\dfrac{5}{13}$

D) $\dfrac{5}{18}$

5

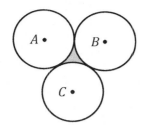

In the figure above, congruent circles A, B, and C, have a radius of 6 and are tangent to each other. What is the area of the shaded region?

A) $9\pi(\sqrt{3} - 2\pi)$

B) $18(2\sqrt{3} - \pi)$

C) $9\sqrt{3} - 2\pi$

D) $24\sqrt{3} - \pi$

6

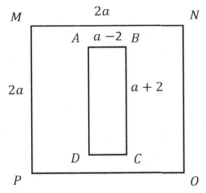

In the figure above, the rectangle $ABCD$ is inscribed in the square $MNOP$. The dimensions of the rectangle are $(a - 2)$ by $(a + 2)$, and each edge of the square is $2a$. In context of the given dimensions, what could $3a^2 + 4$ represent, where a is a constant greater than 0?

A) The perimeter of the square.

B) The perimeter of the inscribed rectangle.

C) The combined area of the inscribed rectangle and the square.

D) The area of the square not covered by the inscribed rectangle.

7

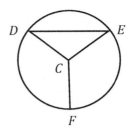

Note: Figure not drawn to scale.

Point C is the center of the circle shown in the figure above. Angle $EDC = 30°$ and points D, E, and F lie on the circumference of the circle. If the length of $\overline{CF}$ is 4 inches, what is the area of triangle CDE, in square inches?

A) $\sqrt{3}$

B) $4\sqrt{3}$

C) 3

D) 16

8

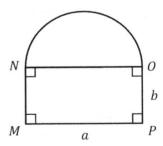

Note: Figure not drawn to scale.

The figure above shows a wall design created by an architect in the shape of a rectangle with a semicircle on top. The length a of the rectangle is twice the width b. If the radius of the semicircle is 2 feet, what is the total area of the rectangle, in square feet?

9

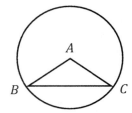

In the figure above, A is the center of the circle and points B and C lie on the circumference of the circle. If angle A is $\frac{5}{9}\pi$ radians and the degree measure of angle B is x, what is x?

10

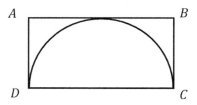

The figure above shows a semicircle inscribed in the rectangle $ABCD$. $\overline{CD}$ is the diameter of the semicircle and the length of the rectangle. If the area of the semicircle is 18π, what is the area of the rectangle?

11

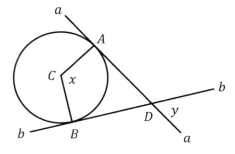

Note: Figure not drawn to scale

In the figure above, point C is the center of the circle and lines a and b are tangent to the circle at points A and B, respectively. If the measure of angles x and y is in degrees and $x = 120$, what is y?

12

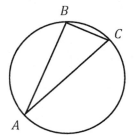

Note: Figure not drawn to scale.

In the figure above, $\overline{AC}$ passes through the center of the circle. The length of chord BC is 10 and the radius of the circle is 13. What is the area of triangle ABC?

13

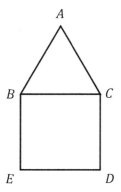

In the figure above, ABC is an equilateral triangle of area $16\sqrt{3}$ square yards and $BCDE$ is a square. What is the perimeter of the square, in yards?

Category 81 – Geometric Shapes in the xy-plane

Key Points

- The (x, y) coordinates of the two end points of a line segment determine its length.

- In a vertical line segment, the x-coordinates of the two end points are same. The length of the line segment is the difference of the y-coordinates of the two end points.

- In a horizontal line segment, the y-coordinates of the two end points are same. The length of the line segment is the difference of the x-coordinates of the two end points.

- The length of a slanting line segment can be determined using the distance formula. If (x_1, y_1) and (x_2, y_2) are the two end points, then the length can be determined as

$$\sqrt{(x_2 - x_1)^2 + (y_2 - y_1)^2}$$

How to Solve

Look out for the ratios of Pythagorean triples, or the side ratio of 45°-45°-90° triangle or 30°-60°-90° triangles.

Example 1:

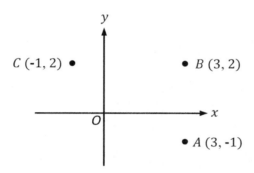

In the xy-plane, points A, B, and C shown in the figure above are the coordinates of a triangle ABC. What is the perimeter of triangle ABC?

Step 1: Determine the length between points

Calculate $\overline{AB}$: $A = (3, -1)$ and $B = (3, 2)$. AB is a vertical line segment.

$$AB = 2 - (-1) = 3$$

Calculate $\overline{BC}$: $B = (3, 2)$ and $C = (-1, 2)$. BC is a horizontal line segment.

$$BC = 3 - (-1) = 4$$

Calculate $\overline{AC}$: Since the vertical line segment AB and the horizontal line segment BC meet at point B, angle ABC is 90° and triangle ABC is a right triangle.

$AB : BC = 3 : 4$ is the ratio of Pythagorean triple $3 : 4 : 5$. Hence,

$$AB : BC : AC = 3 : 4 : 5$$

$$AC = 5$$

Alternatively, the distance formula can be used to determine AC.

Step 2: Determine the perimeter

$$AB + BC + AC = 3 + 4 + 5 = 12$$

Correct answer is **12**.

Category 81 – Practice Questions (answers on page 412)

Calculator Questions

1

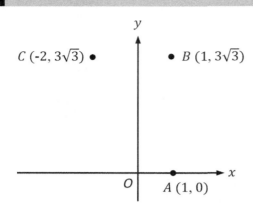

Note: Figure not drawn to scale.

In the xy-plane, points A, B, and C shown in the figure above are coordinates of triangle ABC. What is the measure of angle BAC, in radians?

A) 2π

B) $\dfrac{\pi}{2}$

C) $\dfrac{2\pi}{3}$

D) $\dfrac{\pi}{6}$

2

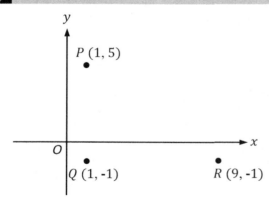

Note: Figure not drawn to scale.

In the figure above, points P, Q, and R form a triangle PQR in the xy-plane. What is the perimeter of triangle PQR ?

A) 9

B) 12

C) 24

D) 26

3

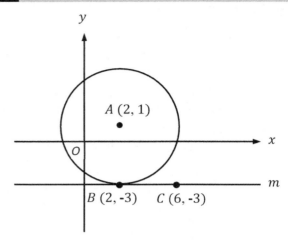

Note: Figure not drawn to scale.

In the xy-plane, a circle with center A is shown above. Line m is tangent to the circle at point B and point C lies on line m. If points A, B, and C are joined to form triangle ABC, which of the following is the degree measure of angle ACB?

A) 30

B) 45

C) 50

D) 60

4

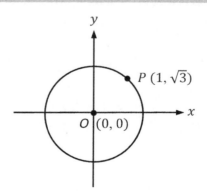

Note: Figure not drawn to scale.

In the figure above, O is the center of a circle in the xy-plane and point P lies on the circle. What is the radius of the above circle?

Category 82 – Geometric Shapes and Percent

Key Points

- A percent increase or decrease in one or more dimensions of a geometric shape will increase or decrease, respectively, the percent area or the volume of the shape.

How to Solve

Refer to Section 9 for further details on calculating the percent change.

Example 1:

If the length of a rectangle is decreased by 25% and the width is increased by 20%, which of the following statements are true?

A)   The area of the rectangle will decrease by 5%.

B)   The area of the rectangle will increase by 5%.

C)   The area of the rectangle will decrease by 10%.

D)   The area of the rectangle will increase by 20%.

Step 1: Determine the area

Area before change: Let length $= l$ and width $= w$.
$$\text{area} = lw$$

Area after change:

Length: 25% decrease $= 1 - 0.25 = 0.75$. Hence, the decreased length is $0.75l$.

Width: 20% increase $= 1 + 0.2 = 1.2$. Hence, the increased width is $1.2w$.
$$\text{area} = 0.75l \times 1.2w = 0.9lw$$

Step 2: Determine the percent change in the area
$$\text{area after change} - \text{area before change} = 0.9lw - lw = -0.1lw = 10\% \text{ reduction}$$

Correct answer choice is **C**.

Example 2:

The edges of a square measure 9 inches. If each edge is reduced by 20%, what is the percent change in the area of the square?

A)   20%

B)   36%

C)   64%

D)   80%

Step 1: Determine the area

Area before change:
$$\text{area} = 9^2 = 81$$

Area after 20% reduction in edge:

20% reduction $= 1 - 0.2 = 0.8$. Hence, each reduced edge $= 9 \times 0.8 = 7.2$.
$$\text{area} = 7.2^2 = 51.84$$

Step 2: Determine the percent change in the area
$$\% \text{ change} = \frac{\text{new area} - \text{old area}}{\text{old area}} \times 100 = \frac{51.84 - 81}{81} \times 100 = \frac{-29.16}{81} \times 100 = 36\%$$

Correct answer choice is **B**.

Category 82 – Practice Questions (answers on page 413)

Calculator Questions

1

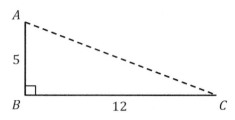

Note: Figure not drawn to scale.

The figure above shows the driving route Adriane takes to work each day, Monday through Friday. Adriane drives 5 miles from point A to B and then 12 miles from point B to C. If a bypass is built from point A to point C that allows Adriane to directly drive from point A to point C, what will be the percent change in the number of miles driven by Adriane each day to work, rounded to the nearest tenth?

A) 8.5%

B) 23.5%

C) 26.2%

D) 47.5%

2

A landscape architect initially designed a square shaped garden with an area of x square meters. In the final design, the landscape architect increased the area by 30%, resulting in a square with each edge measuring 8 meters. Which of the following range could contain the length of each edge, in meters, of the square garden initially designed by the architect?

A) 6.1 to 6.2

B) 6.8 to 6.9

C) 7.0 to 7.1

D) 8.0 to 8.1

3

Johnathan designed a circular garden in his backyard of radius 4 yards. The following year, Jonathan increased the radius of the circular garden by 50%. What is the percent change in the area of the circular garden after the 50% increase in radius?

A) 50%

B) 100%

C) 125%

D) 150%

4

If all the edges of a square are proportionally increased by 40%, which of the following is the approximate percent change in the area of the square?

A) 25%

B) 40%

C) 80%

D) 96%

5

If the length of a rectangle is increased by 10% and the width is decreased by 20%, which of the following statements is true?

A) The area of the rectangle will decrease by 12%.

B) The area of the rectangle will increase by 12%.

C) The area of the rectangle will decrease by 10%.

D) The area of the rectangle will be unchanged.

No Calculator Questions

1

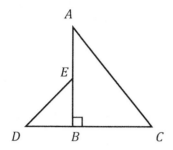

Note: Figure not drawn to scale.

In the figure above, $AC = 10$, $BC = 6$, $AB = 2BE$, and $BD = BE$. The area of triangle DBE is what fraction of the area of triangle ABC?

A) $\frac{1}{4}$

B) $\frac{1}{3}$

C) $\frac{1}{2}$

D) $\frac{3}{5}$

2

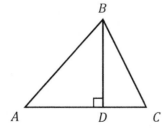

Note: Figure not drawn to scale.

If x is the area of triangle ABC shown above and $BD = 10$, which of the following represents $\overline{AC}$ in terms of x?

A) $\frac{x}{5}$

B) $\frac{x}{2}$

C) $2x$

D) $5x$

3

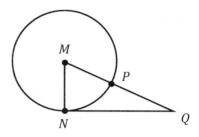

Note: Figure not drawn to scale.

In the figure above, M is the center of the circle and $\overline{NQ}$ is tangent to the circle at point N. If $MN = 1$ and $NQ = \sqrt{3}$, which of the following is the ratio of the minor arc PN to the circumference of the circle?

A) $1:3$

B) $1:4$

C) $1:6$

D) $1:8$

4

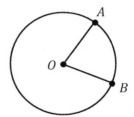

Note: Figure not drawn to scale.

In the circle above, angle AOB is a central angle, the minor arc AB is 2π, and the radius is 5. What is the value of angle AOB, in degrees?

A) 60

B) 72

C) 90

D) 116

5

In the xy-plane, a circle with center $(3, -4)$ is tangent to the x-axis. Which of the following is an equation of the circle?

A) $(x - 3)^2 + (y + 4)^2 = 4$

B) $(x + 3)^2 + (y - 4)^2 = 4$

C) $(x - 3)^2 + (y + 4)^2 = 16$

D) $(x + 3)^2 + (y - 4)^2 = 16$

6

An advertising company hired an artist to create a new company logo in a rectangular shape. The dimensions of the rectangle proposed by the artist are a feet by b feet. The company manager suggested to double the length of a and decrease the length of b by half. Based on the suggestion of the company manager, how will the area of the rectangle, in square feet, change when compared to the proposal by the artist?

A) The area of the rectangle will double.

B) The area of the rectangle will be half.

C) The area of the rectangle will be same.

D) The area of the rectangle will be four times more.

7

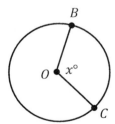

Note: Figure not drawn to scale.

In the circle shown above, the center is point O, $x = 120°$, and the area of the sector enclosed by angle x is 12π. What is the radius of the circle?

Calculator Questions

8

If the length of a rectangle is increased by 25% and the width is decreased by 20%, which of the following statements is true?

A) The area of the rectangle will decrease by 5%.

B) The area of the rectangle will increase by 5%.

C) The area of the rectangle will decrease by 20%.

D) The area of the rectangle will be unchanged.

9

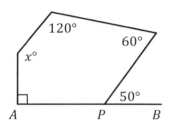

Note: Figure not drawn to scale.

In the figure above, the point P lies on the line segment AB. What is the value of x?

A) 60

B) 100

C) 130

D) 140

10

In the xy-plane, the equation of a circle is $(x - 6)^2 + (y + 1)^2 = 9$. Which of the following points lie on the circumference of the circle?

A) $(3, -2)$

B) $(3, 1)$

C) $(6, 2)$

D) $(7, 4)$

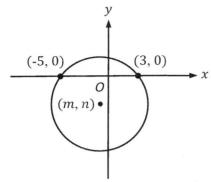

In the xy-plane above, a circle of radius 5 has center at (m, n). Which of the following are the coordinates of (m, n)?

A) $(-1, -4)$

B) $(-1, -3)$

C) $(-1, -1)$

D) $(-1, 3)$

A rectangle with length l meters and width $(5 + l)$ meters has an area of 36 square meters. What is the width of the rectangle, in meters, where l is a positive constant?

A right rectangular prism has a length of l inches, a width of w inches, and a height of h inches. If $lw = 5$, $hw = 6$, and $lh = 30$, what is the volume, in cubic inches, of the prism?

A right rectangular water tank when filled to maximum capacity can hold 2,400 cubic feet of water. If the length and width of the tank are 25 feet and 12 feet, respectively, what is the height of the tank in feet?

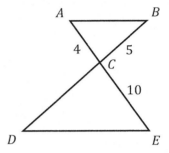

Note: Figure not drawn to scale.

In the figure above, $\overline{AB}$ and $\overline{DE}$ are parallel lines and $\overline{BD}$ intersects $\overline{AE}$ at point C. What is the length of $\overline{BD}$, rounded to the nearest tenth?

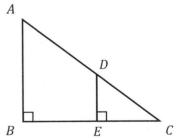

Note: Figure not drawn to scale.

In the figure above, $AB = 7$, $DC = 5$ and $DE = 3$. What is the length of $\overline{BE}$, rounded to the nearest tenth?

17

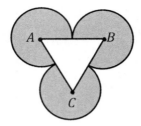

Note: Figure not drawn to scale.

In the figure, three congruent circles A, B, and C are tangent to each other. Points A, B, and C are the center of circles A, B, and C, respectively, and form an equilateral triangle ABC. If the area of triangle ABC is $4\sqrt{3}$, what is the radius of each congruent circle?

18

The graph of $x^2 + 4x + y^2 + 10y = 71$, in the xy-plane, is a circle. What is the diameter of the circle?

19

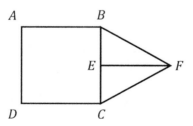

In the figure above, $BC = BF = CF$, $BE = CE$, and $EF = 2\sqrt{3}$. What is the area of the square $ABCD$?

20

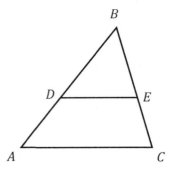

In the figure above, $\overline{AC}$ is parallel to $\overline{DE}$. If angle BDE measures $52°$, angle ACB measures $80°$, and angle ABC measures $x°$, what is x?

21

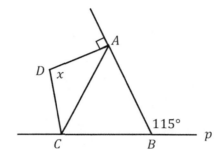

In the figure above, points B and C are on line segment p, $AB = AC$, and $AD = CD$. What is the value of x?

22

If the edge of a cube of volume 64 cubic feet is reduced by 25%, what is the surface area of the cube after reduction, in square feet?

Section 14 – Trigonometry

Category 83 – Right Triangles and Trigonometry
Category 84 – Unit Circle and Trigonometry

Category 83 – Right Triangles and Trigonometry

Key Points

- The trigonometric functions are based on right triangles. A right triangle has one of the angles as 90°, also known as the right angle. The other two angles are known as acute angles and their sum is 90°. In the figure below, triangle ABC is a right triangle with angle B as the right angle. For acute angle x, AB is the opposite side, BC is the adjacent side and AC is the hypotenuse.

- The three main trigonometric functions are the sine (sin), the cosine (cos), and the tangent (tan). The definitions can be remembered as SOH-CAH-TOA.

  - SOH: <u>sin</u>e equals <u>opposite</u> over <u>hypotenuse</u>. For angle x,

  $$\sin x = \frac{\text{opposite}}{\text{hypotenuse}}$$

  - CAH: <u>cos</u>ine equals <u>adjacent</u> over <u>hypotenuse</u>. For angle x,

  $$\cos x = \frac{\text{adjacent}}{\text{hypotenuse}}$$

  - TOA: <u>tan</u>gent equals <u>opposite</u> over <u>adjacent</u>. For angle x,

  $$\tan x = \frac{\text{opposite}}{\text{adjacent}} = \frac{\sin x}{\cos x}$$

- For two acute angles x and y in a right triangle, the following facts are helpful to remember.

  - $\sin x° = \cos y°$ and $\sin y° = \cos x°$ (sine of one acute angle equals the cosine of the other acute angle and vice versa).
  - $\sin x° = \cos (90° - x°)$ and $\sin y° = \cos (90° - y°)$ (sine of an angle equals to the cosine of its complement).
  - $\cos x° = \sin (90° - x°)$ and $\cos y° = \sin (90° - y°)$ (cosine of an angle equals to the sine of its complement).
  - tan of the two acute angles are inverse of each other. For example, if $\tan x = \sqrt{3}$, then $\tan y = \frac{1}{\sqrt{3}}$.

- In similar right triangles, the sine, the cosine, and the tangent at the corresponding vertices are same. For example, in similar right triangles ABC and XYZ, if vertex A corresponds to vertex X, then $\sin A = \sin X$, $\cos A = \cos X$, and $\tan A = \tan X$. Same is true for other two vertices. (See Section 12 Category 72 for further details on similar triangles.)

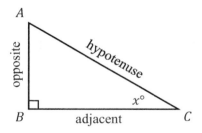

How to Solve

If a question does not give a figure, it can be helpful to draw one. Look out for the side ratios of a right triangle. They may be the ratio of Pythagorean triples and their multiples, or the ratio of a 45°-45°-90° or 30°-60°-90° triangle. (See Section 12 Category 71 for further details on this.)

Example 1:

In a right triangle ABC, angle B is the right angle and angles A and C are the two acute angles.

Question 1

If $\cos A = \dfrac{5}{13}$, what is the value of $\sin A$?

A) $\dfrac{5}{12}$

B) $\dfrac{7}{12}$

C) $\dfrac{5}{13}$

D) $\dfrac{12}{13}$

Step 1: Determine the ratio of sides

See figure below.

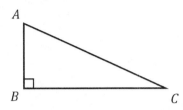

$$\sin A = \frac{\text{opposite}}{\text{hypotenuse}} = \frac{BC}{AC}$$

Determine AC and BC as shown below.

It is given that $\cos A = \dfrac{5}{13}$. Hence,

$$\cos A = \frac{\text{adjacent}}{\text{hypotenuse}} = \frac{AB}{AC} = \frac{5}{13}$$

$AB : AC = 5 : 13$ is the ratio of Pythagorean triple $5 : 12 : 13$. Hence,

$$AB : BC : AC = 5 : BC : 13 = 5 : 12 : 13$$
$$BC = 12$$

Step 2: Determine $\sin A$

$$\sin A = \frac{BC}{AC} \quad \frac{12}{13}$$

Correct answer choice is **D**.

Question 2

If $\cos A = \dfrac{5}{13}$, what is the value of $\sin (90° - A)$?

A) $\dfrac{5}{12}$

B) $\dfrac{7}{12}$

C) $\dfrac{5}{13}$

D) $\dfrac{12}{13}$

There is no need to solve since $\cos A = \sin (90° - A)$. See key points.

Correct answer choice is **C**.

Example 2:

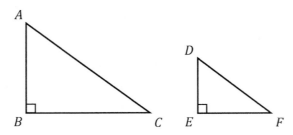

Note: Figure not drawn to scale.

In the figure above, ABC and DEF are similar triangles with vertices A, B, and C corresponding to vertices D, E, and F, respectively.

Question 1

If $\sin A = 0.8$, which of the following is the value of $\sin F$?

A) $\dfrac{5}{4}$

B) $\dfrac{4}{5}$

C) $\dfrac{3}{5}$

D) $\dfrac{4}{3}$

Step 1: Determine the ratio of sides

The question asks to determine $\sin F$ in triangle DEF but gives information on $\sin A$ in triangle ABC.

Since the two right triangles are similar, the value of sin at the corresponding vertices will be same. Since the question gives the value of $\sin A$, use triangle ABC to determine $\sin C = \sin F$ as shown below.

It is given that $\sin A = 0.8 = \dfrac{8}{10}$. Hence,

$$\sin A = \frac{\text{opposite}}{\text{hypotenuse}} = \frac{BC}{AC} = \frac{8}{10}$$

$BC : AC = 8 : 10 = 2(4 : 5)$ is the ratio of Pythagorean triple $2(3 : 4 : 5)$. Hence,

$$AB : BC : AC = AB : 8 : 10 = 6 : 8 : 10$$

$$AB = 6$$

Step 2: Determine $\sin F$

$$\sin F = \sin C = \frac{\text{opposite}}{\text{hypotenuse}} = \frac{AB}{AC} = \frac{6}{10} = \frac{3}{5}$$

Correct answer choice is **C**.

Question 2

If $\cos F = \dfrac{4}{5}$ and $BC = 12$, what is the length of $\overline{AC}$?

Step 1: Determine the side proportion

Since the two right triangles are similar, the corresponding sides are in proportion and $\cos F = \cos C$. Hence,

$$\cos F = \cos C = \frac{\text{adjacent}}{\text{hypotenuse}} = \frac{BC}{AC} = \frac{4}{5}$$

It is given that $BC = 12$. This is three times of 4. Hence AC is three times of 5.

$$AC = 3 \times 5 = 15$$

Correct answer is **15**.

Category 83 – Practice Questions (answers on pages 416-417)

No Calculator Questions

1

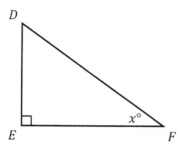

Note: Figure not drawn to scale.

In the right triangle DEF shown above, $EF = 12$. If $\tan x$ is 0.75, which of the following is the length of $\overline{DE}$?

A) 3

B) 4

C) 7

D) 9

2

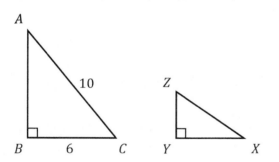

Note: Figure not drawn to scale.

In the figure above, ABC and XYZ are similar triangles with vertices A, B, and C corresponding to vertices X, Y, and Z, respectively. Which of the following is the value of $\tan Z$?

A) $\dfrac{3}{5}$

B) $\dfrac{3}{4}$

C) $\dfrac{4}{3}$

D) 3

3

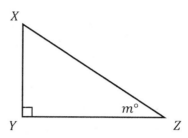

In the right triangle XYZ shown above, the tangent of $m°$ is $\dfrac{1}{\sqrt{3}}$. What is the degree measure of m?

A) 30

B) 40

C) 45

D) 60

4

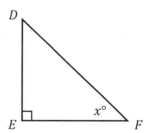

In the right triangle DEF above, the tangent of $x°$ is 1 and $DE = 5$. What is the length of $\overline{DF}$?

A) 1

B) 5

C) $\sqrt{2}$

D) $5\sqrt{2}$

5

In a right triangle, a and b are the two acute angles. If $\sin a = \frac{3}{5}$, which of the following is the value of $\cos(90 - a)$?

A) $\frac{3}{5}$

B) $\frac{4}{5}$

C) $\frac{3}{4}$

D) 1

6

Triangle ABC has a right angle at B. If the tangent of one of the acute angles is $\frac{1}{\sqrt{2}}$, what is the tangent of the other acute angle?

A) $\sqrt{3}$

B) $\sqrt{2}$

C) $\frac{3}{5}$

D) $\frac{5}{12}$

7

In a right triangle, the tangent of one of the acute angles is $\frac{5}{12}$. What is the cosine of the other acute angle?

A) $\sqrt{1}$

B) $\frac{5}{12}$

C) $\frac{5}{13}$

D) $\frac{12}{13}$

8

In a right triangle, x and y are the two acute angles. If the sine of angle y is 0.8, what is the tangent of the other acute angle?

9

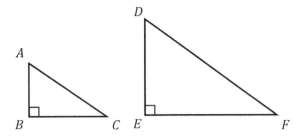

Note: Figure not drawn to scale.

In the triangle ABC above, $\sin C = 0.6$. Triangle DEF is a similar triangle, where vertices D, E, and F correspond to vertices A, B, and C, respectively. If $EF = 20$, what is the length of $\overline{DF}$?

10

In a right triangle, one of the acute angles has a degree measure of b. If $\sin b = 0.8$, what is the value of $\cos(90° - b°)$?

11

Triangle ABC and triangle XYZ are similar triangles, where vertices A, B, and C correspond to vertices X, Y, and Z, respectively. Each side of triangle ABC is half the length of the corresponding side of triangle XYZ. In triangle ABC, the measure of angle B is $90°$, $\tan C = 0.75$, and $BC = 8$ inches. What is the length of $\overline{XZ}$, in inches?

12

In a right triangle, one of the acute angles is k. If $\sin(k + 20)° = \cos(3k + 10)°$, what is the value of k?

13

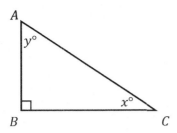

Note: Figure not drawn to scale.

In the figure above, if $x = 30°$ and $y = 60°$, which of the following is NOT true?

A) $\sin x = \cos y$

B) $\sin y = \cos x$

C) $\sin x = \cos 90° - x$

D) $\sin y = \cos 90° - x$

14

Right triangles ABC and XYZ are congruent triangles where vertices A, B, and C correspond to vertices X, Y, and Z, respectively, and angle $B = 90°$. If $AB \neq BC$, which of the following is NOT true?

I. $\sin A = \cos Z$

II. $\tan C = \tan X$

III. $\sin (90° - X) = \cos A$

A) I only

B) II only

C) I and II only

D) I and III only

15

In a right triangle ABC, angle B is the right angle and x is one of the acute angles. If $\sin x° = k$, which of the following must be true for all values of k?

A) $\cos (x^2)° = k$

B) $\sin (x^2)° = k$

C) $\cos (90° - x°) = k$

D) $\tan (90° - x°) = k$

16

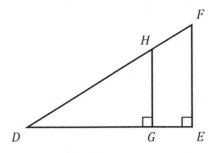

Note: Figure not drawn to scale.

In the figure above, triangles DEF and DGH are right triangles and $\tan F = 1.6$. What fraction is $\overline{DG}$ of $\overline{GH}$?

A) $\dfrac{8}{5}$

B) $\dfrac{4}{3}$

C) $\dfrac{5}{4}$

D) $\dfrac{16}{15}$

17

In the xy-plane, points A, B, and C form a right triangle at point B. If point A is $(4, 2)$, point B is $(1, 2)$, and point C is $(1, 6)$, what is the value of $\sin A$?

18

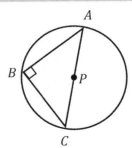

Triangle ABC is inscribed in a circle with center P. Line segment $AB = 12$ and $\sin A = 0.6$. What is the radius of the circle?

Category 84 – Unit Circle and Trigonometry

Key Points

- In trigonometry, a unit circle is a circle with a radius of 1 and the center at origin $(0, 0)$.

- For any angle θ, the (x, y) coordinates of a point on the unit circle are $(\cos \theta, \sin \theta)$.

- For the angles shown in the figure on the right, the coordinates of $(\cos \theta, \sin \theta)$ are a combination of positive/negative values of fractions $\frac{1}{2}$, $\frac{\sqrt{3}}{2}$, and $\frac{2}{\sqrt{2}}$. As seen in the figure, the negative/positive values of $\frac{1}{2}$ and $\frac{\sqrt{3}}{2}$ are a pair and the negative/positive values of $\frac{2}{\sqrt{2}}$ are a pair for the coordinates of $(\cos \theta, \sin \theta)$.

- In quadrant 1 ($0°$ to $90°$), both the coordinates are positive. In quadrant 2 ($90°$ to $180°$), $\cos \theta$ is negative. In quadrant 3 ($180°$ to $270°$), both the coordinates are negative. In quadrant 4 ($270°$ to $360°$), $\sin \theta$ is negative.

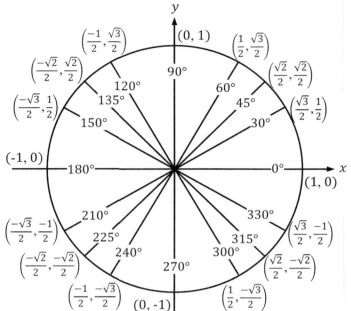

How to Solve

It is important to identify that a question is on unit circle. The question will either mention that the radius of the circle is 1 or the figure will show coordinates indicating that the radius is 1. Remembering the key points will be helpful.

Example 1:

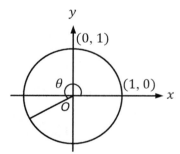

In the figure above, θ is an angle and $\sin \theta = \frac{-1}{2}$. What is $\cos \theta$?

A) $\dfrac{-\sqrt{3}}{2}$

B) $\dfrac{-2}{\sqrt{2}}$

C) $\dfrac{1}{\sqrt{3}}$

D) 2

Step 1: Determine the coordinates on the unit circle

The figure shows that the center of the circle is at origin and the radius is 1. Hence, it is a unit circle.

Since angle θ is in the third quadrant, both the coordinates are negative. Since $\sin \theta = \frac{-1}{2}$, $\cos \theta$ must be $\frac{-\sqrt{3}}{2}$.

Correct answer choice is **A**.

Category 84 – Practice Questions (answers on page 418)

Calculator Questions

1

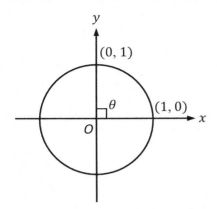

In the figure above, θ is an angle. What is the value of $\cos \theta$?

A) $\dfrac{-1}{2}$

B) $\dfrac{1}{2}$

C) 0

D) 1

2

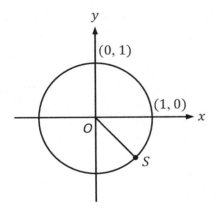

In the figure above, S is a point on the circumference of a circle with a radius of 1 and the origin at $(0, 0)$. If the x-coordinate of point S is $\dfrac{\sqrt{2}}{2}$, which of the following is the y-coordinate of point S?

A) $\dfrac{-\sqrt{3}}{2}$

B) $\dfrac{-\sqrt{2}}{2}$

C) $\dfrac{1}{2}$

D) $\dfrac{\sqrt{3}}{2}$

3

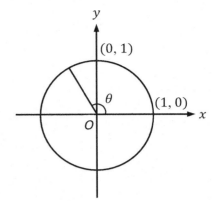

In the figure above, θ is an angle. If $\cos \theta = \dfrac{-1}{2}$, what is the value of $\tan \theta$?

A) $-\sqrt{3}$

B) $\dfrac{-1}{2}$

C) $\dfrac{\sqrt{3}}{2}$

D) $\dfrac{\sqrt{2}}{2}$

4

In the xy-plane, a circle with center $(0, 0)$ has a radius of 1. Which of the following is a possible value of $\sin \dfrac{1}{3}\pi$?

A) $\dfrac{-\sqrt{3}}{2}$

B) $\dfrac{-\sqrt{2}}{2}$

C) $\dfrac{\sqrt{3}}{2}$

D) 1

5

In the xy-plane, a circle with center $(0, 0)$ has a radius of 1. Which of the following is $\sin 180°$?

A) $\dfrac{-\sqrt{3}}{2}$

B) $\dfrac{-\sqrt{2}}{2}$

C) -1

D) 0

Section 15 –
Complex Numbers

Category 85 – Complex Numbers

Category 85 – Complex Numbers

Key Points

- The square root of a negative number does not exist in the real number system. It is an imaginary number that exists in the complex number system. For example, $\sqrt{-4}$ is the imaginary number $2i$ and $i = \sqrt{-1}$ is the imaginary unit. $\sqrt{-4} = \sqrt{4} \times \sqrt{-1} = 2i$.

- i can have any power. Even powers have real number values. See examples below.
  - $i^2 = \sqrt{-1} \times \sqrt{-1} = -1$.
  - $i^3 = \sqrt{-1} \times \sqrt{-1} \times \sqrt{-1} = -1 \times i = -i$.
  - $i^4 = \sqrt{-1} \times \sqrt{-1} \times \sqrt{-1} \times \sqrt{-1} = -1 \times -1 = 1$. Note that every 4th power of i is positive 1.
  - $i^5 = \sqrt{-1} \times \sqrt{-1} \times \sqrt{-1} \times \sqrt{-1} \times \sqrt{-1} = -1 \times -1 \times i = i$
  - $i^6 = \sqrt{-1} \times \sqrt{-1} \times \sqrt{-1} \times \sqrt{-1} \times \sqrt{-1} \times \sqrt{-1} = -1 \times -1 \times -1 = -1$

- A complex number is a combination of real numbers and an imaginary number. It is written in the format $a + bi$, where a and b are real numbers and i is the imaginary unit.

- A complex number in the format $a + bi$ when written with the reverse plus/minus sign is known as the conjugate of that number. For example, $5 + 3i$ is the conjugate of $5 - 3i$ and vice versa.

- Complex numbers can be added, subtracted, multiplied, or divided.

How to Solve

When an expression contains i with only even powers, it can be completely reduced to a real number. For example, $3 + 2i^4 + 3i^6 = 3 + (2 \times 1) + (3 \times -1) = 3 + 2 - 3 = 2$.

When an expression contains i with odd powers or a combination of odd and even powers, it can be completely reduced to $a + bi$ format. For example, $3 + 2i^2 + 3i = 3 + (2 \times -1) + 3i = 3 - 2 + 3i = 1 + 3i$. The value of a is 1 and b is 3.

Example 1:

In the complex number system, $2i(1 + 2i) - (6 + i^4)$ is equivalent to which of the following expressions? (Note: $i = \sqrt{-1}$)

A) $-11 + 2i$

B) $-6 + i$

C) $2 + 2i$

D) $1 + 3i$

Step 1: Simplify the expression

$$2i + 4i^2 - 6 - i^4$$

Step 2: Solve:

$$2i + 4(-1) - 6 - (1)$$
$$2i - 4 - 6 - 1$$
$$-11 + 2i$$

Correct answer choice is **A**.

Example 2:

$$(2 - i^2)(6 + 5i^2)$$

Which of the following is the value of the above expression, given that $i = \sqrt{-1}$?

A) 1

B) 3

C) 11

D) 21

Step 1: Simplify the expression

FOIL.

$$12 + 10i^2 - 6i^2 - 5i^4 = 12 + 4i^2 - 5i^4$$

Step 2: Solve

$$12 + 4(-1) - 5(1) = 12 - 4 - 5 = 3$$

Correct answer choice is **B**.

Example 3:

$$\frac{4 + 3i}{3 + i}$$

If the above expression is written in the $a + bi$ format, where a and b are real numbers, what is the value of b? (Note: $i = \sqrt{-1}$)

Step 1: Simplify the expression

In such questions, multiply the numerator and the denominator by the conjugate of the denominator. This will get rid of i from the denominator. The conjugate of $(3 + i)$ is $(3 - i)$.

$$\frac{(4 + 3i)(3 - i)}{(3 + i)(3 - i)}$$

FOIL.

$$\frac{12 - 4i + 9i - 3i^2}{9 - i^2} = \frac{12 + 5i - 3i^2}{9 - i^2}$$

Step 2: Solve

$$\frac{12 + 5i - 3(-1)}{9 - (-1)}$$

$$\frac{12 + 5i + 3}{10}$$

$$\frac{15}{10} + \frac{5i}{10}$$

$$\frac{3}{2} + \frac{i}{2} = 1.5 + 0.5i = a + bi$$

Correct answer is **0.5** or **1/2**.

Category 85 – Practice Questions (answers on page 419)

No Calculator Questions

1

Which of the following is equivalent to $(2i^2 - i)(5i^2 + 3i)$? (Note: $i = \sqrt{-1}$)

A) $7 + i$

B) $10 - i$

C) $13 - i$

D) $14 + 3i$

2

$$x = \sqrt{-16}$$

In the complex number system, which of the following is equivalent to x in the above expression? (Note: $i = \sqrt{-1}$)

A) i

B) $4i$

C) 1

D) 4

3

In the complex number system, which of the following is equivalent to $\sqrt{-9}$? (Note: $i = \sqrt{-1}$)

A) -9

B) 3

C) i

D) $3i$

4

Which of the following is equivalent to $-(-2i)^2$? (Note: $i = \sqrt{-1}$)

A) -2

B) -1

C) 2

D) 4

5

$$\frac{2(1 + i)}{1 - i}$$

Given that $i = \sqrt{-1}$, which of the following is equivalent to the expression above?

A) i

B) $2i$

C) $1 - 2i$

D) $1 + 2i$

6

In the equation $y = \sqrt{x - 2}$, x is a real number. For which of the following value of x, there is NO real solution for y?

A) 1

B) 3

C) 4

D) 7

7

$$\frac{3 + i}{1 + i}$$

Given that $i = \sqrt{-1}$, which of the following is equivalent to the above expression?

A) 3

B) $4i$

C) $1 + i$

D) $2 - i$

8

In the complex number system, if $2(3 + 4i) - (5i + 3i^2)$ is written as $a + bi$, what is the value of $a - b$, where a and b are real numbers and $i = \sqrt{-1}$?

9

In the complex number system, what is the integer value of the expression $(15 + 6i^2) - (12 + 7i^2)$? (Note: $i = \sqrt{-1}$)

10

$$15i^4 + 5i^2 - 8$$

In the complex number system, what is the value of the above expression? (Note: $i = \sqrt{-1}$)

11

$$\frac{9 + ki}{1 + 3i} = 3 - 2i$$

In the equation above, what is the value of k, where k is a real number and $i = \sqrt{-1}$?

12

In the equation $(11 + 5i) - (5 + 2i) = a + bi$, a and b are real numbers and $i = \sqrt{-1}$. What is the value of $a + b$?

13

$$\frac{7 + ci}{2 + i} = 5 + 3i$$

In the expression above, c is a real number and $i = \sqrt{-1}$. What is the value of c?

14

$$\frac{1}{i^4} - \frac{2}{i^2} - \frac{2}{i}$$

In the complex number system, if the above expression is written in the form $a + bi$, where a and b are real numbers, what is the value of b? (Note: $i = \sqrt{-1}$)

15

What is the value of the expression $2i^2 - 3(-i)^2$? (Note: $i = \sqrt{-1}$)

Answers

Section 1 – Variables and Expressions in Linear Equations

Category 1 – Solving Variables and Expressions in Linear Equations

1. <u>C</u>

Simplify the expression within parentheses:
$$(4 \times x) - (4 \times 3) = 3x - 4 \;\to\; 4x - 12 = 3x - 4$$
Isolate the variables on one side and solve:
$$4x - 3x = -4 + 12 \;\to\; x = 8$$

2. <u>B</u>

Simplify the expression within parentheses:
$$y + 1 = (-3 \times y) - (-3 \times 3) \;\to\; y + 1 = -3y + 9$$
Isolate the variables on one side and solve:
$$y + 3y = 9 - 1 \;\to\; 4y = 8 \;\to\; y = 2$$

3. <u>D</u>

Isolate the variables on one side and solve: for ease, add the variables and the integers on the left-side first.
$$-b - 2 = b \;\to\; -2 = b + b \;\to\; 2b = -2 \;\to\; b = -1$$

4. <u>C</u>

Cross multiply and solve: for ease, add the variables on the left-side first.
$$\frac{6a}{5} = 2 \;\to\; 6a = 2 \times 5 \;\to\; 6a = 10 \;\to\; a = \frac{10}{6} = \frac{5}{3}$$

5. <u>D</u>

Cross multiply and isolate $\frac{a}{b}$ on one side:
$$2b \times 11 = 5 \times a \;\to\; 22b = 5a$$
$$\frac{a}{b} = \frac{22}{5}$$

6. <u>C</u>

Isolate the variables on one side and solve:
$$\frac{x}{2} - \frac{3x}{10} = \frac{2}{5} \;\to\; \frac{5x}{10} - \frac{3x}{10} = \frac{2}{5} \;\to\; \frac{2x}{10} = \frac{2}{5} \;\to\; x = 2$$

7. <u>C</u>

Substitute the value of y in the equation and solve:
$$(3x \times 4) - 10x = 14 \;\to\; 12x - 10x = 14 \;\to\;$$
$$2x = 14 \;\to\; x = 7$$

8. <u>D</u>

Cross multiply:
$$3x \times 7 = 4 \times y \;\to\; 3x \times 7 = 4y$$
Isolate the variables on one side and solve: Note that if $3x$ is moved to the right-side, the answer can be obtained.
$$\frac{4y}{3x} = 7$$

9. <u>A</u>

Simplify the left-side fraction and isolate $\frac{y}{x}$ on one side:
$$\frac{\left(\frac{x}{7}\right)}{3} = y \;\to\; \frac{x}{7} \div 3 = y \;\to\; \frac{x}{7} \times \frac{1}{3} = y \;\to\; \frac{x}{21} = y \;\to\;$$
$$\frac{y}{x} = \frac{1}{21}$$

10. <u>C</u>

Isolate the variables on one side and solve:
$$x = 11 - 8 = 3$$
Answer choice C when simplified is $x = 3$.

11. <u>C</u>

Isolate the variables on one side and solve:
$$15m - 9m = 24 \;\to\; 6m = 24 \;\to\; 3m = 12$$

12. <u>B</u>

Isolate the variables on one side and solve:
$$5c - 3c = 8 \;\to\; 2c = 8 \;\to\; c = 4$$

13. <u>C</u>

Isolate all terms of the identical expression and solve:
$$4(n + 5) - 3(n + 5) = 38 \;\to\; (n + 5) = 38$$
$$((n + 5) = 38) \times 3 \;\to\; 3(n + 5) = 114$$

14. <u>B</u>

Isolate the variables on one side and solve:
$$\frac{2x}{3} - \frac{x}{5} = \frac{7}{5} \;\to\; \frac{10x}{15} - \frac{3x}{15} = \frac{7}{5} \;\to\; \frac{7x}{15} = \frac{7}{5} \;\to\;$$
$$\frac{x}{3} = 1 \;\to\; x = 1 \times 3 = 3$$

15. <u>D</u>

Isolate all terms of the identical expression and solve:
$$\frac{5}{8}(x - 3) - \frac{3}{8}(x - 3) = 42 \;\to\; \frac{2}{8}(x - 3) = 42 \;\to\;$$
$$\frac{1}{4}(x - 3) = 42 \;\to\; \left(\frac{1}{4}(x - 3) = 42\right)4 \;\to\; x - 3 = 168$$

16. <u>36</u>

Determine the value of n: Plug in $a = 12$ and $b = m$.
$$a = \frac{b}{n} \;\to\; 12 = \frac{m}{n} \;\to\; 12n = m \;\to\; n = \frac{m}{12}$$
Determine a when $b = 3m$: plug in above value of n:
$$a = \frac{3m}{\left(\frac{m}{12}\right)} \;\to\; a = 3m \div \frac{m}{12} \;\to\; a = 3m \times \frac{12}{m} = 36$$

Section 2 – Lines and Linear Functions

Category 2 – Line Equation in Slope Intercept Form

1. **C**

Determine the slope: For every 3 units increase of x from left to right, y increases by 2 units upwards. Hence, the slope is

$$\frac{\text{rise}}{\text{run}} = \frac{2}{3}$$

This eliminates answer choices A and D.

Determine the y-intercept: Plug in the given point $(2, 5)$ and slope $= \frac{2}{3}$ in $y = mx + b$ equation.

$$5 = \left(\frac{2}{3} \times 2\right) + b \rightarrow 5 = \frac{4}{3} + b \rightarrow b = 5 - \frac{4}{3} \rightarrow \frac{11}{3}$$

This eliminates answer choice B.

2. **D**

Determine the slope:

$$\frac{\text{rise}}{\text{run}} = \frac{1}{3}$$

This eliminates answer choices B and C that have negative slope.

Determine the y-intercept:

$$y\text{-intercept from graph} = 1$$

This eliminates answer choice A. Note that equation D when divided by 3 gives

$$\frac{3y}{3} = \frac{x}{3} + \frac{3}{3} \rightarrow y = \frac{x}{3} + 1$$

3. **B**

Determine the slope: Set up the slope equation using points $(-1, 2)$ and $(1, 6)$.

$$\frac{6 - 2}{1 - (-1)} = \frac{4}{2} = 2$$

This eliminates answer choices A and D.

Determine the y-intercept:

$$\text{slope} \times 2 = 2 \times 2 = 4$$

This eliminates answer choice C.

4. **C**

Determine the slope of line p:

Slope of line $l = 2$ (from the given equation).

Slope of line $p = 3 \times 2 = 6$. This eliminates answer choices A and B.

Determine the y-intercept of line p: Since line p passes through point $(0, 2)$, the y-intercept $= 2$. This eliminates answer choice D.

5. **B**

Determine the x-intercept: Set $y = 0$ and solve for x.

$$0 = \frac{2x + 24}{4} - 3 \rightarrow 0 = \frac{1}{2}x + 6 - 3 \rightarrow$$
$$0 = \frac{1}{2}x + 3 \rightarrow -3 = \frac{1}{2}x \rightarrow x = -6$$

6. **D**

Determine the slope: Divide the equation by a.

$$y = -2x + b$$

Since the slope is negative, the line on the graph will slants downwards from left to right. This eliminates answer choices A and C.

Determine the y-intercept: Since $b > 1$, answer choice B can be eliminated.

7. **B**

Determine the slope: Set up the slope equation using points $(0, 0)$ and $(2, 6)$.

$$\frac{6 - 0}{2 - 0} = \frac{6}{2} = 3$$

Divide the equations in answer choices B, C, and D by 2. This eliminates answer choices A and C.

Determine the y-intercept: Since the line passes through origin, y-intercept $= 0$. This eliminates answer choice D.

8. **D**

Divide the equation in answer choice C by 2 and the equation in answer choice D equation by 3.

The y-intercept of the equation in answer choice D is double the slope.

9. **1.5 or 3/2**

Determine the x-intercept:

Plug in slope $= 2$ and y-intercept $= -3$ in $y = mx + b$ equation and set $y = 0$ (remember at x-intercept, $y = 0$).

$$y = 2x - 3 \rightarrow 0 = 2x - 3 \rightarrow 2x = 3 \rightarrow$$
$$x = \frac{3}{2} = 1.5$$

10. **4**

Determine the y-intercept: Plug in the given point $(3, -5)$ and slope $= -3$ in $y = mx + b$ equation.

$$-5 = (-3 \times 3) + b \rightarrow -5 = -9 + b \rightarrow b = 4$$

Category 3 – Line Equation in Standard Form

1. <u>A</u>

Determine the slope:
$$\frac{\text{rise}}{\text{run}} = \frac{4}{2} = 2$$
Look for the answer choice where $-\frac{A}{B} = 2$.

This eliminates answer choices B, C, and D. In correct answer choice A, $-\frac{A}{B} = -\frac{6}{-3} = 2$.

2. <u>B</u>

Determine the y-intercept:
$$\frac{C}{B} = \frac{-5}{-2} = \frac{5}{2}$$

3. <u>C</u>

Determine the x-intercept: Set $y = 0$ and solve for x.
$$2x + (3 \times 0) = 4c \;\to\; 2x = 4c \;\to\; x = 2c$$
The coordinates are $(2c, 0)$.

4. <u>D</u>

Slope is given as $-\frac{3}{2}$.

Look for answer choice where $-\frac{A}{B} = -\frac{3}{2}$. This eliminates answer choices A and C.

Determine the y-intercept: Since the line intersects the x-axis at 4, $(4, 0)$ is a point on the line. Plug this point and slope $= -\frac{3}{2}$ in $y = mx + b$ equation.
$$0 = \left(-\frac{3}{2} \times 4\right) + b \;\to\; 0 = -6 + b \;\to\; b = 6$$
This eliminates answer choice B.

5. <u>B</u>

Solve for a: Plug in the given point $(4, 1)$ in the equation.
$$4 - (a \times 1) = a \;\to\; 4 - a = a \;\to\; 2a = 4 \;\to\; a = 2$$

Category 4 – Points on a Line with Unknown Coordinates

1. <u>A</u>

Set up the slope equation and solve: Set up the slope equation using points $(2, 2p)$ and $(5, p - 1)$ and equate to slope $= -2$.
$$\frac{(p - 1) - 2p}{5 - 2} = -2 \;\to\; \frac{-p - 1}{3} = -2 \;\to\;$$
$$-p - 1 = -2 \times 3 \;\to\; -p - 1 = -6 \;\to\; p = 5$$
Determine $p - 1$: $5 - 1 = 4$.

2. <u>D</u>

Set up slope equations and solve:

To calculate n, set up the slope equation using points $(1, 4)$ and $(5, m)$ and equate to slope $= 3$.
$$\frac{m - 4}{5 - 1} = 3 \;\to\; \frac{m - 4}{4} = 3 \;\to\; m - 4 = 12 \;\to\; m = 16$$
To calculate n, set up the slope equation using points $(1, 4)$ and $(n, 7)$ and equate to slope $= 3$.
$$\frac{7 - 4}{n - 1} = 3 \;\to\; \frac{3}{n - 1} = 3 \;\to\; 3(n - 1) = 3 \;\to\;$$
$$n - 1 = 1 \;\to\; n = 2$$
Determine $m + n$: $16 + 2 = 18$.

3. <u>C</u>

Set up slope equations and solve: Since the slope is not given, set up two slope equations and equate them. Set up one slope equation using points $(1, 3)$ and $(4, a)$ and second slope equation using points $(4, a)$ and $(7, a + b)$.
$$\frac{a - 3}{4 - 1} = \frac{(a + b) - a}{7 - 4} \;\to\; \frac{a - 3}{3} = \frac{b}{3} \;\to\;$$
$$a - 3 = b \;\to\; a - b = 3$$

4. <u>B</u>

Set up slope equations and solve: Set up one slope equation using points $(1, 2)$ and $(5, 10)$ and second slope equation using points $(1, 2)$ and $(s, 6)$. Equate the two slope equations.
$$\frac{6 - 2}{s - 1} = \frac{10 - 2}{5 - 1} \;\to\; \frac{4}{s - 1} = \frac{8}{4} \;\to\; \frac{4}{s - 1} = 2 \;\to\;$$
$$2(s - 1) = 4 \;\to\; s - 1 = 2 \;\to\; s = 3$$

5. <u>D</u>

Set up the slope equation and solve: Set up the slope equation using points $(0, 0)$ and $(3, 3a)$ and equate to slope $= 3$.
$$\frac{3a - 0}{3 - 0} = 3 \;\to\; \frac{3a}{3} = 3 \;\to\; 3a = 9$$
Hence, point $(3, 3a) = (3, 9)$.

6. <u>8</u>

Set up the slope equation and solve: Set up the slope equation using points $(0, 2)$ and $(x, -2)$ and equate to slope $= -\frac{1}{2}$.
$$\frac{-2 - 2}{x - 0} = -\frac{1}{2} \;\to\; \frac{-4}{x} = -\frac{1}{2} \;\to\;$$
$$(x \times -1) = (-4 \times 2) \;\to\; -x = -8 \;\to\; x = 8$$

Category 5 – Slope of Parallel Lines

1. B

Determine the slope: Slope of line k is

$$\frac{\text{rise}}{\text{run}} = -\frac{2}{2} = -1$$

Since line l is parallel to line k, the slope of line $l = -1$. This eliminates answer choices C and D.

Determine the y-intercept of line l: Plug in the given point $(6, -4)$ and slope $= -1$ in $y = mx + b$ equation.

$$6 = (-1 \times -4) + b \rightarrow 6 = 4 + b \rightarrow b = 2$$

This eliminates answer choice A.

2. D

Determine the slope: Slope of line k is

$$-\frac{A}{B} = -\frac{6}{3} = -2$$

Since line p is parallel to line k, the slope of line $p = -2$.

Look for the equation where $-\frac{A}{B} = -2$.

This eliminates answer choices A, B, and C.

3. B

Determine the slope: The slope of line $s = 4$. Since line t is parallel to line s, the slope of line $t = 4$.

Determine the y-intercept of line t: Plug in the given point $(3, 5)$ and slope $= 4$ in $y = mx + b$ equation.

$$5 = (4 \times 3) + b \rightarrow 5 = 12 + b \rightarrow b = -7$$

Since $x = 0$ at the y-intercept, the coordinates are $(0, -7)$.

4. A

Set up slope equations and solve: Since lines l and p are parallel lines, they have the same slope. Set up one slope equation using points $(c, 3)$ and $(6, 5)$ on line l and second slope equation using points $(c, 1)$ and $(8, 4)$ on line p. Equate the two slope equations.

$$\frac{5 - 3}{6 - c} = \frac{4 - 1}{8 - c} \rightarrow \frac{2}{6 - c} = \frac{3}{8 - c} \rightarrow$$

$$2(8 - c) = 3(6 - c) \rightarrow 16 - 2c = 18 - 3c \rightarrow c = 2$$

5. C

Set up slope equations and solve: Since lines p and q are parallel lines, they have the same slope.

Let the x-intercept of line $q = (x, 0)$.

Set up one slope equation using points $(-2, 3)$ and $(0, 1)$ on line p and second slope equation using points $(1, 2)$ and $(x, 0)$ on line q. Equate the two slope equations.

$$\frac{1 - 3}{0 - (-2)} = \frac{0 - 2}{x - 1} \rightarrow \frac{-2}{2} = \frac{-2}{x - 1} \rightarrow -1 = \frac{-2}{x - 1} \rightarrow$$

$$-1(x - 1) = -2 \rightarrow -x + 1 = -2 \rightarrow x = 3$$

Category 6 – Slope of Perpendicular Lines

1. A

Determine the slope: The slope of line $p = 3$. Since line s is perpendicular to line p, the slope of line $s = -\frac{1}{3}$. This eliminates answer choices B and D.

Determine the y-intercept of line s: Since line s passes through the point $(0, -4)$, the y-intercept $= -4$.

2. B

Determine the slope: Slope of line p is

$$\frac{\text{rise}}{\text{run}} = -\frac{1}{2}$$

Since line t is perpendicular to line p, the slope of line $t = 2$.

Determine the x-intercept: Let the x-intercept $= (x, 0)$. Set up the slope equation using points $(x, 0)$ and $(1, 4)$ and equate to slope $= 2$.

$$\frac{4 - 0}{1 - x} = 2 \rightarrow \frac{4}{1 - x} = 2 \rightarrow 2(1 - x) = 4 \rightarrow$$

$$1 - x = 2 \rightarrow x = -1$$

3. C

Determine the slope: Set up the slope equation using points $(-1, 3)$ and $(3, 1)$ on line segment l.

$$\frac{1 - 3}{3 - (-1)} = \frac{-2}{4} = -\frac{1}{2}$$

Since line h is perpendicular to line segment l, the slope of line $h = 2$. This eliminates answer choices A and B.

Determine the range of the y-intercept: The perpendicular line h can be any line passing between the two end points of line segment l.

Plug in each end point and slope $= 2$ in $y = 2x + b$ equation and determine the range of the y-intercept.

For point $(-1, 3)$:

$$3 = (2 \times -1) + b \rightarrow 3 = -2 + b \rightarrow b = 5$$

For point $(3, 1)$:

$$1 = (2 \times 3) + b \rightarrow 1 = 6 + b \rightarrow b = -5$$

Hence, the y-intercept of line h can be any number between -5 and 5. This eliminates answer choice D.

4. D

Determine the slope: Write the equation of line s in the correct standard form before proceeding.

$$9y + 3x = 3 \;\rightarrow\; 3x + 9y = 3$$

Slope of line s is

$$-\frac{A}{B} = -\frac{3}{9} = -\frac{1}{3}$$

Since line t is perpendicular to line s, slope of line $t = 3$.

Determine the y-intercept of line t: Plug in the given point $(-2, 5)$ and slope $= 3$ in $y = mx + b$ equation.

$$5 = (3 \times -2) + b \;\rightarrow\; 5 = -6 + b \;\rightarrow\; b = 11$$

Since $x = 0$ at y-intercept, the coordinates are $(0, 11)$.

Category 7 – Linear Functions

1. B

Determine the slope: Set up the slope equation using points $(-2, -5)$ and $(2, 3)$.

$$\frac{3 - (-5)}{2 - (-2)} = \frac{8}{4} = 2$$

This eliminates answer choices A and D.

Determine the y-intercept: Plug in any given point and slope $= 2$ in $y = mx + b$ equation.

$$3 = (2 \times 2) + b \;\rightarrow\; 3 = 4 + b \;\rightarrow\; b = -1$$

This eliminates answer choice C.

2. C

Determine the slope:

$$\frac{\text{rise}}{\text{run}} = \frac{1}{1} = 1$$

This eliminates answer choices A, B, and D.

3. A

Set up the slope equation and solve: Let the unknown point be $(-2, y)$.

Set up the slope equation using points $(1, 4)$ and $(-2, y)$ and equate to slope $= 3$.

$$\frac{y - 4}{-2 - 1} = 3 \;\rightarrow\; \frac{y - 4}{-3} = 3 \;\rightarrow\; y - 4 = -9 \;\rightarrow\; y = -5$$

5. C

Determine the slope: Set up the slope equation for line m using points $(3, 7)$ and $(4, 9)$.

$$\frac{9 - 7}{4 - 3} = \frac{2}{1} = 2$$

Since line n is perpendicular to line m, the slope of line $n = -\frac{1}{2}$. This eliminates answer choices B and D.

Since line n passes through origin answer choice A can be eliminated.

Note that the equation in answer choice C when divided by 2 is $y = -\frac{1}{2}x$.

4. B

Set up slope equations and solve: Let the unknown point be $(1, y)$.

Set up one slope equation using points $(-2, 6)$ and $(3, -4)$ and second slope equation using points $(3, -4)$ and $(1, y)$. Equate the two slope equations.

$$\frac{-4 - 6}{3 - (-2)} = \frac{y - (-4)}{1 - 3} \;\rightarrow\; -2 = \frac{y + 4}{-2} \;\rightarrow$$
$$(-2 \times -2) = y + 4 \;\rightarrow\; 4 = y + 4 \;\rightarrow\; y = 4 - 4 = 0$$

5. D

Determine the slope: Select any two points from the table and set up the slope equation. Below equation is set up using points $(2, 6)$ and $(4, 9)$.

$$\frac{9 - 6}{4 - 2} = \frac{3}{2}$$

Determine the y-intercept: Plug in any of the given point and slope $= \frac{3}{2}$ in $y = mx + b$ equation. Point $(2, 6)$ is used in the equation below.

$$6 = \left(\frac{3}{2} \times 2\right) + b \;\rightarrow\; 6 = 3 + b \;\rightarrow\; b = 3$$

Since $x = 0$ at y-intercept, the coordinates are $(0, 3)$.

Category 8 – Graph Transformations of Linear Functions

1. C

Left shift by 3 units, changes $2x$ to $2(x + 3)$.
Upward shift by 2 units, changes -4 to $-4 + 2 = -2$.
Hence, $f(x) = 2x - 4 \;\rightarrow\; f(x) = 2(x + 3) - 2$.

2. A

Reflection across x-axis changes $y = 4x + 1$ to
$-y = 4x + 1 \;\rightarrow\; y = -(4x + 1) \;\rightarrow\; y = -4x - 1$.

3. B

The given y-coordinate of the y-intercept $= -5$. Adding 3 units will move it up by 3.
Hence, the y-coordinate will be $-5 + 3 = -2$.

4. A

Reflection across y-axis changes $f(x) = x + 2$ to $f(x) = -x + 2$. This eliminates answer choices B and D with positive slope and answer choice C with y-intercept -2.

Section 2 – Review Questions

1. <u>A</u>

Determine the slope: The slope of line $k = 1$. Since line l is parallel to line k, the slope of line $l = 1$.

Look for the equation where $-\dfrac{A}{B} = 1$. This eliminates answer choices B, C, and D.

2. <u>B</u>

Determine the slope:
$$\frac{\text{rise}}{\text{run}} = -\frac{2}{4} = -\frac{1}{2}$$
This eliminates answer choices C and D.

Determine the y-intercept: $= 2$.

This eliminates answer choice A.

3. <u>D</u>

Change from $5x$ to $5(x - 2)$ is 2 units shift to right.

Change from -2 to 2 is 4 units shift upwards.

4. <u>C</u>

Determine the slope: Set up the slope equation using points $(0, -2)$ and $(-2, -5)$.
$$\frac{-5 - (-2)}{-2 - 0} = \frac{-3}{-2} = \frac{3}{2}$$
Divide equations in answer choices C and D by 2. This eliminates answer choices A and B.

Determine the y-intercept: Since the line passes through $(0, -2)$, the y-intercept $= -2$.

This eliminates answer choice D.

5. <u>C</u>

Determine the y-intercept from the equation:
$$\frac{C}{B} = \frac{4}{-b} = -\frac{4}{b}$$
Determine b: Equate the y-intercept from the above equation with the given y-intercept $= -6$.
$$-\frac{4}{b} = -6 \;\rightarrow\; 6b = 4 \;\rightarrow\; b = \frac{4}{6} = \frac{2}{3}$$

6. <u>A</u>

Since the slope of line p is undefined, it is a vertical line. Only answer choice A is the equation of a vertical line.

7. <u>D</u>

Determine the slope:
$$\frac{\text{rise}}{\text{run}} = -\frac{4}{10} = -\frac{2}{5}$$
Look for the equation where $-\dfrac{A}{B} = -\dfrac{2}{5}$. This eliminates answer choices A, B, and C.

8. <u>C</u>

Set up slope equations and solve: Let the unknown point be $(-6, y)$.

Select any two points from the table to set up slope equations. Below slope equations are set up using points $(-1, -4)$ and $(-3, 0)$ and points $(-3, 0)$ and $(-6, y)$. Equate the two slope equations.
$$\frac{0 - (-4)}{-3 - (-1)} = \frac{y - 0}{-6 - (-3)} \;\rightarrow\; \frac{4}{-2} = \frac{y}{-3} \;\rightarrow$$
$$-2y = -3 \times 4 \;\rightarrow\; -2y = -12 \;\rightarrow\; y = 6$$

9. <u>B</u>

Determine the slope: From the equation of function g, slope $= 3$. Since the lines on the graphs of function f and g are parallel, they have the same slope $= 3$.

Set up a slope equation for function f and solve: Let the unknown point be $(1, y)$.

Set up the slope equation using points $(3, 3)$ and $(1, y)$ and equate to slope $= 3$.
$$\frac{y - 3}{1 - 3} = 3 \;\rightarrow\; \frac{y - 3}{-2} = 3 \;\rightarrow\; y - 3 = -6 \;\rightarrow\; y = -3$$

10. <u>D</u>

Since the two lines intersect at point $(2, 4)$, the point exists on both the lines.

Determine the slope: Set up the slope equation for line m using points $(0, 0)$ and $(2, 4)$.
$$\frac{4 - 0}{2 - 0} = 2$$
Since line n is perpendicular to line m, the slope of line $n = -\dfrac{1}{2}$.

Determine point P: Let point P be $(x, 0)$. (At x-axis, $y = 0$.)

Set up the slope equation using points $(x, 0)$ and $(2, 4)$ and equate to slope $= -\dfrac{1}{2}$.
$$\frac{4 - 0}{2 - x} = -\frac{1}{2} \;\rightarrow\; \frac{4}{2 - x} = -\frac{1}{2} \;\rightarrow$$
$$(4 \times 2) = -(2 - x) \;\rightarrow\; 8 = -2 + x \;\rightarrow$$
$$x = 2 + 8 = 10$$

11. <u>B</u>

Determine the slope: Select any two points from the table and set up the slope equation. Below equation is set up using points $(0, 2k)$ and $(3, 3k)$.
$$\frac{3k - 2k}{3 - 0} = \frac{k}{3}$$
This eliminates answer choices C and D.

Determine the y-intercept: Since $(0, 2k)$ is a point in the table, y-intercept $= 2k$. This eliminates answer choice A.

12. A

Determine the slope: Slope of line s is

$$-\frac{A}{B} = -\frac{4}{2} = -2$$

Since line t is perpendicular to line s, slope of line $t = \frac{1}{2}$.

Determine the y-intercept of line t: Plug in the given point $(4, 5)$ and slope $= \frac{1}{2}$ in $y = mx + b$ equation.

$$5 = \left(\frac{1}{2} \times 4\right) + b \rightarrow 5 = 2 + b \rightarrow b = 3$$

This eliminates answer choices C and D.

Determine the x-intercept of line t: Plug in the slope and the y-intercept in $y = mx + b$ equation and set $y = 0$.

$$0 = \frac{1}{2}x + 3 \rightarrow \frac{1}{2}x = -3 \rightarrow x = -6$$

This eliminates answer choice B.

13. C

Determine the slope: Use any two points from the table.

$$\frac{84.95 - 44.95}{8 - 4} = \frac{40}{4} = 10$$

Determine the y-intercept: Plug in slope $= 10$ and any point from the table in $y = mx + b$ equation.

$$44.95 = (10 \times 4) + b \rightarrow 44.95 = 40 + b \rightarrow b = 4.95$$

14. D

Determine the slope as rise/run:

$$\frac{\text{rise}}{\text{run}} = \frac{2}{1}$$

Determine points on the line: Since the points in the answer choice are higher than $(-1, -1)$, determine the next upward point on the line that is an answer choice. $(-1 + \text{run}), (-1 + \text{rise}) \rightarrow (-1 + 1), (-1 + 2) = (0, 1) \rightarrow (0 + 1), (1 + 2) = (1, 3)$.

15. B

Determine the slope: Slope of line l is given as $\frac{3}{5}$. Since line p is perpendicular to line l, slope of line $p = -\frac{5}{3}$. This eliminates answer choices A and D.

Determine the y-intercept of line p: Plug in the given point $(6, 5)$ and slope $= -\frac{5}{3}$ in $y = mx + b$ equation.

$$5 = \left(-\frac{5}{3} \times 6\right) + b \rightarrow 5 = -10 + b \rightarrow b = 15$$

This eliminates answer choice C.

16. D

Determine the slope: Slope of line p is

$$-\frac{A}{B} = -\frac{2}{4} = -\frac{1}{2}$$

Since line r is perpendicular to line p, slope of line $r = 2$. Evaluate each answer choice: Easiest approach is to check which two points have slope $= 2$. Slope of points in answer choice D $= 2$.

17. C

Determine the x-intercept: Set $y = 0$ and solve.

$$2 \times 0 = 5x - 15 \rightarrow 5x = 15 \rightarrow x = 3$$

18. B

Determine the slope: Slope of graph $f(x)$ is

$$\frac{\text{rise}}{\text{run}} = \frac{2}{1} = 2$$

Since the graph of $g(x)$ is perpendicular to the graph of $f(x)$, slope of the graph $g(x) = -\frac{1}{2}$.

Set up the slope equation for function g: Let the unknown point be $(4, y)$.

Set up the slope equation using points $(0, 0)$ and $(4, y)$ and equate to slope $= -\frac{1}{2}$.

$$\frac{y - 0}{4 - 0} = -\frac{1}{2} \rightarrow \frac{y}{4} = -\frac{1}{2} \rightarrow 2y = -4 \rightarrow y = -2$$

19. C

3 units shift to the left will change $3x$ to $3(x + 3)$.

3 units shift downwards will change 2 to $2 - 3 = -1$.

20. A

Determine the equation of function f:

$$\frac{\text{rise}}{\text{run}} = \frac{1}{2}$$

Plug in slope $= \frac{1}{2}$ and y-intercept $= -1$ in $y = mx + b$ equation.

$$f(x) = \frac{1}{2}x - 1$$

Determine the transformed equation (across y-axis):

$$f(x) = -\frac{1}{2}x - 1$$

21. 14

Set up slope equations: Set up one slope equation using points $(1, 3)$ and $(7, 9)$ and second slope equation using points $(a, 10)$ and $(4, b)$. Equate the two slope equations.

$$\frac{9 - 3}{7 - 1} = \frac{b - 10}{4 - a} \rightarrow \frac{6}{6} = \frac{b - 10}{4 - a} \rightarrow 1 = \frac{b - 10}{4 - a} \rightarrow$$
$$4 - a = b - 10 \rightarrow a + b = 14$$

22. 6

Set up a slope equation and solve: Slope of line $l = 2$. Set up slope equation using points $(-2, -2)$ and $(2, k)$ on line l and equate to slope $= 2$.

$$\frac{k - (-2)}{2 - (-2)} = 2 \rightarrow \frac{k + 2}{4} = 2 \rightarrow$$
$$k + 2 = 2 \times 4 \rightarrow k + 2 = 8 \rightarrow k = 6$$

Section 3 – System of Linear Equations and Inequalities

Category 9 – System of Linear Equations and Number of Solutions

1. <u>D</u>

Evaluate the ratios:

$$\frac{a_1}{a_2} = \frac{2}{-6} = -\frac{1}{3}$$

$$\frac{b_1}{b_2} = \frac{-3}{9} = -\frac{1}{3}$$

$$\frac{c_1}{c_2} = \frac{-4}{12} = -\frac{1}{3}$$

Since all the ratios are same, the system has infinitely many solutions.

2. <u>A</u>

It is apparent from the graph that the two lines have same slope. For both the lines,

$$\frac{\text{rise}}{\text{run}} = 1$$

Hence, the two lines are parallel and have no solution.

3. <u>B</u>

Evaluate the ratios: Convert the two equations to the standard form before evaluating the ratios.

$$y = 3x - 2 \rightarrow 3x - y = 2$$
$$-y = 3x + 1 \rightarrow 3x + y = -1$$

Set up the ratios.

$$\frac{a_1}{a_2} = \frac{3}{3} = 1$$

$$\frac{b_1}{b_2} = \frac{-1}{1} = -1$$

$$\frac{c_1}{c_2} = \frac{2}{-1} = -2$$

Since the ratios of a and b are not same, the system has one solution.

4. <u>A</u>

Evaluate the ratios:

$$\frac{a_1}{a_2} = \left(4 \div \frac{1}{3}\right) = 4 \times 3 = 12$$

$$\frac{b_1}{b_2} = \left(3 \div \frac{1}{4}\right) = 3 \times 4 = 12$$

$$\frac{c_1}{c_2} = \left(3 \div \frac{1}{2}\right) = 3 \times 2 = 6$$

Since ratios of a and b are same but not same as the ratio of c, the system has no solution. The equations are for two parallel lines.

5. <u>D</u>

Evaluate the ratios:

$$\frac{a_1}{a_2} = \left(\frac{1}{4} \div 1\right) = \frac{1}{4}$$

$$\frac{b_1}{b_2} = \frac{1}{4}$$

$$\frac{c_1}{c_2} = \frac{-c}{-4c} = \frac{1}{4}$$

Since all ratios are same, the system has infinitely many solutions.

Category 10 – System of Linear Equations with No Solution

1. <u>C</u>

Equate the ratios: Since the system has no solution, the ratios of a and b must be same.

$$\frac{a_1}{a_2} = \frac{b_1}{b_2} \rightarrow \left(2 \div \frac{1}{6}\right) = \left(12 \div \frac{1}{b}\right) \rightarrow$$
$$2 \times 6 = 12 \times b \rightarrow 12 = 12b \rightarrow b = 1$$

2. <u>D</u>

Equate the ratios: Since the system of parallel lines has no solution, the ratios of a and b must be same. Before equating, convert equations to the standard form.

$$y = 4x + 10 \rightarrow 4x - y = -10$$
$$4y = ax + 14 \rightarrow ax - 4y = -14$$

$$\frac{a_1}{a_2} = \frac{b_1}{b_2} \rightarrow \frac{4}{a} = \frac{-1}{-4} \rightarrow a = 16$$

3. C

Equate the ratios: Since the system has no solution, the value of k cannot result in the ratio of c to be same as the ratios of a and b. Equate the ratios of a and c and determine what value of k makes the ratios same.

$$\frac{a_1}{a_2} = \frac{c_1}{c_2} \rightarrow \frac{3}{9} = \frac{k}{12} \rightarrow \frac{1}{3} = \frac{k}{12} \rightarrow 1 = \frac{k}{4} \rightarrow k = 4$$

If $k = 4$, then all the ratios will be same. For the system to have no solution $k \neq 4$.

4. A

Equate the ratios: Since the system has no solution, the ratios of a and b must be same. Before equating, rearrange $10y + 5x = 16$ to $5x + 10y = 16$.

$$\frac{a_1}{a_2} = \frac{b_1}{b_2} \rightarrow \frac{2}{5} = \frac{-b}{10} \rightarrow 2 = \frac{-b}{2} \rightarrow b = -4$$

5. D

Equate the ratios: Since the system has no solution, the ratios of a and b must be same but different than the ratio of c.

Determine the value of m that will result in the same a and b ratios:

$$\frac{a_1}{a_2} = \frac{b_1}{b_2} \rightarrow \frac{2}{5} = \frac{m}{10} \rightarrow 2 = \frac{m}{2} \rightarrow m = 4$$

This eliminates answer choices A and B.

Determine the value of n that will result in the ratios of a and b to be same as c: This cannot be the value of n. Either a or b can be equated with c. Below is using a.

$$\frac{a_1}{a_2} = \frac{c_1}{c_2} \rightarrow \frac{2}{5} = \frac{n}{15} \rightarrow 2 = \frac{n}{3} \rightarrow n = 6$$

Hence, for the system to have no solution $n \neq 6$. This eliminates answer choice C.

6. B

Equate the ratios: Since the system has no solution, the ratios of a and b must be same.

$$\frac{a_1}{a_2} = \frac{b_1}{b_2} \rightarrow \frac{0.2}{a} = \frac{0.3}{0.6} \rightarrow 0.3a = 1.2 \rightarrow a = 0.4$$

Category 11 – System of Linear Equations with Infinite Solutions

1. D

Equate the ratios:

$$\frac{a_1}{a_2} = \frac{b_1}{b_2} = \frac{c_1}{c_2} \rightarrow \left(k \div \frac{1}{2}\right) = \left(-10 \div -\frac{1}{3}\right) = \frac{c}{2} \rightarrow$$

$$2k = 30 = \frac{c}{2}$$

Determine k:

$$2k = 30 \rightarrow k = 15$$

Determine c:

$$\frac{c}{2} = 30 \rightarrow c = 60$$

Determine $c - k$:

$$60 - 15 = 45$$

2. C

Equate the ratios:

The values of k and t must result in the same ratios of a, b, and c. Evaluate each answer option.

Plug in $k = 1$ and $t = 1$: The ratios are

$$\frac{a_1}{a_2} = \frac{b_1}{b_2} = \frac{c_1}{c_2} \rightarrow \frac{1}{1} = \frac{1}{1} = \frac{2}{2 \times 1} \rightarrow 1 = 1 = 1$$

This is true for infinitely many solutions.

Plug in $k = 2$ and $t = 4$: The ratios are

$$\frac{a_1}{a_2} = \frac{b_1}{b_2} = \frac{c_1}{c_2} \rightarrow \frac{1}{2} = \frac{2}{4} = \frac{2}{2 \times 2} \rightarrow \frac{1}{2} = \frac{1}{2} = \frac{1}{2}$$

This is true for infinitely many solutions.

Plug in $k = 3$ and $t = 6$: The ratios are

$$\frac{a_1}{a_2} = \frac{b_1}{b_2} = \frac{c_1}{c_2} \rightarrow \frac{1}{3} = \frac{3}{6} = \frac{2}{2 \times 3} \rightarrow \frac{1}{3} = \frac{1}{2} = \frac{1}{3}$$

This is not true for infinitely many solutions since all ratios are not same.

Hence, correct answer choice is C.

3. B

Equate the ratios: Setting up the ratio of c is not needed.

$$\frac{a_1}{a_2} = \frac{b_1}{b_2} \rightarrow \frac{m}{n} = \frac{6.25}{1.25} = 5$$

4. 6

Equate the ratios:

$$\frac{a_1}{a_2} = \frac{b_1}{b_2} = \frac{c_1}{c_2} \rightarrow \frac{a}{1} = \frac{5}{1} = \frac{5}{b} \rightarrow a = 5 = \frac{5}{b}$$

Determine a:

$$a = 5$$

Determine b:

$$5 = \frac{5}{b} \rightarrow 5b = 5 \rightarrow b = 1$$

Determine $a + b$:

$$5 + 1 = 6$$

5. 1

Equate the ratios:

$$\frac{a_1}{a_2} = \frac{b_1}{b_2} = \frac{c_1}{c_2} \rightarrow \frac{\sqrt{k}}{2} = \frac{1}{c} = \frac{2}{\sqrt{k}}$$

Determine $\sqrt{k}$:

$$\frac{\sqrt{k}}{2} = \frac{2}{\sqrt{k}} \rightarrow \sqrt{k} \times \sqrt{k} = 2 \times 2 \rightarrow \sqrt{k} = 2$$

Determine c:

$$\frac{1}{c} = \frac{2}{\sqrt{k}} \rightarrow \frac{1}{c} = \frac{2}{2} \rightarrow \frac{1}{c} = 1 \rightarrow c = 1$$

Category 12 – System of Linear Equations with One Solution

1. B

Determine the approach: If the equations are subtracted, the result is $2x - 2y$. This can be divided by 2 to get $x - y$.

Solve for $x - y$:

$$\begin{array}{cc} 9x - 6y = 9 & 9x - 6y = 9 \\ -(7x - 4y = 3) & -7x + 4y = -3 \\ \hline & 2x - 2y = 6 \end{array}$$

Solve: Divide both sides by 2.

$$x - y = 3$$

2. D

Determine the approach: If both the equations are added, the result is $8x - 2y$. This can be multiplied by 10 to get $80x - 20y$.

Solve for $80x - 20y$:

$$\begin{array}{c} 4x + y = 7 \\ 4x - 3y = 12 \\ \hline 8x - 2y = 19 \end{array}$$

Solve: Multiply by 10.

$$(8x - 2y = 19) \times 10 \rightarrow 80x - 20y = 190$$

3. A

Equate the ratios: Since the system has one solution, the ratios of a and b cannot be same. Equate the ratios of a and b and determine what value of b makes the ratios same. This cannot be the value of b.

$$\frac{a_1}{a_2} = \frac{b_1}{b_2} \rightarrow \frac{4}{8} = \frac{b}{6} \rightarrow \frac{1}{2} = \frac{b}{6} \rightarrow 1 = \frac{b}{3} \rightarrow$$

$$b = 3$$

If $b = 3$, the ratios of a and b will be same. For the system to have one solution $b \neq 3$.

4. C

Read the intersection point on the graph: The coordinates of intersection are $(1, 1)$.

5. C

Determine the approach: If the equation $2x - 3y = 4$ is multiplied by 3 and the equation $3x - 2y = 6$ is multiplied by 2, both the equations will have $6x$ that can be cancelled.

Equation 1: $(2x - 3y = 4) \times 3 \rightarrow 6x - 9y = 12$

Equation 2: $(3x - 2y = 6) \times 2 \rightarrow 6x - 4y = 12$

Determine y: Subtract equation 2 from equation 1.

$$\begin{array}{cc} 6x - 9y = 12 & \cancel{6x} - 9y = 12 \\ -(6x - 4y = 12) & -\cancel{6x} + 4y = -12 \\ \hline & -5y = 0 \rightarrow y = 0 \end{array}$$

Determine x: Substitute $y = 0$ in any of the equation.

$$2x - 3y = 4 \rightarrow 2x - 0 = 4 \rightarrow x = 2$$

6. 3

Determine the approach: Since the system of equations is given in the slope-intercept form, they can be equated together. Before equating, the equation $2y = -2x + 6$ must be divided by 2.

$$\frac{2}{2}y = \frac{-2x}{2} + \frac{6}{2} \rightarrow y = -x + 3$$

Determine x: Equate the two equations.

$$\frac{2}{3}x - 2 = -x + 3 \rightarrow \frac{2}{3}x + x = 3 + 2$$

$$\frac{5}{3}x = 5 \rightarrow x = 5 \times \frac{3}{5} \rightarrow x = 3$$

Determine y: Substitute $x = 3$ in any of the equation.

$$y = -x + 3 \rightarrow y = -3 + 3 = 0$$

Hence, the intersecting point $(j, k) = (3, 0)$

Determine $j + k$: $3 + 0 = 3$.

Category 13 – System of Linear Inequalities

1. D

Compare slope, y-intercept, and inequality symbol:

$y \geq x - 1$:

Since the inequality has $\geq$ symbol, the solution set will be on and above the line with a positive slope. This eliminates answer choices B and C that have a line with positive slope but solution below the line.

$y < -2x + 2$:

Since the inequality has $<$ symbol, the solution set will be below the line with a negative slope. This eliminates answer choice A that has a line with a negative slope but solution above the line.

2. B

Graph the inequalities based on slope, y-intercept, and inequality symbol.

The overlapping region is in quadrants II and III.

3. C

Plug points from answer choices: Start with choice B.

Answer choice B: Plug in point $(1, -2)$ in one of the inequalities.

Check $y > -2x + 4$:

$$-2 > (-2 \times 1) + 4 \rightarrow -2 > -2 + 4 \rightarrow -2 > 2$$

This evaluation is false. This eliminates answer choice B.

Answer choice C: Plug in point $(1, 3)$.

Check $y > -2x + 4$:

$$3 > (-2 \times 1) + 4 \rightarrow 3 > -2 + 4 \rightarrow 3 > 2$$

This evaluation is true.

Check $y < 3x + 1$:

$$3 < (3 \times 1) + 1 \rightarrow 3 < 4$$

This evaluation is true. Answer choice C is the correct.

4. C

Graph the inequalities based on slope, y-intercept, and inequality symbol.

The overlapping region is in quadrants I and IV. Hence, the non-overlapping quadrants that do not contain the solution set are II and III.

Category 14 – Solutions of Linear Expressions

1. B

Equate coefficients and constants: The expressions on both sides of the equation must be equal.

Add constants in the left expression.

$$5ax - 5 - 2 = 1.25x - 7 \rightarrow 5ax - 7 = 1.25x - 7$$

Constants on both sides are equal. If the coefficients are made equal, the equation will have infinetly many solutions.

$$5a = 1.25 \rightarrow a = \frac{1.25}{5} = 0.25$$

2. A

Equate coefficients and constants: The expressions on both sides of the equation must be equal.

Since there is no x variable on right-side, $b = 0$.

3. D

Equate coefficients and constants: The expressions on both sides of the equation must be equal.

$$\frac{6x - a}{3} = 2x - 1 \rightarrow 2x - \frac{a}{3} = 2x - 1$$

The coefficients on both sides are equal. If the constants are made equal, the equation will have infinetly many solutions.

$$-\frac{a}{3} = -1 \rightarrow a = 3$$

4. 1

Equate coefficients and constants: The expressions on both sides of the equation must not be equal.

$$0.2kx = \frac{x + 9}{5} \rightarrow 0.2kx = \frac{x}{5} + \frac{9}{5}$$

Constants on both sides are not equal since the left side does not have a constant. If the coefficients are made equal, the equation will have no solution.

$$0.2k = \frac{1}{5} \rightarrow k = \frac{1}{5 \times 0.2} = \frac{1}{1} = 1$$

5. C

Equate coefficients and constants: The expressions on both sides of the equation must not be equal.

Simplify the right expression.

$$4ax + x - 20 = 2x - 4 + 7x + 14$$

Group all terms of x.

$$(4a + 1)x - 20 = 9x + 10$$

The constants on both sides of the equation are not equal. If the coefficients are made equal, the equation will have no solution.

$$4a + 1 = 9 \rightarrow 4a = 8 \rightarrow a = 2$$

6. D

Equate coefficients and constants: The expressions on both sides of the equation must not be equal.

Simplify the left expression.

$$2kx + 2c + 2 = 10x + 2c + 2$$

The constants on both sides of the expression are equal $(2c + 2)$. Determine the value k that makes coefficients on both sides of the equation equal. This cannot be the value of k.

$$2k = 10 \rightarrow k = 5$$

Hence, for the system to have no solution, $k \neq 5$.

7. 4

Equate coefficients and constants: The expressions on both sides of the equation must be equal.

Simplify the left expression and add the constants.

$$5x + 5 + 3a + 1 = 5x + 18 \rightarrow$$
$$5x + 3a + 6 = 5x + 18$$

The coefficients on both sides are equal. If the constants are made equal, the equation will have infinetly many solutions.

$$3a + 6 = 18 \rightarrow 3a = 12 \rightarrow a = 4$$

Section 3 – Review Questions

1. D

Equate the ratios: Since the system is for two parallel lines, the system will have no solution. The value of m cannot result in the ratio of c to be same as the ratios of a and b.

Set up the ratios for a and c and determine what value of m makes the ratios same. This cannot be the value of m.

$$\frac{a_1}{a_2} = \frac{c_1}{c_2} \rightarrow \frac{1}{4} = \frac{4}{m} \rightarrow m = 16$$

Hence, for the system to have no solution $m \neq 16$.

2. A

Evaluate the ratios: Convert equations to the standard form before evaluating the ratios.

$$2y = 3x + 5 \rightarrow 3x - 2y = -5$$
$$y = \frac{3}{2}x + 5 \rightarrow \frac{3}{2}x - y = -5$$
$$\frac{a_1}{a_2} = \left(3 \div \frac{3}{2}\right) = \left(3 \times \frac{2}{3}\right) = 2$$
$$\frac{b_1}{b_2} = \frac{-2}{-1} = 2$$
$$\frac{c_1}{c_2} = \frac{-5}{-5} = 1$$

Since the ratios of a and b are same but not same as the ratio of c, the system has no solution.

8. 2

Equate coefficients and constants: The expressions on both sides of the equation must not be equal.

Simplify the left expression.

$$2cx + 6 + x = 5x + 7$$

Group all terms of x.

$$(2c + 1)x + 6 = 5x + 7$$

The constants on both sides of the equation are not equal. If the coefficients are made equal, the equation will have no solution.

$$2c + 1 = 5 \rightarrow 2c = 4 \rightarrow c = 2$$

3. D

Equate coefficients and constants: The expressions on both sides of the equation must be equal.

Simplify both sides.

$$4x + 6kx + x + 6 = 3x + 3cx + 2c \rightarrow$$
$$5x + 6kx + 6 = 3x + 3cx + 2c$$

Group all terms of x.

$$(5 + 6k)x + 6 = (3 + 3c)x + 2c$$

Equate the constants.

$$2c = 6 \rightarrow c = 3$$

Equate the coefficients.

$$5 + 6k = 3 + 3c \rightarrow 6k = -2 + 3c$$

Substitute $c = 3$ in the above equation.

$$6k = -2 + (3 \times 3) \rightarrow 6k = 7 \rightarrow k = \frac{7}{6}$$

4. D

Equate coefficients and constants: The expressions on both sides of the equation must not be equal.

Simplify the right expression.

$$3x = 4x + kx - 3x \rightarrow 3x = x + kx$$

$$3x = (1 + k)x$$

Equate and determine the value k that makes coefficients on both sides of the equation equal. This cannot be the value of k.

$$3 = 1 + k \rightarrow k = 2$$

Hence, for the system to have no solution, $k \neq 2$.

5. A

Read the graph: The point of intersection $(0, -1)$ is the solution.

6. C

Equate the ratios: For the system to have no solution, the values of m and n must result in the same ratios of a and b but not c. Evaluate each answer option.

<u>Plug in $m = -2$ and $n = 2$</u>: The ratios are

$$\frac{a_1}{a_2} = \frac{b_1}{b_2} = \frac{c_1}{c_2} \rightarrow \frac{1}{-(-2)} = \frac{-1}{2} = \frac{2}{12} \rightarrow \frac{1}{2} = -\frac{1}{2} = \frac{1}{6}$$

The ratios of a and b are not same. This is incorrect.

<u>Plug in $m = 2$ and $n = -6$</u>: The ratios are

$$\frac{1}{-2} = \frac{-1}{2} = \frac{-6}{12} \rightarrow -\frac{1}{2} = -\frac{1}{2} = -\frac{1}{2}$$

All ratios are same. This is incorrect.

<u>Plug in $m = 2$ and $n = 6$</u>: The ratios are

$$\frac{1}{-2} = \frac{-1}{2} = \frac{6}{12} \rightarrow -\frac{1}{2} = -\frac{1}{2} = \frac{1}{2}$$

The ratios of a and b are same but not c. This is correct.

7. D

Equate coefficients and constants: The expressions on both sides of the equation must not be equal.

Simplify both sides.

$$4x + 8ax + 3a - 3x = 3x + 3a + 2x + 2 \rightarrow$$

$$x + 8ax + 3a = 5x + 3a + 2$$

Group all terms of x.

$$(1 + 8a)x + 3a = 5x + 3a + 2$$

Since the constants on both sides of the equation are not equal ($3a \neq 3a + 2$), the coefficients must be made equal.

Equate the coefficients.

$$1 + 8a = 5 \rightarrow 8a = 4 \rightarrow a = \frac{1}{2}$$

8. D

Equate the ratios:

$$\frac{a_1}{a_2} = \frac{b_1}{b_2} = \frac{c_1}{c_2} \rightarrow \frac{2a}{4} = \frac{1}{-2} = \frac{b}{a} \rightarrow \frac{a}{2} = -\frac{1}{2} = \frac{b}{a}$$

Determine a:

$$\frac{a}{2} = -\frac{1}{2} \rightarrow a = -1$$

Determine b: Substitute $a = -1$.

$$-\frac{1}{2} = \frac{b}{a} \rightarrow -\frac{1}{2} = \frac{b}{-1} \rightarrow -\frac{1}{2} = -b \rightarrow b = \frac{1}{2}$$

9. C

Evaluate the ratios:

$$\frac{a_1}{a_2} = \left(2 \div \frac{1}{3}\right) = 2 \times 3 = 6$$

$$\frac{b_1}{b_2} = \left(3 \div \frac{1}{2}\right) = 3 \times 2 = 6$$

$$\frac{c_1}{c_2} = \left(a \div \frac{a}{6}\right) = a \times \frac{6}{a} = 6$$

Since all the ratios are same, the system is for the same lines.

10. 20/8, 10/4, 5/2, or 2.5

Decide the approach: If the equations are added the result is $8x - 8y$. This can be divided by 8 to get $x - y$.

Solve for $x - y$: Add both equations

$$2x - 5y = 11$$
$$6x - 3y = 9$$
$$\overline{}$$
$$8x - 8y = 20$$

$$\frac{8x - 8y}{8} = \frac{20}{8} \rightarrow x - y = \frac{20}{8} = 2.5$$

11. 3

Equate the ratios:

$$\frac{a_1}{a_2} = \frac{b_1}{b_2} = \frac{c_1}{c_2} \rightarrow \frac{a + 4}{3} = \frac{4}{b} = \frac{4}{3}$$

Determine a:

$$\frac{a + 4}{3} = \frac{4}{3} \rightarrow a + 4 = 4 \rightarrow a = 0$$

Determine b:

$$\frac{4}{3} = \frac{4}{b} \rightarrow b = 3$$

Determine $a + b$:

$$0 + 3 = 3$$

12. <u>20</u>

Decide the approach: If both the equations are added, the result is $4x - 6y$. This can be multiplied by 10 to get $40x - 60y$.

Solve for $40x - 60y$: Add the two equations.

$$3x + 4y = -5$$
$$x - 10y = 7$$
$$\overline{4x - 6y = 2}$$
$$(4x - 6y = 2) \times 10 \rightarrow 40x - 60y = 20$$

13. <u>C</u>

Plug points from answer choices: Start with answer choice B. Plug in point $(-2, -1)$ in one of the inequalities.

Check $y < -x + 7$:

$$-1 < -(-2) + 7 \rightarrow -1 < 2 + 7 \rightarrow -1 < 9$$

This evaluation is true.
Check $y < 3x + 4$:

$$-1 < (3 \times -2) + 4 \rightarrow -1 < -6 + 4 \rightarrow -1 < -2$$

This evaluation is false. This eliminates answer choice B.

Next plug in point $(0, 2)$ from answer choice C.
Check $y < -x + 7$:

$$2 < -0 + 7 \rightarrow 2 < 7 \rightarrow 2 < 7$$

This evaluation is true.
Check $y < 3x + 4$:

$$2 < (3 \times 0) + 4 \rightarrow 2 < 0 + 4 \rightarrow 2 < 4$$

This evaluation is true. Answer choice C is the correct.

14. <u>D</u>

Graph the inequalities based on slope, y-intercept, and inequality symbol.

The solution to the two inequalities is not contained in quadrants II and III.

15. <u>B</u>

Decide the approach: Rearrange the equation $3y + 4x = -5$ so the variables x and y can be aligned in the two equations.

$$3y + 4x = -5 \rightarrow 4x + 3y = -5$$

If the above equation is multiplied by 3 and the equation $3x - 4y = 5$ is multiplied by 4 then both the equations will have $12x$ that can be cancelled.

Equation 1: $(3x - 4y = 5) \times 4 \rightarrow 12x - 16y = 20$

Equation 2: $(4x + 3y = -5) \times 3 \rightarrow 12x + 9y = -15$

Determine y: Subtract equation 2 from equation 1.

$$12x - 16y = 20 \quad\longrightarrow\quad \cancel{12x} - 16y = 20$$
$$-(12x + 9y = -15) \qquad -\cancel{12x} - 9y = 15$$
$$\overline{-25y = 35}$$
$$y = -\frac{35}{25} = -\frac{7}{5}$$

16. <u>A</u>

Equate coefficients and constants: The expressions on both sides of the equation must be equal.

Since there is no x variable on the right-side, the coefficient of x on left side must be 0.

17. <u>C</u>

Decide the approach: Rearrange the equation $5y = -x + 3$ so the variables x and y can be aligned in the two equations.

$$5y = -x + 3 \rightarrow x + 5y = 3$$

If the above equation is multiplied by 2 then both the equations will have $2x$ that can be cancelled.

Equation 1: $(x + 5y = 3) \times 2 \rightarrow 2x + 10y = 6$

Equation 2: $2x + 3y = -8$

Determine y: Subtract equation 2 from equation 1.

$$2x + 10y = 6 \quad\longrightarrow\quad \cancel{2x} + 10y = 6$$
$$-(2x + 3y = -8) \qquad -\cancel{2x} - 3y = 8$$
$$\overline{7y = 14 \rightarrow y = 2}$$

Determine x: Substitute $y = 2$ in any of the equation.

$$x + (5 \times 2) = 3 \rightarrow x + 10 = 3 \rightarrow x = -7$$

18. <u>B</u>

Plug points from answer choices: Start with answer choice B. Plug in point $(-1, -3)$ in one of the inequalities.

Check $y \geq 2x - 3$:

$$-3 \geq (2 \times -1) - 3 \rightarrow -3 \geq -2 - 3 \rightarrow -3 \geq -5$$

This evaluation is true.
Check $y < x - 1$:

$$-3 < -1 - 1 \rightarrow -3 < -2$$

This evaluation is true. Answer choice B is the correct.

19. <u>15/6, 5/2 or 2.5</u>

Equate the ratios: Since the system has no solution, ratios of a and b must be same.

$$\frac{a_1}{a_2} = \frac{b_1}{b_2} \rightarrow \left(\frac{b}{5} \div 3\right) = \frac{-2}{-12} \rightarrow \frac{b}{15} = \frac{1}{6} \rightarrow$$
$$6b = 15 \rightarrow b = \frac{15}{6} = \frac{5}{2} = 2.5$$

Section 4 – Word Problems on Linear Equations and Inequalities

Category 15 – Word Problems on Linear Equations with One Variable

1. A

Determine the constant: Entry fee = $10. This eliminates answer choices C and D.

Determine the unknown number/variable: h hours at $5 per hour = $5h$. This eliminates answer choice B.

2. B

Determine the constant: One-time fee = $25. This eliminates answer choices A and C.

Determine the unknown number/variable: t hours at $20 per hour = $20t$. This eliminates answer choice D.

3. D

Determine the constant: Initial balance = d. This eliminates answer choices A and C.

Determine the unknown number/variable: $100 per month in m months = $100m$. This eliminates answer choice B.

4. C

Determine the constant: Fixed service fee = s.

Determine the unknown number/variable: 3 hours at p dollars per hour = $3p$.

Solve:
$$s + 3p = \$360 \;\to\; s = 360 - 3p$$

5. D

Determine the constant: One-time rental fee = $75.

Determine the unknown number/variable: 4 days at $55 per day = $4 \times 55 = \$220$.

Solve:
$$\text{total cost} = 75 + 220 = \$295$$

6. D

Initial number of research papers = 30.

Determine the unknown number/variable:

Unknown number = number of research papers $\times$ 40 minutes.

The number of minutes required to complete the remaining $30 - r$ research papers is
$$(30 - r) \times 40 \text{ minutes}$$
Convert to hours.
$$\frac{(30 - r) \times 40}{60} \;\to\; \frac{2}{3}(30 - r)$$

7. B

Initial number of tickets = x.

Determine the unknown number/variable:

The number of tickets remaining after the first day is
$$x - 400$$

Solve: Number of remaining tickets T to be sold each day for the next 4 days is
$$\frac{x - 400}{4} \;\to\; \frac{x}{4} - \frac{400}{4} \;\to\; \frac{x}{4} - 100$$

8. B

Determine the constant: Initial saved amount = d dollars.

Determine the unknown number/variable: $150 per month in m months = $150m$.

Solve: Total needed = $1,500
$$\text{total} = d + 150m \;\to\; \$1,500 = d + 150m$$
Rearrange the equation to express in terms of m.
$$150m = 1,500 - d \;\to\; m = \frac{1,500 - d}{150} \;\to$$
$$m = \frac{1,500}{150} - \frac{d}{150} = 10 - \frac{d}{150}$$

9. A

Plug in $h = 20$ in the given equation.
$$g = 0.003h + 0.2 \;\to\; g = (0.003 \times 20) + 0.2 \;\to$$
$$g = 0.06 + 0.2 \;\to\; g = 0.26$$

10. C

Determine the constant: Flat fee per month = $25.

Determine the unknown number/variable: 50 calls at $0.20 per call = $0.2 \times 50 = \$10$.

Solve:
$$\text{total cost} = 25 + 10 = \$35$$

11. D

Determine the constant: Entrance fee = $8. This eliminates answer choices A and B.

Determine the unknown number/variable: r rides at $1.50 per ride = $1.50r$. This eliminates answer choice C.

Category 16 – Word Problems on Linear Equations with Two Variables

1. <u>A</u>

Determine the unknown number/variable 1 (morning shift): m hours at \$15 per hour $= 15m$. This eliminates answer choices B and D.

Determine the unknown number/variable 2 (night shift): n hours at \$25 per hour $= 25n$. This eliminates answer choice C.

2. <u>D</u>

Determine the unknown number/variable 1 (working at restaurant): x hours at \$20 per hour $= 20x$. This eliminates answer choices A and B.

Determine the unknown number/variable 2 (working at hotel): 5 hours at \$35 per hour $= 35 \times 5 = \$175$. This eliminates answer choice C.

3. <u>B</u>

Determine the unknown number/variable 1 (snow cones): 4 snow cones for c dollars each $= 4c$.

Determine the unknown number/variable 2 (frozen yogurt): 7 frozen yogurts for $c + 1$ dollars each $= 7(c + 1)$.

Solve: Total cost $= 4$ snow cones $+ 7$ yogurts.
$$40 = 4c + 7(c + 1) \rightarrow 40 = 4c + 7c + 7 \rightarrow$$
$$11c = 33 \rightarrow c = 3$$

4. <u>A</u>

Determine the unknown number/variable 1 (oranges): 100 oranges for \$1 each $= 100 \times 1 = \$100$.

Determine the unknown number/variable 2 (apples): 100 apples for p dollars each $= 100p$.

Solve: Total cost $= 100$ oranges $+ 100$ apples.
$$150 = 100 + 100p \rightarrow 100p = 50 \rightarrow p = 0.50$$

5. <u>4</u>

Determine the unknown number/variable 1 (Crane A): 100 boxes lifted per hour for 2 hours $= 100 \times 2 = 200$.

Determine the unknown number/variable 2 (Crane B): Let the number of hours $= x$. Hence, 75 boxes lifted per hour for x hours $= 75x$.

Solve: Total boxes lifted $=$ Crane $A +$ Crane B.
$$500 = 200 + 75x \rightarrow 300 = 75x \rightarrow x = 4$$

6. <u>3</u>

Determine the unknown number/variable 1 (painter): 4 hours at \$80 per hour $= 4 \times 80 = \$320$.

Determine the unknown number/variable 2 (landscaper): a hours at \$50 per hour $= 50a$.

Solve: Total earnings $=$ painter $+$ landscaper.
$$470 = 320 + 50a \rightarrow 50a = 150 \rightarrow a = 3$$

Category 17 – Word Problems on Interpretation of Linear Equations

1. <u>D</u>

Determine the components of the equation:

$2 =$ Average number of research papers Anika reviews each day of the month.

$58 =$ Initial number of research papers Anika receives at the beginning of each month.

$R =$ Ending number of research papers at the end of each day of the month.

2. <u>A</u>

Determine the components of the equation:

$0.0054 =$ Average increase in the growth of the plant, in inches, in response to each hour of sunlight.

$15 =$ Initial size, in inches, of the plant before exposure to sunlight.

3. <u>B</u>

Determine the components of the equation:

$1.43 =$ Approximate growth rate, in pounds, of baby panda each week after birth for w weeks.

$R =$ Ending growth rate, in pounds, of baby panda after w weeks of birth.

4. <u>C</u>

Determine the components of the equation:

$7.6 =$ Average increase in the population of insects, in thousands, each year after 1970.

$305 =$ Initial population of insects, in thousands, in 1970.

$685 =$ Ending population of insects, in thousands, after t years, since 1970.

5. <u>D</u>

Determine the components of the equation:

$0.0012 =$ Approximate decrease in the barometric pressure, in inches Hg, at each foot above sea level.

$29.92 =$ Barometric pressure, in inches Hg, at sea level.

$B =$ Ending barometric pressure, in inches Hg, at a feet above sea level.

For the barometric pressure to decrease by 1, the value of $0.0012a$ must be 1. Hence, $a = \frac{1}{0.0012}$.

Category 18 – Word Problems on Linear System of Equations

1. <u>A</u>

Identify the two variables:

Number of tickets sold to ages 12 and below $= c$.

Number of tickets sold to ages above 12 $= a$.

Determine the system of equations:

Equation 1: Total tickets sold $= 400$.

$$a + c = 400$$

This eliminates answer choices C and D.

Equation 2: Price of each $a = \$14$ and price of each $c = \$10$. Total tickets sold for $= \$4,600$.

$$14a + 10c = 4,600$$

This eliminates answer choice B.

2. <u>B</u>

Identify the two variables:

Number of spiral notebooks $= n$.

Number of pocket folders $= p$.

Determine the system of equations:

Equation 1: Total of notebooks and pocket folders $= 78$.

$$n + p = 78$$

This eliminates answer choices C and D.

Equation 2: Price of each $n = \$3$ and price of each $p = \$0.50$. Total cost $= \$164$.

$$3n + 0.5p = 164$$

This eliminates answer choice A.

3. <u>D</u>

Identify the two variables:

Number of shirts $= s$.

Number of hats $= h$.

Determine the system of equations:

Equation 1: Total of shirts and hats $= 10$.

$$s + h = 10$$

This eliminates answer choices A and B.

Equation 2: Price of each $s = \$20$. Price of each $h = \frac{1}{2}s = \frac{20}{2} = \$10$. Total cost $= \$140$.

$$20s + 10h = 140$$

This eliminates answer choice C.

4. <u>C</u>

Identify the two variables:

Let number of rooms with 2 beds $= x$.

Let number of rooms with 3 beds $= y$.

Determine the system of equations:

Equation 1: Total number of rooms $= 55$.

$$x + y = 55$$

Equation 2: Each room with 2 beds (x) will have 2 students and each room with 3 beds (y) will have 3 students. Total number of students $= 125$.

$$2x + 3y = 125$$

Solve the system for y (rooms with 3 beds):

$$\begin{array}{l} 2x + 3y = 125 \\ -2(x + y = 55) \end{array} \longrightarrow \begin{array}{l} \cancel{2x} + 3y = 125 \\ \underline{-\cancel{2x} - 2y = -110} \\ \qquad\qquad y = 15 \end{array}$$

5. <u>15</u>

Identify the two variables:

Let Shannon's present age $= x$.

Hence, Shannon's age 3 years ago $= x - 3$.

Let Tina's present age $= y$.

Hence, Tina's age 3 years ago $= y - 3$.

Determine the system of equations:

Equation 1: Total of present ages $= 42$.

$$x + y = 42$$

Equation 2: Three years ago Tina's age $(y - 3)$ was twice of Shannon's age $(x - 3)$.

$$(y - 3) = 2(x - 3) \rightarrow$$
$$y - 3 = 2x - 6 \rightarrow 2x - y = 3$$

Solve the system for x (Shannon's present age):

$$\begin{array}{l} x + \cancel{y} = 42 \\ \underline{2x - \cancel{y} = 3} \\ 3x = 45 \rightarrow x = 15 \end{array}$$

6. <u>D</u>

Identify the two variables:

Number of hours through backroads $= b$.

Number of hours on highway $= h$.

Determine the system of equations:

Equation 1: Equation $b + h = 5$ is given in the question.

Equation 2: Total miles $= 205$.

Since the speed on backroads is 25 miles in an hour, miles in b hours $= 25b$.

Since the speed on highway is 65 miles in an hour, miles in h hours $= 65h$.

$$25b + 65h = 205$$

This eliminates answer choices A, B, and C.

7. C

Identify the two variables:

Let number of fish tacos $= x$.

Let number of chicken tacos $= y$.

Determine the system of equations:

Equation 1: Total number of tacos $= 14$.

$$x + y = 14$$

Equation 2: Price of each $x = \$6$ and price of each $y = \$4$. Total cost of tacos $= \$72$.

$$6x + 4y = 72$$

Solve the system for x (fish tacos):

$$\begin{array}{l} 6x + 4y = 72 \\ -4(x + y = 14) \end{array} \longrightarrow \begin{array}{l} 6x + 4y = 72 \\ -4x - 4y = -56 \\ \hline 2x \quad = 16 \rightarrow x = 8 \end{array}$$

8. A

Identify the two variables:

Let cost of each box of crayons $= x$.

Let cost of each box of pencils $= y$.

Determine the system of equations:

Equation 1: Cost of 6 boxes of crayons and 4 boxes of pencils $= \$16$.

$$6x + 4y = 16$$

Equation 2: Cost of 3 boxes of crayons and 7 boxes of pencils $= \$13$.

$$3x + 7y = 13$$

Solve the system for y (pencils):

$$\begin{array}{l} 2(3x + 7y = 13) \\ -(6x + 4y = 16) \end{array} \longrightarrow \begin{array}{l} 6x + 14y = 26 \\ -6x - 4y = -16 \\ \hline 10y = 10 \rightarrow y = 1 \end{array}$$

9. D

Identify the two variables:

Let the number of 20 ounces bottles $= a$.

Let the number of 50 ounces bottles $= b$.

Determine the system of equations:

Equation 1: Total number of bottles $= 90$.

$$a + b = 90$$

Equation 2: Price of each $a = \$20$ and price of each $b = \$42$. Use the process of elimination. First determine the lowest value of b using the lower total $= \$2,900$.

$$20a + 42b = 2,900$$

Solve the system for b:

$$\begin{array}{l} 20a + 42b = 2,900 \\ -20(a + b = 90) \end{array} \longrightarrow \begin{array}{l} 20a + 42b = 2,900 \\ -20a - 20b = -1,800 \\ \hline 22b = 1,100 \\ b = 50 \end{array}$$

Hence, the value of b is 50 or higher. 50 is not an answer choice. Only answer choice D is higher than 50.

10. 30

Identify the two variables:

Variables a and b are two different numbers.

Determine the system of equations:

Equation 1:

$$a + b = 110$$

Equation 2:

$$3a + b = 170$$

Solve the system for a:

$$\begin{array}{l} 3a + b = 170 \\ -(a + b = 110) \end{array} \longrightarrow \begin{array}{l} 3a + b = 170 \\ -a - b = -110 \\ \hline 2a \quad = 60 \rightarrow a = 30 \end{array}$$11.

11. 24

Identify the two variables:

Let number of dimes $= x$.

Let number of quarters $= y$.

Determine the system of equations:

Equation 1: Total number of coins $= 40$.

$$x + y = 40$$

Equation 2: Each dime $= \$0.10$. Each quarter $= \$0.25$. Total value $= \$7.60$.

$$0.10x + 0.25y = 7.60 \rightarrow 10x + 25y = 760$$

Solve the system for y (quarters):

$$\begin{array}{l} 10x + 25y = 760 \\ -10(x + y = 40) \end{array} \longrightarrow \begin{array}{l} 10x + 25y = 760 \\ -10x - 10y = -400 \\ \hline 15y = 360 \\ y = 24 \end{array}$$

12. 10

Identify the two variables:

Number of muffin trays $= a$.

Number of cupcake trays $= b$.

Determine the system of equations:

Equation 1: Total number of trays $= 18$.

$$a + b = 18$$

Equation 2: Price of each $a = \$10$ and price of each b is $\$6$. Total cost of all trays $= \$148$.

$$10a + 6b = 148$$

Solve the system for a (tray of muffins):

$$\begin{array}{l} 10a + 6b = 148 \\ -6(a + b = 18) \end{array} \longrightarrow \begin{array}{l} 10a + 6b = 148 \\ -6a - 6b = -108 \\ \hline 4a \quad = 40 \rightarrow a = 10 \end{array}$$

Category 19 – Word Problems on Linear Inequalities

1. <u>B</u>

Determine the variables:

Number of hot dogs $= d$.

Determine the conditional relationship:

Cost of daily stand $= \$68$.

Cost of making d hot dogs $= 1.5d$.

Earnings from d hot dogs $= 4d$.

Daily cost of stand + daily cost of making d hot dogs must be less than or equal to daily earnings from selling d hot dogs.

$$68 + 1.5d \leq 4d \;\rightarrow\; 68 \leq 4d - 1.5d \;\rightarrow\; 68 \leq 2.5d$$

2. <u>A</u>

Determine the variables:

Number of cards given to brother $= a$.

Number of cards given to sister $= b$.

Determine the conditional relationship:

Total cards given $= a + b$.

Total cards left $= 15 - (a + b)$.

Total cards left is at least 5.

$$15 - (a + b) \geq 5 \;\rightarrow\; 15 - a - b \geq 5$$

3. <u>C</u>

Determine the variables:

Number of soft pretzels $= p$.

Number of water bottles $= b$.

Determine the conditional relationship:

Cost of p soft pretzels $= 3p$.

Cost of b water bottles $= 2b$.

Cost of p soft pretzels + cost of b water bottles must be less than or equal to 200.

$$3p + 2b \leq 200 \;\rightarrow\; 200 \geq 3p + 2b$$

4. <u>D</u>

Determine the variables:

Pounds of cherry tomatoes $= c$.

Pounds of potatoes $= p$.

Determine the conditional relationship:

Total sold per day must be greater than 12 pounds.

$$c + p > 12$$

Total sold per week must be

$$c + p > (12 \times 7) \;\rightarrow\; c + p > 84$$

5. <u>C</u>

Determine the variables:

Let number of calls $= n$.

Determine the conditional relationship:

Monthly cost of n call $= 0.16n$.

Monthly fixed fee + monthly cost of n calls must be less than or equal to $\$25$.

$$17.99 + 0.16n \leq 25 \;\rightarrow\; 0.16n \leq 25 - 17.99 \;\rightarrow$$
$$0.16n \leq 7.01 \;\rightarrow\; n \leq 43.81$$

Gary can make a maximum of 43 calls.

6. <u>6</u>

Determine the variables:

Let number of candles $= c$.

Determine the conditional relationship:

Cost of 7 napkins $= 7 \times 2 = 14$.

Cost of c candles $= 1.5c$.

Cost of 7 napkins + cost of c candles must be less than or equal to $\$24$.

$$14 + 1.5c \leq 24 \;\rightarrow\; 1.5c \leq 10 \;\rightarrow\; c \leq 6.6$$

The party planner can buy 6 whole candles.

Category 20 – Word Problems on Linear System of Inequalities

1. <u>B</u>

Identify the two variables:

Number of boxes weighing 20 pounds $= m$.

Number of boxes weighing 40 pounds $= n$.

Determine the conditional relationship:

Equation 1: The number of boxes must be less than or equal to 55.

$$m + n \leq 55$$

This eliminates answer choices A and C.

Equation 2: Total weight of all boxes must be less than or equal to 1,850.

$$20m + 40n \leq 1,850$$

This eliminates answer choice D.

2. <u>D</u>

Identify the two variables:

Fiction books $= c$.

Non-fiction books $= k$.

Determine the conditional relationship:

Equation 1: The total number of books must be less than or equal to 50.

$$c + k \leq 50$$

This eliminates answer choices A and B.

Equation 2: Each $c = \$12$ and each $k = \$15$. Total cost of all the books must be less than or equal to $\$680$.

$$12c + 15k \leq 680$$

This eliminates answer choice C.

3. D

Identify the two variables:

Number of on-line hours $= l$.

Number of in-home hours $= h$.

Determine the conditional relationship:

Equation 1: The number of all hours per week must be less than or equal to 20.

$$l + h \leq 20$$

This eliminates answer choice C.

Equation 2: Each $l = \$25$ and each $h = \$45$. Total from l and h must be greater than or equal to $\$600$.

$$25l + 45h \geq 600$$

This eliminates answer choice A.

Equation 3: h must be at least 10 but cannot be greater than 20.

$$10 \leq h \leq 20$$

This eliminates answer choice B.

4. C

Identify the two variables:

Number of songs $= x$.

Number of videos $= y$.

Determine the conditional relationship:

Equation 1: The number of all songs and videos must be greater than or equal to 12 .

$$x + y \geq 12$$

This eliminates answer choices A and B.

Equation 2: Each $x = \$0.99$ and each $y = \$1.99$. Total cost must be less than $\$21$.

$$0.99x + 1.99y < 21$$

This eliminates answer choice D.

5. B

Identify the two variables:

Number of event coordinators $= c$.

Number of stewards $= s$.

Determine the conditional relationship:

Equation 1: Total number of staff members must be greater than or equal to 8.

$$c + s \geq 8$$

This eliminates answer choice C.

Equation 2: c must be at least 1 but no more than 3.

$$1 \leq c \leq 3$$

This eliminates answer choice D.

Equation 3: Each $c = \$495$ and each $s = \$175$. Total pay for all c and s must be less than or equal to $\$2,500$.

$$495c + 175s \leq 2,500$$

This eliminates answer choice A.

6. A

Identify the two variables:

Number of exercise bikes $= b$.

Number of treadmills $= t$.

Determine the conditional relationship:

Equation 1: The number of treadmills and bikes must be greater than or equal to 12.

$$b + t \geq 12$$

This eliminates answer choices B and D.

Equation 2: Each $b = \$1,800$ and each $t = \$2,600$. Total cost must be less than or equal to $\$28,000$.

$$1,800b + 2,600t \leq 28,000$$

This eliminates answer choice C.

Category 21 –Word Problems on Equal Variables in Linear Equations

1. D

Equate the two equations:

$$48 + \frac{1}{4}p = 150 - \frac{1}{2}p$$

Solve for p:

$$\frac{1}{4}p + \frac{1}{2}p = 150 - 48 \rightarrow \frac{3}{4}p = 102 \rightarrow p = 136$$

2. C

Equate the two equations:

$$10.50 + 4.50x = 36.50 + 2.50x$$

Solve for x:

$$4.50x - 2.50x = 36.50 - 10.50 \rightarrow 2x = 26 \rightarrow$$
$$x = 13$$

Solve c: Plug in $x = 13$ in the equation.

$$c = 36.50 + (2.50 \times 13) = 36.50 + 32.50 = 69$$

3. A

Equate the two equations:

$$35 + 3p = 75 + p$$

Solve for p:

$$3p - p = 75 - 35 \rightarrow 2p = 40 \rightarrow p = 20$$

4. C

Determine the equation for manufacturing costs:

Let the manufacturing costs for next quarter $= C$.

$$C = 37,750 + 25W$$

Equate the two equations:

$$37,750 + 25W = 19,646 + 149W$$

Solve for W:

$$37,750 - 19,646 = 149W - 25W \rightarrow$$
$$18,104 = 124W \rightarrow W = 146$$

Section 4 – Review Questions

1. <u>D</u>

Determine the unknown number/variable 1 (Samara): s miles per day for 4 days $= 4s$. This eliminates answer choices A and C.

Determine the unknown number/variable 2 (Chuck): p miles per day for 6 days $= 6p$. This eliminates answer choice B.

2. <u>A</u>

Determine the components of the equation:

$21 =$ Average number of pages the teacher will read each day.

$315 =$ Number of pages in the book.

$p =$ Number of pages left to read at the end of each day.

3. <u>C</u>

Determine the unknown number/variable 1 (walking on treadmill): t calories per minute for 35 minutes $= 35t$. This eliminates answer choices A and B.

Determine the unknown number/variable 2 (running on treadmill): 6 calories per minute for 10 minutes $= 6 \times 10 = 60$. This eliminates answer choice D.

4. <u>C</u>

Determine the components of the equation:

$0.2 =$ Approximate increase in the Body Mass Index of an adult for each pound of weight. (This is same as "for each increase of 1 pound in weight, B increases by approximately 0.2".)

$B =$ Body Mass Index of an adult weighing p pounds.

5. <u>B</u>

Determine the two variables:

Number of packages shipped during off-peak hours $= x$.

Number of packages shipped during peak hours $= y$.

Determine the conditional relationship:

The total number of packages shipped per day at each franchise must be less than or equal to 150.

$$x + y \leq 150$$

This eliminates answer choices C and D.

The number of packages shipped during off-peak hours must be less than or equal to the number of packages shipped during peak hours.

$$x \leq y$$

This eliminates answer choice A.

6. <u>A</u>

Identify the two variables:

Number of hours during morning shift $= M$.

Number of hours during night shift $= N$.

Determine the system of equations:

Equation 1: Total hours $= 10$.

$$M + N = 10$$

This eliminates answer choices B and C.

Equation 2: Each $M = \$18$ and each $N = \$34$. Total earnings $= \$276$.

$$18M + 34N = 276$$

This eliminates answer choice D.

7. <u>D</u>

Identify the two variables:

Number of hours per week teaching Algebra I $= m$.

Number of hours per week teaching Spanish $= n$.

Determine the conditional relationship:

Equation 1: Total number of hours per week must be less than or equal to 15.

$$m + n \leq 15$$

This eliminates answer choice A.

Equation 2: Each $m = \$50$ and each $n = \$38$. The earnings from m and n must be greater than or equal to $500 per week.

$$50m + 38n \geq 500$$

This eliminates answer choice B.

Equation 3: n must be at least 7 per week. Since the maximum number of hours per week is 15, n is between 7 and 15 hours.

$$7 \leq n \leq 15$$

This eliminates answer choice C.

8. <u>A</u>

Determine the constant: Admission fee $= \$40$. This eliminates answer choices C and D.

Determine the unknown number/variable: n rides for $2 per ride $= 2n$. This eliminates answer choice B.

9. <u>B</u>

$g(t)$ is a linear function. The input value of t determines the value of the function $g(t)$.

$g(12) = 19$ infers that in 12 years from 2015, the tree is expected to be 19 feet tall.

10. D

Determine the variable:

Number of miles $= m$.

Determine the conditional relationship:

Miles driven must be less than or equal to the miles the car can go in 3.5 gallons of fuel.

In 3.5 gallons, the car can go $19.5 \times 3.5 = 68.25$ miles.

$$m \le 68.25$$

11. B

Determine the two unknown variables:

$389c =$ total cost of c iPads.

$72d =$ total cost of d desks.

12. C

Identify the two variables:

Let number of nickels $= x$.

Let number of dimes $= y$.

Determine the system of equations:

Equation 1: Total number of coins 50.

$$x + y = 50$$

Equation 2: Each nickel $= \$0.05$. Each dime $= \$0.10$.

$$0.05x + 0.1y = 3.50$$
$$5x + 10y = 350$$

Solve the system for y (dimes):

$$\begin{aligned} 5x + 10y &= 350 \\ -5(x + y &= 50) \end{aligned} \longrightarrow \begin{aligned} 5x + 10y &= 350 \\ -5x - 5y &= -250 \end{aligned}$$

$$5y = 100 \rightarrow y = 20$$

13. A

Form the equations:

Let the number of extra-large burgers $= b$.

Equation for cost is

$$41.50 + 0.45b$$

Equation for profit is

$$29.50 + 1.95b$$

Set the equations equal:

$$41.50 + 0.45b = 29.50 + 1.95b$$

Solve for b:

$$1.95b - 0.45b = 41.50 - 29.50 \rightarrow$$

$$1.5b = 12 \rightarrow b = \frac{12}{1.5} = 8$$

14. B

Identify the two variables:

Let number of tickets sold at reduced price $= x$.

Let number of tickets sold at regular price $= y$.

Determine the system of equations:

Equation 1: Total number of tickets sold $= 240$.

$$x + y = 240$$

Equation 2: Price of each $x = \$9$ and price of each $y = \$29$. Total price of all tickets sold $= \$4,960$.

$$9x + 29y = 4,960$$

Solve the system for y (regular price):

$$\begin{aligned} 9x + 29y &= 4,960 \\ -9(x + y &= 240) \end{aligned} \longrightarrow \begin{aligned} 9x + 29y &= 4,960 \\ -9x - 9y &= -2,160 \end{aligned}$$

$$20y = 2,800$$
$$y = 140$$

15. C

Determine the variable:

Number of teachers $= g$.

Determine the conditional relationship:

The number of teachers to be added per year is greater than or equal to 4 but less than or equal to 9. Hence,

$$4 \le g \text{ added per year} \le 9$$

In 3 years, all possible values of teachers added are

$$4 \times 3 \le g \text{ added in 3 years } \le 9 \times 3$$
$$12 \le g \text{ added in 3 years} \le 27$$

Since currently there are 52 teachers, all possible values of the total number of teachers in 3 years can be

$$12 + 52 \le g \le 27 + 52$$
$$64 \le g \le 79$$

16. D

Determine the components of the equation:

$68 =$ Average increase in the number of the trout fishes each month after January 2020 for m months.

$p =$ Initial population in January 2020.

17. C

Determine the unknown number/variable:

Students enrolled in 2015 $= 176$.

Students enrolled in 2020 $= 236$.

Total increase in 5 years $= 236 - 176 = 60$. Hence,

average increase per year $= \dfrac{60}{5} = 12$.

Average increase in t years $= 12t$.

Determine the equation: Number of students r in t years after 2020 $=$ students enrolled in 2020 $+$ average increase per year for t years.

$$r = 236 + 12t$$

18. **D**

Determine the variable:

Amount in bank account, in dollars $= s$.

Determine the conditional relationship: Monthly deposits must be greater than or equal to $100 but less than or equal to $150.

$$100 \leq \text{monthly deposit} \leq 150.$$

In 12 months, all possible values of savings are

$$(100 \times 12) \leq \text{deposits in 12 months} \leq (150 \times 12)$$

$$1{,}200 \leq \text{deposits in 12 months} \leq 1{,}800$$

Since the beginning dollars in bank account $= 700$, all possible values of s at the end of 12 months can be

$$1{,}200 + 700 \leq s \leq 1{,}800 + 700$$

$$1{,}900 \leq s \leq 2{,}500$$

19. **C**

Identify the two variables:

Let 6-pack container $= x$.

Let 14-pack container $= y$.

Set up the system of equations:

Equation 1: Total number of containers $= 12$.

$$x + y = 12$$

Equation 2: Number of cupcakes in 6-pack container $= 6x$ and number of cupcakes in 14-pack container $= 14y$. Total number of cupcakes $= 104$.

$$6x + 14y = 104$$

Solve the system for y (14-pack containers):

$$\begin{array}{ll} 6x + 14y = 104 & \quad 6x + 14y = 104 \\ -6(x + y = 12) & \quad -6x - 6y = -72 \end{array}$$

$$8y = 32 \rightarrow y = 4$$

The number of cupcakes in 14-pack containers $= 14 \times 4 = 56$.

20. **D**

There is no need of calculation. For $\frac{t}{2.5}$ to equal 1, the value of t is the reciprocal of $\frac{1}{2.5}$. Hence, for the cactus to grow by 1 centimeters, $t = 2.5$.

21. **40**

Form the equations:

Let the number of calls $= c$.

Equation for Casey's monthly cost is

$$24.99 + 0.08c$$

Equation for Lilian's monthly cost is

$$16.99 + 0.28c$$

Set the equations equal:

$$24.99 + 0.08c = 16.99 + 0.28c$$

Solve for c:

$$0.28c - 0.08c = 24.99 - 16.99 \rightarrow$$

$$0.2c = 8 \rightarrow c = 40$$

22. **21**

Solve: Plug in given values of $C = 3{,}965$ and $n = 3$ in the equation and solve for h.

$$3{,}965 = 500 + (55 \times 3h) \rightarrow 3{,}965 = 500 + 165h \rightarrow$$

$$165h = 3{,}965 - 500 \rightarrow 165h = 3{,}465 \rightarrow h = 21$$

23. **50**

Form the equations:

Let the number of bags filled with cookies $= c$.

Equation for 5 cookies per bag

Each bag contains 5 cookies. Hence, the number of cookies in c bags $= 5c$.

4 additional bags are required for the remaining cookies. Hence, the number of cookies for which 4 extra bags are required $= 5 \times 4 = 20$.

$$\text{total cookies} = 5c + 20$$

Equation for 10 cookies per bag

Each bag contains 10 cookies. Hence, the number of cookies in c bags $= 10c$.

1 bag is extra after filling the cookies in bags. Hence, there are $10 \times 1 = 10$ cookies less for c bags.

$$\text{total cookies} = 10c - 10$$

Equate and solve for c: In both the equations, the total number of cookies is same.

$$5c + 20 = 10c - 10 \rightarrow$$

$$10c - 5c = 20 + 10 \rightarrow 5c = 30 \rightarrow c = 6$$

Solve for the number of cookies: Plug in $c = 6$ in any equation.

$$5c + 20 \rightarrow (5 \times 6) + 20 = 30 + 20 = 50$$

Section 5 – Polynomial and Undefined Functions

Category 22 – Polynomial Functions as Equations

1. **D**

Plug in the given value of x in the function:
$$f(-2) = (-2)^4 - 3(-2)^2 - 4 = 16 - 12 - 4 = 0$$
$$f(1) = (1)^4 - 3(1)^2 - 4 = 1 - 3 - 4 = -6$$
Solve for $f(-2) - f(1)$:
$$0 - (-6) = 6$$

2. **C**

Plug in the given value of x in the function:
$$f(2x + 5) = \frac{3(2x + 5) - 7}{2} = \frac{6x + 15 - 7}{2} =$$
$$\frac{6x + 8}{2} = 3x + 4$$

3. **B**

Solve for b: Divide both sides by 3.
$$\frac{3f(b)}{3} = \frac{21}{3} \to f(b) = 7$$
$f(x) = 4x + 3$ can be written as $f(b) = 4b + 3$.
Determine the value of b when $f(b) = 7$.
$$7 = 4b + 3 \to 4b = 4 \to b = 1$$

4. **C**

Plug in the given value of x in the function:
$$f(3) = (5 \times 3) + 3 = 18$$
$$f(9) = (5 \times 9) + 3 = 48$$
Solve for $f(3) \times f(9)$:
$$18 \times 48 = 864$$

5. **B**

Plug in the given value of x in the function:
$$g(20): \frac{20^2 m + n}{2} = 1,500 \to \frac{400m + n}{2} = 1,500 \to$$
$$400m + n = 2 \times 1,500 \to 400m + n = 3,000$$
$$g(10): \frac{10^2 m + n}{2} = 300 \to \frac{100m + n}{2} = 300 \to$$
$$100m + n = 2 \times 300 \to 100m + n = 600$$
Solve for m: Create a system of equations and solve.
$$\begin{array}{r} 400m + n = 3,000 \\ -(100m + n = 600) \end{array} \longrightarrow \begin{array}{r} 400m + n = 3,000 \\ -100m - n = -600 \\ \hline 300m = 2,400 \to m = 8 \end{array}$$

6. **D**

Solve for t: Add the two equations and equate them to 0.
$$(3t^4 - 2t - 4) + (-3t^4 + 5t - 5) = 0 \to$$
$$3t^4 - 2t - 4 - 3t^4 + 5t - 5 = 0 \to$$
$$3t - 9 = 0 \to 3t = 9 \to t = 3$$

Category 23 – Polynomial Functions as Tables and Graphs

1. **D**

Read the value of $g(x)$ from the table: Since $x = 6$ is not in the table, determine a value of x that can give $g(3x) = g(6)$ and can be read from the table.

If x is given the value of 2, then
$$2g(2) = g(3 \times 2) \to 2g(2) = g(6)$$
From the table, $g(2) = 5$. Hence,
$$2g(2) = g(6) \to 2 \times 5 = g(6) \to g(6) = 10$$

2. **B**

4 solutions of c implies that 4 values of x define $y = c$.

Count the number of x values for each value of y given in the answer choices:

Answer choice A: For $y = -3$, there are 2 values of x.

Answer choice B: For $y = -2$, there are 4 values of x.

Answer choice C: For $y = 0$, there are 2 values of x.

Answer choice D: For $y = 1$, there are 2 values of x.

3. **A**

Read the values of x from the graph for $y = 3$:
$$x = -2 \text{ and } 2$$
Hence, $f(-2)$ and $f(2)$ satisfy $y = f(x) = 3$.

4. **3**

Simplify: Divide both sides by 3.
$$3f(x) = 12 \to f(x) = \frac{12}{3} = 4 \to f(x) = 4$$
Read the value of x from the table for $f(x) = 4$: $x = 3$

5. **1**

Read the values of $f(x)$ from the table:
$f(1) = -3$. $f(2) = 1$. $f(4) = 4$.

Solve for $\frac{f(2) - f(1)}{f(4)}$: Plug in the above values.
$$\frac{1 - (-3)}{4} = \frac{1 + 3}{4} = \frac{4}{4} = 1$$

Category 24 – Polynomial Function within a Function

1. A

$g(f(3))$:

Read the $f(x)$ value for the inside function:
$$f(3) = 0$$

Read the $g(x)$ value for the outside function:
$$g(f(3)) = g(0) = 5$$

$f(g(-1))$:

Read the $g(x)$ value for the inside function:
$$g(-1) = 7$$

Read the $f(x)$ value for the outside function:
$$f(g(-1)) = f(7) = 4$$

Solve the equation:
$$g(f(3)) + f(g(-1)) + k = 1 \rightarrow 5 + 4 + k = 1 \rightarrow$$
$$9 + k = 1 \rightarrow k = -8$$

2. C

Read the y value from the graph for the inside function:
$$h(-3) = 1$$

Solve the equation for function g:
$$g(h(-3)) = g(1) = 2(1)^4 + 3 = 5$$

Solve for $g(h(-3)) - 2$:
$$5 - 2 = 3$$

3. B

Plug in the given value of x in $g(x)$ and solve:

It is given that $h(x) = -5$. Hence,
$$-5 = c - g(2) \rightarrow -5 = c - (2^2 + 4) \rightarrow$$
$$-5 = c - 8 \rightarrow c = -5 + 8 = 3$$

4. D

Plug in the given value of x in the nested function $g(x)$:
$$g(3) = 3^3 - 20 = 27 - 20 = 7$$

Plug in $x = 7$ in the outside function $f(x)$:
$$f(g(3)) = f(7) = 7^2 - 7 = 49 - 7 = 42$$

5. C

Plug in the given value of x in all the functions:
$$g(7) = 3f(7 - 1) - 3 = 3f(6) - 3 =$$
$$3((4 \times 6) - 19) - 3 = 3(24 - 19) - 3 =$$
$$3(5) - 3 = 15 - 3 = 12$$

6. 8

Since $f(3) = 5$, $g(f(3)) = g(5)$.

Plug in $x = 5$ in the outside function $g(x)$:
$$g(5) = \frac{(2 \times 5^3) - 98}{19} = \frac{(2 \times 125) - 98}{19} = \frac{152}{19} = 8$$

Category 25 – Polynomial Functions and Zeros

1. C

Determine the points on the x-axis where the graph crosses: The graph crosses the x-axis at 1 and 3. The corresponding factors are $(x - 1)$ and $(x - 3)$.

Determine the points on the x-axis where the graph touches the x-axis and curves back: The graph touches the x-axis at -2 and curves back. The corresponding factors are $(x + 2)^2$.

The factors are $(x - 1)(x - 3)(x + 2)^2$.

2. D

Determine the values of x where $y = 0$.

The two values of x where $y = f(x) = 0$ are -2 and 8.

3. B

Determine the zeros:

For x, the zero is 0.

For $(x - 1)$, the zero is 1.

For $(x - 3)$, the zeros is 3.

For $(x + 2)^2$, the distinct zero is -2.

The distinct zeros in ascending order are -2, 0, 1, and 3.

4. C

Determine the zeros:

For $(x - 4)$, the zero is 4.

For $(x^2 - 4)$, the two factors are $(x + 2)(x - 2)$. The two zeros are -2 and 2.

There are three distinct zeros.

5. 10

Determine the values of x where $y = 0$:

The two values of x where $y = h(x) = 0$ are 2 and 5.

Determine the product of the zeros:
$$2 \times 5 = 10$$

Category 26 – Remainder in Polynomial Functions

1. <u>B</u>

Plug in $x = 2$ in the equation and set equation to 0 (Factor Theorem):

$$p(2) = 3(2)^3 - 3(2)^2 - 2c + 2 = 0 \rightarrow$$
$$(3 \times 8) - (3 \times 4) - 2c + 2 = 0 \rightarrow$$
$$24 - 12 - 2c + 2 = 0 \rightarrow$$
$$14 - 2c = 0 \rightarrow 2c = 14 \rightarrow c = 7$$

2. <u>C</u>

Plug in $x = -4$ in the expression (Remainder Theorem):

$$A = 2(-4)^2 + 9(-4) + 5 =$$
$$(2 \times 16) + (9 \times -4) + 5 = 32 - 36 + 5 = 1$$

3. <u>A</u>

The factor of the polynomial $p(x)$ will result in $p(x) = 0$ (Factor Theorem).

Hence, when $x = 1$ is plugged in the equation, the result should be 0.

Evaluate each answer choice: Plug in $x = 1$ in the equations given in answer choices.

By looking at the equations of answer choices B and C it can be observed that for $x = 1$ the equations will not equal to 0. They can be eliminated.

Evaluate answer choice A.

$$-2(1)^2 - 3(1) + 5 = -2 - 3 + 5 = 0$$

Hence, $x + 1$ is a factor of the polynomial $p(x) = -2x^2 - 3x + 5$.

4. <u>D</u>

Factor Theorem:

Since $p(-\frac{1}{2}) = 0$, $x + \frac{1}{2}$ is a factor of $p(x)$.

$$x + \frac{1}{2} \rightarrow 2x + 1$$

5. <u>B</u>

Plug in the factor from answer choices in the equation and evaluate for $p(x) = 0$ (Factor Theorem):

Start with answer choice B.

$$3x - 1 \rightarrow x = \frac{1}{3}$$

$$p\left(\frac{1}{3}\right) = 3\left(\frac{1}{3}\right)^3 - \left(\frac{1}{3}\right)^2 - 6\left(\frac{1}{3}\right) + 2 = 0 \rightarrow$$

$$3\left(\frac{1}{27}\right) - \frac{1}{9} - 2 + 2 = 0 \rightarrow$$

$$\frac{1}{9} - \frac{1}{9} - 2 + 2 = 0$$

Since $p\left(\frac{1}{3}\right) = 0$, $3x - 1$ is a factor of $p(x)$.

(Note that this equation can also be factorized. However, factorization may not always be easy in polynomials.

$$3x^3 - x^2 - 6x + 2 = x^2(3x - 1) - 2(3x - 1)$$

The two factors are $(x^2 - 2)$ and $(3x - 1)$.)

6. <u>D</u>

Factor Theorem:

When $p(x)$ is divided by $x + 5$, the remainder is 4. Hence, $x + 5$ is not a factor of $p(x)$. Answer choice D is correct.

7. <u>2</u>

Plug in $x = -3$ in the equation (Remainder Theorem):

$$f(-3) = 3(-3)^3 + 8(-3)^2 + 11 =$$
$$(3 \times -27) + (8 \times 9) + 11 = -81 + 72 + 11 = 2$$

Category 27 – Undefined Functions

1. <u>A</u>

Set denominator $= 0$:
$$6x + 2x + 16 = 0$$
Solve:
$$8x + 16 = 0 \;\rightarrow\; 8x = -16 \;\rightarrow\; x = -2$$

2. <u>C</u>

Set denominator $= 0$:
$$3x - 12 = 0$$
Solve:
$$3x = 12 \;\rightarrow\; x = 4$$

3. <u>D</u>

Set denominator $= 0$:
$$(x^2 - 11x + 27) + (x - 2) = 0$$
Solve:
$$x^2 - 10x + 25 = 0 \;\rightarrow\; (x - 5)^2 \;\rightarrow\; x = 5$$

4. <u>D</u>

Set denominator $= 0$:
$$(x + 4)^2 - (16x + 1) = 0$$
Solve: FOIL and simplify.
$$x^2 + 8x + 16 - 16x - 1 = 0 \;\rightarrow\; x^2 - 8x + 15$$
Factorize.
$$(x - 3)(x - 5) \;\rightarrow\; x = 3 \text{ and } 5$$

5. <u>B</u>

Set denominator $= 0$:
$$4x - 1 = 0$$
Solve:
$$4x = 1 \;\rightarrow\; x = \frac{1}{4}$$

Section 5 – Review Questions

1. <u>A</u>

Read the value of y from the graph for $x = -1$:
$$y = t(-1) = -2$$
Hence, $g(m) = -2$.

Count the number of x values from the graph for $y = -2$: Draw a line through $y = -2$ and count.

There are 3 distinct values of x that define $g(m) = -2$.

2. <u>B</u>

Determine the x-intercepts:

For $(x - 1)$, the x-intercept is 1.

For $(2x - 3)$, the x-intercept is $\frac{3}{2}$.

For $(3x + 2)$, the x-intercept is $-\frac{2}{3}$.

This eliminates option II.

3. <u>A</u>

Determine the points on the x-axis where the graph crosses: The graph crosses the x-axis at 1. The corresponding factor is $(x - 1)$.

Determine the points on the x-axis where the graph touches the x-axis and curves back: The graph touches the x-axis and curves back at -1 and 3. The corresponding factors are $(x + 1)^2$ and $(x - 3)^2$.

The factors are $(x - 1)(x - 3)^2(x + 1)^2$.

4. <u>C</u>

Determine the zeros:

For $2x$, the zero is 0.

For $(x - k)^2$, the distinct zero is k.

For $(x + k)^2$, the distinct zero is $-k$.

There are three distinct zeros.

5. <u>D</u>

Determine the x-intercept: Set $y = g(x) = 0$.
$$0 = 3x - 6 \;\rightarrow\; 3x = 6 \;\rightarrow\; x = 2$$
Hence, the x-intercept is $(2, 0)$. This can also be written as $(2, g(2))$, since $y = g(2) = 0$.

6. <u>C</u>

Plug in the given value of x in all the functions:
$$g(8) = 2f(8 + 2) - 5 = 2f(10) - 5 =$$
$$2\big((3 \times 10) - 10\big) - 5 = 2(30 - 10) - 5 =$$
$$2(20) - 5 = 40 - 5 = 35$$

7. <u>B</u>

Determine the points on the x-axis where the graph crosses: The graph crosses the x-axis at -2, 1, and 3. The corresponding factors are $(x + 2)$, $(x - 1)$, and $(x - 3)$.

$(x - 2)$ in answer choice B is not a factor.

8. <u>20</u>

Since $g(b) = 10$, $f(g(b)) = f(10)$.

Plug in $x = 10$ in the outside function f:

$$f(10) = \frac{(17.8 \times 10^2) + b}{3} = \frac{1{,}780 + b}{3}$$

Determine the value of b: It is given $f(10) = 600$.

$$\frac{1{,}780 + b}{3} = 600 \rightarrow 1{,}780 + b = 1{,}800 \rightarrow b = 20$$

9. <u>4</u>

Plug in the given value of x in the function: $f(5) = 8$.

$$2f(3) = f(3 + 2) \rightarrow 2f(3) = f(5) \rightarrow 2f(3) = 8$$

Divide both sides by 2.

$$\frac{2f(3)}{2} = \frac{8}{2} \rightarrow f(3) = 4$$

10. <u>D</u>

Factor Theorem:

Since $p(-\frac{2}{3}) = 0$, $x + \frac{2}{3}$ is a factor of $p(x)$.

$$x + \frac{2}{3} \rightarrow 3x + 2$$

11. <u>A</u>

Read the value of y from the graph for $x = 2$:

$$h(2) = 4$$

Hence, $h(t) = h(2) = 4 \rightarrow h(t) = 4$

Read the values of x from the graph for $y = 4$:

There are two values of x for $h(t) = 4$

$$x = -1 \text{ and } 2$$

Answer choice A is -1.

12. <u>B</u>

Evaluate each answer choice: Plug in the answer choices in the given equation and evaluate for $p(x) = 0$ (Factor Theorem).

Start with answer choice B.

$$p(-2) = 5(-2)^3 + 8(-2)^2 - 3(-2) + 2 =$$
$$(5 \times -8) + (8 \times 4) - (3 \times -2) + 2 =$$
$$-40 + 32 + 6 + 2 = 0$$

Since $p(-2) = 0$, -2 is a zero of $p(x)$.

13. <u>C</u>

Plug in the given value of x in the function:

$$h(4) = 4^3 - a = 64 - a$$
$$h(2) = 2^3 - a = 8 - a$$

Solve for $h(4) - h(2)$:

$$(64 - a) - (8 - a) = 64 - a - 8 + a = 56$$

14. <u>B</u>

Determine from the table the values of x where $y = 0$:

$$x = 2$$

Hence, the factor is $x - 2$.

15. <u>A</u>

$f(g(4))$:

Read the $g(x)$ value for the inside function:

$$g(4) = -2$$

Read the $f(x)$ value for the outside function:

$$f(g(4)) = f(-2) = 9$$

$g(f(4))$:

Read the $f(x)$ value for the inside function:

$$f(4) = 1$$

Read the $g(x)$ value for the outside function:

$$g(f(4)) = g(1) = 5$$

Solve the equation:

$$k = f(g(4)) - g(f(4)) = 9 - 5 = 4$$

16. <u>D</u>

Plug in $x = 3$ in the equation (Remainder Theorem):

$$p(3) = 3^3 - (7 \times 3) + 3 = 27 - 21 + 3 = 9$$

17. <u>C</u>

Set denominator $= 0$ and solve:

$$(x^2 - x - 9) + 3(x - 2) = 0 \rightarrow$$
$$x^2 - x - 9 + 3x - 6 = 0 \rightarrow x^2 + 2x - 15 = 0 \rightarrow$$
$$(x + 5)(x - 3) = 0 \rightarrow x = -5 \text{ and } 3$$

18. <u>116</u>

Plug in the given value of x in the function:

$$g(24) = ((0.2 \times 24) + 1)(24 - 4) =$$
$$(4.8 + 1)(20) = 5.8 \times 20 = 116$$

19. <u>16</u>

Solve for a: Plug in $x = 2$ in the equation and set it to 10.

$$h(2) = a(2^2) + a(2) + 4 = 10 \rightarrow$$
$$4a + 2a + 4 = 10 \rightarrow 6a = 6 \rightarrow a = 1$$

Plug in the given value of x in the function and $a = 1$:

$$h(3) = 1(3^2) + 1(3) + 4 \rightarrow 9 + 3 + 4 = 16$$

20. <u>3</u>

Solve for x: Plug in the definitions of $f(x)$ and $h(x)$ in the given equation:

$$f(x) - h(x) = 9 \rightarrow (9x - 1) - (5x + 2) = 9 \rightarrow$$
$$9x - 1 - 5x - 2 = 9 \rightarrow 4x = 12 \rightarrow x = 3$$

Section 6 – Quadratic Equations and Parabola

Category 28 – Quadratic Equations and Factors

1. <u>A</u>

Determine the roots: Remove multiple of 2 to simplify.
$$2(x^2 + 3x - 40) = 0 \rightarrow x^2 + 3x - 40 = 0$$
$$(x + 8)(x - 5) = 0$$
$$x = -8 \text{ and } 5$$

2. <u>B</u>

Determine the roots:
$$x^2 - 7x + 12 = 0 \rightarrow (x - 3)(x - 4) = 0$$
$$x = 3 \text{ and } 4$$

3. <u>D</u>

Determine the roots: Since the answer choices have square roots, use the quadratic formula.

$a = 1.\ b = 2.\ c = -5.$

$$\frac{-2 \pm \sqrt{2^2 - (4 \times 1 \times -5)}}{2 \times 1} = \frac{-2 \pm \sqrt{4 + 20}}{2} =$$
$$\frac{-2 \pm \sqrt{24}}{2}$$

The two multiples of $\sqrt{24}$ are $\sqrt{6 \times 4}$ where $\sqrt{4} = 2$.

$$\frac{-2 \pm \sqrt{4 \times 6}}{2} = \frac{-2 \pm 2\sqrt{6}}{2} = \frac{-2}{2} \pm \frac{2\sqrt{6}}{2} = -1 \pm \sqrt{6}$$

The two solutions are $-1 - \sqrt{6}$ and $-1 + \sqrt{6}$. Answer choice D is one of them.

4. <u>A</u>

Determine c: The two given roots are -8 and 2. The value of c when $a = 1$ is the product of the two roots.
$$c = -8 \times 2 = -16$$

5. <u>D</u>

Determine the roots: Since the answer choices have square roots, use the quadratic formula.

$a = 5.\ b = -6.\ c = -3.$

$$\frac{-(-6) \pm \sqrt{(-6)^2 - (4 \times 5 \times -3)}}{2 \times 5} = \frac{6 \pm \sqrt{36 + 60}}{10} =$$
$$\frac{6 \pm \sqrt{96}}{10}$$

The two multiples of $\sqrt{96}$ are $\sqrt{6 \times 16}$ where $\sqrt{16} = 4$.

$$\frac{6 \pm \sqrt{6 \times 16}}{10} = \frac{6 \pm 4\sqrt{6}}{10} = \frac{6}{10} \pm \frac{4\sqrt{6}}{10} = \frac{3}{5} \pm \frac{2\sqrt{6}}{5}$$

6. <u>C</u>

Determine the factors: Since $a > 0$, the factorization below is shown using the formula. Note that this equation can be factored without the formula depending on the student's comfort level.

$a = 2.\ b = -5.\ c = -12.$

$$\frac{-(-5) \pm \sqrt{(-5)^2 - (4 \times 2 \times -12)}}{2 \times 2} = \frac{5 \pm \sqrt{25 + 96}}{4} =$$
$$\frac{5 \pm \sqrt{121}}{4} = \frac{5 \pm 11}{4}$$

The two roots are
$$\frac{5 + 11}{4} = \frac{16}{4} = 4$$
$$\frac{5 - 11}{4} = -\frac{6}{4} = -\frac{3}{2}$$

The two factors are
$$(x - 4)\left(x + \frac{3}{2}\right) \rightarrow (x - 4)(2x + 3)$$

Category 29 – Quadratic Equations and Number of Roots

1. <u>A</u>

Determine number of solutions using the discriminant:

$a = 3.\ b = 4.\ c = 7.$

$$b^2 - 4ac = (4)^2 - (4 \times 3 \times 7) = 16 - 84 = -68$$

Since discriminant < 0, there is no real solution.

2. <u>D</u>

Set the discriminant to 0:

$a = a.\ b = 6.\ c = c.$

Since the equation has one solution, the discriminant is 0.

$$b^2 - 4ac = 0 \rightarrow (6)^2 - (4 \times a \times c) = 0 \rightarrow$$
$$36 - 4ac = 0 \rightarrow 4ac = 36 \rightarrow ac = 9$$

3. 2

Set the discriminant to 0:

$a = a$. $b = -8$. $c = 8$.

Since the equation has one solution, the discriminant is 0.

$$b^2 - 4ac = 0 \rightarrow (-8)^2 - (4 \times a \times 8) = 0 \rightarrow$$
$$64 - 32a = 0 \rightarrow a = 2$$

4. A

Set the discriminant to < 0:

$a = 4$. $b = -4$. $c = -k$.

Since the equation has no real solution, the discriminant must be less than 0.

$$b^2 - 4ac < 0 \rightarrow (-4)^2 - (4 \times 4 \times -k) < 0 \rightarrow$$
$$16 + 16k < 0 \rightarrow 16k < -16 \rightarrow k < -1$$

Only answer choice A is less than -1.

5. C

Determine number of solutions using the discriminant:

$a = 7$. $b = -10$. $c = 4$.

$$b^2 - 4ac = (-10)^2 - (4 \times 7 \times 4) =$$
$$100 - 112 = -12$$

Since discriminant < 0, there is no real solution.

6. B

Determine number of solutions using the discriminant:

$a = 9$. $b = -6$. $c = 1$.

$$b^2 - 4ac = (-6)^2 - (4 \times 9 \times 1) = 36 - 36 = 0$$

Since discriminant $= 0$, there is one solution.

Category 30 - Sum and Product of Quadratic Roots

1. B

Use the product formula: All the values of n is referring to the roots of the quadratic equation.

$a = 2$. $c = -20$.

$$\frac{c}{a} = \frac{-20}{2} = -10$$

2. A

Use the sum formula: Since the value of c is not given, use the sum formula.

$a = 2$. $b = -7$.

$$\text{sum of roots using formula} = -\frac{b}{a} = -\frac{-7}{2} = \frac{7}{2}$$

Determine the second root:

It is given that one of the roots $= 2$. Let the second root $= x$. Hence,

$$\text{sum of roots by adding} = 2 + x$$

Equate the two sums of the roots.

$$2 + x = \frac{7}{2} \rightarrow x = \frac{7}{2} - 2 = \frac{7 - 4}{2} = \frac{3}{2}$$

3. C

Use the product formula: Since the value of b is not given, use the product formula.

$a = 2$. $c = -12$.

$$\frac{c}{a} = \frac{-12}{2} = -6$$

Evaluate each answer choice for the product of the two given zeros. Correct product $= -6$.

Answer choice A $= -2 \times -12 = 24$. This is incorrect.

Answer choice B $= -2 \times -6 = 12$. This is incorrect.

Answer choice C $= -1 \times 6 = -6$. This is correct.

Answer choice D $= 1 \times 6 = 6$. This is incorrect.

4. C

Use the product formula: Since the value of b is not given, use the product formula.

$a = 2$. $c = 9$.

$$\text{product of roots using formula} = \frac{c}{a} = \frac{9}{2}$$

Determine the second root:

It is given that one of the roots $= 3$. Let the second root $= x$. Hence,

$$\text{product of roots by multiplying} = 3 \times x$$

Equate the two products of the roots.

$$3 \times x = \frac{9}{2} \rightarrow x = \frac{9}{2} \times \frac{1}{3} = \frac{3}{2}$$

5. D

Use the sum and product formulas:

$a = 3$. $b = 13$. $c = 5$.

$$n = \text{sum of roots} = -\frac{b}{a} = -\frac{13}{3}$$

$$m = \text{product of roots} = \frac{c}{a} = \frac{5}{3}$$

Solve for product of roots $-$ sum of roots:

$$m - n = \frac{5}{3} - \left(-\frac{13}{3}\right) = \frac{5}{3} + \frac{13}{3} = \frac{18}{3} = 6$$

Category 31 – Standard Form Equation of a Parabola

1. <u>A</u>

Determine if the parabola opens upwards or downwards: It is given that the parabola opens downwards. Hence, a is negative. This eliminates answer choices C and D.

Determine the y-intercept: It is given that the y-intercept is negative. Hence, the value of c is negative. This eliminates answer choice B.

2. <u>A</u>

Determine the x-coordinate of the vertex: It is the midpoint of the two x-intercepts.

The midpoint of -5 and 11 is 3. Use the midpoint formula if unsure.

3. <u>B</u>

Determine the x-coordinate of the vertex:

$a = 1$. $b = -8$.

$$-\frac{b}{2a} = -\frac{-8}{2 \times 1} = 4$$

This eliminates answer choices A and D.

Determine the y-coordinate of the vertex: Plug in $x = 4$ in the equation.

$$4^2 - (8 \times 4) + 17 = 16 - 32 + 17 = 1$$

This eliminates answer choice C.

4. <u>A</u>

Determine if the parabola opens upwards or downwards:

Since a is negative, the parabola opens downwards. This eliminates answer choices B and D.

Determine the x-coordinate of the vertex: Since the remaining answer choices have the same y-intercept, determine the x-coordinate of the vertex for further elimination.

$a = -1$. $b = -2$.

$$-\frac{b}{2a} = -\frac{-2}{2 \times -1} = -1$$

This eliminates answer choice C.

5. <u>D</u>

Determine the x-coordinate of the vertex:

$a = -16$. $b = 48$.

$$-\frac{b}{2a} = -\frac{48}{2 \times -16} = \frac{48}{32} = \frac{3}{2}$$

Determine the y-coordinate of the vertex: Plug $x = \frac{3}{2}$ in the equation.

$$-16\left(\frac{3}{2}\right)^2 + \left(48 \times \frac{3}{2}\right) = \left(-16 \times \frac{3}{2} \times \frac{3}{2}\right) + (24 \times 3) =$$
$$(-4 \times 9) + (24 \times 3) = -36 + 72 = 36$$

6. <u>C</u>

Determine if the parabola opens upwards or downwards: Since the parabola opens upwards, a is positive. This eliminates answer choices A and B.

Determine the y-intercept: The graph shows that the y-intercept is -2. This eliminates answer choice D.

7. <u>6</u>

Determine the positive x-intercept: Set equation to 0 and solve.

$$-16(t^2 - 5t - 6) = 0 \rightarrow t^2 - 5t - 6 = 0 \rightarrow$$
$$(t - 6)(t + 1) = 0 \rightarrow t = 6 \text{ and } t = -1$$

Hence, $t = 6$ seconds.

8. <u>40</u>

Determine the x-coordinate of the vertex:

The shoe price is the x-axis. Earnings is the y-axis. The shoe price for which the earnings were maximum is the x-coordinate of the vertex.

$a = -\frac{1}{2}$. $b = 40$.

$$-\frac{b}{2a} = -\frac{40}{2 \times -\frac{1}{2}} = -\frac{40}{-1} = 40$$

9. <u>250</u>

Determine y-coordinate of the vertex:

$p =$ the maximum daily profit is the y-coordinate of the vertex. From the graph, the y-coordinate of the vertex is 250.

Category 32 – Vertex Form Equation of a Parabola

1. B

Determine if the parabola opens upwards or downwards: Since a is negative, the parabola opens downwards. This eliminates answer choices C and D.

Determine the vertex: The coordinates of the vertex (h, k) are $(s, -t)$. This eliminates answer choice A.

2. C

Determine the x-coordinate of the vertex from the graph:
$$x\text{-coordinate of the vertex} = -1$$
Hence, $(x - h) = (x + 1) \rightarrow b = 1$.

3. A

Determine the coordinates of the vertex from the graph: The coordinates of the vertex (h, k) in the graph are $(40, 60)$. Hence, $(x - h) = (x - 40)$ and $k = 60$. This eliminates answer choices B, C, and D.

4. 4

Determine the x-coordinate of the vertex:

From the given equation, the x-coordinate of the vertex is
$$(x - 2) \rightarrow x = 2$$
Determine the x-intercepts:

The x-coordinate of the vertex $= 2$ is the midpoint of the two x-intercepts 0 and b. Hence, b must be 4.

See calculation below using the midpoint formula.

$x_1 = 0.\ \ x_2 = b.\ \ \text{Midpoint} = 2.$
$$\frac{x_2 + x_1}{2} = \frac{0 + b}{2} = 2 \rightarrow b = 4$$

5. D

Determine the coordinates of the vertex from the graph:
$$(2, -10)$$

6. C

Determine the coordinates of the vertex from the graph:
$$(2, 1)$$
Hence, $(x - h) = (x - 2)$. This eliminates answer choice D.

All remaining answer choices have the same vertex. The only difference is the value of a.

Since the parabola opens upwards, the equation of the parabola can be written as
$$y = a(x - 2)^2 + 1$$
Determine the value of a: Plug in the given point $(3, 4)$ in the above equation for (x, y).
$$4 = a(3 - 2)^2 + 1$$
$$4 = a(1)^2 + 1 \rightarrow 4 = a + 1 \rightarrow a = 4 - 1 = 3$$
This eliminates answer choices A and B.

7. B

Determine if the parabola opens upwards or downwards:

Since the parabola opens downwards, a is negative. This eliminates answer choices C and D.

Determine the vertex: The remaining answer choices A and B have the same vertex. The only difference is the value of a.

The vertex of the parabola from the graph is $(2, 2)$. Since the parabola opens downwards, the equation of the parabola can be written as
$$y = -a(x - 2)^2 + 2$$
Determine the value of a: Select a point on the parabola and plug it in the above equation for (x, y). Using point $(1, 0)$ below.
$$0 = -a(1 - 2)^2 + 2 \rightarrow$$
$$0 = -a(-1)^2 + 2 \rightarrow 0 = -a + 2 \rightarrow a = 2$$
This eliminates answer choice A.

8. A

Determine the value of a:

It is given that the graph passes through origin. Plug in $(0, 0)$ in the equation for (x, y).
$$0 = k(0 - 3)^2 - 6 \rightarrow$$
$$0 = 9k - 6 \rightarrow 9k = 6 \rightarrow k = \frac{6}{9} = \frac{2}{3}$$

9. 6

Solve:

$x =$ percent discount offered.

$y =$ quarterly profit $= q$.

To determine the quarterly profit when no discount is offered, plug in $x = 0$ in the equation and solve for y.
$$y = -(0 - 4)^2 + 22 \rightarrow$$
$$y = -(16) + 22 = -16 + 22 = 6$$

Category 33 – Factored Form Equation of a Parabola

1. C

Determine the x-coordinate of the vertex using the midpoint formula: The two x-intercepts are 1 and -1.

$x_1 = -1$. $x_2 = 1$.

$$\frac{x_2 + x_1}{2} = \frac{1 - 1}{2} = \frac{0}{2} = 0$$

This eliminates answer choices A and D.

Determine the y-coordinate of the vertex: Plug in $x = 0$ in the equation.

$$y = -4(0 - 1)(0 + 1) = -4(-1)(1) = 4$$

This eliminates answer choice B.

2. D

The two x-intercepts are -15 and 45. The distance is

$$45 - (-15) = 45 + 15 = 60$$

3. A

Determine the x-coordinate of the vertex using the midpoint formula: The two x-intercepts are 5 and 7.

$x_1 = 5$. $x_2 = 7$.

$$\frac{x_2 + x_1}{2} = \frac{7 + 5}{2} = \frac{12}{2} = 6$$

Determine the y-coordinate of the vertex: This is the maximum annual profit. Plug in $x = 6$ in the equation.

$$y = -3(6 - 5)(6 - 7) = -3(1)(-1) = 3$$

4. B

Determine the x-intercept:

Plug in the point $(-2, -16)$ in the equation.

$$-16 = (-2 + n)(-2 + 6) \rightarrow -16 = (-2 + n)(4) \rightarrow$$
$$-16 = -8 + 4n \rightarrow 4n = -8 \rightarrow n = -2$$

5. C

The two x-intercepts from the graph are -2 and 3. Hence, the two factors are $(x + 2)$ and $(x - 3)$.

Substitute them in the equation for $(x + m)$ and $(x + n)$.

$$f(x) = k(x + 2)(x - 3)$$

Determine the value of k: Read a point from the graph of the parabola and plug it in the equation. Using point $(0, -3)$ below.

$$-3 = k(0 + 2)(0 - 3) \rightarrow$$
$$-3 = k(2)(-3) \rightarrow -3 = -6k \rightarrow k = \frac{3}{6} = \frac{1}{2}$$

Category 34 – Equivalent Standard Form and Vertex Form Equations

1. C

Determine the x-coordinate of the vertex:

$a = 1$. $b = 6$.

$$-\frac{b}{2a} = -\frac{6}{2 \times 1} = -3$$

Since $x = -3$, the factor is $(x + 3)$. This eliminates answer choices A and B.

Determine the y-coordinate of the vertex: Plug in $x = -3$ in the equation.

$$(-3)^2 + (6 \times -3) + 13 = 9 - 18 + 13 = 4$$

This eliminates answer choice D.

2. B

Determine the x-coordinate of the vertex:

Since $a = 0.5$, answer choices C and D can be eliminated.

$a = 0.5$. $b = 4$.

$$-\frac{b}{2a} = -\frac{4}{2 \times 0.5} = -\frac{4}{1} = -4$$

Since $x = -4$, the factor is $(x + 4)$. This eliminates answer choice A.

3. D

Determine the x-coordinate of the vertex:

Since $a = 1.25$, answer choice A can be eliminated.

$a = 1.25$. $b = 7.5$.

$$-\frac{7.5}{2 \times 1.25} = -\frac{7.5}{2.5} = -3$$

Since $x = -3$, the factor is $(x + 3)$. This eliminates answer choice B.

Determine the y-coordinate of the vertex: Plug in $x = -3$ in the equation.

$$1.25(-3)^2 + (7.5 \times -3) + 1 =$$
$$11.25 - 22.5 + 1 = -10.25$$

This eliminates answer choice C.

4. A

Since a is negative, answer choice D can be eliminated.

FOIL:

$$-2(x^2 + 4x + 4) + 1 = -2x^2 - 8x - 8 + 1 =$$
$$-2x^2 - 8x - 7$$

Since $c = -7$, answer choices B and C can be eliminated.

5. <u>B</u>

Determine the x-coordinate of the vertex:

Since a is negative, answer choices C and D can be eliminated.

$a = -1$. $b = 9$.

$$-\frac{b}{2a} = -\frac{9}{2 \times -1} = 4.5$$

Since $x = 4.5$, the factor is $(x - 4.5)$. This eliminates answer choice A.

6. <u>9</u>

FOIL and simplify:

$$(x + 2.5)(x + 2.5) + 2.75 \rightarrow$$
$$x^2 + 5x + 6.25 + 2.75 \rightarrow x^2 + 5x + 9$$

Hence, $c = 9$.

Category 35 – Parabola Intersections and System of Equations

1. <u>D</u>

Equate the two equations:

Convert the equations to the correct form.

$$8x - y = 9 \rightarrow y = 8x - 9$$

Equate and create one quadratic equation.

$$x^2 + 2 = 8x - 9$$
$$x^2 + 2 - 8x + 9 = 0 \rightarrow x^2 - 8x + 11 = 0$$

Determine the values of x: Since the answer choices have square roots, use the quadratic formula.

$a = 1$. $b = -8$. $c = 11$.

$$\frac{-(-8) \pm \sqrt{(-8)^2 - (4 \times 1 \times 11)}}{2 \times 1} = \frac{8 \pm \sqrt{64 - 44}}{2} =$$

$$\frac{8 \pm \sqrt{20}}{2} = \frac{8 \pm \sqrt{4 \times 5}}{2} = \frac{8 \pm 2\sqrt{5}}{2} = 4 \pm \sqrt{5}$$

2. <u>C</u>

Equate the two equations:

Convert the equations to the correct form.

$$y + 4x = 2x^2 + 1 \rightarrow y = 2x^2 - 4x + 1$$
$$y = (x - 1)(x - 2) \rightarrow y = x^2 - 3x + 2$$

Equate and create one quadratic equation.

$$2x^2 - 4x + 1 = x^2 - 3x + 2$$
$$2x^2 - 4x + 1 - x^2 + 3x - 2 = 0 \rightarrow x^2 - x - 1 = 0$$

Determine number of solutions using the discriminant:

$a = 1$. $b = -1$. $c = -1$.

$$b^2 - 4ac = (-1)^2 - (4 \times 1 \times -1) = 1 + 4 = 5$$

$$\text{Discriminant} > 0$$

3. <u>A</u>

Equate the two equations:

Convert the equations to the correct form.

$$2y = 4x + 8 \rightarrow y = 2x + 4$$

Equate and create one quadratic equation.

$$2x + 4 = -ax^2 - 4x - 5$$
$$2x + 4 + ax^2 + 4x + 5 = 0 \rightarrow ax^2 + 6x + 9 = 0$$

Determine the value of a using the discriminant: Since the parabola and the line intersect at one point, the discriminant is 0.

$a = a$. $b = 6$. $c = 9$.

$$b^2 - 4ac = 0 \rightarrow (6)^2 - (4 \times a \times 9) = 0 \rightarrow$$
$$36 - 36a = 0 \rightarrow 36 = 36a \rightarrow a = 1$$

4. <u>B</u>

Equate the two equations:

$$x^2 - x - 6 = \frac{1}{2}x^2 + 2x + 2$$

Create one quadratic equation.

$$x^2 - x - 6 - \frac{1}{2}x^2 - 2x - 2 = 0 \rightarrow$$

$$\frac{1}{2}x^2 - 3x - 8 = 0 \rightarrow x^2 - 6x - 16 = 0$$

Determine the values of x: Factorize.

$$(x - 8)(x + 2) \rightarrow x = 8 \text{ and } x = -2$$

This eliminates answer choices C and D.

Determine the values of y:

For $x = -2$, plug in -2 in any of the equation.

$$x^2 - x - 6 = (-2)^2 - (-2) - 6 = 4 + 2 - 6 = 0$$

This eliminates answer choice A.

5. <u>9</u>

$y = 9$ is a horizontal line. Since it intersects the parabola at one point, it must be tangent to the vertex of the parabola. Hence, the y-coordinate of the parabola n is also 9.

6. <u>4</u>

Equate the two equations:

Convert the equations to the correct form.

$$x = y + 4 \rightarrow y = x - 4$$

Equate and create one quadratic equation.

$$x^2 - 7x + 12 = x - 4$$

$$x^2 - 7x + 12 - x + 4 = 0 \rightarrow x^2 - 8x + 16 = 0$$

Determine the value of $x = s$: Factorize.

$$(x - 4)^2 = 0$$

$$x = 4$$

7. <u>3</u>

Convert the equations to the correct form.

$$y - kx = 1 \rightarrow y = kx + 1$$

The slope of a linear line in the form $y = mx + b$, is the m value (refer to section 1 for further details, if needed).

Hence, the slope of line l is k.

Equate and create one quadratic equation.

$$x^2 - kx + 10 = kx + 1$$

$$x^2 - kx + 10 - kx - 1 = 0 \rightarrow x^2 - 2kx + 9 = 0$$

Set the discriminant to 0 and determine k: Since the two graphs intersect at one point, the discriminant is 0.

$a = 1$. $b = -2k$. $c = 9$.

$$b^2 - 4ac = 0 \rightarrow (-2k)^2 - (4 \times 1 \times 9) = 0 \rightarrow$$

$$4k^2 - 36 = 0 \rightarrow 4k^2 = 36 \rightarrow k^2 = 9 \rightarrow k = \pm 3$$

Since the slope of line l is positive, $k = 3$.

Category 36 – Graph Transformations of a Parabola

1. <u>C</u>

Determine the transformed vertex from the graph:

Read the point that is 4 unit to the left and 5 units up from the vertex in the graph.

The point is $(-3, 2)$.

Hence, the equation of transformed graph is

$$y = a(x + 3)^2 + 2$$

Since only answer choice C has the correct vertex, answer choices A, B, and D can be eliminated.

2. <u>D</u>

Determine the transformed equation:

Reflection across the y-axis is

$$y = 2(x + 3)^2 - 1 \rightarrow y = 2(-x + 3)^2 - 1$$

3. <u>B</u>

Determine the shift in the transformed equation:

$x^2 + 4$ to $(x - 4)^2$ is a shift of 4 units to the right and a shift of 4 units downwards.

This eliminates answer choices A, C, and D.

4. <u>A</u>

Determine the transformed equation:

Reflection across the x-axis is

$$y = -((x + 2)^2 - 4) \rightarrow y = -(x + 2)^2 + 4$$

This eliminates answer choices B and D.

Shift of 2 units downwards of the above equation is

$$y = -(x + 2)^2 + 4 - 2 \rightarrow y = -(x + 2)^2 + 2$$

This eliminates answer choice C.

5. <u>D</u>

Determine the transformed equation:

Shift of 1 unit to the left is

$$g(x) = (x + 1)^2 + 5(x + 1) - 3$$

Shift of 4 units upwards of the above equation is

$$g(x) = (x + 1)^2 + 5(x + 1) - 3 + 4$$

Simplify the equation.

$$g(x) = x^2 + 2x + 1 + 5x + 5 - 3 + 4 \rightarrow$$

$$g(x) = x^2 + 7x + 7$$

Category 37 – Solutions of Quadratic Expressions

1. <u>D</u>

Equate the coefficients and constants of both sides: It is given that both the expressions are equal. Hence,

$$(x + 3)(ax + c) = 6x^2 + bx + 9 \rightarrow$$
$$ax^2 + cx + 3ax + 3c = 6x^2 + bx + 9 \rightarrow$$
$$ax^2 + (c + 3a)x + 3c = 6x^2 + bx + 9$$

Equate.

$$a = 6$$
$$b = c + 3a$$
$$3c = 9 \rightarrow c = 3$$

Determine b, by substituting $a = 6$ and $c = 3$ as below.

$$b = c + 3a = 3 + (3 \times 6) + 3 = 3 + 18 = 21$$

2. <u>A</u>

Equate the coefficients and constants of both sides: The expressions on both sides of the equation must not be equal.

$$5bx^2 + +5x + 2bx + 2 = 5bx^2 + 2bx + 5x + k \rightarrow$$
$$5bx^2 + (2b + 5)x + 2 = 5bx^2 + (2b + 5)x + k$$

If $k = 2$, then the expressions on both sides of the equation will be same. Hence, for the equation to have no solution k cannot be 2.

3. <u>D</u>

Equate the coefficients and constants of both sides: The expressions on both sides of the equation must not be equal.

$$2x^2 + bx^2 + c = 2cx^2 + x^2 + 2x^2 + 1 \rightarrow$$
$$2x^2 + bx^2 + c = 2cx^2 + 3x^2 + 1 \rightarrow$$
$$(2 + b)x^2 + c = (2c + 3)x^2 + 1$$

Equate.

$$c = 1$$
$$2 + b = 2c + 3 \rightarrow b = (2 \times 1) + 3 - 2 \rightarrow$$
$$b = 3$$

For the equation to have no solution, b cannot equal to 3 when $c = 1$. Hence, when $c = 1$ and $b \neq 3$, the equation has no solution.

(Note that the expressions on both sides of the equation have unknown coefficients. To ensure that the equation has no solution, the values of both the coefficients must be evaluated. For this reason, answer choice A is incorrect.)

4. <u>B</u>

Evaluate the coefficients and constants of both sides: The expressions on both sides of the equation must be equal.

$$3abx^2 + 3acx + 4bx + 4c = 6x^2 + 4x$$

Since there is no matching constant in the right expression, $4c = 0 \rightarrow c = 0$. This eliminates answer choices C and D.

Evaluate answer choice A: $a = 1$ and $b = 2$.

$$(3 \times 1 \times 2)x^2 + 0 + (4 \times 2)x + 0 = 6x^2 + 4x \rightarrow$$
$$6x^2 + 8x = 6x^2 + 4x$$

The expressions on both side are not equal. This eliminates answer choice A.

See below that in the correct answer choice B, both sides are equal.

$$(3 \times 2 \times 1)x^2 + 0 + (4 \times 1)x + 0 = 6x^2 + 4x \rightarrow$$
$$6x^2 + 4x = 6x^2 + 4x$$

5. <u>A</u>

Equate the coefficients and constants of both sides: The expressions on both sides of the equation must be equal.

The right-side expression does not contain the variable x. Hence,

$$4cx = 0 \rightarrow c = 0$$

6. <u>D</u>

Equate the coefficients and constants of both sides: The expressions on both sides of the equation must not be equal. Since the constants are same, coefficients must be made unequal.

Equate.

$$0.1a = 1.4 \rightarrow a = 14$$

For the equation to have no solution, a cannot be 14.

7. <u>5</u>

Equate the coefficients and constants of both sides: The expressions on both sides of the equation must be equal.

FOIL the left expression.

$$4x^2 + 2x + 6x + 3 = 4x^2 + 8x + c - 2 \rightarrow$$
$$4x^2 + 8x + 3 = 4x^2 + 8x + c - 2$$

Equate.

$$c - 2 = 3 \rightarrow c = 5$$

Section 6 – Review Questions

1. C

Determine the y-intercept of the parabola:

$$c = 7$$

2. D

Determine the transformed vertex from the graph:

Read the point that is 2 unit to the left and 4 units up from the vertex in the graph.

The point is $(-3, 1)$.

Hence, the equation of the transformed graph is

$$y = a(x + 3)^2 + 1$$

Since only answer choice D has the correct vertex, answer choices A, B, and C can be eliminated.

3. D

Compare the vertex of the two functions:

Vertex of $f(x)$ is at $(1, 2)$.

Vertex of $g(x)$ is at $(-2, -1)$.

Hence, the vertex of $g(x)$ is 3 units to the left and 3 units below the vertex of $f(x)$.

4. B

Determine the x-coordinate of the vertex:

$a = -5$. $b = 10$.

$$-\frac{b}{2a} = -\frac{10}{2 \times -5} = 1$$

This eliminates answer choices C and D.

Determine the y-coordinate of the vertex: Plug in $x = 1$ in the equation.

$$-5(1 \times 1)^2 + (10 \times 1) - 4 = -5 + 10 - 4 = 1$$

This eliminates answer choice A.

The (x, y) coordinates of the vertex are $(1, 1)$.

5. C

The two x-intercepts are -10.5 and 40.5. The distance between them is

$$40.5 - (-10.5) = 51$$

6. C

Equate the two equations:

Convert the equations to correct form.

$$x - y = -4 \;\to\; y = x + 4$$

Equate and create one quadratic equation.

$$x + 4 = x^2 - 5x + 4$$

$$x^2 - 5x + 4 - x - 4 = 0 \;\to\; x^2 - 6x = 0$$

Determine the values of x: Factor out x.

$$x(x - 6) = 0$$

The two values of x are

$$x = 0 \text{ and } (x - 6) = 0 \;\to\; x = 6$$

This eliminates answer choices A and D.

Determine the value of y:

Plug in $x = 6$ in any of the equation.

$$x + 4 \;\to\; 6 + 4 = 10$$

This eliminates answer choice B.

7. A

Determine the roots:

$a = 1$. $b = -5$. $c = 3$.

$$\frac{-(-5) \pm \sqrt{(-5)^2 - (4 \times 1 \times 3)}}{2 \times 1} = \frac{5 \pm \sqrt{25 - 12}}{2} =$$

$$\frac{5 \pm \sqrt{13}}{2}$$

The two solutions are

$$\frac{5 + \sqrt{13}}{2} = 2.5 + \frac{\sqrt{13}}{2}$$

$$\frac{5 - \sqrt{13}}{2} = 2.5 - \frac{\sqrt{13}}{2}$$

Answer choice A is one of the solutions.

8. 0.5 or 3

Determine the roots: Since $a > 0$, the factorization below is shown using the formula. Note that this equation can be factored without the formula depending on the student's comfort level.

$a = 2$. $b = -7$. $c = 3$.

$$\frac{-(-7) \pm \sqrt{(-7)^2 - (4 \times 2 \times 3)}}{2 \times 2} = \frac{7 \pm \sqrt{49 - 24}}{4} =$$

$$\frac{7 \pm \sqrt{25}}{4} = \frac{7 \pm 5}{4}$$

The two solutions are

$$\frac{7 + 5}{4} = \frac{12}{4} = 3$$

$$\frac{7 - 5}{4} = \frac{2}{4} = \frac{1}{2} = 0.5$$

Either solution can be entered as the correct answer.

9. <u>12</u>

Determine the factors:

Divide the equation by 2.

$$2x^2 + kx + 10 = 0 \;\rightarrow\; x^2 + \frac{k}{2}x + 5 = 0$$

The two multiples of $c = 5$ are 1 and 5. Since it is given that $(x + 5)$ is a factor of the equation, the other factor must be $(x + 1)$. Hence, the given equation can be factorized as $(x + 5)(x + 1)$.

$$x^2 + \frac{k}{2}x + 5 = (x + 5)(x + 1)$$

FOIL the right-side of the equation.

$$x^2 + \frac{k}{2}x + 5 = x^2 + 6x + 5$$

Equate the coefficients of x.

$$\frac{k}{2} = 6 \;\rightarrow\; k = 12$$

(Alternatively, the product of roots formula can be used to determine the second root and then sum of roots formula can be used to determine k.)

10. <u>8</u>

Determine the x-intercepts (roots): At the x-intercept, $y = 0$. Hence, set the equation to 0 and factorize.

$$x^2 - 10x + 16 = 0$$
$$(x - 8)(x - 2) = 0$$
$$x = 8 \text{ and } x = 2$$

Hence, $k = 8$.

11. <u>A</u>

Determine the x-coordinate of the vertex:

$a = 1$. $b = -8$.

$$-\frac{b}{2a} = -\frac{-8}{2 \times 1} = 4$$

Since $x = 4$, the factor is $(x - 4)$. This eliminates answer choices B and D.

Determine the y-coordinate of the vertex: Plug in $x = 4$ in the equation.

$$(4)^2 - (8 \times 4) + 13 = 16 - 32 + 13 = -3$$

This eliminates answer choice C.

12. <u>C</u>

Evaluate each answer choice for the midpoint of the two x-intercepts:

Answer choices A and D can be eliminated since both these answer choices have one x-intercept.

The axis of symmetry is the midpoint of the two x-intercepts.

Answer choice B: The two x-intercepts are 1 and -5. Their midpoint is -2. This eliminates answer choice B.

In the correct answer choice C, the two x-intercepts are -1 and 5 and their midpoint is 2.

13. <u>C</u>

Evaluate the coefficients and constants of both sides: The expressions on both sides of the equation must not be equal.

$$6x^2 + 2x + 2x + c = 6ax^2 + 4x + k \;\rightarrow$$
$$6x^2 + 4x + c = 6ax^2 + 4x + k$$

If $a = 1$, then the equation becomes

$$6x^2 + 4x + c = (6 \times 1)x^2 + 4x + k \;\rightarrow$$
$$6x^2 + 4x + c = 6x^2 + 4x + k$$

Hence, when $a = 1$, c cannot equal k for the equation to have no solution.

Note that the values of all the unknown constants and coefficients must be evaluated to ensure that the equation has no solution.

Answer choice A is incorrect since only the value of a is being evaluated. In this situation c and k could be same or different. This does not ensure no solution. Answer choice B is incorrect since $a = 1$ and $c = k$ results in both side expressions to be same. Answer choice D is incorrect since $c = k$ and $c \neq k$ is not a valid evaluation.

14. <u>D</u>

The maximum weekly profit is the y-coordinate of the vertex. The graph shows that the y-coordinate of the vertex is 400.

15. <u>C</u>

Determine the x-coordinate of the vertex:

Simplify the equation.

$$y = -\frac{1}{12}x^2 + 3x$$

$a = -\frac{1}{12}$. $b = 3$.

$$-\frac{b}{2a} = -\frac{3}{2 \times -\frac{1}{12}} = -\frac{3}{-\frac{1}{6}} = -3 \times -6 = 18$$

Determine the y-coordinate of the vertex: Plug in $x = 18$ in the simplified equation.

$$-\frac{1}{12}(18 \times 18) + (3 \times 18) \;\rightarrow\; -27 + 54 = 27$$

16. <u>A</u>

Determine the transformed equation:

Reflection across y-axis is

$$y = (-x - 3)^2 - 4$$

Shift of 2 units upward of the reflected graph is

$$y = (-x - 3)^2 - 4 + 2 \;\rightarrow\; y = (-x - 3)^2 - 2$$

17. <u>B</u>

$x =$ temperature.

$y =$ growth rate.

At the x-intercept, $y = 0$. Hence, k is the temperature at which growth rate is 0.

18. <u>D</u>

Equate the coefficients and constants of both sides: The expressions on both sides of the equation must be equal.

$$abx^2 + 4ax + 3bx + 12 = 10x^2 + kx + 12 \rightarrow$$
$$abx^2 + (4a + 3b)x + 12 = 10x^2 + kx + 12$$

Equate.

$$ab = 10$$
$$4a + 3b = k$$

Get the values of a and b: a and b are two multiples of 10.

The multiples of 10 are 1 and 10 or 2 and 5. Since it is given that $a + b = 7$, the two multiples must be 2 and 5.

Hence, the possible values of a and b are

$$a = 2 \text{ and } b = 5 \text{ or } a = 5 \text{ and } b = 2.$$

Plug in the above possible combinations in the equation $4a + 3b = k$.

For $a = 2$ and $b = 5$:

$$k = (4 \times 2) + (3 \times 5) = 8 + 15 = 23$$

For $a = 5$ and $b = 2$:

$$k = (4 \times 5) + (3 \times 2) = 20 + 6 = 26$$

19. <u>A</u>

Equate the two equations:

Convert the equations to correct form.

$$x = y + 2 \rightarrow y = x - 2$$
$$x + y = 2x^2 - 2 \rightarrow y = 2x^2 - x - 2$$

Equate and create one quadratic equation.

$$2x^2 - x - 2 = x - 2$$
$$2x^2 - x - 2 - x + 2 = 0 \rightarrow 2x^2 - 2x = 0$$

Determine the values of x: Factor out $2x$.

$$2x(x - 1) = 0$$

Hence, the two values of x are

$$2x = 0 \rightarrow x = 0 \text{ and } (x - 1) = 0 \rightarrow x = 1$$

Since none of the answer choices have $x = 0$, this can be ignored.

Determine the value of y: Plug in $x = 1$ in any of the equation.

$$y = x - 2 = 1 - 2 = -1$$

20. <u>A</u>

Determine number of solutions using the discriminant:

$a = 2$. $b = -3$. $c = 6$.

$$b^2 - 4ac = (-3)^2 - (4 \times 2 \times 6) = 9 - 48 = -39$$

Since discriminant < 0, there is no real solution.

21. <u>C</u>

n is y-coordinate of the vertex. Answer choices A and B can be eliminated since n is the coefficient of x^2 in these choices. Answer choice D can be eliminated since n is the value of x-coordinate of the vertex in this answer choice.

22. <u>C</u>

Determine the x-coordinate of the vertex:

Since $a = 2$, answer choices A and B can be eliminated.

$a = 2$. $b = 8$.

$$-\frac{b}{2a} = -\frac{8}{2 \times 2} = -2$$

Since $x = -2$, the factor is $(x + 2)$.

Determine the y-coordinate of the vertex: Plug in $x = -2$ in the equation.

$$2(-2)^2 + (8 \times -2) + 11 = 8 - 16 + 11 = 3$$

This eliminates answer choice D.

23. <u>2</u>

Use the discriminant:

$a = a$. $b = -8$. $c = 8$.

Since the equation has one solution, set the discriminant to 0.

$$b^2 - 4ac = 0 \rightarrow (-8)^2 - (4 \times a \times 8) = 0 \rightarrow$$
$$64 - 32a = 0 \rightarrow a = 2$$

24. <u>4</u>

Determine the x-intercepts of the parabola: Time taken by the ball to reach the ground is the positive x-intercept of the parabola. Set $y = 0$ in the equation and solve.

$$-16t^2 + 48t + 64 = 0 \rightarrow -16(t^2 - 3t - 4) = 0$$
$$t^2 - 3t - 4 = 0$$
$$(t - 4)(t + 1) = 0$$

The two x-intercepts are

$$(t - 4) \rightarrow t = 4 \text{ and } (t + 1) \rightarrow t = -1$$

The correct answer is the positive x-intercept $= 4$.

25. <u>49</u>

Determine the x-coordinate of the vertex using the midpoint formula:

The two x-intercepts are -2 and 12.

$$\frac{-2 + 12}{2} = \frac{10}{2} = 5$$

Determine the y-coordinate of the vertex: Plug in $x = 5$ in the equation.

$$y = -(5 + 2)(5 - 12) = -(7)(-7) = 49$$

26. <u>40</u>

$x =$ percent discount.

$y =$ monthly profit.

The percent discount at which the profit is maximum is the x-coordinate of the vertex.

Determine the x-coordinate of the vertex:

$a = -60$. $b = 4,800$.

$$-\frac{b}{2a} = -\frac{4,800}{2 \times -60} = \frac{4,800}{120} = 40$$

Section 7 – Absolute Value

Category 38 – Absolute Value and Linear Equations

1. <u>A</u>

Move 8 to the right-side of the equation.
$$|x - 4| = 6 - 8 \rightarrow |x - 4| = -2$$
Absolute value cannot be negative. Hence, there is no solution.

2. <u>B</u>

Move 2 to the right-side of the equation.
$$|2x - 7| = 13 + 2 \rightarrow |2x - 7| = 15$$
Solve for the positive value:
$$2x - 7 = 15 \rightarrow 2x = 15 + 7 \rightarrow 2x = 22 \rightarrow x = 11$$
Solve for the negative value:
$$2x - 7 = -15 \rightarrow 2x = -15 + 7 \rightarrow$$
$$2x = -8 \rightarrow x = -4$$
Solve for $|b|$: Since $a > b$, $a = 11$ and $b = -4$.
$$|-4| = 4$$

3. <u>6</u>

Move 1 to the right-side of the equation.
$$|2x + 5| = 6 + 1 \rightarrow |2x + 5| = 7$$
Solve for the positive value:
$$2x + 5 = 7 \rightarrow 2x = 7 - 5 \rightarrow 2x = 2 \rightarrow x = 1$$
Since $s = 1$, this value must be s.
Solve for the negative value: This must be t.
$$2x + 5 = -7 \rightarrow 2x = -7 - 5 \rightarrow$$
$$2x = -12 \rightarrow x = -6 = t$$
Solve for $|t|$:
$$|-6| = 6$$

4. <u>8</u>

Move 3 to the right-side of the equation.
$$|x - 4| = 6 - 3 \rightarrow |x - 4| = 3$$
Solve for the positive value:
$$x - 4 = 3 \rightarrow x = 3 + 4 \rightarrow x = 7$$
Solve for the negative value:
$$x - 4 = -3 \rightarrow x = -3 + 4 \rightarrow x = 1$$
Add the two values:
$$7 + 1 = 8$$

5. <u>B</u>

Solve for the positive value:
$$3x - 6 = 2 - x \rightarrow 3x + x = 2 + 6 \rightarrow$$
$$4x = 8 \rightarrow x = 2$$
Since the question asks for one possible value, there is no need to solve for the negative value.

6. <u>5</u>

Solve for the positive value:
$$2x + 5 = 7 \rightarrow 2x = 7 - 5 \rightarrow 2x = 2 \rightarrow x = 1$$
Solve for the negative value:
$$2x + 5 = -7 \rightarrow 2x = -7 - 5 \rightarrow$$
$$2x = -12 \rightarrow x = -6$$
Solve for $|m + n|$: Either value of x could be m or n. Same results will be obtained with either combination.
$$|1 - 6| = |-5| = 5 \text{ or } |-6 + 1| = |-5| = 5$$

7. <u>2, 4, 8, or 16</u>

<u>Equation $|x + 3| = 1$</u>
Solve for the positive value:
$$x + 3 = 1 \rightarrow x = 1 - 3 \rightarrow x = -2$$
<u>Equation $|2y - 3| = 5$</u>
Solve for the positive value:
$$2y - 3 = 5 \rightarrow 2y = 5 + 3 \rightarrow 2y = 8 \rightarrow y = 4$$
Solve for $|xy|$:
$$|-2 \times 4| = |-8| = 8$$
Since the question asks for one possible value, there is no need to solve for the negative values.

(For the purpose of completion, see below for other solutions.

The other value of x is
$$x + 3 = -1 \rightarrow x = -1 - 3 \rightarrow x = -4$$
The other value of y is
$$2y - 3 = -5 \rightarrow 2y = -5 + 3 \rightarrow y = -1$$
Hence, all other possible $|xy|$ values are
$$|-2 \times -1| = |2| = 2$$
$$|-4 \times 4| = |-16| = 16$$
$$|-4 \times -1| = |4| = 4$$

)

8. 4

Move 2 to the right-side of the equation.

$$|4x - 3| = 7 - 2 \;\rightarrow\; |4x - 3| = 5$$

Solve for the positive value:

$$4x - 3 = 5 \;\rightarrow\; 4x = 5 + 3 \;\rightarrow\; 4x = 8 \;\rightarrow\; x = 2$$

Since question asks for $x > 0$, $x = 2$ meets the condition.

Solve for $|xy|$:

It is given that $y = -2$.

$$|2 \times -2| = |-4| = 4$$

(For the purpose of completion, see below for the second value of x.

$$4x - 3 = -5 \;\rightarrow\; 4x = -5 + 3 \;\rightarrow\;$$

$$4x = -2 \;\rightarrow\; x = -\frac{1}{2}$$

This does not meet $x > 0$ condition and can be eliminated. Hence, there is only one solution of xy.)

9. 1 or 7

Equation $|x + 5| = 3$

Solve for the positive value:

$$x + 5 = 3 \;\rightarrow\; x = 3 - 5 \;\rightarrow\; x = -2$$

Equation $|y + 2| = 3$

Solve for the positive value:

$$y + 2 = 3 \;\rightarrow\; y = 3 - 2 \;\rightarrow\; y = 1$$

Since question asks for $y > 0$, $y = 1$ meets the condition.

Solve for $|x + y|$:

$$|-2 + 1| = |-1| = 1$$

(For the purpose of completion, see below for other possible solutions.

The second value of x is

$$x + 5 = -3 \;\rightarrow\; x = -3 - 5 \;\rightarrow\; x = -8$$

The second value of y is

$$y + 2 = -3 \;\rightarrow\; y = -3 - 2 \;\rightarrow\; y = -5$$

This does not meet $y > 0$ condition and can be eliminated.

Hence, the other possible $|x + y|$ value is

$$|-8 + 1| = |-7| = 7$$

).

Category 39 – Absolute Value and Linear Inequalities

1. C

Determine the solution set:

$$-2 < x + 3 < 2 \;\rightarrow\; -2 - 3 < x + 3 - 3 < 2 - 3 \;\rightarrow\;$$

$$-5 < x < -1$$

The 3 possible values of x are $-2, -3, -4$.

2. A

Determine the midpoint of the two numbers:

$$\frac{100 + 150}{2} = \frac{250}{2} = 125$$

This eliminates answer choices C and D.

Determine the distance of the two numbers from the midpoint:

Both the numbers are at a distance of 25 from the midpoint. This eliminates answer choice B.

3. C

Determine the solution set:

Since the absolute value has greater than inequality symbol, the values of a can be

$$a > 4 \text{ and } a < -4$$

Hence, answer options I and II are correct.

4. D

Determine the solution set:

$$-34{,}000 \leq r - 79{,}000 \leq 34{,}000 \;\rightarrow\;$$

$$-34{,}000 + 79{,}000 \leq r \leq 34{,}000 + 79{,}000 \;\rightarrow\;$$

$$45{,}000 \leq r \leq 113{,}000$$

The maximum value of $r = 113{,}000$.

5. B

Determine the solution set:

$$-4 < x - 1 < 4 \;\rightarrow\; -4 + 1 < x - 1 + 1 < 4 + 1 \;\rightarrow\;$$

$$-3 < x < 5$$

6. D

Determine the solution set:

Since the absolute value has greater than inequality symbol, the values of x can be

$$2x + 3 > 5 \text{ and } 2x + 3 < -5$$

Solve $2x + 3 > 5$:

$$2x > 5 - 3 \;\rightarrow\; 2x > 2 \;\rightarrow\; x > 1$$

Solve $2x + 3 < -5$:

$$2x < -5 - 3 \;\rightarrow\; 2x < -8 \;\rightarrow\; x < -4$$

Hence, the possible values of x can be greater than 1 or less than -4. The integers $1, 0, -1, -2, -3, -4$ cannot be the values. This eliminates Option II.

Options I and III are correct.

Category 40 – Absolute Value and Functions

1. <u>A</u>

Determine the shift in the graph:

The vertex of the graph is below 0 and x-coordinate $= 0$. Hence, the y-coordinate of the vertex must be negative and the x-coordinate is not shifted horizontally. This eliminates answer choices B, C, and D.

2. <u>C</u>

Determine the shift in the graph:

The vertex of the graph is below 0 and to the left. Hence, the x- and y-coordinates of the vertex must be negative. This eliminates answer choices A, B, and D.

3. <u>B</u>

Determine the shift in the graph:

$x - 1$ indicates that the vertex is shifted horizontally by 1 unit to the right. This eliminates answer choices A and D.

y-coordinate $= 1$ indicates that the vertex is shifted by 1 unit upwards. This eliminates answer choice C.

4. <u>A</u>

Determine the change in y values:

All the y values must become positive. Note that not every graph that has positive y values is the correct graph. The negative y values must match the corresponding positive y values (as shown in key points). The correct answer choice is A.

Section 7 – Review Questions

1. <u>C</u>

Determine the solution set:

Since the absolute value has greater than inequality symbol, the values of x can be

$$x - 3 > 5 \text{ and } x - 3 < -5$$

Solve for $x - 3 > 5$:

$$x > 5 + 3 \rightarrow x > 8$$

Solve for $x - 3 < -5$:

$$x < -5 + 3 \rightarrow x < -2$$

Hence, the possible values of x can be greater than 8 or less than -2. The integers $-2, -1, 0, 1, 2, 3, 4, 5, 6, 7, 8$ cannot be the values.

This eliminates answer choices A ($x = |-1| = 1$), B ($x = |-3| = 3$), and D ($x = 6$).

5. <u>B</u>

Evaluate each answer choice: Since $|f(t)|$ is positive, $f(t)$ must also be positive. Hence, for each value of t in the answer choice, check for the value of y on the graph. The correct answer choice will have a positive y value.

Answer choice A: The y value for $x = -4$ is not on the graph of the function.

Answer choices B: For $x = -2$, $y = 3$.

Answer choices C: For $x = 3$, $y = -1$.

Answer choices D: For $x = 4$, $y = -3$.

Only answer choice B has a positive value of y.

6. <u>C</u>

Read the value of $f(x)$ from the table:

$$f(1) = -2$$
$$f(3) = -1$$

Solve for $|2f(1) - f(3)|$:

$$|(2 \times -2) - (-1)| = |-4 + 1| = |-3| = 3$$

7. <u>D</u>

Plug in $x = 5$ in the function g:

$$g(5) = (3 \times 5) - 10 = 15 - 10 = 5$$

Solve for $|f(-2) + g(5)|$: It is given that $f(-2) = -10$.

$$|-10 + 5| = |-5| = 5$$

2. <u>D</u>

Determine the shift in the graph:

The vertex of the graph is above 0 and to the left. Hence, the x-coordinate of the vertex must be negative and the y-coordinate of the vertex must be positive. This eliminates answer choices A, B, and C.

3. <u>2</u>

Solve for the positive value:

$$6 - x = 4 \rightarrow x = 6 - 4 \rightarrow x = 2$$

Since it is given that $s = 10$, t must be 2.

4. <u>A</u>

Determine the midpoint of the two numbers:

$$\frac{40 + 70}{2} = \frac{110}{2} = 55$$

This eliminates answer choices B and D.

Determine the distance of the numbers from the midpoint:

Both the numbers are at a distance of 15 from the midpoint. This eliminates answer choice C.

5. B

Determine the midpoint of the two numbers:
$$\frac{25 + 45}{2} = \frac{70}{2} = 35$$
This eliminates answer choices A and C. Answer choice D can be eliminated since the inequality should be $x - 35$ not $x + 35$.

6. D

Determine the solution set:
$$-3 < 2x - 1 < 3 \ \rightarrow$$
$$-3 + 1 < 2x - 1 + 1 < 3 + 1 \ \rightarrow$$
$$-2 < 2x < 4 \ \rightarrow \ -1 < x < 2$$

7. C

Determine the shift in the graph:

The vertex of the graph is below 0 and to the right. Hence, the x-coordinate of the vertex must be positive and the y-coordinate of the vertex must be negative. This eliminates answer choices A, B, and D.

8. D

Read the value of y from the graph for $x = 3$:
$$y = -3$$
Read the values of x from the graph for $y = -3$:

The two values of x that define $f(3)$ are $x = -4$ and $x = 3$ (given).

Sum of the absolute values of x is
$$|-4| + |3| = 4 + 3 = 7$$
Note that the question is asking for the sum of the absolute values of x not the absolute value of the sum.

9. B

Determine the solution set:
$$-16 \leq l - 38 \leq 16 \ \rightarrow$$
$$-16 + 38 \leq l \leq 16 + 38 \ \rightarrow \ 22 \ \leq l \leq 54$$
The smallest value of $l = 22$.

10. C

Plug in the given values of x in the function:
$$g(3) = 3^2 - (2 \times 3) - 11 = 9 - 6 - 11 = -8$$
$$g(5) = 5^2 - (2 \times 5) - 11 = 25 - 10 - 11 = 4$$
Solve $|g(3) - g(5)|$:
$$|-8 - 4| = |-12| = 12$$

11. 7

Move 1 to the right-side of the equation.
$$|2x + 7| = 4 - 1 \ \rightarrow \ |2x + 7| = 3$$
Solve for the positive value:
$$2x + 7 = 3 \ \rightarrow \ 2x = 3 - 7 \ \rightarrow \ 2x = -4 \ \rightarrow \ x = -2$$
Solve for the negative value:
$$2x + 7 = -3 \ \rightarrow \ 2x = -3 - 7 \ \rightarrow$$
$$2x = -10 \ \rightarrow \ x = -5$$
Solve for $|a + b|$: Either value of x could be a or b. Same results will be obtained with either combination.
$$|-2 - 5| = |-7| = 7$$

12. 3

Equation $|2x + 1| = 3$

Solve for the positive value:
$$2x + 1 = 3 \ \rightarrow \ 2x = 3 - 1 \ \rightarrow \ 2x = 2 \ \rightarrow \ x = 1$$
It is given $x > 0$. The above value satisfies the condition. Hence, no need to solve for the other value.

Equation $|2y + 3| = 7$

Solve for the positive value:
$$2y + 3 = 7 \rightarrow \ 2y = 7 - 3 \ \rightarrow \ 2y = 4 \ \rightarrow \ y = 2$$
It is given $y > x$. Since $2 > 1$, the above value of y satisfies the condition. Hence, no need to solve for the other value.

Solve for $x + y$:
$$1 + 2 = 3$$
(Note that when the negative values for x and y are calculated, they do not satisfy $y > x > 0$. Hence, 3 is the only possible answer.)

Section 8 – Ratio, Proportion, and Rate

Category 41 – Ratio and Proportion

1. D

Set up a proportion:

Let the number of students in music class $= x$.

$$\frac{\text{students in music class}}{\text{students in drama class}} = \frac{2}{5} = \frac{x}{120}$$

$$5x = 2 \times 120 \rightarrow 5x = 240 \rightarrow x = 48$$

Determine total number of students: Since each student must select one of the classes, the total number of students is the sum of the number of students in both the classes.

$$120 + 48 = 168$$

2. C

Set up a proportion:

Total number of trays $= 4 + 7 = 11$.

Total amount of butter $= 5\frac{1}{2} = 5.5$ cups.

Let the cups of butter for 4 trays $= x$.

$$\frac{\text{number of trays}}{\text{cups of butter}} = \frac{11}{5.5} = \frac{4}{x}$$

$$11x = 4 \times 5.5 \rightarrow 11x = 22 \rightarrow x = 2$$

3. A

Determine the ratio:

$GH = 21$. $FG = 6$.

Hence, GH to $FG = 21$ to 6.

4. B

Determine the ratio:

Total of Product A and Product B sold at Company X last month $= 1,212$.

Total of Product A and Product B sold at Company X and Y last month $= 3,016$.

$$\text{Ratio} = 1,212 : 3,016$$

Divide both sides by 1212 to reduce to the lowest ratio.

$$\frac{1,212}{1,212} : \frac{3,016}{1,212} = 1 : 2.488 = 1 : 2.5$$

5. A

Determine the ratio as a fraction:

Product A sold at Company X last month $= 502$.

Product A sold at Company X and Company Y $= 1,506$.

$$\frac{502}{1,506} = \frac{1}{3}$$

6. C

Set up a proportion:

Let the unknown inches $= x$.

$$\frac{\text{inches}}{\text{meters}} = \frac{0.04}{2} = \frac{x}{2,500}$$

$$2x = 0.04 \times 2500 \rightarrow x = 50$$

7. D

Equate the ratios: Since the ratios are equivalent, they can be equated.

Since 24 is double of 12, $2(a : 5 : 12) = 3 : b : 24$. Hence,

$$2a : 10 : 24 = 3 : b : 24$$

$$2a = 3 \rightarrow a = \frac{3}{2}$$

$$b = 10$$

Determine $2(a + b)$:

$$2\left(\frac{3}{2} + 10\right) = 2 \times 11.5 = 23$$

8. A

Note that if $2 : 3$ is multiplied by 10, the ratio of muffins will be $20 : 30$. This gives a total of 50 muffins with the difference $= 30 - 20 = 10$.

Alternatively, proportion can be set up to determine the number of muffins and, subsequently, the difference.

9. B

Regular sugar cookies: Since each packet contains 12 ounces, 48 ounces will be in $\frac{48}{12} = 4$ packets.

$$\text{total cookies} = 4 \times 8 = 32$$

Low sugar cookies: Since each packet contains 8 ounces, 48 ounces will be in $\frac{48}{8} = 6$ packets.

$$\text{total cookies} = 6 \times 12 = 72$$

Determine the difference:

$$72 - 32 = 40$$

10. C

The butter in the second cake is 2.5 times more than the first cake. Hence, the sugar in the second cake will be 2.5 times more $= 2 \times 2.5 = 5$ grams.

Evaluate each answer choice: Answer choices A, B, and D are incorrect. The amount of sugar in grams that must be added to the second cake $= 5$ is half the amount of butter that was added to the first cake $= 10$.

11. A

$\frac{1}{4}$ cup butter + $2\frac{3}{4}$ cups flour batter = 3 cups

Hence, 3 cups will have $\frac{1}{4}$ cup of butter.

Each cup will have one-third of $\frac{1}{4} = \frac{1}{4} \times \frac{1}{3} = \frac{1}{12}$.

(See calculation below using proportion.

Let the butter in 1 cup = x.

$$\frac{\text{number of cups}}{\text{cup of butter}} = \frac{3}{\frac{1}{4}} = \frac{1}{x}$$

$$3x = 1 \times \frac{1}{4} \rightarrow x = \frac{1}{4 \times 3} \rightarrow x = \frac{1}{12}$$

)

12. D

Determine the ratio:

Total number of students = 600.

Number of students walk home = 80.

Number of students go home with a parent = 160.

Number of students take the bus = $600 - (80 + 160) = 600 - 240 = 360$.

go home with a parent:take the bus = $160:360 = 4:9$

13. A

Determine the ratio:

Total number of trees planted 4 or more years ago = $8 + 11 + 2 + 6 + 3 = 30$.

Total number of trees planted more than 6 years ago = $6 + 3 = 9$. (Note that this does not include year 6).

$$\frac{\text{more than 6 years ago}}{\text{4 or more years ago}} = \frac{9}{30} = \frac{3}{10}$$

14. B

Determine the ratio:

Trees planted within last 3 years = $5 + 3 + 12 = 20$.

Trees planted within last 8 years = $5 + 3 + 12 + 8 + 11 + 2 + 6 + 3 = 50$.

planted within last 3 years:planted within last 8 years = $20:50 = 2:5$

15. C

Protein mix A:

Protein in 1 cup = 28 grams. Hence, protein in $\frac{1}{4}$ cup is

$$28 \times \frac{1}{4} = 7$$

Protein mix B:

Protein in 1 cup = 20 grams. Hence, protein in $\frac{3}{4}$ cup is

$$20 \times \frac{3}{4} = 15$$

Determine total protein in 1 cup mixture Laura created:

$$7 + 15 = 22$$

16. 210

Set up a proportion:

Let the distance between airports in miles = x.

$$\frac{\text{inches}}{\text{miles}} = \frac{0.5}{14} = \frac{7.5}{x}$$

$$0.5x = 14 \times 7.5 \rightarrow 0.5x = 105 \rightarrow x = 210$$

17. 90.7

Set up a proportion:

Let the weight in kilograms = x.

$$\frac{\text{pounds}}{\text{kilograms}} = \frac{2.20462}{1} = \frac{200}{x}$$

$$2.20462x = 200 \times 1 \rightarrow x = 90.718 = 90.7$$

18. 30

Set up a proportion:

It is given that the shadow of 8 feet pole = 20 feet.

Let the shadow of 20 feet pole = x.

$$\frac{\text{length of pole in feet}}{\text{shadow cast in feet}} = \frac{8}{20} = \frac{20}{x}$$

$$8x = 20 \times 20 \rightarrow 8x = 400 \rightarrow x = 50$$

Determine the difference:

$$50 - 20 = 30$$

Category 42 – Rate

1. **B**
Use the conversion factors: 1 hour = 60 minutes.

$$10 \text{ minutes} \times \frac{30 \text{ miles}}{60 \text{ minutes}} = 5 \text{ miles}$$

2. **D**
Use the conversion factors: 1 minute = 60 seconds.

$$y \text{ inches} \times \frac{60 \text{ seconds}}{x \text{ inches}} = \frac{60y}{x} \text{ seconds}$$

3. **105**
Use the conversion factors: 1 hour = 60 minutes.

$$140 \text{ minutes} \times \frac{45 \text{ miles}}{60 \text{ minutes}} = 105 \text{ miles}$$

4. **C**
Use the conversion factors:

$$2 \text{ hours} \times \frac{50 \text{ miles}}{1 \text{ hour}} \times \frac{1 \text{ gallon}}{20 \text{ miles}} \times \frac{3 \text{ dollars}}{1 \text{ gallon}} =$$
$$15 \text{ dollars}$$

5. **A**
Use the conversion factors: 1 minute = 60 seconds.

$$\frac{768 \text{ ounces}}{60 \text{ seconds}} \times \frac{1 \text{ gallon}}{128 \text{ ounces}} =$$
$$0.1 \text{ gallons per second}$$

6. **D**
Use the conversion factors: 1 hour = 60 minutes.
Jolie: 10 miles in 60 minutes.

$$15 \text{ minutes} \times \frac{10 \text{ miles}}{60 \text{ minutes}} = 2.5 \text{ miles}$$

Charlie: 18 miles in 60 minutes.

$$15 \text{ minutes} \times \frac{18 \text{ miles}}{60 \text{ minutes}} = 4.5 \text{ miles}$$

Determine the distance between Jolie and Charlie: They are traveling in the opposite direction.

$$2.5 + 4.5 = 7 \text{ miles}$$

7. **D**
Total miles = 3,459.
At the average speed of 526 miles per hour, miles traveled in 4 hours are

$$526 \times 4 = 2,104$$

The remaining miles traveled for x minutes at 420 miles per hour are

$$3,459 - 2,104 = 1,355 \text{ miles}$$

Use the conversion factors to determine x: 1 hour = 60 minutes.

$$1,355 \text{ miles} \times \frac{60 \text{ minutes}}{420 \text{ miles}} = 193.57 \text{ minutes} = 194$$

8. **A**
Use the conversion factors: 1 hour = 60 minutes.
Bird A: 18 miles in 60 minutes.

$$10 \text{ minutes} \times \frac{18 \text{ miles}}{60 \text{ minutes}} = 3 \text{ miles}$$

Bird B: 24 miles in 60 minutes.

$$10 \text{ minutes} \times \frac{24 \text{ miles}}{60 \text{ minutes}} = 4 \text{ miles}$$

Determine the distance between the two birds: The birds are travelling in the same direction.

$$4 - 3 = 1 \text{ mile}$$

9. **C**
Use the conversion factors: 1 hour = 3,600 seconds.

$$\frac{36 \text{ gallons}}{3,600 \text{ seconds}} \times \frac{128 \text{ ounces}}{1 \text{ gallon}} =$$
$$1.28 \text{ ounces per second}$$

10. **B**
Use the conversion factors: 1 hour = 60 minutes.
First 15 minutes: 60 miles in 60 minutes.

$$15 \text{ minutes} \times \frac{60 \text{ miles}}{60 \text{ minutes}} = 15 \text{ miles}$$

Remaining 30 minutes: 40 miles in 60 minutes.

$$30 \text{ minutes} \times \frac{40 \text{ miles}}{60 \text{ minutes}} = 20 \text{ miles}$$

Determine the total miles traveled:

$$15 + 20 = 35 \text{ miles}$$

11. <u>50</u>

Use the conversion factors: 1 hour = 3600 seconds.

$$\frac{180 \text{ kilometers}}{3{,}600 \text{ seconds}} \times \frac{1000 \text{ meters}}{1 \text{ kilometer}} =$$

$$50 \text{ meters per second}$$

12. <u>12</u>

4 miles is one-fifth of 20 miles. Hence, it will take her one-fifth the time = 12 minutes. See below calculation using conversion factors.

$$4 \text{ miles} \times \frac{60 \text{ minutes}}{20 \text{ miles}} = 12 \text{ minutes}$$

Section 8 – Review Questions

1. <u>B</u>

10 kilometers is one-third of 30 kilometers. Hence, it will take her one-third the time = 20 minutes.

2. <u>D</u>

Use the conversion factors:

$$3 \text{ hours} = 3 \times 60 = 180 \text{ minutes}$$

$$180 \text{ minutes} \times \frac{p \text{ pages}}{m \text{ minutes}} = \frac{180p}{m} \text{ pages}$$

3. <u>C</u>

Use the conversion factors: 1 hour = 3,600 seconds.

$$0.2 \text{ miles} \times \frac{3{,}600 \text{ seconds}}{60 \text{ miles}} = 12 \text{ seconds}$$

4. <u>C</u>

Evaluate each answer choice:

$$\text{salt:water} = 20:500 = 1:25$$

Since each proportion will have the same ratio, evaluate the above ratio against the ratio in each answer choice.

Choice I: $1:25$. This matches the given ratio.

Choice II: $3:50 = 1:16.7$. This is does not match the given ratio.

Choice III: $5:125 = 1:25$. This matches the given ratio.

5. <u>A</u>

Set up a proportion:

$$\frac{\text{annual rainfall}}{\text{March rainfall}} \rightarrow \frac{12.4}{3.1} = \frac{r}{\text{March rainfall}}$$

$$\text{March rainfall} = \frac{3.1r}{12.4} = \frac{r}{4}$$

13. <u>50.7</u>

John travels 100 miles per day. In 4 days, John will travel

$$4 \times 100 = 400 \text{ miles}$$

Use the conversion factors:

$$400 \text{ miles} \times \frac{1 \text{ gallon}}{30 \text{ miles}} \times \frac{3.8 \text{ liters}}{1 \text{ gallon}} =$$

$$50.66 \text{ liters} = 50.7 \text{ liters}$$

6. <u>D</u>

Use the conversion factors: 1 hour = 3,600 seconds.

$$\frac{120 \text{ miles}}{3{,}600 \text{ seconds}} \times \frac{5{,}280 \text{ feet}}{1 \text{ mile}} = 176 \text{ feet per second}$$

7. <u>B</u>

Use the conversion factors:

$$1{,}400 \text{ dollars} \times \frac{100 \text{ square feet}}{250 \text{ dollars}} \times \frac{8 \text{ hours}}{140 \text{ square feet}} =$$

$$32 \text{ hours}$$

8. <u>A</u>

Use the conversion factors:

$$3{,}280 \text{ feet} \times \frac{1 \text{ miles}}{5{,}280 \text{ feet}} = 0.62 \text{ miles}$$

The question asks for an approximate answer. Answer choice A is closest.

9. <u>50</u>

Plane A is flying at the speed of 600 miles per 60 minutes. In 30 minutes, the distance will be half = 300 miles.

Plane B is flying at the speed of 500 miles per 60 minutes. In 30 minutes, the distance will be half = 250 miles.

The difference in miles = $300 - 250 = 50$.

(See below calculation for miles in 30 minutes using conversion factors.

Plane A: 600 miles in 60 minutes.

$$30 \text{ minutes} \times \frac{600 \text{ miles}}{60 \text{ minutes}} = 300 \text{ miles}$$

Plane B: 500 miles in 60 minutes.

$$30 \text{ minutes} \times \frac{500 \text{ miles}}{60 \text{ minutes}} = 250 \text{ miles}$$

)

10. <u>6</u>

1 mile is 0.2 centimeters. Hence, 30 miles is $0.2 \times 30 = 6$ centimeters.

(See calculation below using a proportion.

Let the distance in centimeters $= x$.

$$\frac{\text{miles}}{\text{centimeters}} = \frac{1}{0.2} = \frac{30}{x}$$

$$x = 30 \times 0.2 = 6$$

)

11. <u>114</u>

Convert the centimeter scale to miles: For ease, convert the scale to 1 centimeter. Multiply both numbers by 2.

$$\frac{1}{2} \times 2 \text{ centimeters} = 24 \text{ miles} \times 2 \ \rightarrow$$

$$1 \text{ centimeter} = 48 \text{ miles}$$

Multiply the distance given in centimeters by 48 to convert to miles. See table below.

Names of roads and highways	Distance in centimeter	Distance in miles
State Road 27	$\frac{1}{8}$	$\frac{1}{8} \times 48 = 6$
Highway 2	$1\frac{1}{4}$	$\frac{5}{4} \times 48 = 60$
Highway 17	$\frac{1}{4}$	$\frac{1}{4} \times 48 = 12$
State Road 4	$\frac{3}{4}$	$\frac{3}{4} \times 48 = 36$

Determine the total distance in miles:

$$6 + 60 + 12 + 36 = 114 \text{ miles}$$

12. <u>90</u>

Total miles on Highway 2 = 60.

Use the conversion factors: 1 hour = 60 minutes.

$$60 \ \cancel{\text{miles}} \ \times \frac{60 \text{ minutes}}{40 \ \cancel{\text{miles}}} = 90 \text{ minutes}$$

13. <u>1.5</u>

Use the conversion factors:

Total distance on State Road 27 and State Road 4 = $6 + 36 = 42$ miles.

$$42 \ \cancel{\text{miles}} \ \times \frac{1 \text{ gallon}}{28 \ \cancel{\text{miles}}} = 1.5 \text{ gallons}$$

Section 9 – Percent

Category 43 – Percent of a Number and Percent Increase/Decrease

1. A

Convert percent to decimal:
$$25\% \text{ decrease} = 1 - 0.25 = 0.75$$
$$6\% \text{ increase} = 1 + 0.06 = 1.06$$
Determine the final value of k:
$$(0.75)(1.06)(k)$$

2. D

Convert percent to decimal:
$$25\% \text{ decrease} = 1 - 0.25 = 0.75$$
$$150\% \text{ increase} = 1 + 1.5 = 2.5$$
Determine the final value of 76:
$$0.75 \times 2.5 \times 72 = 135$$

3. B

Convert percent to decimal:
$$55\% \text{ increase} = 1 + 0.55 = 1.55$$
$$13\% \text{ decrease} = 1 - 0.13 = 0.87$$
$$117\% \text{ increase} = 1 + 1.17 = 2.17$$
Determine the final value of s:
$$(1.55)(0.87)(2.17)(s)$$

4. C

Convert percent to decimal:
$$20\% \text{ checked out} = 20\% \text{ decrease} = 1 - 0.2 = 0.8$$
Determine the remaining books:
$$0.8 \times 1,040 = 832$$
Determine total number of books at the end of the day:
$$\text{remaining} + \text{return} = 832 + 125 = 957$$

5. A

Convert percent to decimal:
$$35\% \text{ discount} = 35\% \text{ decrease} = 1 - 0.35 = 0.65$$
$$12\% \text{ discount} = 12\% \text{ decrease} = 1 - 0.12 = 0.88$$
$$8\% \text{ sales tax} = 8\% \text{ increase} = 1 + 0.08 = 1.08$$
Determine the final value of p:
$$(0.65)(0.88)(1.08)(p)$$

6. B

Convert percent to decimal:
$$20\% \text{ to brother} = 20\% \text{ decrease} = 1 - 0.2 = 0.8$$
$$35\% \text{ to cousin} = 35\% \text{ decrease} = 1 - 0.35 = 0.65$$
Determine the final number of CDs:
$$0.8 \times 0.65 \times 125 = 65$$

7. A

Convert percent to decimal:
$$25\% = 0.25$$
$$30\% = 0.3$$
$$200\% = 2.0$$
Determine the final value of 60:
$$0.25 \times 0.3 \times 2 \times 60 = 9$$

8. D

Convert percent to decimal:
$$10\% \text{ increase} = 1 + 0.1 = 1.1$$
$$10\% \text{ increase in 2 academic years} = 1.1 \times 1.1$$
Determine the final number of students:
$$1.1 \times 1.1 \times 200 = 242$$

9. C

Convert percent to decimal:
$$160\% \text{ increase} = 1 + 1.6 = 2.6$$
Determine the final number of residents by 2025:
$$2.6 \times 3,680 = 9,568$$
Additional residents $= 9,568 - 3,680 = 5,888$

10. A

Convert percent to decimal:
$$6\% \text{ more} = 1 + 1.06 = 1.06$$
Determine the 2019 bonus: Estimated bonus $= d$.
$$1.06 \times d = 1.06d$$

11. 80

Convert percent to decimal:
$$20\% \text{ decrease} = 1 - 0.2 = 0.8$$
$$25\% \text{ increase} = 1 + 0.25 = 1.25$$
Determine the history grade of the 3rd test:
$$80 \times 0.8 \times 1.25 = 80$$

12. 12

Convert percent to decimal:
$$\text{First stop} = 25\% \text{ decrease} = 1 - 0.25 = 0.75$$
$$\text{Second stop} = 50\% \text{ decrease} = 1 - 0.5 = 0.5$$
Determine the number of remaining passengers:
$$0.75 \times 0.5 \times 48 = 18$$
Since 2 passengers boarded at 2nd stop, total is
$$18 + 2 = 20$$

Category 44 – The Original Number before a Percent Increase/Decrease

1. A

Convert percent to decimal:
$$20\% \text{ decrease} = 1 - 0.2 = 0.8$$
$$5\% \text{ increase} = 1 + 0.05 = 1.05$$
Determine number n: End number = 42.
$$\frac{42}{(0.8)(1.05)}$$

2. D

Convert percent to decimal:
$$27\% \text{ stores close} = 27\% \text{ decrease} = 1 - 0.27 = 0.73$$
Determine the number of stores in 2022: End number of stores in 2025 = 584.
$$\frac{584}{0.73} = 800$$

3. C

Convert percent to decimal:
$$40\% \text{ discount} = 40\% \text{ decrease} = 1 - 0.4 = 0.6$$
$$6\% \text{ sales tax} = 6\% \text{ increase} = 1 + 0.06 = 1.06$$
Determine the original price of shirt: End price = \$15.90.
$$\frac{15.90}{0.6 \times 1.06} = 25$$

4. B

Convert percent to decimal:
$$20\% \text{ increase} = 1 + 0.2 = 1.2$$
$$10\% \text{ decrease} = 1 - 0.1 = 0.9$$
Determine number p: End value = 378.
$$\frac{378}{1.2 \times 0.9} = 350$$

5. C

Convert percent to decimal:
$$30\% \text{ discount} = 30\% \text{ decrease} = 0.7$$
$$5\% \text{ discount} = 5\% \text{ decrease} = 0.95$$
Determine the original price of book: End price = \$5.32.
$$\frac{5.32}{0.7 \times 0.95} = 8$$

6. A

Convert percent to decimal:
$$25\% \text{ increase from 2017 to 2018} = 1 + 0.25 = 1.25$$
$$20\% \text{ increase from 2016 to 2017} = 1 + 0.2 = 1.2$$
Determine the 2016 profit: Profit in 2018 = 10.5.
$$\frac{10.5}{1.2 \times 1.25} = 7$$

Category 45 – A Number Percent of Another Number

1. B

Determine 12 is what percent of 30:
$$\frac{12}{30} \times 100 = 40\%$$

2. A

Percent discount at Store A
$$\text{Discount} = 250 - 215 = \$35$$
Determine 35 is what percent of 250:
$$\frac{35}{250} \times 100 = 14\%$$
Percent discount at Store B
$$\text{Discount} = 250 - 200 = \$50$$
Determine 50 is what percent of 250:
$$\frac{50}{250} \times 100 = 20\%$$
Determine the difference in percent discount:
$$20\% - 14\% = 6\%$$

3. D

Determine the increased value of $p = 72$:
$$25\% \text{ increase} = 1 + 0.25 = 1.25$$
$$72 \times 1.25 = 90$$
Determine 72 is what percent of 90:
$$\frac{72}{90} \times 100 = 80\%$$

4. B

Determine the price of computer at Store B = a:
$$10\% \text{ additional discount} = 1 - 0.1 = 0.9$$
$$a = 1,180 \times 0.9 = \$1,062$$
Determine $a = 1,062$ is what percent of 1,200:
$$\frac{1,062}{1,200} \times 100 = 88.5\%$$

5. D

Determine 3.20 (cost of one ride) is what percent of 40 (initial pass value):
$$\frac{3.20}{40} \times 100 = 8\%$$

6. C

Remove the sales tax from original and refunded prices.

Determine the original price without sales tax:

$$\frac{43.20}{1.08} = \$40$$

Sales tax $= 43.20 - 40 = \$3.20$.

Determine the refunded price without sales tax:

$$36 - 3.20 = \$32.80$$

Determine 32.80 (return price) is what percent of 40 (original price):

$$\frac{32.80}{40} \times 100 = 82\%$$

Category 46 – Percent Change

1. B

Determine the percent change:

Old profit $= 1.2$. New profit $= 1.6$.

$$\frac{1.6 - 1.2}{1.2} \times 100 = \frac{0.4}{1.2} \times 100 = 33.33\%$$

2. C

Determine the percent change:

Old price $= 20$. New price $= 8$.

$$\frac{8 - 20}{20} \times 100 = -\frac{12}{20} \times 100 = -60\%$$

3. B

Determine the percent change: Remove the warranty from the original and reduced prices.

Old price $= 3,200 - 200 = \$3,000$.

Reduced price $=$ new price $= 2,300 - 200 = \$2,100$.

$$\frac{2,100 - 3,000}{3,000} \times 100 = -\frac{900}{3,000} \times 100 = -30\%$$

4. B

Determine the percent change: It is apparent that the change in answer choices A, C, and D is lower than in answer choice B. If unsure, calculate percent change for each answer choice.

5. 25

Determine the percent change:

Old value (February) $= 88$. New value (March) $= 110$.

$$\frac{110 - 88}{88} \times 100 = \frac{22}{88} \times 100 = 25\%$$

Section 9 – Review Questions

1. C

Remaining balance $= 75 - 9 - 17.25 = \$48.75$.

Determine 48.75 (remaining balance) is what percent of 75 (initial value):

$$\frac{48.75}{75} \times 100 = 65\%$$

2. D

Calculate the percent change: Old $= 12$. New $= 14$.

$$\frac{14 - 12}{12} \times 100 = \frac{2}{12} \times 100 = 16.66\%$$

Since the change is positive, it is an increase by 16.66%.

3. A

Convert percent to decimal:

$$15\% \text{ discount} = 15\% \text{ decrease} = 1 - 0.15 = 0.85$$
$$8\% \text{ sales tax} = 8\% \text{ increase} = 1 + 0.08 = 1.08$$

Determine the original price of the scarf: End price $= d$.

$$\frac{d}{(0.85)(1.08)}$$

4. B

Step 1: Determine the end population of Bird A in 2019. This is also the end population of Bird B in 2019.

Step 2: Determine the initial population of Bird B in 2016 using the end population in 2019, from Step 1.

<u>End population of Bird A in 2019.</u>

5% increase from 2016 to 2019 $= 1 + 0.05 = 1.05$

Determine the end population in 2019:

$$6{,}000 \times 1.05 = 6{,}300$$

<u>Initial population of Bird B in 2016.</u>

20% increase from 2016 to 2019 $= 1 + 0.2 = 1.2$

Determine the initial population in 2016: End population in 2019 $= 6{,}300$ from Step 1.

$$\frac{6{,}300}{1.2} = 5{,}250$$

5. C

Calculate the percent change:

Old value $= 2k$. New value $= 0.6k$.

$$\frac{0.6k - 2k}{2k} \times 100 = \frac{-1.4\,k}{2\,k} \times 100 = 70\%$$

6. B

Convert percent to decimal:

$$6\% \text{ decrease} = 1 - 0.06 = 0.94$$
$$19\% \text{ increase} = 1 + 0.19 = 1.19$$
$$22\% \text{ increase} = 1 + 0.22 = 1.22$$

Determine the final value: Initial population $= s$.

$$(0.94)(1.19)(1.22)(s)$$

7. B

Determine the percent of members:

41 and up in yoga class $= 28 + 35 = 63$.

41 and up in karate class $= 15 + 12 = 27$.

Total 41 and up in both classes $= 63 + 27 = 90$.

The percent members in yoga class are

$$\frac{63}{90} \times 100 = 70\%$$

Hence, the percent members in karate class $= 30\%$.

Determine the difference:

$$70\% - 30\% = 40\%$$

8. D

Convert percent to decimal:

$$40\% = 0.4$$

Determine the total members enrolled in the club: Members in yoga and karate class $= 140$.

$$\frac{140}{0.4} = 350$$

9. D

Determine the remaining amount on cashless card:

Since 36 is 12 times of 3, the cost of 36 rounds is

$$0.5 \times 12 = 6$$

Hence, $6 were deducted for 36 rounds of games.

Amount remaining on cashless card $= 20 - 6 = \$14$.

Determine the remaining amount $= 14$ is what percent of 20:

$$\frac{14}{20} \times 100 = 70\%$$

10. 140

Convert percent to decimal:

20% stores close $= 20\%$ decrease $= 1 - 0.2 = 0.8$

Determine the initial number of stores in 2015: End number of stores in 2018 $= 112$.

$$\frac{112}{0.8} = 140$$

11. 30

Determine x: $n = 40$.

$$10\% \text{ decrease} = 1 - 0.1 = 0.9$$
$$x = 0.9n = 0.9 \times 40 = 36$$

Determine p: $x = 36$.

$$20\% \text{ increase} = 1 + 0.2 = 1.2$$
$$1.2p = x \rightarrow 1.2p = 36 \rightarrow p = \frac{36}{1.2} = 30$$

12. 980

Convert percent to decimal:

20% cost $= 20\%$ decrease $= 1 - 0.2 = 0.8$

Determine the initial earnings (x): End earning $= \$784$.

$$\frac{784}{0.8} = 980$$

13. 480

Determine the percent difference:

Students in cooking club $= 40\%$.

Students not in cooking club $= 100\% - 40\% = 60\%$.

Hence, $60\% - 40\% = 20\%$ less students joined the cooking club.

It is given that 96 less students joined the cooking club. Hence, 96 is 20% of the students.

Determine the total number of students: $20\% = 0.2$.

$$\frac{96}{0.2} = 480$$

Section 10 – Exponents and Exponential Functions

Category 47 – Exponents

1. C

Make the bases same: 27 can be written as (3^3).

$$3^2 \times (3^3)^4 = 3^2 \times 3^{3 \times 4} = 3^{2+12} = 3^{14}$$

2. D

Since 16 and x^4 are perfect squares, the square root can be removed.

$$\sqrt{4^2 x^2 x^2} = 4x^2$$

3. A

Make the bases same: All bases are multiples of 3.

$$((3^2)^3)^{n+1} = (3^4)^3 \times 3^{3n} \rightarrow 3^{6(n+1)} = 3^{12+3n}$$

Equate the exponents:

$$6(n+1) = 12 + 3n \rightarrow 6n + 6 = 12 + 3n \rightarrow$$
$$3n = 6 \rightarrow n = 2$$

4. B

Make the bases same: All bases are multiples of 2.

$$(2^2)^{3a-1} = 2^{3+a} \times (2^5)^b \rightarrow 2^{2(3a-1)} = 2^{3+a+5b}$$

Equate the exponents:

$$2(3a-1) = 3 + a + 5b \rightarrow 6a - 2 = 3 + a + 5b \rightarrow$$
$$6a - a - 5b = 3 + 2 \rightarrow 5a - 5b = 5 \rightarrow$$
$$a - b = 1 \rightarrow b = a - 1$$

5. D

Remove perfect squares and write as square root:

$$(4^2 x^4 x y^2 y)^{\frac{1}{2}} =$$
$$4x^2 y(xy)^{\frac{1}{2}} = 4x^2 y \sqrt{xy}$$

6. C

$$(3y)^{\frac{3}{a}} = \sqrt[a]{(3y)^3} = \sqrt[a]{27y^3}$$

7. C

Replace roots with fractional exponent:

$$\frac{5^{\frac{1}{2}} \times a^{\frac{4}{2}}}{5^{\frac{1}{4}} \times a^{\frac{3}{4}}} = \frac{5^{\frac{1}{2}} \times a^2}{5^{\frac{1}{4}} \times a^{\frac{3}{4}}}$$

Move expressions in the denominator to the numerator:

$$5^{\frac{1}{2}-\frac{1}{4}} \times a^{2-\frac{3}{4}} = 5^{\frac{2-1}{4}} \times a^{\frac{8-3}{4}} = 5^{\frac{1}{4}} \times a^{\frac{5}{4}} = \sqrt[4]{5a^5}$$

8. B

Simplify: 27 can be written as 3^3.

$$(3^3 \times a^9)^{\frac{1}{3}} = 3^{3 \times \frac{1}{3}} \times a^{9 \times \frac{1}{3}} = 3a^3$$

9. A

Replace roots with fractional exponents and simplify:

$$r^{\frac{1}{2}} \times r^{\frac{1}{3}} = r^{\frac{1}{2}+\frac{1}{3}} = r^{\frac{3+2}{6}} = r^{\frac{5}{6}}$$

10. D

If the expression $2^a y^4$ is divided by the expression $2^b y^4$, then y^4 will cancel out and 2^a divided by 2^b will give 2^{a-b}.

$$\frac{2^a y^4}{2^b y^4} = \frac{80}{5} \rightarrow 2^{a-b} = 16 \rightarrow 2^{a-b} = 2^4$$

Equate the exponents:

$$a - b = 4$$

11. A

Move the expression in the denominator to the numerator:

$$(x^5 y^{-2}) \times (x^2 y^{-3}) \times (x^{-6} y^6)$$

Add exponents of similar bases:

$$x^5 x^2 x^{-6} y^{-2} y^{-3} y^6 = x^{5+2-6} y^{-2-3+6} = xy$$

12. 5

Since 64 and m^3 are perfect cubes, the cube root can be removed from the left expression.

$$\sqrt[3]{4^3 m^3} = 20 \rightarrow \sqrt[3]{(4m)^3} = 20 \rightarrow 4m = 20 \rightarrow$$
$$m = 5$$

13. 3.6 or 18/5

Replace roots with fractional exponents and move the expression in the denominator to the numerator:

$$\frac{\sqrt{s^{3+5}}}{\sqrt[5]{s^2}} = s^{\frac{x}{y}} \rightarrow s^{\frac{8}{2}} \times s^{\frac{-2}{5}} = s^{\frac{x}{y}} \rightarrow s^{4-\frac{2}{5}} = s^{\frac{x}{y}}$$

Equate the exponents:

$$\frac{x}{y} = 4 - \frac{2}{5} = \frac{20-2}{5} = \frac{18}{5} = 3.6$$

14. 20

$$a^6 = a^2 \times a^2 \times a^2 = 10 \times 10 \times 10 = 1,000$$
$$b^{-5} = \frac{1}{b^5} = \frac{1}{50}$$
$$a^6 b^{-5} = 1,000 \times \frac{1}{50} = 20$$

Category 48 – Linear Versus Exponential Growth and Decay

1. <u>B</u>

In tables A, C, and D the change in the value of y with the change in the value of x is constant. In table B, y increases 4-fold for every 2 increase in the value x. This is exponential increase/growth.

2. <u>D</u>

Since the colonies double every 30 minutes, there are twice more colonies of bacteria every 30 minutes.

3. <u>A</u>

Since the decrease is same each year, it is linear decrease.

4. <u>B</u>

Since the population is projected to grow exponentially each year, it will increase by a certain percent each year than the preceding year.

5. <u>D</u>

Since Team A is ahead of Team B by one-fourth the distance every 20 minutes than the preceding 20 minutes, it is exponential increase/growth.

Category 49 – Exponential Growth and Decay

1. <u>C</u>

Determine the components of exponential growth:

$a = 3.2$. Since a is the initial number, 3.2 is the initial population in 1990.

2. <u>D</u>

Determine the components of compound interest formula:

Since $n = 1$, $b = 1 + r$.

$r = 12\% = 0.12$.

Hence, $k = 1 + 0.12 = 1.12$.

3. <u>D</u>

Determine the components of exponential growth:

$b = 1 + r = 1.16 = 1 + 0.16$. Hence, $r = 0.16 = 16\%$.

Since time interval $= \frac{t}{2}$, the increase is every 2 years.

Hence, every 2 years P increases by 16%.

This eliminates answer choices A, B, and C.

4. <u>A</u>

Determine the components of exponential decay:

$a = 200{,}000$.

$r = 50\% = 0.5$. $x = 1 - r = 1 - 0.5 = 0.5$.

Time interval $= 10$ minutes. In 30 minutes, there will be $\frac{30}{10} = 3$ time intervals. Hence, $t = 3$.

$$y = a(b)^x = 200{,}000(0.5)^3 = 25{,}000$$

5. <u>D</u>

Determine the components of exponential decay:

$a = 150$.

$r = 1\% = 0.01$. $b = 1 - r = 1 - 0.01 = 0.99$.

Time interval is every 4 months $= \frac{m}{4}$.

$D = $ decay after m months.

$$y = a(b)^x \rightarrow D = 150(0.99)^{\frac{m}{4}}$$

6. <u>C</u>

Determine the components of exponential growth:

$r = 9\% = 0.09$. $k = b = 1 + r = 1 + 0.09 = 1.09$.

7. <u>B</u>

Determine the components of compound interest formula:

$P = 2{,}000$. $r = 8\% = 0.08$. $t = 3$.

Since the interest is compounded each quarter and there are 4 quarters in a year, $n = 4$.

Plug the values in the formula.

$$A = P\left(1 + \frac{r}{n}\right)^{nt} = 2{,}000\left(1 + \frac{0.08}{4}\right)^{4\times3} =$$
$$2{,}000(1 + 0.02)^{12} = 2{,}000(1.02)^{12}$$

8. <u>A</u>

Determine the components of exponential growth:

<u>Model M</u>

Time interval is per month for 6 months. Hence, $m = 6$.

$$M = 400(2)^m = 400(2)^6 = 25{,}600$$

<u>Model Q</u>

Time interval is per quarter. Since there are 2 quarters in 6 months, $q = 2$.

$$Q = 2{,}100(3)^q = 2{,}100(3)^2 = 18{,}900$$

Determine difference: $25{,}600 - 18{,}900 = 6{,}700$.

9. C

Determine the components of exponential growth:

$a = a$.

$r = 2$.

Since the increase is every 29 years, time interval $= \frac{t}{29}$.

$y = n =$ trees after t years.

$$y = a(b)^x \ \rightarrow \ n = a(2)^{\frac{t}{29}}$$

10. B

Determine the components of exponential growth:

$a = \$12$.

$r = 8\% = 0.08$. $x = 1 + r = 1 + 0.08 = 1.08$.

$t = 4$ months.

$$y = a(b)^x = 12(1.08)^4 = 16.32 = 16$$

11. D

Determine the components of compound interest formula:

Jenny

$P = d$. $r = 6\% = 0.06$. $t = 4$ years. $A = X$.

Since interest rate is compounded semi-annually, $n = 2$.

$$A = P\left(1 + \frac{r}{n}\right)^{nt} = d\left(1 + \frac{0.06}{2}\right)^{2 \times 4} =$$
$$d(1 + 0.03)^8 = d(1.03)^8$$

Sara

$P = d$. $r = 5\% = 0.05$. $t = 4$ years. $A = Y$.

Since interest rate is compounded annually, $n = 1$.

$A = P(1 + r)^t = d(1 + 0.05)^4 = d(1.05)^4$.

Determine $X - Y$:

$$d(1.03)^8 - d(1.05)^4$$

12. C

Determine the components of compound interest formula :

$P = d$. $r = 10\% = 0.1$. $t = 3$ years.

Amount at the end of 3 years $= A = \$1,331$.

Since interest rate is compounded annually, $n = 1$.

$$A = P(1 + r)^t \rightarrow 1,331 = d(1.1)^3 \ \rightarrow$$
$$1,331 = d(1.331) \ \rightarrow \ d = \frac{1,331}{1.331} = \$1,000$$

Category 50 – Graphs of Exponential Growth and Decay Functions

1. B

Determine the graph that passes through the points $(0, a)$ and $(1, ab)$

$a = 1$. $b = 3$.

$(0, a) = (0, 1)$ and $(1, ab) = (1, 3)$.

Only, the graph in answer choice B passes through the above points.

2. C

The y-coordinate of the y-intercept on a graph corresponds to the initial number. Hence, $a = 575$.

This eliminates answer choices A and B.

Since the function is exponential decay, the value of b will be less than 1 and greater than 0. This eliminates answer choice D.

3. D

Determine the vertical shift of the graph:

In the equation, $a = 2$.

Minus n is a downward shift of a.

In the given graph, the y-coordinate of the y-intercept $= -1$. This is a downward shift of a by 3 units.

Hence, $n = 3$.

4. A

Identify the rate of change:

When m is increased by 1, n increases 4-fold. Hence, in the exponential function $f(x) = a(b)^x$, the rate of change $= b = 4$. This matches answer choice A.

Section 10 – Review Questions

1. <u>A</u>

Determine the components of exponential growth:

$b = 1.03 = 1 + r = 1 + 0.03$.

Hence, $r = 0.03 = 3\% = k$.

2. <u>B</u>

Determine the components of exponential decay:

$a = n$.

$r = 3\%$. $b = 1 - r = 1 - 0.03 = 0.97$.

Since the decrease is every 8 days, time interval $= \dfrac{d}{8}$.

$P = $ population after d days.

$$y = a(b)^x \;\to\; P = n(0.97)^{\frac{d}{8}}$$

3. <u>D</u>

Determine the components of exponential decay:

$a = $ initial number. $x = b$.

Since b is less than 1, the rate of change is exponential decay. Hence, the initial number a will decrease with increase in time t.

4. <u>C</u>

$$(x^3)^{\frac{2}{5}} \times (y^5)^{\frac{2}{5}} = \sqrt[5]{(x^3)^2} \times y^2 = \sqrt[5]{x^6} \times y^2$$

x^6 can be written as $x^5 \times x$.

$$\sqrt[5]{x \times x^5} \times y^2 = \sqrt[5]{x} \times x \times y^2 = xy^2 \times \sqrt[5]{x}$$

5. <u>C</u>

Factorize: $x^2 - 1$ can be factorized as $(x - 1)(x + 1)$.

$$\sqrt[4]{(x - 1)(x + 1)}$$

Substitute $(x - 1) = 16$ and replace root with exponential fraction:

$$\sqrt[4]{16(x + 1)} \;\to\; \sqrt[4]{2^4(x + 1)} \;\to\; 2^{4 \times \frac{1}{4}}(x + 1)^{\frac{1}{4}} \;\to\;$$
$$2(x + 1)^{\frac{1}{4}}$$

6. <u>C</u>

Determine the vertical shift of the graph:

In the equation, $a = 4$.

Minus c is a downward shift of a. In the given graph, the y-coordinate of the y-intercept $= 2$. This is a downward shift of a by 2 units. Hence, $c = 2$.

7. <u>6.75 or 27/4</u>

Replace root with fractional exponent and simplify:

$$(x^6)\left(x^{\frac{3}{4}}\right) = x^a \;\to\; x^{6 + \frac{3}{4}} = x^a$$

Equate exponents:

$$a = 6 + \frac{3}{4} = \frac{27}{4} = 6.75$$

8. <u>1</u>

Replace roots with fractional exponents:

$$\frac{(x^7)^{\frac{1}{3}}}{(x^4)^{\frac{1}{3}}} = x^{mn} \;\to\; \frac{x^{\frac{7}{3}}}{x^{\frac{4}{3}}} = x^{mn}$$

Move the expression in the denominator to the numerator:

$$x^{\frac{7}{3}} \times x^{-\frac{4}{3}} = x^{mn} \;\to\; x^{\frac{7-4}{3}} = x^{mn} \;\to\; x^{\frac{3}{3}} = x^{mn}$$

Equate the exponents and simplify:

$$mn = 1$$

9. <u>D</u>

Determine the components of compound interest formula:

$P = d$.

$r = 10\% = 0.1$. $1 + r = 1 + 0.1 = 1.1$.

$t = 3$ years. $n = 1$.

$A = $ amount after 3 years $= d + 1,665$.

$$A = P(1 + r)^t \;\to\; d + 1,655 = d(1.1)^3$$

Solve for d:

$$d + 1,655 = d(1.331) \;\to\; 1.331d - d = 1,655 \;\to\;$$
$$0.331d = 1,655 \;\to\; d = \$5,000$$

10. <u>D</u>

Determine the components of compound interest formula:

$P = 2,000$. $r = 8\% = 0.08$.

Since interest rate is compounded quarterly $n = 4$.

$$A = 2,000\left(1 + \frac{0.08}{4}\right)^{4 \times t} \;\to\; A = 2,000(1 + 0.02)^{4t} \;\to\;$$
$$A = 2,000(1.02)^{4t}$$

11. <u>B</u>

Determine the components of exponential decay:

$r = 0.5 = 50\% = $ half.

Time interval $= \dfrac{m}{20}$ is once every 20 minutes.

12. <u>A</u>

Since the population decreased exponentially each year, it is exponential decay. The graph will decrease sharply from left to right as a curve. This matches with answer choice A.

Section 11 – Manipulating Expressions and Equations

Category 51 – Fractions with Expressions in the Denominator

1. C

Determine the strategy and solve: Since the denominators have same expression, the numerators can be added.

$$\frac{3(x+1)-(3x+4)}{x-2}=1 \to$$

$$\frac{3x+3-3x-4}{x-2}=1 \to \frac{-1}{x-2}=1 \to$$

$$-1=x-2 \to x=-1+2 \to x=1$$

2. B

Determine the strategy and solve: The two factors of m^2-n^2 are $(m+n)$ and $(m-n)$. The given value of $(m+n)$ can be substituted to solve.

$$\frac{6m-10}{(m+n)(m-n)}-\frac{3}{(m-n)}=\frac{m}{(m-n)} \to$$

$$\frac{2(3m-5)}{2(m-n)}-\frac{3}{(m-n)}=\frac{m}{(m-n)} \to$$

$$\frac{(3m-5)}{(m-n)}-\frac{3}{(m-n)}=\frac{m}{(m-n)} \to$$

$$3m-5-3=m \to 2m=8 \to m=4$$

Determine n.

$$m+n=2 \to 4+n=2 \to n=-2$$

Determine mn.

$$4 \times -2 = -8$$

3. A

Determine the strategy and solve: The two denominators on the left-side of the equation, $(x+5)$ and $(x-2)$, are multiples of the denominator on the right-side equation $(x+5)(x-2)$. Multiplying the numerator and the denominator of the left-side equation with the missing common multiple will make all the denominators same.

$$\frac{6(x-2)}{(x-2)(x+5)}+\frac{3(x+5)}{(x+5)(x-2)}=\frac{7x+9}{(x+5)(x-2)} \to$$

$$6(x-2)+3(x+5)=7x+9 \to$$

$$6x-12+3x+15=7x+9 \to$$

$$6x+3x-7x=9-15+12 \to$$

$$2x=6 \to x=3$$

4. D

Determine the strategy and solve: Multiplying the numerator and the denominator of the left fraction with $(x+1)$ will create same denominators, x^2-1.

$$\frac{3(x+1)}{(x+1)(x-1)}+\frac{k}{x^2-1}=\frac{3x+8}{x^2-1} \to$$

$$\frac{3(x+1)}{(x-1)^2}+\frac{k}{x^2-1}=\frac{3x+8}{x^2-1} \to$$

$$3(x+1)+k=3x+8 \to 3x+3+k=3x+8 \to$$

$$k=3x+8-3x-3 \to k=5$$

5. 3

Determine the strategy and solve: Since the fractions have the same denominator, the numerators can be added.

$$\frac{3a^2+7ab}{(a+b)}-\frac{ab-3b^2}{(a+b)}=9 \to$$

$$\frac{3a^2+7ab-ab+3b^2}{(a+b)}=9 \to$$

$$\frac{3a^2+6ab+3b^2}{(a+b)}=9 \to \frac{a^2+2ab+b^2}{(a+b)}=3$$

$(a^2+2ab+b^2)$ can be factored as $(a+b)(a+b)$.

$$\frac{(a+b)(a+b)}{(a+b)}=3 \to \frac{(a+b)\cancel{(a+b)}}{\cancel{(a+b)}}=3 \to$$

$$a+b=3$$

6. 9

Determine the strategy and solve: Multiplying the numerator and the denominator of the left fraction with $(x+y)$ will result in (x^2-y^2). The given values of $(x+y)$ and (x^2-y^2) can be substituted to solve.

$$\frac{2(x+y)}{(x+y)(x-y)}+\frac{5}{x^2-y^2} \to$$

$$\frac{2(x+y)}{x^2-y^2}+\frac{5}{x^2-y^2}$$

Substitute given values of $(x+y)$ and (x^2-y^2).

$$\frac{2 \times 11}{3}+\frac{5}{3}=\frac{22}{3}+\frac{5}{3}=\frac{27}{3}=9$$

7. 8

Determine the strategy and solve: y^2-9 can be factored as $(y+3)$ and $(y-3)$.

$$\frac{(y-3)(y+3)}{(y+3)}=5 \to \frac{(y-3)\cancel{(y+3)}}{\cancel{(y+3)}}=5 \to$$

$$y-3=5 \to y=5+3=8$$

Category 52 – Rearranging Variables in an Equation

1. <u>B</u>

Rearrange to isolate r:

Multiply both sides by r^2 and divide by F to isolate r^2.

$$\frac{r^2}{\cancel{F}} \times \cancel{F} = G\,\frac{m_1 m_2}{\cancel{r^2}} \times \frac{\cancel{r^2}}{F} \rightarrow r^2 = G\,\frac{m_1 m_2}{F}$$

Remove the square from r.

$$r = \sqrt{G\,\frac{m_1 m_2}{F}}$$

2. <u>A</u>

Rearrange to isolate μ:

Multiply both sides by $\pi \times r^4$ to remove from the denominator of the right fraction.

$$(\pi \times r^4) \times R = \frac{(8 \times \mu)l}{\cancel{\pi \times r^4}} \times \cancel{(\pi \times r^4)} \rightarrow$$

$$\pi \times r^4 \times R = 8 \times \mu \times l$$

Divide both sides by $8 \times l$ to isolate μ.

$$\frac{\pi \times r^4 \times R}{8 \times l} = \frac{\cancel{8 \times l} \times \mu}{\cancel{8 \times l}} \rightarrow$$

$$\frac{\pi r^4 R}{8l} = \mu$$

3. <u>D</u>

Rearrange to isolate h:

Multiply both sides by $\frac{2}{a+b}$ to isolate h.

$$\left(\frac{2}{a+b}\right) \times A = \frac{\cancel{a+b}}{\cancel{2}}\,h \times \left(\frac{\cancel{2}}{\cancel{a+b}}\right) \rightarrow$$

$$\frac{2A}{a+b} = h$$

4. <u>C</u>

Rearrange to isolate s:

Move expressions to one side.

$$\frac{ut + 2u + 1}{u+1} - \frac{us - ut^2}{u+1} = 1$$

Write as one fraction.

$$\frac{ut + 2u + 1 - us + ut^2}{u+1} = 1$$

Cross multiply.

$$ut + 2u + 1 - us + ut^2 = u + 1$$

Move all terms without s to one side of the equation and simplify.

$$us = ut + 2u + 1 + ut^2 - u - 1 \rightarrow$$

$$us = ut + u + ut^2$$

Factor u in the right expression.

$$us = u(t + 1 + t^2)$$

Eliminate u from both sides.

$$s = t + 1 + t^2 = t^2 + t + 1$$

5. <u>A</u>

Rearrange to isolate π:

Divide both sides by $(1+r)$ to isolate $(1+\pi)$.

$$\frac{(1+i)}{(1+r)} = \frac{\cancel{(1+r)}(1+\pi)}{\cancel{(1+r)}} \rightarrow$$

$$(1+\pi) = \frac{(1+i)}{(1+r)}$$

Subtract 1 from both sides to isolate π.

$$\cancel{1} - \cancel{1} + \pi = \frac{(1+i)}{(1+r)} - 1 \rightarrow$$

$$\pi = \frac{(1+i)}{(1+r)} - 1$$

Category 53 – Combining Like Terms

1. <u>B</u>

Simplify and add/subtract like terms:

$$2(x^2 - 1) + 10x^3 - 2x^2 \rightarrow 2x^2 - 2 + 10x^3 - 2x^2$$
$$\rightarrow 10x^3 - 2$$

2. <u>A</u>

Simplify and add/subtract like terms:

$$4x(x^3 + 3x^2) - 3(x^4 - 2x^3) + x^4 \rightarrow$$
$$4x^4 + 12x^3 - 3x^4 + 6x^3 + x^4 \rightarrow 2x^4 + 18x^3$$

$2x^3$ can be factored out.

$$2x^3(x + 9)$$

3. <u>D</u>

Simplify and add/subtract like terms:

$$m^2 + 3n^3 - 2mn - m(m - 2) \rightarrow$$
$$m^2 + 3n^3 - 2mn - m^2 + 2m \rightarrow$$
$$\rightarrow 3n^3 - 2mn + 2m$$

4. <u>C</u>

Add/subtract like terms:

$$s^2 - 3t^3 + 3s^2 + 5t^3 + t \rightarrow 4s^2 + 2t^3 + t$$

Category 54 – Expressions with Square Root

1. <u>D</u>

Square both sides: Move 2 to the right-side before squaring.

$$\sqrt{x+5} - 2 = 3 \;\rightarrow\; \sqrt{x+5} = 3+2 \;\rightarrow\; \sqrt{x+5} = 5$$

Now square both sides.

$$\left(\sqrt{x+5}\right)^2 = 5^2 \;\rightarrow\; x+5 = 25$$

Solve:

$$x = 25 - 5 \;\rightarrow\; x = 20$$

2. <u>B</u>

Square both sides: Move 1 to the right-side before squaring.

$$\sqrt{\frac{27}{x}} + 1 = 4 \;\rightarrow\; \sqrt{\frac{27}{x}} = 4 - 1 \;\rightarrow\; \sqrt{\frac{27}{x}} = 3$$

Now square both sides.

$$\left(\sqrt{\frac{27}{x}}\right)^2 = 3^2 \;\rightarrow\; \frac{27}{x} = 9$$

Solve:

$$9x = 27 \;\rightarrow\; x = 3$$

3. <u>C</u>

Square both sides:

$$\left(\sqrt{x^2+5}\right)^2 = 3^2 \;\rightarrow\; x^2 + 5 = 9$$

Solve:

$$x^2 = 9 - 5 \;\rightarrow\; x^2 = 4 \;\rightarrow\; x = \pm 2$$

Since $x > 0$, $x = 2$.

4. <u>C</u>

Square both sides:

$$\left(\sqrt{5x-1}\right)^2 = \left(3\sqrt{x-1}\right)^2 \;\rightarrow\; 5x - 1 = 9\,(x-1)$$

Solve:

$$5x - 1 = 9x - 9 \;\rightarrow\; 9x - 5x = 9 - 1 \;\rightarrow$$
$$4x = 8 \;\rightarrow\; x = 2$$

5. <u>1</u>

Square both sides: Move $\sqrt{x+26}$ to the right-side for ease.

$$\left(3\sqrt{x+2}\right)^2 = \left(\sqrt{x+26}\right)^2 \;\rightarrow\; 9(x+2) = (x+26)$$

Solve:

$$9x + 18 = x + 26 \;\rightarrow\; 9x - x = 26 - 18 \;\rightarrow$$
$$8x = 8 \;\rightarrow\; x = 1$$

6. <u>11</u>

Square both sides: Move 1 and $\frac{1}{2}$ to the right-side before squaring.

$$\frac{1}{2}\sqrt{x+5} + 1 = 3 \;\rightarrow\; \sqrt{x+5} = 2(3-1) \;\rightarrow$$
$$\sqrt{x+5} = 2 \times 2 \;\rightarrow\; \sqrt{x+5} = 4$$

Now square both sides.

$$\left(\sqrt{x+5}\right)^2 = 4^2 \;\rightarrow\; x+5 = 16$$

Solve:

$$x = 16 - 5 = 11$$

7. <u>B</u>

Square both sides: Move 2 to the right-side before squaring.

$$\sqrt{7-2x} + 2 = x \;\rightarrow\; \sqrt{7-2x} = x - 2$$

Now square both sides.

$$\left(\sqrt{7-2x}\right)^2 = (x-2)^2 \;\rightarrow\; 7 - 2x = (x-2)^2$$

Solve: FOIL the right-side expression.

$$7 - 2x = x^2 - 4x + 4$$

Form a quadratic equation.

$$x^2 - 4x + 4 + 2x - 7 = 0 \;\rightarrow\; x^2 - 2x - 3 = 0$$

Factorize.

$$(x+1)(x-3) = 0$$

Hence $x = -1$ and 3.

Check for extraneous solution:

Plug in $x = -1$ in the equation.

$$\sqrt{7-2x} + 2 = x \;\rightarrow\; \sqrt{7-2(-1)} + 2 = -1 \;\rightarrow$$
$$\sqrt{9} + 2 = -1 \;\rightarrow\; 3 + 2 = -1$$

$x = -1$ is an extraneous solution since both sides of the equation are not same.

Plug in $x = 3$ in the equation.

$$\sqrt{7-2x} + 2 = 3 \;\rightarrow\; \sqrt{7-2(3)} + 2 = 3 \;\rightarrow$$
$$\sqrt{7-6} + 2 = 3 \;\rightarrow\; 1 + 2 = 3 \;\rightarrow\; 3 = 3$$

$x = 3$ is the real solution.

Section 11 – Review Questions

1. <u>A</u>

Determine the strategy and solve: $a^2 - b^2$ can be factored as $(a - b)$ and $(a + b)$. The given values of $(a - b)$ and $(a + b)$ can be substituted to solve the equation.

$$\frac{1}{(a-b)(a-b)(a+b)} \rightarrow \frac{1}{(2)(2)(3)} \rightarrow \frac{1}{12}$$

2. <u>B</u>

Rearrange to isolate a:

Multiply all terms on both sides by 2 to remove $\frac{1}{2}$ from the right expression.

$$2 \times m = \cancel{2} \times \left(\frac{1}{\cancel{2}} am\right) + (2 \times 4) \rightarrow 2m = am + 8$$

Subtract 8 from both sides to isolate am.

$$2m - 8 = am + \cancel{8} - \cancel{8} \rightarrow 2m - 8 = am$$

Divide both sides by m to isolate a.

$$\frac{2m - 8}{m} = \frac{am}{\cancel{m}} \rightarrow \frac{2m - 8}{m} = a \rightarrow$$

$$\frac{2m}{m} - \frac{8}{m} = a \rightarrow a = 2 - \frac{8}{m}$$

3. <u>D</u>

Rearrange to isolate H:

Multiply all terms on both sides by 2 to remove $\frac{1}{2}$ from the right expression.

$$2 \times K = \cancel{2} \times \frac{1}{\cancel{2}}(D^2 + H) + (2 \times D^2) \rightarrow$$

$$2K = D^2 + H + 2D^2 \rightarrow 2K = H + 3D^2$$

Subtract $3D^2$ from both sides to isolate H.

$$2K - 3D^2 = H + \cancel{3D^2} - \cancel{3D^2} \rightarrow H = 2K - 3D^2$$

4. <u>C</u>

Determine the strategy and solve: Since, the denominators have same expression, the numerators can be added.

$$\frac{2y^2 + y - y^2 - 5y + 4}{y - 2} = 3 \rightarrow \frac{y^2 - 4y + 4}{y - 2} = 3$$

$(y^2 - 4y + 4)$ can be factored as $(y - 2)(y - 2)$.

$$\frac{(y-2)(y-2)}{y-2} = 3 \rightarrow \frac{(y-2)\cancel{(y-2)}}{\cancel{y-2}} = 3 \rightarrow$$

$$y - 2 = 3 \rightarrow y = 5$$

5. <u>A</u>

Rearrange to isolate v_o:

Subtract $\frac{at^2}{2}$ and s_o from both sides to isolate $v_o t$.

$$s - \left(\frac{at^2}{2}\right) - s_o = \cancel{\frac{at^2}{2}} - \left(\cancel{\frac{at^2}{2}}\right) + v_o t + \cancel{s_o} - \cancel{s_o} \rightarrow$$

$$s - \frac{at^2}{2} - s_o = v_o t$$

Divide both sides by t to isolate v_o.

$$\frac{s}{t} - \frac{at\cancel{t}}{2\cancel{t}} - \frac{s_o}{t} = \frac{v_o \cancel{t}}{\cancel{t}} \rightarrow \frac{s}{t} - \frac{at}{2} - \frac{s_o}{t} = v_o$$

Add fractions with t in the denominator.

$$v_o = \frac{s - s_o}{t} - \frac{at}{2}$$

6. <u>D</u>

Square both sides:

$$\left(\sqrt{2k + 17}\right)^2 = 7^2 \rightarrow 2k + 17 = 49$$

Solve:

$$2k = 49 - 17 \rightarrow 2k = 32 \rightarrow k = 16$$

7. <u>B</u>

Square both sides:

$$\left(\sqrt{5c^2 - 4}\right)^2 = (2c)^2 \rightarrow 5c^2 - 4 = 4c^2$$

Solve:

$$5c^2 - 4c^2 = 4 \rightarrow c^2 = 4 \rightarrow c = \pm 2$$

Hence, the two values of c are -2 and 2.

Check for extraneous solution:

Plug in $x = -2$ in the given equation.

$$\sqrt{5(-2)^2 - 4} = (2 \times -2) \rightarrow \sqrt{20 - 4} = -4 \rightarrow$$

$$\sqrt{16} = -4 \rightarrow 4 = -4$$

$x = -2$ is an extraneous solution since both sides of the equation are not same.

Plug in $x = 2$ in the given equation.

$$\sqrt{5(2)^2 - 4} = (2 \times 2) \rightarrow \sqrt{20 - 4} = 4 \rightarrow$$

$$\sqrt{16} = 4 \rightarrow 4 = 4$$

$x = 2$ is the real solution.

8. C

Determine the strategy and solve: Simplify the fractions in the denominator first and then solve the equation.

<u>Simplify the denominator.</u>

Create the same denominator using the common multiples $(x - 2)$ and $(x + 2)$.

$$\frac{1}{x + 2} + \frac{1}{x - 2} \rightarrow \frac{(x - 2)}{(x + 2)(x - 2)} + \frac{(x + 2)}{(x + 2)(x - 2)} \rightarrow$$

$$\frac{(x - 2) + (x + 2)}{(x + 2)(x - 2)} \rightarrow \frac{2x}{(x^2 - 4)}$$

<u>Substitute the simplified denominator in the given equation and solve.</u>

$$\frac{2}{\frac{2x}{(x^2 - 4)}} = x - 1 \rightarrow 2 \times \frac{(x^2 - 4)}{2x} = x - 1 \rightarrow$$

$$\frac{(x^2 - 4)}{x} = x - 1 \rightarrow x^2 - 4 = x(x - 1) \rightarrow$$

$$x^2 - 4 = x^2 - x \rightarrow -4 = -x \rightarrow x = 4$$

9. B

Square both sides: Move 1 to the right-side before squaring.

Note that the entire left expression can be squared.

$$\sqrt{\frac{36}{4x^2}} - 1 = 0 \rightarrow \sqrt{\frac{36}{4x^2}} = 1 \rightarrow \sqrt{\frac{6^2}{2^2 x^2}} = 1 \rightarrow$$

$$\sqrt{\left(\frac{6}{2x}\right)^2} = 1$$

The square root can be removed. 1 and 1^2 are same.

$$\frac{6}{2x} = 1 \rightarrow 2x = 6 \rightarrow x = 3$$

10. 2

Determine the strategy and solve: $a^2 - b^2$ can be factored as $(a + b)(a - b)$ and $2a^2 + 4ab + 2b^2$ can be factored as $2(a + b)(a + b)$.

$$(a + b)(a - b) = \frac{2(a + b)(a + b)}{a + b} \rightarrow$$

$$(a + b)(a - b) = \frac{2(a + b)\cancel{(a + b)}}{\cancel{a + b}} \rightarrow$$

$$\cancel{(a + b)}(a - b) = 2\cancel{(a + b)} \rightarrow$$

$$a - b = 2$$

11. D

Simplify and add/subtract like terms:

$$4a(a^2 + b) - 2a^2 - ab \rightarrow$$

$$4a^3 + 4ab - 2a^2 - ab \rightarrow 4a^3 - 2a^2 + 3ab$$

12. B

Simplify and add/subtract like terms:

$$x(2x^2 + y) - 2x(x^2 - y^2) \rightarrow$$

$$2x^3 + xy - 2x^3 + 2xy^2 \rightarrow xy + 2xy^2 \rightarrow$$

$$xy(1 + 2y)$$

13. 5

Determine the strategy and solve: $x^2 - 9$ can be factored as $(x + 3)$ and $(x - 3)$.

$$\frac{(x - 3)(x + 3)}{2(x - 3)} = 4 \rightarrow \frac{\cancel{(x - 3)}(x + 3)}{2\cancel{(x - 3)}} = 4 \rightarrow$$

$$\frac{x + 3}{2} = 4 \rightarrow x + 3 = 8 \rightarrow x = 8 - 3 = 5$$

14. 6

Square both sides: Equate the expression to 2. Move $\frac{1}{3}$ to the right-side before squaring.

$$\frac{1}{3}\sqrt{5x + 6} = 2 \rightarrow \sqrt{5x + 6} = 2 \times 3$$

Now square both sides.

$$\left(\sqrt{5x + 6}\right)^2 = 6^2 \rightarrow 5x + 6 = 36$$

Solve:

$$5x = 30 \rightarrow x = 6$$

Section 12 – Data Analysis and Interpretation

Category 55 – Probability

1. <u>C</u>

Determine the probability:

$$\frac{\text{all blue electric cars}}{\text{all blue cars}} = \frac{311}{516}$$

2. <u>D</u>

Determine the probability:

$$\frac{\text{all District A Yes \& Not Sure + all District C Yes \& Not Sure}}{\text{all responses from Distict A and C}}$$

$$\frac{11 + 5 + 11 + 5}{40} = \frac{32}{40} = 0.8$$

3. <u>B</u>

Determine the probability:

$$\frac{\text{all No}}{\text{all Yes + all Maybe + all No}}$$

$$= \frac{32}{72 + 84 + 32} = \frac{32}{188} = 0.17$$

(Note that the question is excluding the answer choice "Do not wish to answer").

4. <u>C</u>

Determine the probability:

$$\frac{\text{all Yes}}{\text{all Yes + all Maybe}} = \frac{72}{72 + 84} = \frac{72}{156} = 0.46$$

5. <u>A</u>

Determine the probability:

$$\frac{\text{all small green marbles + all small blue marbles}}{\text{all marbles} - \text{all large marbles}} =$$

$$\frac{6 + 9}{100 - 18} = \frac{15}{82}$$

6. <u>C</u>

Determine the number of mystery novels:

$$\frac{4}{7} \times 140 = 80$$

Determine the number of adventure novels: Set up the probability.

$$\frac{\text{all adventure novels}}{140} = \frac{1}{10} \rightarrow$$

$$\text{all adevnture novels} = \frac{140}{10} = 14$$

Determine the number of science fiction novels:

$$140 = 80 + 14 + \text{science fiction novels} \rightarrow$$

$$\text{science fiction novels} = 140 - 94 = 46$$

7. <u>B</u>

Determine the probability x:

$$\frac{\text{all flexible hours + all worked from home}}{\text{all employees}} = \frac{50}{450}$$

Determine the probability y:

$$\frac{\text{all no flexible hours + all did not work from home}}{\text{all employees}} =$$

$$\frac{200}{450}$$

Determine x is what percent of y:

$$\frac{x}{y} \times 100 = \left(\frac{50}{450} \div \frac{200}{450}\right) \times 100 =$$

$$\left(\frac{50}{450} \times \frac{450}{200}\right) \times 100 = 25\%$$

8. <u>3</u>

Determine the probability:

$$\frac{\text{all Team A participants for Coffee Brand B}}{\text{all participants}} = \frac{1}{9}$$

Solve for a:

$$\frac{a}{6 + a + 2 + 5 + 5 + 6} = \frac{1}{9} \rightarrow \frac{a}{24 + a} = \frac{1}{9} \rightarrow$$

$$9a = 24 + a \rightarrow 8a = 24 \rightarrow a = 3$$

Category 56 – Graphs with Line Segments and Curves

1. D
Follow the events from the graph:

Quinn drank the protein shake over 90 mins. This eliminates answer choices B and C that show the entire protein shake finished in 60 and 30 minutes, respectively.

Quinn finished half the protein shake within 30 minutes, and then waited for 30 minutes. The wait is represented by a horizontal line along time. This eliminates answer choice A that shows 60 minutes of wait.

Answer choice D matches the events.

2. C
Read the data points from the graph: From the graph, it is seen that week 8 and 9 will give the lowest total.

If unsure, evaluate each answer choice. See below.

Answer choice A: week 1 + week 2 = 45 + 10 = 55.

Answer choice B: week 7 + week 8 = 25 + 15 = 40.

Answer choice C: week 8 + week 9 = 15 + 15 = 30.

Answer choice D: week 18 + week 19 = 40 + 7 = 47.

3. A
Read the data points from the graph: The graph shows that the greatest difference is from 2 pm to 3 pm.

If unsure, read the data point for each hour and calculate the difference.

4. C
Read the data points from the graph: Since the speed is along the vertical axis, a horizontal line indicates no change in speed. The horizontal lines are from 20 to 35 miles and from 50 to 70 miles.

Hence, the total distance in miles Geeta traveled at a constant speed is
$$15 + 20 = 35$$

5. B
Read the data points from the graph: No need to read all the data points. For each month, check if the two data points are double of each other.

In August, the rainfall in 2018 (8 inches) was twice that of 2017 (4 inches).

(Note that in May the rainfall in 2017 was twice that of 2018. This is opposite of what the question is asking for.)

6. B
Read the population from the graph: The graph shows that the greatest increase was from 1984 to 1988.

If unsure, read the population for each given four-year period and determine the difference.

7. C
Read the number of tourists from the graph:

1984 = 100. 1996 = 200.

The tourists in 1984 = 100 are what percent of the tourists in 1996 = 200:
$$\frac{100}{200} \times 100 = 50\%$$

8. D
Read the number of action figures sold from the graph:

Month 1 = 100. Month 2 = 500. Month 3 = 200. Month 4 = 200.
$$\text{Total} = 100 + 500 + 200 + 200 = 1,000$$

9. A
Determine percent change: Read the data points from the graph.

Old value = Month 6 = 500.

New value = Month 7 = 400.

$$\frac{\text{new value} - \text{old value}}{\text{old value}} \times 100 =$$
$$\frac{400 - 500}{400} \times 100 = \frac{-100}{500} \times 100 = -20\% = 20\%$$

10. B
Read the data points from the graph: Note that the answer choices give each data point as (x, y) coordinate.

The coordinates of the horizontal axis represent the time of the day. The coordinates of the vertical axis represent the number of customers. The graph shows that the greatest number of customers were from 7 pm $(7, 70)$ to 8 pm $(8, 70)$.

If unsure, read the data points and determine the number of customers during each one-hour period.

11. C
Read the initial and the ending weight from the graph: The graph shows that Tony lost greater weight than Sam. See calculation below.

Tony: initial weight = 174, ending weight = 155. Difference = 174 − 155 = 19.

Sam: initial weight = 165, ending weight = 155. Difference = 165 − 155 = 10.

Category 57 – Scatter Plots and Line of Best Fit

1. A

Determine the slope of the line of best fit:

Below is slope using points (60, 80) and (100, 60).

$$\frac{60 - 80}{100 - 60} = \frac{-20}{40} = -0.5$$

This matches answer choice A.

2. B

Draw a line of best fit: See below

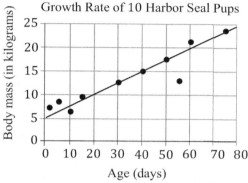

Growth Rate of 10 Harbor Seal Pups

The relationship between the age and the body mass is the slope of the line of best fit. Age is represented along the horizontal axis (run) and body mass is represented along the vertical axis (rise).

Determine the slope of the line of best fit:

Below is slope using the points (20, 10) and (40, 15).

$$\frac{15 - 10}{40 - 20} = \frac{5}{20} = \frac{\text{rise}}{\text{run}} = \frac{5 \text{ kilograms body mass}}{20 \text{ days in age}}$$

Hence, for every 20 days in age the estimated (predicted) body mass increase is 5 kilograms.

3. D

Read the data point on the line of best fit:

2014 (horizontal axis) corresponds to approximately 128 grams of wheat production (vertical axis).

4. A

Read the data point on the line of best fit:

2010 (horizontal axis) corresponds to 110 millions of metric tonnes of wheat (vertical axis).

Read the data point on the scatter plot:

The data point is approximately 114.

Determine the difference:

$$114 - 110 = 4$$

5. D

The time is represented along the horizontal axis and the profit is represented along the vertical axis.

At y-intercept, time = 0. Hence, it is the predicted monthly profit in thousands of dollars when no time is spent on advertising.

6. C

Read the data point on the line of best fit:

k is the profit, in thousands of dollars, when 40 hours are spent on advertising each month.

40 hours (horizontal axis) correspond to $30 = k$ (vertical axis).

7. A

Determine the slope of the line of best fit:

The relationship between weight loss and number of weeks in the program is the slope of the line of best fit.

Below is slope using the points (8, 3) and (14, 5).

$$\frac{5 - 3}{14 - 8} = \frac{2}{6} = \frac{\text{rise}}{\text{run}} = \frac{2 \text{ pounds weight loss}}{6 \text{ weeks in program}} = \frac{0.33}{1}$$

Hence, for every 1 week, the predicted weight loss is 0.33 pounds.

8. B

The weight loss at week 30 cannot be read from the given graph. Let the weight loss at week 30 = y. The coordinates of this data point will be (30, y).

The slope of the line of best fit is known from the above question 7. (If slope is not known, then calculate it using any two points on the line.)

Set up a slope equation using points (8, 3) and (30, y) and equate to the slope.

$$\frac{y - 3}{30 - 8} = \frac{2}{6} \rightarrow \frac{y - 3}{22} = \frac{1}{3} \rightarrow$$
$$3(y - 3) = 22 \rightarrow 3y - 9 = 22 \rightarrow 3y = 31 \rightarrow$$
$$y = 10.33 = 10.3$$

Category 58 – Bar Graphs

1. B

Read the height of each bar:

Medium 1: 20 minutes = 1 colony. 40 minutes = 4 colonies. Since 4 is not double of 1, Medium 1 can be eliminated. This eliminates answer choices A and C.

Medium 2: 20 minutes = 2 colonies. 40 minutes = 4 colonies. 60 minutes = 8 colonies. 80 minutes = 16 colonies. The colonies doubled every 20 minutes.

Medium 3: It is seen from the graph that the number of colonies decreased at 80 minutes. This eliminates Medium 3 and answer choice D.

2. D

Read the height of the top bar:

1 = 10. 2 = 20. 3 = 20. 4 = 10. 5 = 15. 6 = 5.
$$10 + 20 + 20 + 10 + 15 + 5 = 80$$

3. C

Read the height of each sub-group bar for Day 5:

New = 15. Returning = 10. Total = 15 + 10 = 25.

Determine returning patients are what percent of total patients:
$$\frac{\text{returning}}{\text{total}} \times 100 = \frac{10}{25} \times 100 = 40\%$$

4. A

The graph shows that that the greatest change occurred between week 1 and 2.

5. B

The graph shows that Dixie read twice the number of mystery books than Tracy. If unsure, read the height of each bar and compare.

6. D

Read the height of each bar and determine the difference between the top and the bottom bar for each month:

February: Yes = 40. No = 60. Difference = 20.

March: Yes = 35. No = 65. Difference = 30.

April: Yes = 60. No = 40. Difference = 20.

June: Yes = 55. No = 45. Difference = 10.

7. A

Read the height of the top bar for May: Since there are 100 students, the percent can be directly read from the vertical axis.

25 students responded "No" = 25%.

Category 59 – Histograms and Dot Plots

1. A

Count the dots on 3 and 4 times a week and add them:
$$5 + 4 = 9$$

2. C

Determine the total number of calls:
$$(1 \times 5) + (2 \times 4) + (3 \times 3) + (4 \times 6) + (5 \times 2) =$$
$$5 + 8 + 9 + 24 + 10 = 56$$

3. D

Determine the total number of daily servings:
$$(1 \times 5) + (2 \times 30) + (3 \times 15) + (4 \times 10) + (5 \times 5) +$$
$$(6 \times 5) = 5 + 60 + 45 + 40 + 25 + 30 = 205$$

4. B

Read the heights of bars 3, 4, 5, and 6 and add them:
$$15 + 10 + 5 + 5 = 35$$

Determine the percent:
$$\frac{35}{70} \times 100 = 50\%$$

5. C

Read the heights of bars 20-30 and 30-40 and add them:

Bar 20-30 = 20. Bar 30-40 = 10.
$$20 + 10 = 30$$

6. B

Read the heights of bars 30-40 and 40-50 and add them:

Bar 30-40 = 10. Bar 40-50 = 4.
$$10 + 4 = 14$$

Determine the percent:
$$\frac{14}{50} \times 100 = 28\%$$

7. A

Read the heights of bars 70-75 and 75-80 and add them:

Bar 70-75 = 4. Bar 75-80 = 2.
$$4 + 2 = 6$$

8. C

Count the number of dots on each group: The maximum number of students are enrolled in 4 clubs.

Category 60 – Mean

1. **B**

Determine the sum of scores for both the classes:

Total number of students $= 40 + 20 = 60$.

The total score of 40 students in Mr. Daniel's class is
$$40 \times a = 40a$$
The total score of 20 students in Mr. Power's class is
$$20 \times b = 20b$$
The total score of both classes $= 40a + 20b$.

Determine the mean:
$$\frac{40a + 20b}{60} = \frac{20(2a + b)}{60} = \frac{1}{3}(2a + b)$$

2. **104**

Set up the mean:

Count of numbers after adding $y = 6$.

The mean of the 6 numbers $= 134$.

$$\frac{50 + 120 + 230 + 80 + 220 + y}{6} = 134 \ \rightarrow$$

$$\frac{700 + y}{6} = 134 \ \rightarrow \ 700 + y = 6 \times 134 \ \rightarrow$$

$$700 + y = 804 \ \rightarrow \ y = 804 - 700 = 104$$

3. **98**

Set up the mean:

Count of numbers after adding 5th test $= 5$.

Let the 5th test $= x$.

Since the mean of the 5 tests must be at least 90, equate the mean to 90. This will give the minimum score Gina will need on the fifth biology test.

$$\frac{85 + 88 + 87 + 92 + x}{5} = 90 \ \rightarrow \ \frac{352 + y}{5} = 90$$

$$352 + x = 5 \times 90 \ \rightarrow \ 352 + x = 450 \ \rightarrow$$

$$x = 450 - 352 = 98$$

4. **16**

Set up the mean:

Mean of the 2 numbers $= 32$.

Let the lesser number $= x$. The bigger number $= 3x$.

$$\frac{x + 3x}{2} = 32 \ \rightarrow \ \frac{4x}{2} = 32 \ \rightarrow$$

$$2x = 32 \ \rightarrow \ x = 16$$

5. **43**

Determine the sum of numbers:

Since the mean of 12 numbers $= 38$, their sum $= 12 \times 38 = 456$.

After removing 11 and 15, the sum of the remaining 10 numbers $= 456 - 11 - 15 = 430$.

Determine the mean of the remaining 10 numbers:
$$\frac{430}{10} = 43$$

6. **82**

Determine the sum of numbers:

Since the mean of 7 tests $= 92$, their sum $= 7 \times 92 = 644$.

Since the mean of first 5 tests $= 96$, their sum $= 5 \times 96 = 480$.

The sum of last 2 tests $= 644 - 480 = 164$.

Determine the mean of the last 2 tests:
$$\frac{164}{2} = 82$$

7. **10.5**

Determine the sum of weights:

Total number of dumbbells $= 6 + 10 + 4 = 20$.

Total weight of 20 dumbbells is
$$(6 \times 5) + (10 \times 10) + (4 \times 20) =$$
$$30 + 100 + 80 = 210$$
Determine the mean:
$$\frac{210}{20} = 10.5$$

8. **138**

Determine the sum of the 11 integers:
$$(3 \times 210) + (4 \times 148) + (4 \times 74) =$$
$$630 + 592 + 296 = 1,518$$
Determine the mean of the 11 integers:
$$\frac{1,518}{11} = 138$$

Category 61 – Histograms, Dot Plots, and Mean

1. C

Determine the total number of family members in all the households:

$(1 \times 4) + (2 \times 2) + (3 \times 14) + (4 \times 16) + (5 \times 8) +$
$(7 \times 2) + (8 \times 4) =$
$$4 + 4 + 42 + 64 + 40 + 14 + 32 = 200$$

Determine the mean: There are 50 households.
$$\frac{200}{50} = 4$$

2. B

Determine the total number of kittens for all the cats:

$$(2 \times 1) + (3 \times 3) + (4 \times 6) + (5 \times 5) =$$
$$2 + 9 + 24 + 25 = 60$$

Determine the mean: There are 15 cats.
$$\frac{60}{15} = 4$$

3. 4

Determine the total number of times all the buses were late:

$(1 \times 2) + (2 \times 4) + (3 \times 3) + (4 \times 4) + (5 \times 7) +$
$(6 \times 5) = 2 + 8 + 9 + 16 + 35 + 30 = 100$

Determine the mean: There are 25 buses.
$$\frac{100}{25} = 4$$

4. 3

Determine the total number of vacation days for all the employees:

$(1 \times 9) + (2 \times 10) + (3 \times 12) + (4 \times 8) + (5 \times 7) +$
$(6 \times 2) =$
$$9 + 20 + 36 + 32 + 35 + 12 = 144$$

Determine the mean: There are 48 employees.
$$\frac{144}{48} = 3$$

Category 62 – Median

1. A

Sort the numbers least to greatest and determine the middle number:

The middle number = 49.37 inches. The corresponding year = 2010.

2. B

Determine the median: There are 27 employees. The salary range that includes the 14th employee is the median salary range.

There are 15 employees in the first salary range from $40,000 - $60,000. Hence, the 14th employee falls in this salary range. The median salary is any number between 40,000 and 60,000. This eliminates answer choices A, C, and D.

3. D

Sort the numbers in both the sets from least to greatest and determine the middle number of each set:

Since there are 7 numbers in the set, median is the 4th number.

For Set 1 = A, the median is 13.5.

For Set 2 = B, the median is 48.5.

Determine $B - A$:
$$48.5 - 13.5 = 35$$

4. C

Sort the integers least to greatest: Since y is the median, it will be in the middle.
$$5, 8, y, 11, 15$$

Determine the possible values of y: Since y is between the numbers 8 and 11, the only possible integer values of y can be 8, 9, 10, or 11. Hence, option I and option II are correct.

Note that since the set contains an odd count of numbers, $y = 8$ or 11 will not change the median.

5. A

Determine the median: Since there are 49 students, the group that includes the 25th student is the median group. Starting from the top of the table, continue a cumulative count of students till the 25th student is reached.

25th student corresponds to the group with 4 - 6 number of books. The median number of books could be any number from 4 to 6. This eliminates answer choices B, C, and D.

6. 25

Sort the numbers least to greatest and determine the middle number:

Since there are 6 numbers in the set, the median is the average of the 3rd and 4th number.
$$\frac{24.3 + 25.7}{2} = \frac{50}{2} = 25$$

Category 63 – Histograms, Dot Plots, Bar Graphs, and Median

1. B

Determine the median: Since there are 100 households, the bar that includes the 50th and 51st household contains the median car expense.

This corresponds to bar 400 - 500. Any number between this can be a median car expense. Hence, option I is incorrect and option II is correct.

2. C

Determine the median: Since there are 85 adults, the bar that includes the 43rd adult contains the median speed limit.

This corresponds to bar 60 - 65. Any number between this but, excluding 65 could be a median speed limit.

3. B

Determine the median: Since there are 15 baby dolphins, the group that includes the 8th baby dolphin contains the median weight.

This corresponds to baby dolphin = 35 - 40 pounds. Any number between 35 and 40 could be a median weight.

4. 2

Determine the median: Since there are 60 employees, the bar that includes the 30th and 31st employee contains the median number of degrees.

This corresponds to bar = 2 degrees. Hence, the median number of degrees = 2.

5. 3

Determine the median: Since there are 21 quizzes, the bar that includes the 11th quiz contains the median score.

This corresponds to bar for quiz score = 8. Hence, the median quiz score = 8.

There are 3 quizzes with the median score = 8.

6. 9

Determine the median: Since there are 49 newborn babies, the bar that includes the 25th newborn baby contains the median length.

This corresponds to bar for length = 21 inches. Hence, the median length of the newborn babies = 21.

There are 9 newborn babies with the median length = 21 inches.

Category 64 – Box Plots and Median

1. C

Read the median from the box plot:

The median is between 15 and 20 but closer to 20. Answer choice C is the closest choice.

2. B

Evaluate each answer choice:

Answer choice B is correct since the box (middle 50% of data) is from 8 to 18.

3. D

Evaluate each answer choice:

Median = 38. Answer choice D is correct.

4. B

Read the median from the box plot:

Bakery 1 = a: The median is in the middle of 80 and 100. Approximate median = 90.

Bakery 2 = b: Median = 80.

Hence, $a > b$.

5. A

Determine the median: Since there are 192 data points, the median will fall between 96th and 97th response.

Rating 1: 1st to 9th response.
Rating 2: 10th to 59th response.
Rating 3: 60th to 86th response.
Rating 4: 87th to 127th response. Hence, median = 4.

This eliminates answer choices B and C. Remaining answer choices A and D have same $Q1$ but different $Q3$.

Determine $Q3$: The median of the 50% higher numbers fall in rating = 5. This eliminates answer choice D.

6. C

Evaluate each option:

I: Median = $6,000. This option is true.

II: The box is from $4,000 to $10,000. This option is true.

III: The minimum salary is about $1,000. This option is not true.

7. 0.5

Read the median from the box plot:

Median of School A = 3.5. Median of School B = 3.

Difference: $3.5 - 3 = 0.5$.

Category 65 – Mode

1. B
Sort all the numbers from least to greatest:

15.1, 15.1, 17.2, 20.5, 20.5, 20.5, 35.3, 35.3, 47.5 50.1, 50.1, 72.8

Determine the most often occurring number: 20.5.

2. D
Sort the numbers from least to greatest:

8.1, 9.3, 9.4, 9.5, 10.7, 15.1, 15.2, 21.1, 21.2, 21.2

Determine the most often occurring number: 21.2

3. C
Sort the numbers from least to greatest:

1, 1, 2, 2, 2, 3, 4, 4, 5, 7, 7, 7, 9, 9

Determine the most often occurring number: 2 and 7 both occur three times.

4. 10.2
Sort the numbers from least to greatest:

10.1, 10.2, 10.2, 10.2, 10.6, 15.1, 15.3, 15.3, 15.4

Determine the most often occurring number: 10.2.

Category 66 – Standard Deviation and Range

1. B
Compare the range:

Group A: The lowest number is 744 and the highest number is 915. The range is $915 - 744 = 171$.

Group B: The lowest number is 100 and the highest number is 546. The range is $546 - 100 = 446$.

2. C
Compare the standard deviation: The numbers in the set are between 6 and 31.

After adding 52, the numbers in the set will be between 6 and 52. This will increase the spread of the numbers.

3. A
Compare the standard deviation: From 2010 to 2018 the number of students enrolled in the Lacrosse team are between 0 and 55 and the number of students enrolled in the Soccer team are between 41 and 58. Hence, the students enrolled in the Soccer team have a lower spread.

4. 38
Determine the range:

Lacrosse team $= a$: The range is $55 - 0 = 55$.

Soccer team $= b$: The range is $58 - 41 = 17$.

Difference: $a - b = 55 - 17 = 38$.

Category 67 – Comparing Mean, Median, Mode, SD, and Range

1. C
Adding a constant number to each number in a data set will not change the range. The mean and the median will change.

2. B
Original data set is 0, 0, 0.2, 0.2, 1.1, 2.5, 4.8.

Data set after replacing 4.8 with 0.8 is 0, 0, 0.2, 0.2, 0.8 1.1, 2.5.

Since 4.8 is the greatest number in the original set, replacing it with 0.8 will decrease the mean, the range and standard deviation. The median $= 0.2$ remains same.

3. D
In the original data set of 21 plants, 14 inch plant is the shortest plant. After the 4 inch plant is added, it becomes the shortest plant. Hence, the range must increase by $14 - 4 = 10$.

Since the height of all the plants is not given, it cannot be determined if the mean, the median, or the mode will increase by 10.

4. C
Range: Removing the numbers between 50 and 125 will decrease the range by 75 and decrease the standard deviation.

Median: The question is asking for certainty using the phrase "must change". Since the actual numbers of a data set and their frequency is unknown in a box plot, it cannot be determined with certainty how many numbers will be removed and how median will be affected.

For example, if there are only 3 numbers between 50 and 125, and the median number is repeated enough times, then removing the 3 numbers will not change the median. If there are 20 numbers between 50 and 125, and the median number is not repeated, then removing the 20 numbers will change the median.

5. C
10% increase will result in higher mean and median.

6. B

Since 18,000 is the highest number in the 2018 bonuses and farthest from the other numbers, removing it will change the mean more than the median. Note that the remaining numbers are relatively closer to each other than they are to 18,000.

If unsure, then calculate the mean and the median of the bonuses before and after removing 18,000 and compare.

7. C

Mean:

Group A:

$$\frac{15 + 18 + 24 + 26 + 32 + 35}{6} = \frac{150}{6} = 25$$

Group B:

$$\frac{23 + 23 + 25 + 26 + 26 + 27}{6} = \frac{150}{6} = 25$$

Median:

Group A: Average of 24 and 26 = 25.

Group B: Average of 25 and 26 = 25.5.

This eliminates answer choices A, B, and D.

Note that the ranges are different. Group A = 35 − 15 = 20. Group B = 27 − 23 = 4.

8. D

Mean: After adding 5 games, the mean will change.

Median: In 20 games, the 10th and 11th game contains the median score. Median = 3.

In 25 games, the 13th game contains the median score. Median = 3.

The median does not change.

Range: In 20 games, range = 5 − 1 = 4. In 25 games, range = 6 − 1 = 5.

Hence, the mean and the range will change. This eliminates answer choices A, B, and C.

Category 68 – Interpretation of Sample Data in Studies and Surveys

1. B

The school district wants to determine if the teachers in the district schools are satisfied with their salary. The correct sample should be a random sample of teachers from all district schools.

2. C

The 4.5% margin of error indicates it is likely that 52% − 4.5% = 47.5% to 52% + 4.5% = 56.5% shoppers bought at least one item.

3. A

The auto dealership wanted to determine if the visitors were satisfied with the number of cars on display in the showroom. The correct sample should be a random sample of visitors coming to the dealership.

4. C

95% confidence level indicates that the team conducting the study is 95% confident that the results reflect the actual (true) average tusk size of the entire male population of African elephants.

The average size was concluded to be from 5.8 to 6.3 feet.

5. D

An associated margin of 15 minutes indicates that the students probably studied from 80 − 15 = 65 to 80 + 15 = 95 minutes.

6. C

The sample population in the scientist's experiment was miniature hybrid tea roses from a certain geographic region. Hence, the largest sample population is all the miniature hybrid tea roses in the geographic region.

7. A

Margin of error decreases as the sample size increases.

8. D

Since the seniors who took the yoga class were able to walk on a treadmill for 15 minutes without fatigue, there is likely an association between yoga and walking on treadmill for 15 minutes without fatigue but this does not prove that yoga is the cause.

9. A

To generalize the results of an association the samples must be randomly divided into groups. In this study, the groups were determined based on age.

Section 12 – Review Questions

1. A

Determine a:

$$a = \frac{x + 11}{2}$$

Determine b:

$$b = \frac{3x + 5}{2}$$

Determine the mean of a and b:

$$\frac{\frac{x + 11}{2} + \frac{3x + 5}{2}}{2} = \frac{\frac{4x + 16}{2}}{2} = \frac{4(x + 4)}{4} = x + 4$$

2. C

Since the apple production decreased at a constant rate each year over 8 year period, the correlation is negative. This eliminates answer choices A, B, and D.

3. D

Determine the probability:

$$\frac{\text{all 18 to 28 years old in bus} + \text{all 29 to 40 years old in bus}}{\text{all 18 to 28 years old} + \text{all 29 to 40 years old}}$$

$$\frac{124 + 55}{200 + 200} = \frac{179}{400} = 0.4475 = 0.45$$

4. A

Determine the probability:

$$\frac{\text{all 71 and older in car} + \text{all 71 and older in train}}{\text{all in car} + \text{all in train}}$$

$$\frac{45 + 15}{330 + 210} = \frac{60}{540} = \frac{1}{9}$$

5. C

Determine the median: Starting from the top of the table, continue a cumulative count of the number of responses till the median response is reached.

Survey 1 $= x$: Since there are 78 responses, the median age corresponds to the 39th and 40th response. This falls in age group 26 - 40.

Survey 2 $= y$: Since there are 104 responses, the median age corresponds to the 52nd and 53rd response. This falls in age group 41 - 55.

6. 3

Determine the ratio: See the median age group for Survey 1 and Survey 2 from question 5 above.

Survey 1 median age group (26 - 40) has 32 responses.

Survey 2 median age group (41 - 55) has 24 responses.

$$\text{Survey 1: Survey 2} = 32 : 24 = 4 : 3 = 4 : a$$

$$a = 3$$

7. D

Follow the events from the graph:

Since the flat fee is $25 per month, the monthly cost will start at 25. This eliminates answer choice C.

Since 20 visits are included, there will be a horizontal line till 20. This eliminates answer choice B.

Since after 20 visits in a month, each additional visit = $2, the monthly cost will go up. This matches the graph in answer choice D.

8. B

At y-intercept, number of commercials $= 0$. Hence, it is the predicted monthly revenue of a company when no commercial is played on television in a day.

9. A

Determine the slope of the line of best fit:

Below is slope using the points $(2, 20)$ and $(10, 40)$.

$$\frac{40 - 20}{10 - 2} = \frac{20}{8} = \frac{5}{2}$$

This eliminates answer choices C and D.

The y-intercept is between 10 and 20. This eliminates answer choice B.

10. D

Determine the probability:

$$\frac{\text{all 5th and 6th grade students in different color shirts}}{\text{all students}}$$

5th grade students in blue shirt and 6th grade students in green shirt $= 13$.

5th grade students in green shirt and 6th grade students in blue shirt $= 11$.

$$\frac{13 + 11}{32} = \frac{24}{32} = 0.75$$

11. A

Determine the probability:

There are 9 multiples of 11 between 1 and 100 - 11, 22, 33, 44, 55, 66, 77, 88, 99.

$$\text{Probability} = \frac{9}{100}$$

12. B

Determine the total circumference of all the babies:

$(33 \times 2) + (34 \times 5) + (35 \times 6) + (36 \times 8) +$

$(37 \times 6) + (38 \times 5) =$

$66 + 170 + 210 + 288 + 222 + 190 = 1,146$

Determine the mean:

$$\frac{1,146}{32} = 35.81$$

13. C

The company wants to determine the chemicals in the water of 6 lakes in the 200 mile vicinity of a manufacturing plant. Hence, the most appropriate sampling method is to collect random water samples from all the 6 lakes in the 200 mile vicinity of a manufacturing plant. This matches answer choice C.

14. B

Evaluate each answer choice:

Answer choice B is incorrect since Ken's heart rate was static for 5 mins between 10 and 15 mins and for 5 mins between 25 and 30 mins. Total = 5 + 5 = 10 minutes not 15 minutes. All other choices are true.

15. C

Determine the total height of all the elephants:

$(7 \times 4) + (8 \times 1) + (9 \times 6) + (10 \times 2) + (12 \times 1) + (13 \times 6) = 28 + 8 + 54 + 20 + 12 + 78 = 200$

Determine the mean:

$$\frac{200}{20} = 10$$

This eliminates answer choices A and? B.

Determine the median data point:

Since there are 20 data points, the group that contains the 10th to 11th dot includes the median group. This corresponds to group 9. This eliminates answer choice D.

16. A

Read the height of each bar:

Company A:

$$14, 7, 10, 13, 10, 4$$

Company B:

$$10, 4, 9, 11, 12, 10$$

Determine the median: Order least to greatest.

There are 6 numbers. Median will be the average of 3rd and 4th number.

Company A: 4, 7, 10, 10, 13, 14. Median = 10.

Company B: 4, 9, 10, 10, 11, 12. Median = 10.

They are same.

17. B

Sort the numbers least to greatest:

3, 3, 5, 5, 5, 7, 8, 10, 10, 11, 23, 121

Most often occurring number = 5.

18. C

Use the process of elimination for a question like this and determine the median first.

Determine the median: Since there are 30 adults, the bar that includes the 15th and 16th adult contains the median.

This corresponds to bar 5 -10. Hence, the median can be any number from 5 to less than 10. This eliminates answer choices B and D.

Determine the lowest mean: The lowest mean will be the mean of the left corner numbers for each bar.

The total of lowest numbers is

$(0 \times 10) + (5 \times 6) + (10 \times 4) + (15 \times 7) + (20 \times 2) + (25 \times 1) =$

$0 + 30 + 40 + 105 + 40 + 25 = 240$

$$\text{Mean} = \frac{240}{30} = 8$$

Hence, the lowest possible mean is 8. This eliminates answer choice A.

19. A

Compare the measures:

Median: The median of the 100 numbers in the given box plot is around 91.

After adding 127 new numbers, the new box plot will have 227 numbers. The medium will be the 114th number ordered from least to greatest starting from the smallest number 51. Since the first 127 numbers are between 51 and 70, the median of the new boxplot will be a number between 51 and 70.

Mean: Adding 127 lower numbers will change the mean.

Range: Since the numbers being added are not lower than 51 or higher than 111, the range will not change.

Note that this question is different from question 4 in Category 64. This question gives enough information to determine that the median will be changed.

20. C

Count the number of dots below the line of best fit:

There are 8 dots below the line. Note that the dot on the line does not count.

21. A

Determine the slope of line of best fit: The relationship between the increase in temperature and the increase in air conditioning cost is the slope of the line of best fit.

Below is slope using the points (70, 10) and (90, 40).

$$\frac{40 - 10}{90 - 70} = \frac{30}{20} = \frac{3}{2} = \frac{\text{rise}}{\text{run}} = \frac{\text{cost}}{\text{temperature}}$$

Hence, for every 2°F (run), the predicted cost increase (rise) is $3.

For every 1°F, the predicted cost increase is $\frac{\$3}{2} = \$1.50$.

22. **D**

Only the employees in the sales department were asked about their liking. Hence, all employees in the sales department is the largest group the conclusions can be generalized to. This matches answer choice D.

23. **C**

The correct sample should be a random sample of customers that come to the restaurant. Limiting the sample to a Friday night does not represent a random sample.

24. **D**

Order the numbers least to greatest:

$$3, x, y, z, 121$$

Since x, y, and z are in the middle of the lowest number 3 and the highest number 121, the range will not change for any value given to x, y, and z. However, the mean, the median, and the mode will vary depending on the values given to x, y, and z.

25. **4**

Determine the probability:

$$\frac{\text{all seniors enrolled in physics}}{\text{all students}} = \frac{x}{28 + 12} = \frac{x}{40}$$

It is given that the above probability $= \frac{1}{5}$. Hence,

$$\frac{x}{40} = \frac{1}{5} \rightarrow 5x = 40 \rightarrow x = 8$$

Determine the value of y:

Table shows that $x + y = 12$. Substitute $x = 8$.

$$8 + y = 12 \rightarrow y = 4$$

26. **80**

Determine the sum of numbers:

Since the mean of 7 numbers $= 92$, their sum $= 7 \times 92 = 644$.

Since the mean of 6 numbers after removing the lowest number $= 94$, their sum $= 6 \times 94 = 564$.

Hence, the lowest number $= 644 - 564 = 80$.

27. **108**

Sort the numbers least to greatest:

$$41, 44, 87, 90, 126, 127, 135, 139$$

Determine the middle number: Since there are 8 numbers in the set, the two middle numbers are 4th and 5th number. Hence, the median is

$$\frac{90 + 126}{2} = \frac{216}{2} = 108$$

28. **22**

Read the maximum from the box plot:

Maximum $= 22$.

29. **3**

Retail Store A

Median $= a = 12$, from the box plot.

Retail Store B

Determine median $= b$: Read the height of the bar for each week from Week 1 to 10.

$$6, 4, 14, 22, 16, 12, 24, 18, 17, 6$$

Order the numbers least to greatest:

$$4, 6, 6, 12, 14, 16, 17, 18, 22, 24$$

There are total of 10 numbers. The median will be the average of 5th and 6th number.

$$\frac{14 + 16}{2} = 15$$

Determine the difference

$$b - a = 15 - 12 = 3$$

Section 13 – Geometry

Category 69 – Area and Angles of a Circle

1. A

Convert degrees to radians:

$$60° \times \frac{\pi}{180} = \frac{\pi}{3}$$

2. B

$\angle C = 90°$. Since $90°$ is one-fourth of a circle, the area of the sector is

$$\frac{\text{area of the circle}}{4} = \frac{12\pi}{4} = 3\pi$$

3. D

Determine the area of the circles:

$$\text{area of Circle 1 is } \pi r^2 = \pi 5^2 = 25\pi$$
$$\text{area of Circle 2 is } \pi r^2 = \pi 2^2 = 4\pi$$

Determine the ratio of the areas:

$$\text{Circle 1: Circle 2} = 25\pi : 4\pi = 6.25 : 1 = 6.3 : 1$$

4. B

Convert radians to degree:

$$\frac{2\pi}{3} \times \frac{180}{\pi} = 120°$$

Set up a proportion:

$$\frac{\text{area of a sector}}{\text{area of the circle}} = \frac{120°}{360°} = \frac{1}{3}$$

5. D

Determine the inscribed angle:

$$\frac{\text{central angle}}{2} = \frac{150°}{2} = 75°$$

Convert to radians:

$$75 \times \frac{\pi}{180} = \frac{5\pi}{12}$$

6. C

Determine the area of the circles: Since the circles are congruent, the area of the 3 circles is

$$3 \times \pi r^2 = 3 \times \pi 3^2 = 27\pi = 27 \times 3.14 = 84.78$$

Determine the area of shaded region: Total area = 88.

$$\text{shaded area} = 88 - 84.78 = 3.22$$

7. A

Determine the area of the circle: radius = 2.5.

$$\pi r^2 = 3.14 \times 2.5 \times 2.5 = 19.625 = 19.6$$

8. B

Determine the area of the circle: Since the diameter is 12, the radius is 6.

$$\text{area of the circle} = \pi r^2 = 36\pi$$

Determine the area of a sector: All 12 sectors are equal.

$$\text{area of each sector} = \frac{36\pi}{12} = 3\pi$$

9. 4

Determine the radius of Circle B: Area of Circle A = 4π.
Area of Circle B = $4 \times 4\pi = 16\pi$. Hence,

$$\pi r^2 = 16\pi \rightarrow r^2 = 16 \rightarrow r = 4$$

Category 70 – Circumference and Arc of a Circle

1. B

Determine the length of arc $\overset{\frown}{ADC}$:

The angle corresponding to arc $\overset{\frown}{ADC} = 360° - 60° = 300°$. This is five times more than the angle x corresponding to $\overset{\frown}{ABC}$. Hence,

$$\overset{\frown}{ADC} = \overset{\frown}{ABC} \times 5 = 3\pi \times 5 = 15\pi$$

2. A

Determine circumference of the circle: $r = 2$.

$$2\pi r = 2\pi \times 2 = 4\pi$$

Determine the fraction:

$$\frac{\text{Minor Arc}}{\text{Circumference}} = \frac{\frac{2\pi}{5}}{4\pi} = \frac{2\pi}{4\pi \times 5} = \frac{1}{10}$$

3. 22

Determine circumference of the wheel: $r = 0.5$ feet.

Each revolution of the wheel = 1 circumference.

$$2\pi r = 2 \times 3.14 \times 0.5 = 3.14$$

Hence, 1 revolution = 3.14 feet.

Determine the total distance: Total revolutions = 7.

$$7 \times 3.14 = 21.98 = 22$$

4. 8

Determine the length of minor arc $\overset{\frown}{MN}$:

The inscribed angle in degrees is

$$\frac{\pi}{4} \times \frac{180}{\pi} = 45°$$

Hence, $\overset{\frown}{MN} = 45° \times 2 = 90°$. This is one-fourth of the circumference. Hence,

$$\overset{\frown}{MN} = \frac{\text{Circumference}}{4} = \frac{32}{4} = 8$$

5. 75

Use the degrees arc length formula: $s = 5\pi$. $r = 12$.

$$5\pi = 2\pi \times 12 \times \frac{\theta}{360} \rightarrow 5 = \frac{24\theta}{360} \rightarrow$$

$$5 = \frac{\theta}{15} \rightarrow \theta = 5 \times 15 = 75$$

6. 3

Use the radians arc length formula: $s = \overset{\frown}{XY} = 2\pi$. $\theta = \frac{2\pi}{3}$ radians.

$$2\pi = r \times \frac{2\pi}{3} \rightarrow r = \frac{2\pi \times 3}{2\pi} \rightarrow r = 3$$

Category 71 – Equation of a Circle

1. D

Determine the equation:

Since the center is $(-7, 0)$, the corresponding factors are $(x + 7)^2$ and y^2. This eliminates answer choices A and C.

Since $r = 6$, $r^2 = 36$. This eliminates answer choice B.

2. A

Determine the coordinates of the center:

$$x = \frac{1 - 1}{2} = 0$$

$$y = \frac{-2 - 6}{2} = \frac{-8}{2} = -4$$

Hence, the factors are x^2 and $(y + 4)^2$. The equation can be written as $x^2 + (y + 4)^2 = r^2$. This eliminates answer choices C and D.

Determine the radius: Plug in $(1, -2)$ in the above equation.

$$1^2 + (-2 + 4)^2 = r^2 \rightarrow 1 + (2)^2 = r^2$$

$$r^2 = 5$$

This eliminates answer choice B.

3. D

Determine the equation:

Since the center is $(-2, -4)$, the corresponding factors are $(x + 2)^2$ and $(y + 4)^2$. The equation can be written as $(x + 2)^2 + (y + 4)^2 = r^2$. This eliminates answer choices A and C.

Determine the radius: Plug in point $(0.5, -2)$ in the above equation.

$$(0.5 + 2)^2 + (-2 + 4)^2 = r^2 \rightarrow (2.5)^2 + (2)^2 = r^2$$

$$r^2 = 6.25 + 4 = 10.25$$

This eliminates answer choice B.

4. A

Evaluate each answer choice: From the equation, $r^2 = 36$. Hence, any point inside the circle will have $r^2 < 36$ and any point outside the circle will have $r^2 > 36$. Plug each point in the equation and check.

Evaluate $(-2, 0)$: $(-2 - 2)^2 + (0 + 3)^2 = 16 + 9 = 25$. This point is inside the circle.

Evaluate $(-5, 1)$: $(-5 - 2)^2 + (1 + 3)^2 = 49 + 16 = 65$. This point is outside the circle.

Evaluate $(3, 3)$: $(3 - 2)^2 + (3 + 3)^2 = 1 + 36 = 37$. This point is outside the circle.

5. 9

Determine the factors for the complete square: Move 16 to the right-side and divide the equation by 2.

$$x^2 - 16x + y^2 + 6y = 8$$

Factor for x: Coefficient of x is -16.

$$\frac{-16}{2} = -8$$

The complete square is $(x - 8)^2$.

Factor for y: Coefficient of y is 6.

$$\frac{6}{2} = 3$$

The complete square is $(y + 3)^2$.

Complete the equation:

$$(x - 8)^2 + (y + 3)^2 = 8 + (-\mathbf{8})^2 + (\mathbf{3})^2$$

$$(x - 8)^2 + (y + 3)^2 = 81$$

$$r^2 = 81 = 9^2 \rightarrow r = 9$$

6. 0.5

Determine the factor for the complete square for x:

Factor for x: Coefficient of x is -1.

$$\frac{-1}{2} = -0.5$$

The complete square is $(x - 0.5)^2$.

The x-coordinate of the circle $= 0.5$.

Category 72 – Parallel and Intersecting Lines

1. <u>C</u>

Determine x: Since vertical angles are equal, equate the two angles.
$$3x - 5 = 5x - 85 \rightarrow 2x = 80 \rightarrow x = 40$$

2. <u>B</u>

Evaluate each answer choice:

$a + b = 180°$: Since a and b are same side supplementary exterior angle, their sum is 180°. This answer choice is correct.

$a + c = 180°$: Since a and c are angles of a point on a straight line, their sum is 180°. This answer choice is correct.

$b + c = 180°$: b and c are congruent alternate exterior angles. They can only add up to 180 if each of them is 90°. Question does not give this information. Hence, it cannot be concluded that this answer choice must be true.

3. <u>A</u>

Evaluate each answer choice:

$k = y + z$: k and $y + z$ are corresponding angles formed by intersecting line c. This answer choice is correct.

Answer choices B, C, and D are incorrect.

4. <u>D</u>

Evaluate each answer choice for the types of angles:

$a + y = 120°$: Since y and b are vertical angles, $y = b$. Hence, $a + y = a + b = 120°$. This answer choice is correct.

$b + z = 120°$: Since a and z are vertical angles, $a = z$. Hence, $a + b = z + b = b + z = 120°$. This answer choice is correct.

$c + x = 120°$: Since a, b, and c are angles on a straight line, $a + b + c = 180°$.
$$120° + c = 180° \rightarrow c = 60°$$

Since c and x are vertical angles, $c = x = 60°$. Hence, $c + x = 60° + 60° = 120°$. This answer choice is correct.

5. <u>98, 100, or 102</u>

$$x + y + y = 180 \rightarrow x + 2y = 180$$

Solve for x:

Since $38 < y < 42$, the possible values of y are 39, 40, 41. Plugging any of these in the above equation, will give a possible value of x. See below for all possible values.

$$x + (2 \times 39) = 180 \rightarrow x + 78 = 180 \rightarrow x = 102$$
$$x + (2 \times 40) = 180 \rightarrow x + 80 = 180 \rightarrow x = 100$$
$$x + (2 \times 41) = 180 \rightarrow x + 82 = 180 \rightarrow x = 98$$

6. <u>65</u>

See figure below.

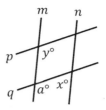

y and a are corresponding angles. Hence,
$$y = a = x + 50$$

a and x are same side interior supplementary angles. Hence,
$$a + x = 180 \rightarrow x + 50 + x = 180 \rightarrow$$
$$2x = 180 - 50 \rightarrow x = 65$$

7. <u>25</u>

a and b are same side interior supplementary angles. Hence,
$$a + b = 180$$

Substitute $a = 3x + 6$ and $b = 4x - 1$.
$$3x + 6 + 4x - 1 = 180$$
$$7x = 175 \rightarrow x = 25$$

8. <u>B</u>

Set up segment proportion and solve:

$AE = 8.1$. $BD = 4$. $DF = 5$. $BF = BD + DF = 4 + 5 = 9$.

The length of CE can be calculated by setting up the following proportion.
$$\frac{AE}{CE} = \frac{BF}{DF} \rightarrow \frac{8.1}{CE} = \frac{9}{5}$$
$$9 \times CE = 5 \times 8.1 \rightarrow 9 \times CE = 40.5 \rightarrow CE = 4.5$$

This falls in answer choice B.

9. <u>9</u>

Set up segment proportion and solve:

$AC = 10$. $CE = 6$. $AE = AC + CE = 10 + 6 = 16$.

$BD = 15$. Let $DF = x$. $BF = BD + DF = 15 + x$.

The length of DF can be calculated by setting up the following proportion.
$$\frac{AE}{CE} = \frac{BF}{DF} \rightarrow \frac{16}{6} = \frac{15 + x}{x}$$
$$16x = 6(15 + x) \rightarrow 16x = 90 + 6x \rightarrow$$
$$10x = 90 \rightarrow x = 9$$

(Note that if a student is good with ratios/proportions, this question can be solved without above calculation. Since, $BD = 1.5AC$, $DF = 1.5CE$. Hence, $DF = 1.5 \times 6 = 9$.)

Category 73 – Polygons

1. B

The sum of interior angles of a quadrilateral $= 360°$.

Solve for x:

$$x + x + 2x + 60 = 360 \rightarrow 4x + 60 = 360$$
$$4x = 360 - 60 = 300 \rightarrow x = 75$$

2. C

Determine n: Each exterior angle $= 30°$.

$$30 = \frac{360}{n}$$
$$30n = 360 \rightarrow n = 12$$

Determine the average degree measure of interior angle:

$$\frac{180(12 - 2)}{12} = \frac{180 \times 10}{12} = 150$$

3. 36

Determine the average measure of exterior angle: $n = 10$.

$$\frac{360}{n} = \frac{360}{10} = 36$$

4. 7

Determine the number of sides: Sum of interior angles $= 900°$.

$$180(n - 2) = 900 \rightarrow 180n - 360 = 900$$
$$180n = 900 + 360 \rightarrow 180n = 1{,}260 \rightarrow n = 7$$

5. 40

Determine the perimeter: Each side of regular polygon is identical.

$$\text{perimeter} = AB \times 8 = 5 \times 8 = 40$$

6. 75

Determine the sum of the interior angles: $n = 6$.

$$180(n - 2) = 180(6 - 2) = 180 \times 4 = 720$$

Determine x: Add all the angles and equate to $= 720$.

$$85 + 145 + (2x - 10) + 60 + 150 + (x + 65) = 720$$
$$495 + 3x = 720 \rightarrow 3x = 225 \rightarrow x = 75$$

Category 74 – Angles, Sides, and Area of a Triangle

1. C

$$x + y + z = 180$$
$$x = 180 - (y + z) \rightarrow x = 180 - y - z$$

2. B

Determine the possible lengths of c: $a = 2$. $b = 5$.

The three combinations for lengths are

$a + b > c \rightarrow 2 + 5 > c \rightarrow 7 > c$.

$a + c > b \rightarrow 2 + c > 5 \rightarrow c > 5 - 2 \rightarrow c > 3$.

$b + c > a \rightarrow 5 + c > 2 \rightarrow c > 2 - 5 \rightarrow c > -3$.

Hence, $7 > c > 3$.

This eliminates Option I since 2 and 3 are not possible values of c and Option III since 8 is not a possible value of c.

3. 4

Determine the length of AC: Since AD bisects BC, $\angle A = 30° + 30° = 60°$. Hence, $\angle C = 60°$ and triangle ABC is an equilateral triangle divided into two equal 30°-60°-90° triangles. In triangle ADC, the side ratio are as follows.

$$CD : AD : AC = a : a\sqrt{3} : 2a = a : 2\sqrt{3} : 2a$$
$$a\sqrt{3} = 2\sqrt{3} \rightarrow a = 2$$
$$AC = 2a = 2 \times 2 = 4$$

4. 120

Determine $3x$: Since $3x$ is the exterior angle of triangle XYZ, it is the sum of the two non-adjacent angles.

$$3x = x + 80 \rightarrow 2x = 80 \rightarrow x = 40$$

Hence,

$$3x = 3 \times 40 = 120$$

5. 8 or 9

Determine the possible lengths of c: $a = 3$. $b = 7$.

c must be less than $3 + 7 = 10$. It is given that $c > 7$.

Hence, $10 > c > 7$.

The possible integer values of c are 8 or 9.

6. C

Determine x: Use Pythagorean theorem.

$$AB^2 + BC^2 = AC^2 \rightarrow x^2 + (2x)^2 = 10^2$$
$$x^2 + 4x^2 = 100 \rightarrow 5x^2 = 100 \rightarrow x^2 = 20$$
$$x = \sqrt{20} = \sqrt{4 \times 5} = 2\sqrt{5}$$

Determine the perimeter of triangle ABC:

$$x + 2x + 10 = 2\sqrt{5} + (2 \times 2\sqrt{5}) + 10 = 6\sqrt{5} + 10$$

7. D

Determine the measure of angles in triangle ABC:

Since $AB = BC$, $\angle A = \angle C = 40°$. Hence,

$$\angle 40 + 40 + \angle ABC = 180$$
$$\angle ABC = 180 - 80 = 100$$

Determine the measure of angles in triangle BDE:

Since the angles at point B add to 180,

$$\angle DBE = 180 - 100 = 80$$

Since $BE = BD$, $\angle BED = \angle BDE = \angle x$. Hence,

$$\angle x + \angle x + 80° = 180$$
$$2x = 180 - 80 = 100 \rightarrow x = 50$$

8. B

area of shaded region = area of triangle PQR − area of triangle MNR

Determine the area of equilateral triangle PQR: Side = 4.

$$\frac{\sqrt{3}}{4}a^2 = \frac{\sqrt{3}}{4}4^2 = 4\sqrt{3}$$

Determine the area of equilateral triangle MNR:

Since MR and NR are the midpoint of PR and QR, respectively, and $MN = 2$, triangle MNR is an equilateral triangle with each side = 2.

$$\frac{\sqrt{3}}{4}a^2 = \frac{\sqrt{3}}{4}2^2 = \sqrt{3}$$

Determine the area of shaded region:

$$4\sqrt{3} - \sqrt{3} = 3\sqrt{3}$$

9. B

Determine the side length of equilateral triangle ABC:

Since the area of each congruent triangle = $\sqrt{3}$, the area of ABC is $9 \times \sqrt{3} = 9\sqrt{3}$. Hence,

$$\frac{\sqrt{3}}{4}a^2 = 9\sqrt{3} \rightarrow a^2 = 9 \times 4 = 36 = 6^2 \rightarrow a = 6$$

Hence, each side of triangle $ABC = 6$

Determine the perimeter of equilateral triangle ABC:

$$\text{side} \times 3 = 6 \times 3 = 18$$

Category 75 – Similar Triangles

1. B

Determine the corresponding sides: AB corresponds to EF. BC corresponds to DE. AC corresponds to DF. Hence,

$$\frac{BC}{DE} = \frac{AC}{DF} = \frac{AB}{EF}$$

This eliminates answer choices A, C, and D.

10. A

Determine the measure of angle A:

Since $AB = AC$, $\angle B = \angle C = 50°$. Hence,

$$\angle A + 50 + 50 = 180 \rightarrow \angle A = 180 - 100 = 80$$

Convert to radians:

$$80 \times \frac{\pi}{180} = \frac{4\pi}{9}$$

11. 6

Determine the side length of the equilateral triangle:

$$\frac{\sqrt{3}}{4}a^2 = \sqrt{3} \rightarrow a^2 = 4 = 2^2 \rightarrow a = 2$$

Determine the perimeter of equilateral triangle:

$$\text{side} \times 3 = 2 \times 3 = 6$$

12. 10

Determine the area of triangle ABC: $b = BC = 5$. $h = 4$.

$$\frac{1}{2}bh = \frac{1}{2} \times 5 \times 4 = 10$$

13. 4

Since $AB = BC$ and angle $ABC = 90°$, triangle ABC is a right isosceles 45°-45°-90° triangle with side ratio as follows.

$$AB:BC:AC = a:a:a\sqrt{2} = a:a:4\sqrt{2}$$
$$a\sqrt{2} = 4\sqrt{2} \rightarrow a = 4 = AB$$

14. 54

Determine the area of right triangle ABC: $h = AB = 9$. $b = BC$.

$AB:AC = 9:15 = 3(3:5)$ is the ratio of the Pythagorean triple $3(3:4:5)$. Hence,

$$AB:BC:AC = 9:BC:15 = 9:12:15$$
$$BC = 12$$
$$\text{Area} = \frac{1}{2}bh = \frac{1}{2} \times 12 \times 9 = 54$$

2. C

Since the two triangles are similar, the measure of their corresponding angles is same. Hence, the measure of angle B cannot be four time the measure of the corresponding angle E.

All other choice are correct.

3. 6

Since $\angle C = \angle E$ and $\angle A = \angle D$ (corresponding angles), the two triangles are similar triangles.

Set up proportion and solve:

Let $CE = x$ and $BE = 2x$.

$BC = BE + CE = x + 2x = 3x$.

The length of DE can be determined by setting up the following proportion.

$$\frac{BC}{BE} = \frac{AC}{DE} \rightarrow \frac{3x}{2x} = \frac{9}{DE} \rightarrow$$
$$3 \times DE = 9 \times 2 \rightarrow 3 \times DE = 18 \rightarrow DE = 6$$

4. 46

Determine $\angle A$: $\angle B = 70°$. $\angle C = 32°$.

$$\angle A + 70 + 32 = 180 \rightarrow \angle A = 180 - 102 = 78$$

Since the triangles are similar, the corresponding vertices will have the same degree measure.

$\angle X = \angle A = 78$ and $\angle Z = \angle C = 32$.

Determine $\angle X - \angle Z$: $78 - 32 = 46$

Category 76 – Squares and Cubes

1. D

Determine the length of cube edge: Surface area $= 96$.

$$6s^2 = 96 \rightarrow s^2 = 16 \rightarrow s = 4$$

Determine the volume of the cube:

$$s^3 = 4^3 = 64$$

2. C

Determine the volume of both cubes:

For cube with $s = 5$, volume $= s^3 = 5^3 = 125$.

For cube with $s = 2$, volume $= s^3 = 2^3 = 8$.

Difference: $125 - 8 = 117$.

3. A

Determine the length of square edge: Area $= \dfrac{b^2}{4}$.

$$s^2 = \frac{b^2}{4} \rightarrow s^2 = \frac{b^2}{2^2} \rightarrow s^2 = \left(\frac{b}{2}\right)^2 \rightarrow s = \frac{b}{2}$$

Determine the perimeter of the square:

$$4s = 4 \times \frac{b}{2} = 2b$$

4. C

Determine the length of cube edge: Volume $= 27$.

$$s^3 = 27 = 3^3 \rightarrow s = 3$$

Determine the surface area of the cube:

$$6s^2 = 6 \times 3^2 = 54$$

5. 20

Since $\angle B = \angle D = 90°$ and $\angle C = \angle E$ (corresponding angles), the two triangles are similar triangles.

Set up proportion and solve:

In right triangle ADE, $AD : AE = 6 : 10 = 2(3 : 5)$ is the ratio of Pythagorean triple $2(3 : 4 : 5)$. Hence,

$$AD : DE : AE = 6 : DE : 10 = 6 : 8 : 10$$
$$DE = 8$$

The length of BC can be determined by setting up the following proportion.

$$\frac{AB}{AD} = \frac{BC}{DE} \rightarrow \frac{6+9}{6} = \frac{BC}{8} \rightarrow \frac{15}{6} = \frac{BC}{8} \rightarrow$$
$$6 \times BC = 8 \times 15 \rightarrow 6 \times BC = 120 \rightarrow BC = 20$$

5. 1/4 or 0.25

Determine the surface area of one face of the cube:

$$6s^2 = 6\left(\frac{1}{2}\right)^2$$

Hence, surface area of one face is

$$\left(\frac{1}{2}\right)^2 = \frac{1}{4} = 0.25$$

6. 150

Determine the length of cube edge: Diagonal $= 5\sqrt{3}$.

$$s\sqrt{3} = 5\sqrt{3} \rightarrow s = 5$$

Determine the surface area of the cube:

$$6s^2 = 6 \times 5^2 = 6 \times 25 = 150$$

7. 80

Determine the length of cube edge: Volume $= 64$.

$$s^3 = 64 = 4^3 \rightarrow s = 4$$

Determine the difference between the surface area and area of one face of the cube:

Since each face is a square, the difference is

$$6s^2 - s^2 = 5s^2 = 5 \times 4^2 = 5 \times 16 = 80$$

8. 125

Determine the length of cube edge: Surface area $= 150$.

$$6s^2 = 150 \rightarrow s^2 = 25 \rightarrow s = 5$$

Determine the volume of the cube:

$$s^3 = 5^3 = 125$$

Category 77 – Rectangles and Right Rectangular Prisms

1. C

Determine the surface area of the right rectangular prism:
$$2(lw + lh + wh) = 2\big((8 \times 5) + (8 \times 3) + (5 \times 3)\big)$$
$$2(40 + 24 + 15) = 2(79) = 158$$

2. A

Determine the width of the rectangle: Area $= 147$.

Let width $= x$. Hence, length $= 3x$.
$$x \times 3x = 147 \rightarrow 3x^2 = 147 \rightarrow x^2 = 49 \rightarrow x = \pm 7$$
Since width cannot be negative, $x = 7$.

Determine the difference:
$$3x - x = 2x = 2 \times 7 = 14$$

3. B

Determine the volume of the right rectangular prism:

Width $= w$. Height $= 3w$. Length $= 2 \times$ height $= 2 \times 3w = 6w$.
$$V = lwh = 6w \times w \times 3w = 18w^3$$

4. B

Determine the surface area of the right rectangular prism:
$$2(lw + lh + wh) = 2\big((7 \times 5) + (7 \times 2) + (5 \times 2)\big)$$
$$2(35 + 14 + 10) = 2 \times 59 = 118$$

5. A

Determine the area of the papers:
$$\text{area of Molly's paper} = 12 \times 16 = 192$$
$$\text{area of Sam's paper} = 2(12) \times 2(16) = 768$$
Determine the percent: Area of Molly's paper is what percent of area of Sam's paper.
$$\frac{192}{768} \times 100 = 25\%$$

6. 1.6

Determine the cube ratio of the volumes:
$$64 : 1000 = 4^3 : 10^3$$
Hence, ratio of the corresponding heights $= 4 : 10 = 2 : 5$.
Determine the proportion:
$$2 : 5 = h : 4 \rightarrow h = 1.6$$

Category 78 – Trapezoids and Parallelograms

1. 320

Determine the area of the parallelogram:

$b = 16$. $h = 20$.
$$16 \times 20 = 320$$

2. 55

Determine the length of the side of the parallelogram:

$DE : AE = 10 : 24 = 2(5 : 12)$ is the ratio of Pythagorean triple $2(5 : 12 : 13)$. Hence,
$$DE : AE : AD = 10 : 24 : AD = 10 : 24 : 26$$
$$AD = 26$$
Since perimeter $= 162$,
$$AD + BC + AB + DC = 162$$
Since the opposite sides of a parallelogram are equal in length, the perimeter can be written as
$$2(AD) + 2(AB) = 162 \rightarrow 2(26) + 2(AB) = 162 \rightarrow$$
$$52 + 2(AB) = 162 \rightarrow 2(AB) = 110 \rightarrow AB = 55$$

3. 10

Determine the height of the trapezoid: Area $= 110$.

The two bases are 6.5 and 15.5.
$$110 = \frac{1}{2}(6.5 + 15.5)h \rightarrow 110 = \frac{1}{2}(22)h \rightarrow$$
$$110 = 11h \rightarrow h = 10$$

4. 12

Determine the length of the side of the parallelogram: Since $\angle O = 60°$ and $\angle Q = 90°$, $\angle M$ is $30°$ and triangle MOQ is a $30°$-$60°$-$90°$ triangle. Hence,
$$OQ : MQ : MO = a : a\sqrt{3} : 2a = a : 3\sqrt{3} : 2a$$
$$a\sqrt{3} = 3\sqrt{3} \rightarrow a = 3 = OQ$$
$$OP = OQ + QP = 3 + 9 = 12$$
Since the opposite sides of a parallelogram are equal in length, $OP = MN = 12$.

5. 270

Determine the height of the trapezoid: See figure below.

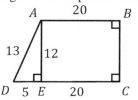

A perpendicular bisector drawn from point A is the height of the trapezoid. It divides the trapezoid into the right triangle AED and the square $ABCE$. Hence, $AB = CE = 20$ and $DE = 25 - 20 = 5$.

$DE : AD = 5 : 13$ is the ratio of Pythagorean triple $5 : 12 : 13$. Hence,
$$DE : AE : AD = 5 : AE : 13 = 5 : 12 : 13 \rightarrow AE = 12$$
Determine the area of the trapezoid:
$$\frac{1}{2}(20 + 25)12 = 45 \times 6 = 270$$

Category 79 – Volume of Cylinders, Spheres, Cones, Pyramids, Prisms

1. <u>B</u>

Determine the volume of the cylindrical cone:

It is given that $h = 3r$.

$$V = \frac{1}{3}\pi r^2 3r \;\rightarrow\; V = \pi r^3$$

2. <u>A</u>

Determine the height of the cylindrical cone: $V = \frac{1}{6}\pi$.

It is given that $r = 2h$.

$$\frac{1}{6}\pi = \frac{1}{3}\pi(2h)^2 h \;\rightarrow\; \frac{1}{6} = \frac{1}{3}4h^2 h \;\rightarrow\; \frac{1}{6} = \frac{1}{3}4h^3 \;\rightarrow$$

$$\frac{1}{2} = 4h^3 \;\rightarrow\; h^3 = \frac{1}{8} = \frac{1}{2^3} \;\rightarrow\; h = \frac{1}{2}$$

3. <u>C</u>

Volume of the ice ball (sphere) is

$$\frac{4}{3}\pi \times 3 \times 3 \times 3 = 36\pi$$

Volume of the water after the ice ball melts is

$$36\pi + 108\pi = 144\pi$$

Determine the ratio: $108\pi : 144\pi = 3 : 4$

4. <u>D</u>

Determine the radius of the cylindrical cone: $h = 12$.

Since the volume should be $\leq 64\pi$, determine the radius for the maximum volume = 64.

$$64\pi = \frac{1}{3}\pi r^2 h \;\rightarrow\; 64 = \frac{1}{3}r^2 \times 12 \;\rightarrow$$

$$64 = 4r^2 \;\rightarrow\; r^2 = \frac{64}{4} = 16 = 4^2 \;\rightarrow\; r = 4$$

Hence, for volume $\leq 64\pi$, r can not be greater than 4.

5. <u>B</u>

Determine the volume of both containers:

Let $x = \pi r^2 h$.

Hence, $y = \pi(2r)^2 2h = \pi 4r^2 2h = 8\pi r^2 h$.

$$\frac{x}{y} = \frac{\pi r^2 h}{8\pi r^2 h} = \frac{1}{8}$$

6. <u>C</u>

Determine the radius of the original circular cone:

Volume = 6π. $h = 2$.

$$6\pi = \frac{1}{3}\pi r^2 \times 2 \;\rightarrow\; r^2 = \frac{6 \times 3}{2} = 9 \;\rightarrow\; r = 3$$

Determine the volume of circular cone with double r and h: $r = 3 \times 2 = 6$. $h = 2 \times 2 = 4$.

$$\frac{1}{3}\pi \times 6 \times 6 \times 4 = 48\pi$$

Change in volume:

$$\frac{48\pi}{6\pi} = 8 \text{ fold increase}$$

7. <u>A</u>

Determine the area of the equilateral triangular base:

Each face the equilateral triangle = 2.

$$\frac{\sqrt{3}}{4}a^2 = \frac{\sqrt{3}}{4} \times 2 \times 2 = \sqrt{3}$$

Determine the volume of the prism:

$$\sqrt{3} \times 3\sqrt{3} = 3 \times 3 = 9$$

8. <u>113</u>

Determine the volume of the sphere: = amount of air

Diameter = 6. Hence, radius = 3.

$$\frac{4}{3}\pi \times 3^3 = 36\pi = 36 \times 3.14 = 113.04$$

9. <u>42</u>

Determine the volume of the cylinder: $h = 6$.

Area occupied = area of base = $\pi r^2 = 7$.

$$V = \pi r^2 h = 7 \times 6 = 42$$

10. <u>14</u>

Determine the edge of the pyramid square base:

$$\text{each edge of square} = \frac{\text{perimeter}}{4} = \frac{12}{4} = 3$$

Determine the height of the pyramid: $V = 42$. $l = w = 3$.

$$42 = \frac{1}{3}lwh \;\rightarrow\; 42 = \frac{1}{3} \times 3 \times 3 \times h \;\rightarrow h = 14$$

11. <u>6</u>

Determine the height of the cylinder: $V = 54\pi$. $h = 2r$.

$$54\pi = \pi r^2 \times 2r \;\rightarrow\; 54\pi = 2\pi r^3 \;\rightarrow$$
$$r^3 = 27 = 3^3 \;\rightarrow\; r = 3$$
$$h = 2 \times 3 = 6$$

12. <u>9</u>

Determine the radius of the cylindrical cone: $V = 27\pi h$.

$$27\pi h = \frac{1}{3}\pi r^2 h \;\rightarrow\; 27 = \frac{1}{3}r^2 \;\rightarrow$$
$$r^2 = 27 \times 3 = 81 = 9^2 \;\rightarrow\; r = 9$$

13. <u>4</u>

Determine the radius of the sphere: $V = \frac{32}{3}\pi$.

$$\frac{32}{3}\pi = \frac{4}{3}\pi r^3 \;\rightarrow$$
$$32 = 4r^3 \;\rightarrow\; r^3 = 8 = 2^3 \;\rightarrow\; r = 2$$

Determine diameter: $2 \times 2 = 4$

14. <u>16</u>

Determine the area of the pyramid base: $V = 32$. $h = 6$.

$$32 = \frac{1}{3}\text{ area of base} \times 6 \;\rightarrow\; \text{area of base} = \frac{32}{2} = 16$$

Category 80 – Combined Geometric Figures

1. <u>A</u>

The ratio of the two sides of the right triangle is $3:5$. This is Pythagorean triple $3:4:5$. Hence, the third side $= 4$. This side is also the diameter of the semicircle.

Determine the area of the semicircle: Radius $= 2$.

$$\text{area of semicircle} = \frac{\pi r^2}{2} = \frac{\pi 2^2}{2} = 2\pi$$

2. <u>D</u>

Since $AE = BE$, $\angle ABE = \angle BAE = 45°$.

Since $BC \| DE$ (opposite parallel sides of a trapezoid) and $\angle BEA = 90°$, $\angle CBE = 90°$.

$$\angle B = \angle ABE + \angle CBE = 45 + 90 = 135$$

3. <u>B</u>

Since $\overset{\frown}{AB} = \overset{\frown}{AC}$, the opposite angles are congruent.
$$\angle B = \angle C$$
Since arc $BXC = 160°$, inscribed $\angle A = 80°$. Hence,
$$\angle B + \angle C = 180 - 80 = 100$$
Since $\angle B = \angle C$, each angle $= \frac{100}{2} = 50$.

4. <u>C</u>

Determine $\angle P$: $\angle P$ is the central angle for $\overset{\frown}{QOR}$.
Since $PR = PQ$ (radii), $\angle R = \angle Q = 40$. Hence,
$$\angle P + 40 + 40 = 180° \rightarrow \angle P = 180 - 80 = 100°$$
Determine the fraction:
$\overset{\frown}{QOR} = \angle P = 100$. $\overset{\frown}{QSR} = 360 - 100 = 260$.
$$\frac{\overset{\frown}{QOR}}{\overset{\frown}{QSR}} = \frac{100}{260} = \frac{5}{13}$$

5. <u>B</u>

Since each circle is congruent, the centers A, B, and C form an equilateral triangle with each side $= 2 \times$ radius $= 2 \times 6 = 12$ and $\angle A = \angle B = \angle C = 60°$.

area of the shaded region = area of triangle ABC – the area of 3 circle sectors. See figure below.

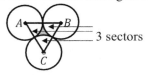

Determine the area of equilateral triangle ABC:
$$\text{area} = \frac{\sqrt{3}}{4} \times 12 \times 12 = \sqrt{3} \times 36 = 36\sqrt{3}$$
Determine the area of 3 sectors:
$$\text{area of 1 sector} = \frac{\theta}{360} \times \pi r^2 = \frac{60}{360} \times \pi \times 6 \times 6 = 6\pi$$
$$\text{area of 3 sectors} = 3 \times 6\pi = 18\pi$$
Determine area of shaded region:
$$36\sqrt{3} - 18\pi = 18(2\sqrt{3} - \pi)$$

6. <u>D</u>

Use the process of elimination:

Since neither the square nor the inscribed rectangle have a square term in the sides, $3a^2 + 4$ cannot be the perimeter of the square or the rectangle. This eliminates answer choices A and B.

The area of the square $= s^2 = (2a)^2 = 4a^2$.

Since $3a^2 + 4$ is less than the area of the square, it cannot be the combined area. This eliminates answer choice C.

7. <u>B</u>

Determine the base and height of triangle CDE:

Since CD and CE are the radii of the circle, CDE is an isosceles triangle. Hence, $\angle D = \angle E = 30°$.

Since all radii are equal, $CF = DC = EC = 4$.

See figure below. A perpendicular bisector divides the triangle CDE into two congruent $30°$-$60°$-$90°$ triangles. Use the side ratio relationship to determine height $= AC$ and base $= DE$.

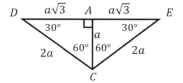

$$2a = 4 \rightarrow a = 2 = AC = \text{height}$$
$$\text{base} = DE = AD + AE = 2\sqrt{3} + 2\sqrt{3} = 4\sqrt{3}$$
Determine the area of triangle CDE:
$$\frac{1}{2} \times DE \times AC \rightarrow \frac{1}{2} \times 4\sqrt{3} \times 2 = 4\sqrt{3}$$

8. <u>8</u>

Determine the area of the rectangle: NO is the diameter of the semicircle.

Since the radius of the semicircle $= 2$, the diameter $= NO = 4$. Hence,
$$NO = MP = a = 4$$
$$b = \text{half of } a = 2$$
$$lw = ab = 2 \times 4 = 8$$

9. <u>40</u>

$$\angle A = \frac{5}{9}\pi \text{ radians} = \frac{5}{9}\pi \times \frac{180}{\pi} = 100°$$
Since AB and AC are the radii, $AB = AC$ and $\angle B = \angle C$. Hence,
$$100 + \angle B + \angle C = 180 \rightarrow$$
$$\angle B + \angle C = 180 - 100 = 80$$
Since $\angle B = \angle C$, each angle $= \frac{80}{2} = 40$.

10. <u>72</u>

The length l of the rectangle is the diameter of the circle and the width w is the radius of the circle.

Determine the radius of the circle:

$$\frac{\pi r^2}{2} = 18\pi \rightarrow r^2 = 2 \times 18 = 36 \rightarrow r = 6 = w$$

$$\text{diameter} = 2 \times r = 2 \times 6 = 12 = l$$

Determine the area of rectangle:

$$lw = 12 \times 6 = 72$$

11. <u>60</u>

Since lines a and b are tangent to the circle, $\angle CBD$ and $\angle CAD$ are 90°.

The sum of the angles of a quadrilateral = 360°. Hence,

$$\angle CBD + \angle CAD + x + \angle ADB = 360$$
$$90 + 90 + 120 + \angle ADB = 360$$
$$300 + \angle ADB = 360 \rightarrow \angle ADB = 360 - 300 = 60$$

Since $\angle ADB$ and $\angle y$ are vertical angles, $\angle y = \angle ADB = 60$.

12. <u>120</u>

Since $\angle B = 90°$, triangle ABC is a right triangle with base = BC and height = AB.

Since $r = 13$, AC = diameter = $2 \times 13 = 26$.

$BC:AC = 10:26 = 2(5:13)$ is the ratio of Pythagorean triple $2(5:12:13)$. Hence,

$$BC:AB:AC = 10:AB:26 = 10:24:26 \rightarrow AB = 24$$

Determine the area of triangle ABC:

$$\frac{1}{2}bh = \frac{1}{2}BC \times AB = \frac{1}{2} \times 10 \times 24 = 120$$

13. <u>32</u>

BC is a side of the equilateral triangle and the square. Since the area of the equilateral triangle is given, the length of BC can be determined.

Determine the sides of the equilateral triangle ABC:

$$\frac{\sqrt{3}}{4}a^2 = 16\sqrt{3} \rightarrow a^2 = 16 \times 4 = 64 = 8^2$$
$$a = 8 = BC$$

Determine the perimeter of square $BCDE$:

$$4s = 4 \times BC = 4 \times 8 = 32$$

Category 81 – Geometric Shapes in the xy-plane

1. <u>D</u>

See figure below.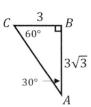

Determine the length between points: AB is a vertical line and BC is a horizontal line. Hence, $\angle B$ is 90°.

Calculate $\overline{AB}$: $3\sqrt{3} - 0 = 3\sqrt{3}$.

Calculate $\overline{BC}$: $1 - (-2) = 3$.

$BC:AB = 3:3\sqrt{3}$ is the ratio of the sides of a 30°-60°-90° right triangle. Hence,

$BC:AB:AC = 3:3\sqrt{3}:AC = a:a\sqrt{3}:2a = 30°:60°:90°$

Determine $\angle A$:

$\angle A$ is opposite to $BC = a$. Hence, $\angle A = 30°$.

$$30 \times \frac{\pi}{180} = \frac{\pi}{6}$$

2. <u>C</u>

Determine the length between points: PQ is a vertical line and QR is a horizontal line. Hence, $\angle Q = 90°$.

Calculate $\overline{PQ}$: $5 - (-1) = 6$.

Calculate $\overline{QR}$: $9 - 1 = 8$.

$PQ:QR = 6:8$ is the ratio of Pythagorean triple $2(3:4:5)$. Hence,

$PQ:QR:PR = 6:8:PR = 6:8:10 \rightarrow PR = 10$

Determine perimeter: $6 + 8 + 10 = 24$.

3. <u>B</u>

See figure below.

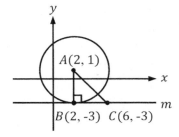

Determine the length between points: AB is a vertical line and BC is a horizontal line. Hence, $\angle B$ is 90°.

Calculate $\overline{AB}$: $1 - (-3) = 1 + 3 = 4$.

Calculate $\overline{BC}$: $6 - (2) = 4$.

Since $AB = BC$, triangle ABC is an isosceles right triangle. Hence, $\angle A = \angle C = 45°$.

4. <u>2</u>

Determine the length between points: Radius of the circle is the distance between points $(0, 0)$ and $(1, \sqrt{3})$. Use the distance formula.

$$\sqrt{(1-0)^2 + (\sqrt{3}-0)^2} \rightarrow \sqrt{1 + (\sqrt{3})^2}$$
$$\sqrt{1+3} \rightarrow \sqrt{4} = 2$$

Category 82 – Geometric Shapes and Percent

1. B

Determine the current distance:
$$AB + BC = 5 + 12 = 17$$

Determine the distance after bypass: The length of bypass $= AC$ is not given.

$AB:BC = 5:12$ is the ratio of Pythagorean triple $5:12:13$. Hence,
$$AB:BC:AC = 5:12:13 \rightarrow AC = 13$$

Determine the percent change:

Old distance $= 17$. New distance $= 13$.
$$\frac{13 - 17}{17} \times 100 = \frac{-4}{17} \times 100 = -23.5\% = 23.5\%$$

2. C

Determine x:
$$30\% \text{ increase} = 1 + 0.3 = 1.3$$

Hence, the area after 30% increase of $x = 1.3x$.

Each edge of the square with above area $= 8$. Hence,

$1.3x = 8^2 = 64 \rightarrow x = 49.23 =$ area in initial design.

Determine the edge before increase:
$$\text{area} = s^2 = 49.23 = \text{approximately } 7^2$$

Since 49.23 is greater than $7^2 = 49$, the edge cannot be less than 7. This eliminates answer choices A and B.

Answer choice D can be eliminated since the area of $s = 8$ is $s^2 = 8^2 = 64$.

3. C

Determine the area before radius increase: Let radius $= r$.
$$\text{Area} = \pi r^2 = \pi 4^2 = 16\pi$$

Determine the area after 50% radius increase:

Increased radius $= 1 + 0.5 = 1.5r = 1.5 \times 4 = 6.$
$$\pi r^2 = \pi 6^2 = 36\pi$$

Determine percent change:
$$\frac{36\pi - 16\pi}{16\pi} \times 100 = \frac{20\pi}{16\pi} \times 100 = 125\%$$

4. D

Determine the area before edge increase:

Let edge $= x$.
$$\text{area} = x^2$$

Determine the area after 40% edge increase:
$$40\% \text{ increase} = 1 + 0.4 = 1.4$$

Hence, increased edge $= 1.4x$.
$$\text{area} = (1.4x)^2 = 1.96x^2$$

Determine percent change:
$$\frac{1.96x^2 - x^2}{x^2} \times 100 = \frac{0.96x^2}{x^2} \times 100 = 96\%$$

5. A

Determine the area of the rectangle:

Let length $= l$ and width $= w$.
$$\text{area} = lw$$

Determine the area of the modified rectangle:

Length increased by 10% $= 1.1l$.

Width decreased by 20% $= 0.8w$.
$$\text{area} = 1.1l \times 0.8w = 0.88lw$$

Difference: $0.88lw - lw = -0.12lw = 12\%$ less

Section 13 – Review Questions

1. B

Determine the area of triangle ABC: $b = BC = 6$. $h = AB$.

$BC:AC = 6:10 = 2(3:5)$ is the ratio of Pythagorean triple $2(3:4:5)$. Hence,
$$BC:AB:AC = 6:AB:10 = 6:8:10 \rightarrow AB = 8$$
$$\text{area} = \frac{1}{2} \times 6 \times 8 = 24$$

Determine the area of triangle DBE: $b = BD$. $h = BE$.

Since $AB = 2BE$, $BE = 4$. Hence, $BD = 4$.
$$\text{area} = \frac{1}{2} \times 4 \times 4 = 8$$

Determine the fraction:
$$\frac{\text{area of triangle } DBE}{\text{area of triangle } ABC} = \frac{8}{24} = \frac{1}{3}$$

2. A

Area $= x$. $b = AC$. $h = BD = 10$.
$$x = \frac{1}{2} \times AC \times 10 \rightarrow x = 5AC \rightarrow AC = \frac{x}{5}$$

3. C

Determine $\angle M$: $\angle M$ is the central angle for $\widehat{NP}$. Since $\angle N$ is a right angle, triangle MNQ is a right triangle.

$MN:NQ = 1:\sqrt{3}$ is the ratio of the sides of a 30°-60°-90° right triangle. Hence,
$$MN:NQ:MQ = 1:\sqrt{3}:MQ = a:a\sqrt{3}:2a = 30°:60°:90°$$

Since angle $\angle M$ is opposite the middle side NQ ($a\sqrt{3}$), $\angle M = 60°$. Hence, $\widehat{NP} = 60°$.

Determine the ratio:
$$\widehat{NP}:\text{circumferenece} = 60°:360° = 1:6$$

4. B

Determine the central angle in degrees, using arc length formula: $s = 2\pi$. $r = 5$.

$$2\pi = 2\pi \times 5 \times \frac{\theta}{360} \rightarrow 1 = \frac{5\theta}{360} \rightarrow \theta = 72°$$

5. C

Determine the equation: Since the center is $(3, -4)$, the factors are $(x - 3)^2$ and $(y + 4)^2$. This eliminates answer choices B and D.

Since the circle is tangent to the x-axis, the distance between the y-coordinate of the center and the x-axis is the radius of the circle. See figure below.

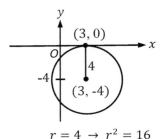

$$r = 4 \rightarrow r^2 = 16$$

This eliminates answer choice A.

6. C

Compare the areas of the rectangle:

$$\text{area proposed by artist } = lw = ab$$

$$\text{area proposed by manager} = lw = 2a \times \frac{b}{2} = ab$$

7. 6

Determine the radius of the circle, using area of sector formula: $\theta = 120°$. Area of sector $= 12\pi$.

$$12\pi = \frac{120}{360} \times \pi r^2 \rightarrow 12 = \frac{1}{3} \times r^2 \rightarrow r^2 = 36 = 6^2$$

$$r = 6$$

8. D

Determine the area of the rectangle: Let length $= l$ and width $= w$.

$$\text{area} = lw$$

Determine the area of the modified rectangle:

Length increased by 25% $= 1.25l$.

Width decreased by 20% $= 0.8w$.

$$\text{area} = 1.25l \times 0.8w = lw$$

The area remains same.

9. D

Determine the sum of the degree measure of interior angles: $n = 5$.

$$180(n - 2) = 180(5 - 2) = 180 \times 3 = 540$$

Determine x: The unknown angle at point P mut be determined first. Since the angle at point P add to 180°, the unknown angle $= 180 - 50 = 130$.

$$\angle x + 120 + 60 + 130 + 90 = 540$$

$$\angle x + 400 = 540 \rightarrow \angle x = 540 - 400 = 140$$

10. C

Evaluate each answer choice: The distance between a point on the circumference and the center of the circle is the radius of the circle. Plug each point in the equation and check for $r^2 = 9$. Start with answer choice B.

Answer choice B: Point $(3, 1)$.

$$(3 - 6)^2 + (1 + 1)^2 = (-3)^2 + (2)^2 = 9 + 4 = 13$$

Since $r^2 = 13$, answer choice B can be eliminated.

Answer choice C: Point $(6, 2)$.

$$(6 - 6)^2 + (2 + 1)^2 = (0)^2 + (3)^2 = 9$$

Since $r^2 = 9$, answer choice C is correct.

11. B

See partial figure below.

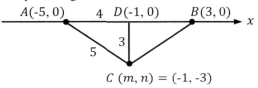

$$C\,(m, n) = (-1, -3)$$

Determine m: A perpendicular bisector from the center C to the x-axis is the midpoint of the two points shown on the x-axis. The x-coordinate of the midpoint D is the x-coordinate of the center of the circle.

$$\text{midpoint } D = m = \frac{-5 + 3}{2} = \frac{-2}{2} = -1$$

Determine n: The length of CD will give the position of n on the y-axis. See below using triangle ACD.

$AC = 5$ since it is the radius.

$AD = -1 - (-5) = 4$

$AD : AC = 4 : 5$ is the ratio of Pythagorean triple $3 : 4 : 5$.

$$CD : AD : AC = CD : 4 : 5 = 3 : 4 : 5 \rightarrow CD = 3$$

n is 3 units below 0 on the y-axis. Hence, $n = -3$.

12. 9

Determine the width of the rectangle: Length $= l$. Width $= l + 5$. Area $= 36$.

$$36 = l \times (l + 5) \rightarrow 36 = l^2 + 5l$$

Form a quadratic equation and factorize.

$$l^2 + 5l - 36 = 0$$

$$(l + 9)(l - 4) = 0 \rightarrow l = -9 \text{ or } l = 4$$

Length is greater than 0. Hence, $l = 4$

$$\text{width} = l + 5 = 4 + 5 = 9$$

13. <u>30</u>

Determine the volume of the right rectangular prism:

$lw = 5$. $hw = 6$. $lh = 30$.

Multiplying the given dimensions will give the square of the volume.

$$lw \times hw \times lh = 5 \times 6 \times 30 \rightarrow llwwhh = 900$$
$$(lwh)^2 = (30)^2 \rightarrow lwh = 30$$

14. <u>8</u>

Determine the height of the right rectangular tank: Filled to capacity is the volume of the tank.

Volume $= 2,400$. $l = 25$. $w = 12$.

$$V = lwh \rightarrow 2,400 = 25 \times 12 \times h$$
$$2,400 = 300 \times h \rightarrow h = 8$$

15. <u>17.5</u>

Since $AB||DE$, $\angle A = \angle E$ and $\angle B = \angle D$. Hence, triangles ABC and CDE are similar triangles.

Set up a proportion: $AC = 4$. $BC = 5$. $CE = 10$.

$BD = BC + CD = 5 + CD$.

The length of CD can be calculated by setting up the following proportion.

$$\frac{AC}{CE} = \frac{BC}{CD} \rightarrow \frac{4}{10} = \frac{5}{CD}$$
$$4 \times CD = 5 \times 10 \rightarrow 4 \times CD = 50 \rightarrow CD = 12.5$$
$$BD = 5 + 12.5 = 17.5$$

16. <u>5.3</u>

Since $\angle B = \angle E$ and $\angle C$ is shared, triangles ABC and CED are similar triangles.

Set up a proportion: $AB = 7$. $CD = 5$. $DE = 3$.

In triangle CED, $DE: CD = 3:5$ is the ratio of Pythagorean triple $3:4:5$. Hence,

$$DE: CE: CD = 3: CE: 5 = 3:4:5 \rightarrow CE = 4$$

Hence, $BE = BC - CE = BC - 4$.

The length of BC can be calculated by setting up the following proportion.

$$\frac{BC}{CE} = \frac{AB}{DE} \rightarrow \frac{BC}{4} = \frac{7}{3}$$
$$3 \times BC = 4 \times 7 \rightarrow 3 \times BC = 28 \rightarrow BC = 9.33$$
$$BE = 9.33 - 4 = 5.33 = 5.3$$

17. <u>2</u>

Determine the radius:

Area of equilateral triangle $= 4\sqrt{3}$. Hence,

$$\frac{\sqrt{3}}{4}a^2 = 4\sqrt{3} \rightarrow a^2 = 4 \times 4 \rightarrow a = 4$$

Each side of the triangle is comprised of two radii. Hence,

$$\text{radius} = \frac{4}{2} = 2$$

18. <u>20</u>

Determine the factors for the complete square:

<u>Factor for x</u>: Coefficient of x is 4.

$$\frac{4}{2} = 2$$

Hence, the factor is $(x + 2)^2$.

<u>Factor for y</u>: Coefficient of y is 10.

$$\frac{10}{2} = 5$$

Hence, the factor is $(y + 5)^2$.

Complete the equation:

$$(x + 2)^2 + (y + 5)^2 = 71 + 2^2 + 5^2$$
$$(x + 2)^2 + (y + 5)^2 = 100$$
$$r^2 = 100 = 10^2 \rightarrow r = 10$$

The diameter is $10 \times 2 = 20$.

19. <u>16</u>

Determine the sides of the square:

Since $BC = BF = CF$, BCF is an equilateral triangle. Since E is the midpoint of BC, EF is a perpendicular bisector that forms two equal 30°-60°-90° right triangles. Use either triangle to calculate BC.

$$BE: EF: BF = a: a\sqrt{3}: 2a = a: 2\sqrt{3}: 2a$$
$$a\sqrt{3} = 2\sqrt{3} \rightarrow a = 2 = BE$$
$$BC = BE + CE = 2 + 2 = 4 = \text{side of the square.}$$

Determine the area of square $ABCD$:

$$s^2 = 4 \times 4 = 16.$$

20. <u>48</u>

Since $AC||DE$, $\angle A = \angle D$. Hence,

$$\angle A = \angle D = 52$$
$$\angle A + \angle B + \angle C = 180 \rightarrow 52 + \angle B + 80 = 180$$
$$\angle B = 180 - 132 = 48$$

21. <u>100</u>

See figure below.

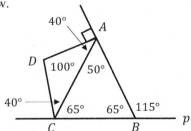

22. <u>54</u>

Determine the edge of the cube: Volume $= 64$.

$$s^3 = 64 = 4^3 \rightarrow s = 4$$

Determine the surface area of reduced cube:

25% reduction $= 1 - 0.25 = 0.75$.

$$\text{reduced edge} = 4 \times 0.75 = 3$$
$$6s^2 = 6 \times 3^2 = 6 \times 9 = 54$$

Section 14 – Trigonometry

Category 83 – Right Triangles and Trigonometry

1. D

Determine the ratio of sides:

$$\tan x = \frac{\text{opposite}}{\text{adjacent}} = \frac{DE}{EF} = 0.75 = \frac{75}{100} = \frac{3}{4}$$

Determine the proportion: It is given that $EF = 12$. This is three times of 4 (from above). Hence, DE is three times of 3.

$$DE = 3 \times 3 = 9$$

2. C

Determine the ratio of sides:

$$\tan Z = \tan C \text{ (similar triangles)}$$

$BC : AC = 6 : 10 = 2(3 : 5)$ is the ratio of Pythagorean triple $2(3 : 4 : 5)$. Hence,

$$BC : AB : AC = 6 : 8 : 10 \rightarrow AB = 8$$

$$\tan Z = \tan C = \frac{\text{opposite}}{\text{adjacent}} = \frac{AB}{BC} = \frac{8}{6} = \frac{4}{3}$$

3. A

Determine the ratio of sides:

$$\tan m = \frac{\text{opposite}}{\text{adjacent}} = \frac{XY}{YZ} = \frac{1}{\sqrt{3}}$$

$XY : YZ = 1 : \sqrt{3}$ is the ratio of the sides of a $30°$-$60°$-$90°$ right triangle. Hence,

$$XY : YZ : XZ = a : a\sqrt{3} : 2a$$

Since $\angle m$ is opposite XY (the smallest side a), $\angle m = 30°$.

4. D

Determine the ratio of sides:

$$\tan x = \frac{\text{opposite}}{\text{adjacent}} = \frac{DE}{EF} = \frac{1}{1}$$

$DE : EF = 1 : 1$ is the ratio of the sides of a $45°$-$45°$-$90°$ right triangle. Hence,

$$DE : EF : DF = a : a : a\sqrt{2} = 1 : 1 : \sqrt{2}$$

Determine the proportion:

It is given $DE = 5$. Hence, $a = 5$.

$$DE : EF : DF = a : a : a\sqrt{2} = 5 : 5 : 5\sqrt{2} \rightarrow DF = 5\sqrt{2}$$

5. A

$$\cos(90 - a) = \sin a = \frac{3}{5}$$

6. B

Tangent of the two acute angles is inverse of each other.

Hence, if $\tan A = \frac{1}{\sqrt{2}}$, then $\tan C = \sqrt{2}$.

7. C

Determine the ratio of sides: See figure below.

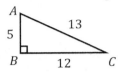

$$\tan C = \frac{\text{opposite}}{\text{adjacent}} = \frac{AB}{BC} = \frac{5}{12}$$

$AB : BC = 5 : 12$ is the ratio of Pythagorean triple $5 : 12 : 13$. Hence,

$$AB : BC : AC = 5 : 12 : 13 \rightarrow AC = 13$$

The other acute angle is A.

$$\cos A = \frac{\text{adjacent}}{\text{hypothenuse}} = \frac{5}{13}$$

8. 3/4, 6/8, or 0.75

Determine the ratio of sides: See figure below.

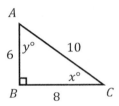

$$\sin y = \frac{\text{opposite}}{\text{hypothenuse}} = \frac{BC}{AC} = 0.8 = \frac{8}{10}$$

$BC : AC = 8 : 10 = 2(4 : 5)$ is the ratio of Pythagorean triple $2(3 : 4 : 5)$. Hence,

$$AB : BC : AC = 6 : 8 : 10 \rightarrow AB = 6$$

$$\tan x = \frac{\text{opposite}}{\text{adjacent}} = \frac{AB}{BC} = \frac{6}{8} = \frac{3}{4} = 0.75$$

9. 25

Determine the ratio of sides:

$$\angle \sin C = \sin F \text{ (similar triangles)}$$

$$\sin C = \sin F = \frac{\text{opposite}}{\text{hypotenuse}} = \frac{DE}{DF} = 0.6 = \frac{6}{10}$$

$DE : DF = 6 : 10 = 2(3 : 5)$ is the ratio of Pythagorean triple $2(3 : 4 : 5)$. Hence,

$$DE : EF : DF = 6 : 8 : 10 \rightarrow EF = 8$$

Determine the proportion: It is given that $EF = 20$. This is 2.5 times of 8 (from above). Hence, DF is 2.5 times of 10.

$$DF = 2.5 \times 10 = 25$$

10. 0.8, 4/5, or 8/10

$$\cos(90 - b) = \sin b = 0.8$$

11. 20

Determine the ratio of sides: See figure below.

Side XZ corresponds to side AC (based on the vertices).

$$\tan C = \frac{\text{opposite}}{\text{adjacent}} = \frac{AB}{BC} = 0.75 = \frac{75}{100} = \frac{3}{4}$$

$AB:BC = 3:4$ is the ratio of Pythagorean triple $3:4:5$.

$$AB:BC:AC = 3:4:5 \rightarrow AC = 5$$

Determine the proportion: It is given that $BC = 8$. This is twice of 4 (from above). Hence, AC is twice of 5.

$$AC = 2 \times 5 = 10$$

Determine XZ: It is given that each side of triangle ABC is half of the corresponding side of triangle XYZ. Hence,

$$XZ = 2AC = 2 \times 10 = 20$$

12. 15

sin of one acute angle and cos of the other acute angle add to 90°.

$$(k + 20) + (3k + 10) = 90$$
$$4k + 30 = 90 \rightarrow 4k = 90 - 30 = 60 \rightarrow k = 15$$

13. D

Answer choice D is incorrect, since $\sin 60° = \cos(90° - 30°) = \cos 60°$ is not true.

14. B

Evaluate each answer choice: $\angle A = \angle X$, $\angle B = \angle Y$, and $\angle C = \angle Z$.

Option I: $\sin A = \cos C$ and $\cos C = \cos Z$. Hence, $\sin A = \cos Z$ .This is correct.

Option II: Since $AB \neq BC$, $\angle A \neq \angle C$. Hence, $\angle X \neq \angle Z$ and $\tan \angle X \neq \tan \angle Z$. Since $\tan \angle Z = \tan \angle C$, $\tan \angle C$ cannot be equal to $\tan \angle X$. This eliminates option II.

Option III: $\sin(90° - X) = \cos A \rightarrow \sin(90° - A) = \cos A$. This is correct.

15. C

Evaluate each answer choice by replacing $\sin x°$ for k: The answer choices must be true for all values of k.

Answer choice A: $\cos(x^2)° = \sin x°$ is not correct.

Answer choice B: $\sin(x^2)° = \sin x°$ is not correct.

Answer choice C: $\cos(90° - x°) = \sin x°$ is correct.

Answer choice D: $\tan(90° - x°) = \sin x°$ is not correct.

16. A

Set up proportion: Triangles DGH and DEF are similar triangles. Hence, the corresponding sides are in proportion.

$$\tan F = \frac{DE}{EF} = \frac{DG}{GH} = 1.6 = \frac{16}{10} = \frac{8}{5}$$

17. 4/5 or 0.8

Determine the length between points: See figure below.

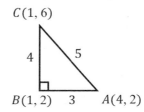

AB is a horizontal line and BC is a vertical line.

Calculate AB: $4 - 1 = 3$.

Calculate BC: $6 - 2 = 4$.

$AB:BC = 3:4$ is the ratio of Pythagorean triple $3:4:5$.

$$AB:BC:AC = 3:4:5 \rightarrow AC = 5$$

$$\sin A = \frac{\text{opposite}}{\text{hypothenuse}} = \frac{BC}{AC} = \frac{4}{5}$$

18. 15/2 or 7.5

AC is the diameter of the circle as it passes through the center.

Determine the ratio of sides: See figure below.

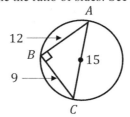

$$\sin A = \frac{\text{opposite}}{\text{hypothenuse}} = \frac{BC}{AC} = 0.6 = \frac{6}{10}$$

$BC:AC = 6:10 = 2(3:5)$ is the ratio of Pythagorean triple $2(3:4:5)$. Hence,

$$BC:AB:AC = 6:8:10 \rightarrow AB = 8$$

Determine the proportion: It is given that $AB = 12$. This is 1.5 times of 8 (from above). Hence, AC is 1.5 times of 10.

$$AC = 1.5 \times 10 = 15 = \text{diameter}$$

Determine the radius:

$$\text{Radius} = \frac{AC}{2} = \frac{15}{2} = 7.5$$

Category 84 – Unit Circle and Trigonometry

1. <u>C</u>

Determine the coordinates on the unit circle:

Angle $\theta = 90°$. The (cos 90°, sin 90°) coordinates in a unit circle are (0, 1).

Hence, cos 90° = 0.

2. <u>B</u>

Determine the coordinates on the unit circle:

Since point P is in quadrant 4, angle θ is also in quadrant 4. Hence, the x-coordinate = cos θ is positive and the y-coordinate = sin θ is negative.

Since $\cos \theta = \frac{\sqrt{2}}{2}$, sin θ must be $\frac{-\sqrt{2}}{2}$.

3. <u>A</u>

Determine the coordinates on the unit circle:

Angle θ is in quadrant 2. Hence, cos θ is negative and sin θ is positive.

Since $\cos \theta = \frac{-1}{2}$, sin θ must be $\frac{\sqrt{3}}{2}$.

Determine tan θ:

$$\tan \theta = \frac{\sin \theta}{\cos \theta} = \frac{\sqrt{3}}{2} \div \frac{-1}{2} = \frac{\sqrt{3}}{2} \times -\frac{2}{1} = -\sqrt{3}$$

4. <u>C</u>

Convert radians to degrees:

$$\frac{\pi}{3} \times \frac{180}{\pi} = 60°$$

Determine the coordinates on the unit circle:

$\theta = 60°$ is in quadrant 1. All coordinates are positive in this quadrant. This eliminates answer choices A and B.

1 is not a coordinate of $\theta = 60°$ in a unit circle. This eliminates answer choice D.

5. <u>D</u>

Determine the coordinates on the unit circle:

The (cos 180°, sin 180°) coordinates in a unit circle are (−1, 0).

Hence, sin 180° = 0.

Section 15 – Complex Numbers

Category 85 – Complex Numbers

1. C

$$(2i^2 - i)(5i^2 + 3i) = 10i^4 + 6i^3 - 5i^3 - 3i^2 =$$
$$10i^4 + i^3 - 3i^2 = 10(1) + (-i) - 3(-1) =$$
$$10 - i + 3 = 13 - i$$

2. B

$$x = \sqrt{-16} = \sqrt{(-1) \times (16)} =$$
$$\sqrt{-1} \times \sqrt{16} = i \times 4 = 4i$$

3. D

$$\sqrt{-9} = \sqrt{(-1) \times (9)} = \sqrt{-1} \times \sqrt{9} = i \times 3 = 3i$$

4. D

$$-((-2i)(-2i)) = -(4i^2) = -(4 \times -1) = 4$$

5. B

Multiply the numerator and denominator by $(1 + i)$.

$$\frac{2(1 + i)}{(1 - i)} = \frac{(2 + 2i)(1 + i)}{(1 - i)(1 + i)} = \frac{2 + 2i + 2i + 2i^2}{1 - i^2} =$$

$$\frac{2 + 4i + 2i^2}{1 - i^2} = \frac{2 + 4i + 2(-1)}{1 - (-1)} = \frac{2 + 4i - 2}{2} = \frac{4i}{2} = 2i$$

6. A

For y to have a real solution, the number within the square root cannot be negative. When $x = 1$, $y = \sqrt{1 - 2} = \sqrt{-1}$. Hence, when $x = 1$ there is no real solution for y.

7. D

Multiply the numerator and denominator by $(1 - i)$.

$$\frac{3 + i}{1 + i} = \frac{(3 + i)(1 - i)}{(1 + i)(1 - i)} = \frac{3 - 3i + i - i^2}{1 - i^2} =$$

$$\frac{3 - 2i - (-1)}{1 - (-1)} = \frac{3 - 2i + 1}{2} = \frac{4 - 2i}{2} = 2 - i$$

8. 6

$$2(3 + 4i) - (5i + 3i^2) = 6 + 8i - 5i - 3i^2 =$$
$$6 + 3i - 3i^2 = 6 + 3i - 3(-1) = 6 + 3i + 3 = 9 + 3i$$

Solve for $a - b$:

$$a + bi = 9 + 3i$$
$$a = 9 \text{ and } b = 3$$
$$9 - 3 = 6$$

9. 4

$$(15 + 6i^2) - (12 + 7i^2) = 15 + 6i^2 - 12 - 7i^2 =$$
$$3 - i^2 = 3 - (-1) = 3 + 1 = 4$$

10. 2

$$15i^4 + 5i^2 - 8 = 15(1) + 5(-1) - 8 = 15 - 13 = 2$$

11. 7

Cross multiply.

$$9 + ki = (1 + 3i)(3 - 2i)$$
$$9 + ki = 3 - 2i + 9i - 6i^2$$
$$9 + ki = 3 + 7i - 6(-1)$$
$$9 + ki = 9 + 7i$$

Determine k: Both sides of the equation are in the $a + bi$ format.

$$b = k = 7$$

12. 9

$$(11 + 5i) - (5 + 2i) = 11 + 5i - 5 - 2i = 6 + 3i$$

Solve for $a + b$:

$$a + bi = 6 + 3i$$
$$a = 6 \text{ and } b = 3$$
$$6 + 3 = 9$$

13. 11

$$7 + ci = (5 + 3i)(2 + i)$$
$$7 + ci = 10 + 5i + 6i + 3i^2$$
$$7 + ci = 10 + 11i + 3i^2$$
$$7 + ci = 10 + 11i + 3(-1)$$
$$7 + ci = 7 + 11i$$

Determine c: Both sides of the equation are in the $a + bi$ format.

$$b = c = 11$$

14. 2

Create a single fraction with i^4 as the denominator. This will cancel out the denominator, since $i^4 = 1$.

$$\frac{1}{i^4} - \frac{2}{i^2} - \frac{2}{i} = \frac{1 - 2i^2 - 2i^3}{i^4} =$$

$$\frac{1 - 2(-1) - 2(-i)}{1} = 1 + 2 + 2i = 3 + 2i$$

$$a + bi = 3 + 2i \rightarrow b = 2$$

15. 1

$$2i^2 - 3(-i)^2 = 2i^2 - 3(-i)(-i) =$$
$$2i^2 - 3i^2 = -i^2 = -(-1) = 1$$

Mapping of Categories to SAT Practice Test 10 Math Sections

SAT Practice Test 10 can be accessed from the Resources menu of the website.

Section 3

Question Number	Category Number
1	1
2	15
3	7
4	7
5	47
6	51
7	50
8	72
9	3
10	31
11	71
12	83
13	28, 33
14	54
15	10
16	16
17	38
18	49
19	12
20	51

Section 4

Question Number	Category Number
1	5
2	16
3	56
4	1
5	22
6	53
7	68
8	56
9	50
10	68
11	67
12	44
13	63
14	63
15	79
16	43, 44
17	52
18	55
19	32
20	67
21	16
22	48
23	3
24	57
25	12
26	50
27	1
28	33
29	17
30	74, 80
31	19
32	74
33	60
34	1
35	14
36	35
37	42
38	41

Printed in Great Britain
by Amazon